ITALO CALVINO
LETTERS, 1941–1985

ITALO CALVINO

LETTERS, 1941–1985

Selected and with an Introduction by
Michael Wood

Translated by Martin McLaughlin

To Tristan, Buona lettura, July 2013, Martin

All v best Michael

PRINCETON UNIVERSITY PRESS
PRINCETON AND OXFORD

Published by Princeton University Press, 41 William Street, Princeton, New Jersey 08540
In the United Kingdom: Princeton University Press, 6 Oxford Street, Woodstock, Oxfordshire OX20 1TW

press.princeton.edu
Jacket illustration: *Italo Calvino*, 2012, by Michael Molloy. Illustration based on photograph *Italo Calvino*, by Jerry Bauer.

Library of Congress Cataloging-in-Publication Data
Calvino, Italo.
[Correspondence. Selections]
Italo Calvino : letters, 1941–1985 / selected and with an introduction by Michael Wood ; translated by Martin McLaughlin.
pages cm
Includes bibliographical references and index.
ISBN 978-0-691-13945-6 (hardcover : alk. paper) 1. Calvino, Italo—Correspondence. 2. Authors, Italian—20th century—Correspondence. I. Wood, Michael, 1936– editor. II. McLaughlin, M. L. (Martin L.), translator. III. Title.
PQ4809.A45Z48 2013
856′.914—dc23
2012038719

British Library Cataloging-in-Publication Data is available

Translation is supported by a bequest from Charles Lacy Lockert (1888–1974)

This book has been composed in MVB Verdigris Pro

Printed on acid-free paper. ∞

Printed in the United States of America

10 9 8 7 6 5 4 3 2 1

Contents

Introduction

MICHAEL WOOD

ITALO CALVINO WAS DISCREET ABOUT HIS LIFE AND THE LIVES of others, and skeptical about the uses of biography. He understood that much of the world we inhabit is made up of signs, and that signs may speak more eloquently than facts. Was he born in San Remo, in Liguria? No, he was born in Santiago de las Vegas, in Cuba, but since "an exotic birth-place on its own is not informative of anything," he allowed the phrase "born in San Remo" to appear repeatedly in biographical notes about him. Unlike the truth, he suggested, this falsehood said something about who he was as a writer, about his "creative world" (letter of November 21, 1967), "the landscape and environment that . . . shaped his life" (April 5, 1967).

This is to say that the best biography may be a considered fiction, and Calvino was also inclined to think that a writer's work is all the biography anyone really requires. In his letters he returns again and again to the need for attention to the actual literary object rather than the imagined author. "For the critic, the author does not exist, only a certain number of writings exist" (November 24, 1967). "A text must be something that can be read and evaluated without reference to the existence or otherwise of a person whose name and surname appear on the cover" (July 9, 1971). "The public figure of the writer, the writer-character, the 'personality-cult' of the author, are all becoming for me more and more intolerable in others, and consequently in myself" (September 16, 1968).

Such assertions begin to conjure up what came to be known as the death of the author, although still only as a prospect or a principle, and in a lecture called "Cybernetics and Ghosts," Calvino explored the notion with great polemical and theoretical panache. This was in 1967, a year before Roland Barthes made the theme notorious in France and the English-speaking world. He also uses the specific metaphor of authorial death in a letter of that year (November 24, 1967), and in several other letters. "And so the author vanishes," Calvino said in his lecture, "that spoiled child of ignorance—to give place to a more thoughtful person, a person who will know that the author is a machine, and will know how this machine works." We note that a machine replaces a myth, but a real (thoughtful) person replaces an unthinking illusion, and Calvino adds that we shall get a "poetic result . . . only if the writing machine is surrounded by the hidden ghosts of the individual and of his society."[1]

This last sentence makes clear that Calvino is talking about a finished work and its life in the world, and not about some sort of unattainable impersonality: self and society may have become ghosts, but they are essential. The death of the grandee author in no way implies the disappearance of the writing person, and any appearance of contradiction vanishes as soon as we understand that for Calvino and many others, writing *is* life. "We are people, there is no doubt, who exist solely insofar as we write, otherwise we don't exist at all" (August 24, 1959). The death of the author may indeed be the liberation of the writer, and for Calvino there is also an ethical element in this disposition. "Books," he says, "in the end represent the best of our conscience" (July 22, 1958). They are not always what we wish they were, but they show us what we ourselves could be. Books are unavoidably personal for Calvino, but not confessional, and not only personal.

But then what are we to make of the letters of such a writer, and what are we doing reading them? In part we are, I'm afraid, ignoring his warnings and careful distinctions; peeping into his privacy. These letters were not written for us or to us. We see "that young man," as Calvino later calls his earlier self (May 26, 1977), in all his unruly literary excitement, his half-hearted agricultural studies, his worries about conscription, followed by his departure to join the partisans. He returns from the war a declared Communist but still a diverse and witty stylist. The letters reflect his encounters with the writers Elio Vittorini and Cesare Pavese, both of whom meant a great deal to him, and record many of his exchanges of thoughts with friends and critics. He travels to Russia and America, reporting in detail on his impressions; resigns from the Communist Party; continues to work at the Turin publishing house Einaudi. He marries the Argentinian Esther Singer and they have a daughter, Giovanna, who appears in the letters as happy, alert, and admirably resistant to education ("she speaks three languages . . . and has no wish to learn to read or write" [March 1, 1972]). Calvino moves to Paris; then Rome, a place "that young man" once swore he would never set foot in. There are kindly letters to scholars and schoolchildren, quarrelsome exchanges with figures like Pier Paolo Pasolini and Claudio Magris. Calvino "discovers" the Sicilian writer Leonardo Sciascia, makes clear his admiration for Carlo Emilio Gadda, thinks about film with Michelangelo Antonioni, and collaborates on opera with Berio.

There are dramatic moments, albeit quietly evoked. He dates a letter to his friend Eugenio Scalfari "the first night of the curfew imposed by the Germans" (September 12–13, 1943); sends a message on a notepad to his parents from a partisan hiding place; in another letter mentions his parents' being taken hostage and then released ("my father was on the point of being shot before my mother's eyes") (July 6, 1945). Calvino is constantly exercised by Italian politics. We have his letter of resignation from the Italian Communist Party (August 1, 1957). He witnesses the events of May 1968 in Paris. He thinks about Brazilian prisons, Palestinian poets, the war in Vietnam. In Cuba he meets Che Guevara.

And again and again, we encounter Calvino the voracious reader: as a young man catching up with Ibsen and Rilke and what seems to be the whole of western literature, paying attention to contemporary Italian writers of all stripes; as a prolific reviewer "reading books to review immediately," as he says (January 16, 1950); as a man who spent most of his adult life working as an editor in a publishing house. A collection of his letters in Italian is called *I libri degli altri* (*Other People's Books*), a phrase itself taken from a casual, generous remark of Calvino's: "I have spent more time with other people's books than with my own." He added, "I do not regret it."[2] Perhaps not coincidentally, this avid reader sometimes halts as a writer, wonders whether he is finished, whether his present pause will become permanent. He is always discreet, but the distress is palpable as he evokes, for instance, a "period of depression and writer's block which . . . has gone on for some time now and maybe won't ever unblock" (January 11, 1976), or tells a correspondent that he has "only progressed towards rarefaction and silence." "In recent years," "he says wryly, "I was very satisfied playing the dead man for a bit: how clever I am at not publishing! . . . Whereas now I am starting again to realize that the one thing I would like is to write . . . but . . . I have managed to lose all love for images of contemporary life" (May 6, 1972). He regains this love, but the loss was real while it lasted. All the late work, beautifully written as it is, shows a greater and greater attention to what cannot be said.

The selection of letters in this volume—a little less than one third of those that appear in Luca Baranelli's magnificent *Lettere* (2000)—seeks to reflect this history and Calvino's place in it. We have not scanted the Italian dimension but have taken care to retain letters that have an international dimension. The focus is on literary and political matters rather than family—although we have just seen there is no safe way of keeping these elements separate—but even the complete *Lettere*, which especially in the early years represents family life more roundly, does not give us access to a secret, second Calvino, a person concealed behind the writer, so to speak. It is true that Baranelli's collection, containing close to a thousand items, presents as he says only "a modest percentage" of the letters Calvino wrote, and "obvious reasons" of reserve and privacy must take some letters off the table (something Calvino himself thought was right in the cases of Pavese and Vittorini). But a private life, whatever our current eagerness for gossip may suggest, is not necessarily a buried life.

What is more striking, perhaps, is that the creative writer doesn't dominate this correspondence as we might expect. There are interesting exceptions—occasional sketches and descriptions, an outline for "The Motel of Crossed Destinies," which Calvino never wrote (August 20, 1973), the letter on paradise I mention later, which appeared as an article—but on the whole the letters are not being used as practice for fiction or essays. And finally, since he is not thinking of us, Calvino does not have any sort of eye on posterity, as André Gide and so many other modern letter writers do. He is living in the present, not constructing a future monument.

These aspects of the letters may therefore offer something of a surprise to the reader who comes to them from the fiction and who may at first miss the expected intricacy and play. It's not that there is no fun in the letters (there are plenty of humorous and ironic moments) or that Calvino is ever solemn or pompous; nor am I suggesting that the letters are serious while the fiction is not. But the sense of direct communication, of a man being as clear as he can about a host of matters, complex and simple, is quite different from that created by the artistic density of Calvino's prose fiction and indeed of many of his essays. In his art, the wit and the irony are ways of reflecting the difficulties of the world while hanging on to his sanity—instruments of reason in a world of madness. "I am in favor," Calvino says in one letter, "of a clown-like mimesis of contemporary reality" (January 18, 1957). Clowns are often sad and all too sane; but their relation to reality is oblique. Calvino's writing is part of a great literary project of hinting and suggesting, making memorable shapes and images, rather than giving information or offering explanations. In his letters, Calvino tells rather than shows his correspondents what he means—with great and often moving success.

For this reason, although we invade Calvino's privacy by the mere fact of looking at these letters, it is a very special privacy that appears: not the writer's real self—why wouldn't his writing represent this self, as he thought it did—but his plain self. We eavesdrop not on his secrets but on his devotion to clarity. Of course Calvino is too thoughtful not to register the possibility that the very idea of a plain self is a fiction. But it could be a truth-telling fiction, like the story of being born in San Remo. Consider sentences like these. "I am not a passionate person," Calvino writes in a letter when he is manifestly very angry. He insists, I'm sure rightly, that "hatred, resentment at insults, wounded dignity" are not his "cup of tea" [literally bread for my teeth]. "I think one ought to feel mortally offended. . . . I can't do it." But he is still angry, and needs both to keep calm and to let his feelings show. "Maybe diligence is my way of being passionate," he says finally. "That is why I manage to be diligent only in odd, very brief moments" (March 20, 1964). There: he's found the right tone, and a faint touch of self-mockery helps to maintain the balance.

Calvino's clarifications cover many diverse topics—he has no unified theory of literature or anything else—but they often converge in their effect. We now understand what we half-understood before; we see that what looked like a quirk was a policy; we realize that our puzzlement and Calvino's are one and the same. There is an excellent example of this effect in the cluster of closely related questions concerning the representation of reality in literature, the notion of paradise, and the travails of Italian Communism. Perhaps surprisingly, each of these questions turns out to be in part a version of the others.

A "clown-like mimesis" of reality will picture the world as sad and laughable, perhaps scarcely to be lived in—"always in the background," Calvino says in one letter (November 13, 1979), "there remains the impossibility of accepting the world as it is." But we are living in it, and that is why the laughter is essential. It is a sign that we are not mere victims, that we are still thinking. This is how we attempt to get the starkest sort of grasp on the real—"in order to hate the Tower of Babel we have to have the Tower of Babel totally tangible in front of us" (March 3, 1958)—while recognizing that only indirection will work. This is how literature becomes at times a "kind of game, which does not require allegories to be looked for, though at the same time suggesting them" (August 7, 1952), and this is why closure in Calvino is always ironic, a neat simulation of what is not available. "The conclusion has to seem meaningful while still remaining a purely formal element" (December 16, 1967). "For me . . . writing has always meant setting out in one direction, staking everything on one card, yet with the awareness that there are others" (March 2, 1950).

All this is part of what Calvino calls his Enlightenment mentality, belated, self-conscious, aware of the troubles reason has got itself into but faithful to lucidity all the same. "Enlightenment rationalism has for two centuries done nothing but be beaten about the head and been on the receiving end of denials, and yet it continues to co-exist in the face of all its critiques: and perhaps I express this co-existence" (October 26, 1964). Here's an old/new Enlightenment idea: "Man is simply the best chance we know of that matter has had of providing itself with information about itself" (July 7, 1970). We may also think of Calvino's epigram in a list of writers he likes: "I like Chesterton because he wanted to be the Catholic Voltaire and I wanted to be the Communist Chesterton."[3]

Clowns and rationalists do not—cannot—believe in paradise, and more important perhaps, are endlessly troubled by the fact that everyone around them does. The left, the middle, and the right are as bad as each other in this respect. What chance is there for those "who have always wanted people no longer to think in terms of hell and paradise" (March 2, 1969)? Well, they can argue their case, as Calvino does in 1950 in a long letter to Mario Motta, later published in the short-lived magazine *Cultura e realtà*. Responding to Motta's suggestion that "each one of us can hope for a supernatural paradise," Calvino says that the very term "paradise," let alone "supernatural," is "totally foreign" to his "usual way of thinking." This doesn't mean he won't try an unusual way of thinking, but it doesn't help. The thought of paradise for Calvino, however he takes it, gets in the way of the work that needs doing on earth: "a host of things to do, of responsibilities, of 'troubles' . . . What pushes me in this direction is not, it seems to me, a 'paradise' to be reached, but the satisfaction of seeing things gradually starting to go the right way, feeling in a better position for solving problems as they emerge." Even Dante, Calvino says, in spite of the otherworldly locations of his great poem, is concerned with "men as they are, on the 'earth'" (July 1950).

But will anyone listen to such arguments, if even Calvino talks about hell in what are perhaps his most famous sentences? The answer will depend on how we read those sentences. *Invisible Cities* ends in this way:

> The inferno of the living is not something that will be; if there is one, it is what is already here, the inferno where we live every day, that we form by being together. There are two ways to escape suffering it. The first is easy for many: accept the inferno and become such a part of it that you can no longer see it. The second is risky and demands constant vigilance and apprehension: seek and learn to recognize who and what, in the midst of inferno, are not inferno, then make them endure, give them space.

It's clear that we have not left the earth even if the imagery has, and Calvino's language is in an important sense more direct than that of the translation. "Apprendimento," as Martin McLaughlin reminds us, means "learning" rather than "apprehension," and so suggests work and persistence rather than fear combined with conceptual grasp. We are still very close to the unmystified Enlightenment.

Calvino says he has noticed that "critics dwell on the final sentence . . . as if that were the conclusion." It is the conclusion, but faithful to the idea of there always being another card to play, Calvino adds that his book "has two conclusions, both of the same order of importance: one on the ideal city . . . and the other on the infernal city" (January 20, 1973). The irony is that the ideal city does sound like a paradise, however tentative and disjointed its appearance. Marco Polo says:

> I will put together, piece by piece, the perfect city, made of fragments mixed with the rest, of instants separated by intervals . . . If I tell you that the city toward which my journey tends is discontinuous in space and time, now scattered, now more condensed, you must not believe the search for it can stop.[4]

Still, we get the point. We can (just about) talk of paradise as long as we realize we must not give up looking for it, and too many people take the invitation as heading in precisely the opposite direction: toward the end of all searches.

What provoked Calvino's long initial reflection on paradise was Motta's review of a book called *The God That Failed*, and this is where the paths of writing and paradise cross with Communism. The God in question was either Marx or Revolution, and Calvino can't bear the thought that politics is a matter of faith, or has any relation to religion. Such an assumption "has always been at the farthest pole from everything I have written done said thought" (March 21, 1960). Politics, as in the above quotation regarding "things to do," is about making conditions better on earth (or trying to), or it is nothing. The very idea of an ex-Communist in this theological sense (as distinct from the mundane sense of no longer being a member of a Communist Party) seems shabby to Calvino, a proof only of delusion.

> The "ex-Communist" is one of the dreariest figures of the postwar period: with behind him that sad air of wasted time, and ahead of him the squalid existence of someone redeemed by the Salvation Army,

> going around the streets with the band and its choir, shouting out that he's been a drunkard and a cheat. (July 1950)

It's not that Communism itself doesn't have its dreary sides and worse. Calvino himself is willing to say that "a witty and communicative Communist" is "a rare thing" (April 10, 1954), and to admit that "the Party card (along with all the contradictory network of relations it brought with it) often took the place of my conscience" (August 9, 1957). But it didn't take its place often, and "in fact the very poverty of Communism's official literature acted as a spur to me to try to bring a touch of creative felicity to my work as a writer; I believe I have always managed to be, inside the Party, a free man" (August 1, 1957).

In order to understand Italy (and indeed many other countries) in the twentieth century, we need to see how a Communist Party could be a representative progressive force in its intentions and sometimes its achievements; and also fatally flawed by its dependence on Moscow. It was not a God that failed but a deified dictator called Stalin—or more precisely, an unquestioning allegiance to Stalin's success was the ruin of European Communism. Calvino does not deny this allegiance, which he came to see as "schizophrenic," the split adherence of well-intentioned persons to a "tragic and ferocious system.[5] But he never becomes an ex-Communist except in the narrowest sense. Or perhaps we should say he never becomes an anti-Communist. It is possible, and Calvino does this very delicately in his letters and in his essays, to get a clear view of one's errors without believing that one's former life was nothing but a mistake. It is in this sense that the contemplation of the Tower of Babel rather than the Garden of Eden is instructive for a writer.

For an instance of how the clarity of these letters relates to the transposed, ironic clarity of a fable, we could look at one of Calvino's earliest stories, "Making Do." The location is a town where everything is forbidden except playing the game of tip-cat. No one complains, everyone enjoys the game. Then a thaw comes, or a moment of liberalization, and the constables of the town decide "there was no longer any reason why everything should be forbidden." Now the people are allowed to do whatever they want. What they want, however, is to go on playing tip-cat, and when the constables try to prevent this, we are told, "the people rebelled and killed the lot of them." The last words of the story are, "Then without wasting time, they got back to playing tip-cat."[6]

This tale, with its respect for a hostility to change and its implied invitation to do better nevertheless, has a close resemblance to the much later story "Becalmed in the Antilles," where Donald Duck, who once sailed with Francis Drake, is pestered by his nephews for his account of the time when the crews of an English and a Spanish ship, rather than fighting each other, just watched and waited—for the wind or perhaps the invention of the steam engine. That's all that happened: nothing. Calvino was thinking of the Italian Communist Party in the mid-1950s, but also more generally of the Cold War, and the antagonism between Russia and China. And both of these stories, of course, can be taken as alluding to a range of realities Calvino himself could not have known, because as with his birth in San Remo, the instances are fictitious but their echoes in the world are actual. Calvino's objection to the French translation of the title of his *Non-existent Knight* as *Le chevalier irréel* makes this point impeccably: "I never say that the knight is unreal. I say that he does not exist. That is very different" (June 9, 1961).

Translator's Note

MARTIN MCLAUGHLIN

THIS TRANSLATION OF A WIDE SELECTION OF ITALO CALVINO'S letters is based on the following edition: Italo Calvino, *Lettere 1940–1985*, edited by Luca Baranelli (Milan: Mondadori, 2000). The notes are sometimes translations of those in Baranelli's edition, but on other occasions they are supplied by the translator in order to assist the non-Italian reader with certain names and events that need no explanation to an Italian reader but do require one for the Anglophone reader. At the opening of each letter I have retained Calvino's various forms of address, whether formal or informal or indeed jocular (as in the first letter to his school friend Eugenio Scalfari where "Dear Eugenio" is written as one word "Deareugenio"). One nuance that is difficult to express in English is the Italian custom of addressing even quite close colleagues and acquaintances by their family name: so in these cases I have retained this form in English, e.g., "Dear Micheli," "Dear Venturi" rather than "Dear Silvio," "Dear Franco," etc. Naturally when the author does use first names to his correspondents, I have respected this in the translation. I have also respected the various different ways Calvino has of dating his letters, along with other variations, such as signing off or closing a paragraph without end punctuation. Each letter is followed by information about its source, with references also to any previous publication of the whole or part of the letter.

The translator would like to thank all the people who have generously helped this translation project. First, thanks to all those who know most about the background and meaning of the letters, namely Chichita Calvino, Luca Baranelli, Mario Barenghi; second, to the two helpful readers contacted by Princeton University Press; and last but not least, thanks to those who helped me with various linguistic or other specialist problems: Stefano Adami, Helen Anderson, Guido Bonsaver, Chichita Calvino, Cristina Demaria, Robert Gordon, Peter Hainsworth, Andrew Kahn, Tom Kuhn, Cathy McLaughlin, Mairi McLaughlin, Graham Nelson, Ritchie Robertson, Michael Sheringham, Elisabetta Tarantino, Michael Wood.

Oxford 2012

Abbreviations

The following abbreviations are used for works by Calvino:

ILDA = *I libri degli altri. Lettere 1947–1981*, ed. Giovanni Tesio (Turin: Einaudi, 1991)

RR = *Romanzi e racconti*, ed. Claudio Milanini, Mario Barenghi, Bruno Falcetto, 3 vols. (Milan: Mondadori, 1991–94)

S = *Saggi*, ed. Mario Barenghi, 2 vols. (Milan: Mondadori, 1995)

1941–1945

To Eugenio Scalfari—Rome

San Remo, 16 Dec. [1941]

Deareugenio,

Writing to Scalfari is very fashionable these days. Maiga's written, Pasquale's written, dammit, I really must sit down and write to him as well![1] He's a good guy that Scalfari: talks a bit too much nonsense, too many people from the P. C. Ministry in his head,[2] but on the whole a good guy. I really must write to him. I must inform him of the fact that, after a month's residence in Turin, I felt it my duty to take my holidays and return to this cheerful Mediterranean town which, even though it was not my birth-place, was nevertheless the cradle of thousands of my chimerical hopes and ambitions. I could also tell him that I am horribly bored and think that I could have stayed on in Turin for a bit longer: but these are banal topics and I don't want to seem always to be harping on about the same thing. I am the first San Remo person to migrate back from Turin, alongside the likes of Donzella. The engineers, weighed down by mountains of work, have to wait in fear and trembling for exams on mathematical analysis which force them to stay up there all this week. The medical students (in other words G. Pigati) will come back on Wednesday. Here life is the same as usual, Corso Vittorio is as it always was, the usual numbing monotony, the usual silviodian is there, a bit wasted for having spent a whole month walking up and down Via Vittorio on his own. I've not seen Cossu yet: he's employed in the town hall finance section and is vegetating in an office. Godiasco has written to me from Aosta: he's at the main school for the Alpini. Francuccio, more pissed off than ever, is a poor bloody infantryman in Piacenza.[3]

. . . (At this point the author of the present missive flings the pen far away from himself, sneers, gets up and . . . oh, miraculously, a pair of white wings have popped out from his shoulders, his body has become more diaphanous, his sneer more Mephistophelian. He opens the window, hovers in flight, crosses—braving the threats of anti-aircraft fire—most of the Italian peninsula, and arriving above an important town in Lazio plummets down upon a house in Corso Mazzini.)[4]

In a bedroom plunged in the most mysterious penumbra sleeps a young man. On the walls hang the sacred images of people who occupy the highest echelons in the Ministry of Popular Culture, images which the young man, with religious zeal, adorns every day with garlands of wild flowers. Scattered everywhere, on bookshelves and stands, are important bound volumes on which stand out titles such as *I Love the Tripartite Pact More than my Aunt!*, or *Alfredo Oriani, Now There Was a Man!*, or *Ethical Foundations of Vegetable Rationing*, or *Menenius Agrippa, Precursor of the Battle against Dem . . .* , etc.[5] Italocalvino, as diaphanous and silent as a specter, places himself at the young man's pillow, barely manages to restrain the temptation to caress his dark, wavy hair, and with a solemn gesture points an accusing finger at him, calling out in a guttural voice: "Eugenio!" The young man, interrupted right in the middle of an erotic dream, yawns, rubs his eyes and, thinking it's the maid that's wakening him, stretches out a hand to touch her breasts. But instead of the maid's breasts what he touches is the accusing (and rather dirty) finger of Italocalvino who with an even more solemn voice continues: "Eugenio! What has become of you? How have you let yourself be led astray by bad company? See what comes of having contact with certain people? How could you have stooped so low? Do you not know, dear innocent creature, that these volumes that you naively pretend to appreciate, are the fruit not of faith or conscience but of greed for high office and money? Do you not realize that their words are forced and squeezed out of them like those of an essay in class? That those who wrote them are even less sure of them than I am, and now enjoy the leisure afforded by the high office they have obtained, and are squandering their wealth on courtesans and dissolute young men? Do you not understand that what you think can give you living strength is nothing but aridity, sterility and rhetoric? Your lungs, like mine, need much healthier air![”]

. . . And so saying, with a voice full of emotion, the specter of his distant friend starts to speak of flights of butterflies, the smooth curves of women's hips, the sea breaking against the rocks, of workshops, vines, men working and loving without thinking about mysticism or ethical precedents. “Here lies true inspiration,” concludes the specter and in a manly fashion disguises the sob escaping from his mouth with a belch, a healthy manifestation of joyous vulgarity. Then the young man, now repentant, makes as if to kiss the specter's feet, but, on reflection, holds back from this unwise gesture which could cost him his life, and, seizing the books, makes a great pile of them, on top of which he places the portraits hanging on the walls, and to the cry of “Savonaro’,” “Savonarola!” sets fire to it all and then relishes the spectacle of the flames. Next, once the fire has gone out, he strips and dances for a long time over the ashes. Then, encouraged by the ghost, he runs completely naked, apart from beach mules on his feet and the ashes covering his head, along Via dell'Impero. At that point, the specter, who deep down is a bit of a lad, claps his hand on the shoulder of the catechumen, speaks to him of catharsis and says: “If you don't hurry and come to San Remo, you'll soon find out what'll happen to you!” Terrified at this obscure threat, the young man hurries to pack his suitcases and rushes for the first train towards that well-known climatic resort where he finds waiting for him his unforgetting friend

Italo

[Handwritten; with the addressee.]

To Eugenio Scalfari–Rome

Today is the seventh of March [1942] and I am in Turin
an elegant and original way of writing the date

POLEMICAL EPISTLE TO HIS FRIEND EUGENIO

A FINE THING IT IS TO HAVE A DISTANT FRIEND WHO WRITES long letters full of drivel and to be able to reply to him with equally lengthy letters full of drivel; fine not because I like to plunge into captious polemics nor because I enjoy getting certain ideas into the head of some idiot from the Urbe, but because writing long letters to friends means having a moral excuse for not studying. If I wasn't writing to you, I'd be staring hatefully and diffidently at the cover of my textbook on crystallography, thinking with regret that, according to the study plan drawn up on the first day of the month, I should already be on p. 276, whereas instead I haven't even tackled the introduction. That is sad. For that—and not for any other—reason I am replying to you with alacrity and enthusiasm.

I got the letter meant for me and have read the one sent to Maiga. Right then, Turi Vasile?[6] OK. Turi Vasile is a name, even though he has not yet emerged from the shapeless mass of pale arts-page hacks. (What have you read of Turi Vasile, I hear you say? Well, OK, nothing, but dammit, you don't expect me to take note of every name that appears in print anywhere; he does something like radio plays on a rural theme, if I'm not mistaken.) At any rate, for his information, I would ask you to notify him that the great hope of Italian theater, the one that all writers and critics say is going to emerge any moment now, is not him. It's someone else. Modesty prevents me from supplying further enlightenment. In short, if you really haven't worked it out, see the footnote at the end of this paragraph.* You can also tell Vasile that it is in fact himself and all his colleagues who make me certain of this. Well, I mean, what are you doing with this Turi Vasile? The business about the "talent pool" is not very clear.[7] Don't write so much nonsense, give us facts and cliques and people. Now you tell me that the journal does not belong to the talent pool, but to Azione Cattolica: what a disaster! I bet it's one of those parish propaganda sheets, full of miracles, gifts to charity, stories of missionaries in China, and Confirmation names for girls. It is sad to think that one who claims to have been forged at my school has fallen so low. But, that's life! Still, if you've broken through, keep going. They'll all turn out to be so many idiots anyway . . . Don't trust the big names that support youth movements: it's fashionable to show you're favoring youth. But, for example, a few days ago Betti published a letter in *La Stampa* or *La Gazzetta*, quite pissed off because at the Genoa conference people claimed he was the leader of a literary school.[8]

*It's me. (But don't tell anyone, OK?)

By the way, how important and original was the outcome of the Genoa conference! What a contribution to the art of the nation! At least as far as I can make out up here—at second-hand, reading the newspapers—they are apart from anything else complete ignoramuses if they thought that Cantini was on the same level as Viola, and Viola on the same level as Tieri and could not come up with any better models than Betti and Lodovici.[9] There's this advantage in the whole business, namely that by moving in those circles, you feel stimulated to widen your knowledge in this area. Fine: that way, I'll have someone to discuss these things with in the leisure of summer. We've got to study, graft, grind away. The more you know the better it is. Intelligence is not enough. I too am seized with a hunger for culture, in all fields. Unfortunately, stuck as I am here in this unknown city, I have no possibility of satisfying this hunger, but I try to compensate for it as much as I can in the rare parentheses in San Remo. I too saw *Six Characters* with Ricci.[10] Here it was a great success: only a group of agitated youths in the balcony booed him. Amongst those agitated youths was myself. Booed that big clown Ricci, of course, not Pirandello. Pirandello is hard, I've read him again and again, and reflected on him, though I've not yet properly digested him but few people can claim to have digested him fully. But however much I continue to discover some new plus point in him, I can't quite reduce the distance that separates us. Dentone too says he's seen him but adds: philosophy is not poetry and does not provide us with dreams. Maybe he's got something. But this is a digression: what I have to tell you is something quite different, much more serious is the rebuke I have to address to you. When will you stop pronouncing in my presence phrases such as "all methods are fine as long as you succeed," or "follow the current," or "adapt to the times"? What do you mean by "adapting to the times"? Are these the ideas of a young man who ought to face life with pureness of intentions and clarity of ideals? And then you think you can claim to have understood me, to have taken me as a model? No, that deluded youth of Via Bogino, the prisoner of his dreams in Villa Meridiana does not think along those lines. A different heart beats beneath the pigeon chest of the cloud-catcher of San Giovanni.[11] Asserting oneself—he says—doesn't mean asserting a name and a person. It means asserting oneself with all that one has inside, and what he has inside, underneath that pigeon chest, is taking on more and more precise contours. And it is precisely in that that my certainty lies: this something does not represent today, it represents tomorrow. And it is this something that I want to assert, not italocalvino; italocalvino will die and won't serve any purpose any more; the something will remain and will provide good seed. As for you, stop flaunting your concepts: they are based on fragments of stars and bits of illusion. Do you know you've become boring? That's what you've become, Eugenio: Pasquale and I were talking about this just this morning underneath the colonnade in Via Roma. Every idea you have, you become a fetishist of it, you think it's the greatest and most original idea that any human mind ever had, you turn it into a philosophy of life and bore the backside off your friends. But you're also a well-meaning sort, and you'll be happy because you see the world only as you like to see it.

I accepted the praise you gave me at the start of your letter with barely restrained grunts of satisfaction. Although I am small, ugly and dirty, I am highly ambitious and at the slightest flattery I immediately start to strut like a turkey. The accusations you make later on are completely without foundation: the idea that there were thousands of youths with literary ambitions was something I knew even in the irresponsible days spent behind our school desks, and this thought has always filled me with terror: that I might be one of those people, that I might be only one of those people. And if I have decided to be merely a modest agronomist this was not just because my family's destiny forbade me the contemplative life, but also and principally because I was terrified by the thought of one day meeting a crowd of people like me, each one convinced that he and only he was a genius. Up here in Turin I know only students of agriculture, medicine, engineering, chemistry: all good guys who are thinking about getting a job, without a head full of nonsense, no mirages of glory, often without much intelligence. And as far as they are concerned, I am one of them: no one knows who italocalvino is, who he wanted or wants to be. With these people there is little talk of dreams and the future, though they too certainly think about such things. This is what I am for the people of Turin, Pigati included, but except for Roero and Maiga, of course. Only in this way can the deluded man of Via Bogino live. I don't know how you feel in the environment you say you've moved into. Apart from the fact that the literary or pseudo-literary world has always aroused a certain dislike in me, for me it would only be discouraging. But instead, living like this, I feel happy in the knowledge that I am different from those around me, that I see things with a different eye to theirs, that I know how to appreciate or suffer from the world in my own way. And I feel myself superior. I prefer being the obscure, isolated figure hoping for the victory that will see his name on everyone's lips rather than being one of the pack just following the destiny of a group. And you certainly can't say that this kind of behavior of mine is accommodating. I may be accommodating in life, I'll let myself be carried away passively in the course of my actions, but I will not prostitute my art. Eh, am I not good?

8 March: I found this letter that I had started to write yesterday evening and I reread it with interest. Dammit, what a lot of drivel I managed to write! In the end it's impossible to understand anything in it. But better that way: the less one understands the more posterity will appreciate my profundity of thought. In fact, let me say:

POSTERITY IS STUPID

Think how annoyed they'll be when they read that!

But let's change subject: I read that you go to symphony concerts. As long as you're not doing this to give yourself intellectual airs, then that's fine. I've never been able to understand what symphonic music is and how one can distinguish one piece from another (and perhaps I'll never manage to), but I've always thought that knowing how to appreciate music must be wildly satisfying. Still, don't snore too loud: the men and women in the neighboring seats may not appreciate it.

I now have to talk to you on the subject of Pasquale.[12] And I have to say that you are a really good guy, the best kind of guy in the world. The concern you showed for our mutual friend's grief moved me, already in your earlier letter, and it also moved him: I told him to write to you to reassure you. Dear Eugenio, you have to realize that even the greatest, most inconsolable grief is sooner or later followed by a feeling of resignation. The refrain "The king is dead, long live the king" is one of the laws of life. And Pasquale laughs and has fun just like in the old days, maybe more so than before in order to prevent memory from grazing him with her black wings. Just sometimes I, who know him and who can read his mind as though it were my own, notice through a barely perceptible change in his features, a blink of his eyes, a sudden silence, that he is thinking about his grief. And there is nothing I can do, nothing I can say. Sometimes when we are walking on our own, we will happen to talk of his dear dead brother, of his death, of the sad events of those days, of a thousand reflections on life and death. And we talk about it coldly, as one should talk about things that have happened and are now irreparable, and also sadly, because the death of a brother and a friend unites us in a single grief. For the rest Pasquale is as usual, cheerful and carefree, a skeptic and a poet, platonically in love with women, dogs, and cars. And if one thing can be of comfort to him amid the enormous grief, this cannot but be having felt close to him the thoughts of his friends, of his real friends. For if sincere friendship is to be considered a form of wealth, we in the "gang" can consider ourselves millionaires.

And now I have to speak to you about another friend: about Godiasco, infantry corporal, at his camp, in Pogno (province of Novara), 54th Infantry Regiment, University Battalion. This is a Godiasco who is so changed as to seem unrecognizable. His illness, his having come close (it seems) to the Final Comrade, the contact with harsh reality have all made of the fierce warmonger a mild and Arcadian dreamer. Do you recognize the Dentone of the old days in someone who now writes "I think it would be much better to make dolls not rifles, to make cars and not cannons"? He is down, weary of the life he is leading, and feels very much alone. Write to him. That will comfort him. It's your duty as a friend. It's sad to think that this year's holidays will be the last ones I'll have as a civilian. When I come back, if I come back, I'll be a grown man, worried about finding a job, without all this drivel in my head, and my youth will be at an end. Oh well, let's enjoy it! And what does that mean to me, enjoying it? Certainly not writhing in a bed with one of these sluts that hang around my little hotel, or having my reproductive organs covered by the saliva of some prostitute from a brothel. No. In that sort of thing one can see the misery of humanity, as the chaste Pigreta would say. I know how to enjoy myself watching a cloud, or waiting in the snow for a woman who'll certainly not turn up. My life with the animal Pigati offers me constant material for study and reflection on this extremely strange man and on man in general. Merry and absurd, Giannozzo eternally tortures my eardrums and those of everyone else in the hotel with his falsetto singing displays. At times he seems to me a brute, when I think about his conceptions of life, at other times a sublime philosopher when I compare him with all those narrow-minded and superficial people around us, and I admire how he tortures himself with his highly idiosyncratic line of reasoning. And I am already imagining a play about this figure in which I'll put Diogenes, the man who sees every ideal as unreachable and pointless, alongside Alexander the Great, Pascoli's Alexandros, the man who has followed ambitions and ideals and has realized their vanity and yet is still enslaved by them. I will give new poetic form to the legend and the anecdote. And already I can feel my grey cells swarming with new ideas. And springtime . . . Last year's spring brought me ideas for a dozen short stories which I wrote, a dozen I didn't write, and a score of plays and novels that I forgot or abandoned. What will the new spring bring me? I will revolutionize art and the world. Hurrah!

But Turi Vasile won't do all this!

AGRONOMUS SED FIDENS

[Handwritten; with the addressee.]

To Eugenio Scalfari–Rome

Turin—your country's birthday [21 April] '42

My dear Eugenio

I had a good long wait in San Remo, almost a month, waiting for a reply from you! It was lying in the bottom of a wardrobe in a filthy bedroom in a cheap Turin hotel: I found it there on reaching that destination yesterday evening. Moral of the story: you're an idiot, as ever! Sending me letters to Turin when you know I'm in San Remo is not an indication of great genius.

As soon as *Gioventù italica* comes out, send me the issue containing your baptism by typographer's ink. Since you'll have written a lot of nonsense, I'll have a go at you. What remains a great mystery to me is how the various *Gioventù & Progenie*, *Roma & Ischirogeno* proliferate where you are. And, what's even more important, where they get the money to give to wretches like you, whereas youths of much greater merit and more outstanding genius lie in the most abject poverty tormented by losses at poker and by exams in the Agriculture Faculty.

Talking of which, it will perhaps please you to know that, as regards the famous italcalvinian dualism, the agronomist is about to lose out, and the poet will emerge as the clear winner. My revision for the exams is still today in a deplorable state and offers no hope of recovery. The Easter holidays, which were filled with the pleasures of cheerful cycling trips along the Via Aurelia and daring but unsuccessful pursuits of Riviera Amazons, have long disappeared. The poet, on the other hand, has been more productive: he has finished the famous *Brezza di terra* (*Land Breeze*) and would now do well to go off and hide. The work is solemn rubbish and I don't think I'll have the courage to present it, not even in Florence. Rhetoric, artifice, and trite Pirandellian ideas grafted onto pompous D'Annunzian language. But also daring, warmth, enthusiasm and, what counts above all, real poetry.

In one of your previous letters you said some unpleasant things about poetry and made proclamations such as "We've got enough poets," which sounded like blasphemy to my ears. Even although poetic drama was a utopian idea, now unfashionable, my favorite authors, my only models, are those who took poetry as their only means and end: Rostand, D'Annunzio, Benelli.[13] Others who influenced my work directly or indirectly are Ibsen, whom I have intuited rather than understood, and Pirandello who cannot but influence us who come after him. For me the history of theater finishes with these names and links back directly to myself. Of the trio of laureates applauded by your clique I only know, slightly, Betti (and even then only his latest works, which according to what people say should not be taken as models) and I am completely ignorant of Lodovici and Landi.[14] I will try to fill these gaps and let you have my view. My brain is swarming with great ideas for the theater. But I don't know if I will dedicate myself to it. I must convince myself that the theater is not yet my cup of tea and that the time wasted on plays and comedies could be more satisfactorily if not more profitably dedicated to fiction where I clearly succeed better.

I am curious to see what you come up with for Florence. Dentone is now a sergeant at Rivoli, near here, so we hope to see him. That's all. I've sworn not to start another sheet

Italo

[Handwritten; with the addressee.]

To Eugenio Scalfari–Rome

[Turin, 10–11 May 1942]
REPLY TO THE LETTER, TO THE POEM THAT ACCOMPANIES THE LETTER, TO THE POSTCARD THAT FOLLOWED THE LETTER AND THE POEM

Friend,
HERE WE ARE COUNTING THE DAYS THAT SEPARATE US FROM OUR return home. Damn these professors who won't sign you off until the final days, these labs that go on through the month of May, this militia thing. Your exams start on the 15th? Ours probably much earlier, but they'll go on until the end of June. I start to salivate when I think about the juicy conversations we'll have when we're back together again.

The fact that your journal only comes out when it can could make it seem somewhat down-at-heel in the eyes of the malicious, but one shouldn't pay attention to them. When one knows that Giuseppe writes for it! Gianni said that he'll write to you because it's time you stopped boring us all with these articles, journals and all that nonsense: so you'll have his opinion at first hand. As for your article on tragedy, he made a very appropriate observation: it's like reading Lamanna . . .[15]

MAJOR NEWS

Gianni has been suspended for a month by Bregliano . . . because he was out of uniform on 23 March. There's talk of an anonymous letter to Bregliano denouncing Gianni, Silvio, and myself. Silvio is now a Gerarca in place of Vigo.

EXTRAORDINARY NEWS

Emilio, overheard in discussion by the Torinese Bregliano, has been expelled from the youknowwhat, had his whatsitcalled taken away, and been chased from the position he was in.[16] All this has no bearing on our studies and exams. Pasquale and myself want to resign. Do you realize what a victory that would be? To think that that wretch who not even a year ago was firmly on your side, has gradually become a martyr for our cause and if he goes on like this he'll end up planting a bomb!

As for Pasquale, he's in heat: he chats up a woman every day, naturally without getting anywhere. He continually urges me to wake up, to do just like him, so that with a Eugenio of an artistic bent on one side and a Pasquale of strong sexual proclivity on the other, I'll have no peace or time to draw breath.

I've read your poem. I too, if you remember, wrote a Hermetic poem in my early youth. I know that gives enormous satisfaction to the person who writes it. But whether the person who reads it shares this enthusiasm is another matter. It's too subjective, Hermeticism, do you see? And I see art as communication. The poet turns in on himself, tries to pin down what he has seen and felt, then pulls it out so that others can understand it. But I can't understand these things: these discourses about the ego and the non-ego I leave to you. Yes, I understand, there's the struggle to express the inexpressible, typical of modern art, and these are all fine things, but I . . .

Going back to your poem, there are a lot of good things in it, let's be clear about that, it could even be a masterpiece of its kind, I'm not an expert. The willing reader's effort in reading your verses and trying to reconstruct the state of mind that inspired them is rewarded by a number of clear, luminous sensations, and some images that work well. In addition the idea is fine and lofty compared to so much empty Ungarettian, Montalian, and Quasimodan absurdity. Well, I realize that I'm paying you tons of compliments whereas I had started off writing to you to tell you you'd written a lot of drivel.

Do you know what I think? That when in the school toilets we said "I see Saturday as red, Tuesday green, and Thursday how do you see it?" we were unwittingly laying down the foundations of modern art.

What is modern art but the attempt to pinpoint vague, incorporeal, inexpressible sensations? What is modern art, I would add, but the most solemn pile of nonsense that ever appeared on earth?

I'm a regular guy, I like well-defined outlines, I'm old-fashioned, bourgeois. My stories are full of facts, they have a beginning and an end. For that reason they will never be able to find success with the critics, nor occupy a place in contemporary literature. I write poetry when I have a thought that I absolutely have to bring out, I write to give vent to my feelings and I write using rhyme because I like it, tum-tetum tum-tetum tum te-tum, because I've got no ear, and poetry without rhyme or meter seems like soup without salt, and I write (mock me, you crowds! Make me a figure of public scorn!) I write . . . sonnets . . . and writing sonnets is boring, you have to find rhymes, you have to write hendecasyllables so after a while I get bored and my drawer is overflowing with unfinished short poems. I'll send you one, a finished one. You judge.

Byee

Santiago[17]

To Eugenio Scalfari
This impressionist sonnet
Like the nostalgic lament
Of a motorcyclist crocodile

TURIN NIGHTS

I've got a bottle of Nebbiolo inside me,
In my brain an iridescent cloud.
There are so many people around: and I'm alone.
There's so much noise: and I can't hear a thing.
I hear a record creaking out a song,
Between my lips an unlit fag hangs.
A slow vortex of music and smoke
Drowns out my tiny hotel room.
A couple then abandon themselves
To a weary dance and another couple on a sofa

Turn to lazy kisses. Everyone mutters a quiet
Whispered song. Meanwhile I pant for
A valley in the light of dawn,
A barking that fades away in the distance.

Italo
The eternal Crepuscular poet

Record of a drunken night
Turin, March 42
[Handwritten letter, undated, on squared paper; with the addressee. The letter and sonnet are followed by another letter to Scalfari, extending over two handwritten pages, signed "Argo IX (Pigati)"]

To Eugenio Scalfari—Rome

San Remo twenty-first December [1942]

Eugè,

Pack your suitcases straight away and come at once to San Remo. At once, do you understand? If not, we'll come down to you and boot you up the backside to make you come back. Are you not ashamed of yourself? A young man of your age and of your ambitions, who's afraid of getting on the train to reach San Remo, his spiritual home, that place where he was brought up and educated and whence he would set out again refreshed in body and soul, having discovered the best part of himself in that town? Here, where there is a Calvino, who for long months has been forced to talk of nothing but billiards, women, politics, and who can't wait for the moment when he'll be allowed to decant the product of long months of rumination into a healthy, profound, and profitable conversation. Here, where a Pasquale has become a professional player (we are not to be seen in Via Vittorio any more: those who don't play at billiards, snooker, or pool become so dehumanized they spend hours playing dice for pastries) and shouts out at every lucky shot which goes against Lanero or Garbarino or Davella: "If only Scalfari was here!" Here where—every time the talk turns to our current brutalized state—a Silvio-Dian has been moaning for months, with tears in his eyes and a choking voice: "Still, when Eugenio comes, we'll organize a good orgy . . ." SO THAT'S SETTLED THEN, THAT YOU'LL COME HERE FOR CHRISTMAS AND STOP FOOLING AROUND. You're starting to get on our nerves with this business of replying after a fortnight. I've already sent you a postcard asking about it. Silvio was surprised and a bit offended at the official tone, the "Dear Friend" stuff, in your letter. You're starting to sound like a Commendatore: you really need a bit of San Remo.

Down with Tilgher and to hell with Pirandello![18] O'Neill is primitive because he's seriously primitive, because he's American etc. Whereas we are refined types. At most we can "want to be primitive" but that's quite different and by now rather banal. At any rate there is someone (Pinelli) who has tried to paraphrase *Streetcar* changing the Puritan spirit into a pagan one.[19] Read his *The Etruscan Fathers*: it's good.

It's the same old story: you think that one can be primitive or religious just by wanting to be so. On this latter point read the excellent *Introduction to the History of Literature in our Century* by G. Sotgiu (published by Augustea). Tell me what you know and think of EVOLA and his nonsense about Aryan thought.[20] These are things that are really boring but that cannot be ignored and have a certain fascination, so much so that from reading the odd article by him I have had more than one inspiration for a play. Has this man written a book? I see him quoted very often.

I've read all the Lodovici imaginable that I can lay my hands on. There's a lot to learn as far as dialogue (he's a god there!) and the art (like Chekhov) of saying and not saying are concerned, summed up in the magnificent motto: TO NAME IS TO DESTROY—TO SUGGEST IS TO CREATE. The rest is shit, so much shit. I'm not talking about WHEEL which is still for me the masterpiece of masterpieces, even though it is—in terms of profundity and complexity—inferior to NOBODY'S WOMAN.

I've read terrible things about the Teatroguf in Rome.[21] They've stirred up everyone against them. I didn't choose a good moment to make my debut.

I'm awaiting a rapid reply about the outcome from the radio and the newspapers. Will *Atlante* be on sale here too? Will there be one of your articles in the first issue? Crepuscularism is my "commercial" style (by the way, are rich pickings envisaged?) and it has to be said that I've got a certain knack for that kind of thing. But in WIND IN THE CHIMNEY there was also (you don't understand anything) a certain profundity: illusions that are no longer considered romantically preferable to reality but as dead weights that we cannot detach ourselves from *out of habit, through a kind of vice*. All this is very important for political and religious ends, as well as for the oil-producing industry.

I've finished THE EGOIST. Very labored and not good. But very interesting. Do you want me to send it to you? Even for Vasile it is too much. But I'd like THE PEOPLE'S COMEDY to be performed first.

And in any case all you need to do is catch the train that takes you to San Remo straight away and I'll read it to you.

GOSSIP: the Visci woman says you're wearing glasses with tin [sic] frames.

Whereas when O'Neill stops wanting to be primitive he writes *The Great God Brown*.

TELL ME HOW GOOD I AM: I've read Daveglia, a high-school economics textbook.

At Turin University they're not giving the OK for transfer to other universities and I don't know how I'll manage when the courses for the Militia start and I'll be forced to attend. If I manage to change university I'll go to Perugia. I've not got a precise idea of where it is but if it's near Rome I might come and see you.

Here there is great and general discontent over the obligatory enrollment in the you-know-what of all the whatdoyoucallthems, both old and young. Silvio and Giovanni have signed up so as not to lose their youknowwhatImeans.[22] They'll remove Pasquale's. Milio and I being etc., will escape it. Gianni has not yet been called up.

An article of mine (1), a ruthless and brutal political piece (entitled "New Europe"), where I denounced all the platitudes of religion as foolish illusions, had a sentence censured where (without pressure from Scalfari) I claimed that even social unity was rubbish.

(1) for the famous GUF journal which apparently will be published in Imperia in January.

BOOK AGENT BUSINESS

Right. If you come, you'll get hold of the following books and bring them to me. If you don't come (idiot), send a registered postal package, or get one made up for you since it's too hard for you, and send them to me that way. If you can't find them but have them yourself, post them to me: I promise to return them to you using the same method. Then you can send me a note of what you spent. Hang on a second. I'm broke at present. So, if the EIAR business goes well for me, then this should be alright as well.[23] If it doesn't, wait for me to write to you. I feel I've been somewhat confused but I'm hopeless at any kind of transaction.

Right then, look at this:

T. S. Eliot, *Murder in the Cathedral*
U. Betti, *Frana allo scalo nord*
Crommelynck, *Cocu magnifique*
Joyce, *Dubliners*
All the Tilgher you can lay your hands on, preferably not on loan
at least as regards *Contemp. Theater*.
Others: give me some advice here.
Women: we no longer remember what they're like.
Read Zavattini: if I'd read him before now, I'd maybe have written
better everything I wrote in my youth.

Rosetta pees everywhere and then says it was the dog (what a liar)

Italo

PS. If you don't come, you're an idiot.

TO EUGENIO SCALFARI: A LITERARY CHRISTMAS GIFT 1942

SPACE

There are some boys
—me—
who know
a terrifying game:
thinking about infinity.

Better if my house cancels the mountains
And if the balustrade above the square
Of my garden
Flew over the city.
Catapulted out of my deck-chair
I will drown in the blue terror
Of the sky's stupid yawn.

Plunging slowly amid distant
Impassive worlds;
Feeling myself ahead behind above beneath
Weighing opaque eternities of void;
And asking the inexorable abyss
Without walls
For the salvation of the bottom of a valley
To crash down in peacefully.

To be able to stretch out to the extreme
My brain which—terrified—soars aloft
On the banks of nothing,
To manage—only for a second—
To imagine myself outside space!
Then to run: and open wide my eyes
So that things enter in by force
All of them together;
And to cry out to fill the vertigo
Of my ears.
But to know how to conserve
In all the little things
(some people call them "life")
a little bit of that terror.

***

Afterwards someone comes who closes
The world all around
And sets up unthinkable

Obstacles for my game.
Perhaps he thought he would placate my anguish?
Let us go, sad prisoners,
Our shoulders bent under curved space
And let's suffocate the crazy
Need for the infinite.

* * *

Giacomo does not know.
On his lonely hill
He is waiting for arcane shivers.[24]

Italo Calvino

WRITTEN IN SAN REMO NINETEENTH OF DECEMBER NINETEENHUNDRED42
[Handwritten; with the addressee.]

To Eugenio Scalfari—Rome

Florence, 7-3-43

Comrade,

With a February exam out of the way, I am living through days that are not very enjoyable and rather lonely, but they are intense and profitable. The free time I am left with after what is taken up by the hateful duo of "schola atque militia" I spend in large part visiting Florence like a good tourist, with the Touring Club guide in my hand. The rest of my time I divide between reading, exhibitions, lectures. Yesterday your friend Jacobbi was speaking about the necessity of tragedy,[25] but because of Militia duties I couldn't go and hear him and I was sorry about that as I would have liked to speak to him. The point is that here the National Theatre has sent out to the experimental theaters only the title of my play, plus my name and address. So if I don't sort out something myself, I'll have a long time waiting for them to get round to asking me for the script. Consequently—leaving aside the fact that I don't want to have anything more to do with *The People's Comedy*—I have to bear in mind that supposing that this year—for one reason or another—I don't manage to write anything decent, the small ray of light cast on my name would be cancelled out by time and I'd have to start again from scratch. So if you who have a copy of my script and have the chance to talk to those people can ask them to take a look at it, you'd be doing me a favor. If it's a chore (I realize that if it's a chore for me to do this for myself, doing it for someone else must be even worse), let me know and I'll send it directly to Vasile myself (let me have the address to send it to). The proposal you made about *N. O.* is flattering,[26] but given the financial nature of this flattery, I think I'll resist their advances: I'm still too ignorant to write articles and as for my output of short stories, a famous summer of overproduction has been followed by years of crisis.

I've started work on a new play: *Filippo and the Universe*. But I doubt if I'll complete it.

All the ideas currently in my head are subject to a strange phenomenon: while I work on them and perfect them continuously from the philosophical point of view, they stay rudimentary and barely sketched on the dramatic and artistic side. In my creativity thought has the upper hand over imagination.

Another thing: quit saying in that contemptuous tone that economic articles don't interest me. I study and am interested in those things as well. If you want to keep your articles to yourself, hold onto them (I imagine that—given the increase in your output—you'd spend a fortune between making copies and postage costs), but if when you come to San Remo you bring your Opera Omnia with you (I suppose you have a bulging album full of cuttings or other such things) I might perhaps deign to cast an eye over them. Meanwhile thanks for the Neo-Occidental offer if you send it to me. (Send it to San Remo.)

For want of anything better to report: the only person I've introduced myself to in Florence was Cipriano Giachetti (he was also on the jury this summer) after a horrendous lecture on the history of theater at the drama school. Very nice but he couldn't remember a damn thing.

TRAVEL PLANS: On Wednesday I'm leaving for San Remo and won't be back here until the 22nd. So you should send your next letter (which I hope will be quite soon) to San Remo, bearing in mind that when I come back to Florence I'll almost certainly have a different address which I'll let you have as soon as I know for definite what it is. Let's leave our next rendezvous till then. I'll write to you about our San Remo friends from there: the little I know about them at present is that Pasquale is getting skinned at billiards, Gianni flits to and from Turin luckily escaping the bombings, Milio is at Acqui, Birone is a recruit somewhere or other. Gianluigi tells me he has written you a long letter and that he hopes he remembers to post it.

RUMOURS DOING THE ROUNDS: that the class of '24 is being called up in April, including students. Bye. For myself outlook very bleak: I'll surely be failed at the exam to become a sergeant, since I'll be coming from the Militia training course therefore as such highly underprepared. I'll stay a corporal all my life, which perhaps will be very short, depending on whether they fling me to the front immediately or not. With that kind of future in front of me my view of the overall situation can't ever be very objective and you can imagine where my aspirations are tending.

Reading

I've read Vittorini's *Conversations*[27] and you who know me will realize at once how it has enthused me. Magnificent (apart from the injections episode) not just for the American style but also for the profundity of thought. Pity he allows himself to play the fool too much, to spin things out with the injections and the knife-grinders, so much so that at times it's like reading Simili in *Bertoldo*.[28] (Read the horrible story in the latest issue of *Tempo*.)

I've read *The Sea Plays* and *The Emperor Jones* by O'Neill (it's a rather rare edition, by Frassinelli in Turin). I've finally managed to "penetrate" the nucleus of O'Neill's theater, to discover the mechanism that determines all his plays that are in appearance so disparate and empirical: it's the contrast between self-control and instinct, between Emerson and Freud, Puritanism and life-forces, all this with a world-view that is so tragic and pessimistic that it rescues it from any accusations of Romanticism that such a position might incur. Now I feel at ease with him and can place him alongside Ibsen and Pirandello amongst the great dialectical dramatists. (Just think, I even manage to appreciate *Mourning Becomes Electra*.)

Another good book you recommended to me and that I've now read is the one by Huizinga.[29] Magnificent in the negative, critical part; puerile, utopian, contradictory in the positive, constructive part with the usual nonsense: he even manages to identify the return to reason with a return to faith. My curiosity was aroused by his critique of Existentialism, so I decided to deepen my knowledge of the subject and got through Jaspers and Abbagnano (in Bompiani's "Idee Nuove" series), very interesting, especially the former.[30] But it's an Existentialism that has nothing to do with the one that Huizinga meant or the one we were familiar with.

Now I'm reading Burzio, *Il demiurgo e la crisi occidentale* (*The Demiurge and the Crisis of the West*), very good though a bit mad. Read it (published by Bompiani, in the "Panorama del nostro tempo" series).

See if you can find in Rome these two plays by Andreyev: *The Life of Man* and *To the Stars*: I can't find them here.

Dammit: you're not going to complain now that nobody writes to you!

Italo

[Handwritten; with the addressee.]

To Eugenio Scalfari—Rome

San Remo. 19 March 1943

Now don't *you* start getting me angry as well: I ask you, the one time the Easter holidays are from 20 April to 10 May, why do you need to come to San Remo at the beginning of April? I'm still in Florence for a month, 20 March till 20 April. Then permanently in San Remo until the exams. It seems to me that if you have no engagements you can choose for your San Remo stay a period which coincides at least for a few days with my time there. Still, who gives a damn? You're not so handsome that I'm desperate to see you! Before I forget: Addressus Florentinus:- c/o De Ponti, 11 Via de' Cerchi—and stop writing "I'll send you this, I'll send you that as well" and then you send me nothing.

I, on the other hand, am sending you a sample of my new experiments in fiction. (It's not stuff for *N. O.* but maybe for *R. F.* and the like.)[31] It's a vision of humanity sunk to the lowest level of its downward curve, humanity as an ant-hill, for whom only a latent and confused memory remains of its ancient individuality. It's also rubbish. If you don't like it or don't want to do anything with it, send it back to me.

EDMONDO that is to say "De Amicis" (in other words, "About Our Friends": ha ha, yes, that's a really good one!). Pasquale: yesterday finally found out from Gianni, his special envoy in Turin, that his leave application form from the Polytechnic has not been lost, he'll apply soon to enroll in the first year of agriculture; at present he's doing nothing but silently loving Maria Camilla. Gianni: makes little trips to Turin without ever running into an alarm. Giovanni: a bersagliere in Gradisca, they're giving him a helluva you know what. Milio: he's at Acqui for a bit, San Remo for a bit, liked *Labbra serrate* (*Sealed Lips*). Silvio: organizing the *Littoriali del lavoro*.[32] Dentone: second-lieutenant in Salerno. Me: fine thanks, and you?

Then there's Chekhov. You say he's not relevant and I get mad. Because Chekhov's theater is the theater of modernist positivism, the tragic conception of a pointless universe, people whose desperate "Why?"s are left without an answer, who try to disguise the pointlessness of existence in fictitious ideals. This is my (and your) theater. And the style of his work, this style that makes it almost unperformable and soporific, that too is part of this modernism that is taken to its ultimate consequences and which leads precisely to a squalid realism in its extreme objectivity: impressionism. Beyond this limit it is impossible to go: there will be reactions, forms of idealism in philosophy, of expressionism in art, but they'll all be palliatives, things built in the void; the torment of Chekhov's characters is immanent in our thought because it has never been solved.

Now you get excited and you tell me I have to write an article for *Nuovo Occidente*. I have to say that it's a journal that intimidates me a bit, I don't know, it's not like a university review where you can stick in all the baloney that springs to mind. But it's not beyond possibility that I'll write the article, and precisely on this theme of relevance. For instance: *Little Eyolf*, which was performed at the Quirino some time ago (ah, what a paradise for the theater Rome is; in Florence there's a dearth that is quite frightening), the top critics saying that it is not relevant today. For God's sake, what on earth is relevant then about Ibsen? *A Doll's House* perhaps? Man's aspiration towards blending in with the absolute, abandoning himself to the forces of nature, in contrast with the thought of death and of our mortality pushing us towards activity, social duties, responsibilities. You will understand that if someone who is composing a work on this same topic (*Filippo and the Universe*), a work that by chance (I thought of it before reading Ibsen's play) also contains analogies with *Little Eyolf* in the denouement, if that person hears people claim that this is not a relevant theme, he will say: Nonsense! Hey, come on, are you mad?

These days I'm crazy for philosophy. You must be joking if you think I'm revising Lamanna and Bignami. Recently I've read Rensi's *Apologia dell'ateismo* (*Apologia for Atheism*) but it didn't enthuse me. Maybe because I'd just finished reading Rainer Maria Rilke and the leap was a bit too brusque. And then if you are the kind of person that gets enthused by our "intelligence," when you read the Notebook of my Thoughts, you'll kiss my feet and call me "Caliph"!

Good News: tomorrow I'll buy a new pen, which is good for me who has to write—and for you who have to read—my letters.

Sad Refrain: if they boo Chiavarelli, what on earth will they do to me?[33]

Little Cautious Question, in the Pacchiaudi Style:[34] Erm, this Chiavarelli, can you tell me, is he better, ehm, than me . . . ?

Since your trip to Florence is probably off, I'll wait for you. If I have some money left on my return I'd come down to Rome: it would be handy also from the point of view of the trains, but in any case I'm sure I'll have none left, and if I do, I'd better buy some books.

Italo

[Handwritten; with the addressee.]

To Eugenio Scalfari—Rome

Today is Florence
I'm in Fourth
And it is April
The time is 1943

IT IS NOT THAT I ENJOY WRITING TO YOU; NOR THAT I HAVE anything interesting to say to you; but I like getting mail, all alone in the world as I am, and in any case I always hope that you have something interesting to tell me. Consequently I'm replying without delay so that you feel obliged to do likewise. First of all let me congratulate you on youknowwhat.[35] The day is not far off when this will be considered a merit on your part. Events are moving by the hour.

I can't be in San Remo before the 20th or 21st for Militia reasons. I've got the last assembly on the 19th and my absences are now too many (between my move and leave etc., I've missed nearly two months) to allow me to miss anything else. At any rate we'll have ten days in which to talk. If that's not enough, we can do round-the-clock discussion with short pauses for meals and sleep and if it's really bad we can both speak at the same time. Make a little plan of the conversations you want to have, divided up into days and give vent to your frustrations by playing billiards until I arrive.

Thank you for finding a place for the short stories.[36] If they are published, send me a copy at the double. More than by Vittorini, they are inspired by a writer who is in my opinion much better: Zavattini. On Gigliozzi: they tell me that at the EIAR they don't even read what is submitted unless it comes with a recommendation.[37] Thought so. Let me explain. On second thoughts, no, it doesn't matter, it was just something that came into my head, if he can't do anything about it, never mind. Whereas if you pester Vasile you'll be doing me a favor, otherwise what am I wasting my time winning competitions for? Maybe tell him that I am one of those people who liked *Arsura*, that I liked the problem of existentialism in it with all that business about limitation as the condition of existence, really serious stuff which I've found even in the Ibsen of *Peer Gynt*. Wow! (At this point a Wow! was just the right word.)

Another thing: I'm sorry to appear ungrateful toward you, but on this point I am not giving in: *I'm for Federico*. Federico Fellini is one of the nicest humorists that I know, and I cannot tolerate him being betrayed.[38] I was disappointed to learn that he is not yet married: his Crepuscular cartoons on the married life of Cico and Pallina had the flavor of autobiographical truth. What for you is an ephemeral source of fun, is for him a source of artistic inspiration, which in turn will be a source of comfort for hundreds of unfortunate people who seek solace in the pages of a comic paper. In any case, if you're head over heels, lucky you. I recall the few moments of my life when I was lucky in love as moments when life seemed clear and sunny to me, devoid of problems and uncertainties. Love is a great explanation of life, it gives you the illusion (and why say illusion anyway?) of being close to understanding the reason for your existence in the middle of the universe. As for me, for some time now women have completely disappeared from my horizon. The ship's binoculars are unable to focus on any woman. And yes I have never seen anywhere such beautiful girls as in Florence. (All insinuations about the efficiency of the ship's binoculars are banned.)

MY BUSINESS: I've met Gianozzi, fellow member of the Militia and organizer of the new theater for Florence's GUF as well as theater critic of *Rivoluzione*. A good guy, of moderate tendencies, so much so that he welcomes even Gherardi and Viola in his repertoire. I'll get him to read *People* even though I'm aware that it is not a suitable work for his theater.

In the last few days I've finished *Filippo e l'universo* and I'm quite pleased with it. Who knows, I might be able to finish in time for this summer's competition. Now I ought to begin studying for the exams and in July I'll have to go to camp (for a month!). By August I'd like to have finished another work as well for the competition: but I'll be thankful just to complete this one. Can you tell me what other rubbish I can write to finish this page?

Shall I write that Bragaglia is the greatest waster in the world, that O'Neill's *Gold* is a mess of what could be a fine one-act sea play, that *Days without End* is an interesting attempt by a bourgeois O'Neill to use a biological background, that Mosca in *Piccoli traguardi* (*Modest Targets*) is the usual stuff, that his *Sommossa* (*Revolt*) is a very daring satire,[39] that I liked Betti's *Diluvio* (*Flood*) a lot when I read it, that my grandmother's name is Maddalena, she's ninety years old and for her age she's surviving quite well, naturally she's got her aches and pains but what do you expect, at her age not many people can say that they've nothing to complain about, isn't that right?

Italo

What's your address in San Remo: Via Giusti or Val del Ponte?
[Handwritten; with the addressee. On the first page an ink stain is used by Calvino as the center of the emblem of the Consociazione Turistica Italiana (CTI), now the Touring Club Italiano.]

To Eugenio Scalfari, Rome

SAN REMO 5-6-43

Explain please,
WHAT IS ALL THIS NONSENSE YOU'RE GIVING ME ABOUT PURE and impure art? As though we didn't know each other well enough and had never discussed the subject. As though you didn't know who Italocalvino is, what he wants, what he has to say. Forget any remorse: my art has been and always will be social while trying to remain art as far as possible, just as in Ungaretti's poetry there is always an immanent ethic even when at his most lyrical: "*tonda quel tanto che mi dà tormento*" (just round enough to torment me).[40] The funny thing is that just about a year ago you were writing me passionate letters on the necessity of a social nature in art and I was replying with even more heated letters on God knows what. We really have to burn this correspondence.

In any case, I'm fed up writing stories. I'm beginning to develop a style, which is maybe a good sign: after having imitated others so much, I can now afford to imitate myself a bit. At any rate these that I am enclosing are the last ones. (One of them I haven't time to type and maybe it's not worth it anyway.) Do what you want with them, maybe even rip them up. Be careful with the one about the game of tip-cat.[41] I've sent it to you anyway but I didn't think it could be published. Watch out because only Garroni could find it in conformity with the legally constituted authorities. If it turns out not to be publishable, don't give the other one either to *N. O.*, it's not worth it just for one story, maybe give it to Gigliozzi, never mind about payment. And what do you mean that its form is slack? Do you know how much I polished it, word by word, to get that unsophisticated, rough and ready style?

A few days ago I read, by chance, an issue of *Commercio*. It's a good journal, full of interesting articles, the cleverest journal you've ever written for.

I don't understand a damn thing in what you say about fever.

I saw *Le Quai des brumes* (Port of shadows) some time ago and we even discussed it.

All in all, your letter was full of nonsense.

My "Acqueforti di Liguria" (Etchings of Liguria) will probably come out—according to what Ronchi has written (I'm in regular correspondence with him)—in an issue of *Patt.* that will be devoted to Ligurian literature.[42]

I'm about to try something irresponsible: sit 4 exams without having studied for any of them. Now I'm studying economics like any ordinary scalfari.

You don't say anything in your letter about when you're coming to San Remo. From the 8th to the 19th I'll be in Florence: Alb[ergo] del Parco, Via Solferino 35. If you leave Rome on the evening of the 19th we can travel some of the way together. Write to me if you're doing this and I'll look out for you.

Here days that are perfect for bathing alternate with cloudy days. We're all shit-scared of the exams. Pasquale has gone to the country and won't be back till July. A new gang is forming whose leaders are Verdun and Lanero. I think they want to collaborate with us. But it won't work. Marisa is solidly chained to her books. Rosetta goes out on her own or with a man. My grandmother is like all old women.

Get in touch soon.

If not, see you in August.

WRITE.

the maestro

[Handwritten; with the addressee.]

To Eugenio Scalfari—Rome

[San Remo, 12–13 September 1943]

Windy Evening

Windy evening. I roam through the rooms
Of my house full of windows.
Outside is the moan and outline of hobby-horses,
Of beaten wings of restless palms.
The rush of air moves through the leaves
And the walls. Does the house sit firm on its ancient
Foundations or rock about on top of its stems
As on obedient pilasters?
Windy evening. I roam through the rooms
Full of mirrors. Sharply delineated images
Silently, never meeting, pursue me.
The chaos of pages closes the open book.
A turn of a handle
Silences the upheaval of music and phrases.
It doesn't calm me or the world.
The torment that shakes and fans
The leaves and me cannot move them from the trunk.
It groans down at the stump. And the singing of a foreign
Anthem goes by in a distant road.
Windy evening. I roam through the rooms
Full of walls, safe from the ceaseless worry
From the death-rattle that stirs
Outside from the throats of trees and houses.
The rising and collapsing of a curtain,
A shutter banging: the wind, the wind!

written the first night
of the curfew imposed
by the Germans. San Remo
between the 12th and 13th September 1943[43]

To Eugenio
Italo

[Handwritten; with the addressee.]

To His Parents—San Remo

[September 1944]

Dearest Mum and Dad,
I'm well. Flori is fine too.[44] We're not far away. Hope to be back soon. Lots of love,

Italo

[Handwritten message from hiding, written on a little piece of square paper; in the Calvino Archive.]

To Eugenio Scalfari—Rome

San Remo 6–7–45

Dear Eugenio,
I was beginning to think you were dead since I had not received any reply to the various missives I sent you, from the Liberation onward, then the other day I finally got your postcard. We're all alive; you "down there" will never be able to understand what this period has been like for us, and how lucky we must consider anyone who has come through it. I have a right to say this more than anyone else, for my life in this last year has been a whirlwind of adventures: I've been a partisan all this time, I've been through an unspeakable series of dangers and discomforts; I've experienced prison and escape, been several times on the point of dying. But I'm happy with everything I've done, with the wealth of experiences that I have amassed, in fact I'd have liked to have done more. In a previous letter I explained my adventures in detail; I'm sorry that that one went missing. Now I'm involved in journalism and politics. I'm a Communist, fully convinced and dedicated to my cause. Tomorrow I'm going to Turin to finalize my collaboration with a weekly up there. But I'm coming back soon and I'll be happy to see you. I imagined you'd be a big shot in the Par-

tito d'Azione or something similar, but I learn with horror that you've spent this whole period in pastoral idylls. All our old friends are still alive. None of them covered themselves in glory, apart from Gianni who has to his credit a year spent in the mountains where he was commissar of a Garibaldini detachment. Now he's extremely busy criticizing everything and everyone: previously he had just one party to speak ill of, now he's got five or six to badmouth! Silvio was stuck for the whole period in a hospital, Pasquale—who's just come back—in his castle. Milio was organizing Badogliani troops last summer. The "gang" is just a memory from bygone days.

San Remo is in a real mess from the constant naval and aerial bombardments. Yesterday and today I went to your house, but nobody's answering. On the door is written "Minaglia." From the outside it looks badly damaged but not destroyed.

Say hello to your parents: mine send their best to you. They too have been through quite a lot: each of them was arrested for a month and held as hostage; my father was on the point of being shot before my mother's eyes.

See you soon and write to me.

Italo

[Handwritten; with the addressee. Previously published in "Autoritratto: Autoritratto di un artista da giovane (Self-portrait: Self-portrait of the artist as a young man)," *Mercurio*, Weekly Supplement of *la Repubblica*, 59 (11 March 1989).]

1946–1950

To Silvio Micheli—Viareggio

Tu[rin] 8–11–46

Dear Micheli

I've read the riot act to loads of people,[1] especially that idiot Nicosia, because nobody told me when you were up here.[2] I'd like to have seen you personally, and discuss things with you and argue with you, for God's sake, and maybe even fought with you (!) because I believe that the two of us together will end up hitting each other. If you come again to Turin, *demand* that they run me to ground and let me know you're here.

I know you get through tons of writing a day, that you write novels with plots, with incest-plots, crime-plots, hot novels, lukewarm novels, novels with hot and cold running water.

This fills me with envy because I'm still here just wasting time. I was hoping to put together a small book of short stories, all nice and neat and taut, but Pavese said no, that short stories don't sell, that I have to do a novel.[3] At present I don't feel that great necessity to write a novel: I could write short stories for the rest of my life. Stories that are nice and spare, that you can finish off as soon as you start them, you write them and read them without drawing breath, rounded and perfect like so many eggs, stories that if you add or remove a single word the whole thing goes to pieces. A novel, on the other hand, always has some dead moments, bits where you are linking one section to another, characters that you don't feel are truly rounded. The novel requires a different approach, one that is more relaxed, not all holding your breath with clenched teeth the way I write. I write biting my nails. Do you write biting your nails? Writers divide into those who write biting their nails and those who don't. Some writers write licking their finger.

Now you mustn't think that I don't have any ideas for novels in my head. I've got ideas for ten novels in my head. But with every idea I have, I already foresee the wrong novels I would write, because I also have critical ideas in my head, I've got a full *theory of the perfect novel* and that's what stumps me. That idiot imbecile Nicosia is writing a good novel. On the Sicilian separatists, it'll be a success, and in addition he has a style that is decisive and new. Natalia too is writing a novel.[4] Pavese is writing a novel as well.[5] I've started a novel too: I wrote four pages in a week.[6] Weeks go by in which I can't even add a comma, whole days are spent wondering whether in that sentence "going up" is better than "ascending."

Plus I've got to write articles which really kills me. They want articles all over the place and I write them because it takes half an hour to write an article. To *write* an article not to *do* an article. To do an article you have to read books, find ideas, roll up your sleeves. In addition I'm the kind of guy who goes from the maximum of superficiality to the maximum of fussiness in a trice. For instance, I want to cite a certain name in a particular sentence in a particular article. Let's say: Chesterton. Because it sounds good at that point. Chesterton and an adjective. "Olympian like Chesterton." Or "tormented like Chesterton." But I've never read a line of Chesterton: I don't know whether he's Olympian or tormented, whether he has anything to do with what I'm writing. So what do I do? I roll up my sleeves and start looking until I find Chesterton's works. And I read them. All Chesterton's works. And I read them. And everything that's been written about Chesterton. And I read that too. So I can write in that particular sentence: "Olympian or tormented or cataleptic or schizophrenic . . . like Chesterton." That's it. Meantime two weeks have gone by for three words.

In addition I'm also doing features for weeklies like *Omnibus*. Features with photographs. Something that's really complicated for me: liaising with the photographer, dealing with people, interviewing, travelling around, making enquiries. A terrible job for me since I'm above all a lazy and shy person. But necessary because it forces me to see people, study human beings and their problems, get to know a slice of real life. Now I have to do one on the Salvation Army, and one on clandestine emigration.[7] Every time I've had to do journalistic investigations I've cursed, but later I discovered that it had helped me enormously with writing fiction. It's the one thing that can save me from becoming an academic writer.

Just like that![8]

"You grabbed a bunch o' reeds, full o' spray as well as rooted, drained and—why not?—burnt sepals. Don't you hear rubbish? I don't."

Don't write like that again!

But the publisher Tatra is really "waik and febill" because he's not paid me for "Fear on the Footpath."[9]

You'll have seen my Rangoni piece, horribly cut just when I was trying to ingeniously give a diplomatic shape to my hatchet job.[10] In any case it's rubbish. Why do you like the people of Viareggio so much? I piss on the people of San Remo.

Ciao and write to me,

Calvino

35 Via XX settembre, Turin
[Handwritten; in the Archivio del Novecento, Faculty of Letters, University of Rome "La Sapienza."]

To Marcello Venturi—Fornovo Di Taro (Parma)[11]

San Remo, 19/1/47

Dear Marcello,

I already sent you *l'Unità* with my article about you and me as soon as it came out, and I've now resent it, this time in an envelope, as soon as I got your letter. I hope that this time it's arrived.

I'm leaving for Turin tomorrow. My address in Turin is: 35 Via XX settembre.

Thanks for the information about the Premio Mondadori. It's very difficult to get the only person who can really tell me about it, Ferrata, to write.[12] I had already thought of Del Buono as one of the favorites amongst the likely candidates. Now in my view various people like Gotta, Brocchi, Moretti, will be in the final jury to select the winner, not in the committee that selects the three short-listed candidates. Have you got any precise information about this? My novel is a rather bitter mouthful to swallow for conservative, right-thinking palates, but it's not something that can be passed over in silence, and I think they'll be forced to include it amongst the three short-listed titles, or to explain why they've excluded it.[13] Naturally just to have it published would be more than enough for me. I'll get Pavese to read it and see if he'll make me some sort of proposal on behalf of Einaudi. Deep down I'd be much happier if it came out with Einaudi, and this only for sentimental reasons, since apart from the obvious economic advantages, political tactics also would suggest I give it to Mondadori. But none of this is important: the important thing is that I'm sure I've written *a novel*, a novel which, apart from a few dead moments here and there, runs confidently from the first page to the last.

Vittorini has written to me, saying he really liked one of my stories, "The Crow Comes Last,"[14] though I can't work out where he read it. Maybe in the Milan edition of *l'Unità*, and in that case you'll have read it too. This was a story that I considered amongst my more second-division tales: but Vittorini is totally enthusiastic because it is "all narrated." We're having an argument in our letters, Vittorini and I, because I've got this fad for essay-like stories (I got fed up with the usual short story ending with a final gunshot) and V. says I'm not cut out for them. I suggested to Vittorini the idea of doing a collection of *Politecnico* writers in the series *Politecnico-Biblioteca*, with different stories by each of us.[15] He agrees but says he also had in mind a selection from all of *Politecnico*, and wonders whether to do one or the other, or both. I think that doing a selection from all of *P.* is tantamount to saying the journal's dead, and this would be like exhuming it; I think it's more important to continue publishing *Politecnico*. I was a great fan of *Politecnico* despite all its faults; the end of the journal was a great source of sadness for me.

Dear Marcello, you say that you are wasting your energy when you write. This is serious. Writing is always useful. If you write things that are wrong (and of course if you notice they're wrong), you learn to avoid those mistakes. If you write things that are good, they'll stay as good things and if you publish them today or in five years' time it makes no difference (I'm not saying more than five years because otherwise they could be out of date). But if we think that we are writing things that won't even last five years . . . Well, in any case something that is genuinely good can never be overtaken by anyone, it stays unique throughout the course of time. The important thing is to keep at it, keep banging your head against the wall—I'm still making mistakes with two stories out of every three—and to read well those few authors who are really important (there can't be more than twenty or thirty of them), but also to live as well, to observe, and the rest will come on its own.

Then you ask me whether the fact that prizes are awarded in advance makes you lose the desire to write. But these things have always happened, and one day it could happen to you too, and in any case Mondadori is the most unpleasant publisher in Italy, and in addition our time will come. Despite all that you still want to complain: in a year you have gone from being a completely unknown writer—like me—to becoming one of the most well-known and well-published names of your generation. What more could you want? If we were able to continue at this rate we'd be up there with Piovene and Moravia.[16] But it's better if we slow down, since success that comes too early comes at a price.

The fact is that apart from the various editions of *l'Unità*, nobody knows where the hell to write. I fought with *Omnibus* over a low trick they pulled on me (in which my eternal rival Del Buono was involved!). I contribute also to *Agorà*, a rich Christian-Democratish journal in Turin which publishes me with great fanfares.[17] Maybe I'll get as far as *Mercurio*, the only journal able to survive in Rome against the awful *La Fiera*. OK, that's what the journal would like, but if a Communist does a good piece for *La Fiera*, he puts on a good show all the same in spite of *La Fiera*. I would advise you to take part in the contest: you'll have seen that they didn't award the fiction prize the last time they held the competition because there was no entry good enough. But send in something very good, something that will maybe *épater le bourgeois*.

This is a wonderful town where you can still bathe at this time of year, and there are pigeon-shoots, a sport not for the rich but for the very rich (they calculate that someone who comes pigeon-shooting spends a minimum of 20 thousand lire a day). If I was able to use the bourgeoisie as subject matter for fiction, there would be a lot to inspire me here. But I've never been able to create a bourgeois character: perhaps because I don't even hate them, they're simply from another world that is astronomically distant from me. In Turin it's all cold and hunger but there are people that are more intelligent and a work rhythm that gives me more satisfaction.

Ciao, Marcello, and write to me.

Your Calvino

[Handwritten; in the Archivio del Novecento, Faculty of Letters, University of Rome "La Sapienza."]

To Marcello Venturi—Fornovo Di Taro (Parma)

Tu[rin] 23–4–47

Dear Marcello,

It's been some time since I last wrote to you so I'll try to make amends now. Right then: you wrote saying you had been unwell; I hope you're now fully recovered. I'm in Turin for just a few days, so I can't invite you to come here as planned, let's see if we can manage it in May: when I get back I'll write to you again.

So, then, my novel will be published by Einaudi "immediately," in other words before the end of '47. Just as well because Ferrata did a hatchet job on it for M.[18] He wrote me a letter with a total demolition of my work, defining it as lacking in invention, too much "tranche de vie," and too full of slang. All criticisms which don't convince me at all; I can well understand that my novel is to be torn apart but the reasons put forward by F. seem distinctly far-fetched to me. In any case I'm happier with things the way they are: you know that I had already repented of my decision to send it to the Mond. Pr. (which by the way I don't know who won).[19]

I've read two of your stories recently: "La mia famiglia (My Family)" and "È passata la guerra (The War Passed By)," both of them good. You already possess a good level of polished language and of narrative know-how, a very precious and rare achievement. What you lack most is the development of your themes, something new to say, but this will come to you as you mature and you mustn't force it.

Man, you really must get away from Fornovo and come to a city that could allow you to have encounters that are more formative from every point of view. There is a job going that I think you could do and that would allow you to live away from there: to be the producer of ADEL (Amici del Libro). This is a firm that sells books paid for by installments (Einaudi books mostly, but also those of other publishers): it's a question of going round factories and offices and persuading people to buy books they pay for in installments and later going back to pick up the payments and giving other books. You get paid on commission and there's a lot of money to be made, that's what everyone tells me. (I'm a bit lazy, I still have to study quite a bit, I'm a bit of a nomad and I've not yet got into it; but I believe I would like the work too, because it allows you to speak with lots of people and to get into lots of different environments.) If you like, you could come here to Turin, or to Genoa where the agency is run by my very dear friend Nicosia. Either that or you could do it near where you live, where I don't think ADEL exists yet, and go round the whole of that area. If you fancy it, write to me and I'll give you further particulars.

Natalia Ginzburg told me that she was going to write to you and I told her to send you some books. I suggested she send you Sherwood Anderson, *A Story-Teller's Story* and *Black Boy* by Richard Wright. I'm telling you, the Anderson book is really great and you'll like it as much as I did, because it's the story of a narrator who has a tremendous love for our wretched job, for the techniques of the job. And something else I like (I'm going to write an article on this) is a literature coming to life from a soil that is not yet literary but rather low-level journalistic writing, a more commercial literary output. And this too is a bit like us, we who still have so much enthusiasm for the adventure yarn, the "world of the novel."

Dear Marcello, do you know about the Festival of Youth in Prague this summer? Do you know there's also a competition run by the FDG for the best short story?[20] Make sure you get involved, and get them to send you there. I'm going to try everything to get to Prague with the Turin FDG delegation, or via the competition, and I'll do coverage for *l'Unità*. If you come, we'll do it together.

In one of your letters you asked if Nazahariand or whatever the hell he's called had written to me.[21] Yes, he wrote me a hilarious letter talking about the Omnipotent and the infinite, along with a letter from that awful Capasso.[22] I wrote: "Dear Brother, You speak to me of the hidden divinity but I need to know if your journal pays. May the Omnipotent be praised. Yours etc." He replied saying the journal doesn't pay, which is what I knew already, and I told him to go to hell. The hidden hell, of course.

OK, then, Marcello, apply yourself, study, work hard. You'll see, we'll make it. If I think that only two years ago I was still a totally louse-infested, down-at-heel partisan, I can't complain about the progress I've made. And you must feel the same, I believe. And I'm happy most of all because with this job I've been able to prolong some of the drive of the previous one, the louse-ridden, down-at-heel existence, which in any case has now been lost everywhere.

OK, ciao, write to me

Italo

Write to me in San Remo
[Handwritten; in the Archivio del Novecento, Faculty of Letters, University of Rome "La Sapienza."]

To Silvio Micheli—Viareggio

Tu[rin] 20-6-47

Dear Old Silvio,
It's been a long time since we last wrote. I've not yet read *Unfiglielladisse* (*ASonSheSaid*), except the odd furtive glance at the proofs on Natalia's desk. As soon as it comes out, I'll do you the usual lengthy review.[23]

As for my *Sentierodeinididiragno* (*Pathtothespidersnests*), nobody knows when it'll come out: the boss refused to commit to a date on the contract, says it will go to the printers in August and that it could come out as easily in October 1947 as in March '48. But I hope it appears before Christmas and I think Giulio's waiting for some other N. C. to have them both come out together, so I'm really counting on your *Poverocane*.[24]

Meantime I've got the satisfaction of having two publishers queuing up outside my door. Mondadori, having awarded its prize to three of its acolytes, asked if they could publish my book and, realizing they were too late, said they are ready to publish any future novel of mine. Unfortunately I've not been able to persuade them to publish my short stories, which no publisher wants these days. And I've now got a nice volume, *The Crow Comes Last*, containing about twenty stories which I want to publish, and which I'll end up giving to some minor publisher since in three or four years' time I'll have others ready so what am I keeping these for?

Meanwhile I've entered the Premio Riccione with *The Path*, but I haven't the slightest idea who's on the jury.[25] Do you know anything?

Opinions on my novel from those who've read it up till now vary enormously: according to Pavese it's very good, also according to Natalia, for Ferrata it's a mistake, lacking imagination, full of slang, full of conventions and God knows what else, according to Vittorini it's so-so, for Balbo it's the first Marxist novel, and as far as my parents are concerned it's a collection of filth and they can't understand how their son managed to write such a thing.

Meanwhile I've got six new novels in my head. But now I'm busy since I've got to patch together my graduating thesis which I'll hand in by October, but as soon as I've finished it, I'll write the novels.

What about you: what are you doing? *Via del confino* (*The Road to Exile*)?

I must tell you that Nicosia is in Genoa, cursing because he has to work so hard and earn so little. Pavese is studying ethnology and reading Aeschylus in Greek. Natalia is agonizing because she can't write novels about society. Alfonso Gatto is in Turin now between one Giro d'Italia and another and is writing lapidary poems.[26] Vallone is presenting classical dance spectacles.[27] *Ça c'est Turin.*

As for me, I shall shortly be going away from here to get my belly in the sun. In August I'm going to Prague for two weeks. This autumn I'll begin working and earning my keep, I'm not exactly sure how yet. This year with my obsession for staying in Turin I've tightened my belt so much that if I've not got consumption now I'll never have it.

Ciao, and write to me at length about yourself. If you write immediately, send it to Turin, if in a week's time, send it to San Remo. But the post always gets to me in the end. Warmest regards,

Calvino

[Handwritten; in the Archivio del Novecento, Faculty of Letters, University of Rome "La Sapienza."]

To Elio Vittorini—Milan

Turin, 12 December 1947

Dear Vittorini,

I'm sending you a short note on Hemingway which I think contains some things that have not yet been said about him.[28] All things which should be said less superficially, I know, and I've been meaning for some time now to write a major essay that should take as its starting point the central point of this piece, where it speaks about Malraux and Koestler. However, it would be something more wide-ranging, taking in Sartre as well, and maybe you too, it would go further back to the point when writers began to pose the problem of man's responsibility in the face of history, today's real problem. And it would clarify as it went down this route the meanings of the terms "crisis" and "decadence" and "revolution," articulating in the end a *morality within commitment*, a *freedom within responsibility*, since these seem to me to be the only morality and freedom possible.

But these are all things that I still need to chew over for who knows how long. Just as I need to chew over for a long time the things I'd like to say if I intervened in your Great Polemic:[29] I'd need to define clearly all these terms such as "decadence" and "avant-garde." But I also believe that I'd end up being closer to Balbo's position than to yours.[30] We all have a common motive, however in leaping forward we don't want to break our arms or legs, but to acquire new ones. The problem is to make ourselves grow new arms and legs by transforming them. But maybe you believe you can still jump on your old ones.

You must have several of my short stories. Try to write to me about them even if you've binned them.

Warmest regards.

[Typed copy; in the Einaudi Archive, Turin. Also in *ILDA*, p. 7.]

To Silvio Micheli—Viareggio

Turin, 11–6–48

Dear Micheli,

Sorry if it's been a long time since I wrote to you. When you're working you get buried, drowned under things. You've no more friends nor art. Only when you've an evening or afternoon free can you roam the streets or court a girl. That's all. In short, working is pointless. I mean, from the point of view of education. But it's essential. I cannot—and I don't want to—live the writer's life, that is to say write for a living. The novel I was writing, which for months and months had sucked all my blood (because, stubborn as I am, I was determined to finish it even though I no longer felt it was going anywhere), is dead, awful, full of wonderful clever things but desperately bad, forced, it'll never work and I *must* not finish it.[31] And I must not write for some time now otherwise I'd make more mistakes. I hope that Einaudi will publish my short stories eventually, they're the only thing I believe in and which I believe are useful.

As for you, I've asked *l'Unità* to send you the newspaper again as if you were a subscriber, but don't count on it: the managing director is as miserly with free gifts as he is with his own blood, and if he does send it you for a few days, he'll cut it off again. Vallone is a young actor in a film by De Santis on the rice-workers and I think he'll do well.[32] I don't know anything about your "malign paradises":[33] I've also got little time to hang around Einaudi. I'd take some of your short stories, but as long as they're genuine stories, not fragments of a novel and without so many difficult words and swear-words.[34] I mean it because here I'm heavily criticized by all the other editors who can't stand me, and if I print stuff that is open to criticism then I've got real problems. It'll pay 2,000–2,500 lire. Just think that I don't get a cent for contributing to the paper because I've got a salary and when all's said and done I'm actually more in debt than before.

Ciao, dear Silvio, get in touch. Yours,

Calvino

[Handwritten on headed paper of the Turin edition of *l'Unità*; in the Archivio del Novecento, Faculty of Letters, University of Rome "La Sapienza."]

To Silvio Micheli—Viareggio

Turin, 11 Oct. 48

Dear Silvio,

I'm pleased we're arguing. It's a healthy symptom, for goodness' sake! It means there's life and movement and dialectic. Your story's been accepted and we're waiting for others. But you have to understand the needs of the newspaper page, which is not a page of avant-garde literature but a people's page which has to be able to be read by the worker just as much as by the housewife and the rural laborers. I do my utmost to obey this criterion, also because I believe it is not a limitation but has the potential to help us grow. I understand that at times we also have to write pages of "research," and so the question then is where to publish them? This is a real problem because "research" journals in this sense don't exist in Italy today. But a daily is a daily. And you know that, because you spent years on one before me, and I've been doing it for six months now and I already feel I can't take any more of it. I spent a lovely few days at Stresa with Hemingway, along with Natalia and Giulio Einaudi. And I got a real nostalgia for "being a writer." Bah! Ciao.

Calvino

[Handwritten on headed paper of the Turin edition of *l'Unità*; in the Archivio del Novecento, Faculty of Letters, University of Rome "La Sapienza."]

To Franco Venturi—Moscow

Turin 26-1-49

Dear Venturi,

Thank you for your letter and for the piece of news that gave me much pleasure, especially since it proves that in the USSR they're interested to a certain extent in what's being published in Italy.[35] Every week I see, or rather show to those who can read Russian, *Ogonëk*, but the publication of my story wasn't mentioned; now I've also received the issue in question. I would be really grateful if you could forward the enclosed letter to the editor of *Ogonëk*; and if you know the translator, thank him on my behalf.

News from Italy: I expect you get as much there as we do here, and suspect it's not necessary to give you any. The current situation is one that does not suggest any major shifts of position except in the long term, accompanied by an immobility that we have not been used to. The general outlook has been more optimistic for the past few months, and the word "peace" is heard with as much regularity as previously the word "war." The victories in China have impressed public opinion, more than is evident from the papers, and Mao is one of the most popular figures amongst the masses.

I'm editing the cultural page of *l'Unità*, which is much improved, under the direction of Montagnana and with input from some editors who have come up from Rome. *Sempre Avanti* is defunct, and *l'Unità* is the only paper that can compete today with *la Stampa* and *la Gazzetta*.

There are a lot of new and exciting things brewing at Einaudi. Amongst which is a series entitled "Testi e opuscoli" (Texts and short works) which ought to be full of interesting and surprising things, and another series "Biblioteca Popolare" (The People's Library). You'll have seen *Antologia Einaudi 1948*, which was really very good. Pavese's new book *Prima che il gallo canti* (*Before the Cock Crows*) is proving quite a success with non-specialist critics;[36] and he's already written another one entitled *Il diavolo sulle colline* (*The Devil in the Hills*). Natalia is learning Russian and writing short stories; Cicino is writing essays on Marxism and religion for the *Rivista di filosofia*, while the Pope has placed an interdict on Rodano;[37] Serini is vice-editor of *la Stampa* and every now and again writes a good "opposition" editorial.

Soviet culture is on everyone's lips. Discussions abound in every field, from novelists to biologists. The big problem in every sector is whether or not to accept the Soviet viewpoints and what to accept or reject. And this frenzy of arguments, when they are sincere and not forced, is a positive thing from many points of view; and it keeps in motion kinds of language that were already about to become fossilized before their time.

Stay in touch and if I can help in any way please do take me up on the offer. Best wishes and give my best regards to your wife,

Calvino

[Handwritten; with the heirs of the addressee.]

To Cesare Pavese—Turin

San Remo, 27 July 1949

Dear Pavese,

FRA [*SIC*] *SOLE DONNE* (*AMONG WOMEN ONLY*) IS A NOVEL THAT I immediately decided I would not like.[38] I'm still of that opinion even though I read it with great interest and enjoyment.

I decided it was one of Gulliver's travels, a voyage amongst women, or rather amongst strange creatures, half-woman half-horse; a kind of journey to the land of the Houyhnhnm, Swift's horses, horses with sudden human similarities, horribly disgusting like all the peoples Gulliver encounters. It's certainly a new way of seeing women and of taking your happy or sad revenge on them. And the thing that is most disconcerting of all is that hairy horse-woman, with the cavernous voice and breath that stinks of pipe-smoke, the one that talks in the first person and right from the start we know it's you with a wig and false breasts, saying "Look, a real woman should be like this." The most feminine phrase uttered by the horses eulogized above is the one involving "prick," a word that has the same weight on the page as when it is pronounced by a lady's lips. It is not by chance that she who utters it is the queen of the horse-women, the sum of all possible horsiness, Momina.

But nobody believes in the lesbianism in the book. It's simply a magic word indicating something obscure and forbidden practiced by the horse-women. It makes you think not so much of Sappho as of Pasiphae, or of strange rites involving horse penises in beech-wood. In any case the story is all about this circling around a morbid secret that is lurking there in the middle, and gradually getting closer to it. And it is carried out perfectly: à la *Heart of Darkness*, in short.

Then I discovered that *Fra sole donne* and *Paesi tuoi* (*The Harvesters*) are the same: two journeys by "civilized" people into the world of "savages." Talino and Momina are the same symbol. The rural world and the decadent bourgeois world are equally savage, and are judged, or rather seen (who can aspire to the position of judge in the case of cannibals?), by someone who stands outside them, who has a job that transcends their ambience and institutions (the patriarchal family, salon society): namely someone who works on farm machinery (and not someone who simply works the land), and someone who makes clothes for the horse-women (and not someone who paints or constructs houses, but someone *from inside*).

And the real message of the book is a deepening of your ideas on solitude, with in addition something new on the sense of work, on the solitude-work system, on the fact that relationships between human beings that are not founded on work become monstrous. You offer us a fresh discovery of the new relations that emerge from work (and this is the best part, the relation between Clelia and Becuccio, this woman who finds her rule of life in being a *bacheloress*, and she takes a man just as we men take women). The only people to be saved are the communities of friends, which are governed by unwritten rules of purity and solitude: the male friends in *Diavolo sulle colline* and the Clelia-Momina-Rosetta trio in *Fra sole donne*.

All this will have shown you that in this "unliked' book I have sampled all its possible moral references; and I could tell you the same about its narrative structure. What does not convince me, and I've already had other occasions to say this to you, is your portrayal of bourgeois characters. Already in *Il compagno* (*The Comrade*) the weak link was Lubrani and the Torre Littoria. If there was a flaw in *Il diavolo* (but it's better than this book, in my view), it was because the rich friends were not as solidly realized as the other characters. Here the others are more implied than brought onto the stage: and the bourgeois characters are seen and speak in an obvious, journalistic way. To write well about the elegant world you have to know it and experience it to the depths of your being just as Proust, Radiguet and Fitzgerald did: what matters is not whether you love it or hate it, but only to be quite clear about your position regarding it. You haven't got a clear position; you can tell this by the insistence with which you return to the theme, and it's not true that you don't care about it, but you have not yet, it seems to me, discovered the tone you need to have when you represent chic people. More patient than Zola among the miners, will you re-immerse yourself in your in-friends' salons?

And another thing: I've not quite understood what that buffalo-architect does in bed with the two horse-ladies. Does he masturbate with the pillow? I've read the bit carefully several times and it's not clear.

Nevertheless, if spending a few days by the sea doesn't disgust you, you are officially invited to my house. I'll be here until around 10 August. Write to me when you're arriving and I'll come and get you at the station. I'll introduce you to my poetic world in its raw state.

I roam around beaches and rocks with *Il cannibalismo* in my hand.[39] I'm going easy before reading it but the title makes women curious: they ask for explanations, and then I start to show them the illustrations. The rest follows naturally. It's the ideal Einaudi book for the holidays.

Ciao, tribesman!

Calv.

Warm greetings also to the nataliage, balbiage, fonziage, scassellage etc.[40]

Casella Postale 102
San Remo
(postal address)

Villa Meridiana
San Remo
(house-name address)

[Handwritten; in the Centro Studi Guido Gozzano-Cesare Pavese, Turin. Partially published in Cesare Pavese, *Lettere 1945–1950*, ed. Italo Calvino (Turin: Einaudi, 1966), pp. 408–9; and in Cesare Pavese, *Tra donne sole* (Turin: Einaudi, 1998).]

To Geno Pampaloni—Ivrea

Turin, 2 December 1949

Dear Pampaloni,

I read with pleasure your fine review of *The Crow*, the fullest and most flattering notice I've had so far.[41] I can tell you that I recognize myself totally in what you say, or rather I recognize my books: my problem today is how to escape from the limits of these books, from this definition of me as a writer of adventures, fairy-tales, and fun, in which I can't express myself or realize myself to the full. For me this means writing my second book: I don't consider *The Crow* as that book since it is a collection of marginal stories and minor works, moreover mostly written before *The Path*. The second book ought to have been the novel I finished last spring but which maybe I'll keep in the drawer since it doesn't seem to me to be fully realized.[42] So you see that I've still to pass the test of the second novel. Still, I've rarely found so much empathy for my thematics in a critic (apart from your allusion to the social polemic which I didn't grasp fully).

Thank you very much. With best wishes

Calvino

[Typewritten on Einaudi headed paper; with the addressee.]

To Mario Motta—Rome

Turin, 16-1-50

Dear Mario,

If I didn't reply straight away it was because I was going through a moment of terror—a check-up for military service, the third one in eight months.[43] Now it's over—postponed for four months again, but since this is now the third time it should mean there's a strong chance that I'll be exempt and my "de-kafkaization" can go ahead. I would like this to signal the end of "wasted angst" in my life: I've never regretted anything so much as having particular individual worries, in a certain sense anachronistic ones, whereas general worries, worries about our time (or at any rate those that can be reduced to such: like your problem in paying the rent, for instance) are so many and so vast and so much "my own" that I feel they are enough to fill all my "worryability" and even my interest and enjoyment in living.

So from now on I want to dedicate myself entirely to these latter (worries)—but I am already aware of the traps in this question and that's why for some time now my first need has been to "de-journalistize" myself, to get myself out of the stranglehold that has dominated these last few years of my life, reading books to review immediately, commenting on something even before having to time to form an opinion on it. I want to build a new kind of daily program for myself where I can finally get into something, something definitive (within the limits of historical possibility), something not dishonest or insincere (unlike the way today's journalist always behaves, more or less). For that reason I make several plans for myself: even to lead the party political life, which is something I'd abandoned for some time, at the grassroots level, working with party branches, the party's schools, in order to maintain my contacts with reality and the world, but being careful, of course, not to get lost in unnecessary activities; and also to set up my own individual work not as a "journalist" any more but as a "scholar," with systematic readings, notes, comments, notebooks, a load of things I've never done; and also, eventually, to write a novel.

I can already see you twisting on your chair reading this letter, full of worries (worries more about "our time" than ever) about getting this journal out, and me coming out with New-Year resolutions.[44] Hang on: this was all just to tell you that things being as they are (in other words, I being as I am), I can only consider contributing to your journal as a point of arrival, an end result, not a commitment or point of departure. In short, in order not to torture you any more, I'll probably be able to deliver in May (or April?) = in short, I'll probably begin working in March on the article on Hemingway. I'll say more, the journal is at this point I'd almost say essential for me to establish the themes that interest me and commit myself to work. Only I'd like you to know—though you don't care about this at all, since it's my business and you've got plenty of other things to think about—that if I keep my word regarding the Holy Year resolutions I mentioned to you, in a year or two or three I'll be able to be a good contributor to the journal. Otherwise, no; and before then, no. The thing is that at present my efforts cannot be focused—like yours—directly on the journal—though I care an awful lot about it and I rely on it too—but on my managing to work in that particular way. (Which would still mean, I'm under no illusions, being a journalist again, being a better one than I have stutteringly managed to be so far and certainly better than I could manage at present in my current state of being almost unable to speak.)

Right, let's talk about the journal. Ubaldo told me the latest news.[45] I've read the little additional sheet outlining policy, which I approve: you certainly know how to do these general things. I approve the format too. The "Cultura" in the title sounds a bit vague, a bit weak; but I don't know, I might be wrong about this; think carefully about it.

Hemingway. More than an article on H. it will be something on our encounter with H., the way our generation of Italians approaches him, on H.'s usefulness to us (as well as our utilization or use of him). It's a serious business; I've not got my ideas clear yet. I think I'll have to start first with an exhaustive account of the meaning of America for anti-Fascist intellectuals who grew up under Fascism. I've been thinking a bit about these things, about America, about "that' America, reading and discussing the writings of Giaime Pintor (at present through Valentino's introduction, then later I'll read them when they're printed).[46] This is perhaps something that would deserve a separate essay, to explain so many things [Pavese, Vittorini, Balbo (on "technique," on "heroes without glory"), Pintor (the Pintor of *Americana*) and then the whole *Politecnico* phenomenon]. The Russian-American alliance was the fundamental condition for the "communistization" of Italian intellectuals in the avant-garde, and the end of that alliance has also counted for a lot. Now both "Russia" and "America" represented a collection of Italian data and aspirations, they were two utopian countries, two incomplete and complementary utopias, and the sum "Russia" + "America" ("that" Russia + "that" America) added up to the great country of utopia that was, I believe, for many people, and certainly not solely intellectuals, the true objective of the Resistance. (Was that a phenomenon that was an end in itself, or did it contain a historical truth which we must continue to take account of?) In H. one finds almost all of what was meant by America. The virginity of its history, its technique (knowing how to do things), freedom and fullness of love, the open air, a direct democracy in human relations, courage. And, as writing, one finds in it the maximum help for developing one's technique: H.'s language is technical and functional, in which there is nothing that is without immediate, rational utilization, there is no abstraction, solipsism or fanciness (as had previously been the case in the great but obscure Faulkner). But H. is an "America" that fails to find its "Russia." It finds instead (and the problem is it goes looking for it) its "Europe." This is H.'s decadentism. And he finds it on the basis (and as a diversion and explanation) of the elements from the worst side of America (which is as real as the other side) that are in him: alcoholism, ignorance, emptiness. And, as a barbarian, he has highly refined intuitions regarding European barbarism-civilization; he enters the

Olympus of our most refined irrationalism, he the "technical" writer: but what is that to us now? We could have sent any old Montherlant to see bullfights.[47] It was something else we wanted from him, something else now that what comes back more and more to our eyes—to the point of covering the aspects we sought and loved in him and still seek and love in him—now that what comes back, as I was saying, are the other aspects (the now hackneyed contrast between the barbarous and the civilized: see Pintor's writings on the Nazis—yes, Nazis, for God's sake!—but see also how they live on in Pavese's countryside and ethnology). These matter to us less and less now, so it is something else, then, something that is now beyond him (*A Farewell to Hemingway*),[48] beyond him (where?) that we are looking for now. As you can see, these are very difficult ideas to express. And note that these things came to my mind as I was writing, and every time I've begun writing about this damned man what came to mind were different things, and certainly when I come to write this article I'll write things that are different again, and now I need to keep the rough copy of this letter otherwise I'll forget everything.[49]

Novel. I believe that to confront this question of the novel in the same way you want the other questions to be approached—namely how to proceed "post-Marx" following the line of historical development of a particular discipline or art—we would first need to establish a definition of this particular line, in the same way you want to do, you said, for painting. The point is that there have been so many debates on the novel in the last thirty years, both by those who claimed it was dead and by those who wanted it to be alive in a certain way, that if one conducts the debate without serious preliminary work to establish the terms of the question as it has to be set up and as it has never been set up before, we'll end up saying and making others say a lot of commonplaces. Now I basically wouldn't mind this kind of work, but in order to move with a certain amount of ease I'd need to have at least double the amount of knowledge I could manage at present, so I could promise to do it for you for ten years from now.

OK? No? Never mind. In order to raise the question "tangentially" as you say—and I've warned you of the dangers—all you would need is a review of certain books that are being published now in Britain and America on the technique of the novel (one has been translated and published by Bompiani: Warren Beach).[50] Or take up any reasonably intelligent comments on the novel (there are always plenty coming out) in the Italian or foreign press (I've got some here to hand). Otherwise, also from my article on Hemingway something can certainly come out.

Reviews. Yes, I can review the Seghers: better if I've read a couple of other books by her that we have here in translation.[51] And other books to review will certainly come out. Now I've run out of things to say and I've had enough. Adiós, señor.

Calv.

[Handwritten; with the addressee.]

To Elsa Morante—Rome

Turin, 2 March 1950

Dear Elsa,[52]

I'M REALLY HAPPY YOU WROTE TO ME. A HABIT I WOULD LIKE to develop and which instead I lack completely—and perhaps we all lack, in our generation, unlike the *ancients*—is that of, at a certain point, hey presto! having an idea and instantly wanting to put it in writing to a friend, and then writing it. But receiving letters gives me great pleasure; especially if they come from one of those very few people, like you, with whom I can *say something*.

Ever since returning to the publishing house I've been traveling less,[53] however I hope to have to come to Rome soon, and I'll certainly come and see you and Alberto as well as the owl Ulisse that Natalia spoke to me about.[54]

I've not sent you *Il Bianco Veliero* (*The White Schooner*) yet because I'm full of doubts about it and maybe I'll never decide to publish it, and I'm no good at correcting and rewriting things. It represents a forced movement in my writing in the direction of the fairy-tale and caricature, but done in the full knowledge of this coercion, and hence too mechanical and cold. All this is evident especially in the character of the protagonist: she is reduced to a cipher of wonder and innocence, and is unable to develop flesh and blood, in other words to have her own independence so that she can move on her own without needing *something always to happen to her*. And the language is quite precise but all of it sounds a bit *falsetto*. All in all, I think it's quite an amusing book, a kind of contemporary version of *Guerrin Meschino*,[55] full also perhaps of good things but good *only when taken bit by bit*, like a collection of short stories, and, *like all collections of short stories*, with a fair amount of stuff that can be discarded.

The fact is that I already feel I am a prisoner of a kind of style and it is essential that I escape from it at all costs: I'm now trying to write a *totally different* book, but it's damned difficult; I'm trying to break up the rhythms, the echoes which I feel the sentences I write eventually slide into, as into pre-existing molds, I try to see facts and things and people in the round instead of being drawn in colors that have no shading. For that reason the book I'm going to write interests me infinitely more than the other one.

Maybe you don't like hearing an author discuss one of his books with a kind of hostile detachment, you who tie yourself to the bitter end to the things you do, and who almost identify yourself with them. But you see, you have this gift of being able to unify the most disparate elements, always getting everything to work out, you have a very strong capacity for synthesizing things, a rare quality in a woman (rare? well, maybe synthesizing is the female gift par excellence). At any rate, you synthesize in a way that Natalia for instance does not, because for her the problem doesn't exist; she lives, sees, and expresses herself in a single, very powerful direction and manner, even though she too lives in a world that has been torn apart like ours. You feel that the world is torn to pieces, that the things to keep hold of are very many and actually incompatible with each other, yet with your lucid and affectionate obstinacy you always make things turn out. For me, on the other hand, writing has always meant setting out in one direction, staking everything on one card, yet with the awareness that there are others, the awareness of risk and of not being able to exhaust all I have to say. For that reason my writing is always problematic.

I'll send you *Il Bianco Veliero* all the same. I want a dispassionate, detailed, rigorous verdict from you and I'll set great store by it.[56]

Working in publishing gives me more satisfaction than journalism, but takes up much of my time. The fact is that in these last months I've not been able to set up a work project of my own that is attractive enough to act as a counterweight to the office. As a result, I realize that I kind of abandon myself to office work because it is *easier*, hoping that it *will be enough for me*, and that outside the office I'll let myself be tempted by every opportunity, though still with that deafening remorse at the bottom of my heart which is for the writer the specter of his own desk waiting for him with the pile of immaculate sheets of paper.

Say hello to Alberto for me and tell him I'm an avid reader of his articles in *il Mondo*. I've been thinking a lot recently that Italian criticism, which consists entirely of marginal notes and comparisons with vague echoes of favorite books, is something that is absolutely superfluous and unsatisfying. Alberto's book reviews instead are full of ideas and promptings and guides to setting up frameworks and systematizing things; I believe that today, with the chaos that we all have in our heads, his reviews are amongst the best pieces of non-fiction that can be written.

Write to me often, and tell me lots about yourself. Warmest regards,

Calvino

[Handwritten; with the addressee's heirs.]

To Mario Motta—Rome

[Turin, July 1950]

Dear Motta,

Your note on *The God That Failed* has prompted me to some considerations.[57] I will not discuss the debate surrounding the book, which I have not read nor do I think I will read it. (The "ex-Communist" is one of the dreariest figures of the postwar period: behind him one senses that sad air of wasted time, and ahead of him the squalid existence of someone redeemed by the Salvation Army, going around the streets with the band and its choir, shouting out that he's been a drunkard and a cheat.) What I'm interested in are the things you say about paradise:

> In fact each one of us can hope for a supernatural paradise, without necessarily damaging either himself or others, but not for a paradise on earth: hoping for the latter means losing all real understanding of history, choosing a paradigm devoid of sense to evaluate history, condemning oneself voluntarily to never finding a homeland in which he doesn't feel a foreigner sooner or later.

As often happens in such cases, before even formulating a verdict on your statement, I spontaneously asked an "auto-critical" question: what about me, do I believe in a paradise? But I had to struggle a bit to focus the question, to create an "image' of it for myself; all that came to mind were literary examples, second-hand ideas, things gleaned from elsewhere. I realized that this concept of a "paradise"' that is—I won't say supernatural, for I'm not accustomed to reflect on that plane—but even "terrestrial" was totally foreign to my usual way of thinking.

I'll try to go back to the specific case from which we started: how I "see" the revolution, socialism, the society I hope for and for which, "in my humble way," I am working. What came to mind were images dictated by that small amount of experience I have of moments of democratic awakening and organized and efficient activity. I mean moments when interests in all aspects of life, communication with others, and ability and intelligence all increase in each of us; all this taken to the utmost degree and become non-provisional, but with effects that are anything but "paradisiacal"; a host of things to do, of responsibilities, of "troubles": you who are convinced I'm lazy, might laugh. What pushes me in this direction is not, it seems to me, a "paradise" to be reached, but the satisfaction of seeing things gradually starting to go the right way, feeling in a better position for solving problems as they emerge, for "working better," having greater clarity in my head and the sense of being more in my right place when I am amongst other men, amidst things, in the world of history.[58]

Now I believe that this is modern man's achievement (or rather the achievement for which he should strive): to shed the myth of a teleological "paradise" (whether metaphysical or on earth) as man's true homeland, and to find this human homeland instead in the heart of his own works and days, in a dialectic between himself and everything else that is extremely difficult to acquire and maintain. This is possible only for those who have very clear ideas on the direction they must be going in, for those who know—more and more clearly—what they want, what they must want; but more than the succession of points of arrival[59] what counts is seeing the world being transformed by the little that each of us does, that each of us gets involved in during the process of transforming it. That was why socialism emerged from "utopia" (from "paradise") when it started to be a "science" and hence a "praxis"; for this reason the Communist fights even though he knows that the results of his sacrifices will be enjoyed only by future generations. That is why one cannot imagine a "contemplative" Marxist (ouch! What a piece of auto-criticism for the lazy fellow you believe I am!).

The "paradise" to be reached (with its little angels, or its sausage-tree: it's all the same) is the wrong way of posing the problem of man who does not feel he has the keys in his hands to allow him to fit in the world. Instead of looking for these keys, of learning to use them, he dreams of (or makes this the myth of his activity, wasting his time and labor) a world without locks, a non-world, a non-history, an "absolute human state." Whereas the problem is precisely that of being aware of one's own relativity, of becoming master of it, and knowing how to deal with this relativity.

Ever since I started reflecting on this, I notice that I've started classifying historical figures, writers, cultural movements into "paradisiacal" or not. As happens with these juxtapositions invented on the spot (which also have their own auxiliary usefulness, as long as one doesn't dwell too long on them), the system always works out: the "paradisiacal" ones are all those that I systematically distrust, the "non-paradisiacal" are those from whom I believe I've gathered some concrete teaching.[60]

How many paradises there are, for instance, in recent literature! What can be more "paradisiacal" than Surrealism? And psychoanalysis? And Gidean irresponsibility? But even more significant, it seems to me, is the fact that the most coveted myth in modern literature is a regressive paradise: memory. And what can one say about the gelid paradise of the Hermeticists: absence?

Behind all this there always lies Romanticism, that great river of paradisiacal incontinence. And behind that again, Rousseau, the inventor of one of the most beloved ways of writing about paradise. (However, I believe we should go carefully with Rousseau's myths: just because someone likes the South Seas—at a time when one could still believe in such things, of course—it is not necessarily the case that he has to be an unthinking escapist. If instead one goes there seriously, maybe one feels good there, and finds just what he wants: that's what happened to Gauguin and Stevenson.)[61]

And as far as I am concerned, "infernal" writers are also a subspecies of "paradisiacal" writers: they have the same preoccupation with some human absolute to be reached, which for them is the antihuman absolute, the terrifying God or his terrifying absence (or rather Absence). Kafka is the one who travels furthest in this infernal direction, because he is the one who suffers it in concrete terms right to the end and wants to find out if there really are no ways out, and invents (or discovers as he looks around) certain Infernos that not even Dante would have ever dreamed up. (By the way, I don't want to talk rubbish about Dante, but it seems to me that he is not "infernal" or "paradisiacal" at all, given that concern of his for men as they are, on the "earth.") The French Existentialists instead are more inclined to act like children, to cultivate the inferno: the gelatinous, hairy inferno of "existing," in Sartre; the coldly insensate inferno, but with nearby beaches and parasols, in Camus.

I am certainly not looking to such people for examples of what I mean by "exit from paradise," but to men who have as their homeland the things they do and see—a homeland that is constantly fraught with obstacles and has to be regained—these are "to the extent that" men, men who are impervious to marvelous hopes as much as to marvelous despair.

On their side (I'll continue to cite names of writers because they are more familiar to me; you might be able to replace them with names of philosophers since you know them better) there is Conrad, with his dark vision of the universe and his confidence in man, his morality which stems from the practicing of a skill, a job—working on sailing ships—(and this makes a rigid conservative of him, but who if not revolutionaries now learn from him?), his refusal to make a paradise of the tropics, the sea, which he sees as a test of man's moral strength and technique. On their side is Chekhov, who gnaws pitilessly to the bone every proud presumption of petit-bourgeois man (of human petit-bourgeois mentality), but he does so in order to discover beneath it, in each of us, that there is a man to be saved, in other words to test the historical utility of every man, which is—setting aside all the individual failures—the only human dignity and salvation. And as for the failures he recounts, what remains in your mind is the "positive" loophole that stays open despite everything, just as in his landscapes, in the loopholes of nature that he lets us glimpse every so often, you get a wonderful sense of breadth from the harmony of minute, scattered fragments. On their side is Hemingway—notwithstanding (or rather precisely because of) the fundamental American emptiness that he notices all around him and of which he too is a part—Hemingway who feels the need to go back to the basic relationships of man with things: fishing well, lighting fires well, establishing relations between a man and a woman well, and between men and other men, blowing up bridges well (except that he lacks the general perspective, and becomes futile and gets bored; what do bull-fights matter to us, even when well done?).

I could go on, but I would like to point something out to you: I've provided the names of three atheists, and this is no accident. Actually these considerations can be expanded; that presupposition of a "paradise" (of the angelic or sausage variety), of man continually on the threshold of a kingdom that is his alone (and not belonging to him and the stone, say, or to him and the lizard, him and hydrogen, mold, whales, hail), that presupposition that the virtues that derive from things are separate from things themselves, I now think I realize that this is what you call religion. Whereas this burying the rewards of one's own actions in the furrow of one's own duties and jobs, which have been established with science and confidence, would instead be the attitude toward the world that often in oral discussions with you I would uphold with the definition of *atheistic atheism*.[62] You say that such a position cannot hold philosophically, but what does that matter? We have so many centuries ahead of us to think about it.

Only by going down this route, I believe, can one avoid "losing all real understanding of history," "choosing a paradigm devoid of sense to evaluate it."

Forgive me this garbled letter and for having chosen an (apparently) marginal topic to enter into discussion in your journal, but the mouse starts gnawing the cheese from the sides.[63]

Italo Calvino

[Handwritten; with the addressee.]

To Isa Bezzera—Milan

San Remo, 16 July 1950

Dear Isa,

I AM WRITING TO YOU FROM THE PARENTAL HOME, SITTING AT the desk on which I did my homework as a young boy. It's a place that is still the same, and sitting here (I was about to say "sitting here and gazing" Leopardi-style)[64] I can hear again the same old sounds, which are stuck still in time like the decorations in this room: roosters and turkeys in the neighbor's coop (maybe a different neighbor but still the same roosters and turkeys; maybe also the peacock that I used to spend so much time staring at?), birds in the garden, drops in the fountain, the old folk from the Home walking up via San Pietro, and the little girls playing ring-a-ring-a-roses in the nuns' garden. The "search for lost time" is a cheap sport; all you need is a house and town you were born in, to live away from it and come back every so often. Or maybe not; it's really a sport for the well-off; if I had grown up in an alley or in a working-class area, the poetic effects would all be different; if Proust had not grown up in villas and palaces he would certainly not have invented Proustism. When we were very small, this room was called "the spare room"; as far as I remember, there was absolutely nothing in it, or at most some chest or folded camp-bed. Occasionally we would manage to get in to play and that seemed something wonderful to us; but maybe we got bored with it after a bit. Then it became "the boys' study." Now it is once more "the spare room" more or less, with the few bare bits of furniture and various objects brought here haphazardly as though into a closet. And from here one can reflect on how the world changes as we pass through it: rooms, people we meet, everything leaves a mark on us and we leave a mark on them. But enough of that. It's morning. I've not been down to the sea yet. I got here last night by train but I'd come as far as Varigotti by car, where I had a warm bath in the darkness about nine in the evening in a sea that was as gentle as could be. I did the driving as far as Mondoví. I got my license the Saturday you left. I'm glad you like Chekhov. He is a very great writer, immense. He picks all human arrogances clean to the bone but has an unshakeable confidence in the future of humanity. And he tells his stories with that inimitable tone that is as one with the story but is also detached and discreet and sensitive and impassive all at once. I always remember you. I sometimes go up the hill to eat and you're not there. Now I'm off to the sea. Tonight I'm going back to Turin. Ciao

I.

[Handwritten; with the addressee.]

To Elsa Morante—Capri

San Remo 9 August 1950

Dear Elsa,

I'm taking advantage of the tranquil rhythm of the holidays to reply to your letter. Your letters, so few and far between, are always very welcome; even if, as in this last one, they contain severe criticisms. Criticisms which, as you know, I anticipated and fully agreed with. The "cold" construction you found in *Il Bianc. Vel.* derives from the fact that the heat of "inspiration"—too thin anyway—with which I'd started out writing it cooled along the way, and I decided to finish the book more out of the pigheadedness of not wanting to leave anything unfinished than because I was really keen on it.[65] Apart from the odd chapter or scene that has the dimensions of a short story, I think that the only thing that can be salvaged from the novel is the landscape, in other words a few sober annotations. But read in this way, there is a "San Remo—Turin journey" inside it which I still like.

My new book, which you think has already appeared or is about to appear, is in the phase of labored expansion. And if I get there, that will be *my first book*. But gone are the days when I could write straight off, "like an apple tree produces apples," to use an image which defined Maupassant (whom I'm rereading to write an article for the centenary of his birth). I've got less stamina than before, or more problems in my head that stay as problems and don't become images and narrative rhythm, and I have to digest them bit by bit. You will understand, then, how much I agree with you and share your worries. I realize that it was the pressure of history that carried me forward and then dumped me there. Now when we really feel the necessity for writers too to put pressure on history!

I've come away to San Remo for the holidays, because it is the one place where I have a house and where I can build a certain solitude around myself. I need it because these last months in the publishing house have been full of upheaval and distraction, full of trips, tourism, seaside baths, good company: happy months, but ones that are dangerously empty. Here I am trying to rediscover landscapes and memories of my childhood, very precious things, and to avoid as far as possible adolescent memories, toward which I still retain some leftover rancor.

I wish you a summer full of full pages and sunny days. Say hello to Alberto. I think that in the autumn I'll have occasion to come to Rome and we'll meet up. Warmest regards,

Calvino

Casella postale 102
San Remo
[Handwritten; with the addressee's heirs.]

To Natalia Ginzburg

San Remo 14 August [1950]

Dear Natalia,

I'VE BEEN WANTING TO WRITE TO YOU FOR A LONG TIME AND now I'm writing to you. How are you? How are things going?

I've come to San Remo to escape from the tourist frenzy that has seized the publishing house, because this is the only place in the world where I can live in studious and fruitful peace and solitude. However, I've been here ten days and am now bored to death, and I discover that I have more need to be sociable than I thought.[66] I spend the afternoons on some rocks here, belly in the sun, reading Thomas Mann, who writes very well about many things that are completely incomprehensible to me. San Remo is overflowing with people on holiday and that's enough to keep me locked up at home or to send me out on walks in the country. Writing is very difficult, it really is not the joke it once seemed to me. If I ever manage to write something serious it will be after much labor and study. Meanwhile: the only completed work to appear in this period is a very short story for *l'Unità*, "Storia di un soldato che si portò un cannone a casa" (The story of a soldier who brought a cannon home), but it's a bit stupid.[67] The work that's a bit more fun (only fun for me writing it, for the moment) is gathering material for an article on Maupassant. I wrote a tiny piece for *l'Unità* for the centenary of his birth and noticed that I had various ideas,[68] so I brought to San Remo all the Maupassant I could find (including some of your books: I'll bring them back to you later, don't worry) and I'm busy reading what I've not read before, and also rereading the rest, making notes on what I want to say. This is a way of working which I enjoy a lot (and for which I've never had enough time), even if in the end nothing finished emerges from it. Also in order not to lose contact with things, I've bought a sketch-pad, a pencil, and a sharpener, promising myself I'd do some drawing. In the house I found an old collection of shells and I've begun to draw shells. They're very difficult, especially the nautilus shells, and I'm not good at it. If some day you happened to want to draw shells, don't start with the nautilus shells, otherwise you'll get discouraged immediately. But I'm not discouraged at all, let's be clear about that. I'd like also to manage to translate my favorite four lines from Baudelaire, but this is difficult too.

Dans une terre grasse et pleine d'escargots
Je veux creuser moi-même une fosse profonde,
Où je puisse à loisir étaler mes vieux os
Et dormir dans l'oubli comme un requin dans l'onde.[69]
(In fertile earth full of snails
I want to dig myself a deep grave,
Where I can stretch out my old bones in peace
And sleep in oblivion like a shark in the waves.)

Say hello to Gabriele for me.[70] Give my greetings also to our mutual friends there and stay happy and well,

Calv.

[Handwritten; with the addressee's heirs.]

To Isa Bezzera—Milan

Turin 3 September 1950

Dear Isa,

I think that this letter of mine will reach you in England and will find you happy and intent on making wonderful discoveries as always. I have just spent the last few days in great sadness, and only now can I manage to write to you. I'd like to have written to you from San Remo, where I spent quite a pleasant three weeks' holidays: silent, homely, seaside holidays just as I wanted them, managing to avoid the excessive numbers of people at the beach or at the dances. But I didn't have your address. On my return to Turin exactly a week ago, the night of 27–28 August, I found waiting for me on the chest of drawers your postcard from The Hague with the excellent Holbein and your letter from Haarlem. I started reading it feeling very happy and I can tell you that those were the last happy moments I can remember. While I was reading it, they came to tell me that something awful had happened and that I should go to a friend's house. There I found out about Cesare Pavese's suicide.

I don't know if you can get the Italian newspapers, and you probably missed the news and Pavese is maybe little more than a name to you. But for me Pavese meant a lot: not only was he one of my favorite writers, one of my best friends, a work colleague for many years, a person I spoke with every day, but he was one of the most important people in my life. He was someone to whom I owe almost everything I am, who had been crucial in me becoming a writer, had always guided and encouraged and followed my work, who influenced the way I thought, my tastes, even my life habits and attitudes. It really took me some time to recover from the shock and to take proper stock of the living and the dead. All the places and bits of paper and work that I live among have all been drenched in his presence; now I—like all the friends and colleagues who were closest to him—am trying to fill this terrible void. It was a sad week, as I said, but we can now say we are over the worst, that we're on the road to recovery. The first few days were very painful, all taken up with preparations for the funeral and with our minds working over all the details we could trace of his last days, and with receiving friends who came from all over Italy, and every encounter with them renewed the grief. Then it was all about going back to the publishing house after the funeral without him, going through the many unpublished manuscripts he left, then trying to overcome the [dismay][71] into which his disappearance could throw our publishing activities, and starting again to work and make plans.

You, like everyone else, will ask: "But why did he kill himself?" Those who knew him are horrified but not surprised by the news: Pavese carried this suicide around with him ever since he had been a child, with his loneliness, his crises of despair, his dissatisfaction with living, all disguised by that mask of bashfulness and resentment that he wore. But I thought he was, despite all this, very hard and unbreakable, entrenched; the kind of person you bore in mind every time you were tempted to despair yourself, to encourage yourself: "But Pavese's holding firm." Instead he didn't make it. That's why his death was such a tough blow. Just when he was at the apex of his literary fame (and I was deeply mistrustful of his euphoria in the last few months) he went into a depressive crisis and his nervous system, for all its toughness, couldn't support him any more and collapsed. This is all we can understand: everything else you might read or hear is gossip or speculation. His decision was already irrevocable in a poem he wrote last April, and in many of the things he said to us in the last few months: only now do we realize that. But it is his whole life and oeuvre that have now taken on a new significance; new at least for us: he, perhaps, knew it already.

Dear Isa, I'm sorry to have written you such a sad letter, but I still don't know how to write in any other way, and yet it really was necessary for me to write to you. However, I already feel that a period of powerful renewal and of renewed interest in life has begun for me. It's still my unfortunate friend who's pushing me in this direction, teaching me about the despair of those who cannot escape their loneliness and connect with the world that surrounds them and with life. Your lovely letter from Haarlem which I've read and reread two or three times in recent days, has helped me a lot. You're kind of the opposite of Pavese, you have this gift of being able to be at ease in any corner of the world, of having a spontaneous relationship with anyone, of learning instinctively the most disparate life lessons. I am maybe a bit like him and a bit like you. So we must take the good with the bad. Oh well, I have other things too I'd like to write to you: the day before yesterday I went to the hospital in Ivrea to see Togliatti—you'll have heard, I presume, about the car accident, fortunately nothing serious. But I'll write back to you soon if you write to me. Ciao.
[Handwritten, unsigned; with the addressee.]

To Valentino Gerratana—Rome

San Remo 15 October 1950

Dear Valentino,
To reply to your letter I wanted to wait for a day in which I could write to you, not just in a bit of spare time, but when I could be fully relaxed. And that day arrived only today when I'm underneath my parents' roof on the day of my twenty-seventh birthday.

Your letter is good and important: I'd say perhaps the most important thing I've read until now concerning the search for a morality, a way of being in the world. This search is perhaps the thing that interests us most. It seems to me that here you manage to expand and clarify many concerns which I share too and which I cannot but subscribe to. But at the same time I curse your damned nit-picking which pops out all over the place, particularly in your style, in your extremely long premises, in all your parentheses and ifs and buts which you use to protect yourself from the slightest possibility of misunderstanding what you say. You always move as though you were in a china shop whereas I believe that one can also fling ideas into the air or on the ground or against the walls, too bad about those that end up in pieces. I believe that one can also write just to set something in motion, to provoke a reaction, to keep an unsolved problem still open, etc., and not solely to give normative definitions like those in a penal code. It's clear that this stems from the difference in our jobs: my way of understanding writing is through literature; yours, I think, is a scientific approach. The problem is to make them each participate in the other. At any rate it seems to me that certain points in your letter can actually show you a way of going forward: basically the real book you must give us would be a kind of history of these generations via a series of moral and critical portraits of their best and most significant exponents. I think this is more useful than teaching Marxism to Bontempelli.[72]

Right then: first of all I want to reply about what you call my "tendency to justify his death in some way, or even to ennoble it, to see it as the inevitable conclusion etc." Giving a judgment on a human event that is important and difficult and regrettable must be carried out in two phases, in my view. First: the search for the subjective reasons for this deed, for what it must have meant in the intentions of the person who carried it out, in other words to try to go through the thoughts that brought him to the stage of thinking it necessary. Second: the search for the opposite motives, in other words for reasons that would have made Pavese continue living, as he certainly could have still decided to do (certain writings of his, such as "L'arte di maturare" (The Art of Maturing) in the last issue of *Cultura e realtà*, also provide evidence of this: it is quite different and perhaps auto-critical compared with the other writings; also the note on "literature inspired by Marxism" which I find strikingly close to my letter on "paradise"),[73] the search for why these motives were not strong enough etc. Now without the first of these it is not possible to arrive at the second (just as a novelist must first have *understood* a character down to the bone in order to *judge* him) and the first phase means *taking* his act *seriously*, not trying to minimize it (and I know you're very far from doing that), but also not allowing it to become an accident, a hurdle as you call it. It means going through and beyond this act; in order to continue our lives *afterwards*, we need to go through it as a kind of tragic catharsis which will anchor us again more securely to a life which we now know can contain, and does contain, tragedies such as this as well. I hope I've succeeded in explaining to you the reasons—not so much for the letter—for the tone which you criticized in my piece in *l'Unità* and in what I wrote to you—and see also the piece in the *Bollettino del sindacato scrittori* (*Bulletin of the Writers' Union*), which you'll easily find in Rome.[74] You'll say that what I lack is that "second phase": and I'll reply that it will come later and that I'm more susceptible to the succession of inspirations and impulses than you rational debaters. But what is certain is that the study of this element of will and active morality is what is most interesting, it's what counts most in understanding Pavese, that element without which he would not have been who he was.

With that premise, I enthusiastically agree with your statement against absolutism and perfection and in favor of a morality that is a practice of life and of perfection. In my letter to Motta I wanted to keep my examples on the level of a literary digression, but I would prefer the real models for such a position, and the ones closest to us, to be Gramsci and Pintor. In this context your letter interested me considerably and I took the liberty of reading some extracts to Balbo and discussed them with him; and I think this helped diminish a certain animosity toward you that perhaps he retained after your article. From your quotation of Pintor and also from the general context of your letter I have learnt more about the meaning of Giaime's oeuvre and the moral lesson you draw from it—perhaps more than I had gained from reading *Il sangue d'Europa* (*The Blood of Europe*) and your introduction to it.

And here we come to another criticism that you direct at me, namely what I wrote to you concerning your article on Balbo: in other words, the fact that a quotation, an explanation of a classic passage known to everyone, at a certain point seemed to me to be a discovery, whereas I ought to have known it a long time ago and it should have been second nature to me. The fact is that (apart from the lacunae in my studies which I condemn and am far from justifying) I'm not inclined to seek solutions for problems in philosophical or at any rate theoretical texts: what needs to happen is for these texts to conjure up lives and history and people and imagination before they come into my hands and then, once connected to everything else, they become of use to me. And I think I have some reasons for this: because I do not believe in solutions that are reached solely by means of reasoning, or through solitary study. Better to remain an enfant du siècle with all the contradictions still open but to have contacts and contributions from everyone that passes by in the street. But if I see a comrade, a girl,—or a novel, a film, because those too are life, made up of people and things—moving in one direction or another, then I react and counter them or go along with them or try to shift them, and at that point it'll come natural to me to find the theories I need—if they exist already—and I manage to read and understand them; and if they don't exist yet, I help them to emerge. The fact is that if certain decisive points of Marxist thought are not recognized even by people like me, this means that in practice, in historical reality, one does not take enough account of them, that we are not used to making them work or using them. And this can lead to very serious consequences. At this point you, persnickety as you rightly are, will ask me to clarify this and give examples; but I will tell you to go to hell: you give the examples, I've done my bit.

To conclude: I don't trust solutions that are done by force of will, done with the head. One can say that moral progress has been made only when this has been carried out in real life, and often the encounter with reality leads us constantly to correct our intentions. For that reason what you call the "attempt to bring along part of one's ailment" is sometimes better than deciding by force of will that one is cured, just because *the concept is clear*; and amongst our intellectual comrades we can recognize several of these "imaginary cured." I'll tell you something else: someone who claimed to cure himself through reflection and rejecting experience was Pavese himself (but also, though, through his one means of contact with reality: work). Hence his periodic relapses because he was not actually cured at all (hence his despair when he thought that his work too was at an end). You are quite a different case: because you take good care not to proclaim yourself healed, and you are full of attention toward yourself and others in this regard. But you always believe that healing resides in reasoning, in having clarified the problem theoretically, whereas instead *the awareness of the road toward the solution of a moral problem can only be achieved at the same time as its actual solution in practice.*

And me? Clearly I'm at the opposite extreme. I live from day to day. I systematically refuse to see clearly into my stances and never trust any definitions that are given of me if by any chance I happen to be judged by someone or judge myself. For some time now I've avoided judging others, or even getting involved with them, since that would force me to get involved in my own affairs too. You know this, since you've seen me distancing myself more and more from any confidences. And this is wrong, of course. For months I almost avoided Pavese, because I knew he was full of private worries, though I still followed them with anxiety. Now I can't get rid of the remorse that perhaps even from a conversation with me he might have had—by pure chance, maybe—an idea that would have borne fruit, a discovery of "the broken mesh in the net."[75] So, apparently, "I watch myself live," "waiting to see how it will end."[76] Apparently, because I'm anything but drifting. In every area of my life there is always something that is moving in a direction I consider positive, even though I let other things move in the opposite direction; and I am always on the lookout for the chance to make an intervention that I think might be positive and fruitful. I don't talk about my private life. In my public life here's a very recent example: for four days I managed to feel very closely tied up with and in a certain sense essential to the working-class struggle, something that has not happened for some time now. It was when I went to the Vercelli region and off my own bat I wrote two pieces on the police harassment during the laborers' strike.[77] These were pieces which I'm sure were very useful, both to the paper (which is usually inadequate in terms of information and its capacity to inform), and to the Party and public opinion, and, to a certain extent, to the success of the general strike in solidarity with the laborers. I can't explain this to you properly. But for me this means having accomplished, if only for four days, a practical model of how to be in the Party. I don't know when or how I'll manage to achieve something similar again: but now I know how to reach my optimum level of political output, after years of willing efforts and deliberate attempts and retreats and omissions. Things like this happen if one keeps open the road to make them happen. Send me a reply. Ciao.

Calvino

(finished copying the letter in Turin, the next day)
[Handwritten; with the addressee's heirs. Partially published in Paolo Spriano, *Le passioni di un decennio (1946–1956)* (Turin: Einaudi, 1986), pp. 17–18, 43–44.]

To Valentino Gerratana—Rome

Turin, 18 October [1950]

Dear Valentino,
I'VE JUST RECEIVED YOUR SECOND LETTER AND IN FACT yesterday I just sent off my reply to your first; I hope you'll forgive me for having delayed so long.

I'm very pleased that you liked my letter to Motta: I was in fact hoping you would write something about it to me. I'm very interested in the things you say about "spontaneous Marxism." In my letter I explained to you, in reply to your previous criticisms, my situation as regards texts. (This does not, I repeat, excuse a certain recidivist negligence on my part . . .) Now I find the things you wrote very much in agreement with what I was saying to you. But this word "spontaneous," would it not make Sereni sit bolt upright in his chair?[78] For some time now I've been struggling with the problem of "spontaneity" in literature and in general. And I'd like to do a study of it, a proper study with all the rules, looking at classic texts.

However, I know that my limitation, in theoretical discussions, is that of the literary digression, almost of paradox. The important point here is that this too can be something serious, if it discovers or articulates some things, and it must have citizenship in the Party literature (or rather—in today's society—in literature tout court). Today it does not. Today there is the tendency toward the Official-Party-Writer, like Fadeyev, like Aragon, who end up not saying anything because they say what the Party, as the Party, has already said. But I believe that writers who make their own experiences, who sniff the wind, and provide announcements and alerts as subjects of study and work for the Party, are of more immediate *usefulness*.

I tell you, I think our Catholic friends also belong to the category of writers of digressions and intuitions. And they should be discussed on this level. Except that they consider themselves to be expert and accomplished theorists; hence the difficulty in discussing with them, and their inaccessible attitude which makes you bitterly indignant.

I'll reply to you "officially" on the rights of the Czechs.

Ciao *Calv.*

[Handwritten; with the addressee's heirs.]

1951–1955

To Geno Pampaloni—Ivrea

Turin, 22 June 1951

Dear Pampaloni,

For some time I had wanted to write you an enthusiastic letter about your excellent article on Vittorini; subsequently I wanted to make it less enthusiastic after reading your essay on Orwell; now I've read your polemical piece on Pavese and I'm starting to organize my ideas and think I'm in a position to write you quite a comprehensive letter.[1]

I'll start right away by informing you that as far as the Pavese book is concerned, you're completely mistaken. Einaudi has not done anything wrong against Pavese by publishing his poems; they've respected his wishes without any possibility of doubt. For those who knew Pavese, and knew how keen he was on those poems as he was writing them, and those who found his typescript all neat and ready on his office desk, ready to go to the printers, with the title *Verrà la morte e avrà i tuoi occhi* (*Death Will Come and Will Have Your Eyes*) written in his own hand on the cover (and not chosen by us!), there could be no doubt: it was Pavese's wish that this should be his first posthumous volume.[2]

Naturally before publishing it we thought: "But isn't it too soon, after all the gossip in the papers, to give the public these poems that are so closely bound up with his final desperate crisis?" But we didn't want to wait, both because we knew we were carrying out his tacit intention, and because we think they are very fine poems (as you will discover when you read them less hurriedly), and also in any case they are very far from providing titbits for any journalistic elaboration, and finally because in order to educate the reading public you have to show confidence in them. In this way they can learn that one doesn't go nosing about in the private lives of writers, or turning up one's nose at them, but rather one respects and studies the testimony of their life which must serve everyone: for the writer is someone who tears himself to pieces in order to liberate his neighbor.

It must be said that the majority of readers have shown themselves to be able to meet the challenge: they knew how to read Pavese as a classic. But the reaction of others has worried us and made us reflect whether we should not still wait a number of years before publishing his diary. Some have found this book too near the bone, because of their own immaturity as readers. And now we find your outburst, something we never expected, from a reader who is as highly informed and sharp as anyone.

The most inexplicable thing is that you, after being shocked by the publication of these poems, are now asking for the diary to be published; and you recommend that no cuts be made. Clearly you don't realize that the diary treats in a much more intimate, searing way the more strictly personal of Pavese's problems, in amongst many reflections on his poetics. I think that you are expecting a political diary as opposed to a book of love poems; well, I'm sorry to tell you that in the diary there is only the odd allusion to politics—and even then nothing from more recent times—which we'll be very careful not to cut out. With his diary Pavese wanted to give us this testimony to an ancient tragicness in human life which is ineluctable. As for theorizing on contemporary crises, there is no one further from that than him. If the book is published soon—but it won't be before next year, however—we will have to make some cuts out of respect for people involved in his private life, and also at some points where he cries out his pain in words that could offend his own memory; nothing else, unless we want to distort the structure and meaning of the diary. But if there are those who are protesting at the publication of his poems, what will happen when the diary is published? Perhaps it's best to wait about ten years.

But the problem I was interested in solving is a different one. You are undoubtedly one of our finest critics, you combine a rigorous philological *habitus* with a very sharp sensibility, you have given us exemplary demonstrations of "how to read" an author. How on earth can you veer so suddenly and throw yourself into praising a second-rate pamphleteer after an occasional glance at a translation, and fire off a totally groundless polemic against an author when you have all the time in the world to get up-to-date documentation on him?

It seems to me the answer could be this: you have not immunized yourself adequately against infection from one of the greatest and most hackneyed malaises of our time: anti-Communism. This tendency probably developed in you as a defense mechanism against a certain number of things that were not going well for you; but it soon became aggressive and has reached fever pitch. As long as you are analyzing texts and questions that don't come into this polemic you are all precision, sharpness, and good taste; but if, directly or indirectly, you step into the terrain of Communism/Anti-Communism, you get emotional, and forget your critical *habitus* and you just make one mistake after another.

For now this is just a risk I seem to see in you and that's why I've taken the liberty to warn you about it, because you certainly possess enough strength to resist such a damaging and vulgar ailment.

Best wishes.

[Typewritten copy; in the Einaudi Archive; published in *ILDA*, pp. 45–57.]

To Elio Vittorini—Milan

Turin, 20 December 1951

Dear Elio,

Delighted that you like *The Viscount*.[3] I am a bit reluctant to publish it as a book: would that not mean giving it too much importance? Or perhaps labeling myself as a writer of minor things, writing for "amusement"? Let's talk about it.

Now I need to ask you to supply the text for the blurbs for the books in the Gettoni series that are about to come out.

I enclose the small amount of biographical data that each of the three writers has sent me.

Ciao, and best wishes

[Typewritten copy; in the Einaudi Archives.]

To Michele Rago—Rome

Turin, 7-6-52

Dear Michele,

Thank you for your kind letter which has put into a state of total confusion my Ligurian uncouthness: I mean the fact that I am always clumsy when it's a question of expressing or responding in affectionate terms. In any case, you certainly will be able to understand me more than I am able to make myself understood.

I'm happy that the impalpable "moral" ease of Turin has conquered you too; and I hope it will attract you here more often.

Thank you also for what you write about my private life. On my private life one cannot write in terms of happiness and perfection, but as one does of every living thing, in terms of a trial overcome in every single moment, of greater or lesser success in continuing to be oneself while not betraying the implicit human commitments that every action, every relationship with others involves. In short: I don't want to let these things impinge on me, I want to impinge on them. For me happiness consists in willingly participating in pushing forward the opportunities in life which continually assembles and unravels things, but at the same time always staying faithful to the principle of never doing others' evil nor my own, or doing as little of it as possible.

This is a period in which I'm working quite a lot: I've written quite a clever but slightly gratuitous story, so I'm not very happy with it; it will come out in *Botteghe Oscure*.[4] Now I'm doing short stories along the lines of certain others I've written previously, grotesque, antimilitarist tales, which is the vein that is easiest for writing "useful" stories; I'll publish them in *l'Unità*, and hope to write enough to make a whole volume. But then I've also got many other ideas, as well as the will to work, if the summer didn't inveigle me into going to bathe at the pool or in the Po and then spend the evening in some cool cinema.

Many affectionate greetings also from my girlfriend,

Yours

Calvino

We're waiting for the Rousseau which E. would like to publish as soon as possible.[5]

[Handwritten; with the addressee.]

To Michele Rago—Rome

Turin 27–6–52

Dear Michele,

THANK YOU FOR YOUR LETTER, FULL OF GOOD, SHARP INSIGHTS, as always. And there is no need for you to justify your tone; otherwise I'd have to justify my tone and apologize for it, and it would never end.

I agree especially on *being* which must always be implicit in *acting*; it's the only way to overcome "spontaneity" without strangling it and reducing ourselves to an abstract voluntarism.

Now let's talk about my typescript.[6] I'm pleased you liked it. You're just about the first person who has said that to me. But the criticism you make of it is right. The last few times I went back to look at it I was put off by this effusive, rhetorical tone, which clearly isn't my own, it's not a tone I know how to use. The novel started off as being entirely epistolary; but seeing that an exchange of letters with such minutiae of narrative was improbable, I reduced the letters to intermezzi of comment, and put the rest into the third person; but that false note remained. I'm no longer able to revise it, to put any more effort into it. I don't believe in it enough: what I mean is that the plot seems too insignificant for the questions it attempts to raise and articulate. The contrast between, on the one hand, reason, history, ethics, the working class, the city, the machine etc., and, on the other hand, nature, immediacy, woman, Rousseau etc. has for the first group symbols that are only dimly glimpsed and are a rhetorical aspiration, and for the second group symbols like the river and the girl that are too limited and fatuous to stand up against the first lot. In short, I'm beginning to realize that it really is a failed work and if I don't find anyone who can rekindle my affection for it, I'd be more inclined to keep it in the drawer. Gerratana wrote to me saying that in his opinion it was not publishable, but he didn't specify why. In short, I'd like to discuss it in a little more depth before making my mind up, but I've not managed to do this with anyone so far.

We'll talk about it again. Tell me whether you think that these doubts I have are right, and if you have some other reader close by whose judgment is important, let them read the typescript too. I'd like to make my decision on a broader platform of views.[7]

Don't forget the Rousseau.[8]

Warmest regards also from my girlfriend,

Your Calv.

[Handwritten; with the addressee.]

To *l'Unità*

[Turin, 26–30 June 1952]

Sir,

I have been following in recent days in *l'Unità* the news of the escapees from Devil's Island in Brazil. I have to tell you that I felt that there were a number of things in the coverage of these events that did not sound right to me. The escapees are considered to be "madmen, with a thirst for blood" (22 June); the headlines refer to "ferocious torturing of the prison governor and prison officers" (24 June); there is reportage of "atrocious scenes beyond all imagination," the escape is described as a bestial brawl in which the strongest fling the weakest overboard from the lifeboats and they are then devoured by sharks (26 June).

I have no information regarding Brazilian prisons nor that prison in particular; I do know, however, that Brazil has a fascist-style regime and it seems to me that *l'Unità* cannot blindly accept news reports that clearly come from Brazilian governmental agencies.

Probably many of the escapees are genuine criminals for whom we cannot show solidarity, but we can take as certain a number of points: (1) a revolt of this kind only flares up in order to crush a cruel prison regime, of the kind we know exists in various parts of the capitalist world, and certainly exists in Brazil; (2) we can never consider as criminals en bloc the detainees of a capitalist country, indeed of a fascist one: amongst these there will also be oppressed workers, victims of the social system, and very probably political detainees;[9] (3) in events of this kind brutal and cruel episodes necessarily take place, but we Italians have too much experience of libelous campaigns and the false reporting of atrocities to accept these at face value; (4) a movement of this kind, holding huge army forces at bay, does not succeed unless it is organized, so the hellish scenes of men being thrown to the sharks are improbable. The fact that the wives and children of the functionaries and the soldiers have been respected and made to shelter in a special pavilion, contradicts this scene of uncontrolled violence; (5) I read on 26 June that several Brazilian MPs have taken action against the entire prison regime; this is the line we must follow and we must not forget that these things are happening in the country that is putting on trial Carlos Luis Prestes.[10]

To conclude,[11] I would like agency news to be reported with greater caution in *l'Unità*.

Correct me if I am wrong.

Yours fraternally,

Italo Calvino

[Undated typewritten copy, unsigned; in the Calvino Archive. Published in *l'Unità*, 1 July 1952, under the title "I brasiliani evasi dall'isola di Anchieta" (The Brazilian escapees from the Island of Anchieta).]

To Ernesto Travi—Milan

Turin, 9 July 1952

My Dear Mr Travi,

I read your review of my book in the *Ragguaglio librario*, and while not being able to share any of your judgments, I thank you for the kind interest you have shown in it.[12] That a reader can find in a book things which the author never thought of saying is a sign of the vitality of that book; but I have to tell you that yours is often not so much arbitrary interpretation as total misunderstanding. I think you read my book in a tremendous hurry: that's the only way you can have perceived "nausea" in my depiction of the Huguenots. Actually, mine was simply a critical, ironic view of them, but also at the same time one that was warm and fully sympathetic, in the limited extent to which I too feel similar to them. Speaking very broadly, I can say that I wanted to depict (in this aforementioned critical and yet still slightly involved way) moralism in the Huguenots and hedonism in the lepers; and if one wanted to attribute a more precise allegory to the lepers, I will say that I was thinking of contemporary decadent artists (and of that small part of myself that still shares that spirit). What can your reference to the proletariat have to do with all this?

This reference of yours strikes me and saddens me not just because it is irrelevant but for the way in which it is expressed: "that proletarian mass that creates such a sensation over its own misery." This is a phrase of blind, fanatical cruelty, of the kind that one would have thought impossible to write nowadays in Italy; I would like to think that it was written in a moment of distraction; that it expresses a way of feeling that is not your own personal one; that when you reflect on this phrase you can understand how much a position of blind conservatism can remove you from Christianity and the very notion of humanity.

I would like to think that all this is the case: because really it would grieve me that a person who reads and appreciates, albeit in his own way, the things I write, is a person who thinks he can blithely cultivate his soul in the midst of so many torments inflicted on his fellow human beings.

Yours sincerely,

[Typed copy; in the Einaudi Archive, Turin.]

To Carlo Salinari—Rome

[Turin,] 7 August 1952

Dear Salinari,

I'VE READ YOUR ARTICLE ON MY BOOK.[13] I AGREE WITH THE EXternal definition, if we can call it that: a literary *divertissement*, a bravura piece, a nod to those in the know, something for a restricted circle of readers, and all the limitations that such a definition involves.

On the other hand, I cannot concur with your definition of the book's central motif. The fact that man is a mixture of good and evil actually mattered very little to me; that is old hat and predictable, as everyone knows. What I was interested in was the problem of contemporary man (or rather the intellectual, to be more precise) who is divided, that is to say incomplete, "alienated." If I decided to split my protagonist down the line of the good-evil fracture, I did so because that allowed me a greater clarity of contrasting images, and it was connected with a literary tradition that was already something of a classic (for instance, Stevenson) so that I could play with it without worrying. Whereas my moralizing winks, so to speak, were aimed not so much at the viscount as at the frame characters, who are the real exemplifications of my argument. In other words, the lepers (i.e., decadent artists), the doctor, and the carpenter (science and technology detached from humanity), those Huguenots, seen with a bit of sympathy and with a bit of irony (they are in a sense an autobiographical allegory of mine portraying my family [a kind of imaginary, genealogical epic of my family],[14] and also an image of the whole line of bourgeois idealist moralizing from the Reformation to Croce).

You will say: but none of this can be understood from the text. And on this score all I can do is say you're right. The "anti-historicism" of the book, in my view, is not in its thematics, but is actually in its nature as a kind of game, which does not require allegories to be looked for, though at the same time suggesting them, whereas the books we most need are those that are explicit and devoid of allusions. That does not take away from the fact that one can still write books like this; it's just that we also have to write the other books too, the real ones.

I had written another book that was completely different,[15] one which had cost me a lot of effort; now it's with Michele Rago, and

I've written to him to let you read it too.[16] Up until now it has not met with any good fortune and I think I'll have to resign myself to leaving it unpublished, even though I was very keen on it. Instead, *The Cloven Viscount*, written to give my imagination a holiday after punishing it in the other novel, has enjoyed a success that I would never have expected for it. I thought of publishing it in a journal like *Botteghe Oscure* because publishing it as a book would have seemed to give it too much importance; but basically "I Gettoni" also have a public the size of a journal and I published it in that series. I know that the success it has enjoyed is out of all proportion and partly ambiguous, and I don't trust it; in fact I can't wait to make some people eat their own words of exaggerated praise. But I think the forbidding faces of some comrades are also exaggerated. This is a story in a genre where I could write another ten or twenty such tales, and without much effort, if I weren't completely taken up with the desire to write things that I believe are more important. And my ideal would be to manage to write in equal measure, and ideally with equal facility, "useful" things and "amusing" things. And possibly things that are useful and amusing at the same time.

That's my plan of work for the next ten years at least.

Ciao

Calvino

[Handwritten on Einaudi headed paper; in the Calvino Archive. An almost identical typed copy in the Einaudi Archive, Turin. Also in *ILDA*, pp. 67–68.]

To Alberto Carocci—Rome

Turin, 15 October 1952

Dear Carocci,

Thank you very much for your invitation to contribute to *Nuovi Argomenti*:[17] I was already looking forward to the journal with baited breath, so much so that I was sorry to learn from your letter that things are still in a preparatory phase and I will have to prolong my wait as an impatient reader. I would be very happy to contribute; but I have to tell you that for some time now I've imposed a rule on myself not to write any more criticism, essays, or theoretical articles. I realize I do not have my ideas sufficiently clear to start pontificating. At once both unsatisfied with and involved in all the problems I see moving around me, I try to solve them on a practical level, on the level of life and creative activity, but as for theorizing about solutions—or the problems of the century—I'm not up to it: I listen to everyone but I do not do what they say; and I have to tell you I find this suits me very well. You see basically I am the ideal reader for *Nuovi Argomenti*. And too much of an ideal reader to be a contributor to the journal, at least for the first number. In the course of time it may be that the critical power of the journal will be such as to make me break my vow of essay-writing chastity . . . I don't know. As far as fiction is concerned, certainly, as soon as I have a short story of the right size, and one that seems worthy of being submitted, I'll send it to you;[18] but for the time being, I don't have anything.

With best regards

[Typed copy; in the Calvino Archive.]

To Carlo Salinari—Rome

[Turin,] 22–12–52

Dear Salinari,

I AM VERY PLEASED THAT YOU LIKED *I GIOVANI DEL PO* (*YOUTH in Turin*). You, along with Rago,[19] are, it's fair to say, the only ones who have given a positive verdict on it, of all those who have read it so far, whether comrades or not.

I would be in favor of giving it to "Edizioni di Cultura Sociale,"[20] but I've passed on your proposal to Einaudi who of course has "option rights" over everything I write: and he said that if I want to publish it there's no reason for me not to publish it with him. So I have to decline your kind offer. I feel a bit embarrassed at publishing it with Einaudi (that is to say, having it come out at my own request, since all the verdicts inside the publishing house were negative), but I'll end up bringing it out (in the PBSL series, I think),[21] because I'm keen on documenting the work I have done in this area, even though it cannot be considered complete.

This is a book that I'm very keen on even if I am convinced that it is not a success—and a recent rereading, along with new attempts at cutting and polishing, has confirmed this to me—but it is still a book *that I would like to write*: in it there is not so much a finished product as a program of work, an attempt to organize my imagination and style and ideas. But I am aware that there's a gap between the problematic commitment and the narrative which means that everything sounds false. In it the working class is little more than a symbol, a moral appeal, it's not something real (it's unlikely that workers will identify with it); the love story too has an allegorical function, and the disparity between these two terms is in the end disproportionate. As a result I had thought of circulating it in typescript amongst friends who might be interested in the effort I had made. Now your proposal from Cultura Sociale has reawakened both my interest in seeing it published, and along with that, my doubts.

DE JACO: it was I who informed De Jaco that V. would like to exclude his "party political stories," which, as far as I am concerned, are his best, whereas I don't appreciate so much the more "Neapolitan" ones, which V. prefers.[22] However, I'm not despairing of V. changing his mind. In the Gettoni series he has the last say; and if he sees himself being obstructed, he retreats into his tent like Achilles. Now De Jaco has sent him other longer stories and I hope a good little collection can be put together. This De Jaco is a talented guy and we need to keep an eye on him: no one has ever been able to describe as he does the world of the party's local branches, their moral relationships etc. with his sharp and discreet sureness of touch.

I'll read that manuscript you sent me and I'll write you the letter you need.

With my warmest regards and best wishes for the New Year.

Calv.

[Handwritten draft on Einaudi headed paper; in the Calvino Archive.]

To Raffaello Brignetti—Rome

Turin, 11 June 1953

Dear Brignetti,

Stop being a journalist at once, it's a job that is incompatible with being a writer; or rather, you can even work in a newspaper but as long as you don't write for it. You can be an editor, a reporter, but never a correspondent or at any rate in any job where you have to write articles. Being a journalist is a job of enormous social importance, and one which requires exceptional talents, but which cannot be cultivated alongside literature, because you cannot use the same instrument—language and writing—in two completely different ways.

But even more important is that you immediately give up traveling: travel serves no purpose whatsoever, except that of offering you a good time and preventing you from writing. It is impossible to write about anything except what one has lived through for years and years and which far from amusing and interesting us has bored us and made us suffer.

I'm saying this to you as one who regularly and happily travels and is a journalist. In fact I am someone who could not live without traveling and being a journalist every so often; but who could not write a line unless he forbade himself from traveling and being a journalist for a large part of the year.

I'm sending you back the cutting: it's an incident like countless others that take place in our country; and if you feel this is the case, it can be, like everything else, good material. But is that Gogolian style really yours? Careful you don't betray yourself.

Work. Stay in touch.

Best wishes

[Typed copy; in the Einaudi Archive, Turin. Also in *ILDA*, p. 91.]

To Alberto Carocci—Rome

Turin, 29 July 1953

Dear Carocci,

I WOULD GLADLY SEND YOU ANOTHER STORY BUT I REALLY don't know when.[23] I have little time for writing and always have a queue of journal editors to whom I've promised something. It seems that the short story has become a rarity: who would have thought it? At any rate, as soon as I have something "decent," I'll put *Nuovi Argomenti* at the head of the queue.

Meantime I can give you some useful addresses:

Anna Maria Ortese—c/o Burnet—Via Vigoni 5—Milan (she can supply excellent things and ones that suit *Nuovi Argomenti*'s line).
Renzo Biasion—Corso Sommellier 15—Turin (he has already published a book and will publish a collection of very good stories with us on the war in Greece;[24] you could ask him for one of those, if you can get it out in time before our volume which will come out in September–October).
Aldo De Jaco—Via Mancinelli 10—Naples (a young Neapolitan, rather good).

Another thing: I'd like to suggest we do a survey for your journal, which I'm working on with a friend.[25] It's about the factories in Turin: the dignity of the worker and the management systems. (Now I'll work on how to get a better title.) This is a subject that up until now has only been treated in the Party's press, but which deserves to be studied from a more broadly human viewpoint as a sign of the involution of social relations in Italy today. By now public and cultural opinion is sufficiently well informed on the persecution of Pentecostalists and on cinema censorship; but people end up by not thinking about these other matters which are considered the domain of technical experts from the world of politics or trade unions, whereas they are actually fundamental questions. And information is *quite* easy to get hold of (I say "quite" because many won't want to have their name made public etc.): ranging from strip-searches on entering and leaving the factory, to the monitoring of the toilets, and the use of spies in various departments etc. All of this, of course, will have to be treated with a language that is not political or vindictive. What do you think?[26]

We'll talk about it again at the end of August. I'll be in England for about twenty days.

Best wishes

[Typed copy; in the Einaudi Archive, Turin.]

To Severino Dal Sasso—Rome

Turin, 23 September 1953

Dear Dal Sasso,

I agree, P. is inside Decadentism, he lives in it, he works on it.[27] But since at a certain point Decadentism becomes everything, there is a way of existing within it, of living it through to the bitter end which is already something else. (And then how can you say it's impossible "to isolate and identify [non-] decadent cultural strands in his work"? They are there, plenty of them, if being non-decadentist today means anything: and they come out clearly particularly in his essays on American literature.)

In any case I am not in the ideal position to engage in these debates as my current reading has thrown everything I thought into chaos: Lukács.[28] Read it at once (you'll have received a copy): I advise you to begin with the second part. From those other two books of his I did not really get an idea of him: I thought he was a clever transformer of aesthetic questions into problems in the history of culture. Instead he is—perhaps—the first Marxist I've read who when he talks about literature deals with the flesh and blood of works, and he sets out the problems before you in a way that leaves you gasping. So then literary genres are really something important? So then a novel's plot is something fundamental? But then . . . I'm here and I don't understand a thing.

I got them to send you those Gettoni books. But what is the point in writing another article on the series? Do you want to criticize Vittorini's taste through that series? But the poor authors will lose out, authors who—whether good or bad—deserve to be considered one by one, not collectively through the series. And Vittorini's blurbs are too easy a target.

Best wishes

[Typed copy; in the Einaudi Archive, Turin.]

To Giuseppe Cocchiara—Palermo

Turin, 15 January 1954

Dear Cocchiara,

Ever since I got back from Sicily I've been wanting to write to you to tell you how pleased I am to have met you, to have had the chance to discuss things with you, and to thank you for the more than kind welcome you gave us in your house and for the wonderful tour round the Museum.[29]

I take the opportunity of this letter to send you and your kind wife all my warmest greetings for the New Year.

For some time we've been meaning to reply to a letter of yours to Einaudi, a letter full of interesting proposals.

The first proposal, that of a collection of Sicilian folk songs, would immediately be absorbed by a project for which we have an explicit commitment for some time now: a collection of folk songs from the whole of Italy. We are not sure what point the editors of the collection have reached; but for the time being we cannot commit ourselves to other initiatives of this kind.

As for Novati's essays, this is not a propitious moment in the world of publishing for collections of miscellaneous writings, especially ones that have to be exhumed.[30] And our Essays series has a program that is full all the way through 1955, and in this program any books that are not of pressing publishing interest and which don't lose their topicality are postponed from year to year or rejected.

On the other hand we are very interested in the project to collect the Italian folk tales (or popular novellas or stories, however you want to call them).[31] This is also an idea that we began to discuss a few months ago, that is to say from the moment our publication of Afanasiev, following that of Grimm, made us realize we had to develop an organic plan for fables from all over the world.[32] As for the Italian tales, which have not yet had their Grimm or their Afanasiev on a national scale, this is a huge problem, and we would be very happy to receive any preliminary advice you may have. There is the problem of the collection of the material which for some regions has already been published and for others is almost non-existent. There is the question of the dialects. There is the problem when assembling material from different collectors of giving a stylistic unity, and unity of method to the book. Some time ago one of our colleagues sent us a proposal from Prof. Vidossi for a volume containing the Tuscan, Umbrian, and Veneto tales in the original and the ones from the other regions in Italian translation. But Einaudi's intention is to do something that is as far removed as possible from a university text-book, but which is instead fresh reading for a non-academic public, though carried out with all the criteria of Italian folklore research. Consequently, Einaudi's view is that the publishing house should take responsibility itself for the editing of the work, making use of the advice and material offered by specialists, and should "unify" the volume. In a word, keeping a sound philological basis but adopting criteria that are essentially artistic. In fact he actually proposed that I—poor me!—should take on this work of unification, in other words choosing from amongst the variant versions, translating where things need to be translated, rewriting in Italian things that have already been written down. From the sketchy survey I have been able to carry out so far—completely devoid of expertise as I am in this field—it seems to me undoubtedly absurd, for instance, to rewrite Imbriani's Tuscan: that would destroy the spirit of those tales.[33] We ought therefore to adopt a mixed criterion, along the lines proposed by Vidossi, in other words reproduce part of the material exactly as the collectors have handed it down to us, but translate other parts of it; and here too the work of the "writer" (whoever he is) must be accompanied by the work of the philologist, the scholar of dialects. In short, we're still up in the air. Tell us what you think.[34]

Warmest regards and I hope to read something of yours soon.
With best wishes

[Typed copy; in the Einaudi Archive, Turin. Also in *ILDA*, pp. 109–10.]

To Luciano Pistoi—Turin

[Turin,] 17 February 1954

Dear Pistoi,

Will you forgive me if I take the luxury of arguing a bit with you as well? The thing is that in your article, "Un critico d'arte senza 'repubblica'" (An art critic without a homeland),[35] there is a point I do not understand. This point precisely: "And the complex problem of the separation that has really taken place between contemporary figurative art and the public, which is the problem of the crisis in a society and a culture . . ."

I too believed in this "separation" for a long time, but not any more. I hope I can manage to explain to you why. But above all: is "separation" ever possible, dialectically? I don't think so. Nevertheless, since it is you—a Communist—who uses the term, I naturally start to doubt my own reasoning and prefer to talk to you about it, as I'm doing.

I'll start by saying that I'm trying to set up the question in the context of a contradiction; but, in order to do this I think it is wise to start by establishing what we mean by another term you use, namely "crisis." For me crisis means: the moment of encounter of two opposing and interdependent forces, in other words the moment when the two horns of the contradiction enter into direct conflict, preparing us for the "leap." What are these two opposing forces? Jumping to the final analysis, I would have no hesitation in calling them action and reaction.

And now to begin: what is art? Is it not perhaps the greatest exemplification of the present? If so, contemporary art (and in a more obvious way figurative art, then) cannot help representing today's crisis, hence the clash between the two forces. By representing this clash, what does art show us and what does it consist in? It consists precisely in the two distinct but not disconnected forces. (I'm explaining things in this way because Picasso is a Communist artist—even though he does not paint realistically—since he portrays the two horns of the contradiction. Tomorrow he can become a realist painter, thus taking the "leap," but the work he does today can never be inferior to future work, because it is just as real. However, in order to be a realist painter—I won't say writer—nowadays, in Western Europe, some preliminary conditions still seem to me to be missing, amongst which there is, primarily, the widespread knowledge of the importance of *living*, which means transforming things—for the sake of using them—and not just understanding them in a contemplative way.)

But to go back to the two distinct but not disconnected forces: when faced with a painting by, say, Picasso, what does the public see? What does it not see? It sees the crisis, without understanding it (= what it does not see). What happens to them as a consequence? They take up a position of resistance (*not* of "separation"). Are they wrong to behave like this? First and foremost, since what happens is that they react like this, in the final analysis this cannot be "wrong"; secondly, why should they behave differently? How could they behave differently?

Behaving differently would mean they had understood the crisis and therefore solved it, and in that case Picasso would not be an artist because he would not be relevant. The public's opposition thus remains, in my view, rational and active—inasmuch as it rehearses the action in order to overcome it—even though it shows itself as in reaction to the spectacle of crisis, and for that very reason. Consequently, Picasso cannot be "seen" today by those who have taken the "leap": for the masses he remains "unknown," because the masses—the healthy part of them—demand the "leap" from themselves and from the artist, since they cannot stay simply at the stage of "passive" contemplation of the person who has already made the "leap."

But the masses are made up of the proletariat—the healthy part—and the bourgeoisie. What do the bourgeoisie oppose or rather resist? They too are opposed to the spectacle of the crisis. Why? Because the crisis (= imperialism) is the final phase of capitalism (their resistance is thus experienced passively). What would they want, in fact? They would like to go back to "artistic" reproduction, which is peculiar to capitalism, and would guarantee them a reality that was by this stage superseded by the development of the revolution (= evolution, if I'm not mistaken). Hence the impressionists, with their dialectical materialism, were the first great "representatives" of the looming crisis.

That is how I explain to myself, amongst other things, how on earth the proletariat and the bourgeoisie find themselves in agreement in *resisting*, no matter how active this is for the former and how passive for the latter.

In conclusion: I would not talk of the "separation," but of the "resistance" of the spectator who thus does not seem to me to be uninterested in his own problems. In fact deriding and repudiating contemporary art does not mean, in my view, that the public has become "detached," but rather it articulates a clear stance taken by the public itself. It would be "detachment" if such a position did not exist.

In every period when the two forces—action and reaction—are not in crisis, the artist is followed; every time there is a crisis, the artist is opposed. But whether he enjoys public approval or is the target of disapproval, the artist can never find himself in a situation of detachment, otherwise he would not be one. For the fact is that art cannot detach itself from life—nor man from art—since art is the form, the image of current thought, or rather is reality itself revealed.

What do you think? If you prefer, we can talk about it in person. Best wishes to you, Sesa and Spriano.[36]

[Typed copy; in the Calvino Archive.]

To Domenico Rea—Naples

Turin, 13 March, 1954

ON BEING LACONIC

Dear Rea,

You ask why I am laconic. For several reasons. First, out of necessity, since I write in an office, where I am a slave to the frantic rhythm of industrial production which governs and even shapes our very thoughts. Second, out of stylistic choice, since I try to adhere—as far as I can—to the lessons learnt from my favorite authors. Third, for reasons of character: I am continuing the heritage of my Ligurian ancestors, who are a people more contemptuous of effusiveness than any others. In addition, and most important of all, out of moral conviction: I believe being laconic is a good method for communicating and learning, better than any uncontrolled and deceptive expansiveness. And finally—I would add—out of a polemical and proselytizing spirit, because I would like everybody to convert to this approach, and want all those who talk about themselves and about "my soul"[37] to realize that these are pointless and inappropriate utterances.

Laconically yours,

[Typewritten copy; in the Einaudi Archives. Also in *ILDA*, p. 125.]

To *Il Contemporaneo*—Rome

[Turin, end of March 1954]

Dear Salinari, Antonello, Cesarini, Valentino,

IT'S HORRIBLE![38]

It exceeds all my most pessimistic forecasts!

The squalor of it is horrendous. It looks like *Idea*.[39] It is even more squalid than that since one senses that you cannot even fill the pages.

I've not read any of it yet. I felt the need to write to you after my first impression. Ok, you may be disadvantaged as far as typography is concerned. But it's also true that the pagination could not have been set up more drearily.[40]

The first page has nothing interesting. On pages two and three putting two landscape drawings opposite each other is one of those mistakes that even a novice learns to avoid immediately.[41]

The rubrics, the famous rubrics that were to denounce and inform turn out to be flawed and non-existent right from the start.[42] And on this point you can't start complaining about your collaborators not working, here it was you people in Rome who should have got involved.[43] This is a paper that immediately gives the impression that it is not worth reading. There is nothing which makes you say: this I must read immediately! Nothing even in italics. You're no good even at choosing a shot from a film, for God's sake! You put in a photograph that every other editorial board would have chucked in the bin as soon as they saw it![44]

A weekly must give the impression of being full of things. Vicari's *Il Caffè* is marvelous by comparison![45]

Now I'm going to read it and then I'll write you another letter and haul you over the coals again![46]

As a comrade addressing other comrades, I say to you: you are useless, amateurs, improvisers!

[Draft and typed copy; in the Calvino Archive. The footnotes to this letter provide some of the variants in the draft.]

To Carlo Salinari—Rome

Turin, 10 April 1954

Dear Salinari and dear colleagues,

I received Salinari's letter and I'm glad that you agree with my criticisms, but I'm a little bit worried that I find you so ready to accept them, so devoid of any fighting spirit or any counter-attack. For goodness' sake, if it was so clear that that first issue was so horrible, why did you publish it? Maybe in this submissiveness to criticism lies one of the roots of the journal's weakness: in other words in its not having a clear enough identity and therefore not wanting to make anyone unhappy.

I'm formulating this opinion after word reached us here in Turin too about Cases's article being sent back to him with red and blue underlining and question marks every time he used "bourgeois decadence',", "bourgeois corruption," etc. This is a story that will make people fall about laughing and will be handed down as an anecdote and in a century's time people will say: "Just think that in 1954 some Communists, having decided to set up a 'broad-based' journal . . ."

These are things that one should not really need to say: a journal is "broad-based" when everyone supports its line with their own words and not with official jargon. Otherwise you'll end up like so many comrades who at the local committee for peace or some other mass organization make their little bureaucratic speech, replacing the word "comrades" with "friends," and "Communists" with "democrats," and what comes out is something that is as cold and artificial as can be. (A few days ago, at a union meeting at the Labour Centre in Turin, a comrade said: "As secretary of a democratic circle, I found myself the other evening doing my duty as a democrat, when etc.") Now Cases seems to me to be precisely that rare thing, a witty and communicative Communist. Let's allow him to speak badly of the bourgeoisie just for once!

Taking up Salinari's invitation, I'll continue with my critique of the journal, a duty that is not yet difficult and still quite pleasant. I didn't have time to write to you about issue no. 2: I'll do it now before moving on to no. 3.

Issue no. 2 was a bit better than the first issue because there was more material and there was an attractive piece in the interview with Sartre. However the most important problem that issue 2 started to tackle was the question of relations with Soviet culture (the editorial and the article by G. Berlinguer). And it did not approach the problem well. For the editorial avoided the real poison of Scelba's law,[47] namely his phrase "the countries where cultural activities too are in actual fact a state monopoly," and there you really needed to explain as briefly as possible what relations between culture and the state mean there and what they mean here. Only in that way can you attack the Scelba formula of "reciprocity" and not with a vague, liberal-sounding lament. In addition Berlinguer's article is a journalistic polemic against another journalistic polemic, and an American one at that. Whereas one needs the journal to provide direct information on Soviet culture and polemics on this matter with the best of Italian culture, going into the specifics of the topic as much as possible. As in fact you do in issue no. 3.

No. 3. It's better than the first two. Here at last we begin to confront problems that really are of interest and on which there is an expectation of hearing our answer, like the recent discussions about aesthetics in the USSR. Salinari's article as a way into the topic works very well. The editorial on a serious problem of principle such as that of self-censorship is important. The atomic article: very interesting.

The journal's structure has improved, with the larger number of small rubrics, the shifting of the economic page to p. 10, leaving a more dynamic page on p. 5 which also contains Bandinelli's *Lunario*.

The Valentino-Fortini dispute: we're there, well more or less. It seems to be just a flat refusal to admit that a problem exists. The substance of the article is: "Us? For goodness' sake! Look you're wrong about this! Who told you?" Which is also a more than legitimate way of responding to a polemic, by denying that the basis of the polemic exists. An article like that in *Rinascita* would be perfectly in its place, it would become an official reply by the Communists to a mistaken opinion about them. But here we need to make it different, I'm not sure exactly how, because I can't remember that piece by Fortini and I've got no time to reread it. But I know what he's like, he bristles with problems, he's a collector of the century's ills, and if you reply to him: "But I'm fine and quite healthy," it's the same as not replying to him at all. You start to reply to him when you start searching in the midst of all his rubbish, his delight in playing the role of the provocateur etc., searching for what he is really getting his teeth into, seriously dealing with the century's problems, namely that unfocused need buzzing in many people's heads though not in bad faith etc. This is one of the duties of a cultural weekly, I believe.

Vespignani's cartoons. You've already had a lot of criticism about the ones in the first two issues (especially on his insistence on funerals) and I see you've changed tack. I've got a soft spot for Vespignani because I like those cartoonists who draw things in a minute and complicated way. But he's not yet found the formula for the front-page cartoon. The first one was too strong, too Grosz like, for the journal's tone, which, as we've seen, is so polite with everyone. Then the second one was in the style of expressionist cartoons à la Mittel Berg; that's already an old format, one which doesn't frighten anyone any more, and doesn't even catch the eye any more. (This really is an example of a language that is already "official" and which is not suited to the paper. Better if Vespignani really did tell us *his* impressions of what the EDC means:[48] for instance being called up and finding a German officer at your medical: that could have been a cartoon.) In issue 3 we've moved to specialist, internal, caricature à la Bartoli even though it's more intelligent—but that would not have been difficult.[49] It's fine but I would say it's not suitable for the front page, also because it is not topical.

Frascione's drawing has already been published recently, I can't remember where.

Fiore's survey seems good: certainly the best so far, because it's the first that's been properly "written."

Page 7 is a problem. The fact that the survey begins on p. 6 deprives it of a headline, which is always a disaster for an odd-numbered page.

The poem on p. 7 livens it up a bit, but you'll get into awful trouble with poets.

That short story in issue 2 seems weak and superfluous to me.

The cinema page is still one of the best.
The two reviews in this issue (by Gallo and d'Amico) are both good.
I see that in the short notices you're moving from a brief review to merely giving bibliographical information. Why?

Best wishes from your

Calv.

[Draft (with minimal variants) and typed copy; in the Calvino Archive.]

To *Il Calendario del Popolo* (*The People's Calendar*)—Milan

Turin, 19 May 1954

Sir,

If I have not replied yet to the two letters from readers of *Il Calendario* (Carletti and Fregonese) on the blackberries in my story "L'aria buona" (The Good Air) this is because I do not want to get into trouble with my mother.[50]

The bane of my life is that I was born the son of an agronomist father and a mother who was a botanist, and yet I grew up obstinately ignorant of anything to do with plants. When my mother discovers a botanical mistake in one of my stories (and it's already happened several times), she writes me letters full of disappointment. Consequently when Mr Carletti accused me of making blackberries ripen in spring, I was seized by the fear of having made another blunder, and I promised to ask my mother about it, but at the same time I was reluctant to bring to her attention a mistake which she had missed. Then Mr Fregonese intervened in my defense, explaining that maybe I was talking about mulberries. I am grateful to him, but the words in the story are quite clear: these were blackberries.

A few days ago, finding myself in my mother's house, I delayed no more and asked her the question. It turns out that in fact the blackberry (*Rubus Fruticosus*) ripens in summer/autumn, while the mulberry (*Morus Alba*) becomes ripe in spring/summer. Some books say that blackberries can ripen as early as June, and this tallies with my childhood memories which are about guzzling very early blackberries, memories which I was clearly drawing on in the story. (But I spent my childhood in the Riviera where everything ripens earlier, and the seasons are mixed up; whereas the story was set in a Northern city like the one I've been living in for years but whose flora I don't know very well . . .)

There, that's the story of the blackberries.

The moral of the story: don't trust poets, short-story writers, or novelists as scientific describers of reality.

What kind of reality do they describe, then, these people? That's a long story and would take us far from the blackberries.

Yours sincerely,

Italo Calvino

[Typed copy; in the Calvino Archive. Published in *Il Calendario del Popolo*, 118 (July 1954), p. 1780, under the title "Calvino e le more (Calvino and the Blackberries)."]

To Elsa Morante—Rome

[Turin,] 17-9-54

Dear Elsa,

I found your card from Sils when I got back from holiday and it gave me great pleasure.[51] Your judgment is very important for me—you've followed all my work closely—and this book also means a lot to me; so your letter was doubly welcome. This is a book that is so full of things that are personal to me and—for the first time—is in an explicitly autobiographical format. As a result, I always feel a bit uneasy seeing it circulating in public, unless I find someone who instantly appreciates it in its entirety. For me autobiography is always something that one writes by doing a kind of violence to oneself. Now I would like to manage to transfer this minute and complex sense of things and emotions—this *truth* you talk about—over to an invented story where I can express myself with total freedom.

I hope to come to Rome soon and to see you.

Alberto will have told you that we saw each other at the Lido.[52]

Warmest good wishes

Calvino

[Handwritten on Einaudi headed paper; with the addressee's heirs.]

To Alberto Carocci—Rome

Turin, 8 October 1954

Dear Carocci,

I am enclosing a piece by a primary school-teacher from Racalmuto (Agrigento) which seems very impressive to me and interesting for *Nuovi Argomenti*.[53]

The author, Leonardo Sciascia, a primary school-teacher, is a young, very intelligent writer who is editor of a small, well-run review down there (*Galleria*) and of slim editions of poetry.[54]

With best wishes,

[Typed copy; in the Einaudi Archive, Turin. Also in *ILDA*, p. 146.]

To Ippolito Pizzetti—Rome

Turin, 22 April 1955

Dear Pizzetti,

I tried to phone you some time ago in Rome, but I never got you in so I've not been able to talk to you about your essay on Hemingway,[55] and up until now I've not found the time to write to you.

I wanted to say to you (apart from thanking you for quoting me) how much I agree with you, and to discuss the new, absolutely accurate ideas I found in it: namely the contrast between a classic adventurer and a decadent one, the link between the absolutes of a sporting code and the absolutes of the erotic and the metaphysical, and above all your discussion of the mythical, ritualistic nature of contemporary literature seen as a refusal to situate itself in history, and the taking up of its own private drama as an absolute paradigm. It has to be said that this taking up implies a general historical evaluation of that particular individual experience, of that particular "myth," as an exhaustive or at least typical image of one's own time. But it is in the ritualistic, almost liturgical, insistence, in the self-satisfaction, in writing an apologia for it, that there lies the refusal to adhere to the movement of history, the conversion of one's private myth into an absolute. Here what comes into play is H.'s self-pity, that softness you talk about in a way that perhaps is excessive in its contradiction of that image of a virile and impassive H. which made us take him as a model, as a contrast with a world of literary protagonists who were bloodless and anaemic, but which certainly also exists. This contrast between "the rough bark and the tender centre," as you well put it, really is the thing that gets on one's nerves in H.; the H. of *Kilimanjaro* which I think is the worst side of him. (Whereas I agree with you that *Farewell* is his best book.)

[. . .][56]

Best wishes

[Typed copy; in the Einaudi Archive, Turin.]

To Giuseppe Cocchiara—Palermo

Turin, 9 May 1955

Dear Cocchiara,

It's been a long time since I wrote to you to tell you about my work,[57] but up till March I was unable to do much because I was busy with Einaudi's share subscription, which had a positive outcome, as you will know. So it's only since April that I've been working with any kind of continuity, and I've already read and catalogued almost all the material you gave me. I am very enthusiastic about Pitré's Sicilian folktales, and I have to tell you that since starting to work on Pitré my interest for this project has doubled. The material is very rich, full of variety and moments of poetry, and the only worry is how much of the tales' charm will be lost in my transcription. In my work I proceed as follows: for every tale I read I make a swift note; then I classify it according to numbered types which I've established on my own, according to my needs and which I gradually increase as I encounter each new type. Each type has its own file-card on which I write the title of the tale; when, in the near future I start writing them up, for every type or sub-category I will take the best variant, perhaps blending it with others.

Meanwhile I am trying to get hold of the texts I am still missing. Vidossi has kindly put Imbriani, Corazzini, and a few other collections at my disposal. But there are lacunae I cannot fill because I do not even have bibliographical references for them. For Lucania, for instance, I have not got anything; nothing for Sardinia (Bottiglioni contains only brief legends), and I would really need Mango; I've got very little also for Campania; for Piedmont I'm looking for Ajretti's collection; for Liguria I think hardly anything exists in dialect; for the Veneto I'm missing the essential collection by Bernoni (*Fiabe e novelle popolari veneziane*) (*Venetian Folktales and Novellas*); for Tuscany I've seen almost everything by now, apart from Gradi's works which I think I have to read too.

As for Pitré, apart from the four volumes, there must be other tales that are not contained in them (amongst the translated tales you gave me in manuscript, there are three by Pitré that I cannot find in the volumes). Have you got anything else? For instance, *Otto fiabe e novelle popolari siciliane* (*Eight Sicilian Folktales and Novellas*), published in Bologna in 1873?

One Sicilian collection I'm missing is Cristoforo Griganti, *Folklore di Isnello* (*The Folklore of Isnello*) (two volumes, Palermo, 1899–1909). Do you not have that?

The more my work progresses the more I'll need clarification and advice, and will take advantage of your courtesy. I hope later, in the autumn, to come back and see you.

Warmest regards, and please convey my best wishes to your wife

[Typed copy; in the Einaudi Archive, Turin. Also in *ILDA*, pp. 157–58.]

To Pier Paolo Pasolini—Rome

[Turin, 9 May 1955]

Dear Pasolini,

I'VE JUST RECEIVED MY COPY OF *OFFICINA*, BUT I HAD ALREADY started the draft of this letter, so I'll write to you separately about *Officina* after I've read this issue.[58]

So then: after your piece in *Nuovi Argomenti*, the summary I've read in *Paragone*[59] confirms my opinion that your introduction to Italian popular songs is fundamental not only for sorting out the whole set of problems related to poetry and folklore, but for a critical approach to contemporary Italian literature, which has in fact revolved around its relations with the world and language of the people. It is also fundamental for establishing a link between the most progressive philological work going on in universities (Devoto, Contini) and "militant" criticism.

I have to tell you that from your introduction to dialect poetry[60] (from my memory of it, because I now need to reread it) I had you down as one of the main champions of a refined "descent" into dialect, and from this I drew my motivation for my line of opposition (though I never defined it more clearly) to this attitude, which I felt was so typical of post-hermetic taste. Now the extracts from the introduction to your new book, and in particular this tripartite classification of yours of the attitudes of "realistic" poetry, show how critically aware you are and how detached from any position of mere taste or complacency. However, it seems to me that they also provide us with fundamental tools for classifying and judging contemporary Italian literature. I would like to discuss so many issues with you. For instance, as far as I'm concerned, Jahier is not exactly part of this line of "refined" descent, in other words he is not moved by an aestheticizing or emotional-lyrical attitude.[61] Jahier's "dialect" stems ultimately from a moralistic need (like the poets of *La Voce*, protestant and socialistic in his own way) and so is to be placed in category III rather than II. And if one looks carefully, the dialect polemic in Pavese's *Lavorare stanca* (*Hard Labor*),[62] though it is more directly related to type II, has in common with Jahier's verse a moralistic drive, which sometimes becomes a stylistic affinity. And this is enough to establish a line that lies between type II (the Pascoli-Crepuscolari-Hermetic line) and type III (which seems to me to have given us only decadent results—both before and after—because of its ambiguous setting up of the relationship between the cultured and popular worlds).

However there is one thing that I do not see highlighted in your outline and which seems to me to be a cornerstone. This is the fact that it is particularly from the Counter-Reformation onward that the (paternalistic) taste for the popular and dialectal begins, for the people seen as picturesque, as ragamuffins, piteous and happy at the same time and eternal; a taste that goes from the "painters of reality" to *Pane, amore e fantasia* (*Scandal in Sorrento*).[63] This suspicion so often makes the cult of the dialectal and the down-at-heel hostile to me; this false familiarity, this sentimentality. In your analysis, which is so lucid and "complete," I cannot find any place to classify this historical-aesthetic feeling of mine, however generic it is. And this kind of classification would help me above all to be able to delineate in opposition to Counter-Reformation dialectalism a line—however intermittent—represented by those who depict the people and their language without any empty emphasis on their "niceness," but with that lucid pessimism which alone is able to give the feeling of a strength, of a drama actually taking place in the world of history and in the writer's mind at the same time: as happens in Verga.[64] So I would be tempted to divide the dialectal and para-dialectal poets into "hard-liners" and "soft," with an implicit judgment on their poetic and historical worth.

It seems to me that a different order of observations can flow from your sacrosanct and necessary assertion of the "cultured strand"—in polemic with the rhetoricians of "popular creation"—where I think you deny totally any creative urge from below, even in terms of a simple, unconscious "demand" or "need." (On that topic I would like more clarification on "invention" which is not "innovation.") Certainly linguistic creation from below is not a great thing: it is slang, sometimes witty, and ingenious (for instance, the whole series of metaphors—on the human body etc.—borrowed from automobile terminology by the industrial proletariat of Turin in the last fifty years; or the parodistic neologisms from foreign languages often with obscene connotations used by hotel staff in the Riviera).[65] But it is of limited semantic potential, or at any rate confined to a restricted range of motifs that concern common sense or craftiness. However, if you think how much agricultural or technical terminology derives definitely from the people and how that influences, determines a whole vast world of images, of associations of ideas that become essential tools for more sophisticated culture, you'll see at once that the question is more complex. For songs the problem is circumscribed by the exact terms both of the rhythmic forms and their history, and of the immutable word, but if you move to the popular story suddenly the shifts of something low to high and back to low again of something that initially started out from below become continuous. I can tell you this also from personal experience because the first and most creative period of my narrative work lasted as long as I had to work up material that came from below already in the form of a finished story: the partisan stories I heard being recounted in the evening in the detachments, which had already circulated by word of mouth with their own imprint of the marvelous and the threatening that was typical of the people.[66] These are phenomena that happen rarely now, this taste for telling stories; it only happens, one might say, in times of war, so much so that even today we can still hear people in trains who have not yet tired of telling episodes from the war. However, for fiction this relationship with oral narration was crucial and that changes perhaps the terms of your argument a bit. In short, it seems to me that the picture you draw, which is on the whole accurate, is a bit deficient in conveying the sense of that continual dialectical interaction which is the fundamental law behind such phenomena. In my view, the work of careful definition that Marxism[67] has carried out in the political arena, in terms of the relations between the masses and the ruling avant-garde, between spontaneity and voluntary awareness, is a model for all kinds of relationships between urges from below and "intellectual" operations.

Lastly, I can tell you that your critical framework describing nineteenth-century studies of popular traditions will be of considerable interest to me because I am conducting a study that is in a sense parallel to yours. I am working on the texts of the same authors that were useful to you, as you might already know (but you should not spread the word too much: I am telling you because you are one of the few people with whom I can have a useful discussion). In other words I am working on a collection of Italian folktales—based on poetic, not folkloristic criteria—and on a transcription of them into a style and language that are uniform (a huge problem). Here the problems are different from yours, given the very remote, dark ancestry of the ethnology of folk-tales; but there are many issues in common. And the set of problems that this study stirs up in me most of all is not of a linguistic order, but problems regarding the origins of narrating stories, of giving a sense to human lives by arranging facts in a given order. But for the moment these are only vague ideas. We will have to have a long discussion on the technical and aesthetic questions of how to use the work done by those good but rarely intelligent positivist folklorists. I hope to see you in Rome, if I come—as I think I will—in June. Very best wishes,

Calvino

[Undated, handwritten letter; in the Gabinetto Scientifico Letterario G. P. Vieusseux-Archivio Contemporaneo Alessandro Bonsanti, Florence. Handwritten draft in the Calvino Archive. The date is that of the postal stamp.]

To Giulio Einaudi—Turin

[Rome,] 13-6-55

Dear Giulio,

The meeting of the Cultural Commission was requested particularly by the editors of *Società* to clarify the relationship between *Società* and *Il Contemporaneo*. The opening document was the speech by Muscetta and Manacorda which I enclose. In addition, Bollati and I were invited so that our publishing house could participate in the discussion.

After the papers containing mutual criticisms between *Società* and *Il Contemporaneo*, I took the floor to report on Einaudi's opinion on *Società*. I spoke of the lacunae we notice in areas more connected with topical problems (the economy, political doctrines, legal and constitutional problems), I cited *Il Mulino* as an example of a journal that is creating a group of young scholars who are present in the most active sectors, and I spoke about broadening the editorial board in this direction (Alicata: "Do you want Adorno on it as well?'" "Why not?" Ironic remarks by those present.) I said that the publishing house would be interested in the journal promoting a search to find young people who would foster and renew publishing output (Muscetta then replied that *Società* had discovered some young people already used by Einaudi: Pizzetti, Pasquantonio, and others),[68] and hinted at a possible series entitled "Quaderni di Società" (Muscetta: "A suggestion already put forward by us and rejected by Turin").

After me Spinella gave an excellent paper, around which the whole of the subsequent discussion revolved.[69] Spinella spoke substantially along the same lines as I had, with great ability and authoritativeness in his use of political language, something he's very good at. He bemoaned the absence in *Società* of studies on the economy and problems of political ideology, he criticized Muscetta's "Tagliacarte (Paper-Knife)" column, restated the need for more high-level output from comrades (contrasting the philological depth of Bonfantini's article with the rather imprecise level of Berti's). He went on to criticize the dismissive attitude toward things like Neopositivism and related American philosophical theories, maintaining that there were positive elements in them, that their entry into Italian culture constituted in many ways a progressive factor, and that in any case one cannot deal with cultural phenomena of great importance with a priori exclusions. Like *Il Contemporaneo* did with Thomas Mann, so every important attitude of bourgeois culture should be dealt with (in my opinion Spinella is the best of the young intellectual cadres and has very clear and decided ideas; I think that if we could get him onto the editorial board of *Società* and tie him more closely to the publishing house, that would be an extremely useful accomplishment for us and for those in charge of cultural policy). Gerratana, who had been implicitly criticized by Spinella, intervened with a blunt statement of his closed ideological rigor: why must I show an interested attitude toward ideologies I distrust? Tell me first what these positive elements are and then I will get interested in these things. He too, like Alicata, cited as dangerous and ridiculous the fact that Ryle comes out as a "thinking machine."[70]

Gerratana's attitude reflected the arguments within *Il Contemporaneo* between the Salinari-Trombadori line, with their interest in and utilization of a more varied cultural production in terms of value and scholarly research, as opposed to the rigid Gerratana approach. Antonello came in declaring himself in agreement with Spinella's line and referring to the problems of sociological art history that had been violently attacked by *Il Contemporaneo* but endorsed by the most serious young Communist scholars such as Bertelli and Castelnuovo.[71] For this purpose it was decided to hold a meeting of the Cultural Commission for guidance on Neopositivism, on analysis of language, behaviorism etc. in order to clarify the various positions. At the end Alicata declared himself in agreement with Spinella, recalling the tactical importance of understanding these theories which influence vital nerve-centers of Italian structures today, and mentioning the example of Lenin who in order to crush the Empiriocritics read all their texts and became involved in the heart of all their problems.

Best wishes

Calvino

I only had a brief personal chat with Muscetta where he told me that his resignation had been accepted and that he was waiting for Ossella and Donadio[72] to discuss their [. . .].[73] Alicata told me to invite you to the Conf. of Comm. Intellect. in Milan.
[Handwritten on Einaudi headed paper (Rome office); photocopy of the original in the Einaudi Archive, Turin.]

To Michelangelo Antonioni

[Turin, November–December 1955]

Dear Antonioni,
I am writing to you as a friend of Pavese, and also on behalf of Giulio Einaudi and other friends of Pavese, to thank you for the film *Le amiche* (*The Girlfriends*). We are extremely grateful to you

and your collaborators for having ensured that such an important film as yours is connected with Pavese's name. And we are very happy to have found in your film that moral core that was typical of Pavese, and we are proud to consider ourselves faithful to that ethical kernel in particular.

I will tell you that when I heard that you were preparing to make a film based on *Tra donne sole* (*Among Women Only*),[74] I felt some apprehension: it semed to me that of all Pavese's novels that was the least cinematographic, centered as it is on a dense counterpoint of dialog and sensations left hanging in the air, and on situations too tense and coarse to be brought to the screen without distortion. Your film has clearly overcome my apprehensions; the clever screenplay uses and develops the novel's key points into a fully rounded cinematographic account, which has its own autonomous logic, yet it also maintains a *Pavesian* flavor of its own.[75]

Of course, the first merit of *Le amiche* is that it is important as a film by Michelangelo Antonioni, independently of *Tra donne sole*. The observation of manners, which Pavese used purely as building blocks for giving a lyrical and ethical definition of behavior, here comes to the fore, as is in any case the duty of cinema. And this is consistent with your vocation as a bitter chronicler of a bourgeois generation, a role you formulated in your earlier films with great consistency and it is here brought to its most complete expression. This is the first time that we've seen a film portray the life of groups of middle-class friends, men and women, in a city, the flavor of their evenings and weekends spent together in their cars, the hysterias, the bitterness brewing beneath the witty remarks. We see a whole world that already has its own tradition in literature, but which the cinema has never managed to touch on before, it being suited to handling events full of strong contrasts, individual exploits, rather than the chiaroscuro of life as a community. You have carried this out with your own spare, acerbic style of narration, based on the link between landscapes that are always a bit squalid and wintry, and dialogs with pauses that seem almost casual, a cinematic style that harks back to the model of understatement in so many modern writers, amongst whom Pavese too may be numbered. The merit of your film is that of seeing this world with a look that is sensitive but without indulgence (without the nostalgic-crepuscular tinge of Fellini's *I vitelloni*), but instead putting mercilessly under the spotlight the characters' petty cruelty, superficial sensuality, constant cowardice in the face of more tense ethical situations. Most of all, you did not just provide this depiction of manners, but contrasted it with the presence of another rhythm of life, another rationale and link, the link with work, whatever it may be, whether running a luxury dressmakers' shop or handling bricks and mortar, as long as it is a question of fulfilling oneself in things achieved.

The clarity of this ethical content is such that it manages to impose itself despite the fact that the cornerstone of the novel, the character of Clelia, is the weak point of the film. The screenplay decided to make her younger, less disillusioned and wise, emphasizing that constant temptation of hers to join the world of her "amiche" (girlfriends) that is bound up with their constant rejection of her; and her participation in it becomes youthful solidarity which her difference of experience and morality stirs up to the point of contempt and open polemic. And whereas in the novel her love for the builder is characterized by her shy refusal to abandon herself, here it is given an emphasis that is not only to do with feelings but is also an "alternative" to that world. All these are legitimate operations with the aim of maintaining a clear cinematographic narration, but Clelia's character, which is meant to be problematic (with her hesitation right to the end between different life-styles that are offered her and her "historic" choice to fulfill herself in her work), ends up being confused; and the actress cannot find a way of expressing anything that only a very different face might have suggested. Momina too I had seen in a different way: more bitter and aggressive, with a more open cynicism; and yet, this cat-like Momina you have given us has, I have to agree, a certain force, has her own meaning. The actress who plays Rosetta the suicide is very good and well chosen; and Nene played by Valentina Cortese is really excellent. Although Nene is a character that has almost been created by the screenplay, the role and acting of Cortese are the most "Pavesian" in the film, and if it had been possible to keep everything in that tone it would have been perfect. As for the male characters, the novel left them in the shadows, thus implicitly criticizing them. The film has given them greater emphasis, and the criticism, while not stressed too much, I think comes out more clearly. It is a film which is causing public debate, something rare. And it is a film that gives a fundamentally correct interpretation. For that we are grateful to you. Warmest regards. Your

Calvino

[Published with the title "*Le amiche* e Pavese" (*Le amiche* and Pavese), *Notiziario Einaudi*, 11–12 (November–December 1955), p. 12; later in *S*, II, 1909–11.]

1956–1960

To Pier Paolo Pasolini—Rome

Turin, 1 March 1956

Dear Pasolini,

I am attaching to the official publisher's letter this personal one, because for a long time I've been wanting to tell you how much I enjoyed your *Canzoniere italiano* (*Italian Song-Book*), and how much I believe it is a beautiful and important book. Your selection is really of such high quality it goes beyond all one's expectations and hopes. I read the whole thing bit by bit, and every so often my mouth would just fall open. (How good those pieces from Friuli are!) Your choices show great poetic intelligence. On their own they would be enough to make the book's name.

Then there's the preface: the general ideas I had already admired in the extracts you had published[1] and I am now seeing for the first time all its richness and technical, poetic, historical, and psychological intelligence. Here are those almost mini-portraits of the various regions through their songs, which are wonderful (and they offer an extremely interesting point of comparison for me with the folk-tales). On the one hand I also found—and learned—in your work the procedure which is also one I use in sifting the folk-tale material aesthetically; on the other hand, I who know very little about "how to make poems," how thought is organized in lyric form, learned more from this book than from any other. (But, dammit, why do you have to write in such a difficult style? You people are bringing back into fashion a taste for difficult writing which is not the evanescent taste of the Hermetics because in fact there is an effort to be precise, but behind it lies a Contini-style university game of Germanic origin;[2] however, it has just that amount of affinity with hermetic allusivity to give it an outdated feel. You're a whole team there in Rome, you, Citati, Garboli, and just because you began to publish a few years after '45, bang! you decided you could hark back to the Giubbe Rosse, something that would never occur to any one else now.)[3]

So then, I wanted to tell you that yours is not only an important book on popular Italian poetry, but it is an important book on Italy and an important book on poetry.

It's a distressing thing that the volume is so little discussed. We know that Italian literary culture today finds itself wrong-footed when faced with this kind of study, but over and beyond specialized discussions of it, there is so much to say about a book like this that not to make plain its significance is really a sign of a very low general level of intelligence. Guanda as well is a right old sleepy-head. A book like this ought be launched with big debates, events, radio, television, cinema documentaries, posters on the streets, generally ensuring that people talk of nothing else for months. If I think of the campaign that E. is preparing for the Italian folktales at the end of the year, I am a bit ashamed that a book like yours, more original and more scholarly than mine and which ought to have even more of an impact also on the wider public, doesn't get all the prominence it deserves and ends up being viewed as a topic for specialists. (Vidossi, who in terms of knowing the subject is the one who is most on the ball, likes it a lot, and will write—or has written—a review for *Lo Spettatore*.) But what are those dumplings at *Il Contemporaneo* waiting for before they devote their center page to it?

Ceneri di Gramsci (The Ashes of Gramsci). Astonishing technical brilliance. In addition, it's all linked together in terms of thought like Foscolo's *Sepolcri*. That's the way to write poems! And that sense of Gramsci ending up buried in Rome like an inhabitant of another planet—as Renato Solmi said to me the other day[4]—, is magnificent, and till now nobody has known how to express that. Only you are in favor of Rome in the end, and I'm for Gramsci. Also everything that is "landscape" is very beautifully done. But the real theme of the work seems to me weak and not new: the contrasts between revolution and passion and between logical rigor and vitality are by now really not very dramatic, seeing that we've never had revolutionary puritanism nor will we ever have, and the Italian workers' movement has taken on an image that is very Southern-Roman. Also the dualism of the proletariat as protagonist of history versus the proletariat as nature, is very weak. And Gramsci is something else; we really need to see these and other tensions inside him, and there are several opportunities for this. To set up a Gramsci-Shelley opposition doesn't lead anywhere. There was so much Shelley in Gramsci, in his early tastes, when he was doing *La città futura* (*The City of the Future*), so much neoclassical Romanticism, *Sturm und Drang*, an expression which he liked a lot as Togliatti does today. Togliatti is so full of polemical nostalgias, Togliatti who translated Whitman, Togliatti who writes "Gramsci was a pagan": if ever there were any Shelleyans, those two were. Nonetheless, the poetry is still wonderful and full of things. But are you not insisting too much on these adjectives like "*vizioso*" (vicious), "*lurido*" (filthy)? At a certain point it becomes all too easy for you to rely totally on the adjectives: either you find another route or you'll end up being manneristic.

Ciao. Let's talk about it.[5]

Here I am with the last linguistic hurdle (Friulan) behind me. By dint of flicking through Pirona I can manage to read that as well.[6]

[Typed signed letter, with author's additions, on Einaudi headed paper; in the Gabinetto Scientifico Letterario G. P. Vieusseux-Archivio Contemporaneo Alessandro Bonsanti, Florence. Previously published in P. P. Pasolini, *Lettere 1955–1975*, ed. Nico Naldini (Turin: Einaudi, 1988), pp. 175–76.]

To Mario Cerroni—Udine

Turin, 19 April 1956

Dear Cerroni,

Thank you for the collection. I always liked your poems when I was in Genoa, and they stood out easily from the others. Perhaps the one about the houses was the one I liked best, because it had more thought in it, despite some inelegant lines; the other one is more successful in poetic terms but more "descriptive."

Now I discover that you are also a critic and even though I often seem not to agree with you, I see you have some ideas in your head, which is rare both in poets and in literary critics (many of our friends who are critics and whom you quote with respect or with whom you bother to argue have never dreamt of having an idea in their heads). For this reason I urge you always to write in a more considered and less journalistic way. Elaborate and go into your concept of poetry in depth. I have to confess that I know very little about poetry: for many of the poets that you include in your anthology I would never have thought so many things could have been said about them, because on the whole I see them as always staying the same and all of them being a bit boring and repetitive. But you speak about them as though you are discussing something serious, so much so that for the first time it has made me think that there could be some truth in what you say.

I have to tell you that I don't believe that yours is the right way or the new way forward for poetry. I think that you are the same as the Hermetic poets: it is rare for either them or you to say things that are interesting and not just decorative. The only one who seems to me to be following a serious route (and I am astonished not to find him in your anthology) is Pasolini who writes long poems, with lots of arguments in them, with images that become emblematic of our problems, and with a verse technique that is astonishing. It's not that "I like" his poems: it's just that (as in *Le ceneri di Gramsci*) I find things to discuss in them, maybe I want to take them apart them bit by bit, to show that it's all wrong. But this is the poetry we need: a poetry we can discuss, that touches on the contradictions of the world we move in, that gives us new worries to think about, that gets on our nerves! You poets don't do any of this, you don't say anything we don't know already, you don't irritate, don't get on our nerves, in short you don't do anything useful. You sing. Are you not ashamed of this? You sing about the sufferings and hopes of the people. Are you not ashamed? Do you think that you should sing about subjects like that?

Perhaps you will decide that it is not exactly protocol to attack you like this without even knowing you. But for years now we've been doing nothing but treating each other with mutual politeness, of a formal and indifferent sort. It's really boring. That is why I am trying to establish and spread a new approach to human relations, to see if we can wake up a bit.

Another poet I appreciate is Rocco Scotellaro (I struggled to understand him as a man first before understanding him as a poet, after years when his "folklorism" made him distant from me, and I developed an enormous admiration for his range of activities, alas just a few months before he died); but how can you say he's on the same level as Fiore (even though he is a friend of mine and I also appreciate him)? Fiore sings, Scotellaro has something dramatic inside him, he carries within him the contradictions of our times. Or am I wrong?

In short, I've told you the few things I think about this, from the little I know.

Thank you once again. Best wishes.

[Typed copy; in the Einaudi Archive.]

To *Il Contemporaneo*—Rome

[Turin, 13 June 1956]

Sir,

YOUR POLEMICAL NOTE ON PASOLINI ON THE 23RD GIVES ME the opportunity for a critique of the way in which *Il Contemporaneo* keeps up with contemporary Italian literature.[7]

Some months ago one of the most important events in Italian postwar literature took place, easily the most important event in the area of poetry: the publication (in *Nuovi Argomenti*, nos. 17–18) of Pasolini's poem *Le ceneri di Gramsci* (*The Ashes of Gramsci*). This was the first time for who knows how many years that a large-scale poetic work had articulated, with extraordinary success both in content and form, a conflict of ideas, a set of cultural and ethical problems that a socialist view of the world has to face. *Il Contemporaneo* did not mention it.

Personally I am definitely not in agreement with the conception expressed in this poem (which can basically be reduced to a contrast between revolutionary rigor and Pan-like passion for life, a contrast which does not exist nor must it exist) and I have had an epistolary exchange about this with Pasolini. But at last we have a poem which prompts debate (and there has been much oral discussion of it between young writers especially on the left, and in general amongst what is precisely *Il Contemporaneo*'s readership) and what's more it is a beautiful poem, which summarizes and takes a stage further what we have learnt from the Italian tradition of civic poetry, of verbal skill from the masters of Hermeticism, and of the most recent demands for realism. Precisely for all these reasons I am convinced that *The Ashes of Gramsci* is ushering in a new era for Italian poetry.

A short while afterwards Guanda brought out the hefty volume of *Il canzoniere italiano*, the anthology of popular poetry edited by Pasolini with a preface by him of over a hundred pages in which the historical and aesthetic problems of this extremely important field were addressed, following their development from the Romantics to the Positivists to Croce and Gramsci. This is an essay of tremendous intelligence, both in its general approach and in the individual insights, and it seems to me a fundamental piece in the debate on this subject (a specialized subject, but full of "general" points of interest), forming part as it does of a work of critical revision which we can certainly call socialist (if not Marxist in the strict sense). I would have liked to see a debate emerge from it, precisely in this direction of a socialist critical evaluation (I heard, for instance, severe criticism of Pasolini's selection criteria from friends who are more competent than me in this field). Instead *Il Contemporaneo* made no mention of the preface. After a long delay it published a review by a serious scholar of popular poetry, Vann'Antò, which was a demolition job on the texts and the translations in terms of philological accuracy. Vann'Antò is a scholar who is an expert in the field and his critique of Pasolini's imprecise approach is certainly justified. But was that the review that *Il Contemporaneo*'s readers were expecting? No, what they were waiting for first and foremost was a discussion of the preface and the choice of material. The philological points made by specialists might have been a precious contribution, but the first priority for a weekly devoted to cultural discussion is the assessment of what is new in a literary work.

Now what has happened is that Pasolini has written an article in the Bologna journal *Officina*, no. 6 (an article which is perhaps the least interesting of those Pasolini has written recently—or at least that's the way it seems to me because he is talking about periods and problems which I am not really interested in—though it still seems to me one I rather approve of on the whole). He devotes a dozen lines of polemic to *Il Contemporaneo*. They are rather superficial and banal, I have to say, without the sophistication and knowledge of the subject which Pasolini normally shows. As quick as a flash, *Il Contemporaneo* fires off a column and a half of dense and highly polemical print against Pasolini, adopting the ugly expedient of accusing him of personal motives because Salinari had attacked *Ragazzi di vita* (*The Ragazzi*) (and without indicating which article and journal is being talked about, as if *Officina* was read by half of Italy).

One might say that if Pasolini had not brought *Il Contemporaneo* into it, you would not even have read the article, so much so that as far as you are concerned Pasolini is simply the author of *Ragazzi di vita*, whereas in one year, lucky him, he has published a whole lot of other things. I too am against *Ragazzi di vita*, over questions of "position," of its poetics which I consider mistaken and without room for development, and I believe it is a "minor work" for Pasolini, that the real Pasolini is the poet and the critic, one of the best of the new generation and one who belongs on the "left."

In short, *Il Contemporaneo* mentions *Ragazzi di vita* which is easy to criticize in terms of taste, and says nothing of *Le ceneri di Gramsci* over which one really must face a discussion of ideas. It discusses the little note on "positionalism" where one can indulge in a bit of the usual journalistic backbiting, and says nothing about the preface to the *Canzoniere* which homes in on a network of problems on which we have got work to do for the next twenty years. In an even more naive way Pasolini may believe that this is all due to ideological-tactical "perspectivism," or other such devilry: instead, it is only due to mental laziness.

Leaving Pasolini aside, who will forgive me if I've used him as an excuse to develop an argument of my own, what I wanted to get at was this: *Il Contemporaneo* ought to be contributing to correcting the failings of Italian literary criticism including its failure to inform. Something new will come and will continue to come, in literature as well, from intelligence, from ideas, from a "problematic" questioning of reality: today there can be no happy solutions based merely on instinctive inspiration or taste, or if there can be it is because there is that little imp of historical contradiction lurking beneath them. The critic's duty is to uncover the little imp, and the duty of a journal like *Il Contemporaneo* is to highlight and discuss those few ideas that emerge from creative literature and from criticism. You can be sure that as far as Italy is concerned, these ideas are so few that it does not involve much work.

Best wishes from someone with unshaken and happy confidence in your enterprise.

Italo Calvino

[Published in *Il Contemporaneo*, 26 (30 June 1956), p. 8, along with a letter from Pasolini to the editors and a reply by Carlo Salinari to Calvino, all under the title "La poesia e il dialetto" (Poetry and dialect). The confusion of dates (Calvino's letter appears to precede the note to which it is referring by about ten days) stems from the usual post-dating of the weekly compared to the actual date of publication. On 13 June Calvino sent this letter also to Pasolini, with an accompanying note: "Dear Pasolini, I am sending you a copy of the letter which I sent to *Il Contemporaneo* asking them to publish it. Ciao, Calv."]

To Leonardo Sciascia—Racalmuto/Agrigento

Turin, 12 September 1956

Dear Sciascia,

I'VE READ YOUR "STALIN."[8] WHAT CAN I SAY? IT IS DIFFICULT for me to give you an objective verdict. There's too much of my own life in it, too much Don Calí in me too, for me to be able to provide an "autonomous" reading of it. However much I simply draw out all the paradoxical aspects from the current situation when talking privately or publicly, and outwardly show that I am enjoying the irony of it all, this is for me a time for serious rethinking. In short, caricature seems to me too the most natural way to express these things, as long as it is me that is doing it, and I know I am paying for it personally; when it is done by others, I cannot evaluate it objectively, I feel too caught up in it.

Having said that, it seems to me that your character is still true in historical terms: he corresponds to a very common type of Italian Communist, and I actually would say he's like the typical old Communist cobbler, of the kind we all know, very honest and rigorous and, perhaps for this reason, inclined to interpret every position in politics that he doesn't understand in terms of Machiavellian conspiracies and wheeler-dealing. That was your big card, on which you might have played even more: this dream about Stalin who intervenes to explain things to him just as he wants, despite the official explanations, and basically he's right. The Stalin of the dream ends up being more true to life than the official Stalin . . . In short, by going into this in greater depth, out of these contrasts between the various "souls" of communism, and all this living and suffering experienced by a man who is fundamentally "pure in heart," could come something that is bigger than perhaps you realize.

In addition, in some places there is too much of a mere chronicle of historical events, of an account of what the newspapers are reporting, without this being balanced sufficiently by narration. And perhaps (but in this area everyone has his own way of dealing with it) it needs a bit more sympathetic understanding of the character (look at Cassola) in order to save him from being just a caricature.[9] All in all, it is a book which, if you felt like working a bit more on it, could say much more. As it stands, it is rather superficial, with a hint of being facile.

I will have some other colleagues read it and let you know more.

I understand your idea of doing a book that is a kind of diptych: America-Russia, Sicily between America and Russia.

Very best wishes,

Calvino

[Typed on Einaudi headed paper, with autograph signature and additions; with the addressee's heirs. Published in *ILDA*, pp. 192–93.]

To Elsa Morante—Rome

[Turin,] 25 October 1956

Dear Elsa,

I have read your book with great pleasure and enjoyment and was constantly surprised.[10] I really liked the quality of your imagination, which is richly and constantly inventive and full of images, taking pleasure in nature and human beings. You immerse yourself in a world that is almost visionary, with just a few characters and feelings taken to the extreme, with the barest of landscapes. You make everything real, sufficient unto itself, and direct the characters' game in a way that makes it seem as if it proceeds by itself, so that you communicate to the reader the pleasure you must have felt writing and inventing as you went along page by page. (I cannot forget those wonderful sequences with the arrival of the groom and his conversations with W. G. and Arturo.)

I think it is finer than *Menzogna e sortilegio* (*House of Liars*), which I also liked. You have more success with the images (the hedgehog beneath the shirt!) and the characters, because whereas in the previous book (I think, though I am judging it eight years further on) one could still feel the determination "to write a novel," here one feels that you have given yourself over to pure narration, with a plot dealing with general feelings, fully self-contained!

The description of the house, how Arturo spends his days, are all wonderful things which instantly become part of the reader's experience, creating a world in which one can roam as if in one's own house.

This concreteness in the way you narrate, the way you make things and persons seem alive, makes one also forget how slender your subject matter is, perhaps how it is exceptional in a rather arbitrary way. But what does that matter? You narrate and find real feelings, not cerebral ones. Even the squalid nature of the character Gerace does not communicate any uneasiness, perhaps because of this atmosphere of romantic infatuation that is typical of you. But the secret behind everything is maybe this: that you believe in the human race, you admire it, you have a sense of human beauty and exceptionality—a rare way, these days, of looking at the world.

The ending is not wonderful in itself, we don't care enough about this Silvestro for his intervention to be decisive, but in any case it was right that the story ended there. Your language seems to me to be much simpler, less precious than in *M. e s.* and exudes great pleasure in things and colors. Occasionally there is too much argument, too much ideologizing (for instance, when A. expounds his ideas) but the breadth of the whole plot keeps everything going. The unusualness of the language the boy uses holds up very well, because—and this is one of the major pleasures of the book—you have invented his totally improvised culture. But every so often there is an extra adjective, an adjective too refined and not naïve enough for the boy, I think. (Here are a few examples I noted: *barbaric* triumphal banner, p.79; these are *romantic* legends! p. 80; the *exotic* books of a serene Sybil, p. 83.)

And I really liked the moment when Arturo does his exercises on the bar in front of Nunz., one of the most perfect bits of the book.

I think this is a book that will go down very well.

Long live the Torpedo-boat of the Antilles!

Yours,

Calvino

[Typed on Einaudi headed paper with autograph signature; with the addressee's heirs.]

To Francesco Arcangeli—Bologna

Turin, 18-1-57

Dear Momi,

I have read "A Not Improbable Situation," in fact I am still reading it and starting to write to you in order to put down on paper as I go along my impressions of such a stimulating read.[11] It seems to me to be a very important manifesto of a new romanticism and it has been very thought-provoking for me, even though I am on the other side of the fence—though who can ever say? I am with Stendhal-

Leopardi so on both sides at once. What I mean is I ought to be more on the side of Cesare Brandi,[12] but in actual fact I am much further beyond him since I am in favor of a clown-like mimesis of contemporary reality (Picasso Chaplin Brecht) which you say does not count for anything because it does not have the flow, the plasma, the Sargasso, and that is true. My whole nature is one that is anthropomorphized, Gothicized, maybe we are neo-Goths and, if so, that really would be a disaster. Instead at the head of your article is the name of Faulkner and this helps me understand your whole argument even when it is based on painters I do not know or understand much. The name I do not find, though, is that of Dylan Thomas which ought to be the key name for your whole piece, the poet of your "naturalism" (almost excessively so). Even in terms of his biography he fits in with your self-destructive anarchoholics. So I feel you have identified (or "invented" in its current etymological sense of "discovering") a very precise trend in contemporary literature and art, and particularly in the possibility of creating literature and art; something which no literary critic is capable of doing today, whereas it is the real duty of a great critic, and it is in the fulfillment of that duty that one recognizes his true greatness.

The big thing is that for the first time I have been able to see in this article of yours these concepts of natural flow and unconscious maelstrom freed from the spell of German fads, irrationalism, Bergson, G. B. Shaw's vitalistic prefaces, Lawrence's ecstasies. Instead they find their place in a discourse that is perfectly modern and in which we cannot help but recognize ourselves. You make an evocative point on "the fearful difference of scale between on the one hand us and on the other the new, almost unbearable hum and web of the life of the natural world as well as the world that has been unleashed by modern scientific exploration and mechanics." You write a perfectly justified polemic against archaism (but archaism also meant simplification, a search—falsely set up—for an equivalent of the schematicity of machines), archaism set against the "most modern modernity of the modern world," [. . .][13] Shakespeare and impressionism (a daring juxtaposition but I see the link), things which primitivism has separated us from and with which you (truly acrobatically, I have to say, but I have always been in favor of acrobats) want to ally yourself. The fact is that the two poles of modern intelligence in the field of expression are the tendency toward maximum simplification of reality and the tendency toward portraying its complexity; all the values and high points of literature and art tend toward one or the other pole. (And I have to say that I have not yet fully understood which of the two I tend toward.) You who favor the latter pole, but still having clear in your mind what in your view has to be expressed, you can actually want complexity in simplification or vice versa, in short you are taking the argument in a direction that seems to me to be definitely progressing. Only I remain one of those (those whom you define without specifying your objections) who believe in a "relation of man-to-reality (reality understood in its complete sense, nature plus history)." In short, *anarchy* is something very different for me from what it is for you (someone who is quite sure of the organized civilization that surrounds him goes drunkenly and desperately into the countryside to see a few cells germinating): for me it is the system for organizing committees that will direct industrial and agricultural production from below, eliminating the entire apparatus of the state. It happens that just at this moment, ever since I have been hearing about atomic and automatic production and of the need for planning on a global scale, I feel that if it really goes down this road anarchy will no longer be a utopia but a system that is activated in practical terms. There will be no longer any representatives or people represented, but offices and bureaux which will coordinate the needs expressed by assemblies of producers (social classes will disappear, as well as any non-technical hierarchies) in a form of direct, fully working democracy, and the huge amount of free time will allow men to be happier or sadder depending maybe on a history determined by emotions which for the first time will be autonomous or almost (the realization of idealism). In short, anarchy is for me an ideal of relations between men; in your approach, the claim for a relationship between man and nature is illusory because the relation between man and nature symbolically portrays the relationship between men. That is pure Marxism, but it comes quite spontaneously to me because in my encounters with it I have always tended to portray nature as cannibalistic, Nazi-like, or plague-ridden, poisonous, like the human world around me, despite all my aspirations toward the limpidity and freshness that we would like nature to have. (And you are the same when you theorize about the screeching, spiky nature of Moreni.)[14] Far be it from me to deny man's condition of solitude—social and also, yes, cosmic solitude—but allow me to endow it with a proud, Stoic attitude. If you are looking for the integration of nature as a consolation for the failure in social relations then your atheism, which in other respects is clearly very limpid and neat, takes on religious tones (not *religion* in its etymological sense, as you acutely point out), with a god who is physiomorphic or molecular or chemical or histological. In short, I feel your Neo-romantic naturalism as a possible alternative. Only I am immediately tempted to modify it after the manner in which in Italy a late but not unworthy Enlightenment offshoot was called Romanticism. (And our times, on the whole, are similar.) You will say that this incorrigible humanist or let's say anthropomorphic tendency is a kind of *déformation professionelle* typical of a novelist who deals in stories about men, while the painter deals with chlorophyll and land. But it is essential that our argument stays coherent, and the meaning of your warning to Testori (over which I am in complete agreement with you) is precisely this.[15] But the disagreement between you and Testori is really crucial. You are both offspring of the aesthetic reassessment of the Northern Italian seventeenth century, but Testori maintains its Counter-Reformation intentions (something that to me seemed rather obvious, and in fact I have always distrusted that approach), whereas you situate everything in the direction of the Reformation and this comes to me as a new and stimulating perspective, and the way you say, completely naturally, Reformation-Caravaggio as though one were saying Reformation-Dürer is something that makes me think, especially when you say Reformation-Caravaggio-Shakespeare. Certainly I think the orthodox Longhian is Testori and you are the heretic, or rather the ideological implications of the new borders of aestheticism established by Longhi have been teased out by Testori, and yours is the intuition of something bigger precisely because you reject dialectical discourse but instead situate this provincial area in a European context which is the only true one in historical terms.

Well, these are just the first thoughts provoked by my reading: take them as a confused internal mumbling.

Best wishes.

[Typed transcript; in the Calvino Archive. In a typed letter from Francesco Arcangeli to Calvino, dated "Bologna, 1 April 1960," we find: "I hardly know how to begin, I should be really ashamed because the letter you wrote to me, after I had sent you my almost ancient essay, bears the date 18 January 1957 (I've retranscribed it for you, because you certainly won't remember any more, except in vague terms, what you wrote to me on that occasion)." Arcangeli's heirs have been unable to trace the original of the letter Calvino had sent.]

To Michele Rago—Rome

18-1-57

Dear Michele,

I WOULD REALLY LIKE TO SEE YOU BUT I WOULD ALSO LIKE TO go to Rome as late as possible. I have no desire to talk to those people there.[16] Either I will argue with them or I will allow myself to be inveigled by them to go against my conscience. I do not want to allow myself to be caught up in petty politics any more, where in order to express an idea you have to disguise it, or maintain the opposite, or talk in allusions. I am convinced that we need a break from the past, that all the so-called innovators from Amendola[17] down are the worst supporters of not doing anything and that they are the real enemy, not the old guard which it was so easy to overthrow.

A journal with Muscetta?[18] That would not be the ideal thing for me. Everyone is talking about journals these days. I don't know what the hell to do. I would just like to be on my own and write. But who can manage that? We continue to wrack our brains in this sterile manner.[19]

You are much worse off than I am, with your problem of continuing to collaborate as a party functionary on newspapers and on this *Contemporaneo* which becomes more absurd every day,[20] and I realize that my problems are nothing compared to yours. Write to me.

Warmest good wishes,

Italo

[Handwritten on Einaudi headed paper; with the addressee.]

To Pier Paolo Pasolini—Rome

[Turin,] 18-2-57

Dear Pasolini,

I wanted to write to you about your article in *Ulisse*[21] but I am not going to do so because you have not said anything about the immature, syntactically elementary novel I gave you.[22] Now Leonetti has written to me about it with ill-judged enthusiasm and has sent me a proof of the first page, but he is also worried that the font is too small and he would like to do shorter and more legible extracts. But I am afraid that that would spin it out too much; better if it's in that small format, I think; I am convinced that it is a failed book and that it can be read only out of scholarly interest, and I hope that you share my opinion. Another thing is that in Bologna they don't like the title, because it is too frivolous (if I interpret their objections correctly); I seem to remember that you liked the title; for me that title is closely bound up with the novel and I would not like to change it.

Write to me about it. I won't be coming to Rome for a bit, I don't think.

Your article is good, enjoyable, with acute things in it, and verdicts that are almost all correct. What you say about me I like, and I recognize myself up to a point in your comments, except when you invoke Soldati, someone I had never thought about, and who for me has always been the prototype of the writer who has no language problems and who writes in Italian the same way a French writer writes in French and some English writers write in English.[23]

Yours in Cisalpine vein,

Calv.

Dialog between a priest wearing a berretta and a newsagent overheard at Milan Central Station.

Priest: Have you got Pasolini's *Gioventù bruciata* (*Rebel without a Cause*), published by Mondadori?

NEWSAGENT (after looking in the Medusa Foreign Writers series): Is the series not Il Pavone?
PRIEST: Yes . . . yes . . . Il Pavone.
NEWSAGENT: In that case, I've not got it.
PRIEST: Never mind. (Exit)[24]

[Handwritten letter on Einaudi headed paper; in the Gabinetto Scientifico Letterario G. P. Vieusseux-Archivio Contemporaneo Alessandro Bonsanti, Florence.]

TO FRANCESCO LEONETTI—BOLOGNA

[Turin,] 19–2–57

Dear Leonetti,
MY NOVEL AN ASTONISHING SURPRISE? COME ON! I CONSIDER it a failure from every point of view and I agreed to give it to Pierp. only because it might at least serve as an object of study on a dissecting table. But—as I said to Pierp.—it has to be accompanied by a note, at the beginning, and this is what I am sending to you.[25]

I am in favor of the small font; we can't spin it out too much; and I think it is easy to read like that anyway.

But I would like to see the proofs of the whole of the first installment. It's been such a long time since I reread it, and I don't know if I gave Pierpaolo the corrected fair copy of the typescript. In short, I really would like to see it before it comes out.

I don't want to change the title. When I was writing it, and believed in it, I felt that it could become a title that stood for a generation, for a moral climate, and other such rubbish. None of the frivolity that you see in it. And "youth" means "young" in the sense it is used in the party's youth organizations, in "youngsters' problems," that whole area of boring problems that the book harks back to. In short, I do not feel I can change the title, which would be tantamount to rejuvenating the book, bringing it closer to me, whereas instead I am publishing it inasmuch as it is now when it is totally detached from me. Many thanks for everything. I will reply to you separately about the poems.

Ciao

Calv.

[Handwritten on Einaudi headed paper; with the addressee.]

To Pietro Citati—Rome

Turin, 24 May 1957

Dear Citati,

Your letter was of great importance to me, I have read it publicly to many people, and I have thought about it a lot.[26] If I am late in replying to you and thanking you, it is only because I need to give you a reply I have put serious thought into.

I am really pleased you liked the first part. And the feeling that it is superior to what follows is shared so far by many readers, or at least the unevenness between the first and second parts has been noticed. Vittorini is, I feel, even more accurate when he notes the divergence between two strands, one that is more Stevensonian, and the other that is all full of the grotesque devices there are in the *Visconte* (*Viscount*). He likes both of them but is unhappy about the shift from one to the other.

The book is coming out now just as it is, warts and all. The latter have only been attenuated by the fact that I have stressed the motif of the protagonist telling improbable stories, so the more grotesque episodes are recounted by the narrator exactly as his brother had told him them, and sometimes they are even turned into first-person accounts using his own words (for instance, the war involving the French soldiers in the wood).

In addition I have introduced some further adjustments when I put it all together, following your advice. But I have not cut anything (except for the pointless boar hunt).

I do not agree with all your verdicts. I realize that the brigand is from the other "spool" but it works and everyone likes it. They also like the dog too, even though that's easy.

The fire is structural, for C.'s attitude to collective existence. The pirates are not structural and do not mean anything, but it's a nice story and rounds off the character of the Cavaliere. In the love sections I am only interested in the ideology. The Masonic material was praised by Vittorini as one of the best chapters.

Still, that's it now. I am now writing *La speculazione edilizia* (*A Plunge into Real Estate*), all introspective and psychological.[27] Damned difficult!

Listen, at the start of June we are publishing three new Italian books: Ginzburg, *Valentino*, Cancogni, *L'odontotecnico*, Cassola, *Un matrimonio del dopoguerra*. They are three quite short works in the Coralli series. Would you do us a nice article on all three for the *Notiziario*? Or on the two Tuscans if Natalia is outside your interests? You can then stitch them together again for *Il Punto*: in any case no one reads it. At least in the whole of Northern Italy there used to be only one reader of *Il Punto* and that was me: I bought it to read you and Pasolini, but then quite often you were not in it, so I stopped. I would need it soon, though. Write to me at once and if you're up for it I'll send you the proof copies.

Best wishes,

[Typed copy; in the Einaudi Archive, Turin; published in *ILDA*, pp. 224–25.]

To Elio Vittorini—Milan

Turin, 24 May 1957

Dear Elio,

I WANTED TO INFORM YOU THAT YOUR COMMENTS ON *IL BARONE RAMPANTE* have been extremely useful to me, and I think I have found quite a simple formula for attenuating the stylistic discrepancy that separates the later chapters from the early ones. What I mean is, for instance, I have put into first-person narration the chapter on the war with the French army in the wood, as though it were narrated by the protagonist himself, just like one of the many stories he recounts that are more made up than true. I have done the same thing, or simply hinted at it, at several points, namely where the narrative is more dynamic and improbable. This is a palliative, but it seemed to me to be the only system for reducing the discordance, without a rewrite, something which I did not feel I could do. So the book will come out now, in about ten days.[28]

If by any chance I'm lucky enough to find you in the right frame of mind, and you think that the book could give rise to some observations on your part, and if it was easy for you to write something to introduce it in the *Notiziario Einaudi*, even maybe just a short piece the length of a blurb, I would be very happy. But it is not that I am asking you to do this, I definitely don't want you to get into the state of mind of someone who thinks "Oh, how boring, I have now got to write that thing," I definitely do not want my book to be associated with any thoughts of annoyance. If you get inspiration on the spot, or if you want the proofs to see whether it will come to you, tell me in writing and I will be grateful to you.

Ciao,

Calvino

[Typed on Einaudi headed paper, with autograph signature; photocopy in the Calvino Archive; published in *ILDA*, p. 222.]

To Franco Fortini—Milan

Turin, 28 May 1957

Dear Fortini,

I HAVE BEEN ASKED TO WRITE BECAUSE YOU ARE COMPLAINING to us that *Asia maggiore* did not get the resonant treatment it deserved. Yes, this is in fact one of the many sad experiences of '56, namely that those books that touched on politics somehow did not get reviewed or discussed by the Italian press. In Italy politics comes into the papers as "news" or as up to the minute journalism. Whenever a book wants to go into depths about the topics in the paper, the latter turns its back on it. For *Asia maggiore* we did a launch that was even more elaborate than what we are used to doing for all our new Italian books and you certainly cannot accuse us of negligence. This is a widespread phenomenon, unfortunately.[29] It's pointless talking about *la Stampa*: its editor does not want reviews, and articles by its literary people (apart from Bo, I believe) spend months waiting and then are rejected (Antonicelli is the one who is the worst victim of this situation).[30]

I sense a hint of bitterness in this letter of yours and in a previous one. Excellent: we are living in a dark period, there is absolutely nothing going right, and the only consolation we have is to think about the brevity of life. I have to say that in this situation I am absolutely fine, and I am giving myself up finally to total misanthropy, which I now discover corresponds fully to my true nature.

But you seem to be still anxious about something or other. Ha, ha! Don't worry, it will just get worse and worse.

I have written a book, the one I spoke to you about: *Il barone rampante* (*The Baron in the Trees*), in which I have perhaps managed partly to articulate these concepts. It has turned out to be a terrible book, I can tell you in confidence, as indeed it always should have been. I will send it to you, even though you do not send me your books of poetry. Now I am writing another long novella, something completely different, a cross between Henry James and Silvio Guarnieri.

The worse things get in the world the better* one writes! Hurrah!

Your

Calvino

We are at the end of May and it is still raining. Ha, ha!

* (Better in the sense that one writes and one has nothing else to think about, not in the sense that one actually writes better or usefully. Literature is dead.)

[Typed on Einaudi headed paper, with autograph signature and additions; in the Franco Fortini Archive, Siena; part of a copy from the Einaudi Archive was previously published in *ILDA*, pp. 226–27.]

To Michele Rago—Rome

[Turin,] 22-7-57

Dear Michele,

I WAS HAPPY TO GET YOUR LETTER, HAPPY THAT YOU LIKED the book, and most of all happy that you liked it so much that it prompted you to discuss it, to enter into dialog with the way I am thinking. This is what I aim at when writing rather than some abstract perfection, and that is why I wanted to publish it even though I was already aware both of its flaws, which you are not the only one to reproach me for, and of the fact that the second half is less successful and more mechanical than the first etc. You are the first to make a reference to Giono and maybe you've hit on something there;[31] while I was writing it I never thought about Giono, but when I read his book at the time, I liked it a lot, and I would only have wanted it to have a bit more movement, to be less static; and unconsciously I must have tried to put myself in Giono's situation and make the corrections I felt it needed. You are right not to read the book (any book) on the basis of symbols but on the basis of its ethical substance; that is how it must be read. And to have flaws that I share with Nievo is the best way for me to have flaws . . .[32] The truth is that in the idea for this book that I carried around with me for years it was the political-revolutionary-Napoleonic part that counted; but, as I wrote it, the part that was meant to be merely an introduction took up more space and energy, and I got to the part that interested me most after using up most of my fuel. You mention the name of Conrad. That squares perfectly with an idea of literature that I have been trying to clarify for myself recently. For the first time I have the consciousness that I am able to write what I want, the maximum of what I want, not as had happened to me until recently, when I might have this or that theory about literature, but then on paper I had to restrict myself to just what came to me. Now I hope that more and more things "come to me" that are not too far off the highest level at which I would like to write. This is also because my aims are now clearer and less ambitious and less overawed by strictly political demands (and in this way maybe once I have removed all the "taboos" I will manage also to write about politics). Now I have finished a long novella of about a hundred pages, *La speculazione edilizia* (*A Plunge into Real Estate*) which I think is quite good, even though it may seem another variation on the theme of "the defeat of the intellectual"; but in it there is a whole world and epoch on the move, with real people, and a halfway house between autobiography and objective realism. In short, I do not agree with your "We may as well not say anything," which seems to me to emerge from a struggle with yourself, with a part of yourself which believes that the silence must be broken. I do not see why you do not resume your career as critic and essay-writer and literary polemicist, which is your real profession, your only one. If this is not the moment when could the moment be? We need to hear words that are not just a response to this occasion, but words which are dictated by a rigorous ethical sense, and which look forward, even if they are pessimistic: the main thing is that they do not hide the future.

I am more pessimistic than ever. For these last few weeks we have been struggling to persuade A. G. not to resign, but instead to turn his commitment which is still today very strong into concrete action which will link with the Party's strength, and not just its intellectual strength.[33] But worn out as he was by the horrific meeting where they tried to make him renounce his criticisms, wounded by idiotic attacks, and discouraged because in fact he always found himself isolated, he could not take any more and wrote his letter of resignation. This is a huge tragedy. There is nobody else now in the Party ranks who has the stature and the substance to take on his role of applying pressure for innovation. The situation is bleaker than ever.

I have sent *Il barone* to Mascolo, and I am very grateful to you for having mentioned it to him;[34] but I am under an option from Albin Michel, who is the publisher of *Il visconte* (*The Viscount*). These pricks from Gallimard, who are all friends of ours, have [never] deigned to glance at me in all this time; I am now one of Albin Michel's authors, an anodyne publisher whose books fall into oblivion. I sent *L'entrata in guerra* (*Into the War*) to Sartre. There again, years ago Lucentini had translated "Gli avanguardisti" (The Avanguardisti in Menton) and proposed it to *Les Temps Modernes*, but they did not want to know about it. My love affair with France has always been an unhappy one. Write to me about yourself and your plans. I will be in Turin until around the 10th.

Calv.

[Handwritten, on Einaudi headed paper; with the addressee.]

To the Secretariats of the "G. Pintor" Cell and of the 2nd "A. Gramsci" Section, the Secretariat of the Turin Federation, the Secretariat of the Italian Communist Party, and the Editorial Board of *l'Unità*

Turin, 1 August 1957

Dear Comrades,

I have to communicate to you my carefully pondered and painful decision to resign from the Party.

I renewed my membership for '57 making clear my dissent;[35] this dissent has not at all diminished in the passing months, so much so that I abstained from all Party activity and collaboration with its press, because every political act of mine could not but bear the mark of my dissent, in other words would have constituted a new infraction of discipline after the one that I had already been reproached for.

Along with many other comrades I had hoped that the Italian Communist Party would put itself at the head of the international renewal of Communism, condemning ways of exercising power which have been shown to be a failure and deeply unpopular, giving a boost to initiatives from the grass roots upwards in all areas, laying the foundations for a new unity amongst all workers, and that in this creative fervor it might rediscover its revolutionary vigor and its hold on the masses. I have been amongst those who maintained that only an unambiguous, spontaneous moral boost could genuinely turn 1956 into the year of the "renewal and reinforcement" of the Party, at a time when we were receiving appeals for courage and clarity of purpose from the most diverse parts of the Communist world. Instead, the way followed by the PCI leading up to and after the 8th Congress, toning down innovative proposals in a mood of basic conservatism, placing the accent on the struggle against the so-called "revisionists" rather than on the fight against the dogmatists, seemed to me (especially as regards the part played by our younger leaders in whom we placed most hopes) like the waste of a huge opportunity.[36]

Subsequently I hoped that the traditional centrism of our Secretariat would guarantee the right of citizenship within the Party to those who had pressed for innovation, as it guaranteed it in fact to the more radical dogmatists. The line followed in recent months, up to the last meeting of the Central Committee (a particularly serious meeting since the moment could have been propitious once more to moving forward, but there was no movement), and the drastic and contemptuous elimination of Antonio Giolitti (to whom I am bound by a deep sense of esteem and fraternal solidarity) have removed any residual hope I had of carrying out a useful role even on the fringes of the Party.

I have confidence in the historic movement which will lead socialism from a form of centralized, authoritarian organization to forms of direct democracy and to meaningful participation by the working class and intellectuals in the political and economic direction of society. It is on this road that the world Communist movement is pushing ahead, with or without ruptures depending on the capacity for renewal within the Communist parties of the various countries. It is in this direction that I intend to go on orienting myself politically.

The passions stirred up by our internal debates and the prospects for the future have not made me forget the seriousness of the current political situation in Italy. My decision to abandon the membership of the Party came about only when I realized that my dissent from the Party had become an obstacle to me making any political intervention. As an independent writer I will in certain circumstances be able to take up a position alongside you without inner reservations, just as I will be able to direct criticisms at you fairly and enter into debate (while always conscious of the limits of an individual point of view). I know full well that "independence" is a term that can be illusory and ambiguous, and that the immediate political struggles are decided by the organized strength of the masses and not simply by the ideas of intellectuals; I do not intend at all to abandon my position as a militant intellectual, nor to deny anything of my past.[37] But I believe that at the present moment the particular type of participation in democratic life that can be given by a writer and an opinion maker who is not directly involved in political activity is more effective outside the Party than inside.

I am conscious of how much the Party has counted in my life. I joined it at the age of twenty, in the midst of the armed struggle for liberation; I have lived as a Communist throughout most of my cultural and literary development; I became a writer via the columns of the Party press; I have had the opportunity to know the life of the Party at all levels, from the grass roots to the top, however much that participation might have been discontinuous and include reservations and arguments, but I always derived precious moral and human experiences from it; I have always felt (and not just from the 20th Congress onward) the pain of those who suffer the mistakes made by their own camp, but have constantly had confidence in history; I have never believed (not even with the early zeal of the neophyte) that literature was that sad thing that many in the Party preached, and in fact the very poverty of Communism's official literature acted as a spur to me to try to bring a touch of creative felicity to my work as a writer; I believe I have always managed to be, inside the Party, a free man. That this attitude of mine will not undergo changes when outside the Party can be guaranteed by the comrades who know me best, and know how much I am eager to remain faithful to myself, and devoid of animosity and rancor.

I would appreciate it if, given the amount of reflection that lies behind my resignation,[38] I could be spared the discussion envisaged in the Statute, which would shatter the serenity of this farewell.

I ask you to publish this letter in *l'Unità* so that my attitude can be clear to comrades, friends, and opponents.

I would like to say farewell to the comrades who in their various sectors of work are struggling to affirm principles of justice, and also to those who are further away from my positions and whom I respect as veteran, valorous fighters, and whose respect I hold very dearly, notwithstanding our differences of opinion; and also to all the workers who are comrades, to the better part of the Italian people: of these people I shall continue to consider myself a comrade.

Italo Calvino

[Typed, with the date and signature in the author's hand; in the Archivio della Fondazione Istituto Gramsci. Published in *l'Unità* (7 August 1957) under the title "Le dimissioni di Calvino dal PCI condannate dal C.D. di Torino" (Calvino's resignation from the PCI condemned by the Turin Ruling Committee). Calvino's letter was followed by the communiqué from the Ruling Committee of the Turin Federation of the PCI. In the Calvino Archive there are: a handwritten draft, of four pages; a first typed draft with handwritten corrections; a copy of the definitive typed version. The text published in *S*, II, 2188–91, is that of the first typed draft with corrections and shows some slight variants compared with the final version.]

To Michele Rago—Rome

[Turin,] 1 August 57

Dear Michele,

It is with great sadness that I enclose a copy of my letter of resignation from the Party. But it is also with the conviction that now all my relations with the Party, and all my involvement in politics will be clearer to me.

Of course, now that I have delivered these registered letters to be posted, the sense of disquiet is considerable. There is also the sense of a responsibility that has been increased tenfold, of having to reply in person from now on.

But in reality my position as an ineffective and reticent opponent had become untenable and sterile.

I hope *l'Unità* will publish it: I don't think it is like Muscetta's letter.[39]

I will be grateful to you if you will let Carlo S. and Antonello read it too, explaining to them that I do not want this decision to spoil our friendship.[40]

Now that I am no longer a member, I believe that the moral and psychological reluctance that stopped me from contributing to *Il Contemporaneo* may now fall away; . . . and of course also the reluctance that stopped me from discussing things with you.

Warmest regards

Calv.

I am off to San Remo. Write to me there up until the 26th: Villa Meridiana, San Remo.
[Handwritten on Einaudi headed paper; with the addressee.]

To Paolo Spriano—Rome

[Turin,] 1 August 57

Dear Pillo,

I AM REPLYING TO YOUR SAD LETTER WITH EVEN MORE SADness, enclosing* a copy of my letter of resignation which I sent off today. As you will see, it is very different from Muscetta's; it's a love letter. Maybe now I will manage to find greater clarity and to still be alongside you after months and months when my only political activity has been that of receiving outbursts and confessions from all our despairing comrades. Of course if Antonio had managed to conduct his *battle* staying inside the party, it would have been better; but once he left, I had no position of strength I could look to, I was alone and an *enemy* in enemy territory. And in any case, I have only one voice; I had said that I was not resigning because Giolitti was still there, and once he went I no longer had any justification for staying on, since the other reformers were too hesitant, scattered, and lacking in courage. I do not agree with your letter: your "either stay in the Party or think of your salary and Western pleasures" is a false ultimatum. One is a revolutionary inside or outside the Party depending on the historical circumstances and one's own conscience, and the question of enjoying life is a different problem, which everybody solves in their own way whatever their public position. And one is concerned for the workers if one is really interested in them: this is not something that one can take up or abandon from one day to the next. I understand the mental state you are in, which makes you say confused and unpleasant things; I really cannot give you practical advice; but advice on moral clarity, yes, I would like to give you that.

However, I am not a social democrat, nor a follower of Olivetti, as you know. It is difficult being a Communist on your own. But I am and remain a Communist. If I can manage to prove this to you, I will also have proven that *Il barone rampante* (*The Baron in the Trees*) is a book that is not too far from the things that we are really interested in. Nevertheless, I have at last entered into a period of "realist" literature, and the story I have finished now is perhaps the most Communist thing I have ever written.[41]

My affection for you remains unchanged. I hope to see you and Carla in San Remo (I'll be there until the 26th); unfortunately I have many relations staying in the house and cannot put you up, but maybe I could in September, if I take some more time off.

Calv.

As for money, once more we are broke. But we have high hopes for September.[42]

We will also be delaying till then our reply to your book proposal.
I am leaving this evening.

* Actually I see that I have very few copies so I am not sending it to you, because you can easily see the one I sent to the editors of *l'Unità*.
[Handwritten on Einaudi headed paper; with the addressee's heirs. Published with some omissions in Spriano, *Le passioni di un decennio*, pp. 24–25.]

To Michele Rago—Rome

San Remo 9 August 57

Dear Michele,

I GOT YOUR SECOND LETTER WHICH I WAS VERY MUCH WAITING for, after your first and your article. I understand that you would have preferred me to have consulted with you first, but one has to know how to take the serious decisions on one's own, at least that is the way I have always done it. And in any case this was not so much a decision, more the putting into action of something that could no longer be postponed: I had always stated that I would stay in the Party as long as Giolitti was in it. Certainly, I would have preferred G. to stay, carrying out his *battle* (I did not want him just to remain in the party without speaking out), but now that he has gone there is not even the trace of an "opposition" within the Party, or rather the "opposition" no longer has any spokesman. All of you who are fighting are too few, disinclined to raise your voice, and when you do nobody listens: the odd trade unionist, some who are obliged to stay and study on their own like Leonardi, the odd functionary who embraces double truths even though he is sincerely distraught, others who are constantly forced to accept compromises because they still believe in the political game (Rossana is in this group),[43] others who survive through their exclusive link with a peripheral reality (like Silvio Guarnieri). Then there is you, certainly the only one amongst the writers and serious journalists to see things as they are and to cope with them with full moral responsibility, but it is only now that you have decided to open a public debate. I could have no role if I had stayed in, just as I have had none in these last seven months, apart from that of prolonging a state of ambiguity. I would have had a role if there had been a part of the Party that was fighting and was absolutely sure about our positions, instead of being dispersed among thousands of individual rivulets. Action of this sort has not happened, through many people's fault, through everyone's fault, and also because these are not things that can be improvised. I am not nor do I want to be a leader, so I cannot but adopt an individual position: that way I can reject the moral responsibilities that I do not want to continue sharing, and can take on those I want to take on and be fully responsible for them. The separation between the workers and ourselves, which I became aware of in the days of the Hungarian invasion, is a fact which it is impossible to hide from ourselves. Finding a sense of unity, a genuine unity which will work this time, will be a long process which will depend not only on our willpower but also on the external events in the midst of which we will find ourselves struggling. I left the Party after Giolitti because Giolitti is the man who has shown himself in this crisis to have the most sound moral personality and most independence of judgment and most decisiveness; he may not have great gifts as a theoretician, he is almost certainly not a leader, maybe he does not have a great political future, but I have learned that the first thing one has to do is to look at someone's ethical character. When G. resigned I realized that by delaying my resignation even by a week I would risk being forced to resign in the wake of situations that were morally ambiguous, like another Reale, or as a result of a pre-electoral situation or in any case in other more serious circumstances.[44] No, as you rightly say, this cannot constitute a "liberation" for me: I feel myself assailed as never before by public responsibilities, which previously I could forget most of the time, since the Party card (along with all the contradictory network of relations it brought with it) often took the place of my conscience; now this is no longer the case, I find myself facing history without intermediaries for the first time. I do not know how I will start this new phase of my activity. Maybe I will start working for *l'Unità* again, with literary articles that are connected with politics (I would like to write an article on Sholokhov's stories). But if on the one hand not belonging to the Party any more has released me from the moral reservations I have that by writing for *l'Unità* I am propping up the lies that *l'Unità* prints, on the other hand the paper continues to tell lies and I cannot denounce it every time; so the situation continues to be as contradictory as before. In short, I am still in the same bind: a desire to continue to talk to Communists, to workers (and that is why I decided to resign without a major split and I have succeeded), and the impossibility of doing so except in publications such as the official Communist press which uphold a policy that I know is against the workers and the Communists themselves. Still the new aspect of the situation might be the existence of Communists outside the party, or rather the new way in which this new type of ex-Communist who remains a Communist can structure his relationships today. Naturally, if I can manage this, I owe it to the fact that I have been able to exist for all these years *also* as an independent writer, that is to say as a *producer*—with a public (a "base") that does not identify itself with the Party, and in this sense nothing has changed.

This is what is missing in your case, for God's sake! Now look at the situation you are in. That's why I welcome your return to critical writing (which I hope will be the beginning of something that will continue) as an extremely important fact that can give clarity to your own individual position. (Your problems are not at all negligible in relation to the overall situation.) I have not yet read *La loi* but from what you say it sounds interesting and I will read it soon.[45]

Your political article is the most courageous thing that anyone has read in our (oops! maybe I am not allowed to say "our" any more) press over the last few months: it is only a description of the situation, but for the first time an objective one.[46] However, from the crisis facing all parties that you describe one could draw a conclusion that is completely different from the one you propose, when you conclude more or less that the crisis has to be followed through and resolved within the ambit of existing organizations (in particular, within the ambit of the Communist parties). One could also draw the opposite conclusion, namely that parties are historical formations and once they enter into crisis one has to work (those of us who have "long term" work obligations) to let other parties come into being, especially when we have witnessed their lack of capacity for renewal; or at any rate to work so as to force them out of their immobility, to refuse to accept the rules of the game, to stop them going on as they are, to "deconsecrate" them, since we do not believe they are churches.

This is a dangerous game, I know; but history belongs to those who take risks, to Tito, Gomulka, maybe Mao (I say maybe, it's not all clear to me); not to our timid Amendola. Your article can also be read as an invitation to be patient, to have "belief in history," to be optimistic about problems that develop by themselves: I know that this is not your spirit, that we have already sacrificed too much on this altar of confidence in history; and we know that the only historical confidence can be in what we are doing directly. But today every call of this kind from an official Communist platform takes on this meaning, connives with the general inertia already in evidence. Oh, well. On the other hand, those of us outside the party, by admitting that there are no possible solutions except in the long term, take for granted that today there is no point in doing anything . . . We must be united, must fight . . . without the workers? Would that not end up being a new Partito d'Azione?[47] Well, maybe the years to come will produce a solution sooner than we imagine.

I certainly do not advise you to resign from the Party. It is already a serious enough thing for me, and I care very little about hierarchies, and have always been a "frontier man"; I realize how much it must count for you who have been accustomed to living in that exclusive landscape for so long and so completely. What I want to continue to do is to appeal to your particular strengths, for you to find your own center of gravity within yourself: and then everything will be easy. I believe a lot in the individual precisely because I am concerned with collective history. I am extremely grateful for the affection shown in your letters, and I reciprocate it with all my heart, though I've done it with this lengthy outburst which one can only indulge in with a true friend in grave times.

Your Calvino

[Handwritten; with the addressee.]

To Mario Socrate—Rome

[San Remo,] 10 August '57

Dearest Mario,

Thank you very much for your book of poems, of which I am happy to have been one of the first readers and champions.[48]

I hope that you and your friends are not too angry with me for my resignation. I had worked on Giolitti for a long time urging him not resign, but to no avail; he could not cope—most of all—psychologically, after the pressure they had put on him to get him to renounce his position. Once Giolitti had left, I considered the weakness of our "opposition" which was dispersed, intermittent, devoid of any figure of major standing; and it seemed to me that this was the moment (which maybe would never come again) to take up a position of independence but without a violent split. I succeeded in this (unlike Muscetta, who has ended up in the position of the angry ex-Communist) and I count on continuing my dialog with the Party, in this phase which I think still has a long way to go, during which the Party and my ideals will be two separate things. I know that to whoever is in the Party and is fighting for it (to the limited extent one can do that) resigning sounds like deserting, giving into the Alicatas of this world; but if I have taken this decision, it is because I saw our front crumble bit by bit, and because I think I can in this way be freer to move (I am also reflecting on whether it would not be useful—now that this would no longer mean supporting a whole set of policies—to resume my collaboration with the Party's official press). I know from indirect sources that dark clouds are gathering over your heads and urge you to continue along the road you have embarked on, and I say openly that I am always by your side. I have not seen the issue of *Città aperta* (*Open City*) with my little story, about which I now see the papers are talking.[49] Send me a copy or two to my house in San Remo where I will be until the 26th.

Warmest good wishes to you, Dario, and everyone else,[50]

Your Calvino

[Handwritten on paper headed Villa Meridiana, Sanremo; with the addressee.]

To Paolo Spriano—Rome

[San Remo,] 10 August 57

Dear Pillo,

As you have seen, I have managed to resign without a complete split, and I am counting on continuing my dialog with the party. Thank you very much for what you say in your letter: you know that even if our positions have taken necessarily different routes, I have never considered you a damned soul, and I genuinely hope that you are not damning yourself. Now I have been suddenly seized by the need to do something, to "be a militant," whereas when I was in the Party I did not feel the need for this at all and could live a quiet life. See what a con this is? I really don't know what I will do. On the one hand I think that—now that I am outside the Party and no longer support *l'Unità*'s politics and lies—I might resume my collaboration with *l'Unità* and I am strongly tempted to do so. (I would like to write an article on Sholokhov's stories: literary articles with one foot always in the world of politics, this seems to me to be the best way.) On the other hand it might seem to the workers that my signature—even though it has been solemnly ratified that I am not in agreement with the party line—was being used to prop up the deceptions of policies that are against them, and this would continue to weigh on my conscience. So it's back to square one: my political needs are to talk to Communists and workers, but I cannot do this except from platforms that I do not want to give credence to. Dammit. I'll let you know once I've decided. I'll be here until the 26th, with frequent excursions to the Côte d'Azur (illegal ones too, since I am still an "undesirable").[51] Do you two want to come? Ciao.

Calv.

[Handwritten on paper headed Villa Meridiana, Sanremo; with the addressee's heirs. Published with slight omissions in Spriano, *Le passioni di un decennio*, p. 28.]

To Lucio Lombardo Radice—Rome

Turin, 12–[8]–57

Dear Lucio,

I read your letter with great pleasure (now, just coming back from holiday: so I am sorry for replying so late). It was so open and friendly. What you say about *Il barone* is very welcome not only because it is positive, but because it is very perceptive, because I feel that I have been properly understood (an impression which, reading the reviews of one's own books, even favorable ones, one rarely gets). And I also like the things you say about "La bonaccia" (Becalmed in the Antilles). But I want to thank you as well for the calm way you wrote to me about my resignation (and for the article that Spriano tells me you wrote for *l'Unità*). All you friends of mine who have stayed in the Party have written me similar letters; and in fact they are the same arguments I put to those who left before me, and to Giolitti himself in the weeks before his resignation. Once he had gone, the prospects for continuing to fight seemed too thin, and rather than stay in the Party in ineffectual seclusion—as I explained in my resignation letter—I preferred to leave. The only thing I did not say is that I no longer believe that the Party can save itself without a serious change of course. This is the real point that divides us from you who have stayed in it. But what alternative do we propose? Oh, well. I believe that what we have in common is the awareness that new perspectives will only come about in the long term. And in order to make them come about each of us must find—"inside" or "outside"—the road that allows us to do most.

Will I manage to do more from the outside? I don't know yet; I do know it will be very difficult; just as it is very difficult battling "within." But I also know that it is absolutely crucial that we remain in touch, you and us, not increasing the distance that separates us, that we remain sure that where we are headed is eventually to join up again, and most of all to do this along with the working class which we began to lose long before losing the intellectuals and which we will continue to lose in a dreadful haemorrhage.

In the midst of the general pessimism the calm clarity of conscience you express is a comfort to me and makes me continue to hope.

I do not think I will be able to come to Rome in September. But let's stay in touch. Warmest good wishes

Your Calvino

[Handwritten; in the Archivio della Fondazione Istituto Gramsci, Rome. Through a slip of the pen the date on the original is "12-7-57."]

To Michele Rago—Rome

[Turin,] 27-9-57

Dear Michele,

It's been a long while since we wrote to each other and I can't remember if I was the one who did not reply the last time or you. I read your pieces in *Il Contemporaneo*, when you write (but now I am two issues behind) and I am always anxious to know what you are doing, how you are and what you are thinking. I think that in October I will come to Rome a few times and we will be able to see each other.

Since coming back to Turin I have re-established contact with the best comrades who have stayed in the party here and I try to participate in the struggle from the outside. So I have recovered a bit from that sense of general emptiness that my resignation left me with. Not that I am euphoric or in any sense optimistic: I think things are darker than ever, as everyone does. But it seems to me we can try to obtain a convergence of the forces of those who are inside, those who are on the outside, and those who are going into the PSI (the Italian Socialist Party), and start to work together with a view to bringing about that something which will not be the PCI nor the PSI nor "independence" but something new that will be inclusive of the experiences and needs of all of us. For the time being I will continue to use *Città aperta* as my platform for as long as it survives. After that, I don't know. The various journals in the air are all damnably ideological and I am shunning ideology like the plague.

At Einaudi it's still very much low tide in economic terms. Payments waiting to be made, which had already been promised for September then for October, have been postponed until January. But for a few weeks now there has been an atmosphere of greater euphoria. Here's hoping. I too, who have built up a few credits, have been unable to get a lira out of them. Your name is on the list, waiting along with so many others.

Write to me. And maybe we'll see each other in about ten days' time. Warmest good wishes.

Calv.

[Handwritten; with the addressee.]

To Palmiro Togliatti, Head Offices of the Pci—Rome

Turin, 3 October 1957

Dear Togliatti,

Some ill-wishers are claiming that you were referring to me when you said in your speech to the Cultural Commission (I quote from *l'Unità* of 29 September):

> The man of letters who yesterday refused to write something signifying his political commitment to the Party's noble causes, has left the Party and immediately written the short story to fling mud at the Party and its leaders, at the beck and call of the bourgeois press, in order to heighten confusion, lack of confidence and defeatism.

I think this interpretation is absurd. How could you have spoken of a refusal to commit himself on the part of a writer who has for more than ten years been a contributor to *l'Unità*, to *Il Contemporaneo*, and also to the journal of which you are editor,[52] with writings of every kind, from accounts of working class life and struggle, to ideological campaigns, to comments on current affairs, leading articles during election periods, and satirical stories and fables connected with our struggles? Whoever leafs through the collections of Party journals can rule out that you were talking about someone who like me has clearly been one of the Italian writers who have committed themselves most to the political struggle.

Then you mention a story that the writer in question apparently "has immediately written" after leaving the Party. There is no way this can refer to my "La gran bonaccia delle Antille" (Becalmed in the Antilles). I wrote it and it was published (after much delay as well) while I was still a member of the Party, in the issue of *Città aperta* of 25 July. You say that it was written "at the behest of the bourgeois press" whereas *Città aperta* is written and edited by members of the Party. You say that it was written "to fling mud at the Party and its leaders etc.," which would mean you have not read the text in question, but rather the interpretation of, say, Vittorio Gorresio. That would be tantamount to slandering your spirit of precision and would make people believe that you give credence to tendentious informers.

No, the interpretation of these ill-wishers is absolutely absurd. They do not know that the PCI can criticize someone who, given his disagreements, has preferred to distance himself rather than exacerbating an internal argument, yet it can continue to respect him and discuss things fairly with him. They do not know that certain systems of slanderous polemic whereby either one agrees with everything or one is "at the beck and call of the bourgeoisie," are relics of a political fashion that the PCI wants to put behind it.

However, since these malevolent interpretations exist, circulating both amongst enemies and amongst comrades, and sound like criticism of you, it would be good if you too would do everything you can to dispel them.[53]

Yours sincerely,

Italo Calvino

[Typed, with autograph signature; in the Archivio della Fondazione Istituto Gramsci, Rome.]

To Mario Socrate—Rome

Turin, 14 November 1957

Dear Socrate,

YOU WRITE LIKE CLUMSY HIPPOS![54]

The themes are acceptable and formulated with just the right amount of vagueness that means we do not to have to stop and discuss them. But the language is abominable. I refuse to add my signature on the grounds of both syntax and diction. The first page especially is a shambles, at least three quarters of it. "If an intellectual notices one thing today." How do you mean "if"? Why? Is the intellectual an idiot? Insensitive? And why must he notice one thing and not two? or three? Then the second paragraph: for God's sake! I like "dissolute" clerical activity, though, but I did not understand whether it was to do with Capocotta or Suor Pasqualina.[55]

In short: if you want, I will try to rewrite the "negative" introduction, reducing it to its main points:

> There are many reasons why Italian intellectuals endowed with a democratic conscience and a modern education should feel uneasy and alarmed: the failure of culture to be part of the civic structure of the country; the failure of culture to establish itself as a force driving and stimulating the country's renewal; the fact that once more we are faced with fragmentation into disparate groups, provincial isolation, airtight partitions between disciplines. Over and above all this there is the excessive economic power wielded by monopolies which naturally tend to squeeze culture into the framework of its "functionality' as it serves them. There is also excessive clerical power which with its mix of medieval hesitation and uncontrolled organizational activity is spreading and ramifying everywhere; and all around is the great universal swamp of blackmail and compromise.[56]

Then you can go on:

> This state of affairs touches on the responsibility etc.

As for the rest of it, I'm in agreement. Write to me to say if you agree with this variant of mine.

Yours,

Calvino

[Typed on Einaudi headed paper, with autograph signature; with the addressee.]

To Antonio Giolitti—Rome

[Turin,] 18-11-57

Dear Antonio,

This morning the editor of *L'Espresso*[57] phoned me saying that he has read *La speculazione edilizia* (*A Plunge into Real Estate*), that in it he saw the disillusionment of the ex-Communist faced with a society into which he could not integrate (which maybe is there but is not the main theme of the story, which in any case was written before my resignation), and that he wanted to organize a meeting of ex-Communists to discuss this topic and to record it on tape for *L'Espresso*. I was worried that they might talk of my story in an arbitrary way, so I said yes, on condition that the story appeared as only one of many topics and that you too would take part.

But then on thinking it over I felt that I have nothing I really want to say and that my way of saying things is to write stories and that others can interpret them as they like, and everyone can find what interests him in them, and that my way of taking part in political life is this and I am waiting to have something clear to say before making more direct political statements. I have sent a letter to Benedetti along these lines explaining to him that I prefer not to take part in the debate. This for your information. It might well be that the thing is interesting and that it is in your interest to go along. I don't feel like it also because this business of the tape-recorder makes me clam up.

Best wishes.

Calv.

[Handwritten, on Einaudi headed paper; with the addressee.]

To Lev Veršinin—Moscow

Turin, 28 November 1957

Dear Veršinin,

I AM VERY GRATEFUL FOR YOUR LETTER AND IT GIVES ME great pleasure to deal directly with you and Breitburd and to send you our best books.[58] I am very pleased that Pavese is being published. I will have them send you the volumes you do not have:

Il compagno (The Comrade)
Feria d'agosto (Summer Storm)
Notte di festa (Festival Night)

I am also sending you two of my own books: *L'entrata in guerra* (*Into the War*) and *Il barone rampante* (*The Baron in the Trees*). As for *Ultimo viene il corvo* (*The Crow Comes Last*), it has sold out and I do not even have a copy myself, but a new edition of it will come out maybe next year. Meanwhile, I can send you a series of my short stories in typescript, some of which already appeared in *The Crow Comes Last*, while others were published piecemeal in *l'Unità* and *Il Contemporaneo*. I think that the best way to introduce myself to the Soviet public is a selection of short stories. (Apart from the folktales, which are something separate and not part of my creative work.)

As for the writers you mentioned in your letter, the most important is certainly Elio Vittorini, one of the authors who had most influence on my generation. It is a pity that his creative output has almost dried up in the last ten years, but *Conversazione in Sicilia* (*Conversations in Sicily*) was for us a revolutionary book, and *Uomini e no* (*Men and Not Men*) for all its defects was a high point in the literature of the Resistance in our country. *Le donne di Messina* (*Women of Messina*) too has some wonderful bits, even though it cannot be considered a finished work.

Another writer whose extreme sobriety is highly valued is Bilenchi.[59] Similar to him is Carlo Cassola, who at times reminds one of the limpid sadness of certain of Tolstoy's short stories. (His best story is *Il taglio del bosco* (*The Cutting of the Woods*), published by Nistri-Lischi.)

You should also do Brancati: he was like a small-scale Gogol in Fascist Italy.[60]

Fine for the other names you mention: Tobino is a very whimsical writer (*Il deserto della Libia* [*The Libyan Desert*], which we published, is his best book), Landolfi the best Italian "surrealist," Seminara's *Disgrazia in casa Amato* (*Tragedy in the Amato House*), which we published, seems to me to be his strongest work, and also Bernari.[61]

Have you got the works of these authors? We can send you the books by Tobino and Seminara that I mentioned to you, and almost all of Cassola's works. Tobino is almost entirely published by Vallecchi, as are Bilenchi, Landolfi, and Bernari, while Vittorini and Brancati belong to Bompiani. If you like, I can put you in direct contact with the writers.

In the list of most famous Italian authors that you quote I don't see the name of Italo Svevo. He is certainly a writer who would be very much at home if translated into Russian!

Please give my best wishes to G. Breitburd: I was very pleased to receive his letter. (I do not have his address so I would like to ask you politely to act as go-between.) I was expecting him in Turin when he was in Italy. But I was waiting for him to arrange to see me in any Italian city, and I would have gone to meet him. I travel the length and breadth of Italy regularly, which I like, and it would have been easy to arrange.

I would have liked to have given him the stories that I am now sending to you and which you can look at together.

With all good wishes

Italo Calvino

[Typed on Einaudi headed paper, with autograph signature; with the addressee.]

To Armando Bozzoli—San Felice Sul Panaro (Modena)

Turin, 8 January 1958

Dear Bozzoli,

I AM VERY GRATEFUL TO YOU FOR YOUR LETTER. I AM VERY pleased to hear about your discussion and even more to know that in your village you meet in the library for these debates.[62] Where city and country workers go regularly to the library to discuss books in a spirit of exploration and criticism, there one can be sure is a living center of democracy, a nucleus for the society of the future.

You are right to say that *Il barone rampante* (*The Baron in the Trees*) is not just mere play of the imagination but that I wanted to say something more. But this something cannot be defined by means of simple identification of one image from the story with a topical event or with a theoretical concept as you try to do. It is not an allegorical story. In my view, real poetic creations represent a conception of life, but they represent it in such a way that it cannot be defined except through those images, that plot, those words. To try to define it in another way is always, in some sense, to betray it, because the poetic image contains within itself a multiplicity of meanings, not contradictory meanings, but where one meaning is contained inside another like the leaves of an artichoke.

Now I don't want to claim that I have done something that has this merit. I would like to have done so, and there are those who say that I've succeeded and those who say I have not.

What idea of life did I mean to express in Cosimo? I wanted to put forward the figure of a *committed* man (an intellectual, if you like), who takes a profound part in history and the development of society, but who knows he has to travel roads that are different from ones the others take, as is the destiny of those who do not conform. I also wanted to express a moral imperative of will, of loyalty to oneself, to the law one has imposed on oneself, even when this costs us separation from the rest of mankind. Is this a credo of individualism? I would say that it is the affirmation that in order to be genuinely with others one must not be afraid to find oneself even on one's own. And that it is in one's own strength and individual morality that one finds the strength and morality that make us fight in collective struggles.

Now the book can be criticized (and indeed strongly criticized) both by those who say that if these were my ideas the book does not succeed in articulating them, and it remains instead just pure entertainment, and by those who claim that the moral that emerges from it is a negative, escapist, reactionary one.

Now that I have written you all these things, you must not believe that I am claiming that in the *Barone rampante* I have written a book of great philosophical and historical significance. No, I wanted to write an amusing book, into which I flung a certain amount of my own personal humors and whimsies. This is a *personal* book, I insist on this, written by someone who is talking with friends who know him and who know how to cope also with his game of paradoxes. It is also a story with its own *autonomy* as a story, so that you cannot explain all the episodes and characters by appealing to an outside meaning; so many things happen because it is in the logic of the plot to make them happen. Nevertheless, attributing meanings to a work of art is a more than legitimate operation. If a work is valid, it lends itself to considerations of its relevance not just to the period in which it was written, but also after that, when it is reality itself that will discover new meanings in the artist's images.

Best wishes and thanks,

Yours,

Italo Calvino

[Typed on Einaudi headed paper, with autograph signature; with the addressee's heirs.]

To Lanfranco Caretti—Pavia

[Turin,] 19-1-58

Dear Caretti,

I HAVE RECEIVED THE PART OF YOUR RADIO REVIEW THAT CONcerns me and have read it with great pleasure.[63] I am very happy with what you say about *La speculaz. edilizia (A Plunge into Real Estate)*. It seems to me that your critical approach to all my work is clear and logical, and I would be very happy if the future were to prove you right, in other words that I would succeed in writing a great realist novel. But what counts are the things that have already been written. And, paradoxically, I could also say that you have discovered the simplest system for freeing yourself from this problem: the true line is the one that runs through this and that book, everything that differs from it is merely a marginal deviation. Very neat! (At this moment I am speaking as a marginal spectator, impartially divided between Calvino "the fabulist" and Calvino "the realist"). The line that Sciascia attempts to take in the latest issue of *Il Ponte*, that really is demanding.[64] That is more where I want you, critics!

And another thing, what has *I giovani del Po* (*Youth in Turin*) got to do with *La speculazione edilizia* (*A Plunge into Real Estate*)? In the former there is that jargon-like language, and the distance between author and protagonist which is filled only by a certain Pavesian lyricism and the screen of the uncouth character; in the latter there is psychology, autobiographical elements, narrative of minute detail, elements of intellectual essay-writing . . . Are they both on the line? Which is the more realistic line? And by dint of always talking in terms of realism do we not lose all the nuances that are essential if we are not to fall into generic discourse?

I am glad if I have put the odd flea in your ear, as is the duty of the writer with his critics (our job is basically to raise problems for you to solve), and I send best wishes and friendly thanks,

Calvino

[Handwritten on Einaudi headed paper; with the addressee's heirs.]

To Carlo Cassola—Grosseto

Turin, 5 February 1958

Dear Cassola,

I have reread *Fausto e Anna* (*Fausto and Anna*). You know that I was not a great fan of the book; when I read it I still did not know you, it was the first thing of yours that I had read, and I could not understand it.[65] Now I see how much beauty there is in it, especially in the first part, and that sense of being young; I see how much this really is your book, with the recovery of this simplicity of affections, something you believe is "natural." And yet it continues to be a book toward which I feel more hostile than ever. I am on the side of the early Fausto, the passionate denier: that was when he was in the right, even though he expressed himself in that childish way. And the book stands as a parable of the Italian petit-bourgeoisie, which is unable to give humanity and reality and reason to the force of negation and revolution that is expressed in history, and in order to retreat into conformism finds ready-made justifications in religion even while not believing in it. The partisan war is described very well, it is depicted—as you always manage to do—with astonishing sincerity. And also the reactions of Fausto are *true*; but that does not take away from the fact that I cannot stand them, I do not agree with them. I do not agree even with Zhivago, when he is with the partisans, yet he moves heaven and earth, whereas Fausto only evokes the most obvious and predictable moral reactions.

And it seems to me that the ethical breadth of the book, its meaning, is restricted in the end instead of broadening out. At first there is a fine sense of moral life: the young man who sets off denying everything, then he gradually matures, and the girl who initially cannot but accept traditional values, slowly begins to express her critique of life as it is, to go over to the "opposition." While Fausto conforms, it is she who incarnates the antithesis toward legally constituted society, even though in a very intimate and secret way and though formally accepting her destiny.

In creating a picture such as this, what is the meaning of making the final emphasis fall on Fausto's opposition to violence? It is a fine thing, but earlier the stakes were higher, richer in contrasts. Is the Resistance only useful for that? Only to persuade Fausto that violence is a terrible thing and that consequently it would have been better for him to have stayed a nice petit-bourgeois at peace with the world? The visual picture of the novel, as it were, has broadened out; there is the civil war, a huge touchstone for everyone. But the ethical battle which has been conducted in the novel up until now is reduced to a one-sided meaning, which is—both for those who accept it and for those who don't—a little obvious, not original.*

Or do I still not understand?

All the same, it is a book that has its place, that counts for something now, there is no doubt. And now that I've reread it, at the same time as my first and now second rereading of *Zhivago*, it acquires more light rather than remaining in the shadows.

I have read your observations on *Zhivago*, whose spell enthralls me too. But I see it not as polemical with the rest of the "literature" of our time, but actually as a confirmation of the character of our epoch, a confirmation that comes to us unexpectedly from one of those nineteenth-century writers who have come alive again. A confirmation of modern literature's raison d'être given by the voice of the literature of the past.[66]

My very best wishes.

*The same happens in Pasternak, with the partisan war. At first the moral arc spanned everything, there were the rights of both sides. When he goes off with the partisans, his choice is made, our reading of it becomes one-sided, and consequently the book *says* less.
[Typed copy; in the Einaudi Archive and the Calvino Archive.]

To Alberto Caracciolo—Rome

[Turin,] 24–2–58

Dear Caracciolo,
I HAVE READ CASES'S ARTICLE ON *DÉRY* AND FORWARDED IT TO Guiducci.

I approve of it and like it a lot. The only thing I am against is the anti-Gadda barb at the end.[67] I believe that Gadda's book is one of the very few works that are useful and necessary in this postwar period.[68] It is an epic about Rome with all the horror of the Roman inferno, of Italy that has Rome as its capital, seen for the first time not from the inside, apologetically, but by a Northerner who develops a sort of vertigo from it, and who attempts to represent all the scum and sewage of cultures and sub-cultures that bubble away in Rome, and which Rome transmits to the apparatus of the Italian state. One cannot write about Rome in any other way, after Gadda. I think that attacking Gadda can only have a *reactionary* sense and I would like *P. e P.* not to do it. If it does, I will write a letter of complaint.

I have nearly finished the "Pasternak," which is turning out very long and complicated.[69]

Best wishes

Calv.

In the eighty years since the Unification of Italy Gadda's novel is the first book to take stock of the whole dismal affair, and it puts an end to regionalism [definitively].[70]
[Handwritten draft on Einaudi headed paper; in the Calvino Archive.]

To Cesare Cases—Pisa

Turin, 3 March 1958

Dear Cases,

I agree with your anti-Rinosassic polemic.[71] And I agree also with your description of the *Pasticciaccio* and your desecration of it. But the value of the book is precisely because it is execrable, because in it style and content have become one and are taken to their extreme consequences: precisely because a book lives through the negative without reservation, because it manages to express this as an extreme case, a book enlightens our consciences.

I am however in complete disagreement with your argument that goes "Rome is more than this."

The power of a poetic image is often (I won't say always) given by the fact that the poet peremptorily seizes on some detail of reality as representing the whole and says: that thing, that character, that institution, that society is *all* like that. Clearly one cannot say one thing is applicable to all Romans (just as one cannot say one thing applies to *all* husbands, *all* middle-class men, *all* the Swiss), but the important thing for the writer is to give *one* image of the husband, the bourgeois, the Swiss. The great realist—you will argue—provides instead all the facets of reality. But peremptory, allegorical fiction does not have any less a poetic-historical-moral role than that of all-round fiction which is based on nuances. Leopardi, whom you quote, belongs more to the first than to the latter category. He sees a road in Rome (yes, Rome!) and decides: "Here they are all good, all honest and hard-working!," and with this arbitrary and absolute contrast highlights even more the distinction between light and shadow.[72]

How can you compare Gadda's novel with Moravia's *Racconti romani* (*Roman Tales*) which articulate Roman flabbiness so flabbily? In order to hate the Tower of Babel we have to have the Tower of Babel totally tangible in front of us.

We could perhaps publish this exchange of letters of ours in *P. e P.* but we would have to sweeten them unfortunately.

Best wishes,

[Typed copy with author's corrections; in the Calvino Archive and the Einaudi Archive.]

To Alberto Asor Rosa—Rome

Turin 21 May 1958

Dear Asor-Rosa,

I have read your article which I was waiting for impatiently.[73] Your reading of *La speculazione ed.* (*A Plunge into Real Estate*) is impeccable; having a reader who can catch and evaluate every bit of depth and nuance in a work, without missing anything—every authorial intention and even what goes beyond intention but always sticking to the truth—is the greatest satisfaction one can have as a writer.

I also feel myself to have been understood and interpreted very well as far as my ethical and literary ideals are concerned, in the first part of your essay. Particularly accurate and never before expressed (and never clearly expressed even by me up till now, even though that is precisely what I intended) is your point about "the individual not the character." The whole of the second column on p. 4 and half of the first column on p. 5 are particularly precious to me. And the relationship with Pavese is also perfectly right: myth and history. (Earlier on, I nearly forgot, your contrast with Pasolini is also spot on.)

At that point the problem of the *poetic world* (I would say *poetic world* rather than *poetics*) begins, which you define with a very emblematic example: Pratolini.[74] But he is also a rather convenient example: a writer for whom the whole universe that can be a subject for poetry is enclosed within the microcosm of a municipality or even of a district. For any other writer than Pratolini the problem immediately becomes more complex. I could say to you that for me the equivalent of his Florence is the natural world of my childhood memories: the Ligurian Riviera, from the woods down to the sea, in other words the asocial world. As long as I was writing partisan stories it was all mixed together: woods, adventures, rebellion, and the only society I knew and recognized, namely the partisans. Then, ever since I started seeking out a more complex social reality, I have to feel my way more. The fact that I have become Turinese applied on the cultural level but not on the level of my poetic world. This is a possible interpretative key that can be applied right up to *La speculazione*, in other words my falling back on a story about failing to be assimilated into society, an impossible return to my native landscape. But other approaches are also possible: Cases (in his article in *Città Aperta*) adopts that of the epic; Leonardo Sciascia (in an issue of *Il Ponte* this year) goes for historical-ethical passion. However, that is where the work (and play) of the critic ought to begin: finding a unity amongst things that apparently *each go their own way*. And if that unity does not exist, it means that the author is not a writer, and so these are pointless discourses. A creative writer, whether poet or novelist, is made up of his creative works, and *that is all*; his cultural declarations are valid only if they are at one with his creative work, otherwise they are mere "flatus vocis." I do not want to defend this or that work; in fact I do not want to defend myself at all; only to say to you that you have barely scratched the surface of this part of your enquiry. (Maybe you will be able to complete it with the book of mine that is coming out at the end of the year: a collection of my short fiction.)

However, your choice of *La speculazione* and your pointing out what is my true direction (the crisis of the bourgeois intellectual seen critically from the inside) is in itself correct and rational. But seen from my point of view this has a terribly decadent dimension: autobiography, introspection, egocentrism, all things that I have always hated and fought against. (Yes, while I'm at it: why do you say that *Il sentiero dei nidi di ragno* (*The Path to the Spiders' Nests*)—the most objective story I have ever written—is "semi-autobiographical"? The story of a prostitute's brother? I could take you to court, even though I have no sister's honour to defend!). *L'entrata in guerra* (*Into the War*) and *La speculazione edilizia* were two *concessions* to autobiography: the first in the key of self-exaltation, with an "I" who is the model of all virtues, like the one in Carlo Levi;[75] the second in the key of self-denigration, putting in my place the most disastrous and screwed-up kind of intellectual possible, but apart from this fact it is 95 percent autobiography, so much so that I do not know if I will ever be able to publish it as a book, because the characters are all just like that in reality and highly recognizable and the events almost all true. Must I continue down this road? But you don't know where it will end up, autobiography is subject matter that is difficult to control, the borders of what is poetical and meaningful start to blur, one surrenders to the flow of things that happened, and loses sight of the sovereign prerogatives of art, which are selection and exclusion. As you can see, we are discussing a problem that is perhaps the one that all the problems of modern literature can be reduced to, namely the relationship between subjective experience and the representation of the world.

But we will continue the discussion when we meet.

A marginal observation. "Masera is sickly sweet." Of course! That's the beauty of it! Not that I really wanted him like that, but it came to me that way *naturally*, and I noticed it at once, and I left him like that, good but a bit priest-like. His relations with Quinto are conditioned by this too as well.

Thank you again, many thanks

Warmest good wishes, Calvino

[Handwritten; with the addressee.]

To François Wahl—Paris

Turin, 22 July 1958

Dear Wahl,

It has been a long time since I wrote to you, but what could I say to you during these months when we've all been with baited breath, reading the papers, thinking about France, about what you too are thinking?[76] For the last week now we have held our breath even more because of what is happening in the Middle East.[77] And it is always the news from the latest editions of the papers that determines how we feel; communicating by letters demands another, more detached, rhythm, and who knows when we will ever get it back again?

Let us talk about books, which in the end represent the best of our conscience, our attempt "to do all we can." If only that were enough!

I am very happy that you like Bassani. He is one of the two or three Italian writers of serious worth who have come to the fore in recent years. And *Gli occhiali d'oro* (*The Gold-Rimmed Spectacles*), the sixth story he has published, is the one that is of all of them richest in meaning.

(But also *Una lapide in via Mazzini* [*A Plaque in Via Mazzini*] and *Gli ultimi giorni di Clelia Trotti* [*The Last Days of Clelia Trotti*], in *Cinque storie ferraresi* [*Five Stories of Ferrara*], are very good.)

Bassani is a very cultured writer: a poet, translator, chief editor of the sophisticated journal *Botteghe Oscure*, and a member of the committee that oversees the Italian journal that has been most faithful to pure literature, *Paragone*.

Although he hails from this strictly literary background, all of Bassani's fiction centers on a political topic, which derives from his basic trauma, namely the anti-semitic persecution in bourgeois society in Ferrara. B.'s relationship with Ferrara and its middle classes is twofold: on the one hand there is a nostalgic love for a time when he felt integrated with them, and on the other a mortal hatred for the offense suffered. These two feelings are constantly mixed up and overlaid and give him that peculiar accent of his, which lies somewhere between a nostalgic love for old things (that was typical of our "crepuscular" poetry at the beginning of the century) and a deeply felt resentment.

But the two poles of B's narrative style are Henry James—which however he has abandoned in *Gli occhiali d'oro*, writing for the first time a story in a totally direct and objective style—and Flaubert. There is today, one might say, a strand of Italian literature that I would define (this is still a private, unofficial definition) "neo-Flaubertian," which conjures up effects of metaphysical dismay from a minutely detailed photograph of the Italian provinces with all the melancholy of the anti-Fascist who is disillusioned with the present. Cassola is the most despairing and natural exponent of this strand; Bassani its most self-aware and intellectual representative. (But their neo-Flaubertism, bizarrely, takes them not toward stylistic perfection but to carelessness. Both are defenseless against everyday phrases, linguistic banalities. In Cassola, who does not do so deliberately, this becomes the major attraction of his style. In Bassani, who maybe does do so deliberately, it becomes a grey background against which his stylistic affectations stand out.)

In short, he seems an author of the first rank for you to invest in, since you have the good fortune to still have an option on his translation rights in France.

How was *Le désert et sa splendeur* received?[78] I have not read anything about it. Perhaps amidst the rumble of events the news of the book went unnoticed.

I will send you two books which have non-Italian authors and subjects, but yet were written in Italian and so count as "the latest from Italy." The first (*Ricorda cosa ti ha fatto Amalek* [*Remember What Amalek Did to You*] by A. Nirenstajn) is a horrifying collection of documents on the Resistance and the extermination in the Warsaw ghetto. The author (who was the first to collect the material and translate it into Italian from Hebrew and Yiddish) is a Polish-Israeli writer now settled in Italy.

The second (*La rivolta degli intellettuali ungheresi*, by I. Meszaros)[79] is the history of a decade of cultural politics in the Rakos and post-Rakos era: it contains the first discussions of Lukács, Tibor Déry, and so on down to the Petofi Circle and the insurrection.

For your trip to Italy in September, you can by all means do it through us and pick up the money we owe to Seuil. I shall be very happy to see you again. Send me your plans in advance.

Very best wishes

[Typed copy; in the Einaudi Archive, Turin. Also in *ILDA*, pp. 259–61.]

To Elio Vittorini—Milan

Turin, 5 September 1958

Dear Elio,

I heard from Marguerite (who came to Turin the day before yesterday) and from Giulio that you are back.[80] I will come and see you soon, but now I am working on putting together my collection of short stories which should come out in November, a "Supercorallo" of old and new stories which the publisher "ordered" from me and which I ought to have already handed in some time ago to the Typesetters, but I am constantly riven by doubts about which criteria to follow in selecting them.

I am writing to you about this in order to ask your advice and also to put my ideas a bit in order. The book will contain the old things too, from *Ultimo viene il corvo* (*The Crow Comes Last*), which had a small print run and few readers, not all of the storires of course, just the best ones. The simplest criterion would be just to place the stories one after the other in chronological order; but in my stories there are clearly distinct groups and one cannot just jump from one to the other. So my problem is to find a kind of architecture of the volume that makes sense. (In the index, in any case, every title will have its date.)

So my idea is to divide the volume into three parts. Book I: *Gli idilli difficili* (*Difficult Idylls*). Book II: *Gli amori difficili* (*Difficult Loves*). Book III: *La vita difficile* (*Difficult Life*).

Gli idilli difficili include a selection of stories from *Ultimo viene il corvo* and others written after that but which still follow the same pattern of narration. The general theme is the search for and the difficulty in finding a natural harmony, with things and men.

The second book, *Gli amori difficili*, contains the stories, "L'avventura d'un soldato" (Adventure of a Soldier) (which had already appeared in *The Crow* and whose almost pornographic aspects I have toned down slightly), "L'avventura d'una bagnante" (Adventure of a Bather), "L'avventura d'un impiegato" (Adventure of a Clerk), "L'avventura d'un lettore" (Adventure of a Reader), and two other unpublished stories and maybe others still that I have in mind but which I don't know if I'll have time to write. The general theme is the failure to communicate in love, with a certain progression of intensity from story to story. This is the part that ought to be most "original" and homogeneous, a real "book."

Book III, *La vita difficile*, ought to contain a more complex and general definition of a relationship with the world. That is to say, we move here into the area of the long short story: *La formica argentina* (*The Argentine Ant*]. Alongside *La formica argentina* I thought of closing the book with another long story which would match it, this one set in today's industrial civilization: *La nuvola di smog* (*Smog*). I wrote it this summer; I am quite pleased with it (you will read it in the next issue of *Nuovi Argomenti*). But it has turned out to be a more complex kind of story, you can feel that *La speculazione edilizia* (*A Plunge into Real Estate*) has come in between. I thought that *La speculazione* did not really fit into this book, but it would actually be fine between *La formica* and *La nuvola di smog*. So the volume would in the end collect all my long and short fiction that was of any importance between '45 and '58 (leaving out the three stories in *L'entrata in guerra* (*Into the War*), which I really cannot think how to include in it).[81] But it's true that the difference between some of the stories in the first book and the last ones is enormous. So I'm not sure that it is not better to stop at *The Argentine Ant*.

The selection of stories for Book I, *Gli idilli difficili*, is proving very difficult. I would like to divide it in turn into chapters (which need not necessarily appear as such, but just to give an order): *Nature*, *The War*, *The Postwar Period*, *Nature in the City*, *The World of Machines* (these last two are all new material, that did not appear in the *Crow*, but in that genre I no longer have the sure touch I once had). I have two different selection criteria between which I constantly oscillate: either a criterion of artistic effect, whichever direction they go in, that is to say aiming solely at a book full of *good things*; or aiming at a picture-album of strange little figures, of little stories full of movement and amusement even though sometimes they are a bit cinematographic or journalistic, in short a kind of *Thousand and One Nights* of postwar Italy.[82] I know (and basically I would like you to tell me so too) that the first criterion is the right one, the only one that would allow me not to put together a book that went forward in fits and starts; but with that criterion I end up not knowing whether to include "Furto in una pasticceria" (Theft in a Cakeshop) and many other stories of that kind, whereas the fascination of the *Crow* for its most enthusiastic readers was definitely connected with that second criterion.

Tell me what you think if you have the time and the inclination. If not, at least, as I said, this letter will have helped to clarify my own ideas.

What do you think about a title like *Racconti di bosco e di scoglio* (*Stories of Woods and Rocks*)? Or is it better just to call it: *Racconti* (*Stories*)?[83]

Best wishes,

Calv.

[Typed on Einaudi headed paper with autograph signature; in the Fondo Vittorini dell'Archivio Urbinate, University of Urbino.]

To Mario Socrate—Rome

[Turin,] 18 Sept. 58

Dear Mario,

Thank you for your long letter; I was really keen to hear your news; and I see that things are going their inevitable way. Your exit from the P. has this that's new about it: you are a compact—though small—group, welded together by a period of joint struggle, and I am convinced that you will avoid being split up; and that you are not mere theoreticians but you need to keep a dialog open at a non-specialist level. You have to do all this while remaining profoundly serious, not subject to the moral deterioration of so many former members as displayed in their "journalism." (The confessions of those three idiots in August's *Tempo Presente* were awful!) Now you need to see how you can deal with the problem of the practical possibilities. Meanwhile I will be very happy to collaborate on the new issue of *Città Aperta*. I do not know if I will be able to write a kind of political article that takes stock of my current opinions; I would like to do so and this might be the right time.

On the creative side, the long story you will read in the next issue of *Nuovi Argomenti* (*La nuvola di smog*) expresses quite well my state of mind.

But I need to talk to you about your job worries which I quite understand. Here we are still in a period of cutbacks on expenditure (the economic crisis is having highly unfavorable repercussions on the book trade). It is absolutely out of the question to think about a fixed arrangement with us; you have seen that even a regular payment for translations is unreliable. Send us the bit you have translated from Balzac's *Paysans*, also to show evidence of your current "productivity" as a translator, and we'll see if we can give you some more urgent work which the publisher feels stronger about. (We have several works by Balzac already translated and no one knows when we might publish them.)

Best wishes to you and everyone else

Calv.

[Handwritten on Einaudi headed paper; with the addressee.]

To Franco Fortini—Milan

Turin, 7 October 1958

Dear Fortini,

I imagine you will have returned from your expedition to lands that are now marked *hic sunt leones*. I have had them send you the Proust proofs and I am confidently waiting for your article. Please don't delay it because otherwise I will not be able to paginate it.

I read your article in *Il Ponte*.[84] Is it true that there is nothing in it but "the content of the story" and a "phenomenology of form"? Maybe that is really the case *today*, and I would be the first to say it certainly is for me. But that is the true meaning of decadence. We are living in an Alexandrian period. We can choose freely the most varied forms and we also have a monstrous versatility in that area. But I believe more and more firmly in the morality of style: in the total identification of content (of the truth of the individual) with style. There are epochs when the construction of style is not a matter of virtuoso choice, and those are certainly periods that are outside decadence. There are poets in all ages who can only, and want only, to write in a given way, and they are outside decadence, whether they are primitives—simple in spirit—or whether they do so out of conscious, rational rigor (like Brecht). All the others plunge into the inferno of the exchangeability of styles and they will leave no trace in future centuries: Cocteau, Thomas Mann, me, you. Only Picasso will be exempt, because he has made a sublime tragedy and farce out of the exchangeability of styles.

Warmest good wishes

Calv.

[Typed on Einaudi headed paper with autograph signature; in the Archivio Franco Fortini, Siena.]

To Luigi Santucci—Milan

Turin, 15 November 1958

Dear Santucci,

THANK YOU FOR THE BOOK ON CHILDREN'S LITERATURE WHICH I instantly read at one sitting.[85]

I think that your outline of the characteristics of children's literature in the excellent opening chapters is of great psychological and poetic acuteness. And as I read, I was constantly tempted to extend the categories of this poetics of *children's literature* to *literature tout-court*. (At least the kind of literature that I like.)

As for folktales, your pedagogical-aesthetic study leaves aside entirely all the problems connected with what a folktale is before it becomes literature with Basile and Perrault. I agree that the fairy-tale as an ethnological, or folklore phenomenon has nothing to do with children's literature; but if you leave it out totally you cannot understand anything in the field of folktales. Moreover, all your sub-divisions of the genre (folktale, adventure story, folktale adventure) are arbitrary and simply correspond to the pedagogical prescriptions for readings at various ages. I am not very well up on pedagogy, so I will not pronounce on it.

Your criticisms of Andersen are fine. But I love Perrault while the brothers Grimm frighten me.

We disagree about *Alice*, which I think is a masterpiece (but I only read it when I was grown up), and about *Peter Pan*, which I consider to be false and cloying (but I have not read it again as an adult).

I cannot say anything about Capuana of whom I have only read *C'era una volta* (*Italian Fairy Tales*) recently, and without any great attention, and it seemed good to me but you may well be right.

Fine for *Pinocchio*. And for Kipling.

But I feel wounded for one of my basic loves seeing that you make no mention of the greatest of them all: R. L. Stevenson. And to think that in *Treasure Island* and *Kidnapped* the poetry—and it is seriously great poetry—is all of a piece with a pedagogic spirit which you would have nothing to object to.

As for Mark Twain, you do not even cite his masterpiece, which is *Huckleberry Finn*. I don't know how it works pedagogically but as poetry it is perhaps the greatest book to come out of America.

I shuddered when I saw you putting *Gulliver* in the hands of children, but actually your chapter is highly convincing. (But if you include classics which are fine for children in abbreviated form, then you have to include *Don Quixote* as well as *Crusoe*.)

The chapters on Verne and Salgari are underdeveloped. Good what you say about De Amicis.

All in all, a work that is full of ingenious insights, and it would have been worthwhile (and it still is) working on it a bit more, removing the padding of quotations that betrays its origin as an undergraduate thesis, and the fact that it follows closely in the wake of Hazard.[86]

And now I am waiting to hear something from you about the Christian legends, how that work is going.[87] A few days ago when I was in Milan, I phoned you at home but didn't get you in.

Write to me. Best wishes and thanks again.

Yours

Calvino

[Typed on Einaudi headed paper with autograph signature; with the heirs of the addressee. Previously in *ILDA*, pp. 270–71.]

To Cesare Cases—Pisa

Turin, 20 December 1958

Dear Cases,

Thank you very much for the letter on the *Weltanschauung*.[88] It seems to me to be very appropriate, as a general definition. The discourse about the essence of reality which can only be captured at a distance whereas if you put your nose up against it, it seems monstrous and devoid of sense, is absolutely right. But I would say that this applies not only to me: every writer who wants to see a meaning in reality has in some way to distance it, schematize it, allegorize it; if he wants to give a minute description of life as it is he can only end up in consternation at the void, at the vanity of everything, from Flaubert onwards. For that reason my fiction is rational when it is fantastical, whereas when it is "realistic" it ends up in pure lyricism.

However, watch out because *The Ant* is not "abstractly symbolic," but totally realistic: British critics talked a lot about Kafka in connection with it, probably thinking that the Argentine ant was an imaginary creature. Whoever has been in the Riviera knows that there is nothing exaggerated in my story: the events, characters, systems for fighting against it, different attitudes toward the ants, your life dominated by the ants, form part of the regular experience of my childhood. (Now after the arrival of DDT the situation has changed a bit, but not much.) So it is a realistic story, then, and one which proposes a definition of *nature* and man's attitude toward it. Now you formulate things too drastically by making everything an allegory of capitalism. This relationship is better formulated as follows: I am interested above all in how we consider nature, which is much more important than any capitalism or other passing epiphenomena; but to our eyes nature presents herself as a mirror of history, in it we find the same cruel, monstrous reality that we find in the times in which we live (capitalism, imperialism, Nazism, the Cold War).

Absolutely right when you say that *Smog* is simply *The Ant* rewritten in a different key. That was precisely what I wanted to do, to provide a counterpart to the *Ant*, but situating it in the world of the city. But the poetic intuition is there first in *The Ant*: it's an intuition of the world (the historical and natural world together); and for that reason *The Ant* is undoubtedly far superior to *Smog*. In *Smog* I call "things by their own name"? But what counts is the image not the name. Calling things by their name (images by the historical name that has ultimately determined them) is the critic's duty. And *Smog* is a *critical* story, it steals the critic's job, and it is not entirely successful in poetic terms.

I find your observations on *A Plunge into Real Estate* quite right, it is a less "Calvinian" product than the others.

An excellent analysis, in short, that gave me great pleasure, and which I hope you will work up into a substantial article.

Best wishes,

[Typed copy; in the Calvino Archive.]

To Elémire Zolla—Rome

Turin, 5 January 1959

Dear Elémire,

Only today (now that I am back from holiday) did I see the little portrait of me that you sketched and I liked it very much. It is the nastiest thing I have read about myself, but probably also the most coherent.[89]

Fortini wrote much worse things about me after *The Baron* (which have still not been published) but they were spoiled by his usual moralism. Here, though, you hit hard but with great elegance; your little essay is for its richness, concision, and skill in construction (that wonderful final quotation!), one of the best things you have ever written.

I appreciate very much the touch in the middle about "the peasant acting the fool" and all its corollaries, from the definition of my language to the more subtle jibe about the "good-natured" homage to communism that I had to abandon. I am a bit annoyed that the key to everything for you are the stories in *L'entrata in guerra* (*Into the War*), which I do not much like and which I consider less typical of me than the rest; they smack of that literature of "manners" that one finds in *Il Mondo* which does not interest me very much. Then I don't understand (just as I didn't understand when you said it to me on the phone) the point about *voyeurism*: where does that come in? "The Sly Adventurer," that certainly is relevant to the portrait. And also the risk of the void, ha! ha! that certainly is there, my goodness.

I am sorry I was not in Turin when you and Maria were there.[90] See you again some time.

[Typed copy; in the Calvino Archive and in the Einaudi Archive.]

To Pierre Emmanuel—Paris

Turin, 17 February 1959

Dear Sir,[91]

Thank you very much for the kind invitation to the meeting at Mourmarin. I would of course be very pleased to attend since it is a wonderful opportunity to meet writers from different countries, and to have a discussion on topics that are close to our hearts, surrounded by a beautiful landscape.

However, I fear that I disagree on several points that you have put forward as the basis for the meeting. In the first place, the rather limited conception of Europe: why is Britain not included amongst the countries that have been invited? It is the only European country that can boast a positive experience in this postwar period, both in the social domain and in its wise policy of gradual elimination of its colonial empire. And it is, nevertheless, a country whose culture is in crisis, possibly more than the four others. The British would certainly have some interesting things to say.

I have to confess that European genius, universalism, etc., are words that I understand very little. The positive values that give élan to America and Russia, to the new emergence of the peoples of Africa and Asia, spring also from the European cultural heritage, and we have to recognize them as ours, not as foreign. I do not like the *pure* European spirit, I do not like anything that is too pure, but only what is heavy, whatever is imbued with history. Italy—like Germany in the past, like Spain still today (but I hope France will be spared it)—was for a long time the victim of a paralyzing nationalist ideology. Forgive me if I have a kind of allergic reaction to all words that hint of nationalism, even though it concerns four nations and not one.

Thank you once more, Monsieur, and please accept the expression of my feelings of sincere esteem.

(Italo Calvino)

[Typed copy; in the Calvino Archive.]

To Lucio Lombardo Radice—Palermo

Turin, 17 March 1959

Dear Lucio,

I AM PLEASED BY YOUR SUGGESTION THAT *MARCOVALDO* should be a book for children.[92] I will confess that when I was publishing the Marcovaldo stories in the Turin *l'Unità*, I was already thinking of making them into a book for children. And many of them were written in that spirit. For publishing reasons the book has never materialized; but it has not been ruled out that at a later date . . .

I am thinking about abbreviated versions for children of several of my works, spurred on by the experiences of a number of friends who are also parents (amongst whom I learn with pleasure there is also your wife, whom I thank.)

I am happy, above all, that the encounter between Marcovaldo and your little boy has given us the chance to be in contact again.

Very best wishes.

Your,

Calvino

[Typed with autograph signature on Einaudi headed paper; in the Archivio della Fondazione Istituto Gramsci, Rome.]

To Franco Fortini—Milan

Turin, 13 May 1959

Dear Fortini,

I HAVE READ *CONSIGLI A POCHI* (*ADVICE TO THE FEW*) OVER AND over again, and it has rekindled my inexhaustible passion for discussions of morality;[93] only by having a clear idea of what virtue is can I practice evil with a light heart.

I approve of the general diagnosis, and of your severity and pessimism: but in the end your proposal boils down to keeping one's hands clean, to abstaining (in terms of the "tools" we use), in order to avoid becoming Her Majesty's Opposition, in other words reformists. I think that you are right inasmuch as the pressure to assimilate that is coming from official cultural structures almost always tends toward distorting even one's own technical skills (the writer of books will probably become an awful writer of television dramas; that does not mean that it is not important that good writers of television drama should exist, as there are in America). But Communism's anti-moralistic message—which I have assimilated with perhaps too much alacrity—makes me believe that one should never have taboos about the tools we use, that as long as the thought or images or style one wants to put forward do not become deformed by the medium, one must on the contrary try to make use of the most powerful and most efficient of those tools.

In fact bourgeois cultural structures nearly always distort; for that reason our conclusions end up more or less coinciding; but what does not coincide is the love of purity that you maintain and the love of contamination, of metamorphosis, of regeneration that I uphold. (Going down this road, of course, there are ninety-nine, well let's say ninety-five, chances out of a hundred that one loses one's soul; but that's the beauty of it!)

Your discourse seems to presuppose a literature "of the left" that is indisputable and triumphant. But today we see the outcome of a slow involution of content and styles: Italian literature is *Il gattopardo* (*The Leopard*) and *La messa dei villeggianti* (*The Holiday-Makers' Mass*).[94] What we would seem to need—and the time seems ripe—is a *literary* battle, a clash on the level of form and morality. But what can one do if there are no suggestions, no *presences* to put forward against "Gattopardism"?

It is suggestions of *values* that count. Negation, saying *no*, not accepting things, is the first operation that is necessary in order to *say* something, and for that reason it counts; but today we are feeling again, and more than ever, the effects of a situation where the only valid reasons are negative. Criticism which remains criticism and no more, retains an enormous moral authority, but is not yet dialectical negation. I think that the criticism, for example, of aspects of mass culture made by sociologists, or the critique of Communism made by revisionists, presuppose a persistent, hypnotic love-interest in the object of their own criticism, seen in that particular way; that is what the satire of manners, moralism etc. has always been like. Instead of being consumed by a descriptive-analytical passion for things as they are, one must not accept reality and instead put up against it a reality that maybe does not exist but that solely because you are proposing it acquires a strength and influence of its own. This is the strength of utopia, which is very topical today, while the "scientific" revolution seems to have lost its way. Against this, one must put forward representations of even partial values but ones that can enter into contradiction with things as they are. Either that or one must mimic negativity, forcing oneself to make its mechanism one's own, in order to blow it up. (That is to say try to live negativity positively; and a positive tension today cannot but be paradoxical; or utopian, as we said before.)

The negation of negation is affirmation when, by being the negation of the bourgeoisie, it is called the proletariat; when by being the negation of the proletariat it becomes the revolution.

Paolini's piece on me is unfocused, but the poor guy is trying to say something that is not the usual stuff.[95] And that allows you to counter him with the image of the hammock which is the most appropriate thing that has been written on this subject (and on the current situation in general).

The fact is that as regards the moral values of socialism, its front is not advancing an inch (and my piece on Trotsky is more "history of ideas" than current affairs),[96] while decadence (since it is above all stasis) gallops along like an agile gazelle.

Ciao.

Calv.

I will have them send you the Goytisolo and Adorno. Cocchiara is not ours but belongs to ESE-Boringhieri; I will get them to phone asking them to send it to you.

What do you mean: Trotsky on loan? Schwarz's? But do you not collaborate with Schwarz? Or do you mean ours, Maitan's book? (Which I liked, by the way.)

Perfect if you consult a specialist for Brecht. Who? We could show it to Mila? Send us your versions (and texts) bit by bit, when they are ready, and we'll forward them to him.

For the note on the music and records Mila says he is not competent in that area. Talk to Manzoni about it and then let us know.[97]

14 May. I have just received yours of the 12th. I will notify our Rome office to get them to find you a room. We will reimburse your travel expenses.

[Typed on Einaudi headed paper with autograph signature, corrections and additions; in the Archivio Franco Fortini, Siena. Previously in Italo Calvino—Franco Fortini, "Lettere scelte 1951–1977," ed. Giuseppe Nava, Elisabetta Nencini, *L'ospite ingrato*, Annuario del Centro Studi Franco Fortini (Macerata: Quodlibet, 1998), pp. 101–3.]

To Pierpaolo Pasolini—Rome

San Remo 9 June 59

Dear Pierpaolo,

I'VE READ IT ALL. IT IS MAGNIFICENT.[98] A CLEAR CUT ABOVE all our other books. It is the kind of work that ought to have been written. All (or almost all) of the things that I want to see in a novel are in it. It is a book that I would like to have written (with all those things in it, and in addition they are all so different) and maybe I will never ever write, but I am happy that it has been written, in other words that literature today is not so far off from how I would like it to be.

There is a qualitative leap from *Ragazzi di vita* (*The Ragazzi*), because in *Ragazzi di vita* (though beautiful as a lyric poem) what was missing was the individual tension, the clash with the world, and humanity there was like a mush. Here it is not any old mush, the people are not like a crowd of Chinese, here there is tension, various individual tensions, not so much the character, which we are not interested in, but the parabola of human lives, the sense that is created from the fatuity of each action as one follows another. Lello too. In short there is the violence, the thrust, the epic, that night in chap. 2 is stunning, there was already a great night in *Ragazzi di vita* that was spent wandering around, but it's nothing compared to this, and all the battles are wonderful, that was what we needed, a writer of fights, and I thought you were someone who is always on the point of going all soft, whereas you are a great writer of fights, right up to the one at Forlanini, which works very well and is also a first-class narrative and symbolic solution as well as working in terms of imagery. To sum it up, one races through this book as in Stendhal, with the difference that with him there was always something willed in the middle, an idealizing charge, but here there is a human head that is completely empty, a half-idiot, but all modern literature is like that, with at its center a void that moves, a cavity, but we're still thankful it does move, and in any case what do you want to make him think for? If he started thinking he would think idiotic things so he may as well stay as he is.

All the more so since the only thing I don't like is that story of "the good guy." It seems that you really believe and maintain that [T.][99] is a "good guy," that an education, a human development can have as its objective becoming a good person of a petit-bourgeois type, even though they carry the Communist Party card, and you show yourself to be totally happy when he acts the good guy, and you say: "Well now, see?" Now this is wrong and really bad. That's not where it's going, that possibility is not there. In the end one can only take upon oneself and rationalize all the violence of history and nature in order to live through it with one aim in view: the Communist moral is reached only by living through what is awful with one's eyes open, constantly, because every bit of progress is always accompanied by continual defeats and deteriorations. The person who lives through this, whether a philosopher or an illiterate member of the sub-proletariat, has learnt something. All the rest is nothing, it's all just an edifying attempt worthy of a parish priest or "Communist slush," which is the opposite of true Communist morality. Every now and again you seem to be on the point of unmasking the "Communist sweetly-sick," and to reach the moral truth of Communism, but instead you stay just there, just on the edge of Pratolinizing. In short: virtue must *never* be represented, not under any circumstances. Except to show that underneath it there is even more cruelty and selfishness than in explicit cruelty and selfishness. Or you should represent ruthlessness in order to show how that can be an exercising of virtue if that ruthlessness is pursued with lucidity.

When he is with the girl, it's fine for him to talk one way and to think differently, and one doesn't know which is true or false, fine also the scene of the failed arousal that ends in blows. Because there the virtuous ideal is unmasked, and for that reason truth and true worth emerge.

I don't know what to say to you about the language which, however, is the most fundamental thing. I will say that I don't like chap. 1 at all because being scene-setting it aims entirely at repeating words which have a scene-setting function such as mud, filth, muck, waste paper; there the trick would have been to make all those words there disappear, and insert as keywords, I don't know, words expressing states of mind or movement. The secret is always to conceal the real keywords and to stress others, looking for their equivalents or opposites somewhere else.

Ciao.

Calvino

[Handwritten on Einaudi headed paper; in the Gabinetto Scientifico Letterario G. P. Vieusseux-Archivio Contemporaneo Alessandro Bonsanti, Florence. Previously in P. P. Pasolini, *Lettere 1955–1975, con una cronologia della vita e delle opere*, ed. Nico Naldini (Turin: Einaudi, 1988) pp. xlix–l. In the Calvino Archive there is an autograph copy of the third paragraph, headed "from a letter to Pasolini 9 June 1959."]

To Luigi Santucci—Milan

San Remo, 24 August 1959

Dear Santucci,

For over a month now I have been carrying your cry-of-alarm around with me and mentally formulating the main strands of my reply, but for letter-writing—as you quite rightly say—one needs the holidays, not only that but holidays with rain and—if one is at the seaside—heavy seas to keep me locked up at home. If this kind of delay has affected a letter as fine and stimulating as yours, and one which gave me enormous pleasure at the spirit with which you approached me, you can imagine how slowly my fictional output has been going this summer, you who know how much labor, dissatisfaction, irritability, uncertainty this work costs . . .

However—and this is the point—it is worth it. Or rather: one does not ask if it's worth it. We are people, there is no doubt, who exist solely insofar as we write, otherwise we don't exist at all. Even if we did not have a single reader any more, we would have to write; and this not because ours can be a solitary job, on the contrary it is a dialog we take part in when we write, a common discourse, but this dialog can still always be supposed to be taking place with authors of the past, with authors we love and whose discourse we are forcing ourselves to develop, or else with those still to come, those we want through our writing to configure in one particular way rather than another. I am exaggerating: heaven help those who write without being read; for that reason there are too many people writing today and one cannot ask for indulgence for someone who has little to say, and one cannot allow trade-union or corporate sympathies.

That some critics attack the excessive amount of writing and publishing that is going on these days does not annoy me. They might get their targets and choices wrong, and their flaw is precisely this, that they do this highly useful job in too imprecise a way, that is the job of pruning and discouraging excessive hopes and ambitions. (You are being spoken to by someone who in his publishing job acts as an encourager of young writers; and this is certainly necessary; the only thing is that it is just as necessary, at a later stage, to discourage forty-nine out of the fifty writers one has encouraged.)

Even more annoying are those who theorize that the *novel* has to be like this or like that, that one *must* write the novel, etc. Let them go to hell! How much energy is wasted in Italy in trying to write the novel that obeys all the rules. The energy might have been useful to provide us with more modest, more genuine things, that had less pretensions: short stories, memoirs, notes, testimonials, or at any rate books that are *open*, without a preconceived plan.

Personally, I believe in fiction because the stories I like are those with a beginning and an end. I try to write them as they best come to me, depending on what I have to say. We are in a period when in literature and especially in fiction one can do anything, absolutely anything, and all styles and methods coexist. What the public (and also the critics) require are books ("open" novels) that are rich in substance, density, tension.

All in all, there could not be a better time to fire off your 3–400 page broadside. But are these pages written or still to write? I have not really understood. I would like to be one of the first to read them. I am very curious to see this "turning-point" of yours, which will certainly not just be a quantitative leap. Come on, work, stop looking for excuses not to be at your desk.

Oh God, what have I said! Now I remember what an excuse the Italian folktales were for me, an excuse for not working at anything else for a number of years. And I have the duty to spur you on to work at your Christian legends![100]

Talking of which, I am following with interest what you wrote to me. I am a bit afraid of Giacosa, but I might be wrong.[101] In the literary section the rule ought to be that of choosing according to a criterion of artistry, not of documentation. But I believe that you too are of this opinion.

I await the next bout of rain and your next volley in this dialog. Best wishes

Calvino

[Handwritten; with the addressee's heirs.]

To Mateo Lettunich—New York

Turin, 25 September 1959

Dear Mr Lettunich,[102]

I THANK YOU VERY MUCH FOR YOUR LETTER OF AUGUST 27. Excuse me for my delay in answering you, but I've been for some weeks away from Turin.

I'm waiting for the visa from the U.S. Consulate of Turin and I hope to be in New York punctually at the beginning of November. This date suits me perfectly because in November two books of mine will appear in the United States: *Baron in the Trees* at Random House and *Italian Fairy Tales* at the Orion Press.

I answer the questions of your letter:

1) *Travels*. It's difficult for me to decide right now a schedule of travels. I believe that only when I'll be in New York (where I plan to remain for some time) I'll be able to make up my mind in a defi-

nite way. The cities I would like to see besides New York are: San Francisco and Los Angeles; Chicago; and a town of the South (for instance: New Orleans). I could perhaps spend November and December in New York, travel in the States in January and February, and live through April and March in New York again (with short trips to Washington, Boston, etc.). But it may well be that three different trips to the West, to the North, to the South, with New York as a starting base, is a better solution. Of course, I should like to see more things if there is the time and the occasion: an Indian pueblo, for instance, or to make a trip along the Mississippi. (And I would not mind, remembering that Hawaii are the 50th State, spending a week in Honolulu . . .)

2) *People*. The fortunes of my novel among American literary circles will of course partly determine my encounters. Besides, Random House will sponsor my contacts with American authors. I would be particularly interested to meet the writers of my generation: Jerome D. Salinger, James Purdy, Bernard Malamud, but also J. F. Powers, Nelson Algren, Budd Schulberg, Arthur Miller, Saul Bellow, Penn Warren. And also Vladimir Nabokov. And also James Thurber. Among the critics, Lionel Trilling. And the literary reviews: *Evergreen R.*, *Partisan R.*, *Hudson R.* etc. And the publishers.
3) *Institutions*. I would like to see some Universities. I'm already in touch with some friends of mine, who teach in American Universities (as Mario Einaudi in Cornell, Dante della Terza in Los Angeles) and they will arrange for me lectures in their colleges. I will write also to other professors I know as Renato Poggioli in Harvard University, Giuseppe Prezzolini in Columbia, Scaglione in Berkeley, and I could do a tour of lectures.

Thank you for the *I. I. E. Bulletin*. But I received, together with the copy for me, a lot of copies with other addresses. I sent them back to the I.I.E.

I hope to see you soon.

Yours sincerely.

I was born in 1923 in Cuba from Italian parents. My father and my mother were botanists and spent many years in Mexico and Cuba, but shortly after my birth they went back to San Remo, my father's native town, in the Ligurian coast, where they became directors of an experimental institute of floriculture. I lived there all my childhood and adolescence (so, in my official biographical notes it is often written: born in San Remo, that is more *true*). The scientific tradition of my family was broken by my literary passion. But, for starting in literature, I needed the experience of war. During the German occupation of Northern Italy I joined the bands of partisans on the Ligurian mountains. After the Liberation I published my first short stories about partisans. Elio Vittorini and Cesare Pavese were my first sponsors and my first teachers; then I became friend also of Carlo Levi and Alberto Moravia. Cesare Pavese called me into the editorial staff of Einaudi publishing firm, in Turin. My first book won a prize for unpublished novels in 1947: *The path of nests of spiders*, a rather tough war novel, translated also in the U.S. several years later. I published a great number of short stories (in magazines, in volumes, and now in the complete collection *I racconti*, Bagutta Prize 1959); they were realistic stories but always with a fantastic and sometimes fairy humour. So nobody was surprised when I published in 1952 an entirely fantastic novel *Il visconte dimezzato*. It was only the first of a series; the second one *Il barone rampante* (1957) is a two-years best-seller in Italy and the translation is appearing now in U.S. at Random House. Now I'm writing the third fantastic novel: *Il cavaliere inesistente*.

But the more important work of mine is a big collection of Italian folk-tales (*Fiabe italiane*, 1956), that shall appear in the U.S. (in a shortened edition) at the Orion Press.

With Elio Vittorini, I'm editor of *Il Menabò* a literature magazine (a sort of *New Writing*).

[Typed copy of the letter and of the CV; in the Calvino Archive.]

To Alberto Moravia—Rome

Turin, 16 October 1959

Dear Alberto,

I HAD READ YOUR ARTICLE ON MANZONI THE MINUTE IT ARrived.[103] Then I had to leave for Frankfurt, for the International Book

Fair. Only now have I got back and seen your letter and am now replying to you.

Our opinion as publishers is that it is an excellent article which will be an event in itself and will be much talked about, and that the success of our edition will be based most of all on it since it will be (along with Guttuso's illustrations) the only novelty of the book; it is clear that we have to hold on to it as a surprise and cannot publish it beforehand, otherwise what would attract people into buying the book? For this reason Einaudi has not allowed it to be published in *Nuovi Argomenti*, and has of course also said no to Vigorelli who wanted it for *Successo*.

Since the illustrations are not yet ready, the volume will appear in the spring.

However, you will get proofs soon: they were already waiting to go but they had set them in italics, a font that would have been too cumbersome to read with such a long piece of work, so I have had them reset in roman.

Having got the official messages out of the way, I will now move on to tell you my personal reactions.

I began your essay in a not very receptive and disgruntled frame of mind. To have based what you say on the parallel between Catholic realism and socialist realism seems to me to give a certain rigidity to your argument. And the definition of the novel as "propaganda with poetry or rather with pure representation" seems to me imprecise: either it is propaganda or it is poetry, when it is one thing it is not the other (and Soviet writers are so rarely poetic because they are nearly always propagandistic).[104] Propaganda of an assumption already provided by someone else, I mean, because propagating one's own idea, articulating one's own moral beliefs, can be an act that is both ethical and poetic at the same time.

But I agree I found the definition of the three "layers" of the *Promessi sposi* perfect, just as accurate as your criticism of the abstractness of the bad characters and especially Don Rodrigo. And I agree about the Innominato; actually, for me, it is precisely the whole "Innominato atmosphere" that I cannot take; that is where Romanticism starts to seep through whereas previously—and this is one of the book's great merits—it had not made its presence felt.

So gradually I began to agree with your analysis more and more and in fact I got quite passionate about it when I reached your wonderful observations on corruption, private and public, and the section on Don Abbondio and Gertrude. You are a critic who is all facts and logic and following you, seeing one's own choices and judgments find their place in your very precise and refined totting up of the pluses and minuses, makes for particularly pleasurable reading. I enjoyed even the salvation of Renzo and Lucia, which I (like so many critics) did not like before, but about whom (especially on Lucia) you say very perceptive things.

Is Manzoni's religion, his real religion, to be identified with that of Renzo and Lucia? Well, certainly its sentimental coloring, its positive aspiration is that; but Manzoni's religion seems to me to be more complicated. On the one hand, the good part is sentiment, on the other it is morality in support of a political and economic system: an ideal ordering and utopia typical of an Enlightenment conservative landowner like him. In this sense I see Manzoni in an even less rosy light than you do: his religion is above all politics (you talked very well, with examples, about his highly refined political sense) and his theological bedrock is above all negative. It is a notion of man that comes from his former Jansenism, the certainty that the flesh of Adam is damned unless grace intervenes. So then that wonderful axiom of yours, the one that is densest and most capable of potential development, "purely aesthetic catharses are typical of Decadentism," turns out to be more valid in general than in this specific case; because for Manzoni, as often for Catholic writers (and not only a "Catholic realist") man after the fall is naturally inclined toward sin.

As far as I am concerned, Manzoni is the bourgeois who takes off from eighteenth-century culture (*I promessi sposi* has to be assessed as a late eighteenth-century rather than a nineteenth-century work) and opts for conservative Catholicism in the face of the Revolution. But he tries to do so keeping intact his unflinching gaze, his lofty detachment, his clarity of language, his taste for irony, in short all the intellectual luxuries he has learned to exploit thanks to his familiarity with French literature (the Enlightenment writers, Voltaire above all, much more than Romantic Catholicism).

A fundamental part of his reformist ruling-class attitude is his passion for history, which makes him write magnificent pages like the ones on economic history, on the agrarian crisis in one of the early chapters (I think it was the end of the fourth: I have not got the text to hand), the landsknechts, the plague and also the *historical* chapter on Federigo Borromeo with the foundation of the Ambrosiana Library, which is a wonderful essay on the history of the organization of culture and an exemplification of what he meant by Enlightenment Catholicism, as the duty of a ruling class. Federigo is a character out of a historical essay, not from a novel, hence he never manages to blend with the novel.

These are all points for discussion thrown up by the reading of your essay, and which testify to how stimulating it is.

I'll say goodbye to you for now. I am leaving for the United States where I will stay for six months on a grant from the Ford Foundation. Has Elsa come back?[105]

Best wishes

[Typed copy with autograph corrections; in the Einaudi Archive. Previously in *ILDA*, pp. 327–39.]

To Pietro Citati—Rome

Turin, 21 October 1959

Dear Citati,

"Ideologia e verità" (Ideology and Truth) is perhaps the first theoretical piece of yours with which I find myself in general agreement.[106] It is quite right also because it is contradictory: your negation of our time aims to produce a writer who defines and invents the man of our time. Which is perfectly right. But this can only be done by chewing up and spitting out all the ideological material our age produces; and all the formal expedients for approaching reality: so chew them up and spit them out. Having set out to defend—even though with all your ironic self-defensiveness—"the eternal human heart," you then do nothing but historicize the various human hearts and conclude that in none of them that have been laid bare up to now can one recognize the human heart of today or tomorrow. And I am happy to see that the minute you start to confirm the relevance of the thin Flaubertian line in Italy you rethink and declare that along that line there is nothing more to say. It is true that you also deny the possibility of great distortions of a Romantic-Expressionist kind, despite *Lolita*, but it seems to me that the program you are suggesting for future writers can only be embarked upon with weapons of that kind. (I am in favor of the distorters, of course, even though as soon as I get bogged down in psychology and the representation of our times, damn, I too fall into the Flaubertian category.)

Nevertheless, all your observations depend on a fiercely aristocratic intellectual stratification. The intellectual must not produce ideology because our own time already produces it on its own (that is to say other intellectuals who are considered mere instruments produce it). The separation between the duties of literature and industrialized cultural production is like the difference between two worlds (and here the dividing line will probably be not just between individual and individual but will cut through individuals themselves, through the hours of the working day). Ending up with the magnificent vision of the few dinosaurs (few but not immediately distinguishable from an even bigger crowd than before of big lizards, because the printed paper industry will continue to spew out tons of stuff). I am not at all in disagreement with this: far from it. Only the dialectical relationship between the dinosaur-writers and the little cultural beavers, the robots serving their times, will continue to be what it was at the time of the "literary society" (just as the sacrosanct necessity of solitary defenses and snobberies will continue).

Some parts very well written, like the bit about atrocious ennui.

I am leaving. What a torture these last few days in Europe.

Ciao.

I will get the others to read it and then send it back to you.
[Typed copy with one autograph correction; in the Calvino Archive.]

To Giulio and Renata Einaudi—Turin

New York 22 Nov. 59

Dear Giulio,

Dear Renata,

I AM FOLLOWING UP THE LETTER I POSTED YESTERDAY shortly after receiving yours; I did not want to hold mine up, and here I never know when I'll have time to write; I always keep a sheet of paper in the typewriter, so that when I am in my hotel I can write a little piece even although I have just a few minutes between one engagement and another, whether these are to do with business, tourism, or pleasure. In the early days I wanted to avoid living like a tourist; I wanted to be someone who lives in New York; after a while I noticed that I was not seeing New York at all but only moving through a sequence of business calls (as writer and as "editor"), lunches, cocktail parties, dinners, evening parties, but in general I never left the world of publishing and literature and occasionally the theater and musical world; but now I can say that without having made any special effort to change my life style I am gradually exploring the whole of New York, including the museums, night clubs, and colourful areas that are a must for tourists; certainly I do not have much time for sitting at my desk; my letter-diary (which I write for you and partly for my mother) remains up till now my only activity; the best system is always to keep paper in the typewriter and as soon as I get back to the hotel after a publishing visit or any kind of exploration immediately write my notes; but I do not always manage to keep up with the pace of events and I realize if I start to say: this is not important so I won't write about it, I'll end up writing nothing; (for that reason Giulio's exhaustive letter acted as a great spur to me to continue this detailed account); but I also have to find the time to read the books that I am doing the scouting for (and if I do not think they need instant action they start to pile up here like anything!); and now I have to prepare the lecture they have booked me for on 16 December at the Casa Italiana in Columbia University and which I am counting on repeating subsequently "all over" the American universities, because having a lecture to give is a good excuse for finding people in so many places who will welcome you and ferry you here and there, and for getting to know the university world.

I really enjoyed reading the news about our river;[107] the only thing I regret about having settled in the Village is that I would like to stay in Riverside Drive (which is beside the East River), an area that was very fashionable up to a few years ago but now too many Jews have settled there (in other words the intellectuals have largely moved in) and so now the rents have gone down;[108] or else near the Hudson which is fashionable now.

I also aired Giulio's forecasts on Turin-City-Common Market-Econ. Miracle etc. when there was talk of an atomic center in Turin;

they are attractive prospects but in order to avoid these features being turned into German greyness *we* would really need to take in hand the life of the city, make it our own Ivrea (it's certainly not more difficult because our city is bigger; all you need is a few key initiatives to give a particular tone to a city; in this sense it is not difficult even to take charge of New York; except that here one would also have to bend one's will to New York, accept its tastes).[109]

I came here having set as a first rule of thumb never to take on the traditional anti-American point of view, arguing over mass industrial culture etc. but it is true that I end up finding that everyday practice, publishing houses, their way of looking at literature, all show that general lack of personality, of ingenuity, that we have heard so many complaints about in theory, and when you find yourself surrounded by this day after day, at a certain point you suddenly feel suffocated by it, as it were. You should bear this in mind, Giulio, when you compare American publishers' efficiency with our lack of organizational skills; here the publishers do not have a soul (or they have a false soul, like the Catholic soul behind Pantheon books), they are purely commercial organizations; the only one that has a soul, however immature and off the rails, is Grove, which resembles us a lot in having a kind of editorial board looking to get hold of young intellectuals from all over the place, and also in the atmosphere of their office it is as though Grove has emerged from the hands of a kind of Grigia,[110] and everyone wonders how it manages to survive financially. In short to have a soul you have to pay, on this side just as much as on the other side of the Atlantic. And look, here too the editorial staff is quite numerous, even in a commercial publisher like Random, numerous and highly efficient, though, inasmuch as they tend to present the customer with a product that is perfect from the point of view of consumer needs, in short the role played by artisan work in an American publisher shows no sign of diminishing: it simply gets slotted into a firm organization. The biggest economy is made on translations; they don't decide to translate a book (here one lives practically in a regime of publishing autonomy) unless they are sure the costs can be shared with the British publisher. The scrutiny of European production is done using rudimentary criteria; the readers of It. books for instance are either any editor that happens to know Italian, or some poor souls, almost unheard of, so nobody ever knows what to make of their opinions, and publishers go ahead haphazardly, the choice of a book always comes about by chance; and note that it is not just Italian books that this happens to, but also French books which are often read by the same readers; but the idea never crosses their mind that one could choose major specialists as consultants for each country's literature.

The most precious heritage of a publishing house is its character, its physiognomy. (Which on the commercial level is translated into the capacity to create, maintain and develop its own public.) So each to his own Silerchie: beware of trespassing into spiritualistic lands, in fact we ought to develop anti-Silerchie so as to mark out clearly the difference between our way of responding to those interests and Alberto's and Giacomino's way.[111] Your invitation to launch a counter-proposal is quite demanding and I do not know if I can work it up just like that, on the spot, as an emergency measure, especially being here on my own, without the possibility (that comes from working as a team) of always being able to check one's own ideas. For some time now I have been developing the outlines of what ought to be a series (or anthology) which will provide a moral framework for modern man, a series of texts which exemplify in life and in practical moral terms all that modern man needs to call himself complete and which ideology or organization does not give him or actually denies him (and the collection of modern moralists edited by Zolla for Garzanti gave me the desire to come up with a counter-proposal to that, similar but done in the opposite spirit), but I am not yet at the point of being able to unveil a publishing program which is orientated in that direction. Why do you not get them to send me Bobi's first draft program?[112] I will make my observations on it and this will allow me to formulate some counter-proposals. That seems to me to be the simplest way forward.

As for the Beauvoir series, I interpret it as a need to decouple the "Essays" from the more literary volumes, those on the borders of fiction and at the same time to increase their production seeing that the "Essays" are overburdened.[113] Have I understood the point? But not even stated in those terms is the idea clear to me, also because I cannot see what the published books will be like: will they be thinner books, costing less? (in which case why not think of a kind of paperback "Essay" series that would be an alternative to the "essay" that is now more and more found as a hardback, with illustrations etc.) or will they be hardback volumes that aim at being even more elegant than the "Supercoralli"? In that case it ought to be [the sentence continues after the account of Sunday 22nd and Monday 23rd].

Sunday 22nd: I've been to Westchester, invited by the Knopfs to their house in White Plains, a beautiful little villa in the midst of well-kept woods and fields and with an enormous swimming pool. Mrs Blanche Knopf, who has just arrived freshly back from Europe and very enthusiastic about her meeting with Giulio, would like to publish my books too if I can free myself from Random; I simply refer everyone to my agent and poor Mrs Horsch no longer has any idea what's happening; but it seems to me that the Knopf situation stems from the argument between these two people, who both have very strong personalities, she only thinks about literature, and is hungry for new European authors, while Mr Alfred, an imposing figure with his white moustaches, like one of Franz Joseph's gamekeepers, knows that the basis of his publishing business are the fishing, cooking, and gardening manuals, and doesn't give a damn about anything else. Caught between these two, the son has gone off to the new publishing h[ouse]. In the evening I went to New Jersey, to a party: Mischa was there too (he says he will do the book, but so far he has not made a start);[114] it was at Ruggero Orlando's place: he has a house full of Noldes and even a Vlaminck (his wife is the grandaughter of Max Ophuls and a relation of Kurt Weill and also of Franz Mahler).[115]

Monday 23rd: I've been to Bronxville, to Sarah Lawrence College, a college for girls only, who learn by the Dewey method, where I was invited by Marc Slonim who teaches comparative literature. The students of Italian, about twenty girls, some of them extremely beautiful, all in trousers of various kinds, were waiting for me and they had prepared a surprise for me. One of them has a guitar and starts playing while the others start singing in chorus, and what did they sing? *Eravamo in sette, in sette* (*There were seven of us, seven of us*).[116] I must confess I was astonished. I worked out later that the record brought back by the Momiglianos had ended up in the hands of their Italian teacher.

(back to the letter) a very restricted choice, but all in all they would be a gift-set of essays a bit different from others.

Popular Theater: the question of drama must be approached as a piece of market research (how big its sales capacities are) and as organization (the possibility of producing with the minimum expenditure of resources). Fischer is the biggest drama publisher in Germany and his drama section is one of the most significant ones in his list. It would be worthwhile sending someone to nip over to Frankfurt (but who?) and study Fischer's organizational structure and see whether it is a sector that makes money (it could just be Mrs Fischer's obsession, who is crazy about the theater, and maybe it makes a substantial loss).

I am in favor of Panzieri as an ideological guide because he is someone who has a wealth of interests and culture and staying in the publishing house is reducing his fondness for sects. I am saddened by the persistent lack of spark from Solmi. We must make Lucentini give of his best in the area of encyclopaedias and popularizing the classics (balancing this kind of work with his other precious work as translator). Seen from America, Lucentini is the most representative of a certain image of Europe; we should appreciate him, however much his total lack of contact with society limits his publishing sensibilities. Fortini too must be kept on a leash, and should be contacted frequently because only in this way can his overwhelming excesses be toned down. Frigessi is capable of revealing very positive talents in a number of areas.

Thank you very much for the political news which I very much value, because since over here I have to give up something I have stopped chasing after newspapers, and I am beginning to lose my perspective on politics a bit.

I envy you the skiing, but maybe in January I'll go to Wyoming, where I have been invited by the owner of a ranch, an Italian friend of Al I had met years ago in the Milan Bookshop and whom of course I met here immediately at a party.[117] He is someone who in his spare time writes books on Machiavelli. He is called Boef and stays in Little Big Horn.

If Giulio could come here at the end of March or in April it would be very useful and if you have an important deal already under way (I hope it is in the art area, which is the one that in my view lends itself to big Euro-American deals) all the better. However, it is necessary to affirm our presence more strongly here in any case, because compared to the other Italian publishers we have ended up in the second division. The others are active through their scouts and through a visit from that person this spring (who they say had it organized by a public relations expert because of the way in which he succeeded in getting everyone to talk about him and chase after him). The best time to come is that very period when you can instantly benefit from the network of contacts I have set up during my stay. In March in fact I will be on my way back from my journey across the States, which I will start in January.

Let me know about Devoto whom I respect very much.[118]

In the last few weeks here people have been talking a lot about Olivetti; Adriano has been here, as you will have heard, and he is now in charge of the share-holding that controls Underwood.[119] Now Olivetti will produce goods in America under the Underwood label and its current popularity which is already considerable amongst the elites will become mass popularity (once it gets rid of the obstacle of the Italian name and the customs problems). Naturally, on condition he manages to turn Underwood round, which was going downhill, and to cope with Remington, this time in the internal American market. Still, this seems to be a historic moment for Italian industry. And for Adriano who will go back to his firm victorious.

Put the three series of cultural classics in the Nuova Libreria series?[120] Yes, that seems an excellent solution. My only objections: are we not then loading N. L. with texts that are too precious and rare? (though I am in favor of a certain richness in the N. L.) and the other objection is that of the three series only the "Writers of History" is *already* a nice little collection, whatever happens. But apart from this, I agree. The programme for 1960 seems good to me; at this distance I cannot find any observations to make. Purdy is not the most talked about American writer; seeing that we are only going to do one, I would say Bellow, or amongst the younger writers Malamud.

Keep an eye on *il Menabò*.[121]

Tell me if you've managed to get Ollier's novel that I was recommending to you from the boat and about which I am becoming more and more enthusiastic.[122]

Lucky you who are doing a regular job, I can't find the time to do anything; now I have to write this lecture, continue my visits to publishers and agents, follow up my personal publishing affairs, I have not begun to meet writers except almost by chance, I have to finish my tourist visit to the city etc. etc. Oh the regulated, idyllic calm of the days in Turin

[Typed copy; in the Calvino Archive.]

To Paolo Spriano—Rome

Hotel Grosvenor
35 Fifth Avenue
New York 3*

New York, Christmas Eve 59

Dear Pillo,

I HAVE NOT WRITTEN TO YOU YET, I NEVER WRITE TO ANYONE, New York has swallowed me up like a carnivorous plant swallowing a fly, I have been living a breathless life for fifty days now, here life consists of a series of appointments made a week or a fortnight in advance: lunch, cocktail party, dinner, evening party, these make up the various stages of the day which allow you constantly to meet new people, to make arrangements for other lunches, other dinners, other parties and so on ad infinitum. America (or rather New York, which is something quite separate) is not the land of the unforeseen, but it is the land of the richness of life, of the fullness of every hour in the day, the country which gives you the sense of carrying out a huge amount of activity, even though in fact you achieve very little, the country where solitude is impossible (I must have spent maybe just one evening on my own out of the fifty I have spent here, and that was because my date with the girl that I had arranged for that evening fell through: here you have to order everything in advance, they are buying theater tickets for March now, and a girl, even if she happens to be your girl at present, has to know a week in advance the evenings she is going out with you otherwise she goes out with someone else). But really it is not this I mainly wanted to talk to you about, it's more to say that this country here knows nothing about us Europeans—and Russia here you can feel is part of Europe, and with no great differences either—because they are totally devoid of a sense of history. To put it briefly, I am beginning to understand something about America, but I have not got the time even to think never mind writing. I am leading the life of a business man, because this is the real way to live in this city—I say business, but all I do is see publishers and have endless business lunches with them—I act as ambassador for an imaginary Italian Democratic Republic, because I feel it is my duty and responsibility to do so, being one of the few men of the left who has been given the chance to visit this country for six months. As a result, I have named myself ambassador and have delivered a lecture at Columbia University—at its Casa Italiana, which is a Fascist-government environment (Prezzolini etc.)—on recent Italian literature, where I squeezed in the Resistance, Gramsci, all the forbidden names about whom absolutely nothing is known here, and I will repeat this lecture around the universities: if nothing else it will serve to leave the official government representatives of culture with a bad taste in the mouth. I don't know anything about what is going on in the rest of Italy, I only have a subscription to *L'Eco della Stampa*. Here everyone's sole interest is Russia, nobody talks of anything else, the latest joke is: what is the difference between an optimist and a pessimist? The optimist is learning Russian, the pessimist Chinese. Now I am leaving New York, going to California. There I am going to hire a huge car. I have not driven yet. I am having a great time. I am following the party line, the party that is in the hearts of all of us. Say ciao to dear Carla. Happy New Year

Calvino

* Write to me at this address even though I shall be leaving shortly; I am hoping to get them to forward my mail.
[Handwritten; with the addressee's heirs.]

To Luciano Foà—Turin

San Francisco, 29 January [1960]

Dear Luciano,
I GOT YOUR LETTER OF THE 21ST. THIS GOODMAN, FOR GOD'S sake, in the three months I have been here I have never heard him mentioned.[123] Why do you let three or four weeks go by before asking

me information about something? There are times when I don't understand you Europeans. Now I am here far from New York, cut off from my sources of information. What was I to do? I remembered that one of the most important American literary critics, Kenneth Rexroth, lives in Sfrancisco, but I had never approached him. I called him on the phone, I introduced myself and asked him outright what he thought of *The Empire City*. He started to laugh, said it was a complicated question, and then proceeded to give me a brilliant telephone exposition of the novel for about a quarter of an hour. This is Kenneth Rexroth's view, in summary:

> Paul Goodman is an avant-garde writer who is completely different from all other American writers today. His book is very dense, very deep, a kind of *Tristram Shandy*, but the problem is that although so many writers are gifted with a sense of humour, he totally lacks it. Goodman is a kind of anarchist-pacifist, and he also has a psychoanalytic theory that is all his own. He has written poetry, short stories and various works on the city. He does not belong to any school, which is why nobody has ever spoken to me of him; it is a mystery that he has been published by a very bourgeois publisher. He is seriously avant-garde (no connection with the fake avant-garde of the beatniks) but he really needs Queneau's spirit.[124] He could be compared to Purdy, but Goodman does not have Purdy's lightness, he is a German Talmudic Jew. However, according to Rexroth, he might be better in translation than in the original, if an excellent Italian translator could remove the heaviness from his language and make the book easier to read, because it is certainly not easy in English.

This seems to me a very interesting verdict: I will try to get hold of the book. That is just what America is like: for two months in New York I heard people talk only about Norman Mailer, for or against. If you are not either with the beatniks or with Saul Bellow's group, nobody talks about you.

I am very worried about France, here where news in the papers is very scarce. I will stay in Sfrancisco for another week. Ciao

[Typed copy; in the Calvino Archive.]

To Lanfranco Caretti—Pavia

Los Angeles, 15-2-60

Dear Caretti,

Your letter reached me here,[125] in a city that is as big as one that stretched from Milan to Turin, so huge one can do absolutely nothing because to go from one place to another means a car journey of an hour or an hour and a half. I have been going around America for over three months now and I am only halfway through my stay in this country. I got one of those marvelous grants: for six months, with money from the Ford Foundation (so with no need to thank anyone, except the American taxation system), seven "young writers" from seven different countries have been invited to live and travel in the United States without any obligations whatsoever. I spoke to Poggioli about you, at Harvard. He would like to have you there for six months or a year, and this is an opportunity you should not refuse. Even though Harvard is not America, but a kind of Olympus containing the intellectual cream from all over the world, you would have the chance to see a bit of America traveling around. And one should not let slip any chances of "talking" to the Americans, of doing something to bridge this abyss which divides us, and it really is an abyss: this is a different world, as far from Europe and our problems as the Moon. And the universities are a kind of earthly paradise, so much so that they get on your nerves. Seeing such an abundance of resources for research, and a life so free from any difficulty in these garden cities, can only make us think: but might it not be that the price for all this is the death of the soul? Fortunately America is not all an artificial-natural paradise like California here. A quarter of America is a dramatic, tense, violent country, exploding with contradictions, full of brutal, physiological vitality, and that is the America that I have really loved and love. But a good half of it is a country of boredom, emptiness, monotony, brainless production, and brainless consumption, and this is the American inferno.

Thank you for what you say in your letter. It was I who edited the collection of Pavese's short stories.

As for my new novel, I have to tell you that for the first time I am satisfied with what I have done, I feel presumptiously that I *expressed* myself. No facile writing, letting oneself go, games: I wanted to say things about existence, about life, and I think I have said them; I consider this my first important book in terms of content, the first in which I have *said* something. (But not about politics, as they tell me many stupid critics have written; I never thought about politics directly.) However, here where I am all taken up with my discoveries in traveling and cut off from newspapers and European news, I am blissfully very far away from everything. The book has come out, I have not even seen it, I have not seen a review and I am doing very nicely.

For another month I will be traveling, then I will stay in New York (where I have already spent two months and where I really like living) until early May.[126] If you want to write to me, use this address (it's Einaudi's agent): c/o Franz Horch Ass., 325 East 57 Street, New York 22, N.Y.

Very best wishes. Long live Pavia.

Calvino

[Handwritten; with the addressee's heirs.]

To *Mondo Nuovo*—Rome

New York, 21 March 1960

Sir,

I HAVE BEEN TRAVELING ACROSS THE UNITED STATES FOR THE last three months, and it is only now, on my return to New York, that I have been able to get hold of some press-cuttings about my latest novel, *The Non-Existent Knight*, which came out when I was in America. That is how I came to read, after considerable delay, an article signed by Walter Pedullà, published in your review, in the issue of 31 January, under the title "Il romanzo di un ex-comunista" (An Ex-Communist's Novel).[127]

A critic has the right to interpret any work as he likes; however, I feel I have to warn your readers that the interpretation of *The Non-Existent Knight* as a political allegory is totally arbitrary, does not at all reflect my intentions nor my feelings and completely distorts one's reading of the book.

The Non-Existent Knight is a story about man's various levels of existence, about the relationship between existence and awareness, between subject and object, about our ability to fulfill ourselves and to enter into contact with things. It transposes into a lyrical mode interpretations and concepts that constantly crop up today in philosophical, anthropological, sociological, and historical research. It was written at the same time as my essay "Il mare dell'oggettività" (The Sea of Objectivity), published in *il Menabò*, issue 2, which can be seen as a theoretical counterpart of what I wanted to say in the novel in the form of fantasy. BUT WHAT THE HELL DOES COMMUNIST ALLEGORY HAVE TO DO WITH ALL THIS?

Up until now I have only been able to see a few of the reviews that have come out, but I have read that other critics too actually saw in my character Agilulfo a "party functionary"! It seems to me that interpretations like this of a text that does not offer any foothold for such discourses are the fruit of a dangerous fixation in people who want to see everything in terms of the politics of the moment.[128]

In *The Non-Existent Knight*, as in my two preceding works, fantasy-moral novels or lyrical-philosophical novels or however you want to call them, I did not aim at any political allegory, but only at studying and representing the condition of humankind today, the way in which we are alienated, and the ways to reach a total humanity.

Pedullà writes: "The Knights of the Holy Grail are a grotesque communist allegory." What is grotesque, or rather totally absurd, is Pedullà's interpretation. How can the Communists come into it, at that point, in that context? At that point, in the context of a range of examples of the relationship between the individual and the outside world, I needed to exemplify a particular kind of relationship: a mystic relationship, communion with everything. I explain it, perhaps too clearly, and articulate my opposition to that attitude, and this is one of the chapters of the book which I am most keen on from an "ideological" point of view. Pedullà, on the other hand, sees the Communists and Hungary. Here we really are dealing with an obsession!

It was in that very chapter on the Knights of the Grail that I also placed, by way of contrast, the example of the development of consciousness in a historical sense: the Curvaldian people who gain consciousness of existence precisely at the point where they are fighting for their own freedom. This is the only "political allegory" in the book, but it's not allegory, to tell you the truth, rather an open indication of the people and classes that fulfill themselves through struggle on the level of EXISTENCE.

If I write fantasy tales it is because I like to put a burst of energy, action, optimism into my stories, things which contemporary reality does not inspire in me. Of course, if a critic defines me as "decadent," I can disagree but I cannot protest; that is a verdict to do with literary history in which my intentions count for little. But a definition of my political position is a question of actual data; it is therefore my right to show that it is mistaken and to put readers on their guard against tendentious interpretations. What disturbs me most of all is the fact that someone talks about me in terms of "faith" (in Communism) and of "loss of faith" (with its concomitant anti-Communism), an attitude straight out of *The God That Failed*,[129] which has always been at the farthest pole from everything I have written done said thought.

Sincerely,

Italo Calvino

[Typed copy (unsigned); in the Calvino Archive. Published in *Mondo nuovo* (political weekly of the left wing of the Italian Socialist Party, edited by Lucio Libertini), 3 April 1960, under the title "A Letter from Calvino."]

To François Wahl—Paris

Rome, 5 July 1960

Dear Wahl,

More than a month has gone by since my return and I have still not written to you to tell you how pleased I was with my week in Paris: it was a fitting conclusion to my six months of travel. But here I have been taken up with so many things to do, for the publishing house and on a personal level (amongst which I have started to write down my impressions of America for a weekly magazine), and I still have not settled back into a normal rhythm of life. Now I am in Rome, and will stay here for the Premio Strega (which Cassola will surely win).

The interviews in the Paris papers went well on the whole, especially the one in *France-Observateur* and some others.[130] I hope they have helped the sales of the book a bit.

In Italy there is a volume coming out now which collects my three fantasy novels, under the title *I nostri antenati* (*Our Ancestors*) and containing a preface which I wrote especially for it in the last few days.

Amongst our recent titles by Italian authors the most important one is a new book by Danilo Dolci: *Lo spreco* (*Waste*).

Italy is basically a country which is quite healthy: the anti-fascist demonstrations in the last few days at Genoa and over most of Northern Italy show this.[131] But living here day by day it is very boring. The literary news of the last few days involves a polemical attack by Pasolini on Cassola (who in turn had argued with him) in the form of a parody of Mark Anthony's speech in Shakespeare. Caesar's corpse apparently is realism, stabbed to death by Cassola.

After having tried in vain to keep my vital American rhythm (which had been prolonged by the week in Paris) still going in Italy, I have fallen into a state of discontent which I do not know how I will shake off.

I would like to go back to Paris, but now it is summer, and I do not think I will come before October.

Write to me. I am very grateful to all of you and send best wishes
[Typed copy on Einaudi headed paper, with autograph signature; with the addressee.]

To Michele Rago—Rome

San Remo 18 August 1960

Dear Michele,

THANK YOU VERY MUCH FOR THE FINE ARTICLE AND FOR THE way in which you convey what I am trying to say.[132] I don't agree about the literature of *we* as opposed to the literature of the *I*. Literature is the moment of the *I* and this alone distinguishes it from everything else. It is necessary, though, that this *I* has a *we*, that is certainly so. I hope you, like me, are on holiday and I send best wishes

Italo

Villa Meridiana
San Remo
[Picture postcard from San Remo; with the addressee.]

To Suso Cecchi D'amico—Rome

San Remo, 2 September 1960

Dear Suso,

It is time for me to tell you how I have gone about starting work on *Marco Polo*.

To reach that minimum of arousal of the imagination that would allow me to work on this project, I had to read Marco Polo's *Il Milione* (*Travels*) over and over again, even the bits that least lent themselves to narrative, in order to absorb that visionary charge that is the book's secret. In short, I tried to follow Coleridge's method: by smoking opium and reading Marco Polo he managed to compose in a dreamlike trance "In Xanadu did Kublai Kahn . . ." I don't have any opium to hand and I don't know what will come out of this, but it seems to me that what we have to emphasize is the spectacle of the wonders of the world as they might have been conceived at a time when the world was unknown, in the same way as the film *Around the World in 80 Days* managed to recreate the wonder of discovery that was totally nineteenth century. What I am trying to do is to work my way through your very precious outline in this spirit, an outline which has allowed me to start work with a very solid scaffolding [for the project]. With just this difference, that the tone of your treatment is ironic and disenchanted, whereas I am aiming at something more loaded, still ironic but also enchanted. I am sticking to the episodic structure of your outline, in fact in places I accentuate its fragmentation into scenes. In short I am going for a kind of documentary approach to the text's visionary exoticizing imagination, which I think will suit Vanzi's sensitivity, as far as I can judge from the sense of spectacle loaded with violence and ferment that was found in *Il mondo di notte* (*World by Night*).[133]

Naturally the key to everything has to be Marco's character. Now what do we learn about Marco's character from a reading of *Il Milione*? At first sight, less than nothing, but if you think about it: what are the things that interest Marco in his travels? Two things essentially: rich merchandise (with a distinct propensity more for the marvelous than for the practical), and women, sexual mores. So here we already have his character: young Marco in Venice is a dreamer who goes crazy for everything that has a hint of the Orient. In the back-streets and little squares with all their gossip, he dies of suffocation; he goes round the markets, and every silk border or whiff of spices or glint of precious stones sets him off on a reverie, just as his dreams of the Orient's sexual freedom have him chasing every little Saracen maidservant in Venice. That's why he secretly goes on board his father's and uncle's ship—as you suggested—and gets discovered because of his curiosity. And the film will be the crossing of Asia narrated through a series of episodes of the *loves and wonders of Marco Polo*. He must not be a comic character but rather a romantic-ironic figure, who has to be taken seriously just for the fact that he embodies the insatiability of the new times etc., the yearning in the face of the riches of the world, the sense that nonetheless everything turns to dust, that hidden in that Oriental world there must be some secret truth which he does not understand, and yet etc. etc.

His father and uncle Polo are the two Sancho Panzas of the situation, two old men who are only concerned with business, who travel always thinking about the bottom line, while Marco's fantastic thirst for knowledge causes them constant annoyance.

Another character that has to be highlighted is Kublai Khan, this perfect ruler, full of absolute wisdom and a taste for the pleasures of life. And yet—and this is where we come in—melancholic and with barely perceptible psychological flaws, ambiguous and unfathomable, haunted by something between metaphysical despair and a secret perversity of mind that is still dominated by reason. I want to turn him into an emblem of Shakespearean nobility and melancholy, a prince who is still young, handsome, refined, with a metaphysical sadness, a cross between the Duke in *Twelfth Night* (I think) and Marcus Aurelius. He rides on horseback with a tiger on his saddle and a falcon in his hand.

As for the princess that Marco will accompany to her bridegroom in India, I will make her (taking up one of Vanzi's hints) a sweet incarnation of the Oriental wisdom of not resisting your own destiny: a submissive being, in harmony with everything, in other words the precise opposite of Marco. This contrast characterizes their journey together: princess Cocacin (this is the lovely name from the French text which I am keeping for the time being) is not opposed to Marco loving her and seducing her, but nor does she fight against the fate of her royal marriage. However, if Marco were to steal her away and take her to Venice, she would not oppose that either, and so with this sublime passivity she is a very difficult woman to manage and impossible to save from her unfortunate end.

The other female character is the warrior princess Aigiarne who challenges her suitors to a duel. There is no need to say any more: it's already clear what kind of a woman she is.

The other women are passing adventures, without much characterization.

From the *Brigands* I will take much less than we first thought;[134] I too had thought this was a very precious source; then I realized that that kind of mock-heroic grotesque would take us too far from where we wanted to go.

So the story goes like this:

Niccolò and Marco Polo's arrival in Venice. They hope Marco becomes a friar. Disappointment at finding him as he is. But Marco secretly embarks with them: once at sea, he is discovered. Landing. Battle. The two friars flee. (Up to this point everything follows your outline.)

Episodes during the journey to Kublai Khan's court: (these can even be very brief; all taken from ideas in *Il Milione*; spliced between sequences dealing with the caravan crossing deserts, fording streams etc.)

In a city in Persia Marco comes into contact with the wealth of the Orient.

In another Persian city he gets hold of the notion of Muslim polygamy.

In another city he gets hold of the notion of the plurality of religious cults and reveals his tendency to confuse one with the other (something which, apart from causing local difficulties, worries dad and uncle, who want to present him to the Khan as a friar, in place of the other two).

An episode in a place full of birds.

An episode about crossing a desert, with mirages.

Episode of the Old Man of the Mountains. Marco, taken prisoner, savors the fake paradise of the Huris and becomes a Muslim. (All as you suggested.) A girl who falls in love with him reveals the secret to him. The Khan's army arrives with its elephants. Battle and victory over the Old Man. The Khan wants to meet the young man that allowed him to destroy his enemies, but dad and uncle want him to dress as a friar.

Marco a monk. Dressed as a friar, what does he have to do? He finds other monks and goes off with them to a convent, without realizing it's a Buddhist convent, with ascetics, fakirs, yoga. Meanwhile the old Polos have told the Khan they have brought this famous Christian friar. The Khan wants to meet him. Where is he? He discovers, somewhat to his surprise, that he is in a Buddhist monastery and goes to find him there. It's the day when the new monks have to undergo the test of resisting temptation, in this case to stay motionless in front of a young girl doing the dance of the seven veils. Marco? You must be kidding. He is discovered. Escapes.

The tigers. In the forest Marco ends up amongst the tigers. Kublai Khan goes hunting tigers. Saves Marco who maybe in turn saves the Khan during the hunt. The Khan recognizes the Old Man of the Mountain's prisoner, the fake monk, and above all the son of his friend Niccolò Polo. He doesn't care at all that he is not a monk. He makes a great fuss of him.

The Khan's court and the splendors of the capital. Amongst the wise men of all the nations of the Orient who have gathered at the Tartar court, Marco stands out for his descriptions in which he narrates and mimics the countries he has crossed, while the others merely deliver dry accounts of bureaucracy and business. Princess Cocacin, of the Sung family (the Chinese emperors who had been defeated by Kublai), has been brought up at the Khan's court. An idyll with Marco in the palace gardens. But the Great Khan is wandering through the flower beds. There is something ambiguous in Kublai's attitude: the two lovers find he always gets in the way. It seems that he too is in love with Cocacin. Why does he not marry her then and make her one of his countless wives? A promise made at the death-bed of the Chinese emperor he had defeated demands that he bring her up and respect her like a daughter. Night-time conversation between Marco and the Khan which is in a sense the notional fulcrum of the film. In short we can't quite understand whether he wants to keep this girl as a daughter because of the promise he made or because of some psychological obstacle or for the pleasure of giving up something when you are an omnipotent ruler. The fact is that if he does not take her he does not want Marco to have her either. And he sends Marco on long embassies. (Because he trusts him more than anyone else as ambassador, of course, but also, you would say, to keep him away from Cocacin.)

Marco's embassies (these can even be very short sketches, documentary images, or genuine episodes, taken from moments in *Il Milione*, but you can put in what you want):

to Cangiu, a place where female initiative dominates;
to Camul, where the laws of hospitality oblige husbands to leave their wives alone with strangers;
to Caragian, land of the crocodiles, and where they use shells for currency.

Episode of the King of Ceylon's ruby (optional, length as you wish, to be kept in reserve, it can be grafted onto some other episode). The Great Khan sends Marco to the King of Ceylon to buy his enormous ruby. But the king does not want to sell it for all the gold in the world. So Marco agrees with pirates to steal it. Adventure with the pirates. The plot fails. Consorting with pirates will cause problems for him with the Khan.

Aigiarne, the warrior princess. (First meeting.) Marco ends up in the land where the king's daughter will only marry the man who defeats her in the tournament. Joust in which she unseats many suitors. Marco invited by her to fight, but it's hard to work out what intentions this strange girl has. Marco courts her but is a bit alarmed. He has no desire to be beaten but at the same time beating her and having to marry her is even more dangerous. So he escapes.

The older Polos are still nostalgic for Venice, they would like to go back to their homeland and enjoy the riches they have earned, and not die on foreign soil. But the Khan does not want to lose his precious advisers; and Marco on the other hand never tires of Oriental experiences.

Departure.

An embassy arrives at the Khan's court (it could be Marco that guides it, having run into the ambassadors in one of the previous adventures), an embassy from the Indian king Argon who asks the Khan for a bride of royal blood. Kublai promises him young Cocacin. (Out of generosity toward her? To free himself from temptation? To take her away from Marco? Kublai's usual ambiguity.) And he nominates the three Polos as those who must accompany her. (To give in to the old men's desire to return home? To allow Marco the chance to escape with her? To give Marco a painful duty? It can be any of these.)

Accompanying the bride on her journey.

They leave in a caravan, overland. But who are those menacing warriors appearing on the horizon? An ambush! There, they are now Aigiarne's prisoners.

Princess Aigiarne. (Second meeting with her.) She forces Marco to go back with her. A strange duel in which each of them tries to lose. Until Aigiarne gets angry and throws Marco to the ground. Because of Marco's defeat the caravan loses all its horses.

They leave by ship. Shipwreck off the Fuju Islands, where they are taken prisoners by cannibals. Saved by pirates (who meanwhile might have stolen the King of Ceylon's ruby and given it to Marco). All these ups and downs have separated Marco and Cocacin from the rest of the expedition.

The Maabar Islands where the pearl-fishers live. Marco and the princess in the earthly paradise (using Vanzi's idea), the islands where people live naked, and their love seems to have found a refuge. But Niccolò and Matteo track them down and force them to leave once more for India.

Arrival in India.

King Argon is dead. Marco would like to leave for Venice with Cocacin. But Cocacin has to obey the ruthless law of the land.

Here the two solutions already envisaged are possible, and the choice depends on the climate we have built up thus far: see if it allows us to go for a tragic ending (the bride has to be burned on her groom's pyre) or merely an ending that is somewhere between the heart-rending and the grotesque (the princess is married to a child).

In either case Marco tries to bring about revolution, escape, total chaos, and fails.

His father and uncle force him to take the road back to Venice with them.

All of this has to happen in an irrevocable manner, with Marco still desperately attached to the Orient. But the Orient's borders close behind him: it is a lost world, like Shangri-La.

Return to Venice.

Marco spends all his time telling his tales but is not believed by his fellow-citizens. His obsession with recounting the wonders he has seen, but nobody listens to him, in Venice's squares and alleys life bustles on as usual. (I would make this Venice an unpleasant, mean city.) The two old men (I would make both of them return alive and kicking) think only of enjoying their wealth in peace, in fact they act a bit mysterious about their past activities in all these years. Marco, on the other hand, cannot settle. He takes up where he had left off before starting his journey, but with an even more painful restlessness, raving at every piece of muslin cloth or jade necklace on display in the market, at every little serving girl from the Levant . . .

You can show this letter to Vanzi and the production team, if you like.

I will send you soon a few pages of screenplay I have already written, to see whether that works.[135]

Very best wishes,

I don't know if you are already back in Rome or are still at the seaside. I am sending it to Rome, also because I have forgotten the Castiglioncello address. I will stay maybe another week here at home (the address is: Villa Meridiana, San Remo) then I am off to Turin and as soon as possible I will nip down to Rome.

[Typed copy; in the Calvino Archive. Partially published in *RR*, III, pp. 1264–66.]

To Leonardo Sciascia—Caltanissetta

Turin, 23 September 1960

Dear Sciascia,

I'VE READ *IL GIORNO DELLA CIVETTA* (*THE DAY OF THE OWL*). You can do what nobody else in Italy is capable of: the documentary story, about a real problem, providing complete information about this problem, with visual vividness, literary finesse, skill, highly controlled writing, just the right amount of essayistic writing and no more. You also give just the right amount of local color and no more, and it is set in its historical and national context and in the context of the whole world around it, which saves you from strict regionalism. And all this is done with a moral pulse which never stops beating.

It can be read at one sitting. Toward the end where it becomes almost a bare inquest, it loses a bit of its liveliness. But I like this fact of it being openly almost a "documentary." The finale in Parma is very good.

Best wishes
Your

Calvino

[Typed on Einaudi headed paper with autograph signature; with the addressee's heirs. Also in "Lettere di Italo Calvino a Leonardo Sciascia," *Forum Italicum*, 1 (Spring 1981), p. 64.]

To François Wahl—Paris

Turin, 1 December 1960

Dear Wahl,

I WANTED TO EXPRESS MY TOTAL ENTHUSIASM FOR YOUR PIECE in the *Revue de Paris* (I am late in doing this because I have only just received the cutting: the full issue never arrived).[136] This is the first time

I have ever had the satisfaction of receiving a critical assessment of such intelligence and completeness; because this is the first time that my way of imagining and constructing a story has been analyzed. That is to say that you articulate things that I am not aware of but in which I recognize myself, you explain a mechanism of which I am not completely conscious, but which I recognize as true. (Whereas usually critics either say things that are already known and there is no pleasure in hearing them being repeated; or they say things in which one does not recognize oneself.) You have put together and developed ideas for what could be called my narrative methodology, things I had only hinted at in an unstructured way: namely that my point of departure is the *image*, and that the narrative develops an internal *logic* that is in the image itself. You rightly point out that this logical process, when taken to its ultimate consequences, comes to an end and is nullified in a third phase: that of *contemplation*. This is perhaps my limitation; some critics reproach me for it, using other words: they say I never go right to the bottom, that at a certain point in my stories everything calms down and is resolved, that I lack the tragic element. But what can I say? In actual fact this process must correspond to my psychological make-up, to my relationship with the world, and I cannot express anything else but this whether it is right or wrong. In short, what I tend toward, the only thing I would like to be able to teach is a way of *looking*, in other words a way of being in the world. In the end literature cannot teach anything else.

What you say about the value of *action* in my narratives interests me a lot. This is a problem that I have never asked myself about before. I have always thought I loved action, practical things; but in fact I am not instinctively a man of action, only out of will and a rational urge; and action always constitutes a problem for me. So discovering that all my stories have this problem of pointless agitation and real action is for me a precious new acquisition. It is astonishing how much you manage to say in just a page and a half. Of course I slightly regret the fact that you had to limit your examples within very strict confines (and stories that I do not consider as amongst my most substantial start to take on great importance, like the one about the couple who never manage to sleep together),[137] but I see that the system works for all my output. Your discussion could be expanded into a wide-ranging article.

Pierre F. Denivelle's translation is good on the whole, even if many of the rhythmic effects are lost.

I had hoped for much from *La Route des Flandres* (is the nouveau roman acquiring an epic dimension?) but after a while I got bored with it and could not go any further.[138] I have not yet read Huguenin.[139]

In Italy there is no big news apart from the new Moravia: in general people are critical of it, but I have just started reading it and I actually find it very interesting.[140]

In the world of politics we are following events in France like a slow-motion film.

Best wishes.

[Typed copy; in the Einaudi Archive, Turin. Also in *ILDA*, pp. 350–51.]

1961–1965

To Suso Cecchi D'amico—Rome

San Remo 4-3-61

Dear Suso,

I have started to think about the Monicelli project.[1] I can only think of little solutions a bit like old German expressionist cinema, without much "human depth" or characterization of characters and environments.

Still I am scribbling down a plot, that is to say narrating the story you proposed through a series of images and gags and situations. I will send it to you in the next few days once I return to Turin. It will not be very long or elaborate; but on my own I feel I cannot get much more out of it.[2] To produce a definitive treatment I think you will need someone who knows how to put a bit more human warmth into the industrial world (Arpino would be fine. If not, Ottieri). I can only put in my *Ballet mécanique* stuff.

So I will send you the story early next week.

Ciao

Calvino

[Handwritten; with the addressee.]

To Mario Socrate—Rome

Turin 23 April 61

Dear Mario,

I HAVE NOT YET SEEN YOUR BOOK OF FANTASY-POEMS.[3] I AM pleased to know it has come out; let me have a copy, if you can; if not, I'll ask for it myself from the publisher.

I would like to found a cosmic literary movement. Or rather have it founded by Lucentini who has these ideas firmly rooted in his head, and went to see the eclipse at Recanati. But he has not got time. I don't either. Amongst the names of the very few people admitted as members, yours would be one. I'd be ready to declare myself a follower of the cosmic literary movement for a period of six months, maybe even a year, accepting its directives in a disciplined way (that is to say not only drawing them up but also carrying them out). Not for any longer than that; literary tendencies count only if they are of short duration.

The fact is that until we fight head on *everything* that is happening and being thought about in contemporary Italian literature, the arts, cinema etc., we will not make any progress.

The truth is one really ought to stop for a moment and think. And how can we do that? I came back yesterday from Scandinavia after a fortnight's travel in those countries. But it was not the right season, in all senses. Now I am leaving for Majorca for the Formentor Prize. When I get back I will have to write the treatment for a film about underwater fishing.[4] And then there is the publishing work, which I do badly and it takes up my time, but it least it is something serious and that is why I always say I am going to leave it but I never do.

Recently I have been frittering away my time a lot. The feeling that I am drowning in a sea of pointless activities is grabbing me by the throat. But these are times when what you don't write counts for more than what you do write. I have destroyed that book on America, on which I had worked for many months. It hadn't turned out badly, but for me to go down the road taken by travel writers was opting for an easy way out.[5]

I will certainly come to Rome in May and we can meet. I have now rented a house in Rome but it is still empty and I do not know when I will be there. Very best wishes,

Calvino

[Handwritten; with the addressee.]

TO NATALIA GINZBURG BALDINI—LONDON

Turin, 12 May 1961

Dear Natalia,

I LIKE IT ENORMOUSLY, I READ IT ALL AT ONE SITTING, IT'S the best novel you've written.[6]

This sense of family stories, the intertwining of the families' histories, is something that now only you can do. And the sense of the old people, and of the youngsters growing up, and how they grow up, painfully. Sad, terribly sad. It totally depressed me.

Tommasino's lunch at her house is the best bit. Everything is so clear, her suffering at hearing the whole dialog, without it ever being said.

This mother who looms over the whole book, without us hearing anything else but her oppressive talk, is formidable.

The whole story of the engagement, and that farewell, the way the death of the whole thing is so well narrated, without any introspective or psychological comment. A model of narrative performance, totally rigorous.

A bit behind the times, in terms of style, of rhythm? A little bit like Tornimparte in the old days?[7] Actually no, it's totally up to date, this is the way forward. And I admire you because you have remained faithful to it amidst all the stylistic empiricism of these years.

You have taken great strides down this route, it has to be said. You bring this inner richness to the story, and everything is more mature, more precise, with no more hints of the generic and approximate approach which one still felt even in *Valentino*, in other words in your most mature work.

Purillo is very good as well. So unhappy in being the happiest of them all, and even so still a wonderful person.

There is also one might say a geographical depth. This Piedmont of yours, now that you are far away from it, now comes out everywhere whereas before you tended to be vague and generalize about it. I've never read anything so Piedmontese, Piedmontese enough to make you cry. And the language too, so Piedmontese as to make you feel Piedmont like a kind of tomb, where whoever enters is condemned never to come out again.

And then your objective account of things is truly impartial. I am particularly grateful to you for this, because despite all your passion for playing the poor girl as masochist victim, I for one suffered much more, of course, for Tommasino, seeing him go off to be married when he doesn't want to, because you give each reader the freedom to suffer for whoever they want.

I've forwarded the manuscript to Molina.[8] Ciao. I liked "Le piccole virtù" (The Little Virtues) as well.[9]

As for me, I maybe won't ever write again and am surviving quite well all the same.

[Typed copy; in the Einaudi Archive, Turin. Also in *ILDA*, pp. 366–67.]

To François Wahl—Paris

Turin, 9 June 1961

Dear Wahl,[10]

I HAVE JUST SEEN IN THE *BIBLIOGRAPHIE DE FRANCE* THE TWO excellent pages by Editions du Seuil on Italian literature. I saw that my book is announced as *Le chevalier irréel*. I do not like that *irréel* at all. I do not like it in terms of taste (this is a word that evokes a totally different literary climate) nor of meaning. I never say that the knight is unreal. I say that he does not exist. That is very different. The correct translation is *Le chevalier qui n'existe pas*. I think that with *Le chevalier irréel* one loses everything there is in my book to do with current problems (problems of *existence*) and we shift the emphasis on to problems of reality and illusion (an old hobby-horse à la Pirandello) which have nothing to with what I write about.

Please write to me, and reassure me.

Best wishes
Your

Calvino

This spring's Italian novels? We have published a very good (and very short) Natalia Ginzburg (*Le voci della sera*) (*Voices in the Evening*). Arpino is now with Mondadori (because he is tied to them by a previous contract option).[11] People are speaking about the La Capria book (Bompiani) but I have not read it yet.[12]
[Typed on Einaudi headed paper, with autograph signature; with the addressee.]

To Marco Forti—Milan

[Turin, June–July 1961]

Dear Forti,
I HAVE RECEIVED YOUR WIDE-RANGING SURVEY ON FICTION and industry.[13] You have carried out a huge task, full of very acute critical observations, which offers a first outline of a broad and representative slice of Italian fiction in the last decade.

My only critical note, in general terms, concerns the fact that you spend a long time telling us the plot of the novels and stories. I don't see what use that can be. We all know that the meaning and value of a book does not lie in the plot. At most, one can recount some detail or scene, as a "sample." You will object that this is merely an essay dealing with the sociology of the content, so the story has a lot of importance. I don't agree: what matters is to define the general image that a particular writer offers of industrial civilization. If you cut from your article all the summary passages dealing with plot and leave the critical judgments, your argument holds all the same, and indeed becomes more compact and legible.

I don't think I have any comments to make on your selection and arrangement, apart from my personal view that the less one mentions Testori the better it is. I would remove Bianciardi's *Il lavoro culturale* (Cultural Work), because it has nothing to do with the theme, and I would leave in only the bit that deals with *L'integrazione* (Integration) (but Bianciardi's best things on industry, the wittiest and most relevant pieces on this topic, are the short literary essays he used to write for *l'Unità*). I see that you have left out short stories but often there is more substance there than in a novella or novel (along the same lines and containing the same atmosphere as Buzzi's novel, I remember one of Bigiaretti's short stories which is certainly better).[14] Quite right and intelligent of you to link Bufalari's book to the theme of the article.[15]

Naturally I dwelt on the section that dealt with me (a real essay, that highlights very well motifs in my work on which I am very keen). I am very grateful to you for it, also because what you say provided an opportunity for me to reconsider what I have written from this particular point of view, and to focus some of my ideas. And it also made me want to write to you to discuss some points with you, and also to ask you to do a general restructuring with a view to reducing its length, as well as some corrections. Restructuring because since it is indeed such a lengthy and in-depth section it makes me slightly embarrassed. *Il Menabò* has my name on its frontispiece as co-editor and I do not want to appear as having more advantageous treatment than other writers. Some corrections too because your interpretations, the way you focus on episodes and characters, which are all legitimate from a critical point of view, don't always coincide with my own, whereas appearing in *Il Menabò* it would look as if they came with the support of the author. In short, I would be very happy to see this piece published as an article on its own in a journal, but in *Il Menabò* I would prefer to reduce the section down to a more concise form, without spending time following the plot and defining the characters.

For *La speculazione edilizia* (*A Plunge into Real Estate*) I would use the following definition of its historical-sociological theme:

> In *La speculazione edilizia* (*A Plunge into Real Estate*) Calvino represented the economic boom of Northern Italy in the 1950s in its most striking and characteristic manifestation: the transformation of the Ligurian Riviera's landscape through intense house-building for the middle classes from the industrial cities, a bourgeoisie that wants its "sea-side flat" as its first priority in terms of well-being. As the "belle époque" villas of the turn of the century disappear under the layers of cement, and the traditional bourgeoisie that inhabited them is in crisis and forced to sell (like the story's protagonist, an intellectual who embarks on a dodgy building deal, more than anything else because of his mania for imposing on himself an "economic behaviour" that is at odds with his true nature and education), what dominates the field is a whole new world of small deals and plots and cynicism. This world is represented in the novel by the character of the entrepreneur Caisotti.[16]

And at that point I would start with what you say about Caisotti. I would cut part of the rest, including your remarks on the final meeting between the protagonist and the worker Masera, which I don't think you have nailed properly, since you put the stress on a generic, moralistic meaning. I wanted to say this: in Quinto's view, property speculation was something that was opposed to the ethics of the Party, something that held the (vaguely scandalous, for a left-wing intellectual) fascination of "the economic moment" as opposed to the asceticism of the revolutionary ethic. Instead his comrade Masera tells him: "Well done, you idiot, if you had only said so to the Party Branch, they would have given you a hand." And all of a sudden Quinto realizes that what seemed to him a scandal was not one at all, that there was no morality being violated, that the scandal consisted solely in dealing badly with his own affairs. In other words, he managed his own affairs while following a literary, romantic, individualistic idea of economic honesty, without realizing that there is no separation between morality and economics, and that the interests of a property-owner who has to do a deal also run right through the Communist Party's local headquarters—in short, they have to be integrated into the framework of organized interest.

Now I have couched all this in extreme terms, and of course a comment on the episode ought to be more nuanced, just as the text too is precisely that, more nuanced. But, as I said to you, I don't think there is any need to talk about it in your article since it would divert attention away from the main theme of the story.

For *Smog* I would make some cuts in your essay so as to make just a few points stand out.

The only bit I would correct is the way you define the trade-unionist and worker Omar Basaluzzi, who in the story—contrary to what you claim—represents a range of views on the workers' movement which are completely different from those of "comrade Masera." Here too you talk of moralism. Maybe so, but what moralism? I would try to provide a more specific definition:

The revolutionary workers' movement too, which ought to represent the genuine, invincible opponent of "smog," of the industrial malaise, is portrayed in this story almost as if it is by now of one nature with the smog it breathes. The workers' movement that Calvino portrays for us is one that finds itself in the heart of the most advanced neo-capitalist regime (particularly through the character of Omar Basaluzzi, a young worker and trade-unionist, cultured, elegant, a little bit pedantic, who loves sociological surveys and statistics and who is fighting to replace the party militants' old passionate urges with scientific rigor). It is a working-class movement which has not wavered for a second in its moral intransigence and its own abilities to resist, on the contrary it has transformed them into an internal law which is now remote from any hope of immediate realization, and is not even sure that its own practical victory would signal the end of the "smog," of industrial squalor.

On the level of images, then, not even the working class can offer an antithesis to the cloud that is now looming. And Calvino always needs to close his stories with a counterbalancing of images. Calvino is not a Kafka, who is prepared to document metaphysical horror right to the bitter end; nor is he even a political theorist prepared to formulate out of his negative experience of the world a solution that involves a historical forecast.

That is why the final pages on the suburb of Barca Bertulla etc.[17]

I would not bring in *The Non-Existent Knight*. (Maybe just the briefest of mentions at the beginning in brackets.) There is too little in it that deals with the theme of your article. Gurdulù, for instance, is entirely constructed from ethnological hypotheses; how can industry come into that? And in any case, all the authors and books you deal with are direct narrative representations of today's industrial civilization. Allegories are not relevant. (Here in *Il Menabò*, I mean; whereas in an essay you might want to publish separately on my stories, seeing them from the point of view of "industrial" problems, they would be very relevant.)

I'll let you have the proofs and very many thanks once again.

I am happy about this opportunity which I hope will mean you will write to me.

Calvino

[Typed, no date, on Einaudi headed paper, with autograph corrections and signature; with the addressee.]

To Lev A. Veršinin

Turin, 7 November 1961

Dear Veršinin,

THANK YOU FOR THE GOOD NEWS. AND THANK YOU ALSO FOR your proposal to translate *Smog*. I consider this story much more important than my others and seeing it translated in the Soviet Union would give me enormous pleasure.[18]

You ask me to remove or attenuate some of the reflections contained in the story, on pages 561 and 562. I have to tell you that I feel very strongly about this aspect of my thought. It is a declaration of a *Stoic* morality which ought not to be in contradiction with *Marxist* morality. The way I think is this: just as Christian morality can find its highest realization in someone who acts well without believing in paradise or worrying whether paradise exists or not, in other words in someone who finds his "paradise" in the very act of carrying out good actions, not in a final reward, so Communist morality is valid even if one does not worry about future happiness, about a "paradise" on earth, but one finds one's own happiness in the very fact of behaving like a Communist. Communism is *already* the fact that some men behave as Communists, that some workers tenaciously face up to struggles and persecutions for a just cause etc. I know that this is a highly debatable thesis, and I articulate it in an interrogative, problematic way. But it seems to me that a moral problem of this kind could generate interesting discussions in the Soviet Union. Naturally many would not agree with me and would criticize me: but they would not be pointless debates.

So I would not agree to cut anything on p. 561, none of these sentences: "Mi rendevo conto" (I realized that) etc. "Grane ce ne saranno sempre" (There'll always be trouble) etc. "Cambierebbero vita i santi" (Would the saints change their lives) etc.[19]

If you think it is necessary (because it is convenient or because what I am trying to say does not seem sufficiently clear to you) a paragraph could be cut on p. 562: "E poi studiavo le facce" (And then I studied the faces) etc. down to "sembrare dei primi" (seem to be in the first category).

I hope you have received my letter [in][20] which I replied to your questions on "Furto in una pasticceria" (Theft in a Cakeshop).[21]

Please do thank your collaborator Kin, whose name I had already come across in a translation of a story of mine that had appeared in a journal.[22]

Best wishes,

Italo Calvino

[Typed on Einaudi headed paper, with autograph signature; with the addressee.]

To Primo Levi—Turin

Turin, 22 November 1961

Dear Levi,

I HAVE FINALLY READ YOUR STORIES. SCIENCE FICTION TALES, or rather biological fiction tales, always attract me.[23] Your fantasy mechanism, which always takes off from a scientific-genetic platform, has an intellectual and even poetic power of suggestion, just like Jean Rostand's genetic-morphological digressions, as far as I am concerned.[24] Your sense of humor and your elegance are very effective in saving you from falling into a level of sub-literature, a pitfall into which those who use literary forms for intellectual experiments like this usually fall. Some of your ideas are first-class, like the one about the Assyrian expert who deciphers the mosaic of the tapeworms; and the evocation of the origin of centaurs has a poetic force, a plausibility that is very convincing (and, dammit, you would think that it's impossible to write about centaurs today, yet you've avoided an Anatole France–Walt Disney pastiche).[25]

Of course you still do not possess the sureness of touch of a writer whose stylistic personality is already formed; for instance Borges, who uses the most disparate cultural suggestions and transforms every idea into something that is exclusively his, producing that rarefied climate that is as it were the trademark that makes the works of every great writer unmistakeable. Your work offers intelligent speculation on the fringes of a cultural-ethical-scientific panorama which is apparently that of the Europe in which we live. Maybe I like your stories above all because they presuppose a common culture that is noticeably different from that presupposed by so much Italian literature. And the background of barely perceptible provincialism, reminiscent of the Piedmontese Scapigliatura movement that underlies it, provides a particular fascination also in the slighter pieces in the collection, like the story of the old doctor who collected odors, like a novella by a Soldati converted to positivism.[26]

All in all, this is a direction in which I would encourage you to work, but above all I would say to find an outlet where things of this kind can come out with a certain regularity and establish a dialog with a public that knows how to appreciate them. I really would not know which outlet to suggest. Perhaps you could put together a small collection of unpublished pieces and publish them all together in *Nuovi Argomenti*.

For the stories of a different genre, there are fewer possibilities. Those about the concentration camp are fragments from *If This Is a Man*, which when cut off from the broader narrative, have the limitations of sketches. And I am very keen on your attempt at a Conradian epic about mountain-climbing, but at present that remains just an intention.

We'll talk about all this when we meet. Best wishes from your

Calvino

You wouldn't write a children's book, would you?
[Typed on Einaudi headed paper, with autograph signature and postscript; with the addressee's heirs. Also in *ILDA*, pp. 382–83.]

To Giovanni Arpino—Milan

[1962, later than February]

Dear Arpino,
For a start I have to tell you that I am very happy that you have come back to dealing with things that interest us. I never said anything to you but now I can say it: why the hell did you go off and deal with honor killings?[27] Neither you nor I nor any of the people that you and I know have ever had any doubts about how to judge honor killings. And that is why the tens of thousands of your readers belong to an Italy that has nothing in common with this hangover from medieval morality. The Italy of honor killings (their perpetrators, lawyers, that part of public opinion that agrees with them) will disappear with industrialization and the changes in morality that will come with it; there is no other way. The only form of persuasion that can reach this part of Italy is the cinema. And cinema is right to deal with such themes on a popular level. However, we who write books position ourselves in a state of enquiry and research into facts which are still awaiting a definition, a verdict.

Una nuvola d'ira (*An Angry Haze*)[28] is an important book because it talks of something we can't define properly, namely the attitude to adopt in this civilization of industrial production and mass consumption, and more particularly the attitude to adopt as workers. In other words it deals with what is actually at the core of this civilization, the attitude to adopt as Communist workers, who share a conception that is critical toward this civilization but at the same time is basically optimistic about its outcomes. This attitude—general influential ideas and their repercussions on daily private life—is still a field that needs to be explored; neither you nor I nor your other readers have clear ideas on this subject, nor do the workers or Communists. Consequently writing books like this, books that carry out research in an area that is still unexplored, is work that is useful in itself, the work that needs to be done today is this and not anything else.

We can distinguish three main types of attitude: that of the person who wants to maintain an equilibrium between the traditional, old agricultural world and the industrial world. This is the position adopted by the husband character who lives between the factory and his country pastimes: hunting, fishing, bowls. An old-fashioned worker, he leaves his [Fiat] 600 for his wife to use while he goes to work on his motorbike. In political terms he is by now a skeptic. He keeps his distance, and doesn't understand the times he's living in any more. This kind of white-goods well-being is not to his taste, and the world of politics speaks a language that is more and more incomprehensible. But he is suffering living in these times, more than anyone else: it's no accident he has an ulcer. He is more a kind of old socialist, but he could also be a grassroots Communist, not an activist. This character is very successful, everything to do with him is poetic and true, even the countryside in the end, the step-brother, the silence into which he disappears. One would really want you to say more about him, one would want this wife of his to understand him and love him a bit more in order to be able to say more about him. In the end the story is only his story, the drama belongs only to him. But his point of view is still that of the past, the morality of the countryside, the socialism of country-folk.

Second attitude: that of those who take life in the city with its mass mythology as something good, the son who is grateful and satisfied with the economic miracle, like his friend who is interested solely in football. This element is represented only in passing, but it is the implied background to the whole story. Only its all-pervading presence, the blissful absence of thought in millions of people filling in pools coupons and television spectators, only these things explain the lonely pride of the two protagonists, their superiority in being "different."

Third attitude: that of those who feel they are potentially the ruling class of this world, the inheritors of an ideology that is capable of understanding it fully, and for that reason feel themselves dispossessed of it, and can only manage to think in terms of this claim to power of theirs. This is the position of the wife and of the worker who lives renting a room from them. They become lovers of course because of the similarity between them and the superiority they feel they have over the environment that surrounds them, a superiority that is at one time that of the working-class aristocracy (the woman's 600) and of the political avant-garde that is persecuted (the man is a Communist who is confined to a warehouse). (And let us not forget that they are Piedmontese, in the midst of a working class that is becoming more and more made up of southern immigrants who have to start from scratch both in social and cultural terms . . .).

These are people who are difficult to represent, but you had clear ideas on how to portray them. Your flash of inspiration was your depiction of them: the more they believe they are free and the heirs of a truth and a harmony which does not exist yet, the more they become the most alienated of all the characters, and they end up in a total rage against everything that surrounds them, even against the party (which the man, an opposition person from the left, has started to vituperate and to snub). I don't think you wanted to make them nice, but they have turned out even less pleasant than you intended. Their love for culture, poetry, big cars makes them pedantic; we cannot help thinking that people we like adopt a completely different tone. It is not a question of discussing whether they are *real* or unreal; the motives you had for making them that way are real (or rather one can vouch for the fact that they are "typical," if we want to accept this category) but let us see if they work enough to make it a convincing story, in other words if they are *poetic*.

To sum up, I don't like the way they talk: you want to make them talk a unified language which is representative enough of the spoken language of the people and at the same time expresses their ethical-political-cultural consciousness. Look, when it was a question of making political characters talk in a way that did not sound like editorials or hustings speeches, we were the ones who battered our heads against a brick wall for so many years, all those of us who wrote committed fiction fifteen years ago, starting with Vittorini and Pavese. Pointless: one cannot construct in fiction a *harmonious* language to express something that is not yet harmonious. We live in a cultural ambience where many different languages and levels of knowledge intersect and contradict each other. In terms of language your characters' dilemma could have been expressed by making them come up against this lack of congruity between the various languages: in other words face the dilemma that a particular political statement becomes ridiculous when uttered in privacy to your lover, that the poems on the cultural page of *l'Unità* and the nomenclature of the combustion engine are two different and incompatible linguistic worlds.

In short, it is not enough to want to have a complete, universal humanity in order to believe that we already have it; we have to start to admit that we don't have it today, in order to seek out the road to reach it. You know this so well that you made it the theme of your story, but in order to express this poetically you had two options, as far as I can see: either to plunge yourself into a totally babel-like plurilingualism that could express the ideological schizophrenia in which we live; or using a language of total cultural flexibility to talk like Giovanni Arpino telling a story and trying to interpret the story of the three characters from the outside. To cut a long story short, my objection is to the method of telling the story, which does not distance itself enough from a naturalistic *Verismo*. An objection which must be at least fifty years old by now, but the opportunities for rebutting it have become rarer and rarer.

You already reached a perfect balance between the lyrical and ethical components of your poetical world in *Gli anni del giudizio* (*The Years of Wisdom*), which is still your best book, and which already contains all the basic themes of *Una nuvola d'ira* (*An Angry Haze*).[29] But in it, between Turin and Bra, the centre of gravity was Bra, the more lyrical side, the one that is more yours . . .

[Typed copy, no date, with one autograph correction; in the Calvino Archive. The letter dates from 1962, certainly after February when *Una nuvola d'ira* was published.]

To Umberto Eco—Milan

San Remo, 9-5-1962

Dear Eco,

I'VE READ YOUR ESSAY.[30] THE WHOLE BIT DEALING WITH ALIENation is formidable. I agree wholeheartedly.

Some people might object that you overturn Marx and Hegel too quickly in order to reject everything. There is a disproportion between the analysis of the problem as it was formulated by its founders and the interpretation you give it. In short, you've certainly convinced me (also because I was already thinking along the same lines), but someone will certainly jump up and say that Marx said more than you want to attribute to him and so your discourse does not concern him.

There is a certain mismatch between this first part (sections 1 and 2) and the rest. Watch out because your "cars-Cecilia-stone tools" discourse can also lead to opposite conclusions in the field of poetics.[31] In other words one can say "I use industrial forms—let's say: the thriller, science-fiction, in short the closed forms, the 'machines' for consumer use—and to a certain extent I get alienated by this, to a certain extent I don't, and that's what one has to do in order not to become over-sensitive."

Section 3 is weak, the definition of the avant-gardes, it's too generic and old-fashioned a discourse. Things are more complex than this; there are ten thousand avant-gardes, each different from the next; or rather, we no longer have a tradition and an avant-garde, everything is contemporary. The Proustian novel cannot be rejected as "traditional' but only by dealing with it in detail. In actual fact everything came about at the same time in the space of sixty years or thereabouts; and there is a big dispute between tendencies that can fling at each other the accusation of being *old* and philistinely commercialized. The problem does not lie there. It is inside the work itself.

SECTIONS 5–6–7 GOOD OR VERY GOOD.

You talk too much about popular music: this vulgarizes your discourse. What is this about Claudio Villa? What is the stuff about the San Remo Festival? Never heard of it!

THE FINALE IN FAVOR OF COSMIC RELATIONS: EXCELLENT. For years now I have been thinking about writing a manifesto

"For a Cosmic Literature" but I was waiting to clarify my ideas a bit better.

Best wishes

Calvino

[Handwritten on paper headed "Prix International des Editeurs et Prix Formentor 1961"; with the addressee. The paragraphs that make up the letter are horizontal, vertical, and diagonal and form a patchwork pattern on the page.]

To Geno Pampaloni—Florence

San Remo 30 August 62

Dear Pampaloni,

Thank you for what you wrote about my most recent works (I have only just seen the article in *Epoca* of 12 August), and for the attention with which you follow my output.

Certainly, this is a period when—perhaps in reaction against the general climate of euphoria—I feel like writing only in an interrogative sense.

The collapse of historicism, you say. Or the search for a tighter relationship between the individual and History.

Kind regards,

Calvino

[Handwritten; with the addressee.]

To Michelangelo Antonioni—Rome

Turin, 3 October 1962

Dear Antonioni,

I HEARD THAT YOU CAME TO THE PUBLISHING HOUSE (I WAS IN a clinic for a little operation) and I am sorry not to have seen you.

As far as your book is concerned, the situation is this: the raw material you provided me with (as well as the already published screenplays) is giving us considerable technical problems if it is to be turned into a narration with dialog like the Bergman book.[32] In short, the book is still *all to be sorted out*.

But of course it certainly cannot produce stories to be read like Bergman's treatments. Your artistry is more quintessentially cinematographic, in other words it is not entrusted to the word but to the image, the rhythm, the silences. How to find the equivalent of all this in a book? A written dialog, even although it is not the equivalent of a dialog that is acted out, can give some idea of it; and the same goes for a moment of cinematic action; but a silence, a pause, a moment of stasis or movement, how can these be rendered on the written page? Here a writer would need to fill out what you have entrusted to the image. But no writer has done this work *before* the film (and here lies your greatest claim to fame as a director: namely, you think in images, you do not need to have explained what you mean beforehand on paper, but you are able to make it emerge from your free contact with things). Consequently in order to make a book the only thing would be for you to re-tell the film as you saw it and felt when making it. But I realize that to ask a director to do this is impossible: it would be like asking him to translate his own means of expression into another. And yet, we hoped for something like this from a written version of your screenplays which we thought would be a bit more worked through.

The publication of your screenplays certainly has huge importance for cinema scholars, because it documents precisely how much the "non-written" and perhaps "non-writeable" elements are due to your pure cinematographic intuition, but readers attracted by an Einaudi book would need to be moved by a more direct stimulus to reading. In a book by you they would be looking for something of the emotions that your films produced in them: and they'd be disappointed to find so little.

I have outlined the perplexities that a first look at the material aroused in some of us who have started to study the problem. I am still not in a position to give you any suggestions toward a solution because at present there aren't any.[33] Tell us too what you think about it.

Warmest regards to you and Monica. I hope to see you both soon.
[Typed copy; in the Einaudi Archive, Turin.]

To Leonardo Sciascia—Caltanissetta

Turin, 5 October 1962

Dear Leonardo,
I HAVE READ WITH GREAT PLEASURE *IL CONSIGLIO D'EGITTO* (*The Council of Egypt*).[34] You have managed to make the reconstruction of an environment and a case of philological mystification interesting. You have brought all the characters to life, making each of them human beings with their own lyrical-psychological world, and above all providing a sense of the complex interweaving of themes from political and cultural history. You have managed to blend your passion for researching local history with your taste for satirical comedy to produce a story constructed with great brilliance both in terms of narration and in instructive representation.

We are hoping to publish the book very soon. Don't expect one of those successes that nowadays are making many people's heads turn. Yours is a book for a public that is not the usual one for novels: it is addressed to a reader who is passionate about that period, and the interest for this extraordinary case of the Abbé Vella is historical in nature, not poetic-novelistic. But of course you are well aware of all this and it reflects your intentions for this narrative of yours which has cleverly organized a mass of information that is more powerful than any learned monograph could manage.

I have just one literary comment to make, and a totally marginal one. At a certain point you start to use modern images: the Broadway actor, Malraux, Chaplin. Serious clash of tone. Not because you have to pretend that the book was written then, let's be clear about that: it is obvious that the book was written by you, now. But because in a work of poetic artistry the level of metaphors has to have its own consistency, its own harmony, otherwise it is occasional, journalistic writing. Modern metaphors are justified only if you want to create another plane dealing with contemporary reality as a contrast to the first level of narrative. In other words you play with slipping between the period of the documents you are consulting and the period in which you are writing, but in that case it needs to be a dense and evocative game of allusions, just as in *Doktor Faustus* Serenus Zeitblom removes himself from the narrative every so often and talks of the bombardments under which he is writing.

So remove these modern images, please: they lower the level of your prose which is always so controlled. I think you can do this easily, even at proof stage.

Best wishes.

Your Calvino

[Typed on Einaudi headed paper; with the addressee's heirs. Also in "Lettere di Italo Calvino a Leonardo Sciascia," *Forum Italicum*, 1 (Spring 1981), pp. 65–66.]

To Michelangelo Antonioni—Rome

Turin, 12 October 1962

Dear Antonioni,

You were angry about my letter and you are right to be. And the fault is certainly mine because I did not describe the situation to you in the "dialectical" way in which it stands in reality. You know that your name has the power to ignite the most fiery discussions both in Italy and everywhere else. This is one of the signs that your films strike people to the core, and you can be proud of this. But just as you have enthusiastic supporters so you also have opponents who at the mere mention of your name get mad like bulls faced with the toreador's red rag. I know something about this since I have always been a self-confessed supporter of yours, both in writing and in talk. As a result, I now find myself (especially after *L'eclisse* [*Eclipse*]) embroiled in discussions and arguments that are repeated in every ambience, every evening in friends' houses.

In the Einaudi environment the anti-Antonioni camp is particularly strong. You know that there are no fiercer opponents than those who start from positions that are ideologically close to one's own. My position as regards your films is in a minority but is strengthened by the alliance of Giulio Einaudi, for whom the increasing discussions about your work confirm his conviction regarding its importance.

For this reason we need your book to be presented as a work that is as complete as possible, that does not expose itself to criticisms and underestimations. The material you sent us (I've barely glanced at it; I promise I will look at it as soon as possible) was immediately inspected from the technical viewpoint. The anti-Antonioni group instantly seized on it to uphold their claim that the book did not stand up. When I got back from the clinic I found unfavorable reports, the impression of technical difficulties to be overcome and an atmosphere of hostility to the book amongst colleagues. I thought it essential to put you on guard, and I wrote you that letter.[35] Perhaps I did not choose the happiest of formats, but I have already obtained two results: one from you who in your letter tell me that it was already your intention "to gather any notes, write the preface, etc." something which will considerably enhance interest in the volume and gives me ammunition for a counter-offensive. The second thing is your reaction which has spurred me into explaining to you more clearly in this letter how things stand. Thirdly, I would also add, Giulio Einaudi is more determined than ever to do everything possible so that the book can be published in its most satisfactory form.

I think I have managed to explain to you what the real point of the question is: if yours was a finished book for which there was nothing else to do except to forward the manuscript to the printers, everything would be plain sailing (but it is clear that this cannot be the case). Since it is material that still requires much editing, and in addition here the climate in the editorial office that should deal with the work is riven by the passions that are currently dividing all groups, parties, and families into pro- and anti-Antonioni supporters, the work runs the risk of coming up against a lengthy series of difficulties.

So what is needed is: the maximum amount of collaboration on your part and the maximum amount of collaboration on ours. I know you have more pressing problems since you have to think about your films; but I wanted to let you know that we have our projects to think about. For my part I can guarantee you my total commitment and support; I will now start to take all your material and examine all the points that need to be solved.[36]

I hope to come to Rome soon and see you

[Typed copy; in the Einaudi Archive, Turin.]

To Geno Pampaloni—Florence

Turin, 16 October 1962

Dear Pampaloni,

I've just read in the last few days your article on Pavese in *Terzo Programma*.[37] For more than a month now I have been totally re-immersed in Pavese studies. I am preparing, for Pavese's "Opera Omnia," the volume containing his poems, which I will publish in chronological order, the published poems and the 29 unpublished ones (but still omitting the juvenilia, those that precede "I mari del Sud (*The South Seas*)," which we are keeping for when we decide to undertake what will be the very laborious task of publishing all his youthful writings). I am preparing much fuller notes than those that accompanied the stories. Having set off trying to find the most accurate dates, which was all I had done for the other volumes of the "Opere," the examination of the manuscripts and drafts spurred me on to transcribing the variants that shed most light on the meaning and genesis of each individual poem; not with a view to a critical edition, which is not a feasible publishing possibility, but to provide the maximum in terms of tools that are useful for exegesis.

All this to explain to you that I read your article while I was totally steeped in this material and with a philological tension (which I cultivate only at very distant intervals, but when I get it, it absorbs me totally) that makes me hypersensitive and intolerant of everything in literary criticism that is generic and approximate. And I found that your essay is written with great precision, making fruitful use of all the material that has been published (this is the first time this has happened) and adopting the right perspective on the various elements in Pavese's personality, and with evaluations that in many cases I noticed with pleasure are in line with those I had come to myself. You put more emphasis on the decadent aspect than I would, or rather on a D'Annunzian influence. As far as I am concerned, these things are there but they are part of the building blocks he had at his disposal: what counts, what is his, is the slant that he gives this material. The symptomatic thing is that you end up being in agreement with Moravia, who based his dismissal of him on Decadentism; in you this same element works, by contrast, toward a positive evaluation. The interpretative key of "poetry as absolute" is, however, perfectly correct and acts as a guiding principle for all his poetic choices.

But your article has another characteristic which I am very keen on: namely that finally we have the relationship between Pavese and politics outlined in accurate terms. In these very days I have just written a brief study or rather note on the "political poems" in *Lavorare stanca* (the same four poems you emphasized), and I began the piece complaining that up till now criticism has not been able to define the relations between Pavese and politics properly. I hope to be able to add a reference to your article at proof stage. (My article will come out in a private publication and I'll send it to you.)[38]

We don't always agree in our judgments on single works. I think that Pavese already gave much of the best of himself in the poems of *Lavorare stanca*. Of course, one cannot consider them as *poems* in the sense of belonging to the history of Italian poetry in verse, or any other poetry for that matter. However, the fact that these poems are a unique phenomenon of his, which coincides with a particular period in the author's life (from 1932 to '35; after his exile, this vein dries up), places it on the level of other great "unique" books of twentieth-century European literature. (The love poems of 1940, '45, '50, are worth very little, in my view.)

Judgments on the fiction: in *Il compagno* (*The Comrade*) and also in *La luna e i falò* (*The Moon and the Bonfires*) there are more things I dislike than I like. In my view, the line of high successes in narrative runs through *Il carcere* (*The Political Prisoner*), *La casa in collina* (*The House on the Hill*), *Il diavolo sulle colline* (*The Devil in the Hills*), and also *Tra donne sole* (*Amongst Women Alone*). So I am happy (as well as with your other verdicts which are less controversial) with the evaluation you give of *Il diavolo*.

I do not share your admiration for the short stories, neither for those in *Feria d'agosto* (*Summer Storm and Other Stories*), nor for the unpublished ones (on the whole I agree with the author's criteria in not publishing stories he did not publish himself; and "La famiglia" (The Family) seems to me a story that is not fully written). (But at the same time I am very happy to see my work as editor of the unpublished stories finally appreciated.) As for *Dialoghi con Leucò* (*Dialogues with Leucò*), however, I do not share your reservations (though I have to study the problem in greater depth). It seems to me there is a language there, a fusion between the aphoristic and the lyrical, which also becomes one single thing. I find absolutely right and original your observation regarding the two attitudes: the participatory tone of the dialog, and the detached tone of the introductory note.

What else? I ought to have noted the agreements and disagreements line by line. But the former are more numerous and more important than the latter.

Best wishes

Calvino

[Typed on Einaudi headed paper, with autograph signature; with the addressee.]

To Donald Heiney—Rome

Turin, 5 January 1963

Dear Heiney,

I AM HAPPY TO REPLY TO YOUR QUESTIONS.

(1) The date of that issue of *Il Contemporaneo* containing my article is right. Probably, as you suspect, the journal *Galleria* came out several months late.

(2) When I used the word "innesti" I meant "grafts": an agricultural procedure that is always useful and positive.

Consequently that whole passage on the "inoculations," at least as far as it refers to me, does not seem to work.

Although I was a member of the Italian Communist Party up until 1957, I never found any contradiction between my interest in American literature and the polemics against American policy from Truman's time onwards.

On the contrary, the party's press tried to highlight everything about American culture that seemed positive to us and worthy of its great tradition.

When speaking about Italian Communists, people have to pay attention to the fact that they have always been, even in the worst period of Stalinism, quite independent of the general climate. In other words they always tried not to confuse the language of propaganda with the language of culture. I am well aware that Communist cultural policy throughout the world was horrendously crude; in Italy too people said and did many foolish things, but it seems clear to me that there was a little bit more intelligence here than in other countries. And not just in us who were trying to carry out a campaign for a more open culture inside the Communist Party, but also in our opponent-comrades, that is to say in those who represented official Communist culture.

I do not understand the reference to Pasolini. He is a writer I know and often appreciate, but we have always been very far apart, I would almost say at opposite extremes. We have different backgrounds and models, we have never written for the same journals, nor been part of the same groups. In politics too, we were never close: I was a Party militant, he was always a fellow-traveler, and there is a huge difference there (the fellow-traveler always sees politics from outside, often with a naïve faith; the intellectual who is a party militant sees it from inside, coldly, like a mechanism he is trying to get to move in a certain direction). What's more, in the years when I was politically committed, Pasolini *was not yet there*, that is to say he was still far from that authority in literary and political debates that he acquired after I had detached myself from active politics. In short, I do not think one of my articles could have influenced Pasolini (if he ever read any). Sometimes I wrote well of his books and he of mine, but I think it would be strange to talk of a mutual influence.

I am always at your disposal, for any help I can give.[39]

Best wishes

[Typed copy; in the Einaudi Archive, Turin.]

To Lalla Romano Monti—Milan

Turin, 23 January 1963

Dear Lalla,

It was a great pleasure to get your letter. I was just about to write to you having learned only now from Natalia that you have been ill (I didn't know about this at all) and that you are now thankfully recovered. And now I have the wonderful fresh news that you have written another book. I am waiting impatiently for it. We will publish it as soon as possible with all the honors.[40]

As for the other women writers (although this is a category that does not exist for us: the only thing that counts for us is how good an author is, and whether they are male or female is as important as whether they are blonde or dark-haired), I don't think that there is anything this year that could "put you in the shade." Nobody knows anything about Morante's book except that she stopped work on it almost a year ago and has not yet started writing again.[41] Natalia has written a book which is not a novel but a totally special kind of work, about reminiscences and family memories, and I don't know when she might want to publish it, since *Le piccole virtù* (*The Little Virtues*) came out so recently.[42] There are no other major writers publishing with us this year, not even male ones, as far as I know.

So I'm waiting for your news.

Very best wishes

[Typed copy; in the Einaudi Archive, Turin.]

To Mateo Lettunich—New York

Turin, February 18th, 1963

Dear Mateo,[43]

HAPPY IN RECEIVING YOUR LETTER; HAPPY IN WRITING SOME answers I hope will be useful to the holy cause of your programs;[44] sorry in doing it with so much delay, because I'm always so busy that the free afternoon to answer quickly to correspondence is always rare.

I am doing a lot of things and finally writing. I'm well. I live a bit in Rome and a bit in Turin, I hope to come back to your country and I'll visit first Anita and you.

All my best.

(Italo Calvino)

What a question! The United States are a world. A world of which we in the Continent know everything that it is possible to learn from books, and our first visit is just to get a confirmation or a denial of our previous opinions. What I can say is that in the United States I didn't feel alone in the Lonely Crowd, wasn't persuaded by the Hidden Persuaders, would have liked to organize the Organization Men, found that the Ugly American does not mean the American.[45] So I actually discovered what I was expecting to discover.

I can say that I haven't wasted my time in your country: being completely free I've seen more America than any American (I'm not boasting) and, at the same time, I don't know any country better than yours, my own included. Of course, now, this direct experience of the United States makes me able to participate with more feeling of reality to the everyday European discussion: the good and the evil of "Americanization."

Since my visit, I gave interviews about my American impressions to the main Italian weeklies, wrote a series of about twenty articles for a weekly, and some for quarterlies and monthly magazines. My American experience is often recorded in my lectures. As for my editorial work, my knowledge of today's American literature and my contacts with the American literary world are of course enormously improved. And as for my personal creative work, may I talk of any influence? Not yet; that takes much more time.

1961: a tour of lectures in Switzerland; a tour of lectures in Norway, Sweden, Denmark; a trip in Spain (I'm a member of the Formentor Prize Jury); a trip to Germany for my publishing firm (München and Frankfurt for the Book Fair).

1962: a couple of trips to Paris, a trip to Spain (Formentor); a trip to London as a holiday.

I came back to my job as a literary adviser at Einaudi's publishing firm. Occasionally I wrote for magazines and for the movies. With Elio Vittorini I'm the editor of a literary quarterly *Il Menabò*. I'm a literary contributor of the Italian daily paper *Il Giorno*.
[Typed copy; in the Calvino Archive.]

To Michele Rago—Milan

Turin 21 March 63

Dear Michele,

I CAN'T TELL YOU HOW MUCH PLEASURE YOUR ARTICLE GAVE me.[46] Not only for the things you say about my story (I could not have wished for anything better), but because it marks a point of contact between your work and mine, between our trajectories. And also because it has made me pick up the thread of my discussion with you: for some time I had been bemoaning the fact that this had been interrupted—perhaps through my fault. And also because—though there's no need for me to say this—it is the *Unità* review.

Apart from what you say about my book, what struck me was your definition of the Neo-avantgarde, which considers a work as *the natural product of history* to the point where it becomes enclosed in a *vegetable condition*. That's true, that is the point of the link between avantgardism and historicism. Of course a certain *vegetality* in a natural product of the times is a necessary attribute in a work of art (even in the most labored works there has to remain that sense of spontaneous *felicitousness* without which a work of art would not be that and would just be a kind of act of the literary and intellectual will). But that's it, that is precisely the point: there is too often in the Neo-avantgarde a kind of vegetal voluntarism and not "vegetal felicitousness."

I hope to see you. The fact is that—in my general plan for an existence that was a bit less dispersive than the one I have been leading in recent years—I have cut out many things, and amongst these are also my frequent journeys and stays in Milan. And—if it is true that you have recently changed house—I no longer know where you live,* nor do I have your phone number. Write to me.

Best wishes and many thanks.

Italo

*no, they tell me you are still at the same place
[Handwritten; with the addressee.]

·

To Augusto Monti—Rome

Turin, 30 March 1963

Dear Monti,
YOUR LETTER CONTAINS THE FINEST CRITICAL COMMENT I have had on my little book; and the most complete.[47] I want to convey to you all my gratitude (and also to ask Caterina's pardon for the vocal effort I unwittingly put her to).

First and foremost I was pleased that you assigned it to the illustrious line of "essay-writing" in Italian literature (when I search for my own classics, I look for "books" not "novels"; I still don't bother much about "literary genres," despite the fact that Croce's ban against them has fallen by the wayside), because really I was also trying to write a "manual for the scrutineer," as you say.

You give a total synthesis of the book defining it as a "Touchstone," and it gives me satisfaction to see myself totally understood by you. I am even more interested in the analysis of "maturity," in other words this biography of . . . Amerigo Ormea that you develop from what you know of me.[48] What I can tell you is that this analysis applies to me only in the sense that it is what I *ought* to be. And the comparison with Pavese's experience gives a dramatic emphasis to what you say.

The discovery that I had a vocation in me to be a *teacher* astonished me. I had always thought that I was devoid of a pedagogical spirit. Might this be one of the gains of "maturity"?

Well then let's hope for the best also for what you say in the last part of your letter, about maturity in love. Many critics had already told me that the sections concerning the girl do not square with the rest of the book; but you make a bigger thing of it, in fact you turn it into a sermon which I cannot but accept, grumbling a little but basically agreeing with you.

Yours is a letter that has the length of an article, and I would like it to become one; without changing its epistolary character, perhaps without changing anything. Why don't you send it to a friendly journal like *Il Ponte* or *Belfagor*? I feel I can ask you this without wanting to seem like someone looking for public praise, because there has been praise (more than I could have wished for), but there are also criticisms expressed totally openly.

Your book has gone from Bobbio to Mila and now it is with Fonzi (who will look after the punctuation, the new paragraphs etc., all the refinements one misses when dictating something) and I will wait for him to return it to me.[49]

Warmest thanks (also to Caterina!), and all good wishes

[Typed copy; in the Calvino Archive and in the Einaudi Archive, Turin.]

To Aldo Camerino—Venice

Turin 21-5-63

Dear Camerino,

You are the nicest critic that literary history has ever known. Of all the reviews the one I was waiting for and was afraid of most—of this book that I knew was not made to suit your tastes—was yours.[50] And it was the best review I received. And I am proud of having "pulled it off" with you this time too. Of course the protagonist is fussy and boring and terribly ideological: but the ex-youngsters of my generation and even many more of the youngsters coming up now, are just like that, or even worse (because they are sure of everything and have no nuanced views). And I wanted to write the story of one of them (someone who was also myself at the same time, because characters work only if they are, in some sense, also self-portraits). In any case, just imagine what sort of stuff comes out with characters who are literati or aesthetes: good literature (works of art) can be created only with something that is different from literature (I don't believe much in works of art on the theme of art). Of course I do not intend to continue down this road. You are well aware that I like to change register each time, to alternate my fields of research.

I am writing this letter to you because I do not know if I will come to Conegliano. A week in Corfu on a literary prize jury, then another prize in Lausanne, as a prize-winner, I can't go on like this, the week after that two lectures in other cities.[51] Every now and again I realize how futile it is to waste so much time in official ceremonies. Ciao

Your Calvino

[Handwritten; in the Fondo Manoscritti del Centro di ricerca sulla tradizione manoscritta di autori moderni e contemporanei, University of Pavia.]

To Sylvia Poggioli—Cambridge (Mass.)

Turin, 5 June 1963

Dear Sylvia,

When we heard the news, in the consternation at the loss of a dear friend and collaborator, our first instinct was to contact you and your mother. But we did not know where you were, and the news about your mother's health made us want to wait.[52]

Now a mutual friend (Dante Della Terza) has written to me to say that you have both returned to Cambridge, that you are well and have shown great courage, and that your mother's condition has also improved. I wanted to write then at once to you, so you can also let your mother know, in order to convey all the affection that I have for Renato's memory and for you two.

I will never forget how much your father's friendship meant to me during my stay in the United States. Staying in touch with him as he worked (in the last few months we were in almost weekly correspondence) provided me with an example of inner richness, method and order, of his inexhaustible range of interests.[53]

Your father has left us an example of vital strength: his confidence in the creative spirit, in the perennial life of someone who has been able to express himself. This is the lesson we must look to in order to overcome the anguish of knowing that he is no longer with us.

I send you and your mother my most affectionate wishes for a speedy recovery. Giulio Einaudi joins me in these words of condolence and good wishes.

Yours ever,

[Typed copy; in the Einaudi Archive, Turin.]

To Antonella Santacroce—Sulmona

[San Remo,] 7-10-63

Dear Miss Santacroce,

I have a bad habit of letting the post I receive pile up for weeks and of reading it all at once. So it is only today that I had the pleasant surprise of reading your work which maybe (your letter is not dated) you sent me some time ago.

I like it very much, especially because I found it "similar," I mean similar to what it was my intention to do, and it is only if we find someone who confirms it to us that we can know whether we have succeeded or not.

You define, or rather represent, my "poetic world" in a way that is congenial and sympathetic, both in terms of imagination and in terms of my world of feelings and morality. In your analysis of this moral world you say things that it gives me great satisfaction to see understood, because in general critics do not understand or articulate these things: for instance, that the only "hero" for me is the man who "creates himself," that the lyrical-emotional core, the I-person in a word, in *The Non-Existent Knight* is Rambaldo, whereas the Knight and Gurdulù are side-themes (compared to that core), just like Trelawney or the Huguenots or the lepers in *The Viscount*.

Then there is the fact that "I do not allow myself certain confidences" with my characters: quite right, and this too is an original insight.

But perhaps the thing that interests me most is your observation that for "me the written page is a written page," and your emphasis on the problematics of writing in *The Knight*, on the relationship between the page and the narrated subject matter. (None of the critics has ever dwelt on this though it was the most modern aspect—contemporary with the problematics of the *nouveau roman*—and I have to say I was somewhat disappointed by this.) I am also glad that you are one of the few people who understands and appreciates the final switch between Bradamante and Suor Teodora.

I also find it nice that you reject my contemporary, semi-autobiographical stories. I say nice maybe because at this moment I am once more starting to feel the desire and nostalgia for the "fantastic," and once more feeling less keen on that other approach. But these are periodic oscillations.

Thank you, dear Antonella, and I hope to read your work again soon.

Italo Calvino

I would like your essay to be published. Have you sent it anywhere? Have you any plans or preferences for it? Since it talks about my work, recommending it to a journal is a bit embarrassing for me. The easiest thing for me to do is this: G. B. Vicari's *Il Caffè*, a Rome-based journal, not very famous but not bad either, actually wants to do an issue centered on my work, along with one of my texts and some critical writings on my books. And since he has asked me for this, I could in fact send him your essay.[54]
[Photocopy of the original handwritten letter; in the Calvino Archive.]

To *Paragone*—Florence

[Turin, 10–15 October 1963][55]

Sir,
I AM WRITING IN MY ROLE AS AN EDITOR IN THE EINAUDI PUBlishing house. I have been moved to write this letter by one of Claudio Gorlier's observations (in *Paragone* no. 164, pp. 115–16) on the translation of E. M. Forster's *A Passage to India*, published by Einaudi.[56] I do so not only to do justice to one of our ablest translators, Adriana Motti, but also to provide some general reflections on the duties of critics, coming at the question from the particular point of view of the publishing profession.

Italian publishers print foreign works in translations that are sometimes excellent, sometimes decent, sometimes flawed, sometimes disastrous. The reasons for this variety (which can be found amongst the output of just the one publishing house) are many. To be quite frank about it: amidst the febrile growth in capacity of the Italian publishing world today, not all translations can be excellent. This may be a minor evil as long as we are dealing with minor works, but it is a serious loss and waste when we are talking about a work of great literary value. So there is more of a need today than ever before for critics to enter into the merits of a particular translation. This need is felt by readers, who want to know to what extent they can give credit to the high quality of the translator and to the seriousness of the publisher's name. It is felt by good translators who lavish all their stock of scrupulosity and intelligence on a book and no one ever takes the slightest bit of notice. And it is felt by the people who work in publishing who want the successes to receive the plaudits they deserve, and who want amateurish performances to be ridiculed (one always hope that in a general age of severity that it will be not one's own stable but our rival's outfit that will lose), and think they have everything to gain if the choice and quality control of translators can come about with the collaboration of critics and in public.

Many of us are, therefore, pleased that this type of criticism is starting to come into vogue, and we are following it with interest. And at the same time we maintain that it ought to display unimpeachable technical responsibility. Because if this sense of responsibility is missing, it will only increase the confusion, and cause a sense of dismay in translators which quickly turns into a feeling that anything goes, and into a lowering of the general standard of translation. This is not the first time that we have heard a good translator say: "Yes, exactly, I give my all to solve problems that nobody has ever faced and that nobody will ever notice, and then critic X opens the book at random, his eye alights on a phrase he does not like, and probably without even checking the original, without wondering how else it might be translated, dismisses the entire translation in a couple of lines . . ." They are right to complain. An author always enjoys a range of verdicts: if he finds one critic who trashes his work, there will always be another one to defend him; whereas for the translator's work the judgments made by critics are so rare as to become judicial sentences with no possibility of appeal, and if someone writes that a translation is bad, this verdict enters into common currency and is repeated by all and sundry.

In fact it is not so much with Gorlier that I should have had this discussion as with Paolo Milano. Milano must be given great credit for being perhaps the only critic in the periodical press to dedicate on an almost regular basis a part (sometimes as much as a quarter) of his review to the merits and defects of the translation. He manages to do this with substantial examples despite the space constraints of a weekly magazine, and in such a way as to interest the reader and without any hint of pedantry. In this sense his is a model of criticism that meets the needs of today. Having said this, I have to add that several times I have found myself in disagreement with his judgments. I am sorry I do not have a run of *L'Espresso* to hand, and I do not want to cite from memory, but the fact is that he has slaughtered translations which did not deserve it, and has pardoned others which should have been roundly condemned.

The art of translating is not going through a good phase (either in Italy or elsewhere; but here let us restrict ourselves to Italy, which however, in this particular field, is certainly not the country that has most to complain about). The recruitment base, namely the young people who know a foreign language well or fairly well, has certainly increased. However, what is dwindling day by day is the number of those people who when they write Italian move with those essential gifts of agility and sure-footedness in the choice of words, economy of syntax, and sense of the various linguistic registers, in short with an understanding of style (in its double aspect of understanding the peculiarities of the writer to be translated, and of knowing how to come up with Italian equivalents in a prose that one reads *as though it had been thought up and written directly in Italian*): the very gifts in which the unique genius of the translator resides.

Along with these technical skills, moral skills are also becoming rarer: that kind of doggedness that is necessary to concentrate on digging in the same tunnel for months, a scrupulosity that is liable to disappear at any moment, a capacity for discernment that could suddenly become warped, start to drift, and become prey to hallucinations and distortions of one's linguistic memory, that obsession with perfection which inevitably becomes a sort of methodical madness, and has all the ineffable pleasure and wearying desperation of madness . . .

(The author of this letter is someone who has never had the courage to translate a book in his life; and in fact is hiding behind his lack of these precise moral gifts, or rather his lack of methodological and nervous stamina; but already, in his role as torturer of translators, he suffers enough, both at the torments of others and his own, and with good translations as well as bad.)

(Once upon a time writers did translations, especially young writers. Nowadays it seems as if they all have other things to do. And in any case, are we sure that the Italian of established writers would be any better? Sensitivity to style is becoming rarer and rarer. It could be said that the dwindling commitment to words in young writers and the diminishing appeal of translation as a calling are two sides of the same coin.)

In this situation where the true translator ought to be encouraged, supported, and valorized in every way, it is highly important that the periodical press and literary journals offer judgments on translated works. But if critics adopt the habit of dismissing a translation in a couple of words, without realizing how the most difficult passages have been worked out and how the stylistic features have been dealt with, without asking themselves if and what other solutions there might have been, then it would be better if they did not deal with translations at all. (Let's take the most common case: a minor error. Of course mistakes must be attacked. But that is not enough to form a judgment on a translation. A mistake can lurk in the pages of an experienced, authoritative translator who, everyone believes, has no need to have his translation checked by copy-editors, who corrects his own proofs etc., whereas possibly no mistakes are found in the first attempt by a first-time translator, for whom one has tried to correct every single comma, and which arrives at the printers corrected from top to bottom . . .)

A critical assessment of a translation must be conducted methodically, sampling extracts that are quite substantial and that can act as crucial litmus-tests. Moreover, this is an exercise which we would like to recommend not only to critics but also to all good readers: as is well known, authors are only read properly when they are translated, or one can compare the original text with its translation, or compare different versions in more than one language. (Another excellent method for arriving at a verdict: a three-way comparison between original text, Italian version, and a translation from another language.) A technical judgment rather than one based on taste: on this terrain the margins of subjective variation in tastes within which literary judgment always oscillates are much more restricted. If I maintain that Adriana Motti's translation is excellent and Gorlier only finds things to criticize in it, this is not a subjective question or one of "points of view." One of us must be wrong: him or me.

I quote Gorlier's passage, or rather parenthesis, where he deals with the translation:

> (Let us say [a] decent [version], but no more. In fact this *Passage to India* published by Einaudi leaves one slightly perplexed, starting from the

title itself, *Passaggio in India*, which sounds odd and ambiguous in Italian. And another thing: how is it possible for someone to use "*affatto*" in a negative sense [meaning "not at all"] when only a student from a poor school could be forgiven for it, or to write "*cosa*" instead of "*che cosa*?" [meaning "What?"], or not to know that in most cases "dissolved" means "*sciolto*" not "*dissolto*"?)

I will deal first with the question of the title, for which Adriana Motti is not responsible: sole responsibility here lies with the publisher. We discussed it for months before reaching a decision. In general, in Italy, it has been customary to make radical alterations in titles that are difficult to translate. This was the case up until about twelve years ago; but for some time now, thank goodness, everyone is agreed that not translating a title faithfully is really a highly arbitrary act. To have entitled it *Viaggio in India* (*A Journey to India*), however, would have served the book very badly indeed. It is not solely the fact that in these very months there have been three or four books with more or less this same title in bookshop windows, written by Italian authors who had been to India and had duly written up their little travelog. The fact is that in any case in Italian the title *Viaggio in qualche posto* (*A Journey to Somewhere*) immediately suggests the genre of travel literature (and is this not the case in English for the word "Travel"?). Well then? *Una gita in India* (*A Trip to India*)? *Un soggiorno in India* (*A Stay in India*)? These would have diminished or flattened its meaning somehow; they would have eliminated that hint of symbolic allusiveness that I think "Passage" has. And which the Italian *Passaggio* has too, since it is a word with many resonances—do we not say "*La vita è un passaggio*" (life is just a passage)? Gorlier says, "it sounds wrong"; and I feel that many think he is right. In my view, I have to say, *Passaggio* is a word I like enormously, also when it is used in other phrases, such as "*di passaggio*" (passing through), a lovely, typical Italian phrase. It sounds "ambiguous," Gorlier adds. Exactly: I wanted a word that contained an unrestricted range of meanings, an aura of symbolic ambiguity, corresponding precisely (as Gorlier instructs us very clearly) to the character of the book. However, I see that on this point everyone thinks I am wrong, and I have to give in. If the publisher wants to change the title in a future reprint, we will make amends. End of the self-defense of the title.

Gorlier finds no serious errors in the translation. (He uses substantial sections of it for all his quotations.) He makes three points concerning the translator's Italian, including the one about the word "*dissolto*" (dissolved). On p. 353 (since he does not give numbers for the incriminating pages, I had to go through all 355 pages of the book) what is in fact said is this: "*quando ebbe finito, lo specchio del paesaggio si era frantumato, il prato dissolto in farfalle*" (When he had finished, the mirror of the scenery was shattered, the meadow disintegrated into butterflies)'.[57] Would Gorlier have preferred: "*il prato sciolto in farfalle*" (the meadow melted into butterflies). I am sorry, but here Adriana Motti was perfectly correct to use "*dissolto*" (dissolved).

I too dislike "*affatto*" used on its own as a negative, though it does not bring out in me the schoolboy scandal evoked by Gorlier. On p. 247: "*Temo che per te sia molto scoraggiante.*" "*Affatto, non me ne importa.*" ("I'm afraid it's very upsetting for you." "Not the least, I don't mind.")[58] Could she have used "*Niente affatto*" or "*Per niente*"? Either would have produced a rhyme with "*sconvolgente*": this is the usual no-win situation translators face. Could she have tried "*Per nulla*"? Well, perhaps she was being (excessively) scrupulous about the proximity of a "*non*" that came immediately afterwards. In her letter of grievance to me, the translator stated: "Even in the Rigutini-Fanfani dictionary (Florence, Barbera, 1832, p. 32) the word 'affatto' is given with a negative sense with just a very gentle caution, which amounts almost to allowing it to be used." I am not a devotee of dictionaries: what counts for me is the victory of the internal harmony and logic of the phrase taken as a whole, even if this comes about with the little act of violence, the pull that the spoken language tends to impose on the rule. And the phrase in question, to my ears, sounds fine: the "*non*" of "*non importa*" impinges on "*Affatto*" anyway, embraces it. The spirit of Italian resides precisely in things like this: this is its unequaled richness, and its curse (since it makes Italian literature largely untranslatable) and its difficulty (woe betide anyone who thinks they can write ungrammatically without paying attention to ear and logic: only those to whom the difficult Grace of Language has been given can sin and still be saved!).

"*Cosa?*" for "*Che cosa?*" (What?). Here I really do lose patience. After all the work that creative literature has done to give written Italian the immediacy of a living language, and after all the movement of ideas which modern linguistics has stirred up in every field of culture making "language" an ensemble that is mobile and organic, with its mutual exchanges between the spoken and the written, its higher and lower registers, we have been convinced for some time now that the cultivators of puristic obsessions were confined to the Bouvards and Pécuchets of the rant columns of certain newspapers or weeklies. "*Cosa?*" is used regularly for "*Che cosa?*" and it is a sacrosanct rule to use it, because it is shorter, it helps eliminate a "*che*" (the repetition of "*che*" is the curse of every Italian who writes), it does not diminish the clarity of discourse, and above all it fits with the logic of simplifications that have taken place gradually over the centuries in Italian and other neo-Latin languages.

Before entrusting a translation to someone (I think I can speak collectively on behalf of the editors of the various publishing houses), we check primarily that their Italian has these very qualities of fluency and spontaneity and lack of pedantry or preciosity. What Gorlier is criticizing here is then precisely what we call "good writing," which is the sine qua non for being a translator.

For being a translator. The fact is that one can be a serious scholar, and a critic with clear understanding, and still "write badly." (I do not want to broach the thorny question of authors, some of them even great authors, who "write badly," since that would take us too far from our subject.) "Writing badly" means moving uneasily in a language, as in a jacket that is tight on the elbows, without freedom, without ready reflexes. Can one criticize an art critic for not knowing how to hold a paintbrush? Of course not. Similarly, we do not want to attack the literature scholar who, at the end of the very page in which he has been giving us lessons on language, writes "*contenuta dal risvolto*" (contained by the blurb)—is this a typo? Everything suggests otherwise—who writes "*sensibilizzarsi e acutizzarsi*" (to become sensitive and sharpened), that is to say someone who has no defense against the most evil—yes these certainly are the most evil—journalistic-bureaucratic brutalizations of the language. This person is devoid of that sparkle which at the moment when he falls comes to the aid of the sinner loved by the gods, and flashes before him, in a halo of light, the one perfect word "*acuirsi*" (to become sharp)! before darkness falls again. If his essays are sustained by robust ideas, they will be written and appreciated even though badly written. But he has to beware of one temptation: transforming this linguistic unease of his (which is not even a venial flaw, but is one of the infinite peculiarities of the individual) into a misguided love for an abstract, immobile language, which he imagines, because of its very immobility, can be possessed also by him. Love of language is something else and stems from a totally different aptitude of the mind, and throbs with a very different and more acute neurosis.

(This is my official pronouncement, in an indulgent key. In secret, and in silence, I give vent to my rage when I see words, the raw material of every literature, being used with such awkwardness, laboriousness, and insensitivity by new critics, and I wonder what can have pushed these young people into studies that are so difficult and uncongenial to them. And in secret I second the view recently expressed by Emilio Cecchi, in the *Corriere della sera*, of 4 October 1963: "In a critical essay the quality of the prose is a guarantee of the truth and vitality of the impressions and ideas expounded—in fact it is an intrinsic part of those impressions and ideas." And secretly I dream that soon, once the kingdom of literature has been divided between the two opposing factions of traditionalists and innovators, who are united by a common and equal insensitivity to words, I will be able finally to write works that are clandestine, pursuing an ideal of modern prose to hand down to the generations which eventually, God knows when, will understand . . . But look, I have strayed beyond the confines I had set myself: this was meant just to be a letter from a member of the editorial staff replying to critics. I will go back to my subject.)

Gorlier takes publishers to task for neglecting or delaying the entry into Italy of first-rate Anglo-Saxon authors and publishing instead young second-rate writers. The names he gives for the first group of authors are nearly all writers who are gradually being published by a range of Italian publishers, writers mostly with a subtle stylistic commitment, and for whom we should wish only that people wait until they have genuinely good translations before publishing them. (Why so many authors have not been published before is not difficult to understand: the productive and assimilative capacity of Italian publishing has increased only in the last few years. It is natural that in this new climate, the latest crop of writers from abroad should enjoy the lion's share, and that the recovery of those that have been neglected in previous decades should proceed more slowly.)

As examples of second-rate authors who have in fact been published, Gorlier cites Purdy and Sillitoe. "A Sillitoe regularly appears." Well. So far only Sillitoe's first book has been translated, *Saturday Night and Sunday Morning*, a good novel, interesting, not run-of-the-mill. After it four other books (by my reckoning) by Sillitoe have been published in Britain, which have not yet come out here; some of them (some are very good, others less so) will come out in Italy, without excessive "regularity" but also without any intention of neglecting or underestimating this author.

If Sillitoe is appreciated and translated all over the world, Purdy's case is different. He still has not enjoyed success in America, neither with the critics nor with the reading public. He is to a certain extent a discovery of ours. It was one of the finest and least indulgent palates in Italian publishing (who, thanks to his skeptical snobbery, has now converted to mass culture, and flown off to interplanetary shores) that homed in on Purdy out of the thousands of writers of American short stories, all equally decent and witty but devoid of exceptional flashes. Purdy is a small discovery of ours of whom we are quietly proud. We have not yet published *Malcolm*, his darkest and most delicate book, but we hope to do so soon.

In short, it seems to me that Gorlier sees the publisher's duty as being that of the person who records the values consecrated in the various world literatures, the hierarchies established by age and reputation, and transports them here lock, stock, and barrel. We, however, see it differently: what enthuses and amuses us in the job of publishing is in fact just this very establishing of perspectives that do not coincide with the most obvious ones. Thus, while we listen to our sources of information and foreign critics and the blandishments of publishers, we are always careful not to be taken in by other people's evaluations, but to choose on the basis of *our own* reasoning, and to ensure that our choices have repercussions on an author's reputation at an international level. Choosing foreign books is a two-way exchange: a foreign literature gives us an author and we give it our choice, our confirmation, which is also a "value" to the very extent that it is the outcome of different tastes and a different tradition.

Having got to this point, I must say: just as a translation must not be judged on the basis of a few isolated lines, even less must a critical essay be judged by this parameter. And Gorlier's observations on Forster's book are extremely rich and stimulating and sharp. And I find very fair his critique of the blurb of the Einaudi translation, which in fact diminishes the value of the book. The art of the blurb is also a difficult art: for an important book and one which resists reductive definitions (as Gorlier's whole essay proves) nobody wants to take on a twenty-line presentation, when even the pages of the most learned experts rarely have the necessary force.

While I am on the subject, I would like to be allowed a final digression, not aimed at Gorlier, with whom I agree on this point, but at critics in general. We have seen that it has become almost de rigueur for critics and reviewers to organize their piece around a dialog with the publisher's blurb or publicity strip (or for the laziest and shyest, to paraphrase the blurb). In short, the publisher's blurb has a power which seems to me excessive: that of setting the parameters for critical discussion. Critics might agree with it or disagree, but discussion never gets away from those themes, from those ideas. You might argue: it is only a pretext to start the discussion. Yes, but the real object of criticism, the book, seems to me to end up being overlooked. We lose the true sense, the real thrill of every critical bull-fight, the critic taking on the book-bull, the author-bull by the horns. Instead of battling with the author, the critic fights . . . with whom? At best with that new institution in our literary world, the "Series Editor," but more often simply with the anonymous "Editor," which means those who work in the press office and in publicity. These are usually people who are on the ball and up to date, but who tend through a natural sort of *déformation professionelle* to simplify and take a rough and ready approach to things. It seems to me that as far as readers are concerned too, it would be more instructive to teach them instead to approach the book by opening it at the first page. So much so that I almost start thinking: might it not be more instructive to publish books that are bare of blurbs, bare and spare, as happens (or used to happen) in France?

I apologize for the length of this letter. People are continually writing about literature, but these matters from the publishers' shop floor, as it were, are never discussed, yet they occupy so much of our time and worries. That was why I had so much to say. Thank you.

Italo Calvino

[Published, with the title "Sulla traduzione [On Translation]," in *Paragone. Letteratura*, 168 (December 1963), pp. 112–18; later in *S*, II, pp. 1776–86.]

To CLAUDIO VARESE—FERRARA

[Turin, Autumn 1963]

Dear Varese,

I HAVE ONLY NOW READ *LA NUOVA ANTOLOGIA*. AT LAST A REVIEW which is a serious examination![59] I am extremely grateful to you for it. You homed in, the first person to do so, on the "real theme" of the story, and that reference to *The Non-Existent Knight*, which I had never thought about, is also absolutely right. And you are the first person to have defined what Lia is doing in this tale, an element that the majority of critics rejected as extraneous to it, while I am convinced that without it there would have been no story. And I am also inclined to agree with you on the limitations of the tale: all I know is that I tried to gain on one side what I was well aware of losing on the other. Do I run the risk of "mistrusting fantasy"? For so many years I ran the risk of entrusting myself to it without any caution: I am trying to restore the balance.

On the parentheses: you provide an in-depth analysis of them, which leads you to conclude that—since I use parentheses in so many different senses—I am slightly lacking in rigor. Now this "need" for parenthesis that I had in this story (*need*, not a stylistic option, which would be a really overused kind of virtuosity) came from the desire to see more and more levels in every concept and thought. In other words, this links with what you say so well after that, when you talk about the research of a "semantic" nature that underlies this kind of writing. On pp. 14–15, in order to explain the word "Communist," I needed a very long sentence in which all the meanings were articulated in a syntactic structure where logic and complexity were preserved together. That is why I began using parentheses and then I ended up continuing to need them.

I am sorry but I cannot come to Ferrara. I want to reduce to the minimum this frittering away of the weeks in official ceremonies, even though each one has very nice and worthy motives and leads to pleasant meetings. This week Einaudi managed to send me as far as Modena. Sorry about this, but now I have to finish this season's activities: I will come some other year to Ferrara. Best wishes, and thanks once more.

Italo Calvino

[Handwritten, undated; with the addressee, and a copy in the Calvino Archive. The hypothetical date offered is based on the opening phrase "I have only now read . . . ," and on the mention in the penultimate sentence of "some other year," which suggests the end of the year.]

To Sebastiano Addamo—Lentini (Syracuse)

Turin, 10 December 1963

Dear Addamo,

Your excellent article (I am now reading a clipping from *La Sicilia* of 27 November) gives me satisfaction for two sets of reasons.[60] First, because it confirms what I was trying to express and communicate (the style, the relationship with the world as the unifying element, the involvement with history and historicism, the dialectic between imagination and reason, the "reality that is composed of works and fierce, grim energy, in which intelligence also can be involved": all this could not be better expressed). Second, because it tells me things I had never thought about and which give me pause for thought (that nothing is more distant from me than destiny; that I do not have a *universe*; that I know about detachment but I don't know about wisdom—damn, just when I thought I was aiming at wisdom! But I am actually afraid you might be right: no, I'm not afraid, I am convinced of it because all this forms part of an image of myself which sounds right. That I want to represent this world not the world: that's true! That I do not reject this world even if I distort it or mock it but I accept it: in this too you have been able to understand me perfectly).

Absolutely right about the symmetry between *The Argentine Ant* and *Smog*: that was part of the idea. As for *A Plunge into Real Estate* and *The Watcher*, I was not thinking of either symmetry or opposition, but I am glad that some can be found. (Or rather, I was well aware there was a common denominator: the protagonist; and I am glad that they turned out to be two characters that are a bit different and to some extent contrasting.)

In short, this is an excellent critical essay, one of those rare occasions when one realizes that being a writer is a worthwhile job, one that provides genuine satisfactions, over and above the trivial, ambiguous ones connected with a "success" which leave one feeling cheapened and dubious.

Thank you.

Italo Calvino

[Typed on Einaudi headed paper, with autograph signature; with the addressee.]

To Eva Mameli Calvino—San Remo

Havana 27 January 1964[61]

Dear Mamma,

This afternoon I went to Santiago de las Vegas. It was lovely and very moving.[62] I had already got them to phone some days ago from the Casa de las Americas to Doctor Roig, to say I was coming. Roig cannot speak on the phone because he is deaf, but he had been informed at once by Beba, who is the daughter (now I don't want to get these names wrong) of Luis Gonzales, and Roig was moved and happy and wanted me to go to see him immediately, but then decided it was better to plan the visit when it was a normal working day, to see the Center functioning. We went today, Monday, Chichita and I, along with a guy from the Casa de las Americas. Roig had already been waiting for half an hour to greet me at the door of the Center's main building. He is eighty-six and is considered by everyone to be "el gran sabio de Cuba"; the celebration of his 85th birthday was a huge national celebration, with Fidel making a speech. He is in fine form, he took me all round the Center, he's just a little bit hard of hearing and has a bit of difficulty coming down stairs. A calm person, possessed of great humanity, he exudes serenity and kindness, but also confidence in his drive and passion for showing the plants. He immediately asked about you—as has everybody who knew you—and before I leave he wants to give me some seeds for you and the new edition of the *Diccionario Botánico*. He immediately took me to where our house was (it was destroyed by the cyclone in 1926) near the long avenue of royal palms, planted by Mario Calvino. (This is an almost legendary point of reference here: I constantly heard people repeating "planted by Calvino," "built by Calvino," "introduced into the country by Calvino"). Nowadays the place where our house was and the row of buildings next to it has instead a lawn and a great pile of *Conjea tomentosa*, an extremely tall, endless bush of lilac flowers.[63] Beyond that there is still the building they call the Club. The Center buildings, built of brick, extend—if I've got it right—as far as before, with the big patio in the middle. There to meet me apart from Juan Roig and Beba was Dr Julian Acuña, who in your days was a student whom Dad chose and launched on scientific work, and who worked with you, and who now—they say—comes immediately after Roig as one of the main figures in Cuban culture. Also there were Adela Fortun (I think she's the widow of Fortun), Sotero, the daughter of Agustín Casada (now I hope I'm not getting confused from my hurried notes taken at this first meeting), and the analyst of the Departamento de Botánica, Teodoro Cabrera. The people that accompanied me throughout the whole visit were Roig, Acuña, and the enthusiastic Beba, who had come with an album of photos. They immediately started to talk about the surprise they wanted to give El Cubano, and so this legendary figure El Cubano began to take shape, the person you trusted totally, and they showed me photos of him as a young man. That was how they prepared me for the meeting with this mythical character. In the meantime two old workers came up: Rafael Amador—a funny chap, a mulatto or Indian, who was taken on at the Center by Dad, and who went off to prepare a bunch of very beautiful tropical flowers, remembering that Dad did that whenever women came to visit the Center—and Juan Casada, an employee, and José, another employee. We did the round of all the old people at the Center: old Santamaria, very nice and funny, we came across him as he was shaving, with his face covered in soap. The minute we mentioned Dad, everyone remembered him exclaiming "Sacramento!" Roig says that with those two words alone, "Sacramento!" and "macché!" Dad was able to express everything, since he used them both to express enthusiasm and disapproval. Everyone remembers you and sends fondest greetings: the first thing they did was to take me to see the herbarium, which is now much bigger than when you were working on it: it now has 150,000 exemplars. The *Flora de Cuba* is nearly finished. Then we got back into the car to go to the house where El Cubano worked, but they hadn't said anything to him, so he would not get too worked up. When El Cubano started to work with Dad, he did not know how to read or write, but he was famous for his extraordinary memory. He works at I don't know how many things, amongst which is vanilla essence, which Dad began to grow at the Center and which is all round this house or laboratory or nursery at the end of the field where he spends his days. They called him, he came out, Beba told him to prepare himself for a big surprise and to guess who I was. And then she pretended to pull on a goatee beard and said: "Sacramento!" El Cubano immediately said: "Calvino!" or rather "Carbino!" and realized who I was. "*El hijo de Carbino*!" He is a very handsome old man, with a sweet smiling Indian face, incredibly serene like all of them here at the Center. He was so moved and surprised that he did not know what to say; he started showing me plants that had been introduced here by Dad and bottles of vanilla essence. And then he insisted that we went to his house to meet his wife who had seen me as a child, and he came into the car with us. The old house where El Cubano lives is at a spot in the field that is thickest with vegetation and fruit, with an enclosure where they cultivate roses. When Old Rita found out that I was "*El hijo de Carbino y de Eva*," she alternated "Sacramento!" with "Alabado!" and "Maria Virgen!" Everyone also asked about Flori, some of them even remembered his name, in short they have always kept the memory of our family alive. Old Rita is very devout, especially to Santa Barbara and San Lazaro, and every corner of their three rooms is taken up with a little altar crowded with statuettes and saints and shells and lamps and flowers and various votive offerings: a welter of objects from an indescribable Catholic-pagan cult; as well as the doll and cradle and toys of a daughter who died twenty-five years ago. All in all, a rural Cuban house which could not be more typical, where everything is in very vivid colors, like the flora in which the house is immersed. El Cubano made us drink star-fruit wine, took us to see the plant it comes from (Averroa carambola), and gave us two of the huge yellow fruits; and he took us to see the cocoa plant, and orchids growing on trees. After taking El Cubano back to his place of work, Roig and Acuña took me to see other plants: lychees, drachaenas, pochote trees, bixa orellana with its red velvety fruit, holmskioldia sanguine with very complicated little flowers. The plants that Roig is keenest on are two exemplars, one male, one female, of Bonete (Jacarantia mexicana) which is a kind of boba fruit. (I have seen boba or papaya fruit ever since I came and I often eat and drink it.) In the field where our house once stood, Chinese plants with a little white flower grow spontaneously ("sinensis" or some name like that): they have come here mysteriously, maybe seeds mixed with other seeds. Then we took Roig to the door of his house in the pueblo. And still the indefatigable Beba insisted that we go and see her mother who had held me in her arms when I was a baby (her father died two years ago). This Beba person is five years older than me and has always lived and grown up at the Center. Her mother too, with great enthusiastic cries of "Ave Maria!" and "Maria Santissima!" remembered you and Dad. And her house too was full of saints and madonnas and little altars. Then Beba went to gather some torrancas.

This letter has been entirely about my return to the place I was born. I will tell you about the other things I saw in Cuba in another letter.

Abrazos y besos

Italo

If you want to send a telegram, always use the Casa de las Americas address because we might change hotels. In seven or eight days we will be leaving for Oriente.[64]

[Handwritten; in the Calvino Archive.]

To Franco Lucentini—Turin

Turin, 20 March 1964

Dear Lucentini,

I AM NOT A PASSIONATE PERSON. HATRED, RESENTMENT AT INsults, wounded dignity, none of that is my cup of tea. I never know quite how I should react in such cases: for instance, when a friend suddenly sends me a letter full of insults. I think one ought to feel mortally offended, in other words one should arouse in oneself a passion that is the same as or greater than that which determined the offensive act. I can't do it. Or should one stay quiet, shaking one's head at such irrational outbursts? That would be an attitude of superiority which I don't think I can take on. I am sure I am more rational than you, but knowing that I too have my fifteen minutes of irrationality, I cannot ignore the failure of a rational man as though it was something that did not concern me.

So I am writing you a letter too.[65] I do so to prove to you that this whole outburst of yours is wrong, in flagrant contradiction with the clear, precise mentality that you often show you have, and that this is to be considered a one-off episode, a mistake, so it does not have any real impact, either for you or for me.

On Monday evening, at your request, we discussed the preface which you co-authored and I expressed views which were opposite to yours. As a result, the next day you wrote me a letter full of insults. When it's put like that, you too will recognize this, that this is absurd. Let us try to understand more clearly what this is about.

The preface in question is a very aggressive piece of writing, in many senses, written deliberately to stir up polemics and disagreements. You both wanted to do it that way, so naturally you were not expecting smiles and compliments all round. From your reaction one might say that you thought, on the contrary, that I would be able to countersign your work. Why?

I had expressed a positive opinion on the pages I read in the sample, that is true. And on the basis of those pages I had judged F. Pivano's reaction exaggerated and irrelevant. I then read, at your suggestion (I remember a telephone conversation we had), the whole preface to the volume. And I changed my opinion. Is this change of mine justifiable?

Before starting this letter I reread and compared the two texts. (Maybe diligence is my way of being passionate: that is why I manage to be diligent only in odd, very brief moments.) And I can confirm: my change of mind is perfectly justifiable. The cuts in the sample were perfect (those—I would say—that I would have advised you to make if you had let me read the preface in manuscript, like when we worked together). And not only the longer, "ideological" cuts of pp. v–vi, x–xi, xiii–xiv, but also the tiny cuts where you removed expressions such as "no one will be so bovine as to be either indignant or happy about this," which are enough to give the work a peremptory and intimidating tone, the kind of tone that makes me say: "Hang on, if you put it like that, I'm not happy."

The point is that as long as you are writing about a particular dimension of American literature, which the two of you have very clearly identified (and you are the first to do so) and you represent its philosophy with a brilliant, paradoxical discussion, and you also include polemical points against the literature of the 1920s and '30s, against the writers that "represent novelty," against committed literature, this fits in with our common interest in outlining literary tendencies that are different from what one might expect, and in finding the weaknesses in past and present movements. Things are different if you put in front of me a kind of literary manifesto, if you place this image of Mr Smith as an *exclusive* image of what literature has to be today, putting me up against a choice: either you are with us or with the little local paper and the provincial intellectual!

In that case no, I have to be with the little local paper and the provinces. If every time the subject comes up I have always repeated that I was born into the world of literature through the America that you condemn (Pavese's and Vittorini's America), this must mean that that image is still important for me, however much it is open to all kinds of criticism. And the same goes for the fact that I continue to maintain that I have never loved any writer as much as Hemingway, even though his character can be vulgarized. And the same can be said about my links with committed literature: I went through it, I criticized it, I still criticize it, but I still cannot move except in that direction, basically that's all I have ever done. And I prove my detachment from the current literary climate by restating that I am a disciple and partner of the most isolated man in Italian literature: Vittorini. Otherwise what is the point in my putting my name alongside his on *Il Menabò*? Naturally the journal remains almost entirely his, and I can't always have a dialog with him, but I have confidence in him because I know that he always ends up by moving in the right direction, that his general idea of literature will never be impoverished or restricted. Furthermore, moving from the great optimist to the great pessimists, to those who are anguished by the atomic threat or mass culture or revolutionary morale, I am always at odds with these people, but I feel the need to listen to them, to reflect on what they say, they are people who count for me as a constant term of comparison: here too my position is different from yours.

I am well aware that having been born and having grown up under these auspices has led me to do many stupid and pointless things as well, but it has also saved me from many useless mistakes, first and foremost that of chasing after "legibility" and "bravura" as decisive values. This argument is the key point of your preface (in the *editio major*) and you on Monday evening dwelt on it considerably. And I didn't say anything to you because if I'd said to you that I don't believe that one can judge literature with that criterion, you would have asked me: by what criterion, then? And I would only have been able to answer with things that might seem obvious or pompous, but which in the end are the things I usually write when I try to put my ideas about literature in order.

So if we are in the realm of professions of faith, how could I say that I am on the side of Mr Smith? That would be like having two different roles in a play. It seems to me that it was to be expected that I would not be in agreement with your preface. Did you not write it deliberately so as not to be in agreement with anyone?

But in your letter I see that you were offended above all by some things I said. The first is my point about the panning you might expect. When I had only read the specimen, I was astonished that Pivano had brought up Vittorini's *Americana*.[66] I said to you, I remember, that time on the phone: what does *Americana* have to do with it? Yours is a tendentious anthology like all your others, with a whimsical preface: that this is not *American Literature* as we normally understand it, everyone is well aware. Afterwards, reading the note to your preface I saw that it was you who had brought in *Americana*, and along with it the claim that you cover American literature of the last twenty years. No, I'm afraid this will not stand up. You could expect to be panned not only because of your "ideological" polemic, where you fired blindly at everyone in all directions, but also from the point of view of historical exactness, of "how things really are." What I said to you along those lines on Monday evening was thus something predictable and not such as to merit your reaction.

Another statement that offended you: that Fruttero's influence was felt more than yours. You retort: "What rubbish is this? Where are the texts showing a previous critical personality of mine that I have apparently betrayed?" There may not be any writings or discourses [showing it], but for me you are the Borges and Robbe-Grillet man, the one who is always looking for a way for science and literature to come together, you were the one always making plans for a "cosmic literature."

This particular kind of absolutism that you pursued with daring gambles is less in evidence here. Only the odd quote from "your" authors manages to imply what the majority of the preface tends to deny: that there must exist a possibility of a literature that develops other images, other dimensions of the world.

Instead, in these pages what one hears is pure Fruttero. He too has few works and discourses to his name but he has a personality that we have seen develop and acquire a very clear outline: the demystification of all literary myths, the anti-intellectual snobbery, his preference for not doing rather than doing things through trial and error, the certain pleasure in a good artisan product, the only sure ethic of giving something to the reader *pour son argent*. The fact that all this stemmed ultimately from André Gide—from some facet of Gide—is something I had never reflected on and in this sense the preface is a wonderful literary autobiography by our friend.

In short, one can talk of a well-defined and new literary personality for both of you, as you are both people who know how to combine various experiences into a single line, you want what you want, and exclude everything else. (If only I could say the same about myself! Instead driven by the desire to understand and incorporate, I end up getting involved in too many things. But of course I don't have the temperament of the great rigorous writers; and in any case it is not up to me to define myself.) The vast terrain mapped out in common by you two is dictated above all by the ruthlessness of what you exclude. In the preface to the *Fantasmi* one could hear more Lucentini (with all the stuff about Pliny) than Fruttero;[67] here we certainly hear more Fruttero. I hope not only for the development of both your personalities, but also for the development of an internal dialectic in your collaboration.

At this point I could conclude: that everything I have said is right, or rather: it's what is right is what I say; that therefore, whether you think it is right or wrong, it is impossible for you to be offended because one cannot be offended by what cannot exist in any other way; that being unable to be offended by this, your reaction and your letter were—like everything else that does not fit into a logical scheme—something incidental; that as a result you don't have to repent or feel any remorse for this (far from it) but simply regard it as irrelevant, something that almost didn't happen, which is the way I look at it too.

Goodbye.[68]

[Typed copy with autograph corrections; in the Calvino Archive.]

To Mario Boselli—Genoa

[Turin, 1964]

Dear Boselli,

What I want to write to you is not so much my opinion on the article that you had the goodness to dedicate to the language in my story *Smog* (*Nuova Corrente*, 28–29, 1963), but rather a series of reflections on stylistic criticism which your essay prompted in me.[69] I should warn you that I have no theoretical training in this area and so my notes are dictated only by empirical common sense which might be methodologically dangerous, and by that wholly particular and subjective experience that one has of a text when one is the person who has written it.

I have been helped by the fact that I recently reread *Smog*, a story written six years ago, rereading it very carefully along with my French translator, and revising the translation. It was hard work. All human languages have something in common, even Finnish and Bantu, but there are two which totally prevent you from establishing any equivalence, and these are Italian and French. What is thought in Italian cannot in any way be represented in French: you have to rethink it from scratch, using a formulation that will by its very nature not admit all the meanings of the Italian original or will admit others which the Italian had not foreseen. As far as I am concerned, this was a chance to really *read* what I had written, to understand the intention behind every syntactic twist and every lexical choice, and to decide finally whether there really existed or not a thread, a necessity, a sense in the way I write. After a few weeks of this work, which was carried out on a number of stories, I managed to find out many things about the way I write: things positive and negative. Naturally it's not my job to tell you this: it's not up to me to tell the critics what to say. But now, heartened by this experience, as they say, I shall try to deduce from it some general reflections that may be useful for our discussion.

Your essay begins with a list of the series of stylistic features you found in *Smog*. The first thing to do in this type of analysis, I would say, is to establish for each feature the context in which it occurs, in other words to establish whether it is peculiar:

only to the work being studied;
or to the author in the whole of his oeuvre;
or if it extends to a whole literary school, tendency or period;
or whether it can be found in all the literature of that time and place.

For instance, it is obvious that when you put as the first stylistic feature of my story "obedience to the rules of traditional syntax," you are not saying anything that characterizes my work, since everyone who has been to junior school has studied syntax, and every day one reads books and papers written, for good or ill, using that particular syntax. In practical terms what you are saying is that I do not do automatic writing or stream of consciousness, writing styles that are very rare in Italy, at least in 1958, the year when the story was written. But let's start reading the story. First sentence: "Era un periodo che non m'importava niente di niente, quando venni a stabilirmi in questa città (That was a time when I didn't give a damn about anything, the period when I came to settle in this city)."[70] You see how here a whole discussion opens up about what is meant by traditional syntax in Italian literature from halfway through the twentieth century, a discussion very rich in history and allusions which this first sample of syntax already presents you with.

But let us turn to the second feature in your list: "use of a rather impoverished and unadorned lexis, in any case chosen from the least literary diction." Here you touch on an important point, because the choice of the "impoverished and unadorned," of the "least literary" in terms of diction, and indeed in terms of everything regarding expression, the "downbeat" tone—as you say later—full of "greyness and squalor": all these elements characterize (programmatically, I would say) a broad swathe of contemporary Italian literature. This would be a wonderful topic for an essay: "The 'grey tone' in contemporary Italian literature," which would move from the stylistic to the level of the imagination and from this to the psychological tone and to moral commitment. Of course such an article would find its most obvious and obligatory example in Moravia, indeed it ought to define the extent of a "Moravianism" that has never been charted by our literary cartographers. And on the other hand it would have to situate the different greyness of the Tuscan writers, with Bilenchi's rigor at the forefront, and after him Cassola's (I remember an excellent short essay by Bassani, some years ago, on Cassola's grey, "railway-worker" language). And what would still have to be defined would be other, equally extreme poetics of reductive language: Natalia Ginzburg's, for instance. Only when you have sorted out this geography of the grey style, and situated it for example with respect to the coloring of dialect, in the two opposing directions of dialect as the backbone of the language (from Verga to Pavese) and of plurilingualism (from the Scapigliatura to Gaddism) and seen what the relations might be between the grey area and these which are the most colorful areas today; only when you have decided in what context Bassani's writing, for example, has to be considered (his enveloping the most trite expressions of bourgeois language in a kind of continuous falsetto which takes second place to the "high" writing of the thread of his discourse, a falsetto which could in its own way be another kind of coloring) and before him Soldati's; only when you have completely defined the terms to use and the area and the data, only then can you go on to examine this particular case.

Consequently I would divide up your articulation of the second element into three propositions:

(a) there exists a vast area of Italian literature whose stylistic ideal moves toward a bare, impoverished language;

(b) if you take his oeuvre as a whole, Calvino is distant and indeed extraneous to this kind of poetics (give examples);

(c) yet in the story *Smog* he appears to approach this style. In what way?

And here the analysis of this text can start, that is the examination and classification of the various lexical and stylistic choices.

We have already cited above the opening sentence, very much the spoken language and full of colloquialisms. A little further on we find the phrase: “il nervoso” (his nerves [grow taught]). If we started with, let’s say, Moravia as a paradigm, we realize that with these examples we are already a good bit further on, in terms of characterization and coloring: we are already more in Pavese territory. And a sentence like this, at the start: “Per uno sbarcato dal treno, si sa, la città è tutta una stazione” (To a young man who has just got off the train, the city—as everyone must know—seems like one big station),[71] reminds us of certain predictable, compact, short-range images that were typical of Pavese.

But already in the third line there was this proposition: “Di stabilità non avevo alcun desiderio” (I had no desire to be settled in any sense),[72] which took us toward a loftier, more reflective tone; and in the lines that follow we find: “fluido, stabilità interiore, squallide, frantumato” (flowing, inner stability, squalid, fragmented), in other words we are moving more and more toward a critical, literary vocabulary.

It seems to me that the only solution is to fall back on a formulation like this (which is valid, I believe, for many of my stories but probably also for many other authors who have nothing to do with me): a consistent style, with an elasticity that allows it to reach peaks of loftier, lyrical or essayistic language without altering its consistency, and with frequent use of the pedal of the spoken language and of colloquialism, which is also used (and this is certainly intentional) to suggest nonchalance and contrast.

Using this sort of formulation you can account for a sentence such as this, which seems to me to be a fairly typical sample: “Lavoro nuovo, città diversa, fossi stato piú giovane o mi fossi aspettato di piú dalla vita, m’avrebbero dato slancio e contentezza” (A new job, an unfamiliar city—had I been younger or had I expected more of life, these would have pleased and stimulated me).[73] Basically the entire analysis could be reduced to this sentence: within it you find all the possible movements of the various levels of language used in the story.

At this point, I would no longer be happy with the sampling of random expressions where elements of conscious choice mingle with unconscious choice and things that are not dictated by choice at all. (Maybe for the scholar these all have the same significance, but as far as I am concerned it seems strange for me to watch you put under the lens of your microscope with equal zeal some particles to which I entrusted all the secret treasures of expression and others where I placed no expressive intentionality at all but which are there solely because I wanted to say that thing and nothing else.) And I would then move on to the examination of more complete and compact blocks of writing, in other words what I would call "image-writing" blocks which are actually the *more intensely written* bits, whether long or short.

In every piece I write, I believe, one can see parts that are *more written* and parts that are *less written*, the former where the commitment to writing is at its maximum and the latter which are like bits that have been merely drawn beside bits that are painted. (This, I believe, happens to me just as it does to all other writers, except for Flaubert—and even there I wouldn't swear to it—and to Manzoni, who is a totally different case; naturally this has not got anything to with Croce's distinction between "poetry" and "structure," indeed it could be the opposite in some cases.)

The written page is not a uniform surface like a piece of plastic; it is more like the cross-section of a piece of wood, in which you can see how the lines of the fibers run, where they form a knot, where a branch goes off. I believe that the duty of criticism is also—or perhaps is primarily—to study these differences in the written text: to examine those parts that are "more written" and those that are "less written."

Now in these more written parts there are some I call *written very small* because when writing them it happens that (I write with a pen) my handwriting becomes very small, with *o*'s and *a*'s that have no hole in the middle, and are reduced to tiny points; and there are others that I call *written big* because here instead my handwriting becomes broader, with *o*'s and *a*'s where you could put your finger in the loop.

These parts *written very small* I would say are those where I tend toward a verbal density, toward the minutely descriptive. For instance, the description of the cloud of smog (*I racconti*, p. 547) or the window in the boss's office (p. 552) or the gala evening that turns into an image of destruction (p. 560), or the brasserie that contrasts with the mist outside (p. 544).[74] When examining these bits, you will see that in terms of verbal density, striving for lexical precision etc. etc., we are further than ever from the definition etc. etc. And all this descriptive minuteness etc. etc. tends to configure (as in other books by Calvino anyway, etc. etc.) not so much images as kinds of abstract visions or rather etc. etc.

In short, sort it out yourself, I don't want to know anything about it. The only thing I can tell you is that I suspect that it is from that kind of approach, precisely through the examination of my writing, that one can reach some understanding of the ultimate meaning of what I write, if there is one.

The parts *written big* on the other hand are those which tend toward verbal rarefaction. For instance, very brief landscapes, almost lines of verse: "Era autunno; qualche albero era d'oro" (It was autumn; some of the trees were golden, p. 523, a passage cited by you too).[75]

There are many of these brief landscape descriptions also in the *Difficult Loves* stories which are stylistically and conceptually very close to *Smog*, and these are the points that gave me most trouble with the French translation, because when you translate them nothing stands out. In those cases, in order to explain to my translator what I meant, I started quoting Leopardi: "e chiaro nella valle il fiume appare" (and clearly in the vale the river appears),[76] and improvising lectures on the importance of the individual word in Italian lyric poetry from Dante and Petrarch onward; all things that when you are in Paris you can get away with but when you get back to Italy you no longer have enough of a brass neck.

All in all, the outline could be this: the great stream of verbal rarefaction in twentieth-century Italian literature—both in prose and verse—somehow also runs through what I have written. In the stories under consideration this is accompanied and contrasted with an opposite element, verbal density. How much is there of one and how much of the other? What does this inheritance mean? I don't know; but still, this appears to me to be a relevant question in terms of both stylistics and history.

Let us go back to the starting point: the impoverished, unadorned, squalid, grey. Where will we put this? It seems to me that we should put it as an (objective and psychological) content that the protagonist (or the lyric "I," or the author in his narrative projection) *wants* to select, *wants* to keep constantly before his eyes, *wants* to identify with himself, but (and this theme is already evident in the first lines) through an act of will, a choice. The proof of this is precisely the language that applies instead a range etc. etc. to the description of this greyness etc. etc.

What is the most obvious proof of this situation? It is the frequent use (which you too noticed) of the words "grey," "squalid," "greyness," "squalor." In a language that is grey and squalid one cannot use the words "grey" and "squalid," because in that case what we have is a language that judges the greyness and squalor from the outside. (In language that is grey, the word "grey" can only be used to say that a grey suit is grey; and as for "squalid," this is quite a lofty, learned term, if one ignores its recent, almost over-exploited popularity in journalistic and bourgeois circles.)

Also on the level of content, if in order to represent a grey and squalid theme a writer uses the words "grey" and "squalid," it is clear that he is a poor writer, in other words one who names rather than represents. So what? Well, either I'm a poor writer or this was not really my theme. And what could this theme have been? It could have been not the "greyness" (if we want to continue calling it this) but one's relationship with the "greyness."

Thus from the definition of the story's language you can move on to the definition of its content. But in a more global manner, not seeking confirmation of the relationship between signifier and signified on each occasion. We have then not so much a real story (because there is no story: about this man we are not told, nor are we interested in, what happened to him before in order to make him *choose*—it seems—that life and that attitude, probably in contrast with another life and another attitude which never appear. Nor can his story be discerned even afterwards, except in the minor details of his employment which we know from the start does not count for anything). Not so much a real story, then, as a lyrical-symbolical narrative about the relationship of a man with a (historical-social-existential etc.) reality which culminates in the image of the cloud of smog (define it as you wish), and together with this a range of other kinds of possible relationships with it: his boss, his colleague, his girlfriend, the landlady, the trade unionist. (Also for this type of structure you can find a series of analogies in other stories of mine that are constructed in this fashion: they have at the centre a relationship *ax*, which is given as exemplary, and around it a radius or range of other relations *bx*, *cx*, *dx*, etc. etc.)

All this with continual hints at discussions inside the story. (There, that's the direction in which you could develop the theme of the essay-type story you mention at the outset.) Every now and again essay-type language crops up (here you can take your choice of quotations): maybe inside the story an essay lies hidden, but it is totally erased, and there remain only chipped fragments of it. Even the dialogs relating to content—which could perhaps have been philosophical dialogs—have been eliminated (pp. 557–58; pp. 560–61),[77] and one can read only the vague outlines of words underneath the scoring out of the eraser.

Then comes the question of the poetic value that a story can have which delegates its meaning to an essay which however remains hidden. Is this a failed story? Failed because what underlies it is a confused, hesitant poetics? What poetic value can the simple elimination of the essay dimension have when it ought to have acted as the support for a tissue of images? But is this essayistic dimension just erased or is it contrasted with an active movement of the writing that certainly can constitute a poetic motif, either in itself or in the contrast it effects? There, this is the moment when you, the stylistic critic, can pull out a whole series of materials: quotations to show how a measured but continuous reductionist technique comes out on the level of language, a technique that underplays, understates, ironizes, and renders everything comic. All this directed against what? Against the character who says "I," in other words the intellectual conscience of the story, the paradoxical hypothesis of taking the negative for positive, which is thus constantly being proposed and dismantled.

We could now move on to applying this same method to your third observation, the one about adjectives. You attribute to me "the use of bare and essential adjectives" which would be the stylistic ideal of the whole of Italian literature since D'Annunzio. And of course it would be wonderful if you were right. But the question of adjectives is a topic which I am so fond of that if I start talking about it I will go on for another ten pages. I had better keep it for another occasion. For a long time now I have wanted to prove that the evils of Italian prose stem from the fact that the decisive meaning of a phrase is constantly deferred to the adjectives, while nouns and verbs become more and more generic and devoid of meaning. This removes all strength from the prose: one ends up not by representing the world but reviewing it. But this would be a polemic also against myself, because in this case too things are not quite as straightforward as you make out. Just open the story at any page: p. 525 "il mio sguardo trionfante, il mio sguardo trionfante e disperato" (my triumphant eyes, my triumphant and desperate gaze).[78] The psychological precision is entirely based on the adjective, indeed on the famous counterpoise of two adjectives of opposite meaning! On the next page, "una tristezza nasale e rassegnata" (a nasal, resigned melancholy).[79] Is that badly written? No, the problem is it's written very well, I don't think you could find better adjectives than that, and yet I'd prefer to be able to write without them.

That's all, I'll stop here: I think I've given you enough examples of what I wanted to say to you about stylistic analysis. In a nutshell it was this: I would want there to be behind every affirmation a historical outline of the phenomenon. I am not fanatical about methodology but I don't think I'm committing the crime of inciting eclecticism. I think that by doing it like this you stick to the texts, whereas if you go looking for confirmation in the author's theoretical essays the operation seems to be methodologically more spurious. Once you have drawn your conclusions from your examination of the linguistic material, you will be able—as a curiosity, at the end of your study or in a note—to compare these results with the ideas expressed by the author in his statements of poetics or aesthetics. And all this with the intention:

either of finding him in contradiction with himself, which is always more amusing and more in keeping with your duty to check things by actual sampling;

or of finding him perfectly consistent with himself, as you do with me, something that fills me with satisfaction and also with amazement, seeing that every time I write a story, I am very careful not to think about my essays and every time I write an essay, I am very wary of thinking about my stories.

This time I have made an exception to the rule, taking advantage of your patient attention to what I write, for which I thank you once more.

Italo Calvino

[Original handwritten letter and typed copy with some autograph corrections; in the Calvino Archive. The letter was written in 1964, as can be deduced from the second paragraph: "*Smog*, a story written six years ago [1958] . . . ," and was published in *Nuova Corrente*, 32–33 (Spring–Summer 1964), and later in Calvino, *La nuvola di smog e La formica argentina* (Milan: Mondadori, 1996), pp. vii–xvi. In the letter of 29 November 1963 cited in note 69, Calvino had informed Boselli about this lengthy letter-essay, which he probably wrote between the winter and spring of 1964. Subsequently—perhaps when he was thinking of including it in a collection of essays—he gave it a title, as is evident from a handwritten page in the Calvino Archive: "Letter to a Critic about *Smog*," and he also added the following brief note: "This letter comments on an article by the editor of *Nuova Corrente*, Mario Boselli, on my story entitled *Smog*: "Il linguaggio di attesa" (The Language of Waiting), *Nuova Corrente*, 28–29 (Spring 1963). Boselli replied point by point to my letter in issue 36 of the journal (1965). This work of mine is important for me not so much for its polemic against the new critical methodologies that *Nuova Corrente* was one of the first journals in Italy to champion (in his reply to my letter Boselli rebuked me for having defined him a "stylistic critic," thus confusing "stylistic aesthetics" with textual criticism, linguistic stylistics, and semantic criticism), but more as a totally objective rereading of my work (which had been prompted by having to revise a translation of *Smog*).]

To Antonella Santacroce—Sulmona

Turin, 22 April 1964

Dear Miss Santacroce,

I have read your letter and your stories. Your stories, in their "youthfulness," bear witness to the sensitive eye, devoid of literary prisms, through which you view the world. All that one can say is that you are "on the right track." Is that not much? That is a huge amount.

Your letter brings up a problem that surfaces I think every time a reader wants to know the *author* of a book they liked. It is always a disappointment. Because the *author* does not exist: that is to say he exists only in his works; outside them (unless he is a D'Annunzian writer or some other kind of windbag) he is an everyday guy, who is very careful not to "identify" himself with an ideal character.[80] Like many of my generation, I have an extra chance to deal with other people, apart from the one an author has (which can be accomplished only through his works) and the one an individual has (which takes place in the routine of everyday life): for I am someone who works (apart from on my own books) in order that the culture of my time can move in one direction rather than another. I believe profoundly in this aspect of my life and I am sorry you feel rejected if people like Michele Rago (who dedicates a humanity and sensibility much greater than mine to this ideal)[81] or myself are interested in your work from this point of view. There are no Mysterious Machinations by the Cultural Industry to Stifle Humanity behind all this, believe me.

I hope we can stay friends as before. Best wishes.

[Typed copy; in the Einaudi Archive, Turin. Also in *ILDA*, p. 465.]

To Renato Nocito—Milan

Turin, 24 April 1964

Dear Renato and all my friends in first year,

I RECEIVED YOUR LETTER WHICH GAVE ME LOTS OF PLEASURE because Baron Cosimo di Rondò is always happy when he finds other boys who like to climb into the trees.

Watch out, though, because Alessandro Manzoni, apart from being a much more serious writer than me, wrote a book nobody should miss out on: the more you read it when you're young, the more it will keep you company for the rest of your life.[82] And it is not boring at all: it has very amusing chapters written in an unbeatable style, and other chapters which can be boring and which usually people skip, but which later, as time goes by, they decide to go and read and they then find them wonderful.

All in all, *The Betrothed* is a book which you will continue to carry with you: loving it, or arguing with it, or maybe detesting it. As for *The Baron in the Trees*, well, we don't know how long it will last. It was written only a few years ago (not even seven), and so it has not been possible yet for it to "stand the test of time," in other words the test that helps distinguish books that entertain you at the time but are then soon forgotten, from those that—for complicated and often mysterious reasons—however much they age, have always got something to say to all ages and generations.

For the moment I know that you liked and were entertained by my book. The letter by the excellent Renato proved this to me, and this is an enormous source of satisfaction for me and it is I who should thank you for having given me this pleasure. Best regards to your teacher who chose my book for you to read. And many thanks to Renato's sister for having typed the letter.

Best wishes.

[Typed copy; in the Einaudi Archive, Turin. Also in *ILDA*, pp. 467–68.]

To Norberto Bobbio—Turin

Turin, 28 April 1964

Dear Bobbio,

Alright, then, yes, I'm a reformist.[83] Or more precisely: I believe that today (and perhaps only today) one can begin to consider a reformism that does not fall into the trap so often condemned by revolutionary polemics, namely being absorbed into the system of the ruling class. In order to save itself from this trap, such reformism has to be able to count on the strength of the international workers' movement, in other words that strength that could at any moment be flung into a "catastrophic" game, caught between the revolutionary pressure of the masses and the strategy of States with a revolutionary government. In plain words, reformism will succeed if it is led by Communists. At present they are not capable of this: when forced to move in that direction, they do so clumsily; and on the other hand, the problem is not solely that of the choice of a line to adopt, but to ensure that the choice of that line does not involve the loss of everything else.

In short, I am worried that this approach might make one forget the *universal* value of the workers as antithesis in the way that Marxism set it up. (And this worry can only increase now that an authoritative but elementary spokesman has started to theorize "Goulash Socialism.")[84] In short, I'd like to have the cake of proletarian universalism and be able also to eat historical and technical rationality: the two halves of an ideal humanism which now seem more irreconcilable than ever.

For this reason, the formula you infer from my essay—a working class that is no longer an "antithetical" but a "mediating" force—is legitimate and also suggestive; but I am reluctant to employ it because I am afraid that it will make me lose sight of the aspiration toward the *universal* objective.

There, I've brought you up to date with my ideological-political position. If it cannot be articulated in more cogently rigorous terms, I do not think this is just my fault but also the fault of the objective data which I am trying to put into some kind of order (more to try to get it clear in my own head than for anything else).[85]

Thank you very much for your letter, which was the most relevant commentary that I have received on my essay. Best wishes.

Yours,

Italo Calvino

[Typed on Einaudi headed paper with autograph signature; with the addressee. Excerpts from this letter were quoted by Norberto Bobbio in his article "Italo Calvino. Ebbene sí, sono riformista" (Italo Calvino: Alright then, yes, I am a reformist), *L'Indice dei Libri del Mese*, 8 (1985).]

To Despina Mladoveanu—Bucharest

Turin, 8 June 1964

Dear Mrs Mladoveanu,

I'll deal at once with the question of the proper names in *The Non-Existent Knight*.[86]

Names from the chivalric epic tradition: many names belong to the cycle of the Paladins of France, in the forms in which they were Italianized in the popular epic poems from the thirteenth century onward, right down to the sixteenth-century literary re-workings of the material (Boiardo, Ariosto). These names are not only the most well-known ones of Ariosto's heroes (Bradamante, Orlando, Astolfo, Rinaldo of Montalbano, Guidon Selvaggio), but also: Solomon of Brittany, Ulivieri (or Olivieri), Bernard of Mompolier (Montpellier), Sansonetto, Dudone and so on, all the names of Charlemagne's knights; and the names of their enemies (Saracens or giants or other supernatural creatures): Fierabraccia, Brunamonte, Galiferno etc.

Durlindana is Orlando's famous sword and Fusberta is Astolfo's equally famous sword.

Orlando and Charlemagne's knights have a tradition that is perhaps even stronger in Italy than in France, because particularly from the time of Andrea da Barberino (end of the fourteenth century) they became the great literature of the people and have profound roots in folklore. In both the popular and literary traditions these names crop up in various forms: I often chose the strangest and most ancient version. *They have no lexical meaning*; the reasons behind the choice of name in these cases are purely phonetic and musical. The problem that all translators face is how to render them, because since the Carolingian cycle is of French origin, there is no reason to give the names Italian endings (except in some cases, as an homage to Ariosto). I do not know if there was in Romanian literature an epic tradition of the Carolingian cycle as there was in Italy: if there was, one could find the equivalent for every name ("lists" of warriors always form part of epic poems). If there were no ancient Romanian translations of the *Chanson de Roland* or of French romance epics, one could simply use the French spelling of the names. (Rambaldo di Rossiglione, for instance, should be translated Rambaut de Roussillon.)

Agilulfo: this is not a name from the Carolingian tradition, but one we study in Italian history, since it was the name of a famous Lombard king. I would suggest leaving it as it is, with a Romanian ending.

Agilulfo's titles: these are a bit of nonsense, a string of weird words. Fez is the Moroccan city: by all means use the Romanian spelling. The names of the other cities I think I made them up myself: I can't remember whether there is a Spanish city called Corbentraz, but probably not. Selimpia does not exist and Citeriore does not mean anything.

The Others means the others: just a bit of irony as regards these strings of noble names.

Isoarre: an Arabic name Italianized (probably Isoar), I can't remember if I found it in some ancient epic or invented it myself.

Gurdulù: just a pure sound. Translate it the best way you see fit as regards spelling but without departing from the original's sound.

Gurdulù's other names: some are vaguely dialectal (Omobò could come from Omobono, an ancient Italian name; Martinzul is from Martino with the suffix -zul which I think exists in certain Venetian dialects; Paciasso or Paciugo are dialect words, Piedmontese and Ligurian respectively, meaning "bog" or "concoction"; but everything is based on sounds rather than sense), others vaguely Arabic (an invented Arabic).

San Colombano: a very famous saint, founder of a religious order. *The Voyage of Saint Columbanus* is one of the most curious medieval legendary texts.

Khar-as-Sus: Arabic words I think I found in the *Arabian Nights* and which are translated in the reply that follows.

Mushrik: as above, but I can't remember what it means. Arabic words should be left as they are.

Sozo! Mozo! Escalvao!: this is a line from a thirteenth-century poem, which is largely made up of insults traded between a Provençal man and a Genoese woman. Leave it without translating it.

Torrismondo of Cornwall: a name without a precise reference. Romantic literature is full of Torrismonds.

Sofronia: this too is a name heavy with tradition in Italian literature, particularly because she is a character in Tasso.

Curvaldia: imaginary name.

In "Fear on the Footpath":

Vedetta: this is a misprint for *vendetta*. (I realized this only because you drew attention to it.)

Vendetta, Pelle, Serpe, Guerriglia, Fegato: these are nicknames (or "battle-names") of partisans.

Castagno, Perallo, Creppo etc: place names.

From "Theft in a Cakeshop":

Dritto: nickname meaning crafty, cunning.

"The Sea of Objectivity" was published in *Il Menabò*, no. 2, which is now completely sold out. I am sorry I haven't even a copy of it to send you.

I did not receive *Racconti italiani contemporanei* (*Contemporary Italian Short Stories*). Maybe it has not had time to arrive yet.

Thank you so much for "Viaggio con le mucche" (A Journey with the Cows).[87]

I am always happy if I can be of help to you,

Best wishes.

[Typed copy; in the Einaudi Archive, Turin.]

To Leonardo Sciascia—Caltanissetta

Turin, 26 October 1964

Dear Leonardo,

I've read *L'Onorevole* (*The Honourable Gentleman*).[88] For the first two acts I admired your skill in developing the most convincing and pointed satire about civic morality inside a plot which moves along without ever jarring or seeming forced. This is a talent of yours that we've known about for some time and which has not changed now that you've switched from narrative to theater: you are perfectly at home there, and operate like a real playwright, helped by that bit of tradition that you are perfectly familiar with.

At the same time, I found myself saying: "Hang on, can this blasted man who is always so controlled, so conscious of what he's doing and so adept at his mission as a civic moralist, can he himself ever step forth in the flesh with his own daimon, his own lyrical and private moment to counterbalance the public and historical dimension, with his own 'myth,' his own folly?" This is not the first time I have asked myself this question about you. On this occasion the question cropped up more spontaneously than ever because for the first two acts your play follows its natural course, far removed also from that game of truth and imposture—of Pirandellian origin, as some critic rightly noted—which is the true driving force behind *Il Consiglio d'Egitto* (*The Council of Egypt*) and perhaps also most of your work.

So I got to the third act: and there finally the spring recoils all at once and the substance of the plot, which had been contested only from the inside and with satirical underlining up to that point, is tackled from the outside from all directions, flinging against it feelings, the irrational, literature, Cervantes, Calderón, Pirandello, the soul, the carabinieri, existential morality. I can't complain any more, my points have been richly answered. The problem is that this attack on all fronts is conducted by a character who does not have the shoulders to carry such a weight: this nice Signora Assunta whom you have almost hidden from us for two acts, now has to become the organ for your discourses, speaking as a literary essayist, a sociologist of mass culture and a Jansenist reformer. Serious error? Of course but it is precisely because of this mistake that the play comes alive, and marks—over and above the essential civic polemics—a step forward in your career as a writer and in the project we have in common.

For the fact is that the problem that still has to be solved is how to give artistic life to the elements that are at present only articulated in the discourse that has been put into the mouth of this one-woman chorus. And this could only have been done in one way: by making these elements come alive, right from the start, alongside the satirical sideshow of the first two acts. What was needed was a character or a series of characters (or themes, or plot turns, or different registers of languages etc.) that could express this Cervantes-Unamuno-Pirandello-style critique, this reversal of the way things are. In short, Don Quixote needed not only to be the title on a frontispiece but to ride onto the stage. In *A Midsummer Night's Dream*, the worlds of power and of the mechanicals as well as the anti-world of the elves all intersect: something similar needs to be done today.

Often when I read what the critics write I find myself reflecting on my and your "Enlightenment." As for mine, who knows to what extent it can be defined precisely as such, and is not just an element of taste—stylistic and moral—which is there alongside other highly diverse elements: the fantasy-romance tale, nonsense, sending things up. In short, Enlightenment rationalism has for two centuries done nothing but be beaten about the head and been on the receiving end of denials, and yet it continues to co-exist in the face of all its critiques: and perhaps I express this co-existence. You are much more rigorously

"Enlightenment" than me, your works have a quality of civic struggle which mine have never had, they have their own distinct tone, typical of the political pamphlet, even though on the level of plot, like every work of art, they cannot be reduced to one type of reading. But you have Pirandello's relativism immediately behind you, and Gogol filtered through Brancati, as well as the Spain-Sicily continuity: a series of explosive charges beneath the pillars of the poor old Enlightenment and compared to these my own are merely pathetic fireworks. I am always expecting you to light your powder keg. And it is difficult for this to happen without an explosion in terms of form, in terms of your smoothness of composition. I would like to see finally the real face of your daimon, hear its real voice. (The individual's daimon will also be the expression of a force in history, if we are genuine historicists.) But in this case it is not Enlightenment but the Manzonian smoothness you have to shatter (Manzoni had learned very much from Voltaire and Diderot; but Voltaire and Diderot each had their own daimon, my goodness they did; but not Manzoni). It is no accident that Manzoni is one of the authors Frangipane reads alongside Cervantes. And nice Signora Assunta sees things clearly: providence-justice-carabinieri, and she is almost on the point of summoning up—if I'm not mistaken—the protagonist of *Il giorno della civetta* (*The Day of the Owl*). Through the self-awareness of Assunta you are thus on the verge of freeing yourself from the Manzonian (and therefore foreign) stamp, a sine qua non if Cervantes has to be the winner. Push your Hispano-Sicilian and even Arabic-Sicilian sides to the limits and you'll see you'll be universal.

And what about me, with all this preaching? Well, I'm talking about you in order to try to see things clearly for myself.

Best wishes,

Your Calvino

[Typed on Einaudi headed paper, with autograph signature; with the addressee's heirs. Also in "Lettere di Italo Calvino a Leonardo Sciascia," *Forum Italicum*, 1 (Spring 1981), pp. 66–68; and in *ILDA*, pp. 490–92.]

To Gian Carlo Ferretti—Milan

Turin, 12 November 1964

Dear Ferretti,

YOUR ARTICLE GAVE ME MUCH PLEASURE.[89] I AM GLAD YOU consider that I am beyond the "dangerous crossroads": the way things are, the discussion that is now taking place within Italian literature is becoming more and more crazy.

Your definition of the generation (or literary "class") to which I belong, or at least the one with which I identify, is spot-on: the "cultural void" behind us, the position of posthumous head of a generation that Giaime Pintor took on, and so on.

Your readings were as precise and congenial as could be. And your final questions—giving the lie to my pessimism—sound all the more flattering to me.

The problem of *nostalgia* is a theme I ought to have dealt with in the preface. Is it right to be nostalgic about the Resistance? Analyzing what this nostalgia means, and the false image it ends up casting on that period, the correct answer is no. I am pleased that you say that I have gone beyond "the most passively nostalgic moment," but you are probably right even when shortly afterwards you say that in my preface the moralistic-sentimental trap of consolatory nostalgia resurfaces.

In fact, ever since I published this elastic preface I constantly think of other things I should have put in it. The already troubled process of its gestation is not over yet, I feel. I could already publish an enlarged edition of it, but I am afraid of becoming obsessive.

Thank you once more, and best wishes.

Your Italo Calvino

[Typed on Einaudi headed paper, with autograph signature; with the addressee's heirs.]

To Michele Tondo—Bari

Rome, 25 January 1965

Dear Tondo,

I've read *Itinerario di Pavese* (*Pavese's Journey*).[90] It gave me for the first time the satisfaction of seeing how my work in establishing a chronological order for Pavese's poems, and indeed in dating all his works, has not been pointless. You have the merit of being the first critic to have studied the development, one might almost say, day by day, of the poetics versus works nexus in Pavese. Your methodology finally gives full valorization to every single moment and at the same time sheds light on how Pavese's work is an organic whole, with its own rigorous internal logic. I can't tell you how much I appreciate a criticism that is based, like yours, on a close reading of the text, and how fed up I am at the generic nature of the "closed-book" criticism which continues to dominate in Italy.

Your book fills a gap in the (alas, up to now so inadequate) bibliography on Pavese. It re-establishes the link between Pavese the poet and Pavese the intellectual that a certain kind of criticism (Moravia, Salinari) had destroyed, and at the same time it defines Pavese's historic "commitment" as an internal fact inside his literary oeuvre, something which cannot be judged on the basis of an assessment of the activism in his political behavior (*pace* Lajolo), but on the contrary something that was historically useful precisely in its establishment of an impossibility.[91] It puts the biographical moments back in their appropriate place (again *pace* Lajolo), giving us once more the outline of Pavese's life in his itinerary as a writer. Furthermore it underlines how Pavese's creative experience is indivisible, dictated as it is by an aesthetic-ethical-existential quest which is certainly far removed from any concern for a naturalistic representation of society (this is where your polemic against Piccioni comes in) but also substantially different from other examples of twentieth-century lyrical-ethical prose writing (which is what Pampaloni tends to assimilate it to).

In short, yours is a Pavese who is explained exclusively through Pavese. This is the great merit of your study but also its limitation.

For the fact is that today when we study Pavese we really need to check first and foremost the meaning of all his most important terms: *solitude*. What does *solitude* mean (for Pavese and for us)? You accept this notion of *solitude* as the key concept of Pavese's whole itinerary as a writer but do not define it. And the same could be said for *maturity*. And *construction*? And also two terms which on the surface seem obvious such as *country* and *city* ought to be analyzed with precision. (Not to mention *myth*, *symbol* etc.: but there one would need a specialized study on all this terminology of Pavese's which is part of a European network, moving between D. H. Lawrence, Eliot, Mann's biblical novels—that is the only side of Mann he is interested in, I think that is clear—to what extent Pavese can be placed amongst Jung's disciples, etc.)

Of course, this is not a point I am making regarding your work, which was not aimed at research of this type. It is an observation I have made on several occasions, that Pavese remains such a *solitary* figure (that key word again, inevitably) in the culture of his time, even while being very much inside that culture, that when one deals with him one goes into a kind of tunnel and it is extremely difficult to study him both from within and from without, to keep contacts with the rest of Italian and other cultures, that network of references and comparisons with what was written about him then and with what was written afterwards.

On the subject of "Pavese and politics"* I would like to send you something that might interest you. When I was preparing the edition of his poems, I assembled a "montage' of some of my notes into a continuous piece, which I then used for a non-commercial publication.[92] If I find a copy, I'll send it to you.

Next month an edition of *Dialoghi con Leucò* (*Dialogues with Leucò*) will come out, and for it I have annotated the date of each dialog, drawing on the manuscripts. You will see that they all go from the end of '45 (in Rome) to the beginning of '47, and that will enable you to eliminate your doubts in that chapter.

Of course I think that your study should be published as soon as possible. I will try to discuss this with Einaudi, but I fear that the line we have held hitherto—doing as much as possible in terms of editions of Pavese's texts but allowing books *on* him to be published elsewhere—will continue to hold, without exceptions. And yet, some day, we will have to do a book on Pavese. Still, if it is not possible to publish it with Einaudi, we will need to think about proposing it to another publisher.[93]

Best wishes.

Italo Calvino

*One topic on which I have tried to get my ideas straight is that of Pavese and politics. Your study goes back to the notion of Pavese as a descendant of Turin in the post-Gobetti period, of Professor Monti's school, and anti-Fascism. All of this is true. But we will never understand Pavese until we see that he is defined, yes, by belonging to that climate, but also by being in opposition to it. In the midst of the sea of Fascism, on the little island of Crocean ethics and politics in Turin, Pavese is the anti-political opposition: this is the situation of solitude "in spades" which has still not been studied. What did Pavese[94] owe to the Turinese Croceanism of his friends? And what does he put up in opposition to it? By studying these relationships we will see how alongside the progressive diagram of his aesthetic-ethical-existential "knowledge," that you chart, there is another graph with highs and lows, which is traced by the greater or lesser importance that politics (his acceptance of political discourse, which is something external to him) has in this process of his. And so then we will see that there are peaks of greater aversion to politics and history (one is probably during the period of exile, which is something he ends up enduring, furious that he has suffered through someone else's fault; and above all the other such peak, of great intensity, comes during the German occupation when—probably out of resentment at the ineptness of the anti-Fascists during the forty-five days[95]—he pushes his anti-historicism in a Nietzschean-religious direction.[96] Thus things are in a certain sense more complicated than in Lajolo's simplistic interpretation). And remember that his discovery that he is a Communist at the Liberation is explained like this: this is the dialog and opposition to political ideologism that is continuing, because he is under the illusion of blending his own "construction" of himself (his head-on struggle with the irrational) with Communism.

[Typed on Einaudi headed paper, with autograph signature; with the addressee. Also in *ILDA*, pp. 507–9. The postscript on "Pavese and politics" is in the Calvino Archive (handwritten pages numbered 4 and 5) with this heading: "Fragment of a letter to Michele Tondo which I did not send him 23-1-65."]

To Ornella Sobrero—Rome

Rome, 27 January 1965

Dear Ornella Sobrero,

THANK YOU VERY MUCH FOR YOUR ARTICLE.[97] I FOUND SOMEthing very well worked out in it: the parallel between Gurdulù and the hero of Sercambi's novella, Ganfo.[98] There is really a perfect parallel here: and I didn't realize this, and no critic has ever discovered it. Really this was an ingenious idea. It all goes to show that "comparative" criticism, which has been so neglected in Italy for the last sixty years or so, has its own raison d'être, and should continue to have its practitioners.

For this reason I would like to see you working in that direction, where you are at your best, I think (I say this thinking also of other works of yours), and without allowing yourself to be tempted into eclectic moves into other critical methods.

Don't you think that ideological, philosophical criticism, for instance, actually has too many adepts in Italy? And are you really sure that the kind of statements that this critical approach (I wouldn't call it a method) leads one to make are securely established, incontrovertible? It may be that I have a kind of allergy toward this kind of criticism, but it seems to me that in it everything gets confused in nebulous generalizations, where just like at night everything is the one color.

What is certainly better is historical criticism which is all focused on literature, on the search for influences, even though this is the most traditional kind of criticism in Italy: at least it allows you to say things that are true and precise. Everything, for example, you say about

Hemingway is perfectly correct: that is an area of influence which I don't deny and which must be understood precisely in the sense that you say.

Another critical method you use is that of identifying a given situation or image in order to trace its presence in the author's other works. This is a method (or a procedure common to a number of methods, from the Jungian to the structuralist) to which I am anything but averse, as long as it gives concrete, undeniable results. Now I have to say to you sincerely that I feel you overstate your case here: I cannot agree with you when you say that every time I have a scene take place on the first floor rather than on the ground floor, there is a premonition of the *Baron in the Trees*. And also the premonition of the *Cloven Viscount* in "Attesa della morte in un albergo" (Waiting for Death in a Hotel) seems doubtful to me.[99] This is a procedure which I would say should certainly not be rejected out of hand, but it must be rendered more rigorous. (I am thinking of Barthes's *Racine*, for instance.)[100]

However, I repeat, I am convinced that you can work better in the "comparativist" direction, moving from one century to another.

Because in any case I'm not sure that it is totally legitimate to go finding connections at any cost amongst an author's various other works. When I write, I always think that what I am writing is something isolated, as though I had never written anything else before. If I thought that everything I write can condition the reading of other things I have written or still have to write, I would be paralyzed. In particular, I am always astonished to see that my theoretical statements, which I make always thinking about other authors—even in the days when I had the naïveté to pronounce on "how one should write"—can be applied also to my own work, which is always unsystematic, empirical, and which proceeds by trial and error. You are not the only critic to do this, but it seems to me that in this process something always gets distorted: either the theoretical statement or the work. Instead, something much more in harmony with the function of criticism would be to highlight the contradictions: which there certainly are, and which always have an importance and significance.

Don't be offended if I have exploited something that gave me pleasure like your essay in order to subject you to a philippic against the habits of criticism and above all against eclecticism. This has become a bit of an obsession of mine. Criticism serves a purpose when it is a rigorous application of a method of research, whatever that method is. It does not matter whether it is partial or not. In any case the work always remains readable in highly different ways. I think that the best results are obtained when one chooses a restricted theme, an aspect of a single work, and one tries to define it using practices that cannot be questioned.

Naturally, I am very pleased at the care with which you have read my books and also many of my uncollected works. On this topic, I would like to send you the new edition of *The Path to the Spiders' Nests*, which has a preface that also touches on some of the points you deal with. If you have not received the book, please write to Einaudi's press office asking them to send it to you. (I think you usually receive all the new literature books from Einaudi; if this is not the case, do not hesitate to contact the press office.)

Thanking you once more very much. Best wishes.

Italo Calvino

[Typed on Einaudi headed paper, with autograph signature; with the addressee.]

To Guido Aristarco—Milan

Rome, 22 February 1965

Dear Aristarco,

I HAVE NOT REPLIED TO YOU BECAUSE THIS IS VERY DIFFIcult. I was not convinced by either *Il Deserto rosso* or *Il silenzio*; as for *San Matteo* (*The Gospel According to Saint Matthew*), I think it is devoid of any meaning and amateurish.[101]

Naturally I don't like dishing out instantly damning verdicts, even less when one is dealing with friends, as is the case with two of the directors in question. I tried to explain to Antonioni in person (with great difficulty, given his sensitivity) what I thought of his film; as for

Pasolini, he knows perfectly well what I think of his cinematic ambitions in general.[102]

Of the films you mention in the note, I have only seen the excellent *Dr Strangelove*, about which so much has already been said, and the awful Bergman. Too little to be able to draw up a table.

For that reason, I am sending you just a couple of lines on *The Servant*, hoping that it is a film of 1964.

I would have liked to say something also (dealing with commercial films) in favor of James Bond, but already there is too much talk about it, and I saw from your article that already so many of my colleagues are pro-James Bond, so I am steering well clear of joining the pack.

Very best wishes.

(Italo Calvino)

The most interesting film I saw in 1964 is Losey's *The Servant*. In fact, it seems to me to be a unique example in the history of cinema of a philosophical film, as well as a rigorously cinematographic account.[103]
[Typed copy; in the Einaudi Archive, Turin.]

To Cesare Lupo—Rome

Turin, 31 March 1965

Dear Lupo,

I am very late in replying to your last very kind message about Ariosto, and most of all in thanking you for the things you said and for the invitation, which is extremely flattering.[104] In partial excuse I will say that I am waiting for a reply from Cetra to whom I immediately set out my requests. After a discussion with our friend Zanoletti last week, we have still not reached a decision but I hope to be able to give you a definitive response soon.

This is a prospect that is both attractive and daunting at the same time. It requires a considerable research commitment; and although

I have declared my love for Ariosto several times, I am far from having the background necessary to carry out an enterprise that will have everyone's eyes—or rather their ears—on it, including those of the most authoritative specialists.

The prospect of spending several months studying Ariosto is not at all unpleasant. However, I have to consider that my diary is already divided up, without any space available for anything else, between my work in publishing and my own work as a writer; I would have to put Ariosto under, let's say, the "intermittent" heading of "extra work." In fact, this heading is almost non-existent in my diary, except as occasional temptations that I regularly manage to stifle, since they are concerned with cinema, an activity which (unlike the one you are suggesting) I find thoroughly uncongenial. It is of no use to me (whereas applying myself to this study of Ariosto would be something that would remain with me "for the rest of my life") but it requires a lot less time and is a lot more financially rewarding.

You will find this comparison between two kinds of work that have nothing in common very strange: you are right, but my life is organized in such a way that I am forced to categorize the Ariosto anthology under the same "heading" so the comparison is inevitable.

I hoped to have a figure from Cetra that was at least equal to what was being offered by RAI: if nothing else, the possibility of percentages on rights. But the run of disks to be produced will be rather limited, since each copy will consist of so many records, which would also limit even my most optimistic expectations. I do in fact have to have a definitive response from Cetra (on the advance and on the number of records envisaged), I hope soon, in order to make my decision.

If we reach a deal, I could start work no sooner than next winter. (I will for the next few months be involved in a substantial publishing project: editing Pavese's letters). In short I would think of the possibility of scheduling the series of RAI broadcasts for September–October–November 1966, in such a way that Cetra can come out with the records at the end of November as a Christmas gift set.[105]

I have given you the outline of the situation up to today. As soon as there are any developments we will be back in touch.

Best wishes.

[Typed copy; in the Calvino Archive and in the Einaudi Archive, Turin.]

To Franco Quadri—Milan

Turin, 1 April 1965

Dear Quadri,

Comment c'est has safely reached harbor: please allow me to congratulate you.

I was not in time to see something I would have liked, namely that in the new series the translator's name should be on the title page. If there is a series where the texts require particular bravura it is this one; and amongst the first volumes there are translations like yours and that by Picco (of Schmidt) which deserve every accolade.[106] But the design for our series is provided by the graphics people and very often we're not in time. There are publishers who make a great fuss of very mediocre translators on the front page of the papers: it's either a feast or a famine.

I hope that you have the time and are willing to work again for us and to take up *Sally Mara* once more.[107] The publishing house is keen on getting it out as soon as possible, and it seems that Queneau too is annoyed about the delay. Can you tell us (write to Davico: I think that's better) if you can get back to work immediately and when you think you can deliver the book? I still have the twenty or so pages you sent me. I will take another look at them now to finalize my reactions.

We also have several old Queneau books to translate, amongst which is the wonderful *Lion de Rueil*. But there is something by Queneau that I am personally keener on than the novels, and that is the *Petite Cosmogonie portative*. I am convinced that it is a great book, about which too little is said, even in France, and yet it is one of the most extraordinary exploits in twentieth-century poetry, and it is a Queneau book like no other. And it is also more translatable than other poems by Queneau (such as those in his latest book, *Le Chien à la mandoline*) because the *essay* element in the poem is every bit as important as the verbal texture. So much so that it would make sense even to provide a literal, informative, translation of it, to help the reader go through the French original on the facing page (which is very difficult to follow unless one numbers the verses and uses the table at the end). I actually think that with certain word-plays it would not be a bad idea to leave some words in French. In short, it would be good to find a way of allowing this book to be read, without demanding that it become a poem in Italian as well.[108]

What do you say? Do you think you could try it? It consists of 229 lines. A job you could do just like that, alongside translating *Sally Mara*, when you pause for breath.

I shall await your reply. Very best wishes.

[Typed copy; in the Einaudi Archive, Turin. Also in *ILDA*, pp. 513–14.]

To Henry Sjöstrand—Gothenburg

Turin, 1 April 1965

Dear Mr Sjöstrand,

In reply to your kind letter of 5 March, I will give you my opinion on *niente* ("nothing") and *nulla* ("nothingness") (hoping that this will not be contradicted by my own writings).

Niente is above all a word from the spoken language (at least in Northern Italy). *Nulla* is a more literary, refined word, and as such corresponds to the metaphysical notion of "nothingness," for instance in existential philosophy ("being and nothingness") and also in commonly used expressions such as "to descend into nothingness."

It could almost be said that the meaning of their etymologies has been reversed: *niente* today means *nullam rem*, it is the negative of "something," that is to say it has a concrete connotation; whereas *nulla* today means *nihil ente*, it is the negation of that which is, and has an abstract, philosophical connotation.

I think that the general tendency in my style is to use *niente* more than *nulla*, because when I speak I always say *niente* and because in my stylistic preferences I tend to prefer the word from North Italian spoken usage to literary words and to words from Central and Southern Italian spoken Italian. However, I am not surprised to learn that in *The Non-Existent Knight* I use *nulla* twenty-four times against the twelve uses of *niente*. For the fact is that the stylistic arrangement in this story is based on a contrast between a high, literary, archaizing stylistic level (where it is natural that *nulla* will dominate) and a level that is emphatically prosaic, modern, spoken (where instead *niente* ought to be more frequent). I would add that the story's theme—the Knight character—is a man made of *nulla*, a man of *nulla* (in this case it is not possible to say a man made of *niente*, or a man of *niente*): all in all, *nulla* is the real thematic word in the story.

I have not got the time to reread the whole of *The Non-Existent Knight*. But flipping through it at random, I see in chapter VI "un uomo che non c'è per nulla" (A man who is not there at all), whereas in chapter IV I find "Neanche Rambaldo ne sapeva niente" (Rambaldo knew nothing about this) (the very common idiomatic phrase is "non saperne niente": to know nothing about it).

However, in chapter VI, I find *nulla* used in cases where *niente* would also have been fine. "Ad Agilulfo non importava nulla . . . Non aveva nulla da dire e non aveva detto nulla" (Agilulfo did not care . . . He had nothing to say and had not said anything). Might it be that when Agilulfo is referred to, the language "rises" in tone and demands *nulla*? Or might it not rather be for reasons of sound? The repetition of *niente* here would have been cacophonous, whereas the word *nulla* is quicker and lighter.

We should therefore always keep in mind reasons dictated by euphony: *niente* is a word that often makes a phrase heavy. Its ending in *-ente* makes it incompatible with the closeness of adverbs or present participles which also end in *-ente*.

I hope these answers are of some use to you. When faced with problems like this, a writer realizes he is not really conscious of what he is doing when he writes . . .

Please pass on my regards to Professor Nilsson-Ehle, whom I remember with affection since my visit to Gothenburg.

Yours sincerely.

Italo Calvino

[Typed on Einaudi headed paper, with autograph signature; with the addressee.]

To Franco Quadri—Milan

Turin, 14 April 1965

Dear Quadri,

I HAVE LOOKED AGAIN AT THE PAGES I HAVE HAD HERE (FOR years now!) from your translation of Queneau.

I will try not to be influenced in my verdict by my conviction that *Sally Mara* is untranslatable. This is only a personal opinion. Einaudi is keen on it, you are keen on it, Queneau is also keen: I am in the minority and I have to yield. In fact this conviction of mine gives even more value to what I will say to you: in other words, although "untranslatable" by definition, the text is more translatable than would appear from this first attempt.[109]

Sally Mara is a book about the use *of French* by someone who speaks English. The method employed in any translation, simply replacing the entire French text with Italian, does not work. The verb *foutre* with all its various domestic uses, which Sally experiments with and comments on, is purely French. A *complete* translation would have to mean writing another book: Sally learning Italian.

My idea of retaining (or rather emphasizing) the character of linguistic pastiche in the translation, with expressions left in French clashing with those in English and Irish, seems to me the only way forward. So I would leave all the uses of *foutre* in French, along with certain quotations of famous lines of poetry etc. I would also use some external expedients: leave *Monsieur* when dealing with French characters etc. But [where] to stop? I am aware of the wide area of arbitrariness in an operation of this type. As you said to me, "In that case one might as well not translate the book." I started to think about a possible theoretical justification for this kind of work, in other words about a method that would allow us to know what exactly we are doing. This is a problem which could constitute a new chapter in Mounin's books.[110] The only formulation possible, I think, is this: let's translate into Italian whatever we consider is not a word written by Sally Mara but rather her pre-linguistic idea. Whenever Sally Mara stops to choose a French word, to study it and play with it, in those cases the word or expression ought to be left in French as far as possible. I think that this goes with the experience we all have: when I think about something I have to say in a foreign language, fragments already in French or English come to mind, connected with bits thought out still in Italian, or at any rate in a neutral mental language of mine. The same thing happens when I remember a conversation that took place in French or English, or a passage in a book I've read: there are points where I have in mind the expression in its exact linguistic form, but there are others where I remember only the gist and whose linguistic form, as it fades, gives way to my native tongue. So with Sally we can pretend to translate not her French, but a pre-language which once in its written form can be French as much as English or Italian.

Having said this, I will add that I do realize that this is all very well in theory, but then in practice the difficulties are enormous all the same.

The difficulties are, first, of recognizing, and then of conveying, the constant *intentions* of linguistic usage. I will attempt to classify these:

(a) *obscenity*: I can't manage to recognize all the instances, but I have the feeling they are everywhere (or is it my obsession?);

(b) *use of slang* which in Italian is always hard to translate, but this is a difficulty everywhere in Queneau, not this book in particular. In general, I would say to adopt a light touch, not to waste colorful interventions except in the most important instances. (For instance: when he says *M'sieur*, there is no need for us to go for the unacceptable *Siore*.)

(c) *literary quotations*: one would need a knowledge of French poetry that I do not possess to recognize all the quotations that one feels crop up, for instance, in landscape descriptions, and sometimes they pop up one after another, mixed up with proverbs, such as Aragon's "Bordel pour bordel." What should we do? Leave them in French? If we don't, we lose the spirit of it;

(d) *phrases based on phonetic or onomatopoeic play*: we really need to convey these somehow. For "le buvard de brumes a bu le bateau (the blotting-paper of mists absorbed the boat)," which sounds like a phrase from a spelling manual, or language exercise book, I would suggest: "il bibulo di bruma ha bevuto il battello." It's not great but it keeps the series of b's.

(e) *phonetic spelling*: the usual problem in Queneau. Deal with these case by case. If we adopt the method I suggest, we have the chance to leave in French *Kéxé*, whereas *Coz'è* is clearly inadequate.

Etc. etc. Now I believe there is just one system: read the text with a French person who has a very sensitive ear for all the obvious and hidden intentions, in order to *know* everything there is in each sentence and then it will be possible to decide what to try to translate and what to just leave. The ideal solution would be for this collaborator with the highly tuned ear to be Monsieur Queneau himself. Here it is not my experience as editorial reviser speaking but my experience as an author who has been translated. My writing is very far from Queneau's complexity, but when I do not have the chance and the time to explain to the translator what I put in every sentence (in other words, always: only once did I manage to do this), only 45 percent of what I write gets translated.

Other things: for *rampe*, I would be more for *ringhiera* than *sbarra*, but I have not checked whether that would work everywhere.

Segnorine: absolutely not!

As for mistakes that make you bite your tongue, I've only spotted one: "le clergé est tout à fait opposé à ça." And then also: why on earth *nomino* for *petit nom*?

In short, from being opposed to the translation of this book, do I have to admit that I have ended up getting enthusiastic about it? Well, it would be a tour de force, but in my view it's not worth the candle.[111] Enough of this: I have to be encouraging, not defeatist!

For the contract, talk to Davico.

Best wishes.

PS. I'm really sorry but I can't get round to the questionnaire on the theater. For some years now I have decided not to reply to surveys (the one on the novel: what a bore!) and all this thorny question of the difficult relationship between literature and theater, why I for instance do not write for the stage, I have thought about it often, asked myself about it, replied to questions, questionnaires, interviews and I always end up back where I started. Bah! That's just the way it is, I don't understand why. If one day I should write for the theater, I could try to explain it, but not before.

[Typed copy; in the Einaudi Archive, Turin.]

To Francesco Leonetti—Bologna

[Turin,] 22-4-65

Dear Leonetti,

Elio will already have told you that I have read your piece for *Il Menabò*, which I liked as a position, as a corrective to the flattening out of the last decade or two in literature thanks to the work of the new critics, and as the start of a new scale of individual evaluations of the most recent literary works.[112] (Even though there I am not always able to say whether I agree or not.) However, I was not able to follow the last section properly and it seems to me that it is still a discourse you have to develop, even if I am certainly not opposed to the direction you are moving in.

As a general observation, I'd like to say to you that you are too quick in *declaring* yourself a "structuralist." *Do* some structuralism first and then we'll see. (And then maybe there won't be any need to say it.) It seems to me that there are already too many saying "I am a structuralist" before trying it, both those who are definitely serious such as Barthes (who perhaps is starting to become one now, as a "semiologist," though as a literary critic he has not yet tried), or D'Arco Avalle, as well as youngsters who want to be up to date like Aldo Rossi. Meanwhile, in terms of literary criticism, the only people who have done structuralist work are L.-S. and R. J. with *Les Chats*.[113] That's it, I think. Nobody has had the courage to follow such a rigorous path as this, which is the only one—I think—that allows a *total* reading of a text. Of course, we would need to change our vocabulary and our mental processes. It would be ridiculous for me, for instance, to start doing so: one needs a special vocation for a particular kind of intellectual asceticism. But what stucturalism can give us is some modification of our vocabulary and mental practices, some specific acquisitions. So the particular comments I would like to make about your piece (but I do not have the text to hand), and which are comments about linguistic emphasis and adjectivization (which then become points of judgment), I could summarize by saying: be more structuralist, profit from the lesson of structuralism in its descriptive dryness, in its lack of emotionality.

Ciao

Calvino

[Handwritten on Einaudi headed paper; with the addressee.]

To Kitty Alenius—Stockholm

Turin, 17 May 1965

Dear Miss Alenius,

I HAVE READ YOUR THESIS AND I WILL NOT HIDE MY EXCITEment and embarrassment at seeing two names constantly put together, "Ariosto and Calvino."[114]

I have to say that you are very clever to have shown such a light touch in dealing with this comparison which can only be placed, I believe, on an extremely generic level.

Since I wanted to tell the story of an empty suit of armor, it was natural that I should use the conventional *décor* of the Carolingian cycle. For Italian literature the Carolingian chivalric epic is what the Western is for the Americans: when the "literati" (Pulci, Boiardo, Ariosto) began to work their "variations on a theme," already for over a century those themes had moved from the French *chansons de gestes* to the Italian *cantari* written by anonymous authors, and to the romance compilations of Andrea da Barberino. This success at a *popular*, almost folkloristic, level continued throughout the whole of the last century (the most widely read book—often the only book—in the Italian countryside was *I reali di Francia* [*The Royal House of France*]), and still today in Sicily the "puppet theater" reworks the stories of Orlando in an almost ritualistic series of performances which lasts the whole year. Thus the choice of such a traditional setting cannot be said of itself to be

"Ariostesque." And you rightly try to establish links that are more subtle than just the simple use of the same topic.

I remember that when writing *The Non-Existent Knight*, as a reference book for finding names etc., I used not Ariosto but a volume of *Cantari cavallereschi dei secoli XV e XVI* (*Chivalric Poems of the XVth and XVIth Centuries*), edited by Giorgio Barini (Bologna, 1905).

I am pleased that you want to continue writing on this topic and I am very interested in reading what you write. Perhaps you might find useful an annotated edition of *The Baron in the Trees*, which I prepared this year for use in schools. The notes and commentary appear under a false name, but I wrote them.[115]

You ask me two questions. On the *Italian Folktales* I cannot tell you anything more than what I wrote in the long introduction to the volume. Since then I have never returned to the topic. (Perhaps this was a mistake not to continue studying them; but maybe the chance to do so will come back.)

As for American literature, the author who had most influence on my early work was Hemingway. I will send you an article of mine on this author, from 1954.[116]

Thank you once more and best wishes for your studies.

Italo Calvino

[Typed on Einaudi headed paper, with autograph signature; with the addressee.]

To François Wahl—Paris

Turin, 17 May 1965

Dear François,

La poverina is beautiful and good and healthy.[117] So is her mother. When are you coming to see us?

In the meantime you will have received the invitation from Einaudi for a meeting on 4–5 June and I hope to see you there.

[. . .][118]

About *The Watcher*. The sentence that you quote does not work because it has not been translated properly. On a separate sheet* I've tried to explain the thread of the thinking (which is not very original, in any case) that the sentence implies. Please do ask me about any doubts you have.

As for the Cosmicomic stories, I have finally written one which I am happy about: it is the most abstract of all of them. As soon as I have finalized it, I'll send it to you. At present there are now eleven stories.

Palladio: here they will give you a discount of 40 percent just as they do for those who work for Einaudi "internally." If you come here, you can pick up your copy. If not, write to Davico who will have it sent to you.

A bientôt, j'espère.

* "Il negare valore ai poteri umani implica l'accettazione (ossia la scelta) del potere peggiore" (Denying value to human powers implies the acceptance [or choice] of the worse power).[119]

Amerigo has managed to understand "the sense of the vanity of history" typical of religious thinkers: historical, human power (personified by the Onorevole [the Honorable Member]) is something tiny compared to the power of God (personified by the dwarf): man can do nothing whereas "God" can do everything. And if the forms of human power, the historical forms of society, count for nothing before the "omnipotence of God," this means that one form of political power is the same as another. Consequently, the mystic is indifferent in the face of politics; but political indifference implies passive acceptance of the worst forms of power (hence of fascism) which necessarily must triumph amidst political indifference. Accepting fascism is tantamount to choosing fascism. Thus the "kingdom of God" (of the dwarf) and the triumph of injustice in politics (the Honorable Member) are one and the same thing.

I think this can be translated literally. Don't confuse *kingdom*, which is used in a metaphysical, allegorical sense, and *power* which is used in its practical, political sense.

I've looked for the passage that is quoted from Marx's *Economic-Philosophical Manuscripts of 1844*.[120] It is part of the "First Manuscript" of the fragment entitled (by the German publisher) "Alienated Work," folio XXIV.

If these details are not enough to allow you to trace the passage in a French edition, I can lend you the Italian edition I took it from (by Norberto Bobbio, Einaudi, 1949) in order to help you find it.
[Typed copy; in the Calvino Archive and in the Einaudi Archive, Turin.]

To Michelangelo Antonioni—Rome

Turin, 29 September 1965

Dear Michelangelo,
My view of the screenplay is simply (as I mentioned to you) that there is still a lot of work to be done.[121] Of the two strands of the story, the one about the discovery of the crime through the photographs should be amplified to give the film that amount of thriller-like suspense that is needed: you really have to find some coup-de-scène, and create the sense of solving a mystery.

The other strand, the one about the photographer's conjugal life, let's say, is still very much up in the air. We know what it must mean, what its role should be in the film, but on the level of plot we still don't have anything we can consider definitive.

This is what makes me see a full collaboration as something very demanding, both in terms of time and in terms of the concentration needed to think about it. This could also be something exciting for me, but not at a time when I am immersed in creative work of a very different kind (a series of stories which constitute a new experiment and require me to concentrate using a certain kind of logic).[122] If I spend the afternoon working with you on the screenplay, I'll get back home and won't be able to return to that other atmosphere.

Now you are proposing a different kind of collaboration: that of reading and giving views and suggestions on what you're doing. Faced with this display of your understanding and friendship I cannot but say yes, thanking you for the trust you place in my advice.

As for the other screenwriters, I believe that your double-act with Tonino works very well, and guarantees an internal dialectic that is tried and tested.[123]

Naturally if the staff of screenwriters could count on a new input which had something *different* to say, new perspectives would open up. (This was another reason why I hesitated over your invitation: I don't feel I have this *different* input to give.)

Two ideas that are contradictory (but maybe not too contradictory) come to mind. One is to try Cortázar himself who could give to the film (if he accepts it being different from his story) that tension arising from *mystery* which he feels, that sense of tragedy that he knows how to give to everyday things. The rich range of storylines in his works seems to me to be proof that he has no shortage of cinematic ideas. Another kind of collaboration might be one with a . . . "professional" from the world of thrillers, maybe someone non-Italian. His job would be to make the story of the photographs hold up on a level that is purely professional (something that perhaps none of us is equipped to do), as long as it is clear that he limits himself to contributing to the outline of the film (or adding some joint to its skeleton) and doesn't touch the *substance*.

In about ten days I will be back in Rome and we'll meet up.

Best wishes.

[Typed copy; in the Calvino Archive and in the Einaudi Archive, Turin.]

To Emilio Garroni—Rome

Turin, 26 October 1965

Dear Garroni,

In my "formative" readings I try to avoid what is imposed by publishers' novelties and to concentrate together books on similar topics at times when I am dealing with that subject. That is why it is only now that I have read your book, *La crisi semantica delle arti* (*The Semantic Crisis in the Arts*), which you sent to me over a year ago, and I feel I owe you a letter (I think I wrote a quick reply to a letter of yours at the time) to tell you that it was a very stimulating read, it taught me so many things, and that I am still digesting it and will probably go back to it.[124]

I don't want to make any declarations of agreement or otherwise as regards your basic position. It seems to me that the "sign-semantics" relationship, the way you put it, is convincing. But at this time I am trying to accumulate and reflect, and I am avoiding declarations of faith, which cannot be made just like that on the spur of the moment, but in fact only on the basis of serious analyses like yours.

I will tell you immediately what I don't like about your book, so I can get that out of the way and don't have to think about it any more: I don't like the habit of quoting everything that everyone writes, from basic texts to newspaper articles to spur of the moment declarations and academic broadsides. Why this general respect for everything people write? Not that you do not discriminate, on the contrary your polemics are always well aimed, but they give too much importance to everyone.[125] Your book would be much more useful as a summing up of the problems if it quoted only the most essential authors: in other words if it limited the debate to very few voices that were representative of the basic tendencies, and forgot about the rest. (This passion for piling up disparate references is typical of Dorfles's method, so not yours, I would say.) As I said, it seems to me that your attacks are always aimed in a direction I agree with. And your clarification of the notions that the book is based on seems to work.

But what I liked especially are Parts 3 and 4, firstly because I find there a line of argument that is more useful to me (both as clarification and as stimulus) even than Barthes's *Sémiologie*; secondly, because there are some sections that are excellent in the way they are imagined and written. (The passage on the sunset and then immediately the bit on Chaplin; the whole section on the "improper sign" in nineteenth-century art; Borges's gods as an allegory of the Second World War.)

The reading of your book came at the right time for me, since the things I am writing now are stories where I have to deal with "the question of the sign" more than ever (for me this means developing an image I start out with according to a logic that is internal to that image or system of images). In them I also deal with semanticity (for me this is the range of possible meanings of every sign-image-word, mostly historical-intellectual allegorizations, which always present themselves one minute later and about which I must never worry too much if I want to find the perfect organization in which the logic of the sign—which is one and only one—and the semantic logic—which has to have free play on various levels—become one and the same thing). The result is that many of these stories are rewritten several times, because every so often I discover once more "what they meant" on the level of sign or of meaning and so then I adjust them in one direction or another. There is indeed one story where the key word is "sign"— "Un segno nello spazio" (A Sign in Space)[126]—which came out in all "innocence" and then became loaded with inevitable cultural intentions, and so this is a story which I have been constantly rewriting and retouching now for a couple of years, and I only managed to give it the final readjustments (before the volume comes out in November) after reading your book, so you see how it appeared at the right time.

Best wishes.

Your Italo Calvino

[Typed on Einaudi headed paper, with autograph signature; with the addressee. Also in *ILDA*, pp. 535–37.]

To Leonardo Sciascia—Caltanissetta

Turin, 10 November 1965

Dear Leonardo,

I READ YOUR DETECTIVE THRILLER WHICH IS NOT A THRILLER with all the excitement with which people read detective stories, and in addition with amusement at seeing how the thriller is deconstructed, or rather how you prove the impossibility of writing a thriller in the Sicilian environment.[127] In short, this is vintage Sciascia, worthy to be set alongside *Il giorno della civetta* (*The Day of the Owl*), or even to outdo it, because there is more irony here, because the presence of the tutelary deity Pirandello is not at all marginal, because one can see that it comes after *Il Consiglio d'Egitto* (*The Council of Egypt*). The comedy of characters and the historical-literary-sociological essay undergo a fusion for which only you, amongst today's fiction writers, possess the formula.

It will be a popular book and one which will provoke discussion as well. (The thing I find least convincing is the title: a bit too generically Pirandellian, it doesn't stand out enough.)

Seeing that you are so good and sound at this, I've decided, in a bid to match the grim times we are living through, to offer you bitter little titbits in every letter. Otherwise where's the fun? And on this occasion I can tell you this: for some time now I've noticed that every new thing I read about Sicily is an amusing variation on a theme about which by now I think I already know everything, absolutely everything. This Sicily is the least mysterious society in the world. By now, everything in Sicily is clear, crystal-clear: the most tormented passions, the darkest interests, psychology, gossip, crimes, lucidity, fatalism, none of these hold any secrets any more, everything has by now been classified and cataloged. The satisfaction that Sicilian stories give is like that in a good game of chess, the pleasure of the infinite combinations made by a finite number of pieces for each one of which a finite number of possibilities exist. Whereas for every other chapter in human knowledge, for every other entry in the encyclopaedia, we know we will never be able to reach its end, that the more we learn the more something escapes us, the entry "Sicily" gives us the rare pleasure, so rare as to be unique, of being able to confirm at each new reading that our information pack on Sicily was already well-stocked and up to date enough. So much so that we fervently hope that nothing will change, that Sicily will stay totally the same, so at the end of our life we can say that there is at least one thing we have managed to know thoroughly!

I leave you to meditate on this . . . Parthian shot, and await your revenge!

Affectionately,

Your Calvino

[Typed on Einaudi headed paper; with the addressee's heirs. Also in "Lettere di Italo Calvino a Leonardo Sciascia," *Forum Italicum*, 1 (Spring 1981), pp. 68–69; and in *ILDA*, pp. 538–39.]

To *Il Giorno*—Milan

Rome, November [1965]

[Sir,]

It seems to me that it cannot be said enough that the wave of intolerance that has arisen in Rome against "those with long-hair" is an alarming episode of incivility. This is a topic on which it is easy to joke: which one of us is not ready to make fun of "long-haired youths"? But it is no laughing matter when one sees that a small, harmless but unpopular minority, the butt of jokes and sarcasm, gets beaten up and the police just turn their backs or even take it out on those who have been attacked.

It is a serious matter that there are in our country's capital students so uncouth as to attack people because they are dressed differently from them and because they have a mild and vulnerable manner. It is a serious matter that some newspapers incited them. But much more serious is the behavior of the police. The first two phenomena can be explained with the historical and sociological reasons that lie behind so many other examples of "underdevelopment." We can maybe play these down, thinking that the transformation of Italy into a modern country, with a more European middle-class set of values, with less provincial newspapers, will in the end be just a question of years. But the police are not a social phenomenon that has to be interpreted, the police are a service that has to function in one way and not in another. Amongst their first duties, the police have to guarantee everyone's right to wear their hair and beard as they want, and to spend their time as they want, as long as they respect the law and do not annoy their neighbor. To consider some tourists in Italy different from others because they have long hair is already a fact that goes beyond the competence of public administration.

But there is a question of political and civic sensitivity that is even more important: what must the attitude of the organs of the State be knowing that an arbitrary campaign of persecution is being conducted against foreigners in Italy? It seems to me that there are not two possible approaches but only one: the authorities and especially the police must do everything to protect these foreigners, to prove that the incivility of some of our fellow-citizens is the antithesis of the laws of our country, and to do so with the traditional spirit of Italian hospitality. In short, they must see to it that this wave of intolerance does not win out. Just to fail in this duty is a serious enough omission: but here we are actually talking about behavior that goes in the opposite direction. What is happening?

Italo Calvino

[Published in the Letters to the Editor page with the title "L'ondata d'intolleranza per i 'capelloni'" (The Wave of Intolerance against "Hippies"), *Il Giorno* [17 November 1965], p. 17. See the analogous statement by Calvino, from the same period, in his "I capelli dei capelloni (Hippies' Hair)," *Nuova Generazione* (27 November 1965), p. 3.]

To Grazia Marchianò—Rome

Turin, 21 December 1965

Dear Miss Marchianò,

I've read your piece with interest.[128] The correspondence between passages from Zolla and my own works emerges quite convincingly, and although I had never thought about such links—sticking to the more obvious differences between our positions—I do not think I have any objections to the terms in which you set up the parallel.[129]

Absolutely fine to link *Cosmicomics* to *The Non-Existent Knight* (you are the first to do so), and also the link with Nausicaa (again you are the first). I understand perfectly that the former came out when you had already set up your terms of reference, and it was difficult to make it fit in more.

Moving on to criticisms, I'll start by saying that—in my opinion—you should not have begun your article with that first novel by Zolla, which seems to me to be something that (except—as far as I remember—for the chapter on God and the Devil) lies well below the standards of Zolla the essayist.[130]

But apart from this pairing of Calvino and Zolla, which is your thesis, do you not think that the other names are put together rather haphazardly? Are you sure that this Piedmont of yours exists? Do you not think that your argument would hold just as well if you inserted the names of other non-Piedmontese writers? You already do this to a certain extent by putting in a bit of Lombardy for Arbasino's Voghera and Mastronardi's Vigevano (these two places really have little to do with your argument, and it is only the famous Lombard "Scapigliatura" that acts as a common denominator).[131] (I'm leaving aside the fact that it is very debatable to include me, since although I lived for twenty years in Turin, I continued to set almost all my stories in my native Ligurian Riviera; and I specifically chose to commit to the *moral* climate of Piedmont, but it has never had a narrative climate.) In my view what counts are not geographical areas, but actual points in common and reciprocal influences. Why do you include Arpino and not Fenoglio, when they were from nearby towns (although not friends) and they began writing at the same time and in the same climate? Why is there Zolla and not Citati, when they were classmates right from the first years of high school, and even today they continue a discourse that has striking aspects in common? Amongst the older writers you mention, Carlo Levi and Mario Soldati were friends from their schooldays; Emanuelli was younger and emerged from the Novara area which is also linked (via Bonfantini) with Soldati's beginnings. Here are three writers for whom you could establish a common discourse with documents to hand. (And why not include also someone who was a contemporary of the first two, Giacomo Debenedetti?) And why on earth do you submerge Pavese in the midst of minor and indeed minimal names? He is so much greater, more complex and refined and aware, and so much more a poet than the others you name (and he is definitely *Piedmontese*, not just because he was totally rooted in his land, but because he had created a poetics out of having emerged from a non-poetic region par excellence). There you could tap into something that would provide you with a very rich and still untouched seam: discovering the threads of a Turinese Nietzscheanism, which found its most original exponent in Pavese (as you remember, Turin was the city where Nietzsche went mad) and which contrasts with and more often complements the famous Piedmontese rationalism and historicism (about which people have always spoken so much).

In short, either this literary Piedmont does not exist (we are in a period when the characteristics of national literatures are starting to disappear, never mind dealing with regional characterizations!), or if you want to provide an outline of an intellectual environment, the references must be increased and you must aim at a much more detailed historical reconstruction. In the latter case your article could be a good starting point but would need to be broadened and given more depth.

And if you follow that bit of advice, allow me also to say what I think about your style: it is too *written* (especially at the start), too laden with your concern for expression. Critics must impose their ideas, not their voice. That said, I am not arguing that a critic should be allowed to write in a slovenly way like some of our younger writers. But you cite your interest in Roland Barthes, and in fact he is perhaps the contemporary critic I admire the most. He is not only a highly intelligent critic but a fine writer, actually as a writer of prose: and yet notice how he never overloads his words except when he has to establish a new idea.

Please take my observations as proof of the interest your article aroused in me, and of my gratitude for the attention you have devoted to my works.

Best wishes.

[Typed copy; in the Einaudi Archive, Turin. Also in *ILDA*, pp. 544–46.]

1966–1970

To Maria Livia Serini—Milan

Turin, 13 January 1966

Dear Maria Livia,

Thank you for your very kind letter: I heartily reciprocate your good wishes. I am very sorry to hear the news of your problems: I knew nothing about them; I hope you recover quickly and that 1966 will be a happy year for you. I also hope to see you: I will be coming and going between Rome and Turin (but my family will not be moving: only now do I realize what a commitment it is).

I fully understand your reluctance to have your letters from Pavese published. We work as historians, convinced that every piece of paper and evidence on an author has its importance; but there are many cases where it is right to take account of the confidentiality of correspondents, and we always respect it.

Nevertheless, I shall put two ways forward to you which would take account of both your reservations and the completeness of the published letters:

(1) to publish the letters to you without your name, stating only "To a female friend'; in the same way the other names in the letter (or in the extracts from the letter) that might lead to an identification can be replaced by asterisks;

(2) if there are some letters whose content is not exclusively confidential, but which contain literary or other judgments, or

observations or simply bursts of humor, to publish solely the part of the letter that interests us. Square brackets with three suspension dots will signal that we have cut part of it. Using this method, your name could stay.

Both procedures are widely used when publishing correspondence, and I have by now a certain experience in such operations.

For all this you could count on our utmost discretion, ça va sans dire.[1]

Unfortunately we have not been able to find the letter you mention, which was given to Einaudi in September '50. (And we have now ransacked all the archives.)

Best wishes to you and Fabrizio and a hug for Diana.

[Typed copy; in the Einaudi Archive, Turin.]

To Gian Carlo Ferretti—Milan

Turin, 15 February 1966

Dear Ferretti,

I HAVE BEEN MEANING FOR SOME TIME NOW TO REPLY TO YOUR letter.[2] It gave me enormous pleasure for the very intelligent things you say about my book and it also requires a certain commitment from me in replying because of the questions you ask. Yes, in the kind of stories one finds in *Cosmicomics*, I would like to succeed in distilling the results of my ideal form of research, and of my comments on reality; but I would like to do so not solely using symbolic or rather allegorical words with a range of meanings. I would like to be able to express everything by thinking in images, or in word-images, but word-images which have the rigor almost of abstraction which in the *Cosmicomic* stories happens only in "A Sign in Space" and "The Spiral" (and perhaps also "The Light Years"), and from there to succeed in articulating a discourse that is *my* discourse, without it having other layers of meanings. For the time being, at the point where I am at just now, I manage to let the stories organize themselves, on the basis of their own material, *to let them think themselves*, become a discourse of which I take note. However, this business of the objectivity of the story which takes shape by itself is for me only a partial, provisional hypothesis. I am well aware that even this question of proposing signs and following them through their potential organization is a way of thinking, and so the point of arrival must be the abolition of this opposition between the organization of signs and the organization of meanings.

Naturally this emphasis on the *abstract* component in *Cosmicomics* must be accompanied by the constant presence of *representation*, through linguistic and figurative materials which provide the *texture of real life*. That is what defines the *Cosmicomics* for me.

As you can see, I am still too much taken up with characterizing this work, the *Cosmicomics*, from its inside to try to define it in the context of the rest of my work. The things you say on this topic, looking to parallels with *The Watcher*, are highly suggestive (and I hope you have the chance to develop this argument) and it seems to me that Ferrata too has gone down the same road, also with a certain finesse.[3] But for each book I would like to create first of all a void around it, see it how it is on its own, and then put it in context.

I am very grateful for your reading of the book and for the stimulus for discussion and clarification that you have given me.

Best wishes.
Yours,

Italo Calvino

I had left the draft of this letter in Turin; then I left for Rome and have not been back here for three weeks. I am signing it only now, the day after poor Elio's funeral.[4] All this to explain my prolonged silence.
[Typed on Einaudi headed paper, with autograph corrections, signature and added paragraph; with the addressee. Also in *ILDA*, pp. 558–59.]

To Hans Magnus Enzensberger—Berlin

Rome, 22 February 1966

Dear Enzensberger,

We are in the sad process of getting out the last issues of *Il Menabò*, the ones Elio had approved and prepared. The German issue is ready and will appear soon: seeing it all assembled, with your information about every contributor, which complements perfectly the introductory essay, it seems to me a fine and useful volume.

We will also include a piece from the recent play by Peter Weiss, something Elio had personally chosen in the last few weeks when he was able to read. It is the piece (I'm quoting from memory as I do not have it to hand) about the woman who works for Farben (The Ballad of Lill Topper, I think it's called).[5]

Could you write us a brief page of introduction for this piece too? In fact it really is necessary since it is the only item for which we do not have your "introduction." I would be very grateful if you could send it to us as soon as possible, because the issue is already being typeset.

Write and tell me what you are working on, and tell me about *Kursbuch* and your other work. Now that Elio is no longer with us, and so many things that he stood for and embodied are, it seems to me, now gone, perhaps the only thing to do [is] to keep closer contact with his friends who work in a certain way in various countries.

Best wishes

[Typed copy; in the Einaudi Archive, Turin.]

To François Wahl—Paris

Rome, 13.6.66

Dear François,[6]

Today I received your letter of the 2nd. Here the post has been clogged up with a series of strikes. The movement of letters is just starting to take off again, but we have not received any printed matter for about three weeks. That is why I have not seen *La Quinzaine*

(I have become a subscriber because you cannot get it here). I saw the *Observateur* and the *Express*, which were not at all negative, but both far from providing satisfactory reading. Still, long live the inadequacy of critics if it manages to provoke you into writing an article!

Could you please ask the press office to send me, *by letter post*, the clippings of the articles I have not seen?

I have just come back from the meetings of the Gruppo 63 at La Spezia (this year's Reggio Emilia).[7] It was very interesting for me because this was the first time I'd taken part in this kind of event, and the sight of such an austere and severe assembly struck me very favorably for its novelty, both on the level of literary behavior, and on the level of shedding light on the texts under discussion. I learned a lot, I must admit. Having said that, my more mature and critical reflections concern the following:

(1) the weakness of the critics (apart from Sanguineti, whose authority is indisputable; and Manganelli, who develops his ingenious theoretical exploits always several meters above the object of discussion) and the feeling that from the critical point of view the group's work is simply marking time, and that a considerable number of the texts are above the critical abilities of the group;

(2) the implicit (Sanguinetian) terrorism in the name "avant-garde" which places a veto against all attempts at success on the part of the work: Porta, who read bits of a novel that seems to me very good, moving in the same direction as Thibaudeau, I think, was attacked by everyone as championing the restoration of the literature of memory, as a friend of nature, a D'Annunzian, etc. (Try to see his novel as soon as possible.) But at the same time

(3) the terrorism of those (especially the younger members) for whom avant-garde means the refusal of any plan for literary structure: these are Lettrist-Phonetists, Happeningists, Burroughsists, people terrorizing Sanguineti and the other "old" members of the group who cannot control the process.

The prospect of a literature of *illegibility*, as the horizon that is now in sight, dominated the conference.

* * *

In reply to the "film-novel" questionnaire sent by *Cahiers du Cinéma*, I wrote a little *summa* in French.[8]

***

I received a very enthusiastic letter from J.-L. Barrault, which did not seem just part of his "daily routine," where he asks me to write something for his theater.

***

Have a good summer!

Italo

[Handwritten; with the addressee.]

TO GIULIO EINAUDI—MASSA LUBRENSE (NAPLES)

[Rome,] 29 June 1966

Dear Giulio,

AFTER MATURE REFLECTION ON THE LITERARY SITUATION IN Italy, I have come to the conclusion that it is necessary to continue with *Il Menabò*, and that the only way to do so is for me to take over personally as editor, in other words without an editorial board or other forms of collective responsibility. As in the past, it will be only the editor to decide who to invite as collaborators from issue to issue, operating independently of official categories of groups or tendencies, and taking account solely of the interest in developing a common discourse. I think that *Il Menabò* ought to continue without any interruption, using the same format, and stating "founded by E. V., editor I. C."[9] It will still have only one or two issues per year: either anthologies or devoted to a single topic, and either Italian or international in content. In each issue, I will write something, in order to take forward a particular discourse.

This is a decision I have taken after much reluctance, seeing that I had recently considered the "public" side of my activities as at an end, in order to concentrate on my own creative work. But I see today, looking at the map of the various literary tendencies, that one really feels the gap left by what *Il Menabò* (at least potentially) stood for, and so withdrawing from this difficult inheritance would be tantamount to being responsible for ending years of work that had always looked toward the future. I therefore prefer to take on a positive rather than a negative responsibility, even though I hope that the development of younger people's orientation will allow me to leave *Il Menabò* in good hands in the space of a few years; naturally it will mean having to work to make this possible.

Ciao,

Calvino

[Handwritten; in the Einaudi Archive, Turin. Also in *ILDA*, pp. 564–65.]

To Luigi Nono—Venice

Rome 25-9-66

Dear Gigi,

I HAD PROMISED TO WRITE TO YOU WITH MY REACTIONS TO *Floresta*, and I am now doing so, hoping my letter gets to you before you leave.[10]

What I wanted to say to you does not concern the structure of your work which I appreciated in all its force and quality: blocks of solid, total, black sound, contrasting with blocks of luminous, strikingly human music; something constructed in an escalating crescendo both as regards human destruction and human *interrogation*, the *interrogative* value of the voice.

A sequence of reflections of a more, let's say, content-and-expression type was set off by what in *Floresta* is the *representation* of the war, the bombing etc. I found myself wondering: is it right to represent bombing with noise? Would it not be more meaningful to put the emphasis on what is *silence* in the bombing? When you think about it, the dominant element in bombing is silence. During air-raids people stand with their ears straining to catch the approach of airplanes, their descent on the city, the whistle of the bombs, in order to pinpoint where they explode; and there is no more significant moment than the silence that follows the explosion of a bomb. Also on board a bomber I think that the background roar of the engines and the distant descent of the bombs creates an atmosphere of absurd silence. Above all, there is no element of force during an air-raid: bombing consists of weakness and fear. The pilots who release the bombs are more full of fear than their victims, bombing is an act of weakness, bombs fall lazily, exploiting the force of gravity. If we accept that bombing is *force*, we are playing the bombers' game.

Now I would not want the idea I have expressed to become confused with the claim of all celebratory art (including "socialist realism") to depict war not in its horror but as something heroic and non-repellent. I am with you in being completely against this position, with your desire and ability to express war as an atrocity. I'm only saying to study it in its essence, anti-naturalistically and anti-romantically, and *A floresta* made me rethink war in its *acoustic* essence, which is fundamental.

Also in partisan battles—and I believe in all battle conflicts—the essential element for all combatants is what they hear, in the sense of trying to distinguish and localize gunfire and any other noise, isolating it from the general mayhem, and to interpret the sudden silences in the midst of battle, to realize what is happening, how the battle is going, how our comrades and enemies are moving, so as not to be cut off from our comrades etc. The whole of life as a partisan is lived through an amplification of sound, a detailed recognition of noises and silences, especially at night and in ambushes and reprisals. I thought I recognized this acoustic richness in that part of your composition where the forest itself appears, but of course I don't mean these things in the sense of them being an illustration, but rather I am talking of musical images in the broad sense.

I've also thought about everything in *Floresta* that is a positive presence, the world of struggle, of revolution. The historical value of *A floresta é jovem* lies for me, as I said, in this tension of interrogation (which is perhaps typical of the whole work), this being the voice of an epoch of dramatic uncertainty, of losing the revolution in the world.

And I appreciate a lot your choral dimension that embraces different languages, the internationalist setting, seeing the struggle as *one*.

But it is precisely here that I would like to emphasize or offer as contrast a point that seems to me to be essentially part of the moment we are living through, and in particular of the war in Vietnam: the loneliness of those who are fighting. The Vietcong are fighting against the colossus of the United States and they are *alone*, in the midst of a world that believes it is at peace, that is thinking about (or is trying to think about, or has to think about) other things. The other guerrilla wars in Asia, Latin America, and Africa are—compared with Vietnam—sporadic, localized episodes, and recent struggles, even major ones like the Algerian war, soon turned out to be *local* episodes as well, since they never developed a universal dimension. Cuba started out as a local story, then became universal, but is now perhaps forced to going back to being something local. Meanwhile this guerrilla war by poor rice-growers who are holding at bay the most powerful military force in the world is of *world* significance, just as the Resistance in Europe was when it blocked a large part of the German army. But the huge difference is this: that the European Resistance was an episode in a world war and its outcome was linked to the outcome of that war; whereas in Vietnam the war is taking place in the context of what is called world peace, with in the background consumer economies, the rush toward affluence by more or less privileged countries, with everyone standing staring at the tragedy, unable to move a finger because of the prospect of an even more horrific tragedy, the world war that is looming. While the context that European culture had before it from *Guernica* and *Conversations in Sicily* to *A Survivor from Warsaw* was the universality of suffering and struggle in a world of explicit tragedy, today the picture we are faced with is different.[11] The tragic truth of the world is hidden from a large part of that world, everyone to some extent is duty-bound to hide it (even China which has to downplay the tragedy of a total war). How to express all this, make it become a vision of the world, a stylistic procedure? I can't tell you: if only I knew!

Maybe your "Someone Has Been a Traitor" could be developed in this direction. In parallel with the escalation of the bombs there is the escalation of the particularity of individuals' and individual peoples' interests, the urge to see only the "particular," the impossibility for each of us to incarnate the universal.

These are only meant to be notes for a discussion of the work in progress that you are developing. You can see that *A floresta é jovem* has had the effect on me of making me rethink and look for definitions for the most important things.

Chichita and I think with grateful memories of you and Nuria and your Venetian hospitality. Love to your little girls, and have a good trip.

Yours,

Italo

[Handwritten; in the Luigi Nono Archive, Venice.]

To Gian Carlo Ferretti—Milan

[Turin,] 15.3.67

Dear Ferretti,

ARE YOU AWARE THAT THAT LITTLE QUESTION OF YOURS "FOR whom does one write?" is damned difficult? I have begun it again several times and each time I get off on the wrong foot: either I start with my autobiography from '45 onwards, or the history of world literature from the nineteenth century, or a survey of the current positions on the topic, in short I get swamped in wide-ranging discussions and in the end tear everything up. Perhaps I am not suited to being one of those who open the discussion, because I can't manage to say anything clear and trenchant. If I were to intervene either in support of or against others, maybe I'd have more success. Or perhaps replying to the questions in an interview.

I'm sorry, but I'm blocked, and I'm waiting for you to give me a further shove.[12]

Best wishes.
Yours,

Calvino

[Handwritten on Einaudi headed paper; with the addressee.]

To John Woodhouse—Hull

Turin, 5 April 1967

Dear Mr Woodhouse,

I WAS VERY PLEASED TO RECEIVE YOUR LETTER AND TO LEARN that I have in you a keen reader and a friend, and that you are planning to write a study of my books. I will try to help you as much as I can.

1. Of all the biographical information that can be found about me, "born in San Remo in 1923" is the most accurate and correct. I spent my childhood, adolescence, and youth there, up to the age of twenty-four. My father was from San Remo and all his family, for as many generations as can be remembered, were small landowners and farmers in San Remo. It is also true that in my passport it is written "Born in Santiago de Las Vegas (Cuba)," but this is simply a birth-registry detail, and at most is part of my pre-history, not of my history. So, if it is just a brief biographical note, I always say "Born in San Remo." An exotic birthplace on its own is not informative of anything. In order for it to become meaningful I would have to add many things: that my father, a professor of agronomy, born in 1875, spent twenty years between Mexico and Cuba, that he came to Italy in 1920 to marry another professor (she was a professor of botany), that I was born while my father was director of an

experimental agronomy station in a village near Havana, that before I was two my parents returned to Italy, and from that time I never left San Remo until I was a grown-up. I left Cuba too early for its landscape to have stayed in my childhood memories, so from the *artistic* point of view, having been born there does not count for much. In short, Cuba is more a detail from my parents' biographies than from mine. Of course being the child of parents who have traveled round the world is different from being born in an enclosed, provincial environment. My family's exotic, American, tropical background is not an insignificant biographical fact; but the fundamental thing in defining a writer is the landscape and environment that have shaped his life, so "born in San Remo" is more *true* than "born near Havana."

2. Here the most *accurate* statement is "he has lived in Turin for about twenty years." Even though I have lived (and perhaps still live) in other Italian and foreign cities, these have always been temporary stays. The center of my life and of my intellectual formation has always been Turin.
3. See answer 1.[13]
4. Normal. Nothing unusual to point out.[14]
5. Difficult to answer. I have decided not to make any more theoretical pronouncements. (I have never made that many.) See my contribution in the (collaborative) volume, *La generazione degli anni difficili* (*The Generation that Lived Through Difficult Times*) (Bari: Laterza, 1962).[15]
6. Ditto. I find myself in sympathy a lot with [Bertrand] Russell. But when I hear the word "humanist," I think: Oh, for heaven's sake![16]
7. I left the PCI like many other Italian intellectuals who after the 20th Congress wanted to take the process of "de-stalinization" to its logical consequences. For this as well, you should see *La generazione degli anni difficili*.
8. See the book I mentioned, and issues 23–24 of the journal *Il Paradosso* (Milan: 1960), which I will send you.[17] As for *The Path to the Spiders' Nests*, which you mention in your letter, it has no autobiographical references, though some can be found in the

Preface I wrote for the 1964 edition of that novel (I'll send you the book).

9. Another difficult question! I've never asked myself this. I've always tried to be as "cosmopolitan" as possible. (And perhaps this is the only real way of being Italian.) What I have always hated in literature is the exaltation of the "national-popular" dimension.
10. In my early output (in other words, the stories in *Ultimo viene il corvo* [*The Crow Comes Last*]—which were partly included in the collected *I racconti*—and my first novel) objectivity and fantasy were one and the same thing. I soon lost this capacity for objective representation, and I developed a kind of fantasy strand (which continues today in *Cosmicomics*) as well as a kind of autobiographical-intellectual narrative (which I find less and less satisfying).
11. It was not difficult to master the language. As a child I spoke Italian at home. My mother (from a Sardinian family but she had gone to university in Lombardy) spoke Italian and knew no dialect. But right from my childhood I felt that this was a bit of an artificial language and that the truth of language came from dialect in the way it was spoken by my father (though not with us) and by the rest of the world around us. The Ligurian dialect of San Remo is noticeably different from the Genoese dialect. I never knew how to speak it fluently, yet my whole linguistic environment was permeated by it and when I began to write I tried to model phrases and words on the spoken usage of my town, which was completely new to literature. Subsequently perhaps the Piedmontese influence got mixed up with this Ligurian strain. I believe that even when I use a *higher, more cultured* register, one can feel that my linguistic choices go toward the spoken usage that is closer to North-Western dialects. In order to know what kind of Italian I write the only thing to do is to study my collection of *Italian Folktales* from a linguistic point of view. I translated them from all dialects, trying to find a common *Italian* style and at the same time to let something of their dialectal aura come through, where possible; so one can analyze that little bit of my own substance

that is there. However, I think I can categorically state that my style is not *Tuscanizing*; on the contrary, I've always hated Tuscanizing writers.

12. I have never been a journalist (except for a few months in 1948–49, on the board of the Turin edition of *l'Unità*). My collaboration on newspapers has always been rather irregular, though I published quite regular contributions in 1954–55 in the journal *Il Contemporaneo*, whose editor was Salinari.

    You ask me about *Il Politecnico*. At that time I was a young, unknown figure from the provinces. I sent to Vittorini's journal (when it was still a weekly, in 1945–46) two articles on my region and one short story, which got published.

    As for *Il Menabò*, I don't know if you have ever seen it. It was not a journal but a series of volumes a bit like *New Writing*, that came out once a year. This was a very personal initiative of Vittorini's, who was an extraordinary stimulus for Italian literature. I am grateful to Vittorini's memory and proud to have been able to figure alongside him as co-editor of *Il Menabò*; but my role in the journal was very secondary compared to Vittorini's. I published in *Il Menabò* a couple of essays: "Il mare dell'oggettività" (The Sea of Objectivity) (issue 2, 1959) and "La sfida al labirinto" (The Challenge to the Labyrinth) (issue 5, 1962).

13. I do not have Pacifici's book to hand.[18] Pacifici follows Italian literature with close attention, but one cannot always have an accurate perspective from America.

14. I don't remember where the quote from Pacifici comes from. In the years around 1960 I answered dozens and dozens of interviews and surveys, on the problems of the novel etc. At a certain point I decided to stay silent and I no longer reply to anyone (except to you).

15. The essay, "Il midollo del leone" (The Lion's Marrow) appeared in the journal *Il Paragone*, 66 (June 1955).

16. I think this is a reference to "Il midollo del leone."

17. I have no "professional interest" in botany. It was my parents who had a professional interest in it (they ran an Experimental Floriculture Station in San Remo). My childhood was characterized by rebellion against "botany." Of course, I grew up

amongst plants, and in my books plants appear often, but when I want to write the name of a plant, I have to look it up in an encyclopaedia, because as a child I refused to learn their names. On this question, see my story "The Road to San Giovanni," published in the journal, *Questo e altro*, 1 (Milan, 1962), and reprinted in the book, *I maestri del racconto italiano*, edited by E. Pagliarani and W. Pedullà (Milan: Rizzoli, 1963).[19]

18. The lecture on contemporary Italian literature that I gave in various American universities in 1959–60 was published in *Italian Quarterly*, 13–14 (University of California Los Angeles, Spring–Summer 1960).[20]
19. A selection of stories by Saroyan, translated and totally rewritten by Vittorini, came out in Italy around 1941.[21] Vittorini transformed Saroyan into a kind of model for the lyrical-realistic short story which was to have a powerful influence on the young writers of my generation.

    As for Hemingway, he was the absolute god for me and many other young writers of my generation, at the time when we were starting out as writers.
20. *Unorthodox*: I do not know what Pacifici meant by this as I do not have his text. It might be understood in a political sense with regard to the Christian Democrat government, but Italian writers are all more or less "on the left" and therefore *orthodox* and *unorthodox* almost mean the same thing or relate in a religious sense to the Catholic church (but here again the same thing applies) or inside left-wing culture applied to those who do not obey the directives of the Party (even although in Italy cultural Stalinism has never been as rigid as in other countries).
21. The inventor of the *guillotine*? I thought it was Dr Guillotin. I do not recall ever having heard of Tobias Schmidt.[22]

I realize that you have been making me work for more than three hours now. It only remains for me to send you my best wishes, to wish you all the best for your work, hoping to read your essay soon.

Yours sincerely,

[Typed copy; in the Calvino Archive, and in the Einaudi Archive, Turin.]

To Élise Pedri—Paris

Turin, 24 April 1967

Dear Miss Pedri,

Vittorini did not publish any more novels after *La Garibaldina* but continued to write some, except that he always decided not to publish them because for him the crucial commitment lay in the formulation of an idea of literature and culture, in his tireless work as a literary animator, in his discussions with young writers. His research led him to develop theories which always went much faster than his creative work. For that reason, if he managed to finish a novel (or fragment of a novel which could "become a book"), he thought that this book would be taken as an example of his current idea of literature whereas his idea had already moved on by then, and he would not be able to defend the book critically: on the contrary, he would have to enter into a polemic with himself. That was why he did not publish; he preferred to express himself as the presenter of other writers' works rather than his own.

I am sending you the volume of *Il Menabò* which has just come out, dedicated to Vittorini's memory. There is an article of mine in which I discuss this question also.[23]

Yours sincerely,

[Typed copy; in the Einaudi Archive, Turin.]

To Benvenuto Terracini—Turin

Turin, 24 April 1967

Dear Professor Terracini,

I had heard several months ago, to my surprise and joy, that you had written something on *Cosmicomics*, and I was waiting impatiently for it to come out.

Now, having received the offprint from *Archivio*, I am happier than ever because you dwell on the story that I am keenest on, "A Sign in Space," and you read it highlighting the "scientific" allusions as well as the lyrical or personal dimensions.[24] Certainly, the story became "a writer's confession" even though when I started writing it I had no idea it would come out as that, and even though this is not the only key in which to read it but just a backdrop which surfaces occasionally. I was struck by your linking of the theme of "remorse" with what emerges in my prefaces (and it does not matter whether I am referring to Neo-realism or any other specific moment: it is the sense of what stays and what dies in a "style," the constant dissatisfaction that one has when one writes). This is a theme that would give a psychological critic food for thought, but you have outlined it with perfect restraint and sureness of touch. And everything you say about me, in terms of a psychological portrait, seems to me—even though it is not up to me to say this—to be true. I am very happy that you have uncovered, especially in the endings, a structure that has something in common with the Marcovaldo stories.

All in all, I am very pleased, and grateful.

I always hope there will be a chance to see you when I come to Turin, but I am always afraid of disturbing you.

Please accept my warmest thanks and best wishes from your

Italo Calvino

[Handwritten; in the Fondo Manoscritti del Centro di ricerca sulla tradizione manoscritta di autori moderni e contemporanei, University of Pavia.]

To Amelia Rosselli—Rome

Turin, 17 May 1967

Dear Amelia,

I HAVE NOT REPLIED TO YOUR LIST OF PROPOSALS BECAUSE IT was not what I was expecting. I wanted to know from you if there was a poet that you would particularly like to translate, in other words

someone on whom you have been working now for some time. Translations of poetry, as you well know, are a bit like writing one's own poems; one has to carry an author around with one for a long time and then every so often try out a sample. Instead you have sent me a list of books of poetry which are very different from one another, even including anthologies. You understand that I cannot present this list to my colleagues. It would qualify you instantly as an eclectic translator, who works in terms of quantity; whereas, knowing you as I do, I am aware that you are the opposite of such translators, who do however exist even in poetry, and from whom we try to keep our distance. Something that is dear to your heart, even if it's a minor author or not of huge substance, in other words a translation that is also to a certain extent *your own* book, will always be a serious proposal: the publisher might be interested, or not, but it would be something concrete which could be discussed. I would advise you to orientate yourself toward proposals of this kind.
[Typed copy; in the Einaudi Archive, Turin.]

To François Wahl—Paris

Turin, 5 June 1967

Dear François,[25]

[. . .][26]

I have written the best story of my life, and I will send it to you.[27]

This morning I was wakened by the news of the outbreak of war, but it has not yet been announced by the newspapers or radio at the time of writing.[28] I am busy writing letters in order to overcome my anxiety as I wait for news.

Our removal has been fixed for 20 June if the world does not explode first.[29]

With warmest good wishes,

Calvino

[Handwritten; with the addressee.]

To Francesco Leonetti—Bologna

[Rome,] 15.6.67

Dear Leonetti,

You no longer believe in literature? Well, that's the thing I believe in most. (But "believe" is an ugly verb.) That is to say, I am keen on that something extra that literature can give in terms of *ideas*. For this reason I think your book *consists of* its first part. The rest, the ideas, are useful as well, as long as you bear in mind that they change every now and again, and they are always generic, always untrue, always imposed by someone else, and yet they too are indisp . . . to hell with it! There, I too am starting to grind out ideas.

Mascolo phoned me today from Paris about that petition, asking who could collect signatures in Italy.[30] Seeing that you were talking to me about this in your letter, I said maybe you were the person. I still have not had time to read anything. But I'll sign it, I think; I've already signed so many, even without reading them, we'll die signing things.

I am writing to you also to warn you not to send things to Rome any more, because we're leaving our house and the city the day after tomorrow.[31] For a while, the safest address for me will be c/o Einaudi, Turin.

You must believe more in literature, which will be the only thing that remains for us in the terrible times we will have to live in.

Very best wishes.
Yours,

Calvino

[Handwritten; with the addressee.]

To Pietro Citati—La Castellaccia, Giuncarico (Grosseto)

Ronchi, 31 August [1967]

Dear Pietro,

I've read the chapters in *Paragone*, getting Vittorio Sereni to lend me the issue, and I liked them a lot.[32] That shift from the realm of form to the mineral lack of form via the Duomo of Milan, and then the move from mercurial lightness to coal combustion: I talked about all that with Fortini as well, who of course disagrees about Valmy and the rejection of history. Well, all in all, I who know nothing about this subject, I've understood (I seem to have understood) a little of who Goethe is. I have not seen Einaudi again at Bocca di Magra to ask him if he had seen your letter which must have arrived when the publishing house was closed for holidays. Now we're getting back to work and your letter will certainly be fished out of the pile of correspondence not dealt with. In any case I'll be in Turin next week. These have been the most sedentary of all holidays. I've realized that the never-changing rhythm imposed by the family suits me down to the ground, so much so that every upheaval involving the family becomes a problem for me, which is why I don't know when we will be able to take up your very welcome invitation. I see from your last article that you are becoming more and more brutal with the ideologizers. Just think: I happened to be asked by *The Times Literary Supplement* to write an article on "Literature and Philosophy" for a special issue, something which has slightly ruined my summer because after trying to get them to change my topic, I ended up doing it just for the fun of talking about something I know nothing about and to cite as an example *Alice in Wonderland*.[33]

Warmest good wishes from all of us to you and Elena,

Calvino

[Handwritten; with the addressee.]

To Gian Carlo Ferretti—Milan

Paris, 22 October 1967

Dear Ferretti,

HERE IS MY REPLY TO THE SURVEY FOR *RINASCITA*.[34] I'VE spent several days on it and it's turned out longer and more demanding than I expected, because I found myself having to rethink and define, for myself first and foremost, a whole network of problems. But now I'm happy with it because—even if it arouses perhaps even bitter reactions—I feel I can defend what I have written word for word.

The debate (the first installment) is at a very high level. I've not seen this week's issue; if you have a copy, send it to me.

I'll send a copy of my piece to Ottavio Cecchi in Rome, to save time.[35]

Very best wishes,
Yours,

Calvino

I am now nearly always in Paris:
12 Square de Châtillon
Paris 14[e]
[Handwritten on Einaudi headed paper; with the addressee.]

To Guido Davico Bonino—Turin

Paris, 29 Oct. 1967

Dear Davico,

YOUR LETTER ON THE COMPLETE WORKS OF PAVESE ARRIVED just as I was writing a reminder to myself to reorganize Pavese's works.

My editions of the poems and stories in chronological order, which put together works published by Pavese and those found amongst his unpublished items, are undoubtedly useful for scholars, but they dismantle the construction of those books to which P. attributed a meaning precisely as constructions, such as *Lavorare stanca* (*Selected Poems*), *Feria d'agosto* (*Summer Storm*). Seeing my editions cited every time and not the original texts, and seeing that abroad they translate the former and not the books as they had been conceived by the author, made me repent of the criterion I followed. I was waiting for a chance to reassemble *Lavorare stanca* and *Feria d'agosto*, and to follow them with, respectively, the other poems and the other short stories. Now you write saying we'll do an edition in 15–16 volumes: in that case we will divide into separate volumes the books published by Pavese and our posthumous collections. (The same applies to our editions of the novels in chronological order, which meant that we dismembered *Gallo* [*Before the Cock Crows*] and *Estate* [*The Beautiful Summer*], the two books put together by Pavese that contained more than one novel.)

Volumes still to do:

Essays: we urgently need a re-edition of my 1951 collection which has been out of print for some time now and is much in demand.[36] I don't feel up to doing it. If you can do it, excellent.

The Graduating Thesis on Whitman: I've never read it (at some point it disappeared from the papers in Pavese's house; we would have to have it photocopied at the university). I don't know if it's worth publishing and if it is, whether to add it to the essays or publish it separately.

A Volume of Translations from Greek: we had already suggested this to Codino, who gave a negative reply. I would still ask Carena the question.

A Selection of Juvenilia: ask Mondo.[37] But let's remember that it's all very poor stuff, that it would be better to publish it as a curiosity for Pavesologists or Piedmontologists in an ephemeral edition, rather than keeping it with us for eternity as part of the complete works. (And Mondo would be better doing Fenoglio first.)

For the abbreviated volume of correspondence, tell me how many pages it has to be and I'll carry out the abridgement.

I attach a draft program in about fifteen volumes: the books published by P. exactly as they were, the posthumous works, plus three volumes which it is probably better not to put in the complete works.[38]

The only immediate problem in dividing things up is what to do with *Paesi tuoi*, which is very short. Put it with *La spiaggia* (*The Beach*)?

Or with *La spiaggia* and *Il compagno*, thus collecting in one volume the narrative works that are "minor" (both in terms of size and success)?[39]

Ciao

Calv.

[Photocopy of the original; in the Calvino Archive and in the Einaudi Archive, Turin.]

To the Pupils at Coletti Middle School—Treviso

Turin, 21 November 1967

Dear Pupils of Class 1F,

I AM PLEASED THAT YOU ENJOYED MY STORY "IL GIARDINO INcantato" (The enchanted garden).[40] I wrote it exactly twenty years ago; at that time I was living in San Remo, where I spent all my childhood and early life up to the age of twenty-five. My father, grandfather, great-grandfather and probably all their forebears were from San Remo. The Ligurian Riviera and its hinterland are present in many of my works. The anthology you are using is not wrong in saying "born in San Remo," because in a writer's life it is only important to know facts that are relevant to the writer's works, in other words what is usually called his "creative world."[41]

In actual fact, though, I was born in a little village near Havana (in Cuba): Santiago de las Vegas, which means St James in the Fields. At that time my parents were living in Cuba; my father was an agronomist and worked for Central American agricultural companies and research institutes. But I do not remember anything about this tropical childhood; I was still under two when my parents returned definitively to Italy.

So the UTET Encyclopaedia is also right: indeed, its statement is more accurate from the point of view of my birth certificate. However, this detail about my birth is of no use in explaining where "The Enchanted Garden" is set, whereas "born in San Remo" does explain it, even though it does not correspond precisely with my birth certificate.

As for the anthology that says I was born in Santiago in Chile, that is clearly a mistake. The authors of that anthology will have read somewhere that I was born in "Santiago" and will have immediately thought of the Chilean capital rather than of an unknown village on the island of Cuba like Santiago de las Vegas.

So that is how this mystery is explained. This helps to show one thing: what is written in books can be true up to a point and mistaken up to a point. One must never trust books totally, instead one must check what is right and wrong in them, as you have rightly done. I congratulate you and your teacher on this and send my warmest greetings and best wishes.

(Italo Calvino)

[Typed copy; in the Calvino Archive and in the Einaudi Archive, Turin.]

To Maria Pia Ghiandoni—Arcevia (Ancona)

Turin, 24 November 1967

Dear Miss Ghiandoni,

I AM AFRAID THAT AT THIS POINT I CAN NO LONGER HELP you—and this because of a question of method. What use is it to the critic (you in this case) if the author issues judgments or statements regarding his own works? The critic cannot take as reliable anything the author writes; so this new declaration would have to be subjected to criticism. But if the critic is not sure of his critical tools, he will go back again to the author to ask for further clarification; the author will reply, the critic will have to criticize these new replies, and so on ad infinitum. In my view, the starting point should be to regard the author as dead; to draw up a list of the extant writings and work on them; for the critic, the author does not exist, only a certain number of writings exist. It is with my works that you have to establish a dialog, not with the author in his real-life person. If the author replies to you, that's a sign that he's a chatterbox and that what he says does not count for anything.

That is why I cannot agree to an interview; as it is, I already try to avoid as far as possible newspaper interviewers.

When, on the other hand, you ask me for factual details (dates, bibliographical information), then I will do my best to satisfy you. So now I will try to have those replies of mine to that survey photocopied and send them to you.

Yours sincerely.

[Typed copy; in the Einaudi Archive, Turin.]

To Gianni Mantesi—Milan

Turin, 1 December 1967

Dear Mantesi,

I HAVE READ YOUR ADAPTATION FOR THEATRE OF *THE NON-Existent Knight*. I am full of admiration at the way you have managed to transform my *entire* text into theater, and to make it flow without interruption right to the end. It is genuinely a display of bravura that leaves me open-mouthed.

However, the way you make everything come one after another, one scene after another, creates a rhythm that is cramped, dense, stifling; whereas my text is full of pauses, interrupted by rests, moments which broaden out or become hazy. This is my first reservation regarding your work: very faithful to the letter but not to the rhythm of my text. And rhythm is highly important, because—I believe—that is where the "lyrical," rather melancholy tone of my story comes from.

Another major reservation I have concerns the frame: these puppeteers. Partly because of the artificiality of it, partly because we are already fed up to the back teeth with these "epic" frameworks, partly because the speeches of commentary are too long, and partly because—basically—I don't feel it works. And another thing: when one goes straight to the action, as I do in the novel, the discovery that a warrior is nothing but a suit of empty armor has a certain effect; if on the other hand we're dealing with a puppet play and the suit of armor is a puppet, the effect is considerably lessened. On this point I must say that I do not agree with your solution.

Then there's the Teodora question. This was already a complex operation (and not appreciated by all critics), introducing a nun as the scribe of the story and at the end showing that the nun was the warrior Bradamante.

Here you add another Chinese box: the nun is the same person as the woman puppet-master. Here I think the whole effect is ruined: the little ludic element that there was in bringing out a nun enclosed in a convent as writing a story of war and bloodshed, is totally lost, because we already know that the nun is not a nun, but actually belongs to a company of puppeteers, so the war-convent contrast disappears.

And it is Bradamante's whole character—the least dialogic character in the novel—that is thus attenuated, she no longer has the role of contrast that she had in the story.

This is what I have to tell you while appreciating very much your work: literal fidelity can sometimes turn out to the detriment of a more profound fidelity. For this reason I do not feel, at this point, I can state that this adaptation is "approved by the author." I enclose your typescript and hope to hear alternative proposals from you.

Thank you, and best wishes.

[Typed copy; in the Einaudi Archive, Turin.]

To Michel David—Padua

Paris 13.12.67

Dear David,

Thank you for giving me an advance look at your article.[42] I am very happy with the way you read *Time and the Hunter*, saying the things I most wanted to hear. Did you know that Zeno's Achilles was to have been the subject of a story in the final section, which in the end I did not manage to write?

Also your choice of the stories from *Cosmicomics* coincides broadly with the ones I myself would choose.

The interesting and—I think—original critical point you make concerns the projection of just a single conscious ego, a reasoning reason: seen as a limit or as a limitation that is overcome. I am not able to give my own opinion on this point, but it seems to me to be an interpretation that touches something true.

As for the little barbs, which are the necessary condiment in every decent article, I would like to come back on just one point. When you say: "these stories are also symbolic of the writer's activity and C. thus shows he has brought himself up to date as regards the latest buzzwords," I would like to point out that in the conclusion of *The Baron in the Trees* (1957), the whole forest dissolves into writing and that in *The Non-Existent Knight* (1959) the theme of writing runs through the whole narrative. (Also in some of the final stories—from 1958—in the collected *I racconti* this motif appears: for instance, in "Adventure of a Poet.") These facts show that my relationship to the problems of *scripturalisme* (to use the term recently coined by Ricardou) precedes the current period of theorizing, *Tel Quel* etc. (but of course I cannot be classed with their extreme absolutism because for me this set of problems remains just one element, one level of consciousness that coexists alongside others). At the time when I began to feel—I would almost say—a moral obligation while writing to warn: "Watch out, I am writing," this tendency was present perhaps solely in Butor.[43] (I would say that Robbe-Grillet is not directly involved in this question about writing symbolizing itself.)

It is not that I am annoyed to see my work considered as being an update on current research (after all, one writes most of all in order to take part in a collective enterprise), but it seems to me that these facts prove that it is not the case that I "have brought myself up to date": this was actually the *logical development* of my work, which coincided with what was coming to the fore through different routes in other areas of the European literary map.

Your image of Borges's portrait replacing Hemingway's is very good and has a lot of truth in it. Yet it is precisely my most Hemingwayesque (consciously, intentionally Hemingwayesque) stories from *Ultimo viene il corvo* (*The Crow Comes Last*) and others from the early postwar period that are the ones based on a geometrical structure, on a pattern of abstract lines, a combinatory procedure, a game involving full and empty sequences. It was clear that as soon as Borges would become known in Europe I would like him, and that he would come to be one of my models. In short, in the portrait I had on my wall, my Hemingway already had some of the features of Borges who was unknown at the time . . .

Furthermore, you rightly mention Bontempelli.[44] Italian critics have completely forgotten Bontempelli, whereas in the years immediately preceding the war and in the first years of the war (the period of my early education), the Italian writer who had most authority as a model was Bontempelli, and the literary climate of the time (I'm talking about the literary pages of the dailies and weeklies, because at that time I did not read literary journals) was steeped in his influence: Buzzati, Nicola Lisi, Zavattini etc.[45]

I have written you a very long letter, but your writings always invite discussion (discussion about facts—discussion of ideas is not my forte). So I would have liked very much to discuss these things with you after reading your book.[46]

My best wishes, and thank you once more.
Yours,

Italo Calvino

[Handwritten; with the addressee. A handwritten draft is in the Calvino Archive.]

To Cesare Milanese—Rome

12 Square de Châtillon
Paris 14

Paris, 16.12.67

Dear Milanese,

I have read and reread and reflected on your "guide to reading" and "notes" on *Time and the Hunter*.[47]

Rarely (not to say never) does one come across a critical article which stirs up so many ideas, all of them different from the usual rehashed notions, and forces us to rethink everything from scratch. Your article is a real event and I think it deserves to be so not only in the microscopic field of criticism on my books.

I will tell you my impressions (not for publication, just for discussion between ourselves, for the moment). I will start at the end, from the "third note" on the "endings" as "*false*" *conclusions*, as *mere technical needs*, a point which seems to me fundamental as a preliminary. You say that it is a *genuine professional conscience* (but I would say it is the pleasure of an artisan, a craftsman's need to deliver a finished, "closed" product) that leads me to like above all a story structure where the conclusion has to *seem* meaningful while still remaining a purely *formal* element, whereas the real "nucleus of meaning . . . is always found elsewhere.". Absolutely right and this has never been said before—I believe—by anyone, even though I feel it has always been clear. And this is a first essential point in reading *Cosmicomics* and the "Altri Qfwfq" (More of Qfwfq) tales.

The different discourse starts with "The Spiral" (in *Cosmicomics*) and continues in "Blood, Sea" (which is probably the story where this linguistic operation works best) and "Priscilla." Your observations on this point, the "formalization which is entrusted to pure schemes of reasoning" and all the rest that follows, seem to me to constitute the basic critical nucleus of your article and the one that I am keenest on. At last we have moved away from the generic formula of my "rationalism" (quite right to define as a "strategy" "the rejection of the irrational") and toward a critical sense as regards the Enlightenment. (It is no accident that your "notes" begin by citing Vico and the Pre-Socratics and end up quoting Leopardi.) It seems to me that this is an excellent way to begin this discourse, much better than anything I could do: every time I have to explain theoretically my philosophy, I end up "cheapening" it.

What I most like to hear discussion of is the third part of my book, also in order to know how far I can go down that road.[48] And this "logical description of the logic of an event" is, I think, an extraordinary definition and program. The same applies to "reasoning as structure" and "System" as opposed to "Fact."

As for the "immemorial moments" and the "archetypes," this would open up a completely different discourse, which so far I have not tried to do even with myself. But it seems to me that you have already established a fundamental point: the immemorial moment and archetype not as "myth" but as a void, which one circles around but never reaches.

These notes of mine tell you how I am slowly working through your article, which is certainly very dense, with pronouncements condensed to the point of being short-circuited, and I am not always successful in tracing all its ramifications, for instance in that passage about the "aristocratic" world, which also interests me.

You suggested that I should reply to your article by publishing my own response in *Il Caffè*. But to do so now seems too soon, would it not seem like something cooked up between us? What I hope is that there will be a chance to do so later, perhaps if there were some sort of debate. For instance, the point where you note the fact that my work is contemporary to that of the Gruppo 63 and at the same time you point out the difference of method that distinguishes us: on that topic I cannot be the one to judge, but certainly it interests me, and I would like it to be developed.

In short, I would like—as I said at the outset—others to appreciate the character of an *event* that this article of yours has for me, in that it is a general discourse on the possibilities for literature today. So, I agree we should continue the discussion: let's see if I have to respond immediately myself (with the totally illusory authority of the author who believes he is the one that has the right to say: "the critic is right"!) or someone else.

Best wishes.

Calvino

[Handwritten; with the addressee.]

To Michele Rago—Rome

12, Square de Châtillon
Paris 14

18 December 67

Dear Michele,

Only now have I received your article of Wednesday 13th and my wait has been compensated by a sense of great satisfaction.[49] The central point about the relationship between knowing and doing which you bring out—also through two very relevant quotations—is precisely a definition that I feel suits perfectly my ultimate intentions and—even before that—my and our "condition."

You make a very good point about the *allegory of our condition* which you see in the imprisonment of Dantès, the decodification of the universe, the geometric, abstract painting with planes that multiply and overlap, the progression of a *secular discourse*.

I am glad to have caused such a serious, highly dense discourse, certainly not an easy one, but I prefer it that way rather than seeing my work defined with simplified formulae which always have—yes they certainly do—a wide margin of obscurity and ambiguity.

As for the abandonment of the essayistic-problematic story, the fact is that for some time now I have felt that was too easy a path, all "downhill," with no resistance offered. The story with an intellectual protagonist, an autobiographical-critical-ethical-lyrical hero, is a swamp into which you can sink down indefinitely, as happens in much of contemporary Italian literature. (Not only in fiction, maybe, because also a certain amount of poetry follows this route, running the same risks.)

(See what happens even to those who propose changes, like the latest Leonetti: although he is so fertile in his subjects and metaphors, he falls down in his essayistic-intellectual claims; whereas Sanguineti is exempt from it and provides us with a historically new image of death-as-white-goods, but also in him the autobiographical limitation restricts terribly the horizon of this Inferno of his.)

Here I can't tell you much about my life in relation to my new landscape because I am living a very isolated life, caught up as I am in various publishing and other projects I have to finish, and I spend my weeks in my study in a tranquility that I could certainly never have had in Italy.

Your article on Vittorini's *Le due tensioni* (*The Two Tensions*) was very good, the only good one I have read so far, I think.[50]

That thing I phoned you about this summer seems to have fallen through. They made so much of a mess, they made me look foolish to you, so much so that I quarrelled with them over it and I stirred up a lot of bad feeling for myself.

We send you our best wishes, also from Chichita. And write to me.

Yours,

Italo

[Handwritten; with the addressee.]

To Luigi Baldacci—Florence

Turin, 15 January 1968

Dear Baldacci,

I am happy that, as with *Cosmicomics*, so with *Time and the Hunter* one of the finest reviews I have seen has been yours.[51] It is an analysis which I find is spot on, and I could not be happier with your list of references: Bontempelli Landolfi Leopardi Beckett. As for the Kafkaism in "The Count of Montecristo," when I wrote: "Everything that is unclear in the relationship between an innocent prisoner and his prison continues to cast shadows etc.,"[52] I was intentionally referring to Kafka, suggesting a total depersonalization as the only way out. However, your warning about "symbols that are too humanized" is a source of great support to me amidst the many critics who reproach me for the opposite. In the stories of the third section I went back to representing "human" cases reducing the story and its language to a logical mechanism that is absolutely neutral (especially in the first three tales of the group). By developing this line I believe that you can overcome the perplexities aroused by these last stories, which probably point the way forward for my future work. (Moreover, Ceresa is not a negative point of reference for me:[53] hers is a rigorous experiment, which makes sense, a rarity amongst the many experiments of these last few years.)

I am happy, dear Baldacci, not to have given the lie to the critical idea that you have been upholding for a number of years now, namely my descent from Bontempelli, and to have proved (by moving closer—I believe—to the author of *Donna nel sole* [*Woman in the*

Sun]) that the Bontempelli line is not without further development.[54] Certainly just as in the years of my earliest literary education, before the end of the war, Bontempelli was the number 1 Italian novelist and everything that one read—in terms of fiction—had that atmosphere of magic realism, so in the postwar period it seemed that that discourse was completely rejected, and he, Bontempelli, hovered around with his unflappable kindness—even before his long illness—with the air of a weightless, white ghost; now it seems to me that the moment for a Bontempelli revival—as forecast by you—is ripe.

Best wishes.

Italo Calvino

[Typed on Einaudi headed paper, with autograph corrections, signature and additions; with the addressee.]

To the Zanichelli Publishing House—Bologna

[Turin,] 2 February 1968

Dear Salinari,
Dear De Mauro,
Dear friends at Zanichelli,

I am sending this letter in three copies to bring you up to date with my part in the work.

STORIES OF THREE TO TEN PAGES

ADVENTURE STORIES. I have sent Salinari and De Mauro a wide selection of adventure stories, a largely original selection compared with other anthologies. Still to be decided is to what extent this selection has to be used in the first volume and to what extent in others.

SCIENCE FICTION STORIES. I have already photocopied and will send you in a few days a rich selection of science fiction, which is totally original compared to other anthologies. The problem, apart from that of a certain level of parodic sophistication which is always present, is that of the length of the stories, however much one tries to shorten them and reduce them to the essential. Probably these are not suitable for the first volume; have a look and see.

HUMOROUS STORIES. I have put together a wide choice even though I've not succeeded in getting away much from the selections in other anthologies.

CHILDHOOD MEMORIES and fiction with child protagonists. One can make a good selection of passages, even if we restrict ourselves to the major authors, with excerpts of whatever length you want.

FOLKTALES. I have already got a good, quite original, selection of folktales, especially ones by famous authors, to which one can add some from the Grimms and other collectors of the popular tradition. Here too the only problem is how many to include. I see that some anthologies adventurously include folktales from beyond Europe; I have a little reluctance about amateurishly having to deal with an endless bibliography.

ANIMAL STORIES by famous names, children's literature that is neither folktales nor fairy-tales. I have selected a few while trying to avoid the sugary atmosphere that infests the opening pages of nearly all the anthologies.

SHORT PIECES

FABLES of a classical type, ancient and modern. Here there is simply the problem of deciding how many we want.

BRIEF STORIES AND ANECDOTES. Ditto. However, here I found myself with the problem of everything written by an Italian author from the *Novellino* to the sixteenth and seventeenth centuries (let's say, up to but not including G. Gozzi). Can we put in this section, which will be one of the ones at the beginning of the book, texts that are in such difficult Italian?[55] How does one overcome the contrast between the legibility of the pieces that have been translated (also from ancient Greek and Latin) into modern Italian and the pieces in Italian but which are in the archaic language?

STORIES OF SCIENTISTS. I would like to put together a series of anecdotes from a variety of sources, but so far I only have a few and I don't really know where to lay my hands on more. I feel we should chart a kind of history of science through anecdotes.

OBSERVATION AND DESCRIPTION. Avoiding the typical "descriptions" you find in anthologies, the purple passages etc., I am looking for examples of genuine observation, and here a wonderful, rich, and new collection of pieces could emerge, without the trite seasonal offerings that infest other anthologies. The only problem is that this section is turning out to be a bit haphazard and not organic.

KNOWING HOW TO DO THINGS. A similar section to the previous one, where one gives an account of some operation or job. Here too I am choosing on the criterion of literary value (or literary honesty) and therefore as far as the content is concerned what is emerging is a rather haphazard collection.

IDEAS OF MINE I HAVE GIVEN UP ON

The last two sections above were the ones from my original suggestions that I think can work. Others, though, I see in actual practice that they will not work out or at any rate I am not able to bring them to fruition. For instance, I tried to do a section "Adults Talking to Children," starting to put together a typical selection from the Tolstoy of *Russian Books for Reading*, in order to organize it into a discourse on Tolstoy's realistic pedagogy, and so on for all the writers treated. It could still work out but would become an essay on the various ways of understanding children's literature, more interesting for those who deal with pedagogy than for kids, as well as difficult to do, at least for me.

So the parallel section, "Children writing," is not developing well, I don't think, both because of the paucity and relatively poor quality of the material, and because it would make sense if it was organized by someone interested in pedagogy who had a criterion to defend. The most significant pieces here are those from the San Gersolé material, which can usefully go into the section on observation.[56]

It is also very difficult to develop the theme of "What I will do when I grow up" through an anthological selection, without falling into an anachronistic outline, or one that is futile compared to the responsibilities of vocational direction in the modern world.

THEMES OF AN ENCYCLOPAEDIC OR INFORMATIVE NATURE

This last topic takes us back to a function of the anthology that I did not feel I could face. Apart from the historical and geographical sections entrusted to De Mauro, which have quite clear characteristics in that they are linked to school syllabuses for history and geography, there remain some sections of a didactic or encyclopaedic nature which are present in almost all anthologies and are done in a rather approximate and casual way, because there are no precise criteria for their presence in an *anthology of passages for reading*. We would really need to clarify our ideas here by having a discussion amongst ourselves; and here Zanichelli could be a major help with its experience in the field of encyclopaedias and popular knowledge books.

WORK INDUSTRY FARMING PRODUCTIVE AND PROFESSIONAL ACTIVITIES. SCIENCE AND TECHNOLOGY.

SPORT (games, pastimes, etc.). It seems to me that the way this section is usually done is a fake, demagogic way of opening out to the world of children, without a clear idea of what might interest them in terms of reading, nor an idea of how to carry out an educative action in this field.

CINEMA AND SPECTACLE: These sections crop up in some anthologies in an equally gratuitous and demagogic way.

CIVIC EDUCATION. The problem perhaps only concerns the 3rd volume but I'm already dreading it.

STRICTLY LITERARY PASSAGES (FOR FUTURE VOLUMES BUT ALSO FOR VOLUME I)

FAMOUS BOOKS. Ripping out chapters from novels is always a sacrilegious and cruel operation. I've tried to do it but my conscience is against it; I would make an anthology only of complete stories. And yet there remains the problem of how to represent classic books also as classics of youth, such as *Don Quixote*, *Gulliver*, *Crusoe*, etc. I think the best way is to present not a couple of isolated passages in the middle of a great sea of other things, but to present the book through a series of selected chapters linked together by summaries and in the context of an organic discourse, just as is done with epic poems. Of course it would be wrong to put *Don Quixote* and *War and Peace* in the section of "epic readings" (as we agreed at our meetings), but in parallel to this we could have a section entitled "Famous Books" and in each of our three volumes present three or four of these great novels of world literature just as one does for epic poems.[57] Also the great Italian books that most lend themselves to reading, from *Bertoldo* to Cellini's *Autobi-*

ography and Nievo. So we really need to agree on a list and on the number of pages to select from each text.

(In the second volume there will also be the problem of the masterpieces of theater.)

CLASSIC ITALIAN NOVELLE. As I've already said, the choice of Italian novelle from the *Novellino*, Boccaccio, Sacchetti etc., means the problem of reading archaic Italian in a school system where it no longer functions as a bridge between the spoken language and Latin. In which volume will we deal with this problem?

CONTEMPORARY ITALIAN STORIES. I have started making a selection using criteria of taste as well as of legibility. In the first volume?

I would like to have your observations and advice on all this and to know how far you have got.

But perhaps this is now the moment to set up a meeting, before the deadline for the delivery of the material, in other words say around 10 February. I should be in Italy until around that date, then I go back to Paris.

Best wishes.
Yours,

Italo Calvino

Write to me at this address:
Via Santa Giulia 80, Turin
Tel. 884259
[Typed, with autograph signature; in the Zanichelli Archive, Bologna.]

To Helen Wolff—New York

Turin, 11 March 1968.

Dear Mrs Wolff,
Please forgive my late reply to your very kind letter of 7 February.[58]

I agree to a volume containing the three novellas.[59] Of course it makes sense to detach the novellas from the short stories.

The fact that I wanted to give priority to the short stories was for a precise reason. In the United States I am known above all for my fantasy stories, and in the short stories readers find themselves not too distant from the climate of fantasy they already know: there is the theme of childhood, there is an almost geometric construction of the story. In short, any reader can recognize my style in them.

The novellas have more substance but precisely for that reason they are more difficult, especially *The Watcher*, which requires a knowledge of Italian life in all its political and cultural etc. nuances. I have already had this experience in France publishing the translation of *The Watcher* on its own: critics and public alike found themselves a bit disoriented; there were too many things that they did not expect from me.

In Italy too, I have to say that I had more success with the fantasy works (in terms of sales; but critics here would like me to deal only with "serious" subjects).

The fact that you *believe* in *The Watcher* gives me courage and confidence again. Let's try it.

Warmest good wishes and thanks.

[Typed copy; in the Einaudi Archive, Turin.]

To Guido Fink—Florence

24-6-68

Dear Fink,

Your review of *Time and the Hunter* in *Paragone* gave me the rare satisfaction of finding a critic who is highly attentive and who knows how to *read* (and quote), someone for whom nothing is lost in the page.[60] The three sections of the volume are described very well, both in the analysis of the individual stories, and in your overall definitions, like the excellent one you give of the second section. (And that is how your style-sensitive ear makes unexpected discoveries such as the Pavesian assonances in the *Cosmicomics*: I would never have thought it, but your quote is very convincing.) However, I would not like you to see the value of the third section only in relation to a polemic with the other experimental narrators. In other words my work—which is autonomous, and naturally I am keen that this is recognized—moves in a space that is not decided by me, but which is the literary context in which I find myself working at any given time, and which always poses new problems. Naturally, I come from different experiences from those that dominate today in literary discussions, but this different climate that has been created has led me to deepen aspects which were already present in my work, and of which I was more or less obscurely aware.* So I am happy that you find *Time and the Hunter* "nice"; yet the more books are "not nice" (in other words difficult to digest for our habits of thought and tastes) the more they count; the more laborious it is to absorb them, the more important they are. Now, however, I have to be more detailed. Judging this phase of my work in relation to and in opposition to avant-garde European literature does not seem relevant to me, because it is clear that I remain a writer of the artisan school, I like constructing things that close well, I have a relationship with the reader that is based on mutual satisfaction. By contrast, the avant-garde is a human attitude first and foremost not a literature, it involves a different relationship with the work and the reader (and one judges it according to the categorizing, heroic nature of this attitude); if someone, say, "is not born to it," in other words does not have this as his fundamental vocation, it would be ridiculous for him to start. But what I wanted to say was this: I make artisan products but in a period when the avant-garde does this, that and the other; and even though these different fields are not adjacent, they influence each other (just as every field of writing cannot be indifferent to other fields). For instance, now I am reading Heissenbüttel, and I discover that he also explains the things I am doing: I see with interest—and I would like to emphasize this—an analogy between my position (on the level of artisanal products) and his (on the level of the avant-garde).

In short, what counts for me is my participation in a collective enterprise, not the "genuinely major results" which you complain I never reach. All that counts is one's contribution to that complex thing that is culture. What are "major" results? It is only a cultural situation that is *beyond* this one that can give the value of "major" to a result. And even that is only a symbol of a whole combination of results, maybe minuscule but important. I believe that this is a criterion that does not lead anywhere: let's leave it to the weeklies that deal with literary news and interview writers on the possibility of writing "masterpieces." I have to say that I have never bothered with major results. As a young man my aspiration was to become a "minor writer." (Because it was always those that are called "minor" that I liked most and to whom I felt closest.) But this was already a flawed criterion because it presupposes that "major" writers exist.

Basically, I am convinced that not only are there no "major" or "minor" writers, but writers themselves do not exist—or at least they do not count for much. As far as I am concerned, you still try too hard to explain Calvino with Calvino, to chart a history, a continuity in Calvino, and maybe this Calvino does not have any continuity, he dies and is reborn every second. What counts is whether in the work that he is doing at a certain point there is something that can relate to the present or future work done by others, as can happen to anyone who works, just because of the fact that they are creating such possibilities.

However, I have to say that your search for the real Calvino—although I do not approve of it in methodological terms—leads to the establishment of a common denominator that I like: "aggression and clear opposition." If this comes out also in stories where I intended to be as detached and impersonal as could be, then there must be some truth in it and in that case I am happy about this. For that reason your article has given me great satisfaction—as you can see from the passion for discussion it has aroused in me—and I am infinitely grateful to you.

Yours,

Italo Calvino

*Talking of cultural situations that one does not choose but finds oneself working in: it is quite right that you define as "Bassanian" stories such as "Gli avanguardisti a Mentone" (The Avanguardisti in Menton) etc., because without Bassani I would never have written stories like that, with their particular focus on autobiographical material—with that focus on one's own individuality of experience in a provincial, middle-class ambience. Bassani was important for me in order to escape from the impasse that my first postwar style had run into. (Whereas I was not able to appreciate Bassani's real value at that time and which he too immediately lost: his attempt at a Jamesian ghost story for the Italian middle class.) In the case of those stories there, however (and precisely because I lacked that outlet I spoke of just now), I ended up falling right back on an area of minor Italian literature typical of *Il Mondo*, full of moralistic smugness, facile wisdom, nostalgic lyricism. So those stories of mine (perhaps they are more successful than others, but what does that matter?) form part of an involution on my part and on the part of the Italian literary climate of that time, and I am sorry that you remember them so well and actually quote them twice.

[Handwritten letter, not found by the addressee. Published by Guido Fink with a foreword, under the title "Lettera di uno scrittore 'minore'" (Letter from a "Minor" Writer), *Paragone*, Letteratura, 428 (October 1985), 7–9; later in *S*, II, pp. 1787–89. Fink wrote this about the letter he transcribed: "The letter was written by hand, with corrections and changes of mind: I have also tried to respect certain inconsistencies, like titles which are sometimes underlined or with inverted commas or inserted without any typographical marking, but obviously I cannot reproduce the additions between lines or in the margins, for instance the one on books that are 'not nice,' or on the heroism or otherwise of the avant-garde, which for convenience I have turned into a parenthesis. Just one quite substantial inserted passage [marked here with an asterisk] seems to me self-explanatory.")

TO THE EDITOR OF *TEMPO*—MILAN

[Turin, 26 July 1968]

[Sir,]

IN THE ISSUE [NO. 31] OF *TEMPO* DATED 30 JULY PIERALDO Marasi informed your readers of my refusal of the Viareggio Prize and said: " . . . this was something that had to be done at a certain point. . . . The fact that he waited until the last minute was perhaps the action that was most likely to attract the broadsides and resentment of the critics. On this topic a clarification from Calvino himself would not be inappropriate."

I have no difficulty in responding to an invitation formulated in such polite terms.

The moment I chose for withdrawing from the prize was the only point at which I could do so in order not to distort the sense of my gesture. As is well known, one does not compete oneself for the Viareggio Prize. The jury makes its selection from all the books published in that year. The fact that my book was amongst those shortlisted for the prize did not in any sense authorize me to presume that I had any probability of winning. Given that situation, declaring my withdrawal would have been an ambiguous gesture; it would have sparked polemics anyway; my withdrawal could have been confused with those of others who stand for different positions from mine.

The only moment at which I could announce to the jury (and to the juries) that they must not count on me to save the sinking ship of the prize system was thus immediately after an eventual verdict in my favor, and if possible before any announcement to the press. In the text of the telegram I sent, there is a sentence which the account in *Tempo* omitted: "To avoid any sensationalist cover in the press, I beg you not to announce my name amongst the winners."'[61] But the timing of the operation did not go according to my prediction: I was not able to avoid the publicity given to my "gesture," publicity which does not really suit my temperament, but instead there was a general showdown where all the parties involved provided a sample of their own style.

On top of the damage that I had already anticipated in making my decision, I had to suffer the outbursts of the jury, the distortions of the press, and this gesture being linked to other incidents. But this is only my own personal loss, which takes nothing away from, on the contrary it gives further confirmation of the worth of the deed as a public event. Going along with the game of literary prizes is behavior that honest writers (and there are some) indulge in out of habit, because they feel down, through misplaced good manners, of fear of scandal or loneliness. But actually by now the justifications that could have been valid up to yesterday ("it's like a family lottery," or "certain prizes are worth more than others," or "let's try to improve them by remaining in the system") no longer hold good, because a prize awarded rightly acts as an alibi or a salving of conscience for other prizes which are awarded because of interests and systems that are extraneous to judgements based on the value of the work. It was on the cards that someone sooner or later would break this tired *omertà*; it was the right time to do it; as luck would have it, the opportunity to do so fell to me; it would have been a grave omission on my part to let the chance go by.

[Italo Calvino]

[Typed copy; in the Calvino Archive. Published with slight modifications in the weekly *Tempo* (13 August 1968), pp. 3–4, under the title "Calvino accetta l'invito (e chiarisce)" (Calvino Accepts our Invitation and Explains). The place and date in square brackets are not in the typed copy: apart from the signature, which one presumes is authentic, they seem to have been added by the editors of *Tempo*. It is, however, certain that Calvino sent the letter not from Turin but from Cinquale, where he had been on holiday from the end of June (see the following letter to Michele Rago).]

To Michele Rago—Milan

Cinquale, 27.7.68

Dear Michele,

I AM SORRY ABOUT THE MISUNDERSTANDING REGARDING THE Chianciano Prize. After repeatedly explaining my position to you, at your last assault—if I remember correctly—I just fended you off with a shrug of my shoulders or a sigh or a grunt. Is that what you took as a sign of my assent? Seeing the list of members of the jury, I thought they had taken as valid the list of names to invite without checking whether they had accepted or not, as often happens. I was a bit angry with you too, naturally, but I did not mean in any way to be rude to you. You are one of the few real friends I have in the world, and I don't want these bureaucratic affairs to interfere in any way with our friendship.

I thought a lot about you in the very unpleasant days of the Viareggio Prize, remembering that you rightly would have liked me to refuse that prize back in 1957, when they gave it to me and eleven other people including a minister, a publisher, and a magazine editor. These are very disagreeable situations for anyone who does not want to be bothered with such things at all, and who wants to discuss them as little as possible, and whatever one does turns out to involve major damage.

Today I was already preparing to write to you when your letter of the 17th reached me, having been forwarded from Turin. Can you believe that it was only the day before yesterday that I got your letter of *15 May* which had been sent on from Paris? Signs that the backlog of post caused by the strike is only now starting to be sorted out.

Let me now give you a quick run-down of our life in the last few months. During the days of the first barricades I was on a lecture trip to Holland with Chichita. Marcelo was fighting on the barricades but was unhurt.[62] We got back to Paris in the wonderful days of the occupations of the Sorbonne and of the first factories. Then a quick trip to Italy to pick up the baby (whom we had left with a former baby-sitter during our trip) and to vote. The transport strike meant we were stuck in Italy; worrying days of waiting in Turin. Meanwhile Marcelo was arrested and kept for twenty-four hours in Beaujon, then released, but by that stage moving around was dangerous for foreign students. In Turin I hired a car that had to go back to France and we drove back to Paris with a load of petrol cans for the trip there and back. There we lived through the extraordinary days of the car-less and metro-less city, with the queues outside the shops. Then there was De Gaulle's speech, the Gaullists' cars going round, horns blaring, trying to penetrate the Latin Quarter and getting sent back, the Sorbonne like a fortress under siege, with mercenaries from Katanga lying in wait, and the young people expecting the worst and cursing the Communists. Nights during which no one did anything but go around on foot, amidst constant alarms, in a climate of amazing excitement. In the atmosphere of debacle that soon took over, we left with my car and the cans of petrol, taking Marcelo to safety. We were constantly expecting to see the famous armored cars which were said to be surrounding Paris and which soon turned out to be the hyped-up story that all sides (the official and traditional sides of the old political game) were relying on. We followed the sad finale on the radio from Italy. From the end of June we have been here in a house we rented for the summer. We will go back to Paris in September (as long as the wave of xenophobia does not create any obstacles for our stay).

It seems to me that something really is changing in Europe. We are certainly moving toward a new revolutionary force, which also includes the workers, whereas by now the road the Communist parties are on is as irreversible as the one taken by social democrats on the eve of the First World War. The question as to how far the reaction will move down the road toward fascism does not seem to worry the young revolutionaries. Who knows, maybe that is right, since we are living through a period that is so different from any in our past and things constantly turn out differently from however we imagine them. I cannot formulate any prediction: I know that all I can say either follows old schemes or is totally up in the air. This is the situation that is common to our generations: this was in evidence in France where the only ones out of tune were the writers, even with the best will in the world. Basically I find myself in the ideal position of being a spectator: things are happening that interest me profoundly, that correspond in general terms to what I wanted to see happen (even though I would have been unable to foresee them clearly) and my participation in them is not called for, in fact it is ruled out. This is something that salves my conscience and allows me to relax fully; what more could I ask for?

It would be lovely if you could come here and see us. We have no telephone. The house is not far from the right bank of the river Cinquale; it is difficult to explain where it is but if you ask, for instance, in the little food shops you'll be able to find it. Come with Ninetta. We can put you up (if that's OK with you).

With warmest good wishes.

C/o Alma Cherubini
Via Marietti 52
54030 Cinquale
[Handwritten; with the addressee.]

To John Woodhouse—Hull (England)

Paris, 16.9.68

Dear Mr Woodhouse,

I felt tremendous excitement on seeing that you had written a book about me.[63] This is the first time this has happened. (I don't want to consider that Italian volume that you quote several times, giving it undeserved honor, and which seems to me a mess. It is devoid of method and ideas, written to take money away from poor students to whom university lecturers now assign exercises on contemporary authors.) And I am happy that this first book on my work comes from England: my literary formation owes so much to English literature.

It seems to me that you have really read everything that there was to be read of mine. And you manage to embrace everything in a unified discourse, always based on quotations and matters of fact. Naturally, in such cases the author is always the first to be amazed seeing relations being established between things he wrote many years apart and often forgot. But it is always satisfying to see that I have remained loyal to certain basic themes. So I looked closely at the chapters that you dedicate to my polemic against military vainglory, to the difficulty of communicating, and to the relationship between the individual and nature. It cannot be said that these are personal themes: they reflect choices that I made between attitudes that were already present in the cultural milieu in which I took my first steps, choices that were ethical before they were literary, and which now seem obvious to me, given that they are common to part of my generation and to part of contemporary literature. But your quotations bear witness to the fact that the working out of each of these points made me commit totally to them. All in all, what emerges from your analysis is an impression of seriousness as regards the *moral* efforts pursued by the generation that emerged from fascism and the war, and this seems to me to be an excellent outcome from your study.

The most interesting chapters in terms of literature seem to me to be chapters IV and V, which deal with stylistic questions, and not just content. You say quite rightly—and you are the first to have noticed it—that I feel the necessity to filter the narration through the screen of a naïve narrator, and the quotes you give are very well chosen. As for *The Non-Existent Knight*, I can tell you that I had started it as direct narration, and the need to introduce the nun narrator came to me at a later stage—and this is further proof, it seems to me, of what you claim. Chapter v is also excellent—and original—the accumulation of detail in order to give verisimilitude to something entirely improbable (with your references to *Crusoe* and the tradition that stems from it).

As for a school edition for British students of Italian, are you aware that one already exists in the USA edited by a woman professor from the University of Michigan? I have just received a copy of it: *Il visconte dimezzato*, edited by Ilene T. Olken (New York: Appleton-Meredith-Crofts, Division of Meredith Corporation, 1968). If you want to do *Il barone rampante*, the British publisher will have to send a proposal to Einaudi.

As for a monograph for Oxford University Press, I am of course moved by this, but I really don't know what to say to you. Life and works? I'm afraid I don't think I really have a *life* on which something can be written. All I have is a series of works that form part of the general context of literary works in our time. I am more and more convinced that literature is made up of works, genres, schools, discussions, problems, collective work in order to solve certain problems, and not of the individual personalities of authors. Of course authors exist and are necessary, but the study of literature author by author seems to me to be less and less the right way forward. The public figure of the writer, the writer-character, the "personality-cult" of the author, are all becoming for me more and more intolerable in others, and consequently in myself. In short, if a critic writes about a problem and makes reference to one (or more) of my works in relation to that problem, this gives me the sense that my work is not pointless. Whereas the prospect of my bust crowned with laurel appearing along with the other busts in the hall of famous writers gives me no joy at all.

I would be very happy to meet you. Perhaps you are not aware that for more than a year now I have been living with my family in Paris. If you happen to come over here, do come and see us. I'm counting on it. Do write to me.

Warm and grateful regards from your

Italo Calvino

12, Square de Châtillon
Paris 14[e]

The quotations from Ariosto are very good and appropriate. Did you know that for Italian radio I have done a summary of the *Orlando Furioso* to accompany a reading of excerpts? I will send it to you. (It is published in a booklet to accompany the recording disks.)

There is one misprint in a quote on p. 12, note 1: it should be "affettivo" (not "effettivo"). That seems to be the only error. I will also send you a rather paradoxical lecture I gave last year.

[Handwritten; photocopies of the first two pages are in the Calvino Archive; pp. 3–4 with the addressee.]

To Issa I. Naouri—Amman

Turin, 10 October 1968

Dear Mr Naouri,

I HAVE READ THE POETRY OF THE PALESTINIAN RESISTANCE that you kindly sent me. They seem to be poets of powerful expressive force, full of sincere poetic and human warmth.

The best thing would be to find a journal to publish these poems. I will try to contact a friend to bring them to a journal's attention. Of course, in us Europeans the trauma of the persecution of the Palestinians has a special resonance because their current persecutors suffered—in themselves and in their families—persecutions that were amongst the most horrific and inhuman in centuries, both under Nazism and also a long time before that. That the victims of the past should turn into the oppressors of today is the most distressing fact, the one which I think it is necessary to emphasize. I am sorry that none of these poets deals with this motif.

Personally I think that the only solution to the Palestinian problem lies down the revolutionary road both in the Arab world and amongst the Israeli masses. A revolution by the Israeli poor (to a large extent of Middle Eastern and North African origin) against their colonialist and expansionist rulers; but also a revolution by the popular masses in Arab countries against their reactionary and militarist oligarchies (even although these call themselves more or less socialist) who exploit the Palestinian problem for nationalist demagoguery. The real Resistance is not only a struggle against a foreign invader: it has to be a battle for a profound renewal within the society of one's own country.

I wanted to clarify my thoughts in order to confirm my solidarity with the oppressed Palestinians and their Resistance fighters in the context of a general political and human vision.

Thank you so much, and best wishes.

[Typed copy; in the Einaudi Archive, Turin.]

To Guido Piovene—Milan

Turin, 10 October 1968

Dear Piovene,

In the next few days Einaudi will send you the translation of Michel Tournier's *Vendredi ou les limbes du Pacifique*, a novel that came out two years ago in France, which seems to me to be ideal material for an article by you. I don't know if you've read it or heard of it (in any case it did not get the literary resonance it deserved in France): it's *Robinson Crusoe* retold with almost total fidelity, but reinterpreted according to the awareness that we have today of everything that makes up anthropology, history of religions, archetypes, economy, colonialism etc.[64] As far as I am concerned, this is not just a very interesting book as a rereading of *Crusoe* and also in itself, but also something that offers a new solution to the literature-culture nexus. The author maintains that every writer should rewrite his own *Crusoe*. I would go further and say that each writer should rewrite his own *Hamlet*, his own *Quixote* etc. In other words the time has come when the great modern myths can start to function just as classical myths have done throughout so many centuries of literature. Tournier's suggestion (totally different from that of the linguistic avant-gardes even though its roots belong in the same terrain, the "sciences humaines") is very dear to my heart and for that reason I wanted to be the one to write to you about it.

Your article on *Americana* was very good and precise.

If you two are ever in Paris come and see us.

Best wishes.
Yours,

Italo

[Typed on Einaudi headed paper, with autograph signature; in the Piovene Archive, Biblioteca Civica Bertoliana di Vicenza.]

To Michele Rago—Rome

Paris 31 December 1968

Dear Michele,

Our correspondence has been languishing, and it must be my fault because I think you were the last to write. I'll make amends for this and try to rebuild our bridges.

I've heard that you've started a job at university, but I don't know the details. I have not read your articles now for some time, but it's rare for me to buy *l'Unità* here in Paris because it arrives irregularly and always late.

I spend a few days every month in Italy and am following Italian events quite closely. What's happening in France still stays more remote even though I'm living in the middle of it. You'll have received D. M.'s bulletin, honest as a diary of those glorious days but always based on a naïve and ambitious relationship with politics.[65] These people are admirable because they persist even in the current climate and are amongst the few ready to take risks like young people do. Yet, to have started off as writers seems to make less and less sense because the duties are now no different from those carried out by whoever engages in militant activity, outside the organizations, and this they accept but this makes their specificity fade in the cauldron of tendencies where the discourses that count are not theirs.

Moving on to the fields of more rigorous studies, structuralism, despite the journalistic commonplace that it died in the month of May, is at the height of its powers. I say this, judging from the weighty and ever more difficult publications that follow hard on the heels of each other without giving us time to read them, and from the crowds that squeeze into Lacan's and Barthes's seminars (the former's seminars in particular are of such difficulty that this mass attendance can only be explained in terms of a cult). The problems surrounding the events of May have surfaced even in these seminars, in fact have themselves become an object of study. May-ology shows no sign of abating at any level of the intellectual sphere, whereas reaction against it has massively occupied the field in practical terms.

In these last few months I've been taken up with practical work without much time for a break. Despite this, the projects I talked to you about this summer, about a literary journal, have come to something in the shape of discussions with Guido Neri and with a mutual friend from Bologna, Celati.[66] Guido Neri will be able to inform you about this, but we are still in the phase when we are trying to establish a platform for the problems we will deal with, and when we have something more precise I'll let you know.

Meanwhile, write to me. Chichita and I send all our best wishes for the New Year to you and those closest to you.

Italo

[Handwritten; with the addressee.]

To Gian Carlo Ferretti—Milan

Paris 3 February 1969

Dear Ferretti,

I READ YOUR BOOK WITH THE INTEREST THAT YOU CAN IMAGine, being directly concerned.[67] I read it for its general discourse as well as for the chapter you dedicate to me and the context in which you situate my work. The chapter on my output I feel is very accurate because it is the history of a long crisis that I refuse to accept as such, the story of a series of blind alleys caused by a cultural situation whose immaturity you have now clearly identified. This comes out when comparing my programmatic statements—too many of them and too bold—with my works and with my inability to construct through them a discourse that had any impact. In short, my famous "rationalism," today, when faced with the way things are in the world, really seems something to be put on the scrapheap, were it not for the fact that it does actually serve to indicate something precisely in its attempt to put together its "disiecta membra" every time it is taken to pieces. In this sense I like your reading of *Cosmicomics* and *Time and the Hunter* very much. And I am happy to be in the place you put me in, even if it is maybe a siding in the history of postwar Italian literature.

Perhaps for the first time your book analyzes this history with (historical-political as well as literary) categories that explain what happened. You identify tradition in the two strands, the pre-twentieth century (and pre-fascist) naturalistic strand, and the twentieth century's lyrical-evocative one. Then you note the attempts to open up to a new literature in opposition to both of them, with its own limitations—which are connected with the general cultural situation of the time—limitations which prevented it from following through to its conclusions, and the rapid return to a pre-fascist literary climate, a regional *verismo* that did not engage with the European crisis, and which if anything shaded off into a twentieth-century haze. The fact that you name Jovine in this context seems highly relevant to me; he was the writer that Vittorini used to cite as regards the years around 1950.[68] Then came the immobilizing restoration carried out by the "generation in between." All this sits very well alongside the discourse regarding the successive phases of left-wing criticism in your introduction. But I would have liked to see your discussion here too being full of names. This would be the time to write a history of left-wing criticism, or militant criticism in general, and you are the person to do this. You've already supplied the general outlines, but only in passing. The historical picture will come alive when you have the various positions inhabited by real people—many of whom are as full of personality as the writers—those who succeeded one another as critics mainly in the left-wing press. You have already done this minute work on newspapers and journals for the authors you are interested in, but why make the writers shoulder all the cultural and critical responsibility when their discourse only forms part of a collective discussion?

The part which seems to me to explore the most original theme in terms of criticism is the one you devote to the moralist poets of the Milan school (and in parallel those of *Officina*). In recent years I have entered into polemic with the intellectual-autobiographical tendency of the Milanese poets. I detest so many things that it presupposes, from the elegiac mode of forty-year-olds to conventional morality, which is always a bit complicit with it, but this certainly is an area of Italian literature which has its own compactness and is worth exploring.

So this is the right time to start to approach, as you have done (and you are the first), a history of the neo-avant-garde, analyzing its various strands.

I've read the sections dealing with Pasolini, who is still your hobbyhorse, because certainly in his works the comparison between explicit and implicit ideology produces more results. For some time now I have stopped considering P. as anything other than a character in the papers, and I don't read his works (nor see his films, which arouse delirious enthusiasm here in Paris), but I can see that you manage to pursue a persuasive discourse even as regards his latest works.

The other day in Turin I saw Mondo and I mentioned your book to him: he would like to write about it but his paper allows him little space for literature.[69] As for the other Turin critic you mentioned to me, good old Count Gigli, I have not been in touch with him for years, so I don't know whether I'll get a chance.[70]

Best wishes,
Yours,

Italo Calvino

[Handwritten; with the addressee.]

To Gianni Celati—Bologna

[Paris, 2 March 1969]

Dear Gianni,

I HAVE READ THE PREFACE TO FRYE.[71] THE CRITICISMS THAT were made, about it being (a) obscure and (b) extraneous to the book, are partly debatable and partly justified.

(a) Your essay contains points that are truly difficult (I too struggled to get my head round it) alongside others that are actually as easy to understand as conversation. The difficulties are to do with lexis more than anything else, and with some further research you can make it more readable and accessible, as a preface should be.

(b) Your piece has all the air of providing an exhaustive account of the book's subject matter (so it seems to me, though I have not read the book), and of taking the opportunity to bring us up to date with the situation all the way up to Lévi-Strauss, but it cannot be said that this has the shape of a preface. In other words, the Italian reader who knows nothing about old Northrop would feel that he has come across a theoretical book with a preface that is a theoretical chapter that belongs to the same genre as those in the book. Read Valesio's preface to Sapir and you will see a model preface, in other words a model way of presenting an author and his ideas in a different cultural context.

Moral of the story: prefaces too have their *strategies*, and I who wanted to carry out a strategic operation with your preface was defeated by the strategic plan that lies inside your preface. But I'm not giving up and I want to press you again for an article presenting Frye in *Libri nuovi*, the Einaudi bulletin which, as you will have seen, accepts lengthy and weighty articles. If the article you wrote for *Lingua e stile* was more "article"-like—and if you could finally track it down—I could put it forward.

II

Leaving aside these practical considerations on how to use your preface to Frye, I want next to give you my general, private reflections on Fryeism-Celatism, after what I have read. Have my hopes for finally finding a basic, exhaustive method of reading risen? No, I can't say they have. I start to feel a sharp sense of dissatisfaction, in other words the same feeling that takes hold of me after a bit—or rather: that takes hold of me pretty quickly—when considering any method of reading. Inevitably, after appreciating the new things it gives me, I begin to find it partial, and to fear that what remains outside its net is more than what I find in it.

We are back to square one: this index of archetypes and figures does not tell me anything about the work. The words themselves, where the substance of the work lies, remain remote and unfathomable. I can only know whether there is the belly of the whale or not in a work, or the earthly paradise or not, if I can recognize belly-of-the-whale language or earthly-paradise language. Whether the conventional figure is recognizable or not does not tell me anything yet. There are always conventional figures, but they don't convey anything more than the existence of a convention, *even when that existence has become unconscious*: it is only when from this dead language the green shoots of a living language spring up that something happens.

At this point I feel how important it has been for you to have had as your first fundamental literary horizon, that of poetry—just as it was for those of us who began to exercise our literary attention in the Forties: it is only in poetry that there are no tricks, or at least the (thematic, topical) tricks are more difficult. If Bodkin's season-related archetypes consist merely in what you say here, I am very disillusioned.[72] I was expecting a semiotics of the *lyric language* of winter, spring etc. at the level of verse, of lexis, meter, rhythm, and I would say of phonetics, not just such generic topoi.

You can find winter or springtime archetypes everywhere, just as you can with infernal or celestial ones, or comic or tragic movements, just as the Marxist critic does with the bourgeoisie. But we have to see whether these are distinctive traits. You can't tell me that in Dante's *Inferno* the first two canti are the "tragedy" and the following thirty-two are the "satire." These are the typical constructs of philosophers who, as long as they can make their theory stand up, in the end lose sight of the text they have before their eyes. If there is "tragedy" in the *Divine Comedy* it has to be searched for canto by canto, tercet by tercet, distinguishing it from the many other things there. It is precisely in that sample of analysis of the *Divine Comedy* that the discourse you had developed up to that point grinds to a halt: when faced with an actual work—even one which seems tailor-made to fit in with those categories—it is clear that things don't add up.

But what things? What are we trying to prove? Let's us take up our discussion again from the start. If we clearly thematize (finalize, functionalize) the objective of our research, everything will become more obvious to us. I can see that if we start off by looking for the genuine critical method, the one that is most scientific and least subjective, it will be a disaster.

Right then: by proving that every work—let's say every piece of narrative—has a structure that recalls religious iconography, for instance a relationship between a heavenly world and an earthly one, what are we trying to prove? In other words: what importance can this approach have for us who have nothing to do with that religious iconography and who have always wanted people no longer to think in terms of hell and paradise? What does the permanence and unlimited extension of this (or any other) mythical structure mean for us?

That there is a natural religion to which all texts refer? That all of literature is therefore a Sacred Scripture?

That is not our point.

Are we saying that neither religion nor literature exists but just an algebra of conceptual operations or rather a (biological? ontological?) structure that conditions human imagination and informs all mythopoetic activities with its own imprint?

This is Lévi-Strauss, or at least a popular image of him. We do not identify totally with him, or at least this image of him does not satisfy us.

That (and this is a possible aesthetic corollary of the previous one) only literature that somehow reworks structures/archetypes has any value, whereas all the rest is linguistic deposit?

I get the impression that you tend toward evaluative criteria of this kind; but it would be wrong to force you into such a limiting definition. Let's try to see things in more detail.

Are we saying that there exist problems that the primitive imagination responds to through mythical, elementary configurations and that these are the real problems that continue to face man even if he has forgotten or suppressed them, and that literature expresses their continued existence for man, and that the human languages that are not aware of them find themselves in some way falsified or mutilated?

This is the real theme we argued over—I think—and the one that is the backdrop to our common discourse. However, I am still not satisfied and I want to try out yet another formulation.

Is it that human imagination (or let's say thought, elementary logic) continues functioning by ordering the categories of the earliest human experiences into structures of images: above, below; inside, outside; winter, spring etc., even when it knows that an above and below do not exist, that there are no longer winters and springs but that agriculture will be from now something that happens in greenhouses kept at variable temperatures and humidities etc. Is it that literature is the space where the mythical structures of primitive man and one's childhood continue to impose their logic and *to be discussed on their very own terrain*, and this is the only ground where one can in some way contest them and revolutionize them, the only area in which something changes, in other words where the archetypes also can have a history, even if it is only a history that has to be gone over again from scratch, precisely because every human life starts from childhood?

There, that is what our interest in mythical models means for me, and—I would like to add—for us.

With this aesthetic corollary: literary value is given to something when and only when something so powerful happens that it *blows up* or *deforms* or *inverts* the old, "natural" mythical structure. I say "natural" in the sense that Valesio rehabilitates the "naturalness of languages" (in "Intorno ai segni" [Concerning Signs]). The mythical archetype-structure-model has itself become "nature," second nature, after having been the first victory of culture over nature. In literature the primeval struggle between culture and nature continues to play out on layers that overlay each other.

There, that is, in crude terms, the way in which I align myself with Fryeism-Celatism and I await optimistically its future development as Fryeism-Celatism-Calvinoism.

III

This is the place where Bakhtin's discourse on Menippean satire and Carneval fits in well. You had recommended I read that chapter and it was very important for me.[73] Not so much for the definition of Menippean satire as a genre, which seems too wide to me, so much so that all non-classical literature can be squeezed into it, if we took a strictly legalistic point of view. For instance, all the examples in Auerbach's *Mimesis* would still be for Bakhtin Menippean satire. (To compensate, I don't think Plato's dialogs would qualify at all.) But it is the Menippean attitude, as Bakhtin defines it, which in my view is as one with literature (or rather with literary value tout-court). Literary value is conferred when a mythical-archetypal structure clashes with Menippean-Carnivalizing aggression. Not when the structure feeds quietly on itself, nor when the Menippean-Carnivalesque does not grind against anything, goes around in neutral, without anything to rub against it or resist it.

I'm not sure how far this idea of Carnival—I mean the alternation between Carnival and austerity in medieval society—corresponds to historical truth, but it is certainly a great *model*. It is not just a literary model but a model of society, an ethical-political-economic model, it is the most explosive thing that has been written so far in the USSR, the first time that from that country an alternative model to their own society has been suggested to us, and not by chance Bakhtin hides it in a chapter with an anodyne title, in a terribly boring book about an author who has nothing to do with it like Dostoevsky.

It seems to me that this model is today the only model that one can propose for a revolution whose duty it is to reconcile the anti-authoritarian/anti-repressive/anti-productivity urge with the Socialist-Bolshevik necessity for a military discipline in civic and productive life. Instead of the seasonal-agricultural rhythm, it could be the rhythm of industrial economic cycles and five-year plans that will mark out the alternations between periods of semi-forced labor, austerity, pedagogic literature, and periods of subversion, waste, cultural revolution, and comic-expressionist-demystifying literature. At the point when supplies are about to run out, the Bolshevik-productivist party takes the situation in hand again, and establishes an even more severe period of repressive discipline and censorship.

I really want to write a pamphlet about this project. Naturally I would propose that the entire military-productivist ruling class be ritually tortured to death and killed off in great popular festivals during the protest phase. And I would also be unable to avoid in any way the slaughter of the protesters and poets at the start of every new productivist phase.[74] What guarantees the perfect functioning of the system is the escalation of the intolerability of living conditions in both phases: this will make the switch into the next phase inevitable. Thus the life of society, balanced between two phases with equal advantages and atrocities, phases that are equally necessary and intolerable, will find the only harmony possible.

[Typed copy; in the Calvino Archive (the date was provided in a handwritten addition by Calvino). Also in Italo Calvino, Gianni Celati, Carlo Ginzburg, Enzo Melandri, and Guido Neri, "*Alí Babà*": *Progetto di una rivista 1968–1972*, ed. Mario Barenghi and Marco Belpoliti, special issue of *Riga*, 14 (1998), pp. 79–83, where it is dated 2 January 1969.]

To Maria Corti—Pavia

12, Square de Châtillon
Paris 14

Paris, 11 April 1969

Dear Maria,

If I have not yet thanked you for your letter of 27 February, which I found extremely interesting and which clarified the whole problem for me, it is because I wanted to see your book first, but I have not yet managed to get hold of it.[75] Could you get Feltrinelli to send it to me *here in Paris*? (In Turin they regularly steal all the books that arrive for me at Einaudi.)

The history of your researches and the confirmation of your hypotheses, as you described them to me, is fascinating. The extraordinary fact is that the linguistic inventiveness, the verbal raptus in *Il partigiano Johnny* (*Johnny the Partisan*) was actually Fenoglio's first direct way of expressing himself even though he was from the country and totally isolated, and that he intended his move toward "literariness" as a process of relative linguistic normalization. (Precisely the opposite of what any up-to-date writer would presume today!)

A well-documented edition of this "proto-novel" really needs to be done, as well as of *Una questione privata* (*A Private Affair*).

Now Einaudi is going to bring out *La paga del Sabato* (*Saturday Pay*).[76]

Best wishes, and a friendly thank you once more.

Italo Calvino

In your letter you talk of two distinct versions, as it were, of the capture of Alba, the one in the *Racconti della guerra civile* (*Stories of the Civil War*) and the one that appeared in the Gettoni series. But the manuscript that was published in the Gettoni that had as the title of the short story "I ventitré giorni della città di Alba" (The Twenty-Three Days of the City of Alba) actually had as the author's title *Racconti della guerra civile* (*Stories of the Civil War*).

[Handwritten; in the Fondo Manoscritti del Centro di ricerca sulla tradizione manoscritta di autori moderni e contemporanei, University of Pavia. The Calvino archive contains the draft of the letter that follows. Although there is no date, one can hypothesize that what follows was a first reply, which Calvino later decided not to send, to Maria Corti's letter of 27 February and/or to those works by her on Fenoglio that Calvino knew.]

[March/April 1969]

Dear Maria Corti,

I HAVE THOUGHT A LOT ABOUT YOUR THESIS ON FENOGLIO'S protonovel. Your stylistic proof is convincing; according to it, the passages of the posthumous text that you cite must have been written even before *I ventitré giorni della città di Alba* (*The Twenty-Three Days of the City of Alba*). Is it possible that a novel of such dimensions, and about which Fenoglio spoke to nobody, existed already then?

Before his first short stories (or at the same time as them) Fenoglio had submitted to Einaudi a short novel, *La paga del Sabato* (*Saturday Pay*). That was when I met him. This was the story of a partisan who after the Liberation does not adapt to life in peacetime and becomes a bandit. I remember it as very good, even though a bit cinematographic toward the end. I immediately wrote to Vittorini about it.[77] (The letters must be in the Einaudi archive, it was probably 1951.)[78] Vittorini replied, saying that in the meantime he had read the short stories, which he liked more than the novel, and he wanted to publish them under the title *Racconti barbari* (*Barbarous Tales*). In fact the stories were published and a section from *La paga del Sabato*—the beginning, if I'm not mistaken—was detached and published as "Ettore va al lavoro" (Ettore Goes to Work).[79] (I remember that there were two pieces, but I can't recognize the second one; maybe it was two chapters conflated into one short story.)

So my conjecture would be this: after the Liberation Fenoglio starts work on a rough copy of his partisan experiences, but probably at that stage he goes no further than the capture and loss of Alba. Then he starts writing short stories or polishing pieces from his draft (as he did for *I ventitré giorni*) or working up postwar or non-war themes, up to *La malora* (*Ruin*). Meanwhile he has never abandoned the idea of a vast narrative about his partisan memories, but has thought of starting the story before the Resistance, from the beginning of his military and moral biography. The problem that remains to be clarified is whether he wrote his half-English right from the start or if this happened only at this stage. And in order to prove this, all that is needed is an examination of the manuscripts. It was at that time that once when I saw him in Alba he confided to me ("something that if I tell you it, you will not believe me") that he wrote first in English and then translated it into Italian. (I can work out the date with a certain confidence: autumn 1956.) He must have said the same thing to Citati as well around that time; I can't remember if he already knew Citati then (or Garzanti who went to see him with Citati and persuaded him to move to his publishing house) or if this happened later.

I think that Johnny the English scholar is the backdating of a situation which F. only got to later, in the mid-1950s. Fenoglio had probably learned English at school, but his practice in the language only happened later, especially through his friendship with an Englishman with whom he corresponded for business reasons, and who was also his mentor in the world of English literature, the one who got him the books etc. He mentioned him to me once, and it would be important to track him down. My conjecture is that *Il partigiano Johnny* has three layers, namely a first manuscript in Italian, before *I ventitré giorni* and which goes as far as point x. After *La malora* (*Ruin*), Fenoglio, fired with enthusiasm for the works he has read in English, starts work on it again, and what does he do? He rewrites it, anglicizing it; this must have been an intermediate phase, in order to elevate the language, before arriving at the third stage, that of "retranslating" it from "English" for the definitive Italian version. I can date this with some confidence: autumn 1956, the time I saw him in Alba and he confided . . .

This confidence seemed really unbelievable to me, because I had in mind *La malora*, but I think that his adoption of this method was probably a reaction to Vittorini's comment on *La malora*.[80]

The biggest questions start after this. Why does F. interrupt Johnny's memoirs shortly after the 8th September and have his protagonist die?[81] I think I remember that at the time either he or Citati told me that the story went on, but it was not very good and that consequently it had been decided to end the book at that point.[82] Today we can say that the beginning of *Il partigiano Johnny*—the return to Alba after the 8th September, political discussions, [first] stay with the Garibaldini (part of this in—it seems—a more polished draft)—is the weakest part of the book, which only acquires its epic thrust after that. So this could be a plausible explanation for the fact that he preferred (or was advised) to publish *Primavera di bellezza* (*Springtime of Beauty*) on its own.

However, there is another element, which strangely did not emerge in the discussions: *Il partigiano Johnny*, in the way Mondo published it, clearly shows that at a certain point F. discovered that the novel he really wanted to write was a different one, in other words *Una questione privata*. At a certain point the plot, which seemed to chart extremely faithfully the author's autobiographical experiences in the [ongoing flight] of the partisan who is being hunted down, changes register. It becomes the story of the attempts at capturing a living enemy to be used in an exchange of prisoners, in other words an active, adventurous story, where the novelistic dimension grafted onto his transformed autobiography takes the place of the linguistic-expressionist tension that had been applied to a faithful autobiography. In *Il partigiano Johnny* the part that corresponds to *Una questione privata* represents a fall in tone in the book after the splendid pages about his wanderings and the difficulties of surviving.

There it is clear that F. cannot develop the new narrative structure he has come across. He interrupts *Il partigiano Johnny* and starts writing *Una questione privata* (where he manages to insert a polemical picture of the Communist partisans which is much more successful than the many pages devoted to that experience in *Il partigiano Johnny*). But *Una questione privata* does not allow him to progress: at a certain point (as in *Primavera*) he has his protagonist die in a rushed finale.

But it is certain that *Una questione privata* is the last thing the sick F. was working on. After the publication of *Primavera di bellezza* ('59), F. got annoyed with Citati and Garzanti and wanted to come back to Einaudi. He gave us the book of short stories, *Un giorno di fuoco* (*A Day of Fire*) (still without *Una questione privata*) but Garzanti protested because he still had the option on the book and we had to abandon it. F. wanted to let the option deadline pass in order to give us the book he was writing and which it seems certain to me was *Una questione privata*.

To sum up, the proto-novel that you hypothesize, in the three versions of it that I hypothesize (pre-English, "English,"and post-English), was a kind of matrix or reservoir from which stem[83] the various definitive (but always unfinished) texts.

I would be glad to know what you think of these [hypotheses].[84]

To Maria Corti—Milan

Turin, 28 May 1969

Dear Maria,

I HAVE READ YOUR NOTE ON *LA PAGA DEL SABATO* (*SATURDAY Pay*).[85] It is very good and useful. The history of the book and of Fenoglio's beginnings in publishing terms emerges clearly and very interestingly.

However, I have one doubt: it shows Vittorini to be wrong and me right in a way that makes me a little uneasy, especially as the book is coming out with the publisher that I work for.[86] This is a question only of expressions and nuances that could be slightly modified. Certainly Vittorini's choices were drastic to the point of high-handedness, but that was the spirit in which they were made, the invention of a "line" that was never easily definable, on the basis of materials that happened to come his way.

In short, my worry is that your note might be used for anti-Vittorini purposes by Vittorini's enemies, whereas he can no longer defend himself. (We can also try to reconstruct his defense: his diffidence toward everything that led toward a novel that was constructed and predetermined, and in this case probably the fear of encouraging the "generational" novel with pretensions toward a sociological thesis, and also on the other hand the fear of encouraging the "novelistic" novel, the novel about the most journalistic aspects of the postwar period such as bandits etc., both tendencies that were in the air.)

Best wishes.

[Typed copy; in the Einaudi Archive, Turin.]

To Beatrice Solinas Donghi—Genoa

Turin, 30 June 1969

Dear Miss Solinas Donghi,

I read your article on Cinderella with great satisfaction.[87] One could say that for almost a century now nobody in Italy has been doing comparative studies of folktales: so I hail your excellent article as a real event in our culture. I who had started studying these things fifteen years ago, then got bored with being on my own and dumped everything there and then. And in this field of study it has to be said that the erudition on display makes us enthusiastic but real intelligence is rare. Instead in your article the great range of reference is useful for a discussion that is intelligent and spirited. From the history of the various incarnations of the motif through folklore, literature, popular novel, melodrama and cinema, you manage to pull something out. (On the other hand, that Marc Soriano is a disaster, he follows every clue eclectically, he makes a complete mess of things.)

As for that sentence you cite from me, heaven knows whether it was in my source (Zanazzo, or another one of those cited in my footnotes) or whether I had made it up myself. Moreover, I notice that you do not exploit the references in my notes, though they cost me so much effort and maybe nobody has ever consulted them. Of course, the texts I was quoting are almost all of them irretrievable so it's not worth it. Now in the abbreviated edition for the Oscar series I've placed the notes at the end of every folktale, so at least they are visible.

On the fall-from-on-high/ascent-from-below, Northrop Frye (*Anatomy of Criticism*) reviews practically the whole of world literature seen from precisely that angle.

I am sending you a piece of work I happened to finish recently and which also deals with popular tales, even though it is not relevant. And I am also sending you an extravagant essay which is maybe slightly more relevant.[88]

Very best wishes.
Yours,

Italo Calvino

[Typed on Einaudi headed paper, with autograph signature; with the addressee. Previously in "Sei lettere di Italo Calvino" (Six Letters by Italo Calvino), *Nuova Corrente*, 100 (vol. 2 of special issue *Italo Calvino*, ed. Mario Boselli) (July–December 1987), pp. 411–12.]

To Vito Amoruso—Bari

Turin, 18 September 1969

Dear Amoruso,

I apologize for being a not very punctual correspondent. I spend months without writing a letter (especially when I have a project I'm working on) and when I decide to write one I find a mountain of correspondence to reply to, I panic and shelve everything. Please do not get angry: be patient.

I received your letter at the time, and later the book on the *Beat Writers*, for which I thank you very much.[89] I intended to write to you after a thorough reading. From my first samples it seemed to me full of "critical detachment," something that is right in itself but which tends to make things less exciting. The thing is that I (who deep down am not interested in the *Beats* and maybe even hate them, or at any rate don't understand them) would like to read a book on the *Beats* written by an enthusiast, by someone who comments on them from the inside, because then it would help me to understand, to get into them. Either that or a violent attack on them, but by someone for whom it is a question of life and death. In your case I am afraid that what you offer is the tried and tested Italian wisdom which—since I myself have always had it in my blood and bones—I feel it is my duty to avoid and fight against like the plague.

As for Frye, I find myself—within the limits in which I was writing about him[90]—more and more uplifted by his richness, and also his finesse. I believe that the high road for criticism is the one that starts from anthropological functions.

It is on the level of anthropology (let's say of pre-history rather than history) that literature is not a *closed universe*.

That is why Frye pleases me in comparison with many French structuralists. Because I can only make comparisons (as an empirical reader, or if you prefer, as an ex-historicist who has taken on board his own defeat) with things that are. If something new emerges tomorrow from the by now cold ashes of historicist criticism, I shall be the first to rejoice at it; but for the time being I see no signs of it anywhere.

You have been very good in discovering and encouraging and following Ventrella.[91] In person he confirmed the remarkable impression made by his writings. I hope that with the new things he will write Einaudi can launch something of his.

Thank you very much for introducing him to me. It is good to know that the provinces can still surprise us with educated people from remote areas such as this.

Best wishes,

(Italo Calvino)

[Typed copy; in the Einaudi Archive, Turin. Also in *ILDA*, pp. 580–81.]

To Franco Maria Ricci—Milan

[Paris, autumn 1969]

Dear Mr Ricci,

HERE IS MY CV. I WAS BORN IN 1923 UNDER A SKY IN WHICH the radiant Sun and melancholy Saturn were housed in harmonious Libra. I spent the first twenty-five years of my life in what was in those days a still verdant San Remo, which contained cosmopolitan eccentrics amidst the surly isolation of its rural, practical folk; I was marked for life by both these aspects of the place. Then I moved to industrious and rational Turin, where the risk of going mad is no less than elsewhere (as Nietzsche found out). I arrived at a time when the streets opened out deserted and endless, so few were the cars; to shorten my journeys on foot I would cross the rectilinear streets on long obliques from one angle to the other—a procedure that today is not just impossible but unthinkable—and in this way I would advance marking out invisible hypotenuses between grey right-angled sides. I got to know only barely other famous metropolises, on the Atlantic and Pacific, falling in love with all of them at first sight: I deluded myself into believing that I had understood and possessed some of them, while others remained forever ungraspable and foreign to me. For many years I suffered from a geographical neurosis: I was unable to stay three consecutive days in one city or place. In the end I chose definitive wife and dwelling in Paris, a city which is surrounded by forests and hornbeams and birches, where I walk with my daughter Abigail, and which in turn surrounds the Bibliothèque Nationale, where I go to consult rare books, using my Reader's Ticket no. 2516. In this way, prepared for the Worst, and becoming more and more dissatisfied with the Best, I am already anticipating the incomparable joys of growing old. That's all.

Yours sincerely,

Calvino

[Handwritten; with the addressee. Published in facsimile in "Notizie su Italo Calvino" (Information on Italo Calvino), in *Tarocchi. Il mazzo visconteo di Bergamo e New York* (Parma: Franco Maria Ricci, 1969), pp. 161–62; later in *Eremita a Parigi. Pagine autobiografiche* (Milan: Mondadori, 1994), pp. 180–81; English version in *Hermit in Paris: Autobiographical Writings*, tr. Martin McLaughlin (London: Cape, 2003), 157–58. The date is conjectural and is based solely on the date of printing of the book *Tarocchi*, which is given as "November 1969." There is a French version of the same letter written by Calvino in *Eremita a Parigi*, pp. 181–82.]

To Mario Boselli—Genoa

Paris, 23.10.1969

Dear Boselli,

I LIKED YOUR ARTICLE ON *TI CON ZERO* (*TIME AND THE Hunter*) very much.[92] I have read it and reread it with interest and with an increasing stimulus for discussion each time I reread it. This seems to me at last to be a critical approach which enters into the process of imagination and writing, and explains it—explains it first and foremost to the author himself, helping him to be aware of the operations he carries out when writing, to emerge from the empirical, and to move forward.

It seems to me that you define very precisely both the process of "rationalization of the imaginary" which starts out from the ludic, and also "linguistic precision as a particular form of abstraction" and the "linguistic network" which places reality "at a distance," in other words the series of mutations undergone by an original event "under different linguistic registers."

My position today is probably to be found in that frightening core of desperation caused by the unliveable nature of the contemporary world and of the impossibility of active participation, because all roads to a desirable future are closed off. And I say "probably" because I know that if I were to decide "to think it through" right to the end, to enunciate it more explicitly, make a programmatic declaration (in other words to "ideologize" it), this desperation would become something else, it would maybe lose the *active* strength it can have (active toward what? I don't know), it can have only if I allow this to emerge from the process of writing.

It seems to me that you define very well in section 5 the overcoming of the "nostalgia-anguish" phase (this is very important: I do not think there are any pre-technological paradises to be regained), and in section 6 you clarify what I would really want the effect of my use of language to be on individual consciences.

In section 4 some points seem to me to contradict the rest of your argument, and this is an important factor for me because I believe that the finale of "Montecristo" is the real ethical-epistemological conclusion I have reached. In other words I see the conjectural planning of the absolute prison as a profession of faith in deductivity, in the necessity to construct formally perfect theoretical models of the objective reality one wants to deal with.[93] (The epistemologist who has convinced me most is Popper.) It is still indispensable to make use of experiential data (Abbé Faria's attempts) to check the formal model by continually comparing it with empirical reality. Only in this way can one discover the weak points in empirical reality, "in other words those where historical action can find a breach in order to move forward."

You talk instead of the comfort that can be found by whoever is enclosed permanently in a cell, of the "possibility of a second reality, in other words it seems to me that you find a consolatory attitude in it," almost one of escapist illusion into dreams, and I can't recognize myself in that interpretation. On the other hand, you are probably right when you say that my attitude attenuates the "dramatic nature of the language," it "depersonalizes" it. Yes, my Montecristo wants to escape from the existential drama of the prisoner (Kafka's K.), to depersonalize his tension, as a necessary condition for escaping from the prison. And if one looks closely, K. too—or rather Kafka's style of abstract precision—was a decisive step in this direction; Kafka can be read in these two ways: as the "story of a soul" and/or as the description of a network of objective relationships, and I think the latter approach is more important.

In short, it seems to me that in the planning of the perfect prison I take to its extreme consequences that "Enlightenment dimension" that you define so well at the beginning and end of your article (whereas up to now critics have spoken of it in generic and often banal terms), while in section 4 I feel you stress points of crisis. In particular, the "indeductibility of the effect from its cause" (which you quoted also in your article in *Il Caffè*)[94] is certainly a very important point and I would like to see it developed at greater length. Because when put like that, it is an element that is typical of an awful lot of contemporary literature, but in what sense is it typical of the things I write? Perhaps my characteristic is that I arrive at it from the opposite direction, in other words through an obsession for ratiocination which leads me all the way to a false conclusion, though it never departs from this logical form. And yet the form of the stories in the third part is in every case *deductive*: how can we square that?

All in all, in section 4 I find that some contradictions crop up (contradictions with your argument, I think; it is more than probable that you find contradictions in me—given that I have never been able to think systematically—and if you highlight them, you are doing something that interests me and is useful to me). Such contradictions however do not impinge on the general sense of the article, which is extremely clear, or on the conclusion which I believe contains the most precise stylistic and ethical definition that has been given of my work.

This essay of yours fits very well with your article in *Il Caffè*, and I am fully in agreement with this line.

I hope that we will meet again one day and discuss these things face to face.

Please accept my thanks and warmest greetings,
Yours

Calvino

The quotations are very well chosen, with your skill in quoting my pronouncements—taken from the most varied contexts—in order to define literary procedures.

I am pleased you quote Heissenbüttel, who is the author who interests me most in all the current theoretical writing on literature.[95]
[Handwritten; with the addressee. Previously in "Sei lettere di Italo Calvino" (Six Letters by Italo Calvino), *Nuova Corrente*, 100 (vol. 2 of

special issue *Italo Calvino*, ed. Mario Boselli) (July–December 1987), pp. 413–15. In the photocopy of the letter used for this transcription, some of the words and phrases appear to have been underlined by the addressee.]

To Guido Davico Bonino—Turin

Paris, 21.3.70

Dear Guido,

I AM NOT VERY CONVINCED BY THE PROJECTED ANTHOL.[OGY] of young South American poets and even less convinced by the discourse justifying it, but I know too little about this to give a detailed verdict. I know Gelman[96] as the best Argentinian poet for polemical-gnomic poems, but I also know Alejandra Pizarnik who has been left out although she is the best exponent of the poetry of introversion and metaphorical delirium.

If privileging engagé poets is a criterion which we reject in the rest of the world, why accept it here? In the Hispanic American world more than ever now it is from those interested in formal elements in poetic research that major results emerge also in terms of political poetry. If we want to do an anthology called *Poesia e rivoluzione: i giovani poeti sudamericani* (*Poetry and Revolution: Young South American Poets*), then the exercise has some validity. Or better still take a group of poets with affinities, for instance those—cited by the volume editors—working on "anti-poetry" or "conversational poetry." An anthology of a movement or a school would define the *young* in a less mechanical sense than the date of birth limit of those born after 1930.

As for the geographical limits, the reasons adduced for the exclusion of Central America (which has many poets between Mexico and various other smaller states, not forgetting Cuba and what it represents) are convincing only up to a point because it is not clear that the South Americans offer a more homogeneous picture. (It is a serious mistake to forget to specify that these are only poets writing in Spanish and that Brazil has been omitted.)

I am leaving for the Atlantic coast. I will be in Turin after Easter. Then off to a symposium on semiotics in Palermo.

Happy holidays to you and your family

Calv.

[Handwritten; in the Einaudi Archive, Turin.]

To Mario Socrate and Vanna Gentili—Rome

[San Remo,] 26.6.70

Dear Mario, Dear Vanna,

YOUR LETTER GAVE ME ENORMOUS PLEASURE. THE MORE ONE wants to speak with friends, the less one writes, since a letter does not seem sufficient. I always think I will soon be coming to Rome, but although I spend a few days in Italy almost every month, my various commitments always keep me north of the Gothic Line. I am now at San Remo for a few days to pick up my little daughter who has spent a month with her granny. In July (apart from some trips to Turin) I will be with my family in a hotel in Versilia (Hotel La Pergola, Ronchi-Poveromo, Marina di Massa). We still don't know about August. Let us know your summer plans. I am very pleased to have received Vanna's book which I was looking forward to, and which will be one of the things I will read this summer. I already know that it is a book which *will be useful to me* and I will write to you about it as soon as I have read it.[97] I am looking forward to Mario's book of poems, especially the short poems I really liked and the others I don't know yet.[98]

Our life goes on with all the difficulties of family life in a metropolis but without any big or special problems, so we can already count ourselves lucky. Giovanna is five, is growing nicely, speaks three languages, does not know how to read or write or count, is very happy and full of imagination, in short the best we could ever have hoped for and we should be thankful to the gods.

I am working in fits and starts, fragmentarily, just as much as the different distractions and hitches, the general dissatisfaction and individual hypochondria allow me to, and meantime I dream of composing encyclopaedic works, universal histories, theogonies, maps of the terraqeous globe and of the firmament, utopias . . .

The most important work I have done is a substantial selection from Fourier's works, more substantial than any that exists even in France.[99] The translation (not by me) is already finished and I have to write the introduction, but I am late as always with all my deadlines.

As for politics, my position is well summed up by your phrase: "The problem is that one cannot totally identify with any movement." The only difference is that you are living this condition actively, being in the middle of it, whereas for me now the only possibility is the position of the spectator at a distance. This means I generate a lot of bad blood in myself without the satisfaction that doing something always brings, but I know that any immediate discourse I pronounced would be too full of ifs and buts, and I prefer to hypothesize a point in the future (a general context) when perhaps I'll be able to say things that are relevant and clear (also to myself) and useful.

You wonder what about *Il manifesto*?[100] And this question mark is also my own, despite friendship with the people involved and my agreement with the majority of articles in the paper.

If one moves then from politics to literature, this sense of *not belonging* becomes even more absolute.

I really do hope we'll meet soon. Much love to you, the bride and groom and to Francesca, from me and Chichita.[101]

Italo

[Handwritten; with Mario Socrate.]

TO SEBASTIANO TIMPANARO—FLORENCE

7.7.70

Dear Timpanaro,

FOR SOME TIME NOW I HAVE BEEN WANTING TO WRITE YOU A letter on the end of the world, and it is only now that I can find the time to do so, but it has been going on since I read your piece on Engels in *QP* 39—I agree with it in general terms, as well as in broad terms with all your polemic about materialism.[102] In order to avoid human experience becoming irrevocably lost at the point when the solar system becomes uninhabitable, emigrating to planets of other solar systems is not indispensable, only the transmission of information to inhabitants of other planets of this or other galaxies. Fred Hoyle has insisted for some time on the idea that travel on interstellar spaceships is not just probably unrealizable (the fuel problem; and also the problem of the various generations which would have to be born and die on the spaceship, given the length of the voyage). But he says it is also basically pointless, because what is important is to communicate reciprocally the maximum amount of one's own experiences amongst the various human or parahuman species that exist in the universe. And I would add that even if one did not enter into communication with other beings able to receive our messages—an unlikely eventuality in that the time that separates us from the extinction of life on Earth is still quite long, but it could also be that our planet was the most "advanced" in the history of nearer galaxies and there are no valid interlocutors—all that it would take would be for someone to deposit a summa of human knowledge in some distance-projection system—a stock of images of what life on Earth has been, in short our entire *memory*—on some neutral, extinct, uninhabitable heavenly body in order to conserve it there in a safe place, as though in a library or better still in the crypt of a pyramid, and then it will be up to others to think about discovering this global message of ours and decoding it, the other human beings that will be able to go further than us in the exploration of the cosmos. For us the important thing is that we play our part in providing clear information about what human experience has been, and then the others can sort themselves out; this will mean that there will be a discontinuity in human history, maybe even a very long one, but one cannot say that it will be lost. When you look at it closely, this heavenly body that would act as the deposit of human memory could be the Earth itself, on the day when—by the time it was a fossil planet or at least an uninhabitable one—it was visited by extraterrestrial archaeologists, or even without it needing to be visited, just explored remotely by intergalactic reading systems which will be developed sooner or later. And it might be that we ourselves will already be able to do this with others, and we would be enriched by the experience of other human species who had disappeared on other planets. Now I would not want this discourse of mine to sound like a claim for the eternity of the human species or universal humanization or other rubbish. Man is simply the best chance we know of that matter has had of providing itself with information about itself. (I know that that clause, in syntactic terms, precisely because it has "matter" as its subject, lends itself to being interpreted as a metaphysication of matter, as teleological etc., but let me try to explain what I have in mind with the means I have at my disposal.) I tend to see in the "history of matter" (forgive me these terms), from the simplest atom to the most complex, in the history of the universe, in the history of life, of evolution and of man, a relationship between what exists and what exists, which is right from the most elementary levels a process of knowledge/self-transformation/memorization (in other words: *work*). A later stage of this process will be for man, at the end of the human race, to transmit this capacity for knowledge/self-transformation/memorization which matter has acquired through him, to transmit it either to machines which will automatically reproduce themselves, or to other living species in this or other planets. Only at that point will the human story close positively, and history will emerge from its anthropocentric provincialism. In other words, if the objective of man is the humanization of nature, the total mastery of the forces of matter etc., this objective will be reached only when it is understood that these are rhetorical formulae and that in reality it is the memory of matter that organizes itself through man. We must understand that man is a "space" of matter where certain processes of specialization take place provisionally which will be later redistributed throughout all that exists, that is to say when we finally understand or re-understand that it is in the work of the universe that man must of necessity collaborate.

I can afford to share these ideas with you in this disorganized way (and I am not going to make a fair copy of this letter so as not to make people think that my thought has fewer uncertainties than it has) only because having imposed on myself the role of marginal observer who no longer has any public discourse to make, the only thing I can do is to distribute the half-finished products of my reflections privately.

However, I am involved in a "public" work which will certainly interest you: a substantial anthology of Fourier (for Einaudi) which I hope will supply further ammunition for your battle for a materialistic, hedonistic, anti-rigorous ethic.

Best wishes

Italo Calvino

[Handwritten, with the date written after the signature; with the addressee. Previously published under the title "Lettera sulla fine del mondo" (A Letter on the End of the World), *la Repubblica*, special issue of 1 January 2000, pp. 1, 22–23.]

To Pietro Citati—La Castellaccia, Giuncarico (Grosseto)

[Villasimius (Cagliari),] 4.8.70

Dear Pietro,

I HAVE READ WITH GREAT PLEASURE AND CONCENTRATION THE second part, trying not to get lost amidst what is dense and ungraspable, nor to miss anything, and I found tremendous satisfaction actually in the most difficult bits like the essence of Mothers, and Valpurga's biological vision, where what stands out are your patience as a guide and your ability to shed light as you untangle layers and masses of meaning.[103] The things I particularly liked are many: the catalog of clouds, the catalog of monsters, the Cabiri, Lynceus, Helen's style, Hermes . . . And of course everything about Mephistopheles. You constantly open up new interpretative and imaginative spaces from minimal hints in the text, multiplying the text, and as you do so you write maybe the only kind of literature that is possible today: a literature that is both critical and creative. And the "prolixity" that you will find yourself being accused of is a charge you should reject because it is precisely the minuteness of your analysis and your returning time and again to what has already been said that allows you to perform this operation. Rather, the only critique one could make is of the admiring, exclamatory style, a style [not] kept in check (I mean the style of your sentences, whereas the way you construct the critical discourse, the way you organize your chapters, is always one of great elegance). Here what is at play, I would say, is a respect for the humble, ancillary role of critical discourse compared to the text, the ruling out of any thoughts of stylistic competition with the text, keeping yourself in the position of the traveler who is on a visit and offers comments. All in all, a wonderful, very important book, as I never tire of saying to the few people I meet, including those at Einaudi, those for whom the price-sales-rights worries were decisive. It was certainly better for you not to publish with Einaudi, because their poor record in paying is chronic and when friends are involved this becomes the source of unpleasant tensions. Nowadays in publishing there is only room for the very big or the very small. Einaudi cannot become very big, nor can it go back to being very small, and so what it does it does a bit by chance because something suits this or that combination of intentions which take the place of intellectual tendencies.

We are now in the middle of a desert (after a hotel stay in the limbo of an Apuan beach), in one of these Hollywood-bungalow hotel structures which the Milanese transport bit by bit with all their staff to the most far away places. The water is of a clearness we've never seen, the sand and rocks out of this world. We will stay here till mid-August; then in another place like it a bit further North (Hotel Su Sirboni, Barisardo) till the end of the month, or as long as we can stand it.

As for Ovid, I have not yet thought enough about it to give you an answer so I'll wait till my next letter.[104]

In your last letter you mentioned one of Elena's brothers having an operation. Give me an update, and tell me about Stefano.[105]

You also asked me for some French addresses, but your letter got to me when I was in Italy and the only address I have with me is Butor (but he is always on his travels in some foreign university): 28 bis, Avenue de l'Eperon, Saint-Geneviève de B. Damn! In my address-book the name of the village (near Paris) is incomplete and I've not got a guide to complete it. He knows and reads Italian—which Blanchot does not (nor,

I think, do the others). Nor does Foucault, as far as I am aware, know Italian; but I have got his complete address: 13 rue du Docteur-Finlay, Paris xv^{e}.

Best wishes to you, Elena and Stefano from

Italo

[Handwritten on paper headed "Timi-Ama Residence Hotel"; with the addressee.]

To Pietro Citati—La Castellaccia, Giuncarico (Grosseto)

San Remo, 12.9.70

Dear Pietro,

I was planning to come to La Castellaccia for a few days in this period, but because of various minor commitments I will have to go back to Paris next week where the family already are. Maybe in October I'll spend a week in Rome where I have not been for some time. If you will still be at La Castellaccia, I'll come there, otherwise I'll see you all in Rome.

Your piece on Conrad is very good, perfect on the abyss but one must not overlook the role played by order: he always opposes order and the abyss, though the abyss always wins (or if it doesn't win—as in *Typhoon*—it still remains the stronger force).[106] I have also read your article on the English novel, extremely precise, as well as the polemic against Cassola,[107] both of which resonate with the reflections I have been mulling over recently on what constitutes a novel, maybe because of an (at present vague) desire to go back to proclaiming the necessity of "novelistic" ingredients. (Chichita has done nothing for the whole summer except read her favorite Dickens, and I did too though in fits and starts and wondering whether I was wasting my time, but also understanding more Dickens's way of constructing novels, after seeing at the exhibition that's on in London the magazines that he published throughout his life with the installments of his novels and the illustrations which he had a big say in.) Perhaps in all this there is a reaction and dissatisfaction on my part with the work I've started writing this summer, pushing myself as never before toward preciosity, Alexandrinism, the prose poem: a rewriting of Marco Polo's *Il Milione* (*Travels*) all made up of brief descriptions of imaginary cities.[108] I don't know at this stage if it will work out. I'd like to get you to read it.

Warmest regards to all of you from

Italo

[Handwritten; with the addressee.]

1971–1975

To Franco Fortini—Milan

San Remo 12.2.71

Dear Franco,

I am replying only now to your letter of the 27th because for the last month I have buried myself in a project that had been dragging on for some time and which I wanted to put to bed (Fourier) and I have cut off all contact with the world.[1] I have not yet finished but most of it is done, and—now taking advantage of a break in my mother's house—I am getting back to my correspondence.

I read your letter with pleasure—and most of all because you had forgotten that epigram. From my point of view I can see that at that time there were so many things I could have understood but did not. And if now I understand something more, this does not necessarily help me to find a place to situate myself in the map (a place that is both mine and useful to others) nor to feel satisfied with my isolation.

Amongst the positive experiences of the last few months, I have to include that fact that *Faust* has become—thanks to the spirit of your "translation"[2]—one of my "models," as a work that contains all the dimensions we need. It is at once the establishing of a universe, an evocation of new values, and at the same time a form of game. In other words there is in it the consciousness of using language, signs, meter, cultural materials, and that its real sense is in the meanings that reverberate beyond the book.

I hope to see you soon and before Ruth has got tired of telling her China stories.[3] (I have already had some account of the journey there from Lisa Foà.)

Very best wishes.

Calvino

[Handwritten; in the Franco Fortini Archive, Siena.]

To Esther Benítez—Madrid

Paris 29.4.71

Dear Miss Benítez,

I HAVE READ YOUR INTRODUCTION TO PAVESE'S *LETTERS*.[4] IT seems to me a very detailed and substantially accurate biography. In the first section it sounds a bit strange to put together names such as Moravia, Ungaretti, Scipio etc., a grouping taken from a passage in his diary where it makes sense, but here it is hard to understand why these names and not others. And perhaps that letter to Onofri takes on exaggerated importance.

A more general criticism I would want to make is that one can judge Pavese's importance not from the point of view of practical political activity, but from his attempt to renew the Italian cultural climate, its literary language, the way of seeing the world reflected in his novels. The term of comparison is not so much Italian political history (especially the history of the opposition groups which, being a clandestine history, was known alas just to very few people) as Italian literature of the time (D'Annunzianism, artistic prose, Hermeticism etc.). A proper commentary on Pavese's letters should take account of the provincial isolation of Italian culture in that period, the important role that the initiatives of translators and publishers played, in the midst of all the practical difficulties, in order to open windows onto that enclosed atmosphere. This was a battle in which Pavese (like Vittorini, like only a few others to begin with, then more and more) was always in the front line, and which bore important fruit also outside the strictly literary sphere, because everything—at that time—had political resonance, and it was through the reading of those texts that the generation that would fight in the Resistance (I'm talking of course about the young students and intellectuals) came to maturity.

It is only by situating him in what was his *field of combat* that one can understand Pavese's originality and his constant *commitment*, and the fact that after the war and the liberation he was recognized as one of the founders of the new literature.

As for his relationship with politics in the strict sense, one has to bear in mind that in the Fascist period, when the number of intellectuals carrying out an active campaign of opposition was barely *a few dozen*, Pavese, although he was the "literature man" of the group, was the friend of these activists and not of the others. Although he bowed to the necessity of getting the Fascist Party card, without which nobody could get a job, after a short time, once his friendships and ideas were known (. . . and his poems), he was expelled from the Fascist Party, sent into exile and from that point on could no longer teach in state schools.

Compared with his circle of friends, all of whom were highly politicized, Pavese was an "apolitical" person; but compared to the vast majority of Italian intellectuals Pavese was that rare case of a literary man steeped in politics, fully aware of the historical and civic sense of literary operations.

I have taken the liberty of pointing these things out to you in order to define more precisely your correct thesis that Pavese must not be seen as an example of the *committed* writer but something much more complex and contradictory.

I am very grateful for your expressions of friendship, and I wish you every success with your work.

Italo Calvino

I am returning the manuscript to Jaime Salinas, along with the translation of my book that you had sent me.
[Handwritten; with the addressee.]

To Paolo Valesio—Cambridge (Mass.)

[Poveromo,] 9.7.71

Dear Valesio,

I RECEIVED YOUR LETTER, ALL WRITTEN IN CAPITALS. I AM glad that you have a bright female student who is doing research on my fiction. Up until now Italian or foreign university theses on my work seem to me to be very dreary, giving me the impression that it is only the most clueless students and scholars who are interested in my modest output, and in the end this just makes me depressed. I much prefer negative criticism which at least tries to say something instead of benign but insipid critiques. I will be really glad to read your student's work and if it raises points for discussion, so much the better.

You ask me if I think that it is useful for the person writing about a living author to interview the object of study. I know that in several American universities such an interview is almost a ritual element in the paper or thesis, and this is not the first time the question has arisen. My reply is emphatically: no, I believe that *there must be no interview*. If for the better understanding of written texts it was useful to see and hear the physical being who just happened to be—because of a series of largely chance circumstances—their author, that would be the death knell for literature as a relationship between a written text and its reader. A text must be something that can be read and evaluated without reference to the existence or otherwise of a person whose name and surname appear on the cover. (That name could be a group of several people who sign themselves with just one name; it could be a living person who invents a fictitious character very different from himself and tries to imagine the book that this character might write; it could be an author who, after writing a book, is no longer the same as he was before, and therefore is no longer the author of that book: in fact I believe that this ought not to be the exception but the rule, if literature really was a serious experience.)

Another, even stronger argument: if interviewing was methodologically acceptable, this would create a disparity of tools between those studying a living author and those studying Spenser or Guinizelli, and this is clearly inadmissible. The *living* author, I believe, can never be taken into consideration. To be able to study a writer, he must be *dead*, that is—if he is alive—he must be *killed* (or at least he must be considered as being in his dotage, something that with many writers is in fact the case: in every individual full mental faculties last a certain number of years, not usually very many). Furthermore, already the existence of the *work* is a sign that the author is *dead*, happily dead if the work is worthwhile; the work is the negation of the writer as empirical living being. Admittedly, there are authors who are "rich in humanity" whom it is worth meeting anyway, independently of their work. But I am the exact opposite, and when someone comes to talk to me for reasons of this sort, the little I manage to articulate is so discouraging that they quickly change the topic of their thesis.

It is more difficult for me to reply to the other questions you put to me, on the situation in Italy and my own plans. I do not have clear vision on either point. As far as the Italian situation is concerned—in terms of politics, culture etc.—one can have a viewpoint only from inside something, that is a partial viewpoint (in Italy today everything is partial and fragmentary) and one which is not convincing outside that ambience. But I am more outside it than ever, with all the traumas which that brings in its wake. I have no temptation to be inside anything, and this not only in the weeks I spend shut up in a mansard in Paris (or in a seaside limbo as happens during my summers—this is the sixth such holiday since I became a father), but even during the days of every month I spend in the Einaudi publishing house, the navel of the world, which faithfully reflects the crisis—if not of everyday Italy, at least of intellectual Italy. The fact that I have kept myself cut off from processes that have developed spectacularly and then have ground to a halt—on a very small scale, the self-willed collapse of the *Neoavanguardia*; on the macro scale, even though with less self-awareness of their defeat, the incapacity of the student movement and the "new Left" to be anything more than just a symptom—does not make me happy. I don't feel any less burned than those who really did get seared by those events. Since I don't identify except in a partial and sporadic way with any of the sides in the fray, and since I lack that touch of mythomania that is needed for me to invent my own role, it is difficult to make plans. It is not by chance that I worked so much on that Fourier project which in fact nobody made me do. It was not my field, it couldn't give me any satisfaction (and in fact it hasn't given any so far): utopia was for me, from all points of view, the only non-place I could inhabit. The truth is that I find all sorts of excuses to keep me from writing, I do a lot of tiny publishing jobs which I always think is something useful. To go back to what I was saying before, it is not the case that just because at a certain point someone had the idea of being a writer that he then at another point has to continue being a writer. Perhaps there will come a time when it will suit him to be a writer again, or perhaps not, that depends on many factors. I say "at a certain point" in history, but one ought to say: when a certain point in history coincides with a certain moment in someone's individual biography, with a certain moment in the internal development of his means of expression, etc.

The intolerance you feel for the language of critical essays and which leads you to privilege scientific language on the one hand and the language of "fiction" on the other is the right attitude. But it must also be said that a non-abstract, discursive language, which does not claim to impose an authority it does not possess (unlike, for instance, the claims made by generic political jargon which is made up entirely of clichés, or those made by the language of current critical writing in French) and which remains just a language of enquiry, of research, of reflection, well that is still always an essential linguistic space.

In this sense I could go along with the "soft approach" you support, if this implies (as I seem to understand) a certain stylistic eclecticism. But I am not sure if I have properly understood what you are trying to say. And when you then bring in D'Annunzio—for all the attention and good-will that I can muster in order to follow this D'Annunzio revival—that makes me feel allergic.

Write to me again, because these discussions at long distance are still some of the only ones that are still possible.

Yours,

Calvino

Hotel La Pergola
54039 Ronchi—Marina di Massa

[Manuscript; in Yale University Library, Manuscripts and Archives (Paolo Valesio Papers), New Haven.]

To Leonardo Sciascia—Palermo

Turin 14.9.71

Dear Leonardo,

I have just finished reading *Il contesto* (*Equal Danger*): very enjoyable and enthralling. This false detective story, organized like a game of chess in the Stevenson-Chesterton-Borges manner, is a genre I love and you have set it up perfectly (with just one exception which I will explain later). The highly pessimistic and disillusioned political pamphlet in it, against everything and everyone, suits my own state of mind perfectly, it is something that I would like to do as well, but up until now I have not been able to find the right tone whereas you have on the whole managed to maintain it.

In analytical terms I would divide the novel into three phases: the first, in which the mystery of the murders of the judges is outlined in—I would say—what are still Sicilian dimensions, gripped me very much, and the elegance of the abstract construction which one notices immediately compensates for the loss of local color and landscape compared to your other books. The ironic screen works: only in some rare cases does it seem to me that you push too much in the direction of the comic (I remember for instance a female president of an animal protection group), in short the reader must always know he is in a game but must also be able to take it seriously. The literary references that are studded throughout work very well (and they will continue to work well in their crescendo right to the end).

The second phase is when we move to the satire of intellectual behavior: Nocio and Galano. And there I immediately felt that you became more heavy-handed. That poem . . . In short, that detachment between you and the world you are condemning fades and that was the secret of your Sicilian pessimism. This is only a stylistic observation in a broad sense, and I would not even feel like advising you to cut or change anything because I would not like to lose anything of the book's richness, which is enjoyable and engaging just as it is. And in any case everything has a logic because the party at Narco's with the minister and all the implications and interpretations that the policemen's visit unleashes is a very clever and crucial device. So now we move on to the

Third phase, in other words the big power game, where the game again has to become more abstract because your polemic moves on to a more allegorical level where I found full, enthralling enjoyment.

As soon as one finishes reading it, there is of course that slight sense of frustration that the explanation is not set out clearly, but this too is now a rule in the genre, and it is right that the reader should make an effort to think about it again and if necessary to reread it, as I did, in order to see the mechanism clearly. Naturally I do not know if I have understood everything and whether what I have not understood has to stay as a mystery or is something I should have understood, and that makes me a little uneasy. (Now I am no longer talking literary criticism: I am talking about my crossword-puzzle enthusiasm as someone who loves books and films in this genre.) It is clear that Amar was in the plot to overthrow the state and Rogas kills him because that removed all hope for him or because he hopes to stop the coup d'état. (I rejected the hypothesis that it was the Center of Specialized Information that killed both Amar and Rogas—Amar having become involved in the plot as though in a trap—because it was less functional in terms of the aims of the story.) But when is it that Rogas decides to kill him? Did Rogas already know he was in the plot (had he recognized him in one of the unidentified cars at the meeting in Riches's house?) and does he pretend with Cusan so that he will get to Amar and kill him? Or does Amar tell him (why? To make him go over to his side?) and Rogas then arranges the meeting with him in the museum in order to kill him? Or does Amar not tell him, and arranges the meeting with him in the museum in order to have him killed by the CSI, but Rogas realizes anyway (how?)? In that case why does Amar go to the meeting in the museum?

As for the slaughter of magistrates, it seems to me that there is no doubt that this has nothing to do with the conspiracy and it is Cres's individual initiative. Is that right?

And the similarity between Rogas and Cres has only an allegorical function: they are two lone executioners.

I am curious to know whether I am right in all the details or if I have missed something.[5]

Best wishes.
Yours,

Italo

I detected an allegory also in the name of Lazaro Cardenas when put beside Velázquez who was a painter of kings. The victorious Mexican revolutionary who becomes president of a Mexico that is largely stationary prefigures the possible destiny of Amar. Have I got it?
[Handwritten; with the addressee's heirs.]

To Giovanni Falaschi—Florence

Turin 5 October 1971

Dear Falaschi,
I HAVE READ WITH GREAT INTEREST THE SEQUEL TO YOUR essay and your letter.[6] Your critical approach seems to me to be original and fruitful: through the use of philological and historical elements you aim to pick out the nucleus of, let's say, the structures of the imagination. The real title of your article could be: "Space and Nature in I. C." "Realism and Rationalism" is a title which your analysis fully justifies but at first sight, before starting to read the article, it made me cry out: "The same old song!" However, as soon as I got into your analysis I realized that here at last was a critic who does not just say things I already knew. In other words here was someone who studies not just the theoretical concepts that are common to a whole period or cultural area but those other elements that are less definable with anything other than narrative means, such as, precisely, nature, distance, space, and in general my relationship with the "other." Where will you publish this book of yours on the literature of the Resistance? Other colleagues here at Einaudi have become interested in it after reading *Belfagor*, and if you send it to us once it is finished I think they would be happy to consider it for publication.[7]

I am sorry to hear you have published a book in the Castoro series, a series that began with a book on my writings which is a downright fraud, not on the part of the author, poor woman, who was of such incompetence that you could not really hold her responsible—nor help her except by discouraging her, which I did, totally convinced that no publisher would accept her work—but on the part of publishers who speculate on the demand for school texts like this. However, on the other hand, I am very glad that you studied Carlo Levi, an author who is so rich in intellectual elements and who would lend himself to an analysis like yours (some time after that review you mention—which was inspired by the factionalism of the young Communist I was, against the then supporter of a third way that he was—I became a friend of his and we were in close touch for years).[8] So I will gladly read your book.

I have no great competence in the literature of Resistance memoirs. That 1948 survey of mine was a rather approximate article that I had been commissioned to write and was delivered in great haste for the first issue of that bulletin.[9] At that time I had not heard, for instance, of Roberto Battaglia's *Un uomo, un partigiano* (*A Man, A Partisan*) which seems to me the best book in this genre. I met Battaglia at that same time, 1948–49, and I became a good friend of his. I admire very much his elegance as an essayist in describing the spirit and behavior of partisan life on the basis of direct experience, and this is evident also in his "official" works of history. (But it is of course always an intellectual's eye that is observing.)

I can tell you something more about the partisan *short story* and how it was configured in the years you've worked on. The contemporary writer that I recognized as closest to me then—in his particular "style": Hemingwayism, spare stories, with a final shoot-out—was Marcello Venturi, who had been discovered by *Il Politecnico*, and was then joint winner with myself of the Genoa *Unità*'s prize in 1946. (This is an area you could investigate to get documentary material on a rather crude, "mass" output: I think it was in the summer/autumn of 1946 that the Genoa *Unità* published once a week a story by a young writer competing for a prize that was awarded in a ceremony at the port at New Year 1947; I only possess the issue of 5 January 1947 where I make a "theoretical" statement as joint winner.)[10] Venturi's short stories, published mostly in the Milan and Genoa editions of *l'Unità*, are mainly collected in the volume *Gli anni e gli inganni* (*The Years and Deceipts*) (Feltrinelli, 1965). He was slightly younger than me, lived at Fornovo Taro (his father was a station master), and we wrote a lot to each other.

But the young writer who was typical of that time, the one that Vittorini banked on as the real discovery by *Il Politecnico*, was Angelo Del Boca, from Vercelli. Del Boca was lyrical and effusive and I tried to write stories like that but Vittorini just binned them because what he wanted from me instead was—quite rightly—that I should be all facts and movement. Some of Del Boca's stories came out in an Einaudi volume (*Dentro mi è nato l'uomo*, 1948), but many of them you would have to hunt down not just in the weekly and monthly *Politecnico*, but also in Turin's *Sempre Avanti*, the daily paper of the PSIUP[11] (edited by Umberto Calosso), then later in the *Gazzetta del Popolo*, where Del Boca became an editor before soon abandoning fiction for journalism.

Fenoglio appeared on the horizon later, after 1950, and as far as I know he did not work his way up through newspapers and journals. Instead here I was talking to you about those "barbarous" years before Italian literature sorted itself out (before *Il Mondo*, *Paragone*, *Botteghe Oscure*)—and, on the other hand, before the PCI developed a line of cultural and literary policy (and the two lines then found common ground around 1954, with Salinari's *Il Contemporaneo*, on which I collaborated regularly in '54–'55–'56).

I believe profoundly in in-depth studies of any given period, and not very much in generic "critical portraits" of it. Basically I do not believe much in the figure of the *author* as a continuity in time, and I like your article because it discusses a well-defined period, and the texts belong, yes to an author who bears my name, but also and above all to the world around him. (I would actually go so far as to suggest that the quotations in the text be limited to the writings from that period, and those from fifteen or twenty years later be put in footnotes, so as not to create temporal overlaps.)

Let's try to arrange for you to see my archive. I have drawers full of stuff here in my house in Turin; but most of the time I'm in Paris. Meantime, let's see if we can meet up.

Warmest good wishes.

Italo Calvino

What is the 1946 variant of "Andato al comando" (Going to Headquarters)?[12] That story was published in *Il Politecnico*, with the odd cut or intervention by Vittorini. I have not kept the original manuscript but I remember that in the volume *Ultimo viene il corvo* (*The Crow Comes Last*) of 1949 (have you been able to find this very rare edition?), I republished the story, partly restoring the original text and partly accepting Vittorini's corrections. I can't remember if I made further corrections for the 1958 edition of collected *Racconti*.
[Handwritten; with the addressee.]

To Franco Fortini—Milan

[Paris,] 5.11.71

Dear F.,
I FEEL THE NEED TO WRITE TO YOU TO SAY THAT YOUR TWO ARticles in issue number 44–45 of *QP*[13] were for me a fortifying read, the likes of which I have not come across for years. I'm not concerned so much with the one about the "poisonous" elements, where my approval doesn't count (as too obvious coming from someone who has no qualifications to intervene between you and the readers your discourse is aimed at, or too generic if it does not imply all that your discourse implies on a philosophical-anthropological level, or at any rate if it does not discuss or compare it with anything). It is on the article about poetry and morality and quality that I feel I can say to you straight away that I really like it. Here at last is a polemic conducted with an intransigence that is appropriate, because it has foundations and solid arguments that are also clear and indisputable. This is a polemic that goes beyond the subject which occasioned it (I prefer not even mentioning it here), and becomes the basis for a general judgment.

I accept in full your discourse on the order of quality, on the values and models, I recognize in it the rigorous formulation of the need which I myself have been inarticulately mulling over in these years. Here too perhaps my support might seem (to you or to me, or to a part of you or me) facilely self-serving, leading me to identify or justify my silence with your discourse on silence. Yet, perhaps it is valid precisely because it comes to you from someone who now refuses to judge anyone a reactionary or an enemy of any people, with or without quotation marks. I no longer know who is or isn't such an enemy; and at the same time I have antibodies that save me from the laxity of liberal tolerance and therefore try to justify keeping my distance under other labels than those tired old rubrics of bad political usage (and yet here I recognize each term is right both for the context and for the substance of the question).

At last I have discovered a definition that distinguishes between morality and moralism, one that convinces me and is useful to me. Here too the focus on a particular case of moralism is placed in the context of a more general piece of progress: how to hang on to morality while rejecting moralism (and this is useful for everyone, precisely because your clarification comes with it, or rather your self-criticism) and rejecting skeptical tolerance (which is something that is liable to affect those who like me make a principle out of the rejection or punishment of moralism).

I agree with the order of quality which is the model of models (poetry or sainthood or wisdom), and especially agree because we are getting your formulation at the most "untimely" moment, in other words when it is most needed: in other words, now that the awareness of what "blood and tears drip" (to use Foscolo's phrase) from every value tied to the individual (Benjamin's "horror" mentioned in the other article) has spread so quickly as to have become a dubious and lazy little formula for eliminating the worth of things.

Thus we have come back to the article on the "poisonous" which is deep down closely tied to the other one because we cannot imagine this nexus of the change in society-totality-individual in anything other than in terms of poetry or wisdom. In other words, we can imagine it as something lived, but it is only poetry or wisdom that can talk about it (as for sanctity, I don't know; if the parallel between the models works, sanctity would consist precisely in living through this nexus), whereas political language remains partial or metaphorical, an honest language if used with an awareness of its partiality, otherwise it's simply mystificatory.

There are still a lot of things to clarify in your discourse—and in my head—regarding *anthropology*. Because it is true what you say about the diaphragm between liberation along Reich-Marcuse-Laing lines which is claimed in the private sphere and repression on the political front. But it is also true that the most spectacularly new thing in the New Left is the redefinition of the workers' struggles as a struggle *against* work, the fact that "those who don't work don't eat" has now become a bourgeois slogan, the 1st of May as a holiday against work etc. The more I reflect on this attitude (while all the time being aware of its serious and urgent rightness, as a rejection of *this* kind of work, of "look after yourself," and aware of the great truth that it contains in its implications, namely that "after the revolution" work will be a curse just as much as it is now), the more it seems to me that as a theoretical postulate this is the reversal of the fundamental moral value of the workers' movement. Once you remove that, if the moral *superiority* of the worker as worker is annulled in a generic right to be existing in Eden, first of all this is something very different from what we were brought up on (and this may also be irrelevant), but above all it is a mystification in the worst kind of bad faith, of all the bits of bad faith that can be proclaimed in millennial tones, because it will mean working more than before. Thirdly this is clearly an ideology of class, of the parasitical bourgeoisie, of the old, new, and future clerks or tertiary sector, people who are completely unaware of any possible satisfaction in creating something, a bourgeoisie which can easily be led in the new generations to assimilate a revolutionary language, and has realized that in state socialism-capitalism it has everything to gain and nothing to lose. Now I am not thinking about those who become bearers of an ideology: political and ideological roles are distributed according to a combinatory pattern, following the rules of the game; then correspondences are formed between the system of ideologies and the system of class interests or the unconscious needs of class.[14]

If Marx's anthropology (or the anthropology derivable from him) was an anthropology of work, of man as worker, a new anthropological conscience that is needed today has to be aware of the value it attributes to work that has evolved in new directions—to the transformation of work—whether it corrects or integrates or restores or cancels out what has been said hitherto. What man will become means what work will become, in its dual aspect (subjective, as well as the many objective aspects) of work as effort and trial (nowadays mystified to the point of impudence) and of work as pleasure (today a utopian idea, so much so that it sounds like an outrageous mockery for the majority of mankind, but is in principle still possible and able to be tried out—even though this is the case only in the privileged being that is the artist or poet: writing this letter is work, it certainly is, and apart from costing me effort it also gives me pleasure—hence it is the necessary objective of all projects for a future society, hence Fourier cannot be set aside). But in order to redefine labor one certainly has to take account of the concept of progress which you continue to attack in its most obvious and discredited meaning to the point where you maintain the immutability of man. I, on the other hand, prefer to search (still in a confused way) digging inside its Enlightenment and enlightened tradition as well as in the later positivist one. But what I am attempting is to get away from any humanist teleology by seeing man as an instrument or catalyst or chain of I don't know what, of a universe that is also information, of a history or anthropomorphization of matter, and of a world without human beings any more but one where man has realized himself and become resolved, a world of electronic calculators and butterflies. This does not frighten me, actually it reassures me. However, I naturally have not put aside my let's call it local interest in the spatio-temporal province inhabited by man, as long as all the rest is not lost sight of, what for me ought to be the totality. On the contrary it is in man as society and as individual that all the rest is played out, and so then in this sense I can also accept the terms of prayer and communion that you use (and that you ought to explain more if you want to be understood), in other words the individual's interiority as the necessary space for the relationship with everything. Except that for me God's pact with man does not contain any clauses privileging man over any other living thing. Or I would put it rather as the pact with the Gods, without any privilege for any one of the codes that can organize what can be experienced and said, and also without any gnostic binary oppositions . . . but I am straying too far. Ciao

Calvino

[Handwritten; in the Franco Fortini Archive, Siena. Also in Italo Calvino—Franco Fortini, "Lettere scelte 1951–1977," ed. Giuseppe Nava and Elisabetta Nencini, *L'ospite ingrato*, Annuario del Centro Studi Franco Fortini (Macerata: Quodlibet, 1998), pp. 108–10.]

TO PAOLO VALESIO—CAMBRIDGE (MASS.)

Paris, 16 December 1971

Dear Valesio,

WHEN I WAS WRITING *IL BARONE RAMPANTE* (*THE BARON IN the Trees*) and I found myself having to make my protagonist mad (from love), I came up against the problem of a representation of madness that was both iconic and linguistic. Obviously I went about it by trial and error: in chapter XXIV there is an iconic regression toward the animal state (birds' feathers), and also to the exotic (American Indians), and there is a shift to non-linguistic communication (the puzzle made from objects) which in any case fails. But the only way out of this was the linguistic madness at the end of chapter XXII (the fact that in the book this precedes the other forms of madness does not exclude the possibility that it had been written afterwards; I recall that the book was the result of an elaborate montage of subject matter that did not fit well together, of attempts to move things around in different orders): Cosimo attempts a babelic language by jumbling together words from all the ancient and modern languages, mixing motifs from love lyric with obscene allusions. All these are elements analyzed in your essay but the main thing is missing: the folklore element. Well, if you don't tell anybody, I will reveal that when composing the plurilinguistic verse "Zu dir, zu dir, gunaika" I had in mind as the model for its verse the rude Piedmontese song "Diufaus, diufaus, piciassa . . .".[15]

This comparison with my empirical experience in literary bricolage will tell you how sympathetically and attentively I read your article on the fool and folklore (in the photocopy of it lent to me by Gianni).[16] I'll tell you immediately the reflections aroused by my reading of it before they disappear.

It seems to me that you have touched on a network of problems with many ramifications. This is perhaps the first time that the tools of linguistic research in the strict sense have been used for a piece of historical research typical of the Warburg school, and of the history of ideas school, all this in the context of that defunct discipline, much lamented by me, which had and (I see) still has its last bastion in Harvard, [namely] comparative literature.

The emergence of the fool as language from the iconic fool is a convincing and well illustrated discovery.

The fool-folklore link in Elizabethan theater is an equally important discovery and exhaustively proven. Similarly exhaustive is the analysis of the various components of the Elizabethan fool.

The reasons for the emergence of folklore in the sixteenth century as an awareness of the plurality of languages and linguistic levels is another strong point in the article. In fact, this is an idea worthy of sustaining a whole wide-ranging study, a book in which the case of the fool could be just one chapter.

The fool-folklore link in everything that is not the English theater in the sixteenth and seventeenth centuries is only an ancillary piece: the examples are still relevant, never forced, but certainly they are a bit fragile, opening up more problems than they solve.

Especially the *Quixote*: of course, the world of chivalry is by that stage folklore, that goes without saying; in fact it seems to me that you do not even need to bother proving it, it can be taken for granted. One could even say that the chivalric romance has always been folklore, its motifs and characters are the same as in folktales, at certain points it rises from folklore to become a canonical element of refined literature (of religious edification, of dynastic celebration, of military propaganda, of courtly entertainment, of real literature), but it always stayed bound to its matrix in oral narration. There remains the fact, however, that Don Quixote's madness comes from a library (according to your important observation that here it is language that determines the madness and not vice-versa), that the whole book is based on the fact of an outmoded library, which no longer conveys wisdom but only foolishness or madness.

The obsolete library will become from that time on (I don't think it existed before) a major theme in fiction. I am not thinking solely of our Don Ferrante who is a mere copy of Don Quixote, but I am thinking also of Mme Bovary for the obsolescence of romantic literature, of Bouvard and Pécuchet for scientific encyclopaedism.

Is this a library that becomes degraded down to the level of folklore? Careful: Sancho Panza who is the spokesman for folklore at the level of proverb, of the peasant's code of wisdom, rejects the bookish folklore of the Hidalgo. Sancho's is a cultural world that is very compact, which even though it lets itself be infected by his master's *locura* (madness) always offers resistance to it. One cannot define Quixote except in his opposition to Sancho. There is a madness within culture with its aporias and its diachronies, and there is a *simplicitas* that is inherent in a linguistic level that is too low, with its ruses and revenges. In any case even the democratic-progressive culture of the pharmacist Homais is merely folklore for Flaubert, but the sense of the novel resides precisely in its opposition between the various linguistic levels of bourgeois *lore*, and Flaubert begins the critique of mass culture in industrial civilization.

The iconic aspect of Quixote, which you do not dwell on—and yet never was there a character so famous and recognizable *iconically*—is particularly indicative: his regression is not to the natural state of nakedness but to an anachronistic form of dress, it is the choice of *high* (at least in his intentions) but *outmoded* culture, armor cobbled together with rusty bits and pieces, a helmet that is a barber's basin.

If what counts is the Quixote-Sancho relationship, this must mean that what counts—every time we come across madness in a work of literature—is the *field* that madness creates around itself, the system of collapses of reason (madness and foolishness, madness and *simplicitas*, the fool as buffoon and the fool who is really mad, true madness and simulated madness etc.). So your approach, which takes the fool as a single literary category, leaving aside what type of fool is involved each time, is certainly a good methodological point of departure in that it takes you straight to the linguistic fact and clears the field of so many pointless questions (such as the question of psychiatric definitions, where Vanna Gentili falls down too, though elsewhere she is so precise),[17] but then it turns out that it precludes a fundamental fact: madness in literature is always (?) presented as *a system of madnesses*, and it is the oscillation between the various "foolish" languages that creates the language of madness.

The classic example is *King Lear* as an encyclopaedia of figures of madness. There is the professional fool who is the least foolish of all (fool only in name, and it is no accident that he has no name), mad Lear, Edgar who pretends to be mad and who is the real bearer of folkloric language (poor Tom) as a code which he possesses, and, if you like, the analogies: Gloucester's madness as blindness, Kent's madness as unconditional devotion to his sovereign, the absolute denuding of himself, even of his name, all those wandering around in the storm as the madness of the elements. It remains to be seen what all these languages have in common and what they have that is different.

In short my hypothesis is this (which if it seems verifiable to you, I'll let you have it): there is never folly, only ever follies, the fake madness of Hamlet produces the real madness of Ophelia, one figure of folly must necessarily be in relation to other figures if not of folly, then at least of foolishness or at any rate of people who lose their reason.

In Ariosto too? Let's say straightaway that in Ariosto—as also in Shakespeare anyway—there is always implicit a comparison with an ideal of Renaissance values and virtues that are going awry, the loss of reason is—more than in Shakespeare—the rising up of barbarity. It is no accident that the sign that Orlando has recovered his wits is the fact that he starts talking in Latin, with a quote from Virgil. But I see in the *Furioso* a *field* of madnesses in that I see Orlando—a champion of sense reduced to brute—in opposition to Rodomonte, a brute who has been invested with high military dignity and who always assumes sublime commitments though through his foolishness he only causes disasters, and as for direct speech he can only articulate insults and foul language.

However, in Ariosto there is no buffoon-fool, and where there is no buffoon there is no language of madness. This seems to me to be a corollary of your proofs (and of my thesis about plurality): the buffoon fool is the consciousness of linguistic difference and from him it extends to the non-professional fools. At Elsinore the professional fool is dead, but from Yorick's skull the language of the fool invades the court. From this one sees how the language of madness could emerge only with Elizabethan theater.

However, in the Italian context, perhaps even before this, in what are presumed to be texts of popular theater, there is the language of the Zany. Harlequin is—in his iconic-sartorial aspect even before the linguistic one—a figure of folly, of subversion; he is also a figure of popular craftiness etc.; but one would need to establish what his primary message is. In his book on the origins of Italian theater, Paolo Toschi maintains that Harlequin/Zanni derives from the character of the devil in medieval mystery plays: black mask, multi-colored costume, low language. So here the argument comes full circle with the first example from your article: the madman from the Gospels through whose mouth the devils speak, my name is legion, the comedy of the Zanni's as a quarrel amongst devils. The language of the fool is the language of the devil, in other words of the *other*, of what has been expelled, suppressed, repressed, oppressed, beaten.

(Gertrude Moakley in her study of the origins of the Tarot cards from Renaissance carnival Triumphs maintains—brilliantly—the opposite idea (at least on the surface): the Fool is Lent, a character who has been unhorsed, and who ends the procession, threatening with his stick King Carnival who is on his float (the Juggler in the Tarots). Since the procession goes round in a circular space, King Carnival who leads the procession finds himself next to Lent who closes it. But the contradiction is apparent because in the rest of the year King Carnival is dethroned and takes the place of the Fool.)[18]

In short, this language of the Other/the Devil/the Zanni/the Fool, the language of the savage, the chthonic, the obscene, must also have a medieval history. Then in the sixteenth century, for all the reasons you explain, it becomes identified with the language of folklore, and later again with the language of a culture that is *other*, degraded, which always carries along with it encrustations from previous phases. Nevertheless, it remains a hypothetical language, an attempt at linguistic construction outside the rules of rhetoric and logic, the hypothesis of a language of nature not yet subjugated by culture, a language without a speaking subject, language of things, Gurdulù-language . . .

At this point, with a passing quotation from his own work at the end to match the one at the beginning, and ringing out his cry of Merry Xmas, your very affectionate friend calls a halt.

[Typed copy; in the Calvino Archive.]

To Alfredo Taracchini—Imola

Turin, 21 February 1972

Dear Taracchini,

It is always very difficult for me to reply to those who study my books. What special value can what I say in a letter have over and above what has already been said in the things I have published? The letter is another text that adds doubts, problems, contradictions to the others that the scholar has to solve.

The best method is to consider the author as someone dead, or as a person whose identity is only presumed, and his works as archaeological deposits.

It seems much more important to me to study the historical, cultural, and literary *context* in which the work of that author is situated. I think it is essential that you familiarize yourself with Italian literature of the 1940s and '50s, as well as with the general cultural climate, the journals, translations etc. I say this in reference to your question whether the style of *essential* writing was influenced by cartoons.

Such a way of writing was a stylistic model that was common to a large part of Italian—and not only Italian—literature of the 1940s; cartoons did not come into it (and at that time few were interested in them).

As for articles, declarations of poetics etc. from the period when I began writing: in one of the last issues of *Belfagor* there is a study by Giovanni Falaschi, who is actually carrying out research on my collaborations with journals and newspapers in the period 1946–1948.

Your question about Fortini is probably based on a hint in a biographical note (the one I wrote for the volume *Gli amori difficili* [*Difficult Loves*]) which refers to discussions and conversations with friends rather than to anything written.[19]

In order to deal with my departure from the PCI, which was in July–August 1957 (so several months after the events of Hungary), I think it is essential that you read up on this, by examining directly the newspapers from the years 1956–57, the discussions inside the Party, and in particular my letter of resignation which was published in *l'Unità*.

Your question about "Andato al comando" (Going to Headquarters): I am not sure what you are referring to.[20]

Your other questions are a bit too generic to allow me to reply to them precisely in a letter.

In particular, on the Enlightenment, it seems to me that you are projecting a certain critique—which began in our culture not more than a decade ago—of the Enlightenment onto an age when such an attitude would have been anachronistic or simply reactionary. In the struggle for a democratic and anti-Fascist renewal of Italian culture, the Enlightenment was seen, according to the classic Marxist viewpoint, as the best model for cultural action one could aspire to.

Best wishes for your military leave, hoping it comes soon, and good luck with your studies.
[Typed copy; in the Einaudi Archive, Turin.]

To Marcello Venturi–Molare (Alessandria)

Turin, 1.3.72

Dear Marcello,
Really a long time since we wrote—and even longer since we saw each other. Here is what my life is like now: I live in Paris with my wife and my daughter Giovanna who is now seven and is a wonderful child: she speaks three languages, plays the diva a lot, is very spoiled and has no wish to learn to read or write. For about ten days a month I am in Turin—where I have kept my old bachelor flat—and deal with the publishing work; I make the odd visit to San Remo where my 86-year-old mother still lives, and there is also some land which produces nothing, with all the problems that go with it.

With this now quite established rhythm I never manage to organize other trips, however short. To say I live in Paris is a manner of speaking because it is more a family existence there rather than the life of the city: I have a house which ought to be ideal for writing in peace, but the fact is that I write very little and that worries me less and less. On the other hand I always enjoy working for the publishing house—in the relaxed way I am allowed to carry it out—because it is teamwork with other people, whereas one needs to be alone in order to write. Now you tell me about yourself and yours, what you are doing or writing these days. Greetings from your old friend

Italo

My Paris address:
12, Square de Châtillon
Paris XIV
[Handwritten; in the Archivio del Novecento, Facoltà di Lettere, University of Rome "La Sapienza."]

To Giuseppe Bonura—Milan

Turin 6 May 1972

Dear Bonura,

I just received today your *Invito alla lettura*.[21] I have now finished reading it and I am very pleased. The idea that one could write a book on a literary output as dispersed as mine has always terrified me, and similarly the thought of the school-students who are made to write exercises on it and write to me and I never know what to reply, and I certainly could never recommend that weak book published by Il Castoro.[22]

Instead you chart a history where I can recognize myself, you know how to evaluate every element of news and quotation, giving them the right measure of importance. You manage to give a sense of the general cultural context in which my books and pronouncements are situated, to write accessibly but seriously, so that young people, who know nothing about all the elements that surround a text, can understand how literature—even though people usually study it author by author—is always a dialog amongst many voices which intersect and reply to each other within literature and outside it.[23] And the most strictly critical part (chap. III) is full of new ideas, like the one about the "patriarchal timbre" which seems to me a convincing stylistic definition, both as regards "timbre" and as regards "patriarchal." And also the Mondrian-Bosch idea seems spot on to me. I am also very happy at how you have always managed to speak of Enlightenment, rationalism etc., in the right terms, from a problematic angle with which I can identify, something that happens rarely, even with critics armed with the best of intentions who end up always by being rather bland.

Lastly, one other thing that is done very well is the review of criticism, an area where I constantly receive requests for help from these poor school-children that the lazy teachers send out into the perils of a sea of wasted paper. You were quite correct in underlining the importance of Cases's article, which is unfortunately not well known.[24]

With measured perplexity and confident anticipation you keep your discourse open on my most recent output. Certainly faced with a book like yours, as happens every time someone confronts me with my work as though it were something unified (whereas in fact it is more like a beginning that still needs to be developed), when faced with the things I have written as if it were a continuous and programmatic discourse, I feel more stymied than satisfied. Despite all the things I have always said with that tone of "Now I'll show you all!" in actual fact I have only progressed toward rarefaction and silence. In recent years I was very satisfied playing the dead man for a bit: how clever I am at not publishing! How good I am staying silent! Whereas now I am starting again to realize that the one thing I would like is to write, publish, communicate, but by dint of refusing this and turning down that, I have managed to lose all love for images of contemporary life, and I can no longer regain hold of the coordinates of my discourse, which has been put into crisis everywhere. Might it just be a question of crossing a "biological threshold, a threshold of style"? This is the only mysterious phrase in your book (p. 102) and I already feel that I will not get it out of my head, that it has an arcane authority like an oracle.

Just to end on a comic note, I will point out your one slip, which is more than forgiveable because *I giovani del Po* (*Youth in Turin*) is so boring it can only be read keeping one eye open, and the typeface of *Officina* would make people blind: it is not a "little mouse" (un topolino) that gets run over by the police but a "Fiat 500" (una topolino) which is being driven by the girl, a car that has nothing fairy-tale about it. Serves me right!

Did you know that I wanted to write to you a couple of years ago because I had read an article of yours in *Rendiconti* that I liked? I delayed because I did not have your address, then I found out you were writing something about me and I did not want to interfere. I am besieged by those who are writing theses and want to "interview" me (this is a rule with American students). Also the fact that you did all this without saying anything to me adds to your merit.

In short, I do not know how to express my gratitude to you.

Yours,

Italo Calvino

[Handwritten; with the addressee.]

To Franco Ferrucci—New York

Turin, 24 October 1972

Dear Ferrucci,

THANK YOU VERY MUCH FOR SENDING IN ON TIME THE INTRO-duction to *Zadig*.[25] All your observations seemed to me to be subtle and correct and useful even though—if one identifies Voltaire with Zadig—the book appears to elude an overall definition, refusing to provide a unified vision of itself. But from the moment the meditation on the starry sky starts, your relationship with the book becomes fully established and it is in that philosophical-poetic core that I recognize your supreme qualities as an essayist.

To my eyes, the eyes of a hardened morphologist, Zadig is an "anti-hero" in the sense that although (or precisely because) he is an *intellectual hero*, he harks back to a form of popular literature, namely the cycles of stories about the wily character, who by means of his intelligence and wit copes with a series of difficult situations (hence the episodic narrative; and note that these are stories where there is a king, a court, a power like Alboino with Bertoldo).[26] And at the same time *Zadig* inaugurates a modern genre: narration by induction (as you rightly emphasize), and the importance of Zadig for me resides in the fact that he is the first detective-story hero (and he too is a hero of cycles of stories), the direct ancestor of Dupin and Sherlock Holmes.

I was sorry not to see you this summer in Tuscany. I think I'll be in Italy at Christmas as well; but try phoning me in Paris; I am still not sure of my plans.

I have said yes to the New York conference, finally giving in to the insistent invitations (including telegrams), but to tell you the truth I have not given it any more thought and had forgotten all about it.[27]

I will certainly do *Adolphe*, as soon as I find an available translation. *Bartleby* is too short. I had not thought about Bunyan; but is it not rather long?[28]

Tell me if you want the fee in Italy or over there.

Thanks again and many friendly greetings

[Typed copy; in the Einaudi Archive, Turin. Also in *ILDA*, pp. 591–92.]

To Giovanni Falaschi—Florence

Paris, 4 November 1972

Dear Falaschi,

I READ YOUR "PORTRAIT" WITH GREAT INTEREST ABOUT TEN days ago.[29] If I have not written to you until now it is because I wanted to study it in the depth that the philosophical character of your article demanded and up till now I have been constantly busy, trying to finish the new book which will come out in the next few weeks, along with other minor commitments with their deadlines and the constant to-ing and fro-ing between Italy and Paris.[30]

It seems to me that yours is a methodological article, that goes beyond the theme of Calvino, and as such the whole of the first part must be read with its discussion of the relationship between works and situations and with the theory of the "two books" which seems to me to be very fruitful and worth developing and applying more generally.

And the whole of the final section displays similar methodological commitment, with the comparison with phenomenology, and the phenomenological analysis of *Cosmicomics* and *Time and the Hunter*. I am very interested in this discourse because it is a new approach which highlights things that no one else had seen. I find what you say about *Cosmicomics* totally accurate, that there the "other" world is never outside the I's consciousness: when I carried out what I might call "operation Qfwfq" this reflected a precise intention along those lines. That the price to be paid by knowledge is that of objectification seems a correct observation: in other words, in practice, if that is the result one cannot but take note of it, and also of the irrationalist implications that you see as my risk. But seeing that you give the last word to "Montecristo," as I do, who still consider that text my "epistemological testament," I cannot but be happy.[31]

As for the date of "Montecristo," which takes on a particular importance in your article, it is 1967, summer 1967: in other words it was the last story I wrote before handing over the book for printing. But the fact that the "system" had already shown signs of crisis, counts less than the fact that I have always had strong reservations on the

(Frankfurt School/American) theorization of Neo-capitalism as a totalitarian system. With all the interest I also had in this reversal of roles in revolutionary ideology in recent years, I feel I have remained with the imprint of the old Marxist vulgate of the "incurable contradictions of capitalism" and of "capitalist anarchy." I have never wanted to give credence to a rationalistic vocation within capitalism (which carries as its corollary the capitalistic vocation of rationalism), in other words I have never wanted to give up the position of strength that made us once say (maybe wrongly): we are the only rationalists. This is the fundamental ideological crux that kept me far away from theorizing about what would become "the new left," from the very start, from the beginning of the Sixties (I closely followed its origins day by day working at Einaudi with Raniero Panzieri, Renato Solmi, Fortini, Cases). Deep down my silence on the level of theoretical affirmations, which has lasted now for about ten years and perhaps will remain definitive (after a final attempt at clarifying my ideas in the essay "L'antitesi operaia" (The Working Class as Antithesis) which was so trashed by my friends),[32] stems from the fact that I could not put up against their discourse a discourse of my own that was as rigorous and sharp as theirs. Now that the failure of the "new left" is taken for granted, I have even less will than ever to come and say: I was right, since I am defeated like everybody else. However, it is clear to me more than before that imagining the world as "system," as a negative, hostile system (a symptom that is typical of schizophrenia) prevents any opposition to it except in an irrational, self-destructive raptus; whereas it is a correct principle of method to deny that what one is fighting can be a system, in order to distinguish its components, contradictions, loopholes, and to defeat it bit by bit. I realize that my argument now seems quite the opposite of the one in "Montecristo." But that is not so: the "Montecristo" story stems from this context, it aims to indicate the right way in which the absolute system, the perfect prison, should be hypothesized precisely in order to prove that the real prison is not perfect. In other words, the model of a totalitarian, abstract system and the empiricism of the Abbé's experiments must operate at the same time, the deductive system constantly needs the inductive experiment to confirm it or deny it. Bearing in mind that the models of the world that have a rigorous determinism (Darwin, Marx, Freud, Lévi-Strauss) have always worked in a liberating way, it is right that I should be here accepting and employing the model of the neocapitalistic world as a "system" in order to be able to dismantle and deconstruct it. This is also the problem of a utopia (Fourier), of a negative utopia, and I hint at an answer to this in my new book.

This is a network of problems that are still open and developing, which I am unable to articulate except in a very oblique and figurative way (there is also the disadvantage that the readings I really need, like yours, are not so much rare as unique, but there is also the advantage that I avoid being read through banalizing simplifications). For all these reasons I am glad that you privilege the cosmicomic phase of my work. And basically the article would have had the perfect approach if it had concentrated on those two books, instead of having to deal with the other things required when a "portrait" is commissioned. The fact is that you are perfectly correct in putting the need for a portrait in problematic terms. But certainly on the works of the end of the forties you had already written more than enough;[33] and as for the 1950s, they end up being slightly elided, and you take advantage to a lesser extent of the journalistic writings (which however maybe do not hold any more secrets than those you have already found), in other words of what has been up till now your exclusive hunting ground.

However, it seems to me that the general outlines of your picture are valid also for the fifties as well. And I agree with you that *Our Ancestors* is not *a book*: they are three books which are very different from one another, each one came about on its own, and each one requires a different discourse. And if I issued the trilogy a posteriori after publishing the three individual novels, this is because my work is so disparate that as soon as I find some affinities that allow me to bring different texts together, I never let the chance slip. And I like also the observation that the *Italian Folktales* marks the beginning of my "scientific" period.

Individual points: the nun who writes the chronicle of *The Non-Existent Knight*, as you rightly say, was just the objectification of my action (and labor) in writing while I was composing the tale, and I did not at that point think of making the person who says I the same person as Bradamante. This ploy only came to me at the end, at the point when I was writing the conclusion, and now Guido Almansi has proved with convincing arguments in his article in *Paragone*, that this is an arbitrary extra layer, just tacked on.[34] (Bradamante could not have described her own nakedness as in chapter 4; that is true; there's nothing to be said; the relationship I had throughout the whole book toward that character—a relationship of real love, above all else—excludes any possibility of her being identified with the I who writes; I have to admit that this solution seized hold of me on the spur of the moment.)

On page 535 of your article I find "F. Calamandrei and Bertoli" being cited as writers. Calamandrei never wrote fiction, as far as I know. I must have mentioned his name to you as the author of an article in *Il Politecnico*'s weekly magazine, "Narrativa vince cronaca" (Fiction Beats News), which I quoted to you as a kind of compendium of the poetics of *Il Politecnico*. On the other hand I've never heard of Bertoli.[35]

I very much appreciated your program of research for a school edition of *Conversazione in Sicilia*.[36] I have copied that passage from your letter and distributed it to my colleagues at Einaudi as an example of a serious work method.

Fucini's *Napoli a occhio nudo*: Romagnoli (the evening we went to his house together) had already recommended this to me (and lent me the text). I found it very impressive, certainly worth republishing, but I immediately came up against the Trevisini obstacle at Einaudi.

I will have to make the odd trip to Florence every so often in order to talk to the architect who is building our house at Castiglione della Pescaia. If I have a chance to catch my breath between one train and the next, I will phone you.

Best wishes to you and your wife,
Yours,

Italo Calvino

[Typed, with autograph signature; with the addressee.]

To Geno Pampaloni—Bagno a Ripoli (Florence)

Paris 28 Nov. 72

Dear Pampaloni,

I was waiting impatiently for your article, convinced there would be some reservations regarding the book's poetics and a very precise analysis of its achievements.[37] But the pleasure I had in reading you outdid even my expectations, because the elegance of your critical definitions and your sharpness in classifying the individual components are always surprising; and also because your polemic was more implicit than I expected, especially after closely following your attacks on the current "irrealismi" (unrealisms) in the last few weeks.

I find what you say about the stylistic and stylistic-intellectual setup of the book spot on: after the very fine pages you devoted to me in the Garzanti *Storia*, I could not ask for more.

The definition of "Rondiste"[38] is accompanied by the adjective "daring" which removes from the noun the meaning of static composure that it has taken on in current literary journalism, and it brings back into the light the component of musical tension, pushed perhaps in the direction of virtuosity or whimsicality. But this is a discourse that goes beyond my own individual case, and reopens discussion on the history of twentieth-century Italian prose.

As for the desperate secularity, I would like to call your attention to another possible variant, or variant of a variant: in the same series, "Le città e il cielo" (The Cities and the Sky), that contains Eudoxia and Perinthia, there are (at nos. 3 and 5) Tecla and Andria, cities whose origins correspond to the endless emergence of the firmament; man's work as a necessary moment or link in the construction of the universe, an Enlightenment motif, or rather even more an "illuministe" motif, in the old French sense of the word.

These are all facets or possibilities that are present at the one time and juxtaposed, of course. Despite this, the description of my "Borgesism" is the one part of your piece that I was not happy to read. Because it isn't true? No, maybe because it is too true, and fits with an image

I have consciously chosen and developed. But this already gives me a sense of dissatisfaction, as territory that has already been explored. And more than my convergences with Borges—without wanting to diminish the importance of my involvement with him which was inevitable because of our deep sympathy of tastes—it is my differences from him that I am interested in, which stem from our distant points of departure. As you show with a wealth of evidence in your cybernetic finale. In short, I am very happy.

Yours,

Calvino

[Handwritten; with the addressee.]

To Vittorio Spinazzola—Milan

Paris 15.12.72

Dear Spinazzola,

I FOUND YOUR ARTICLE VERY FAITHFUL TO THE BOOK.[39] THE work's derivation from Vittorini's *Città* seems indisputable to me and what you say in comparing the two books is precise.[40] You are the first critic to touch on this point, just as you are the first to study the compositional structure of the book and to succeed in explaining it, with all the little numbers and everything else. That the work is pessimistic is a fact, and if I wrote a book that was even just a little less pessimistic it would not be sincere of me. It is possible that every single declaration you make could be contradicted in the book, maybe the conclusion is not all there but it is sustained by a network of observations that accompany the text throughout, but I understand that the general impression must be as you say, if not as emphasized by the headline-writers, at least as it is articulated in your discourse. One would still need to reflect on what use revolutionary criticism can make of pessimism in literature. This too is not a new problem, but one that crops up each time one comes up again new impasses, new issues requiring a solution . . .

Best wishes,

Italo Calvino

12 Square de Châtillon
Paris XIV
[Handwritten; with the addressee.]

To Antonio Faeti—Bologna

Paris 8 January 1973

Dear Dr Faeti,

I HAVE READ *GUARDARE LE FIGURINE* WITH GREAT ENTHUSIASM.[41] You are extremely good at critical definitions of the illustrators, at bringing out the overall significance of each of them, at defining them in terms of their artistic technique. You are really an excellent critic, you have that critical gift that one can never praise too much, the ability to identify and give weight to minor and even very minor artists, of realizing that art—and literature—live off the small-scale truth of minor and insignificant artists.

I also liked some of your historical contextualizing: the first chapter, on Florence, is a fine chapter on the history of culture. The first two chapters are perhaps the best. But the analysis of the illustrators of *Cuore* is also very good, as are those of the people round Salgari, and Yambo, and Mussino, and Rubino. I notice that you generously gloss over Rubino's Fascism: he was a Fascist, from beginning to end, even though he was also kind and not servile and did not assume any power, in other words he was the complete opposite of a Fascist in terms of temperament.

One comic which I believe you do not look at and which—if I remember correctly—would deserve a whole book from you is *Il Balilla*, which from (I think) 1927 to (I think) 1932 had Rubino as its artistic editor. I had all the Rubino issues bound, in that great collection of comics that my mother subsequently gave away as a present. *Il Balilla* was the comic that *Il Popolo d'Italia* created in order to rival the *Corriere dei Piccoli*. In my memory I now see it as something very interesting even though at the time I believe I found it a bit boring. It had at the time a strong flavor of civil war, allegorically transfigured on the front page by Rubino with the Balilla youth leader Lio leading the March on Rome against the reds who were led by Disorder, who was a man without a head. It was more direct and immediate in the section on children's drawings which portrayed Fascist beatings and burnings of Labour Centres. It was a comic that had an encyclopaedic, didactic tone, and the stories in the comic strips—done by the most famous illustrators you examine—retold classic works: *Bertoldo*, Polo's *Travels*, *Don Quixote*, *Guerrin Meschino*. Rubino had Margherita Sarfatti as an enemy at the *Popolo d'Italia* (I remember this from conversations at our house when he came to see us) because in the polemics of the 1930s he must have belonged to the conservative wing of artistic Fascism (Ojetti), and I remember hearing him make anti-Futurist and anti-Novecento speeches. In the end he fell into disgrace and left *Il Balilla* for a comic run by Rinascente called *Mondo Bambino* (before going back to *Corriere dei Piccoli*), whereas *Il Balilla* became a comic more in line with what was by now Starace's brand of Fascism (but I didn't follow it any more because in our house, apart from *Corriere dei Piccoli*, we bought and kept only Rubino's comics).

I would not put Sacchetti in the Art Nouveau category but before that: he was an impressionist. What I remember about him are the covers of *Le Letture* from the 1910s and the '20s (another of my mother's collections).

Also I would have put the chapter on *Il Giornalino della Domenica* before the one on *Il Corriere dei Piccoli* because it belongs to a taste and a way of understanding children's comics that clearly precedes the *Corriere* even though their dates overlap.

I endorse your revaluation of Bisi and Angoletta. I would have liked to see greater emphasis on Sergio Tofano, an illustrator of great elegance and economy—but placed earlier, immediately after Rubino, as the equivalent of Modigliani in the world of illustrators. But I see that you rightly ignore the illustrators who have been relatively well studied and you devote yourself more to those that have still to be discovered.

Another comic from the 1930s I would put in your excellent chapter on the deformation of the everyday, is the children's supplement from the *Gazzetta del Popolo*, which was extremely popular particularly because of two characters from their comic strips: the journalist Pio Percopo (by Camerini, I think) and the little maid Isolina Marzabotto (by Pompei).

For Bioletto you should have said that before his sketches (and before the Perugina prize-books) came the radio magazines like *The Four Musketeers* by Nizza and Morbelli, which were broadcast every Friday at 2.30 p.m. and were extremely popular.

Once you get onto the professional illustrators of comics I am less of an expert, but I have to tell you that Walter Molino had the ill luck to join the *Domenica del Corriere* on 8 September 1943 as an illustrator for Mussolini's Salò republic (replacing the elderly A. Beltrame),[42] after having been extremely popular with students for the women's legs he drew in *Bertoldo*, rivalling Boccasile's legs (he too ended badly, even worse in fact, doing posters for enrolment in the Italian SS!).

I really enjoyed the final triumph of Gustavino.

I should also tell you about Beppe Porcheddu, whom I knew since he stayed in Bordighera, and in particular I know many people who knew him well and still continue to talk about his mysterious disappearance. He was a very refined, gentlemanly, elegant, and cultured person, he professed a Christian-Communist mysticism and he frequented anti-Fascist circles before, during, and after the Resistance, until the day he disappeared and his relatives heard nothing more of him, and the only explanation one can come up with is that this was a Buddhist-type religious crisis which finally led to a total loss of self.

All in all a wonderful book, which I hope is successful and I am wondering who there is amongst the critics who can review it.

I also liked very much the piece you wrote on the use of television, which I read last summer.[43]

Best wishes for 1973,
Yours,

Italo Calvino

[Handwritten; with the addressee.]

To Giuseppe Sertoli—Milan

Paris, 9.1.73

Dear Prof. Sertoli,

We have not met but I just wanted to say to you that I have read with great interest your article "Su letteratura e ideologia" (On Literature and Ideology), in *N. C.* 57–58,[44] in fact I was very taken with it. That is to say, that having started out with the diffidence I usually have for—let's say—Adorno-style discussions (but I recognize that your approach is not limited to this label), I found your essay not just of very high calibre but also very convincing, and I ended up agreeing almost entirely with your conclusions and with the general picture that flows from it. In particular your exemplification through the four novelists holds up well (with Manzoni and Conrad you go more deeply into their "forms," with Flaubert quite rightly you approach him more from the outside, while I'm not sure whether Hardy's silence can be aligned with the others—as a further step down this road—or whether at that time silence's role in literature was already part of a more widespread and conscious set of problems). I would like to read the "more detailed account" that you mention in the notes. (I would like to read it because of my interest in it as a reader, but also, if it works out, to consider it for possible publication with Einaudi.)

And then something else I meant to say: I am preparing some Conrad titles for the Centopagine series and getting organized to write some introductions myself (Conrad is an author I studied a lot in my youth) but I wondered if there was not some short novel of Conrad's which you would like to write an introduction to (but my series is intended as a "popular" series so we must not write things that are too difficult).

You can write to me in Paris or Turin where I will be going in about ten days' time; in fact, for manuscripts and printed matter it is best to send them to Einaudi in Turin, where I go regularly, because the post is not working well either in Italy or in France.

Kind regards.

Italo Calvino

12 Square de Châtillon
Paris XIV
[Handwritten; with the addressee.]

TO CLAUDIO VARESE—FLORENCE

Paris 20.1.73

Dear Varese,

YOUR LETTER IS EXCELLENT AND THIS IS PRECISELY THE WAY I like people to read me. Yes, I believe this book is no different in spirit from others of mine and that it stays faithful to an idea of literature as a tool of knowledge.[45] Precisely for this reason I do not know if I will succeed in writing a letter of discussion or one that adds anything at all to what you have written. And moreover, I have the feeling that I have written a book that is already very, maybe excessively, sententious: and I would not want to extend the series further by adding pronouncements to my pronouncements. I notice that all critics dwell on the final sentence (and you do it very well) as if that were *the* conclusion[46]—and of course by placing it at the end I myself have privileged it over the other conclusions that the book suggests as it goes along—but I think one can dwell also on other sentences that have an emphasis of this type. The final italic passage itself has two conclusions, both of the same order of importance: one on the ideal city (which is seen as discontinuous and immanent, and no critic has concentrated on this so far), and the other on the infernal city.

The book was written piecemeal, through a successive juxtaposition of separate pieces, and I myself did not know where I was going with it, I only felt the need to continue until I had exhausted everything I had to say. In other words, I could only overcome the incompleteness of each discourse I attempted by adding other convergent or divergent discourses. If the book now seems like a fully worked out and rounded off construction, this construction came at the last minute on the basis of the material I had accumulated. The classifications of the cities too, some of them (those of memory, of desire) were already clear from the start, because that was the way they had turned out, but others were decided on later, after many hesitations, based on thematic nuclei that did not have any clear outlines. So it is not that I do not let people read the chapters one after the other: I think that they must be read one by one because that was how they came into being, and then each should be read in the various series that the book suggests. But the sense the book has to convey is of something dense and overcrowded that you describe so well.

I am pleased to see that you quote Northrop Frye, a literary theorist who has long fascinated me (I wrote an article on him about four years ago: if you have not seen it, I'll send it to you).[47] And pleased that you mentioned Balzac's and Baudelaire's Paris (in the coming days I will be publishing in the Centopagine series Balzac's *Ferragus*, for which I have written the introduction, which touches on this very point; I will have it sent to you). On the other hand, I can't say anything about your most important reference, Hesse, because that is a real gap in my reading which people have often reproached me for recently, and which I shall have to fill as soon as possible.

Very fine too is your figurative contrast between the two poles of Klee and pop art.

In short, you can see that I am unable to write a letter that has the compactness of a "public" statement. Maybe my mature age has made me lose the peremptoriness in my declarations, and this can be felt in the book as well . . .

My thanks once again, with all good wishes
Yours,

Italo Calvino

[Handwritten; with the addressee. Also in *Studi Novecenteschi*, 4 (1973), pp. 126–27; and in Claudio Varese, *Sfide del Novecento. Letteratura come scelta* (Florence: Le Lettere, 1992), pp. 380–81. Calvino gave his permission to the publication of this letter when he wrote to Varese from Paris on 1 March 1973: "Dear Varese, I found your letter on my return from Italy. If you think that my letter merits publication alongside yours, I am happy with that."]

To Pier Paolo Pasolini—Rome

Paris, 7.2.73

Dear Pier Paolo,

Only yesterday did I read your wonderful article and I am happy that writing books can still hold surprises for me, the surprise of a dialog like this, a discourse like yours which is full of a direct approach to the text and lively intelligence, far removed from any of the predictable mechanisms of critical discourse.[48] And happy that my book has provided the occasion for new, ingenious, and focused reflections like the ones you put forward: in all of them I recognize my book from new angles which are already encouraging me to find new developments and links to your discussion. Above all this looms the extraordinary image of the universal future, stretching out in its entirety, where sense is lost, so that knowledge too becomes memory. And look, this is already a Platonic motif and is linked to the Platonism you mention shortly afterwards. You are the first critic to point out this Platonic component in my work, which seems to me to be central. And you rightly move on to explain, in a move that resonates with those in the book, how the subject matter of dreams is real.

A brief word on our having "stopped being close to one another" in the last ten years or so.[49] What you mean is that it is you who have gone very far away: not just with the cinema, which is the thing that is furthest from the mental rhythms of a bookworm, which is what I have become in the meantime, but because also your use of words has shifted to communicating a presence traumatically as though projecting it onto big screens: a mode of rapid intervention on the present that I ruled out from the start. All this on the one hand, whereas the kind of discourse into which you put the best of yourself is made up of extremely minute judgments that are precisely argued, based on a meticulous micro-analysis of words and people (talents you have not lost, as these well-honed critical interventions of yours testify), and this is the type of discourse that can only have indirect influences, after doing the rounds, at a distance of years and years, just like poetic discourse.

By contrast, being present in order to have your say on "current affairs" according to the newspapers, using the newspapers' measure of what is topical, engaging directly with public opinion, certainly gives one a great sensation of being alive, but this is life in the world of effects, not in the world of slow reasoning and reflection. It is thus your "way of having chosen topicality" which has divided us, not mine, which doesn't exist. I quickly realized that I had no place in actuality and I stayed on the sidelines, maybe champing at the bit, but still remaining silent, as you say yourself moreover; in any case, even if I had spoken out, there would not have been anyone prepared to listen and reply to me. Where did you ever see in my behavior any "a priori commitment to the student cause"? As for an "openness toward the Neo-avant-garde," I'll let that go: I would always welcome a change in the mental climate of Italian literature, if ever there were any hint of it, and even though this or that set of poetics does not persuade me, I am always interested in what can come out of the interaction with other poetics. But my reservations and allergies toward the new politics are stronger than the urge to oppose the old politics, and so I no longer had a position to uphold since I had ruled them out one by one, and this also took away my curiosity to know people, follow developments, distinguish positions. And not possessing any competence or qualifications to express my judgments, it is natural that I stayed silent, both publicly and in private, reinforced in this attitude of mine by the lack of success that yours and others' interventions encountered, interventions which in any case I did not feel I could associate myself with at all.

What you say about my image starting to turn yellow and fade matches precisely my intentions. Since the dead are no longer in a place where too many things no longer belong to them, they must feel a mixture of spite and relief, no different from my state of mind. It is no accident that I've gone to live in a big city where I know nobody and no one knows I exist. In this way I have been able to realize a kind of existence which was at least one of the many existences I had always dreamt of: I spend twelve hours a day reading, on most days of the year.

I will always try to read your articles in *Tempo* (your piece on Wilcock was also good). Thank you once more and accept my best wishes as an old friend.

Your,

Italo Calvino

Sent from Turin on 12 February
(I did not have your address)
[Typed, with autograph signature and additions; in the Gabinetto Scientifico Letterario G. P. Vieusseux-Archivio Contemporaneo Alessandro Bonsanti, Florence. Previously published in P. P. Pasolini, *Lettere 1955–1975*, ed. Nico Naldini, pp. cxlvi–cxlviii; and in Nico Naldini, *Pasolini, una vita* (Turin: Einaudi, 1989), pp. 372–74.]

To Geno Pampaloni—Bagno a Ripoli (Florence)

[Turin], 16.5.73

Dear Pampaloni,
THE POSTAL STRIKE HAS LEFT SO MANY MOVEMENTS AND thoughts suspended in mid-air. So I waited before thanking you and commenting on the expanded version of your piece on *Invisible Cities*. As a result I'm now left waiting for the introduction to *Memorie lontane (Distant Memories)* which is now URGENT, and I am full of doubt as to whether you have sent it and fear it is lying in some post office.[50]

The three-dimensional utopia as opposed to the non-Euclidean utopia seems to me a very good idea, and corresponds to the truth as far as I am concerned: I cannot think of the future except in those terms! This is a time when critics reflect an image of myself that never fails to unsettle me, the more I recognize its truth; just as at a certain point one finds a face in the mirror which is not the one we've been used to finding in mirrors and on each occasion it gives us a start.[51]

In the move from the *Corriere* to *Libri Nuovi* your essay has become considerably richer and your placing of my book has been carried out with great precision.[52] The "long shadow" of reality seems to me spot on, as does what differentiates me from the "irrealists" who come from somewhere else.

I look forward to receiving the note on (Guido) Nobili, which the technical office is urging me to pursue in order to make progress with the book. In any case, do give me some news.

Best wishes,
Yours,

Italo

[Handwritten on Einaudi headed paper; with the addressee.]

To Mario Lavagetto—Parma

18.5.73

Dear Prof. Lavagetto,
I have only now read your article in *N. A.*[53] and I liked it very much. You are the first to take as the book's main thread Kublai Khan and the succession of proposals and counter-proposals on reading, and in that way you hit on many key points that others missed. In short, you hold the book by its spine, by the binding; not that one cannot hold it by the page corners and leaf through it like a calendar or a daisy: many critics have read it like that and read it well, but then they got lost when they found all those pages scattered everywhere.

As for the order of the series and numbers of cities, this seemed to me the simplest thing in the world, but so many people thought it was heaven knows what kind of cabala. You manage to explain it with your beautiful trapezium chart. I too made a similar diagram (for an interview to come out in *Uomini e Libri*) but mine turned out to be an ugly oblique parallelogram, whereas your trapezium is much better.

But what is more important, you manage to square the position of my previous books with this one: and this is an important critical outcome, which is useful to me and which orientates me, because lately I have been trying to walk without looking behind.

In general I am happy with the critiques of this book, even the perplexed ones, even the negative ones, because I like to hear things that are not the usual points. However, when faced with certain criticisms I have the feeling as if after a long period of not looking in a mirror, I recognized an image that I cannot say does not resemble me, no, it's definitely me, but I did not expect to be seen—or to see myself—like that.[54] But what comes to me from your article is not the look of an outsider, rather it is the same gaze with which I looked at my own book as I was writing it that comes back from the mirror, and this proves that there is a common mental horizon in the two of us.

I am sorry that we have not met, or rather I am sorry to know you so little. I read your replies to the badly formulated and even more badly thought out questions in the survey, and I agree with you and appreciate seeing a spirit of rare balance in the way you cope with the university existence in these times.

I will gladly read your works. Do send them to Einaudi in Turin.

Very best wishes,

Italo Calvino

[Handwritten; with the addressee.]

TO THE PUPILS OF VALENTINA FAUSTI
MIDDLE SCHOOL—PIACENZA

Turin, 4 June 1973

Dear Friends in Second Year,

THANK YOU VERY MUCH FOR YOUR LETTER AND FOR THE FINE things that you wrote to me about *Marcovaldo*. I've received and continue to receive similar letters to yours from children in middle schools all over Italy.[55]

You ask me if Marcovaldo is a little bit myself. I would say yes, but the odd thing is that I started to feel myself like Marcovaldo only after writing the book. When I was writing it I thought he was a character who was a bit funny, a bit sad, but very different from me. But instead with the passing of time . . .

My thanks also to your teacher and best wishes to all of you.

[Typed copy; in the Einaudi Archive, Turin. Also in *ILDA*, p. 599.]

To Elsa Morante—Rome

Pineta di Roccamare
58043 Castiglione della Pescaia
(Grosseto) Telephone (0564) 52144

5 August 1973

Dear Elsa,

I hear from friends that you are about to finish—you have already finished—your novel.[56] This consoles me because I am very discouraged by this general dearth of books coming out, a desert that also affects me, removes my desire to write, because books cannot grow if they don't find around them the company of other books their same age and that are congenial to them. And so I very much hope to read your book soon because I am feeling the need for something to stir the still air. If you let me read it as soon as you can I will be very grateful to you.

We are here all of August and part of September, we've got a little house in a pine-forest near the sea, a very isolated and quiet place—two hours from Rome. If you're ever passing by . . .

Best wishes also from Chichita,
Yours,

Italo Calvino

[Handwritten; with the addressee's heirs.]

To Antonio Faeti—Bologna

Pineta di Roccamare
Castiglione della Pescaia

20 August 1973

Dear Dr Faeti,

I STILL HAVE TO THANK YOU FOR THE SELECTION OF COMIC strips you sent me. But my project is still up in the air and I think that for the time being I will not be able to complete it. I've had (and am still having) a very busy summer organizing this summer house that we've bought in this pine-forest and that up until now of course only gives me problems and worries.[57] (Luckily at least our little girl really loves it.) Furio Scarpelli has a house near us, son of Filiberto: he liked your book a lot and he said he would like to write to you. He is a very nice person.

Well then, my idea was to create the equivalent—using modern figures—of the combinatory-arbitrary narrative device that I had set up with the Tarot cards. So what I needed was a repertory of figures that was popular and contemporary and so I thought of comics. Maybe the thing is too difficult to succeed and I don't know whether—apart from the idea—I can go any further in carrying it out. But even if I give up, in order that some trace of the operation remains, I am sending you these notes which explain it.

Best wishes,
Yours,

Calvino

THE MOTEL OF CROSSED DESTINIES

A group of people have escaped from a mysterious catastrophe and find refuge in a half-destroyed motel, where there is nothing but a burnt page of a newspaper, the comics page. The survivors, struck dumb by the shock, tell their stories by pointing to the units of the comic strip, but their stories move in vertical columns jumping from one strip to another. I offer the simplest case with three strips, excerpts from different comic stories each composed of three units, but these could be made up of five or more strips.

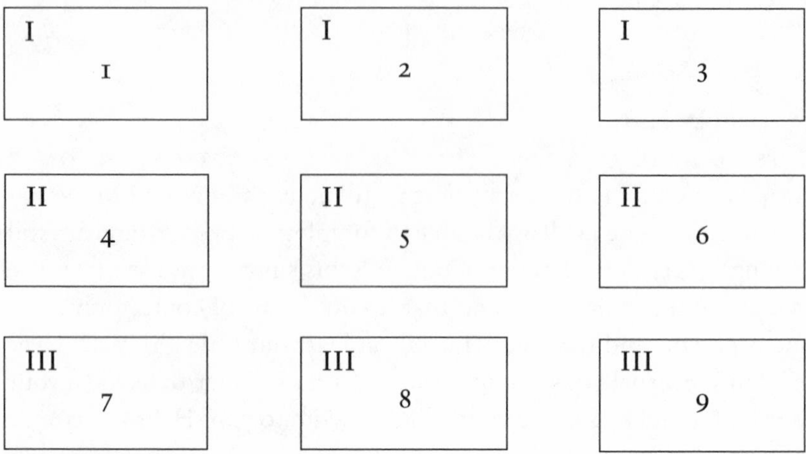

A recognizes his story in units 1, 4, 7
B recognizes his story in units 2, 5, 8
C recognizes his story in units 3, 6, 9
D recognizes his story in units 7, 4, 1
E recognizes his story in units 8, 5, 2
F recognizes his story in units 9, 6, 3
There can even be diagonal narrators: G = 1, 5, 9; H= 3, 5, 7 etc.

The strips must be highly dramatic, a bit terrifying. For that reason it is difficult to find a real newspaper page that will work, because they always have a majority of humorous comic strips, which are not suitable, and only a couple of adventure strips that are not caricatures and these are the ones that will work. But they must be very evocative, anonymous drawings, and at the same time they should have just that touch of the mysterious and the polysemous that the Tarots have. They should not be the kind of super-heroes and fantasy monsters you find in Marvel Comics, because in that case contemporary "verisimilitude" is lost, though of course fine to use science fiction ones involving technology and astronauts, which could be one of the stories. Another could involve gangsters, revolvers, cars. Another still could have wars, machine guns, bomber planes, another one could be sentimental like Tiffany Jones or like a toothpaste advertisement, another could have eroticism, naked women, maybe a bit of sadism, and perhaps also one with a sinister-looking house like the one in "The Addams Family."

Of course the words in the comic strips are disruptive, not in graphic terms, but because they would immediately condition the story; the ideal solution would be to cut out comics from newspapers in languages like Finnish and Swahili.

[Handwritten; with the addressee. Of the two typed pages (with the structures drawn by hand) which Calvino attached to this letter and which are reproduced here, the first paragraph anticipates the conclusion of the final note to *The Castle of Crossed Destinies*, which is dated October 1973; the other two paragraphs were published in *RR*, II, pp. 1379–80 (in the "Note e notizie sui testi," ed. Mario Barenghi).]

To Edoardo Sanguineti—Genoa

Paris 5.2.74

Dear Edoardo,

I FOUND YOUR LETTER OF 11 DECEMBER A MONTH LATER, after my return from Italy. I hear that you will be coming to Shakespeare & Co. on 4 March, so we will see each other then.

Yes, it is true that in my book the Tarot cards do not tell the future only the narratable, in other words what has been narrated, in other words the past. Moreover, in our time, which ought to be the one which knows how to deal with the future, the individual's destinies can be read by deciphering their buried past, and basically as regards collective destinies, one does not know how to imagine them except through comparisons with historical models. Nevertheless, it has to be said that—especially in some stories in *The Tavern*—the Tarots attempt prophecy, and it is always a dark prophecy. It is as though the polysemousness of the cards (which was the first thing I was aiming at, I feel, in that book, which not by accident takes place in an epoch when historic roles are continually reshuffled in constantly changing permutations) had to converge on the cards of ruin and destruction, the only ones which bring meanings together. However you look at it, then, what emerges is fear or rejection of the future: hence my need to change the pack of cards, but I have not yet found the right one. (I have already tried with Utopian cards and the results have not been any more promising.)

But perhaps future and past are false dimensions of the discourse of literature where "the roles are all assigned," as you say. That is an excellent topic of discussion for us two. The state of my ideas today leads me to prefer not the essay—and that amount of peremptoriness that it allows—but the dialog genre, a real dialog, in other words discussing with a non-fictional interlocutor, but at the same time still a fictitious dialog, in other words written while pretending that it is spoken. (Writing up or not a verbal discussion.) I started practicing this genre last year writing fictitious replies spoken to Ferdinando Camon for the reedition of his (actually not very pleasant) book *Il mestiere di scrittore* (*The Writer's Job*), in other words by adapting or inventing his questions or objections to my answers.[58] And I noticed that this is the most suitable system for me to engage in discussions, I mean writing them down but in a way that makes them seem as if I am talking. And I thought that this could be the formula for a possible journal today, a dialog-journal: each issue would have two people discussing a theme, a (fake) recording of a real dialog, and then some texts and documents and supporting material for the discussion.

[Handwritten draft; in the Calvino Archive. In the Archive there is also another handwritten draft with a dense web of deletions and corrections, in several places very difficult to decipher, which now follows. Putting together the allusions in the two drafts that Calvino makes to Sanguineti's poetry reading in the Shakespeare & Co. bookshop, one can conclude that this second note was a first draft at a reply, written in Turin but then never sent. The letter sent to Sanguineti probably corresponds to the draft of 5 February above.]

Dear Edoardo,

YOUR CRITIQUE OF THE VARIANTS IN THE THREE DARK STOries is very accurate and, I have to say, convincing.[59] In arranging (or rearranging, to be more precise: never has a text of mine been subject to [so many] hesitations and I have now lost count of them) the three stories in terms of sequence, the "practical" preoccupation was certainly predominant (I had seen that by putting it first, this muddle discouraged the less methodological readers) not only because of the "higher print-run" but because this[60] would be followed by *The Tavern* and I would have liked to make *The Castle* the locus of regularity and concentrate all the instability in *The Tavern* (but maybe this did not work out). But the principal reason was that I wanted to give emphasis to the story of Faust which appeared in both texts: in *The Tavern* using the same cards as Parsifal, a mixing of two stories that I had loaded with meanings, whereas in *The Castle* Faust linked perfectly with two stories that were much more tenuous in terms of density of meaning; in this way I preferred to offer first a clean Faust, and then a Faust "multiplied by" the Grail.[61] However, all the motifs you mention analyzing the overlapping elements in *The Castle I*, are serious and I realize that (Gothic cathedrals are never completed) if this letter of yours had reached me while I was still at proof stage, it would have thrown me into crisis and pushed me toward hesitating again. But what a pain you are: with erudite nastiness you meticulously praise whatever has disappeared from my text, and minimize all the rest!

(As for the variants in "Tutte le altre storie" (All the Other Stories), they were aimed, if I remember correctly, at valorizing the appearance of the Goddess of Destruction who seemed to me to have been a bit sacrificed.)

You are certainly correct that this book (in the form in which I published it) contains (and is conditioned by) if not a "terrified self-critique" of my own performance in it, at least an attempt at distance. Those two very favorable readers with whom I have spoken so far have both reproached me for the final note with its anti-climax and detachment. You reveal that it is the appearance of the "I" who is already in the text as narrator of his own story that effects this change (and this links with my old ideological obsession about conscience), this "I" that can only define himself as a juggler (and from this the ideological conscience is transformed into a guilty conscience). This is something that has become clear to me only now as I elaborate the sense of your analysis: the fact that in *The Castle* the narrator who says "I" does not find his story narrated in the cards is no accident (I was convinced I had remembered too late, at the end, that having begun the frame-story in the third person, this person had to be one of the narrators), and I tried to make amends for this in *The Tavern* by introducing the writer-narrator. No, the point of assuming the narratable as a combination of cards, of stories that narrate themselves, ends up by canceling the "I," otherwise what point does it serve? Thus your bringing in the "I"[62] sends everything up in the air. And here then one can also explain how this "I" ends up by feeling the need to turn into the Nobody that you mention, and to protest that he has nothing to do with it, that he was just passing by.

In short, your analysis has helped me a lot,[63] if only I had [had] it in the gap between the Ricci edition and the Einaudi one,[64] because I have to say that the consensus that the first volume elicited, both on aesthetic and on structuralist grounds, was not enough to dispel the feeling of isolation in this procedure and my uncertainty about the real meaning of what I was doing. All in all, it is a pity that we have not seen each other in all these years.

The third critical point to emerge from your analysis is that of the feeling of disappointment that something new did not emerge "from this combinatory machine"[65] such as our future destiny and not the stories of the past rewritten and rearranged. This seems to me to be the weakest argument and the easiest to argue against: but I know that you could counter it even better than me.

I have heard little news from you and always with some delay. I never manage to find your articles in *Paese-Sera*: thanks to an old [privilege] I get a free copy of the Friday paper with *Paese-libri*. Only now have I discovered that you write something for it every second Thursday. When I'm in Paris I never [manage to] see them, but when I'm in Italy (and recently I've been more often in Turin than in Paris) I will try to [buy it]. I wanted to write to you to welcome you as another father of a daughter, but that news too I got rather late.

In Paris I discovered that you will be coming (or have already come?) for a poetry reading at Shakespeare & Co. Now that I'm in Paris (I'm leaving this evening), I'll go there and find out the date.

Best wishes to you and yours,

To Guido Almansi—Dublin

Paris 10.2.74

Dear Guido,

I HAVE SUGGESTED TO THE OU.LI.PO THAT YOU BE INVITED, and they are happy to do so. It would be for the May meeting (and lunch)—there were already previous invitees for March and April—date still to be fixed, toward the end of the month, I think. However, you yourself have to contact François Le Lionnais directly: 23 Route de la Reine, 92100 Boulogne-sur-Seine. I said you would talk about "in-imitations" (and mistranslations?) but you ought in any case to prepare examples that can be understood by French speakers.[66] (No question of Italian; English gets a good audience. One of the participants—the only other foreigner apart from myself—is an American, Harry Matthews [*sic*]: I know his Roussel-style novel, which is not bad.) However, erudite allusions to Oulipians avant-la-lettre in various literatures arouse great interest (they call it "anticipatory plagiarism"), and they certainly abound in the seventeenth century or thereabouts in Italy; you will easily be able to satisfy this kind of curiosity, not me.

Chichita mentioned a phone call of yours in which you said you were worried about my reactions to your title *Le città illeggibili* (*Illegible Cities*).[67] I hadn't given it a thought, the title was witty and made one want to read the article (unlike the other two), and seeing that the sense of the article was not that, it worked very well, because everyone read it with the hope of finding a hatchet-job and found instead a positive though unusual and entertaining critique. In fact I have heard of many people round about who have read it and mention it to me, always in positive terms, and I have to say that rarely has a piece of criticism on my work had such success.

I have been thinking about what I might do in Dublin, and I have started to wonder how I can prepare so many (how many?) lectures and I have been seized with panic. The only lecture I have ready is one on Manzoni which would work very well but it certainly can't be the main dish, given its theme. They are also asking me for one (or more?) lectures in English and I don't know how I can manage. I could present *Invisible Cities* with a reading of selected passages, seeing that Weaver has now finished the translation (which is not entirely felicitous). But if I have to read those passages in English, I'll massacre them. We would need someone (an actor?) to read the excerpts, and I could then make some comments on them. I really don't how to manage this. Maybe in dialog with you? As for the date, I've suggested 6 May. But the letter I wrote to Lonergan is very hesitant because I really don't know if I can manage to do everything that they are asking me to do.[68] Ciao.

Italo

[Handwritten; in the Archivio della Radio della Svizzera Italiana, Lugano Besso.]

To Giorgio Viscardi—Rome

Turin, 8 April 1974

Dear Dr Viscardi,

You know about my fierce internal resistance to authorizing a cinema version of *The Path to the Spiders' Nests.* In addition to the reasons that have so far held me back from this should be added, in your case, the fact that you are a beginner, maybe a promising star for tomorrow's cinema but this means me shouldering a large amount of risk.

Nevertheless, I did not want to say no to you immediately, since I found your personality—from the telephone calls and now from the letter you've sent me—interesting. That was why I wanted to wait until I had read some of your ideas about the film before deciding.

And now having read the film-script I realize that the basic objection I had was a different one and I should have made it clear to you from the start. In films on Fascism or the Resistance the thing that most puts me off is when the "historical" setting (though for me that is actually part of my own experiences) is not convincing, does not correspond to reality; and this happens regularly in films made by young directors who have not lived through that period. This is not their fault, you'll say; of course not, maybe it is more our fault, I mean all of us who have transmitted an image of that period which if it is rehashed without that hint, that flavor of immediate testimony that it could have had, reveals and magnifies the element of falseness that it—like all literary images—did in fact contain. Thus I instantly realized that the atmosphere created during an aerial bombardment of a city is very difficult to get across, and you are really very off the mark in this. Similarly, partisan battles (which in my book are not represented directly) are a huge obstacle. (Your idea to deal with the battle by inserting into it my short story "The Crow Comes Last" is not a happy solution: this is a story that is in a different stylistic key, very much distorted from reality, in fact decidedly fantasy; it is totally irrelevant here.)

On the other hand, Louis Malle's *Lacombe Lucien*, which was the object of so much discussion and was attacked by French ex-Resistance fighters, I found conveyed the flavor of those times, and I found the film, to a large extent, believable.

But this fundamental objection to your reconstruction of the climate of that period is not the only problem I have with your scenario. My impression is that it does not create the pattern of a cinematic narrative, with its moments of tension and of relief. Fidelity to the text leads to an excessive use of dialog, where the flaws in this youthful, very immature, novel of mine stand out. On the other hand what does not come across, I don't think, is the sense of pre-ideological progress in a group of human beings who belong to a large extent to the subproletariat. (But this should come across just from the facts, the images.) I would say that your treatment works well when it follows my text in the parts dealing with the child's adventures, and less well when it follows it in the pseudo-ideological discussions which are its weak point. And when it departs from my text it becomes generic, lacks bite, is unconvincing. (That finale . . .)

In short, dear Dr Viscardi, I'm sorry but I have to say no to you as well, just as I have done to others who approached me with treatments of this novel years ago. You are certainly someone with something to say and a strong inner dynamism. My advice is to deal with contemporary subjects, ones that are tied to an almost documentary starting point, just like in the first television rehearsals that you described in your letter to me, and which I hope to have a chance to see.

Please do not be angry with me; you will soon understand that this film would not make anyone happy and would bring you more criticism than praise. I hope to receive news soon about a different, more fortunate film made by you. I wish you every success.

[Typed copy; in the Calvino Archive and in the Einaudi Archive, Turin.]

To Gore Vidal—Rome

San Remo, 20 June 1974

Dear Gore Vidal,

I HAVE STARTED THIS LETTER MANY TIMES AND INTERRUPTED it many times. I was looking for excuses: like I had to find your address, like I did not know whether you were in Rome or New York. I tried to write to you in English, but the things I thought out in Italian did not sound right when translated into English, and the things I thought in English did not sound good when I recast them in Italian. The problem is that you have written a critical essay on me that is as spontaneous and friendly as a letter, and now I would like to write you a letter that is as carefully thought out and analytical as a critical essay in order to convey to you how happy I was at reading it.[69]

Happy not just at being read with such enthusiasm and intelligence and affinity, and not just because it was written by you, in other words by a writer whose biting irony, capacity to transform reality, and precise adherence to our own times had always attracted me, but also for the way in which your review was written, which seems admirable to me for two reasons.

First: one feels that you wrote this article for the pleasure of writing it, alternating warm praise with criticisms and reservations in a totally sincere tone, and with constant freedom and humor, and this feeling of pleasure is communicated irresistibly to the reader.

Second: I have always thought that it is difficult to extract from my books, each of which is so different from the others, a unitary discourse, an overall definition, maybe even just the outline of an author that is not also split up. Now you—despite exploring my oeuvre in the way it demands to be explored, namely in a non-systematic way, moving like someone out for a walk who stops here, but moves on there without looking around, over there wanders about in an occasional diversion—you manage to establish a general sense in everything I have written, almost a philosophy—"the whole and the many" etc.—and I am very happy when someone manages to find a philosophy in the products of my so unphilosophical mind.

The conclusion of your review contains a statement that seems to me to be important in an absolute way. I don't dare to wonder whether it is true if applied to myself, but it is true as a literary ideal for each of us: the aim that each one of us has to reach has to be that "writer and reader become one, or One." And to encompass both your discourse and mine in a perfect circle, we will say that this One is the Whole.

I was keen to convey to you these general considerations that your essay inspired in me. On another occasion perhaps I will reply to you more analytically, point by point. For the moment I just wanted to say this: you note that already in 1958 I was worried about the destruction of the environment, and this recognition makes me happy because it comes from you who have always been in the front line in the defense of ecology. Also on this topic is *A Plunge into Real Estate* which I will send you in Italian. There is a translation of it (by D. S. Carne-Ross) in a paperback anthology: *Six Modern Italian Novellas*, edited by W. Arrowsmith, New York, Permabook, 1964.

I am writing to you from San Remo, from the house where the events in that novella took place—twenty years ago—and since then things have only changed in terms of quantity, in other words, our house is more and more surrounded by a horrible forest of reinforced concrete, and our family is always having to deal with some entrepreneur: this time to sell it for good.

But I am here only passing through, in this Riviera which now only represents the past for me, and which I now no longer recognize. Now I spend the summers with my wife and daughter in a pine-forest in the Tuscan Maremma, two hours from Rome. I have a small house in an estate (alas!) but greenness is respected there more than elsewhere. My address is: Pineta di Roccamare, Castiglione della Pescaia (Grosseto). If you come and see us, I hope to be able to express my thanks personally to you better than by letter.

Italo Calvino

[Handwritten; with the addressee.]

To Elsa Morante—Rome

[Pineta di Roccamare,] 6 August 1974

Dear Elsa,

For me the value of your book[70] is that you start from Italian literature of the postwar period taken as a collective epic, and that you give this material a *novelistic* construction, in other words exploiting the mythical strength that the novel form carried within itself originally. (And in this sense I would have liked an even more novelistic development, as in your other novels. What I mean is that I would have liked the hero to have continued living and having many adventures as the mythical genealogy of his family and his mythical conception promised, this latter being the most intense moment in terms of internal movement and tumultuous language.) But for me the most extraordinary result is that you have given the novel the completeness of an *encyclopaedia*, with all the voices of that literature recreated and inserted into the network of ramifications of the main story, even including the Alpino frozen on the Russian front, even the workers' conditions, even the murder of the prostitute, all of this with the maximum effect in terms of portrayal. My reading of it, in short, can never get away from the skill with which you used those building blocks, in other words my point of view remains that of someone who in his own time participated in that literature and lived through its exhaustion and crisis and now faced with this book feels the crisis, his crisis, opening up again in front of him. And the questions I asked myself when reading it were: in what sense is this a book of today and not of that epoch? In what way is it a book that was impossible then but which makes possible again something of the way we wrote in those days that has now been lost? In what sense is it a book that can solve problems of portrayal or communication or knowledge that we might have ourselves today? Of course, at the center of everything there is the relevance of the thesis of amorous anarchism of the children who are saved and who are the saviours even though victims, but it is on your method of work that I am trying to learn something more. And my first reaction is a confirmation that that literature—and even more that emotion which one feels for the individual and collective destinies—is indissolubly linked to that epoch. Could you have transmitted everything that you have transmitted telling a story set in the present? No, you had to resort to subject matter from that time (with extraordinary results precisely in the things that I feel as a "professional" are the most difficult because of the emotional power already implicit in them, such as the loss of the house during the bombing, and the train full of deportees) because the war years are not only the raw material but also the main theme of the book. In other words, everything starts again from that unrepeatable situation where the writer was in the middle of the life of the people without this relationship having anything unnatural about it, because the author was not there as a writer but as a person in the midst of other people. Here, though, we are now in a new phase where it is the indirect effect of that urge that still is at work in us, and which I have not as yet been able to define fully. But already the mentions I made of the "encyclopaedic" and the "novelistic" will give you an idea of the sense in which I would like to succeed in reading you, the sense of a composition that is totally constructed, where even emotionality is a building block. Yet my reading is certainly a very forced one, I would like in some sense to *dehumanize* you in order to feel you closer, so as not to leave you in the hands of your critics who want you as totally human. For instance, I am happy that the animals have the full dignity of characters, but I would be even happier if I did not feel them smothered in human affection which is expressed effusively, whereas your real achievement is what you convey of the animal rhythm in humans, of the equilibrium of biological energies in living. And so I still have not managed to define the narrating voice, which nevertheless must hold the key to the cognitive operation you carry out, but in your stylistic eclecticism I cannot avoid the obstacle (for me) of that emotional expressivity which remains the basic tone. These personal allergies of mine do not prevent me from admiring the vital heart of the book in the big shelter full of refugees, the possibility of happiness in the midst of the catastrophe, and the sense of the passing of time in that life, like when Useppe feels the place has become different after the departure of the Thousand.

I wanted to put down these impressions of mine because they seem to me to be different from what I have read so far about your book in the papers, things with which I nearly always found myself in disagreement. And I wanted to send them to you because when I publish a book the thing that gives me most pleasure is it being read from different points of view and it eliciting different reactions. I hope that this letter, in which I have tried to give reasons both for my admiration and for my distance, transmits the friendship of your

Calvino

[Typed, with autograph signature; with the addressee's heirs.]

To Cesare Milanese—Rome

Castiglione della Pescaia

18 August 1974

Dear Prof. Milanese,

I read with great pleasure your Pythagorean essay on my book, or rather on the book's index.[71] In constructing that system of alternating chapters for the various series of cities, I tried to put into operation the simplest method for ensuring that the cities were not all either grouped together or separate but rather linked to each other creating a lively and varied movement. To that end I set up the sequence which I represent in the attached diagram. The vertical numbers are the series of cities and the horizontal ones are the chapters designated with

Roman numerals: I mean the normal chapters consisting of five mini-chapters. But since the first horizontal ones are shorter I grouped together the opening "triangle" in an introductory chapter and the final "triangle" in a concluding chapter, and these naturally came out longer, each of them consisting of ten mini-chapters each.

I see that by using an arithmetically more sophisticated and complex procedure you have managed to reconstruct my very own diagram.

What is totally new to me—and full of interesting surprises—is the numerological part, which culminates in the fateful 666.

I am very interested in the direction your work is going in, somewhere between archaic wisdom and futuristic knowledge. I had already noticed this reading your excellent book on Ronconi.[72]

Thank you very much and I hope to see you soon.

Yours,

	1										
	2	1									
I	3	2	1								
	4	3	2	1							
II	5	4	3	2	1						
III		5	4	3	2	1					
IV			5	4	3	2	1				
V				5	4	3	2	1			
VI					5	4	3	2	1		
VII						5	4	3	2	1	
VIII							5	4	3	2	1
								5	4	3	2
IX									5	4	3
										5	4
											5

[Handwritten; with the addressee. From the postmark it appears that the letter was actually sent (and therefore written) on 17 August 1974.]

To Leonardo Sciascia—Caltanissetta

Paris, 5 October 1974

Dear Leonardo,

Yesterday I read your *Todo modo, todo modo, todo modo*, initially a little intolerant of all these priests and masses and theology, then getting really interested from the moment of the crime onwards, both because of the murder element and because of the infernal vision of Christian Democrat Italy which is about the most powerful thing written on that theme.[73] In fact this really was the novel we needed to explain what Christian Democrat Italy has been and still is and no one has been able to do this before you.

In this book too I became obsessed with reconstructing what you leave unsaid, namely the solution of the mystery, and I carefully followed up the web of quotations from literature and philosophy (and also to my pleasure found myself an almost direct interlocutor with the Voltaire-Pascal nexus). In this novel more than in *Il contesto* (*Equal Danger*) the quotations seem to hold the crucial clues; and of course I immediately went to check out *Pensées* 460 to 477. In the edition I have here in the house (a Livre de Poche edition) which is organized by subject matter, no. 460 is not the one you quote but is (I'm not sure whether this is through some surrealist "objective chance" or because it's one of your traps) in fact a eulogy of spectacles, which could have easily fitted in with your digressions on glasses. I rushed to the nearest bookshop to flip through another edition (Garnier) (just as one hunts for a telephone number in the directory in a café): this had another sequence organized by subject matter, a different number system, plus other numbers in brackets. Unfortunately I do not have here the Einaudi edition with its table of correspondences provided by our late friend Paolo Serini which gives a key to the various numbering systems. So perhaps I am missing a theological link to crack the logical-detective puzzle.

This time too I will tell you my theories, or at least those that came to me on a first reading:

(A) The most obvious one, given the way Don Gaetano moves in that marching square, is that the murderer is Don Gaetano, and this fits with his role as "devil in the convent." According to the logic of events he could easily be the perpetrator of the second murder and of his own suicide, but from the psychological-theological point of view his suicide holds up less well. In other words, in this case Don Gaetano is not directly the devil but the person who allows the devil to operate through him and then eliminates himself to take the devil out of the equation. In other words, he would thus be the devil and Christ at the same time and this fits well with his character.

The thing that makes me rethink is the second murder. For the sake of consistency of form, I would prefer all three deaths to be caused by the same weapon. The revolver could have been thrown from the terrace and landed near the mill (this would be the intuition that the narrator has as he does his drawing) where it could be picked up for the third murder. But in that case what is it that the police commissioner found after the second murder? A blunt object covered in blood would break the symmetry of the crimes committed with the same weapon and undermine the significance of its final discovery.

(B) Another hypothesis: the three crimes could be committed by three different people. Don Gaetano would kill Michelozzi (because he's a *goody* who corrupts and as such is more of a corrupter than others). Voltrano blackmails a third party who although innocent of this crime has enough things to hide to be forced to kill him. Here I would want the series of crimes to be longer: the guests at the hermitage would be forced to kill each other in turn until Don Gaetano too is killed.

(C) Alternatively: no crime is committed by Don Gaetano; his diabolical-Christ-like role is to let the blaze spread. With his belated about-turn he sees the person who did the killing, and knows that the chain of crimes will stop only when he too is killed. This is maybe the most satisfying solution in ideological terms, even though it may not be so on the level of the logic of events.

(D) (or B2 or C2) If Don Gaetano did not commit suicide, who killed him? If it is true that that morning none of the suspects left the hotel, Don Gaetano could have been killed by:

(a) the narrator, who knows that Don Gaetano is really the devil, and finally gives vent to his hatred for the corrupt church and his nostalgia for the church of his childhood;

(b) the magistrate, who feels he is being blackmailed by Don Gaetano who could ruin his career ("I know *nothing* about you");

(c) the police commissioner, who just before he retires discovers his vocation to be a revolutionary executioner, which would fit with the well-known Utopia beloved by Sciascia who sees a possible Jacobin role for the forces of order.

(E) One also has to consider the possibility of a more active role on the part of the narrator, who disappears mysteriously into the city (to buy a gun?), has a mysterious relationship with one of the women (he gives her a pistol to shoot Michelozzi, the lover with whom she was arguing? in other words the shot might have gone off from a window? or from the mill in the woods? or is the role of the painter and the women merely to introduce the gun amidst the Christians so they can carry out their latent violence? or might one actually have to think about a tacit plot between Don Gaetano, the painter and the women to make the guests at the hermitage slaughter each other?)

But I am going too far: in other words, in this case you seem to have gone too far, hiding too many clues from the reader, thus contravening one of the primary rules of the detective genre.

Whatever the case, I am sure that like the last time, you will neither confirm nor deny any of my hypotheses.[74]

Best wishes from your

Calvino

[Typed copy; in the Calvino Archive. Also in "Lettere di Italo Calvino a Leonardo Sciascia," *Forum Italicum*, 1 (Spring 1981), 70–72.]

To Primo Levi—Turin

Paris, 12 October 74

Dear Primo,

I have looked at the new version of *Il sistema periodico* (*The Periodic Table*).[75] I've read the new chapters, Iron, Phosphorus, Nitrogen, Uranium, Silver, Vanadium, and they enrich your "chemical autobiography"' (and the moral one as well).

Putting Carbon at the end and making it symbolize the writer's experience is a good idea. And since now the whole structure of the book is more robust, even the heterogeneity of Lead and Mercury does not disrupt the rest.

As for Argon I have always had my reservations about the fact that it is the opening piece (despite its value as a prologue) because it is the only chapter in which the chemical element is metaphorical; here too the structural incongruity would be less obvious if it were roughly in the middle of the book. (For instance: return from deportation; discovering all your relations have survived; reflecting on what this family continuity has meant.) But if the chapters were to follow an order reflecting their atomic weight (with exceptions, I think), I won't say anything more.

All in all, I would say that the book now exists and I am very happy with it.

I hope to see you soon,
Yours,

Italo

[Typed on Einaudi headed paper, with autograph signature; with the addressee's heirs. Also in *ILDA*, p. 606.]

To Giovanni Falaschi—Florence

[Paris,] 17.11.74

Dear Prof. Falaschi,

I AM FOLLOWING UP THE OTHER LETTER TO DISCUSS THE REview in *Belfagor* which I have read (or reread) and for which I thank you once more.[76]

I am pleased that you have gone through and illustrated the construction of the book, the meaning of the chapters and the italic sections, and also the various possibilities in its order and in rereading the book.

However, I do not agree so much about the negative nature of my perspectives when it comes to a hypothesis of knowledge. Certainly Kublai finds beneath the chess piece an empty square, the void, but the italics continue to the end of the chapter and one learns that this apparent void is full of details of real life, and that one can read inside these indefinitely. But you are quite right to say that "the journey serves no other purpose than to indicate the approximations and the errors." I see no other form of knowledge except that which is gained through successive approximations and corrections of mistakes. Certainly your conclusions regarding my "epistemological insecurity" and "lack of confidence in practicality" are absolutely right. But I have to admit this in spite of myself: I would like my experience to bring me other results, whereas instead for the moment that is how things are and I cannot but bear witness to it. You emphasize the presence of the archetypal city of memory, the Venice of Marco's childhood, as the only positive element; and this is certainly in the book. But as I put the book together I was constantly obsessed with this problem of not wanting to give the book (the journey) a nostalgic direction, not wanting to make it a journey back to the past.

The link between *The Castle* and the problematics of *Invisible Cities* and the way you define my operation or attempted operation here seems to me to be convincing and critically relevant.

With all good wishes,
Yours,

Calvino

[Handwritten; with the addressee.]

To Linuccia Saba—Rome

[9–10 January 1975]

Dear Linuccia,

On Tuesday I was not able to get near you because of the crowds. I am writing to you now to try to tell you what I would certainly not have been able to say to you in your presence, what I will certainly not manage to say even now in writing, because the role that Carlo's friendship had in my life makes me go back over all the fundamental principles that were his and start questioning myself endlessly.[77] So I continue to monologue with myself < . . . > and mute,[78] from the moment I saw the news in the Paris papers on Monday,[79] and then in a state of shock during the journey and amidst the crowds at the ceremony[80] which was so unlike Carlo. I continue to try to talk about him to others[81] who might <understand>, and even more I try to find others to talk about him to me.[82] The image of his life, such a full life, of the inner harmony that was his secret, of his being so serenely himself in order to understand others thoroughly[83] through what entered into the range of his <amorous> intelligence, continues to appear to me as an absolute standard[84] before which I feel more than ever the bitterness of my own life which is like trying to hold together bits that are collapsing all over the place.[85] So with this feeling that the world around us has become poorer in a way that really nothing can compensate us for, my thoughts are with you in these days of emptiness that fills everything and I hold your hands tightly in my thoughts. [Handwritten draft; in the Calvino Archive. The angled brackets indicate words that are difficult to decipher.]

To Giorgio Manganelli—Rome

Turin, 22.1.75

Dear Giorgio,

I really feel the need to write to you tell you how pleased I was to read your reply to PPP in today's *Corriere*.[86] You were really good, you found the right tone, and said the most serious things with a lightness of touch that is miraculous. There, that's something I would never have been able to do: when I read that article on Sunday I got so angry that I felt that I would never be able to argue with him without descending to a level that would have played into his hands, and I said: no, with Pasolini, the only thing to do is to act as if he did not exist. Instead you managed to say what needed to be said, starting off by being humorous, then rising to a crescendo and yet always having the necessary guts. (A crescendo that extends beyond halfway through your article: toward the end the discourse becomes a bit garbled partly to follow Pasolinian logic and partly because the tele-printer must have missed out a line.)

In short, I say thank you.

Yours,

Calvino

[Handwritten; in the Fondo Manoscritti del Centro di ricerca sulla tradizione manoscritta di autori moderni e contemporanei, University of Pavia.]

To Claudio Magris—Trieste

[Paris, 3–8 February 1975]

Dear Prof. Magris,

I was very disappointed to read your article "Gli sbagliati" [The Deluded].[87] It pained me a lot not only that you had written it but above all because you think in this way.

Bringing a child into the world makes sense only if this child is wanted consciously and freely by its two parents. If it is not, then it is simply animal and criminal behavior. A human being becomes human not through the casual convergence of certain biological conditions, but through an act of will and love on the part of other people. If this is not the case, then humanity becomes—as it is already to a large extent—no more than a rabbit-warren. But this is no longer a "free-range" warren but a "battery" one, in the conditions of artificiality in which it lives, with artificial light and chemical feed.

Only those people—a man and a woman—who are a hundred percent convinced that they possess the moral and physical possibility not only of rearing a child but of welcoming it as a welcome and beloved presence, have the right to procreate. If this is not the case, they must first of all do everything not to conceive, and if they do conceive (given that the margin for unpredictability continues to be high) abortion is not only a sad necessity, but a highly moral decision to be taken with full freedom of conscience. I do not understand how you can associate abortion with an idea of hedonism or the good life. Abortion is <a> terrifying thing < . . . >.

In abortion the person who is massacred, physically and morally, is the woman. Also for any man with a conscience every abortion is a moral ordeal that leaves a mark, but certainly here the fate of the woman is in such a disproportionate condition of unfairness compared with the man's, that every male should bite his tongue three times before speaking about such things. Just at the moment when we are trying to make less barbarous a situation which for the woman is truly terrifying, an intellectual <uses> his authority so that women have to stay in this hell. Let me tell you, you are really irresponsible, to say the least. I would not mock the "hygienic-prophylactic measures" so much; certainly you will never have to undergo a scraping of your womb. But I'd like to see your face if they forced you to have an operation in the filth and without any recourse to hospitals under pain of imprisonment. Your "integrity of life" vitalism is to say the least fatuous. For Pasolini to say these things does not surprise me. But I thought that you knew what it costs and what the responsibilities are if you bring other lives into this world.[88]

I am sorry that such a radical divergence of opinion on these basic ethical questions has interrupted our friendship.[89]

[Handwritten draft; in the Calvino Archive (four pages, the last of which is almost entirely scored out). The angled brackets indicate words that are difficult to decipher.]

To Esther Benítez—Dakar (Senegal)

Turin, 28 February 1975

Dearest Esther,

I AM VERY GRATEFUL TO YOU AND I ALSO PITY YOU THE EFFORT you have to make to translate my three novels. I will try to clarify your doubts.

Argalif: I remember that other translators had previously asked me the same question, and I could not remember any more whether I had found the name in some Italian chivalric epic or invented it. The Arabic root is probably the same one that "Kalif" comes from.

A number of strange words in the chapter with the battle come from literary texts, but the only source I remember is the one for "Sozo! Mozo! Escalvao!" which is *Il contrasto con la donna genovese*, a Provençal poetic text from the thirteenth century by Rambaut de Vaqueiras.

Crapa: a very common jocular synonym for "head."

Gian Paciasso, *Gian Paciugo*: names invented by me.[90] "Paciasso": in Piedmontese means "marsh." "Paciugo": in Genoese dialect means "concoction." But my choice here was more based on sound than on sense.

In *The Non-Existent Knight* the names from the chivalric tradition, which is common to both Italy and Spain, should be given in their Castilian form. In general I would say that in this novel where there is nothing Italian, all the names must be Hispanized.

Pervinca [*Periwinkle*] is a blue-purple color, but above all it is a nice word. *Vincapervinca* sounds very nice and I would be almost inclined to allow the Spanish reader to imagine green eyes (which would be just as nice) if that word can sound evocative. Otherwise, indigo or another kind of blue, as long as it has a nice name.

Il visconte dimezzato [*The Cloven Viscount*]. The Argentine translation was entitled *Las dos mitades del vizconde*. The problem with this title is that it gives the game away immediately, in the sense that the reader knows from the start that there are two halves and not just one, as he is led to believe reading the first chapters. *El vizconde partido en dos* has the same flaw, and it is also too long. The French translation is *Le vicomte pourfendu*; it sounds good but is imprecise. The English translation is *The Cloven Viscount*; cloven means maimed and is an ancient attribute of the devil.

Perhaps one could find a solution along those lines, a nice adjective that means only "lame" or "maimed" or "mutilated." *El vizconde tuerto*? This would be an interesting case of metonymy: not "the part for the whole" but "the part for the half" . . .[91]

Scorazzare (more correct than the form *scorrazzare*): means to run here and there for fun (particularly used of children).

Gerbidi: non-cultivated (land).

Uva fragola: this must be something like a muscat grape, with a sweet taste.

Il barone rampante: "rampante" is a heraldic term (as in lion rampant) also in Spanish, I believe. I would leave it as it is.

Please do send all your questions to me and I will do everything possible to answer them.[92]

Very best wishes,

Italo Calvino

[Typed on Einaudi headed paper, with autograph signature; with the addressee. Also in "Correspondencia Esther Benítez / Italo Calvino," *Cuadernos de traducción e interpretación* (Escuela Universitaria de traducción e interpretación, Universidad Autónoma de Barcelona, Bellaterra), 4 (1984), pp. 103–4.]

To Jean-Louis Moreau—Paris

Paris, 29 September 1975

Dear Monsieur Moreau,[93]

I DERIVED GREAT SATISFACTION FROM SEEING MY NAME IN the *Petit Larousse*. I am very grateful to you for the present and for your letter.

I have leafed through the dictionary and admired its riches. I explored particularly the domain of Italian literature, which I found very carefully written.

I would nevertheless like to point out two lacunae for which the next edition can easily make amends. One is the name of Eugenio MONTALE (1896–still living) who deserves the first place amongst Italian poets, he is at least on a par with Ungaretti, and certainly a greater poet than the Nobel Prize–winner Quasimodo, two names that figure rightly in the *Petit Larousse*.

The other name missing is that of Elio Vittorini (1908–1966), who should not be forgotten amongst the writers of the generation of

Moravia, Pavese, Buzzati, Pratolini, all of whom are mentioned in the dictionary.

I know that to add names one also has to remove others. That task is less easy. In the area of Italian literature I found only one name that is not indispensable: that of Alfredo Panzini (1863–1939). (I've got nothing against him, but it is a fact that his books have not been reprinted for thirty years and no critic has bothered about him since.)[94]

Please take these comments as proof of my esteem for the quality of the editors' work in the new *Petit Larousse*, and believe, dear sir, that I send you my heartfelt gratitude.

Italo Calvino

[Typed draft, with autograph corrections and signature; in the Calvino Archive.]

To Carlo Cassola—Marina di Castagneto (Livorno)

[November 1975]

Dear Carlo,

I still have to reply to your letter and about your project.[95]

The first objection that springs spontaneously to mind is that Italian writers already express their thoughts in newspapers in a quantity that is now more copious than ever, and in some cases—for instance, Pasolini—actually excessive. One can see that you do not read the newspaper that you too collaborate on where one <continually> finds Pasolini, Moravia, Ginzburg, Parise, myself (more rarely), just as in *La Stampa* you find Sciascia, Soldati, Siciliano, Arpino. All of these writers continually have their say on politics, manners, morality, ideas etc. What's more, every week *Il Mondo* publishes a large number of the names you mention in your list, each of them speaking as they wish even though within the remit of the particular columns they write for. The feeling that comes across from this—that I believe the man in the street has of it—is that these writers talk too much and there is an inflation of what they really have to say.

However, in your *Proposal*, on pp. 5–, there is a point that characterizes the project and to a certain extent demolishes my objection, namely your polemic against *topical news*, which befuddles us and drowns what is essential in a great sea of news. So the weekly you propose (but why make it a weekly, then? Wouldn't a monthly be enough?) would be a tool for intervening in politics that would bypass topical items in order to deal with the major choices in history, its fundamental problems, the ideas that are always understood but never discussed. While newspapers push writers to intervene in topical news (so much so that the minute I write something that is not immediately topical, I feel it is out of place in the *Corriere*), the periodical you suggest would be the place to rethink problems and ideas that are not bound to the situation of that particular week or month, but to our historical epoch. Your own programmatic piece takes for granted concepts such as *revolution*, for instance: it would be interesting to hear what this really < . . . > means for each of us. In that sense, a space for this kind of discussion does not exist, and your project would seem to make sense.

At this point what becomes crucial is the choice of names. Your list is too broad and heterogeneous to be of much use. And you contradict what you said earlier, by including journalists in it. I am not saying this is wrong, even though you put in names haphazardly, but in that case the distinction between journalists and writers put in those terms does not distinguish anything at all: one cannot say a priori that a writer just because he is a writer is more capable of handling ideas and of seeing what is essential than a journalist when we are dealing with a good journalist.

A weekly or journal like this has to have as editor one person or a group of people who are homogeneous, and then you can draw up a list of collaborators as broad as you like, but unless you have someone who has a hold on the situation, <success> is both organizationally and culturally <unthinkable>.

There are no homogeneous groups, but you and Cancogni are there, and you are old friends and make a good team, and what's more Cancogni has wide experience as a journalist.

If you two together manage to set up a weekly or a monthly journal all the others will follow you, including a skeptic and a doubting Thomas like your old friend

Italo

[Handwritten draft; in the Calvino Archive. The angled brackets indicate words that are illegible or difficult to decipher. The letter can be dated to the beginning of November 1975, as is clear from note 95.]

1976–1980

To Andrea Zanzotto—Pieve di Soligo (Treviso)

Paris, 11.1.76

Dear Zanzotto,

I received your letter and the enclosures with great pleasure. The sonnets cheered me enormously. I approve of this return to closed forms: I believe more and more in the necessity of "contraîntes." I appreciated very much the interlocking rhymes and the steadying hold of the language over the whirligig of the subconscious.[1]

As for your article, your justification of the minimalist, depressive, reductive line, using Hermeticism, cannot but sound convincing to the chronic depressive I have now accepted myself as being.[2] Italy is the depressive country par excellence: only the depressed can be neither charlatans nor liars. Of course the scope of poetry in the rest of the world is different and Hermeticism does seem rather limited compared to everything else that was coming to the boil in world literature at the time, but perhaps we Italians have only that truth there to tell ourselves and others too, that there cannot be any other moral except a de-pressive one, even before a re-pressive one. So much so that the line you suggest as a line of separation could turn out to be a line of unification. There have been few genuine euphorias as opposed to absurd ones: euphoric people (the ones who believe we must be euphoric)—unless they are compulsive liars—end up by keeping silent (like Vittorini, who was the "positive" opposite of Hermeticism, just to take an example from outside poetry, since he has no equivalent in poetry).[3] As for someone who fits exactly your polemical target, I would say there is only Pasolini, the only D'Annunzio figure of our times, as the ideologizer of eros and the eroticizer of ideology, and in the same boat are those who hark back to him either on the ideology side (*Officina*) or on the erotic side (I think Testori might be one, though I have never read him, and others still that I have not read either, let's say the poets from *Nuovi Argomenti*). The Novissimi,[4] on the other hand, if you look at them carefully, turn out to be reductivists, minimalists, especially Sanguineti, I mean in terms of substance, even though he has some ambition to edify in proposing a program of agitation. Nevertheless, his is still a reductivist euphoria, as he retreats into a shell that is all school and family (at one stage I rejected this shell of his, and then I realized that at least in the negative all the outside of that shell was right, if not in hanging on to that shell). In short, even if you don't like it, and he doesn't like it, you and Sanguineti remain brotherly enemies even after this declaration of principle.

And then what other groups have there been? The gnomic Milanese writers are not a group but a "tendency" (one I don't like out of principle), and even they can be grouped under your line because their presumptious attempt at defining a moral code (which is sometimes very irritating) is offset by the reductivism of that code, and often of that language.

But here we should look at a point that you do not deal with, and yet it is relevant to your theme, and this is the lowering of language, colloquial poetry. This is on a macroscopic scale, if for no other reason than that these were the years when Montale started writing poems with a pencil, from *Satura* onwards. And they are great poems and no less "difficult" than those in *Le occasioni* (*Occasions*) but in terms of the politics of language this becomes an endorsement of a lowering of the level of poetic language, and ends up by bringing everything down to the most banal levels and even Bassani's get accepted as poems. (But here we are certainly already far from depression and what that guarantees.) So reductivism works if it is backed up by neurosis, and collectively, as you say, by psychodrama.

But one can also hypothesize depressivity as method and basis, cold depressivity. (In any case in politics, Italy as a depressive country cannot identify with any model outside the Moro-Berlinguer one.)

As you can see, in this period of depression and writer's block which I am going through, which has gone on for some time now and maybe won't ever unblock, I have enjoyed having this silent conversation with you. I hope you will come to Paris and we can see each other.

Yours,

Italo Calvino

[Handwritten; in the Calvino Archive. At the head of the first page is a handwritten note: "an unsent letter (only the first few lines were sent)."]

To Franco Maria Ricci—Milan

Paris, 21.4.76

Dear FMR,

It has been a long time since we were in touch. Last month I was in the USA and I did some lectures on the Tarots. I met John Barth, an admirer of this book from the start—even though he does not read Italian—and a great enthusiast of your publications. He is very kind and friendly and in fact I believe he deserves a present of the English edition of the Tarots.

Then I went to Mexico and traveled a bit all over the country. Amongst other things I saw the works of a painter you perhaps already know, who I think would be perfect for one of your books: ERMENEGILDO BUSTOS, a nineteenth-century painter, a naïf artist in mentality and spirit but with a very sophisticated technique, the Holbein of the popular Mexican portrait who goes in for extraordinary psychological penetration and grotesque portrayals of society. His pictures take up a very well arranged room in the museum of GUANAJUATO, a delightful colonial town north of México City. The Museum Director is a terrible painter but a great collector, José Chavez Morado. It would be worth while you going there. It would make a perfect book and you would certainly find one of the big names in Mexican writing to produce the text for you. You could start asking by talking to Juan Rulfo, who has not written anything since his two extraordinary books, at first because he was drinking and then because he had stopped drinking;[5] but who knows, maybe Bustos's characters might break the spell. If not, then Carlos Fuentes who is now ambassador in Paris. Octavio Paz would be the most prestigious name, but perhaps it is not up his alley.

In Mexico your books are in evidence and well displayed in the Italian bookshop owned by a very intelligent and enterprising man called Angelo Baron, who in November is going to do a big exhibition on the Italian Book. I hope to see you soon.

Italo

[Handwritten; with the addressee. Published in facsimile in Octavio Paz, *Ermenegildo Bustos*, con un saggio di Luis González y González (Milan: Franco Maria Ricci, 1995), p. 13.]

To Carlo Minoia—Milan

Pineta di Roccamare
Castiglione della Pescaia

18.7.76

Dear Dr. Minoia,

I HAVE READ ALL THE LETTERS IN THE TWO GREEN FOLDERS.

I think we can already say that the Vittorini Letters constitute a very rich biography and represent the various phases of his activity.[6]

The beginnings are very well documented thanks to the letters to Carocci which follow his departure from Sicily, his collaboratn. [sic] with *Solaria*, the problems with censorship. (It will be necessary to try to establish and document concisely episodes such as the polemic with Titti Rosa.)[7]

Unfortunately there are only a few letters to Malaparte.

The letters to Solmi are very good, in fact all the letters of the period are interesting.

His letters to Guarnieri form one of the meatiest parts of the correspondence, first because it is about friendship, holidays, girls; then there is the flare-up in Spain, which bursts into life very suddenly, after a dark period ([. . .];[8] the proposal to go off as a volunteer to Ethiopia).

The letters to his family are also of great biographical interest.

For the work letters (Bompiani; *Politecnico*) to Bontempelli, Alvaro, Capitini etc., I have marked yes on the most significant of them. For the others, let's keep them on hold and when we get to the stage of putting the book together we'll see which might be useful in covering any period or phase of his work that is less well documented; otherwise let's leave them out.

The letters during his time on *Politecnico* when it was a weekly, for instance, are not many, but already amongst those present here (to his brother, to his father, to Massimo Mila) there are some which are very representative of this type of work. When we have all the material available we'll work out how to give a basic but representative picture of this type of journalistic editorial work.

There are fewer letters, I think, from the time when *Politecnico* was a monthly (those to Debenedetti; but much more interesting ones to Fortini). We'll have to get by with what we've got.

We will also do a selection of letters to young authors (Pirelli, Del Boca) where the Einaudi and Gettoni archives will be very rich, maybe even too rich.

The crisis with the PC is well documented (and this already gives historical importance to the correspondence) especially with the letters to the French (Mounin, Artaud, Mascolo) but also to Pratolini, Fortini, Steiner, and to his brother Ugo.

There are very interesting letters amongst those to Fortini and Mascolo. Arnaud will have to be pruned a bit. Some interesting things also in the letters to Laughlin and Penn Warren.

Now we need to see them in chronological order, in other words to set up the book. And start the notes.

I will return the two folders of photocopies—on which I have made some notes—as soon as I return to civil society, perhaps not before September.

Best wishes for the summer,

Italo Calvino

[Handwritten; with the addressee.]

To Bob Silvers—New York

Pineta di Roccamare
58043 Castiglione della Pescaia

July 26, 1976

Dear Bob Silvers,[9]

THE PACKAGE WITH YOUR LETTER OF JULY 8TH WAS SENT BY train (not by mail) from Rome to the station which is nearest to my place, and there it stayed several days because a part of address was missing (Pineta di Roccamare), so I finally got it only the 20th. Meanwhile I thought it was too late or too early to rewrite my article:[10] too late as far as elections are concerned, too early as for post-election conclusions. We are still without a government, the new positions of the parties are not yet cleared, and it would be better to wait until we get a more stable vision. But the real question I was wondering was and still is: am I the right person to write the article you need?

Now I read your 12 pages analytical criticism of my piece and I admire even more the way you work. This is the only serious method for editing a magazine. Most part of your criticisms are right and interesting; to some of your questions I could answer, to some others not. But the first problems they raise is how so much informations could be contained in a shorter article. Some of those subjects would need a special article, and by a specialist too.

So much has been written about our economic crisis, but even to resume it I should need a knowledge of economics I haven't. I'm sure, by instance, that Italian economists of all the parties don't find any contradiction between State controlled industry and decentralization, but I'm not able to tell what is the point, nor to decide the right and wrong in that matter.

I think that the Union situation in Italy deserves a special article, because the power Unions have conquered in the last years make Italy different from every else capitalistic country (and even more far from every socialist model, in perspective). The important point, more than the salaries (although their indexation is certainly one of the factors of inflation) is the "Statuto dei Lavoratori" (Workers Constitution) which is perhaps the most advanced in the world (but makes some owners of factories run away to Canada). An article on this matter needs researches and interviews among Union men and owners and managers and economists. You are right saying that "autonomous" unions problem is a minor one, but the Alitalia pilots strike which is mainly a strike against the other Unions (because pilots refuse to be represented in a general contract of all airline categories) is a very interesting sample of the situation, and has something in common with Chilean truck-drivers strike.

The Italian Regional organization is also worth of a special study, but one has to say that the regional reform is moving still its first slow steps: it is still undecided what is the extent of Regional power and what are the sources of Regional financing. As for the cities very exactly you put the problem of the catastrophic shortfalls of cities administrations: till the Town Halls were Christian-Democrat, they were covered by the banks (State banks, still directed by CD men) but no more now that the PC-PS administrators inherited the shortfalls. Narrative aspects on that matter are not difficult to find, but a more technical analysis of the problems is needed too.

I'm wondering how the article you ask could be written by somebody who is not a political writer or a political scholar but a literary fiction writer, who since many years is far from every political activity, who doesn't keep an archive of documentation, and just reads one paper every day, or at most two. (If I think that for my article I should be obliged to read *l'Unità* for some months, I feel so sad that I renounce immediately.)

When you called me before the elections I was puzzled by the kind of writing you could expect from me: how should I conciliate the duties of information with a kind of writing which can justify the choice of my signature? I tried a plain anecdotal way with a sort of conversational commentary. Another kind of article I could try is a sort of gallery of portraits of the main political figures, from Moro and Andreotti to Berlinguer, Pajetta, Amendola, Ingrao. Anyway it is something I never did before, and I'm not sure to succeed. In this kind of portraits Vittorio Gorresio is the real maestro, since the post-war years. Now there is a new generation of political men in their fifties, in PCI but also in PSI and DC, who are still to discover as characters (Berlinguer apart). But I think that this generation (my generation) has less striking features, they look a bit as pale faces.

At moment I feel myself better as somebody who gives suggestions about possible articles than as their author. The most important novelty after the elections is surely the increase of power of Parliament, whose commissions seem to become almost important as Ministries and set off for the weakness of the Government. The nomination of Pietro Ingrao as President of the Chamber of Deputies is important, because Ingrao has always had ideas of his own in order to draw new images of democracy, first as some sort of direct democracy based upon local power and mass organizations, then as reform of the Parliament as a real instrument of control. He is the natural antagonist, inside the party, of Giorgio Amendola who is more the man of traditional parliamentary (Southern) policy, of agreement at the summit, while Ingrao has been always looking for ways of influencing the summits from below. (Ingrao was in the last years a bit in the shade, as head of the defeated left wing of the party, but now maybe Berlinguer, very skillful in composing interior contrasts, succeeded in reintegrating him in the general pattern of his policy.)

Anyway, to understand what PCI is and its roots in Italian society, I think it's necessary to start with a historical survey. Why don't you ask, for instance, to Eric Hobsbawm a review of the 4 volumes Paolo Spriano's *Storia del Partito Comunista Italiano*? Spriano's work ends with 1945, but I think it's necessary to start with this underground prehistory to understand the very important years '45–'48, when the commitment of PCI in drawing the general pattern of Italian democracy was at its best. Because this is the point foreigners often miss: the PCI is not conquering something alien, a democracy constructed by somebody else: the general frame of today's Italian democracy was the first task this Party (although a good deal Stalinist, at the time) committed itself to (always through compromises with Christian Democrats, of course), during the Assemblea Costituente of the new-born Republic (Assembly whose President was a Communist: the old Gramsci's companion Umberto Terracini) and after. This sort of Constitutional primogeniture of PCI explains how for so many years the PCI's program could be just the defense and the actualization of the Constitution ("la Costituzione di Terracini" how is called by the militants).

Beside that there are all the most unattractive aspects of every communist Party and of this one in particular, toughness and ambiguities, dullness and machiavelism, a terrific boredom, but the fact remains that a part of the history of Italian society (and not of the worse) is not understandable without the PCI.

Your remark about my *negative* view of Communists is right, but it is difficult to resume what Italian Communists actually are and want. The important point for me is that once only the left wing of the party could be free from Moscow influence, because the strength it looked for was based in the fight of the masses, while the moderate wing needed to be covered by Moscow authority. The big novelty of the last years is that the moderate wing found strength enough in the victories of its strategy to unify an interior strategy and an international one, without the danger of a pro-Soviet schism. I think that the PCI is still pretty centralist but—this is my very personal point—what I care for is that in the Italian general disintegration it will stay a very disciplined and efficient organization vitally interested in the defense and the development of democracy. (The reasons that made me come near to the Communists during the Resistance were the same; now I'm glad to be far from them but also that they are there.) The problem is not to save the souls of the Italian Communists but to save Italian democracy. So I think it's a waste of time counting how many times they protested for Russian Jews, dissent intellectuals or Polish workers and how many times they didn't. The general trend is the only important thing; the way they deal with, it's their business. You speak also of Middle East policy; there I think they have a more ambitious purpose: to have their own diplomatic relations with Arab movements (at government or at opposition), a Middle East policy I don't know how divergent from the Soviet one. In any case, I think one can't expect from the PCI autonomy in foreign policy any relevant pro-Israeli gesture. What PCI most wishes is to exerce [sic] an influence of his own in what is called the anti-imperialist field; its attitude towards Israel can be seen only in that framework.

Many points you found missing to my article are related to questions I have not an answer for. But this doesn't mean that to find the right answer is not possible.

I realize that I'm writing you a long letter, but not the article, and I am not even telling you if I will write the article or not. The fact is that the only article I could write is this sort of letter, but I'm not satisfied with it because as a reader, as a consumer of journalism, I like only exact information and not chattering columnism. I mean that I share your point of view about what an Italian article of *NYRB* has to be.

Yours sincerely,

Italo Calvino

[Typed copy; in the Calvino Archive.]

To Danièle Sallenave—Angers

[Pineta di Roccamare, September 1976]

OPACO AND *APRICO*

The last part of the text is—I would almost say—a vocabulary exercise.[11] *Aprico* (*sunny*) and *opaco* (*opaque*)—in the sense of *ubac* (*shady*)—are very rare words, which nobody uses any more in Italy when they speak: *aprico* exists only in poetry; whereas no Italian knows that *opaco* can also have the meaning above. I would prefer therefore that more unusual words were used in French as well such as *soulane* and *adret*. The sense of what I have done is to create two categories starting with two ancient, technical words. (I know them only because my father was an agronomist, born in 1875.) For that reason it seems to me that *ensoleillé* is a word that is too much in common usage, like the Italian *soleggiato*; so *opaco* would have to be translated <*ombragé*>. And for *opaco* I would <rather see> *ubac* given that it is so close to the dialect word from which I started (the San Remo dialect is a mixture of Provençal and Genoese dialect but words such as *ubago* and *abrigu* were used by my father who had been born in 1875 but now I think that nobody knows what they mean any more). I would use *opaco* only in the following cases: (a) the first time; (b) every time the dialect word *ubagu* is used; (c) when it is used as an adjective: "revers opaque," "points opaques"; (d) in adverbial form: "opaquement"; (e) at the end; (f) in the title (but *De l'ubac* is also a mysterious title that I would not object to).

For *solatìo* and *bacìo* I would say: "soulane" and "ombrée."

[Handwritten draft, undated; in the Calvino Archive.]

To Gianni Celati—Bologna

Paris, 20 March 77

Dear Gianni,

I RECEIVED YOUR LETTER AND ALSO YOUR COUNTER-REPORT. The only thing on which we agree is the verdict on that book on Conrad.[12] I read it when it had already come out and I got ferociously angry, and remonstrated both with Davico and with Melchiori and with at least one of the two authors. And I rushed to publish *Heart of Darkness* in the Centopagine series, with an introduction that went against those essays.[13]

This time, seeing that I was asked my opinion on a manuscript, I immediately wrote what I felt.

I do not agree with many of the things that you say. But I do not agree now with such a large part of the way so many people think that I no longer find I belong to any discourse and I speak only when asked, on very precise questions.

I recognize that the work you do and what you participate in always has an inner necessity and consistency which are not found in many

other places. I hope that, even when not in agreement, we will remain friends, with you and with Anita.
[Typed copy; in the Calvino Archive.]

To Emma Grimaldi—Salerno

Paris, 18.5.77

Dear Emma Grimaldi,

Thank you for your article on *The Path*. (My thanks are late because I have only just returned to Paris where I found the journal.)[14]

I find your symbolic-sexual interpretations—and let's also say your psychological-moral ones—convincing. You use psychoanalytical criticism with circumspection and without being facile. This is a book which I can discuss with detachment because it is difficult for me to identify with the person who wrote it, now over thirty years ago. But the fact that I have always had a difficult relationship with this book, more so than with any other of my works,[15] takes me back to a time in my youth when there were all the preconditions for a classic neurosis. This despite bearing in mind that in the psychoanalytical reading of a work one never knows to what extent one is analyzing the author or the literary code he is using, tied as that is to stereotypes of the period. But let's also say that the choice of a code (exaggerated fear of sex was at that time a typical element in fiction—Faulkner's *Sanctuary* had been translated, I think, in that very year '46) tells us something about the relationship one enters into with one's neuroses. This is even more the case in the first work by a young author who is very immature also in literary terms.

I am happy to have read your essay and feel your work is very serious in its approach.

Italo Calvino

The symbolic interpretations that draw on Bachelard, on the other hand, seem to me to be more generic.
[Handwritten; with the addressee; photocopy in the Calvino Archive.]

To Antonella Peruffo—Pisa

Turin, 26 May 1977

Dear Antonella Peruffo,

I've read your thesis. It seems to me well documented (you have managed to find articles that I had completely forgotten about) and balanced. The historical thread that runs through your work seems to show how a young man at the end of the forties tries to find his way in the worlds of politics and literature.

One must bear in mind—and it should be said explicitly—that that young man was at the time highly ignorant, both in politics and literature, in other words he really should have spent years studying and understanding things in both fields before spewing out opinions with such pomposity. (And also with a rather primitive spirit of factionalism.)

In this sense the ideal thing would be to follow even within the brief period studied the hints if not of maturity, at least of a progressive loss of immaturity, let's say between the writings of '46 and those of '51 or '52.

You highlight very well, especially when analyzing the fictional works, not just the rational determination, but also the huge amount of insecurity that also emerges.

By the way, I think this is the first time that *I giovani del Po* (*Youth in Turin*) has been the object of such a close reading. In short: I thought that when I read an analysis of such a raw image of myself it would have been more *painful*. Instead, I believe that what I was doing was understandable both in historical and individual terms. I don't know what else to say to you: I am too close to the material.

The meticulousness of your research and the attention you pay to the texts prove how much you are capable of doing in the field of historical-critical studies of contemporary literature.

I am returning your thesis with warmest gratitude.

(Italo Calvino)

[Typed letter; photocopy in the Calvino Archive.]

To Franco Fortini—Milan

Paris, 3 June 77

Dear Fortini,

Your letter gave me enormous pleasure. You were one of the ideal readers of those pages—even when I was writing them—and I was very keen to have your verdict.[16] You are one of the few people with whom I continue to have a dialogue—even without us talking or writing to each other—and I have to say that I find myself disagreeing with you less often than in the past.[17] So I quite understand your criticism of my lead articles—which already earned me a lot of criticism from so many friends. The noble father is certainly not a role that satisfies me—and I still envy those people who manage to be witty and light despite being in the midst of the hurricane, something I have not managed to do for some time (I say the hurricane but I know well that it is maybe the complete opposite: stagnant water over shallow, silted up sandbanks)—but the fact is that when writing about topical subjects the strongest urge I have is to talk of the non-topical, distant topics, perhaps to distance myself as much as possible from those who want to stay on the crest of the latest wave at all costs. But I certainly express things better when I am silent, and I end up being dissatisfied with myself all the same.

Best wishes,
Yours,

Calvino

It will be even worse when—soon—the wave of "new philosophers" which is now rampant in France extends to Italy, philosophers of the ineluctability and inevitability of "power," who churn out a Chateaubriand-style prose to celebrate their late discovery of the Gulags, their disappointment with Maoism, the defeat of "desire," while relaunching a spiritualistic religiosity which is just so much rhetoric, just like their Maoism and Althusserism of yesteryear.

[Handwritten; in the Franco Fortini Archive, Siena; also in Italo Calvino—Franco Fortini, "Lettere scelte 1951–1977," ed. Giuseppe Nava and Elisabetta Nencini, *L'ospite ingrato*, Annuario del Centro Studi Franco Fortini (Macerata: Quodlibet, 1998), p. 118.]

To Pirkko-Liisa Ståhl—Helsinki

Turin, 14 September 1977

Dear Miss Ståhl,

I found your letter of 25 August on my return from holidays. I will try to answer your questions.[18]

1. The Nobel Prize plays a role that cannot be underestimated: it is the only institution that is universally acknowledged which establishes literary values *on a global scale* for authors who write in different languages and who come from different traditions. As with all prizes, a certain number of arbitrary decisions are inevitable, but one should ensure that the mistakes also have a significance. It is pointless to bring up the cases of top-class writers who have not received the Prize (there is a *longevity* factor that plays a part) or the cases of the Nobel Prize being awarded to second-class writers while there were more important ones still around (this is particularly serious for "minor" literatures to which the Nobel Prize is awarded at intervals of more than ten years). The accusations leveled at the Nobel Prize in the past—of rewarding careers that were already established officially, and of taking more account of explicit and universally accepted moral content than of more original and harder ideas communicated through the specific means of literary expression—is less justified today, especially after the award of the Prize to a difficult and isolated writer like Samuel Beckett. Similarly the award of the Nobel to Eugenio Montale, even though it came late, is proof that the Prize can play a very useful role in making proper literary values known to the whole world.
2. We should keep alive the idea of a world literature as a whole in which the "minor" literatures must be considered on a level with the "major" ones, and not have a mechanical rotation along United Nations' lines, but taking account only of what is an original

contribution to world literature. And a very rigid scale of values should be adopted as far as quality is concerned, but it should also be flexible enough to accommodate all the manifestations of the art of writing and of the *global* discourse that literature articulates.

3. For those of us who are not Scandinavian, the Scandinavian jury brings both the advantages and limitations of distance. All things considered, I believe that the advantages—in other words the guarantee of being removed from internal polemics and from the rivalry between the publishers of French, American, German etc. literature—are more important than its limitations. The best system would be for the Scandinavian jury to make use of an international, widespread, and differentiated network of advisers (but one that is tied as little as possible to "official" structures).
4. In the last few months Raymond Queneau and Vladimir Nabokov have died, and these are both writers I would have gladly seen receive the Nobel Prize.
5. Amongst the writers who are already recognized as being first rate and who have not yet received the Prize are Borges and Henry Miller. Amongst Italian writers one should not forget Alberto Moravia, for his entire oeuvre, which began in 1929. Of course this would be one of those cases where the Nobel rewarded a largely popular success, but it would be unjust to exclude on these grounds a writer who has thoroughly merited international recognition. At the same time the Nobel ought to seek out writers who are not well enough known, like the Austrian Thomas Bernhard who already has the stature of a Nobel writer. Another correct and courageous choice would be the Mexican writer Juan Rulfo, who is also of Nobel quality even though he has only written two books in his life, but this is in fact a proof of his seriousness.

I apologize once more for the delay, and I am very grateful to you for the kind things you said.

Best wishes,

(Italo Calvino)

[Typed copy; in the Calvino Archive.]

To Guido Calogero—Rome

Turin, 19 September 1977

Dear Professor Calogero,

Your letter of 16 August traveled far and wide with four changes of address before finally reaching me here in Turin. (But I'll be staying here only for a few days: my next address will be: 12, Square de Châtillon, Paris 14[e].)

It is a great pleasure to know that you have read my work with such empathy and attention. (The only wrong you do me is to think that I might not be able to remember who Prof. Calogero is.)

In my article of 15 August, "Gli uomini giusti con le cose giuste" (The Right Men with the Right Things), what you reject is precisely the argument I was keenest on: the man-things continuity, the way in which society, culture is reflected in the things it produces.[19] And I specifically mentioned "objects, tools, buildings, spaces, and similarly signs, representations, writing." (Unfortunately a technical error replaced "buildings"—a crucial element in my idea—with a nonsensical "therefore.")

That it is the use we make of things that is right or wrong—as you remind me—independently of the qualities of those things, still remains true. But our certainty about the neutrality and innocence of things seems to me to have been impaired for a long time now, at least from Rousseau onwards, or rather from before then, from the moment the concept and mode of civilization was called into question, and one saw the values of a culture in its remains, archeological or otherwise, in other words from the time when objects became historicized.

After that, throughout the whole of the nineteenth century, utopians and aesthetes, from Fourier to Ruskin and Morris, rejected the ugliness of contemporary civilization as expressed in urban design and everyday objects, and proposed not only different usage but different things (and houses). This line continues into our own century with the Bauhaus, industrial design etc. Of course these projects were flawed from the outset because of their utopian claim that changing the shape of things changes the world. But trying to read in objects the dilemma of our condition does not seem to me to be a mistaken idea.

So you can see that it was not only institutions that I was thinking of as "right or wrong things" but *things* themselves and that thing par excellence that is the *city*.[20]

(My last book *Invisible Cities*, 1972, is concerned to a large extent with these themes.) In short, what I am saying is something quite obvious and which you will experience each time you leave the house: today's Rome, ridden with property-speculation, bears within it the imprint of the sum of injustices from which it springs, independently of the use one makes or will make of it.

I hope to have clarified my ideas to you if not to have convinced you. I am grateful and happy to have had this discussion.

With all my deferential respect and friendship,
Yours,

Italo Calvino

[Typed on Einaudi headed paper, with autograph signature; in the Archivio Centrale dello Stato, Rome.]

To Daniele Ponchiroli—Viadana (Mantua)

Paris 14 October 77

Dear Daniele,

Thank you very much for the information about Giovanni Rossi and my father.[21] I was completely unaware of this relationship between the two men (moreover, it was only recently I heard about this character Rossi: either in a review of this book, or at one of the Einaudi Wednesday meetings: maybe this was a book that had come as a proposal to Einaudi?). I do not remember ever hearing my father mention him, but then his name was not such as to stick in my memory.

Last month while at San Remo I discovered several letters and newspapers from that period in the house: the next time I go, I'll check if there are any letters or information about Rossi. And I'll get hold of the book immediately.

Maybe it was Rossi who introduced my father to the Russian astronomer Lebenzeff who was hanged as a revolutionary in St Petersburg in 1908 using my father's name, because he had given him his passport.[22] For this episode, which became a cause célèbre, I still have the newspaper clippings from the time, with the conflicting bits of news that came out each day. And I also remember snippets of things my father recalled about it.

Then in 1909 my father left for Mexico.

There is a strange phrase in your letter, that "late for me." What the hell does that mean? From now on I'll call you the late-for-me man!

Best wishes to you and yours from all of us here.

Italo

You didn't show up this year either. Next summer I'll come to see you (if it's not late for me, of course).

[Handwritten on Einaudi headed paper; with the addressee's heirs.]

To Natalia Ginzburg—Rome

Paris 2 Nov. 77

Dear Natalia,

I'VE READ "FAMIGLIA" (FAMILY) AND I LIKED IT VERY MUCH.[23] There is in it the music of events, the rhythm of the private life of so many people in our times, the fragility of relationships, partnerships that are established and then dissolved, people looking for or avoiding each other, in pursuit of something though no one knows what it is because of the collapse of all models of how to live together. This is a story that catches well the way we live now, better even than *Caro Michele* (*Dear Michael*) where the allusions to topical events were more external. And it is one of your best stories with this thing that only you know how to do, piling up events and relationships across time which produce a general sense that is also the shape existence takes—something you managed already in *Le voci della sera* (*Voices in the Evening*)—and with constant humor, which emerges in the precise observations that stand out from the everyday greyness. And it is very well constructed with this encroaching sense of plunging into the void which takes hold at precisely the right moment in order to assess all the little events as values in life and it manages to say this with a lyrical or musical effect that one cannot express in other words. It is life defined in the perspective of death, which is the only way to define life. I've not yet read "Borghesia" but I did not want to delay giving you these initial impressions of mine. I'm not sure about these titles. "Famiglia" is certainly a significant title, I mean it is significant that this story is called "Famiglia," in the sense that the Einaudi *Encyclopedia* could under the entry "Family" refer to this story as a point of reference for the situation today in a significant phase of Western civilization. In this sense "Famiglia" is better than "The Window on Via del Vantaggio" or any other title that springs to mind. I would really like the title "Ciaccia Oppi" but it would not make sense.[24] "Borghesia" as a title frightens me a bit but before judging I need to read it.

Here it is raining and we have been without the telephone for three days and no one knows when it can be fixed because the cable on the wall has perished and they'll have a hellish job to do there. Being without the phone gives a frightening sense of isolation, even though all I get from the telephone are annoyances, like Di Bella who immediately asks me to write a lead article and I don't want to write for newspapers for a while and want to delay every decision—basically thank goodness the telephone is broken.[25]

Best wishes,

Calvino

[Handwritten; with the addressee's heirs.]

To Natalia Ginzburg—Rome

Paris 6 Nov. 77

Dear Natalia,

I'VE READ "BORGHESIA" AND I LIKED IT A LOT TOO, BUT NOT AS much as the other story, it hasn't got its music, its density, its enjoyment.[26] Here what emerges very clearly is the meaning of the place that animals have in the emotional void of life today, the function of animals as a substitute for what has been lost. Already in the installments I had read in the *Corriere*, I was struck by the beautiful phrase "dolori di specie povera" (poor sorts of pain).[27] This is a much bleaker story than the other because in "Famiglia" there was the value of life seen in the awareness of death, whereas here everything collapses toward death, there is nothing more to cling on to. In addition, here there is something that seems to me to be a particular flavor of our times, namely a widespread weakness and sadness in the young, young people as empty sacks, repeated in Aldo and Emanuele. I now understand the title in the same sense as "Famiglia": just as the latter portrays what stands in place of the family that no longer exists, so "Borghesia" represents the void that stands in place of the bourgeoisie. Taken in this way, I'm not against the title even though I do not really like the fact that it is connected to that song, as though it gave the song a particular value.[28] I realize that here, as in "Famiglia," songs have the function of representing the ideological mush in which we are immersed, but the great merit of these two stories is that they portray a world that cannot think about itself without using a crazy intellectual jargon, they portray it outside of that language, as though that jargon did not exist.

Best wishes,

Calvino

I've also read *Fratelli* (*Brothers*) and find it extraordinary.[29]
[Handwritten; with the addressee's heirs.]

To Guido Neri—Bologna

Paris 31.1.78

Dear Guido,

I was very pleased to get your letter. That's how to write a letter, just like in the days when people really did write letters, even though it did not quite make up for the time that has gone by without us seeing each other. I will try to reply to your various points as ideas come to me.

I am very happy with your reading of "La poubelle" in that anthropological Leirisian mode. That story forms part of a series of autobiographical texts which in texture are more like essays than fiction, texts which mostly exist only in the sense of something I intend to write, and partly in versions I am still not satisfied with, and which one day will maybe form a book which might be called *Passaggi obbligati* (*Staging Posts*).

This however is not the series of texts on the Ligurian landscape—"Dall'opaco" ("From the Opaque")—which instead should be made up of more geometrical-descriptive pieces with a more disciplined language—and those texts there will also form a book but one which basically I still have to write.

On the other hand, the hyper-novel I have been working on or trying to work on for a year now (but the first outline for it was three years ago) is in the mysterious, attractive narrative style, but structured in a very complicated way, which means I am constantly stuck and in crisis trying to make it work on the level of structure and on the level of the writing, and always afraid that I am just wasting time in a game which is not worth the candle. It is called *Incipit*,[30] the protagonist is the reader, addressed in the second person, and the reader is trying to read a novel which enthuses him but his reading is always interrupted for some reason or another and when he goes back to his reading he finds another novel which engages him even more, and the book contains N beginnings of novels (maybe 12 or 10) representing so many types of novel styles or rather of ways in which novels are read. It will also include the reflections on reading that you and I and Gianni had ten years ago, but here it will all be on the level of the average reader.[31] In short, once more I am trying to construct a machine which won't stand up and in order to make it work I am complicating it more and more and this has been my neurosis since the time of the Tarot book.

Interview: in that one in *Il Resto del Carlino* I didn't manage to say anything because the interviewer did not stimulate me. Instead there was one in *Paese-sera* on 7 January which is very much an interview in which I say something, I think.[32] I would send it to you but I wouldn't want to be without a copy. If you can't get hold of that issue, the next time I go to Italy I'll try to get it photocopied.

I have stayed in touch with Gianni by letter since he, shall we say, "changed" and I was glad to find him on the mend. Now I have seen him again recently in Paris, passing through on his way from London ten days ago and he seemed to me to be a bit troubled inside.

I see Claudio Rugafiori nearly every week. He has had a very bad time in terms of health because after being poisoned by the anti-asthma cortisone, he had kidney blockage and had to go to the hospital every week to have them unblocked. But the most awful thing is his sight: he has lost the sight in one eye definitively, it seems, and he's been in danger of losing the other one too. He's had to abandon the Chinese because of the strain on his sight and he has to restrict his hours of reading. He recently edited a reprint of *Le grand Jeu* for a publisher of reprints called J.-M Place, and now he'll do a boxed set of Mallarmé (plus other editions of Daumal and company) and is very preoccupied with the philological problems surrounding Mallarmé which he says are all wrong in Mondor's edition for La Pléiade.

I saw Giorgio in Rome during the holidays and as well as "Il Presepio," he also gave me his essay on Experience, full of very interesting things, which he would like to become a book.[33] To have him taken on as a publishing adviser Einaudi would need to see him the next time he goes to Rome, to get to know him a bit. That was what we agreed with Einaudi and Roscioni who was meant to set the thing up, but it's true that the distance between him and the atmosphere in the publishing house is so great that it's doubtful if he'll manage to bring it off.

Of course the journal is a fine thing, but it would be one where the only person writing would be Giorgio while the other potential contributors like you, me and Roscioni or Rugafiori, would never write anything. Secondly, such a review would be very out of place in an environment like Einaudi and in any case even if Einaudi wanted to do it, the publishing house would in its possessive spirit try to turn it into the house journal (for which it feels a need) and so it would be something else. My advice is that Giorgio does the journal, getting a printer to print it, then we could all contribute a bit, and when the journal definitely exists he will certainly find a publisher who wants to distribute it. And in any case I am the last person that can be counted on to undertake an initiative like this and to take it forward. Recently I came across the documents of the discussions I had with you and Gianni in '68–'69 and I thought that it was a real crime not to have done that journal then and what was wrong was that you were confident in my having a role as its promoter, whereas I am only able to say "but . . .".[34] (And Vittorini used to say that I was useful to him precisely for that reason, when he was asked why on earth he involved me in his initiatives.)

I very much appreciated the fact that you acted as publisher and presenter of your student Muschitiello (who seems to me to have an authentic voice) and I liked the reflections on poetry you put in the foreword to his book.[35]

I very much hope you will come back to Paris while I am still here. I think that renting an apartment is expensive and also difficult to find. The best thing is for you to get Ippolito to allow you to stay—he's never here—and I think he's happy to lend his flat to friends in order not to have it always closed up.[36]

I don't know how much longer we will manage to live here in Paris, in economic terms I mean. The worse things get in Italy the more I'll be forced to take the family back there. Here we get by because Chichita has some work every now and again, otherwise with the lire that are halved in value when converted into francs (and what's more you can't transfer them and even if that were possible it's a horrific waste seeing them halved in value like that), and with the cost of living becoming higher and higher, I actually cannot support my family, even though I hardly ever go out, we never go to a restaurant etc. (And I stay in Italy as much as possible: I spent much more of 1977 in Italy than in Paris.)

I followed events in Bologna week by week listening to people of all sorts who had observed or been involved in them.[37] I appreciated the fact that you managed carry out useful work.

On a separate sheet I'll reply to the questions relating to publishing.

I very much hope that I will not have to wait too long to get another letter from you. And even more to see you. Chichita and Giovanna also send their best wishes

Italo

PUBLISHING MATTERS

The problem now with Turin is that there is no longer a contact to go to for all the problems. Naturally the departure of Davico makes everything more complicated. But Carena who is in charge of the whole section dealing with classics is very efficient and active and it would be good if you could regard as many of your authors as possible as classics in order to have him in charge of them.

SCHWOB—a few years ago I was about to do *Les Vies imaginaires* when Adelphi beat me to it. And Ricci has done *La Croisade des enfants*. I don't know *Le Roi au masque d'or* but in principle I'd be very much in favor. If you can follow Muschitiello's translation closely I would say to get the thing going. Meanwhile I'll try to get hold of the book.

PAULHAN—if you want to prepare an outline of the volume, as long as the translation is useable (have you contacted that woman?), excellent. I can't say I've read them: I tried some of them but I wouldn't say they conveyed anything to me. On the other hand, I've read *The Death of Groethuysen* and I was really taken by it and I think it could form a book on its own. (In the Einaudi Letteratura series? Pity the Piccola Biblioteca Adelphi belongs not to Einaudi but Adelphi.)

VALÉRY—of course I'd like to write the introduction, first spending a year studying these works.[38] But in the meantime I need to revise the Queneau essays which have already been delivered to Bogliolo and write the introduction. When will I do it? I hope in the course of this year. Then I'll think about tackling Valéry. Meanwhile please keep nagging Turin so they give Panaitescu the help he deserves. Who should you talk to about it? I don't know, try Carena, but also Bollati. You'll have to be very insistent. I'll keep on at them too.

DARIEN—it would be great if you could give me something of Darien for the Centopagine series. Also this Zola you mention (I don't know it).

PETERNOLLI—it seems to me that what he is doing is something that is at last serious and useful, or rather essential, given the crisis of translators, and I hope I've made the publishing house sensitive to this. In other words, I've put him in touch with Carena for the classics and with Ferrero for contemporary literature. The problem is that on the spur of the moment there was no particular title to suggest to him that would be interesting for them and for us, so that is why I advised him to contact you as well. We suggested that Simon book to him because apparently it had not been assigned to anyone; it's up to you to decide what's best. I agree about what the contract and fee should be: I had already suggested as much to him.

SELVATICO ESTENSE—I don't know anything about this manuscript.

MIZZAU—have the proposal sent to Turin and also to me if you think it appropriate.

QUENEAU—Q's complete works will be published in 3 volumes by La Pléiade though we don't yet know who will edit them. The first issue of *Temps Mêlés II* will come out: this is the first in a series of issues dedicated to Queneau (it's the continuation of a journal with that title that's been coming out for the last 25 years, published at Verviers, but I don't know anything about it). It is run by André Blavier who it seems has set up a Centre de Documentation Raymond Queneau in the central library in Verviers. Addresses: André Blavier, Place du Général Jacques 23, 48000 Verviers (Belgium).

This is all written on a brochure.

The main expert on the Queneau bibliography is: Claude de Rameil, rue Carnot 6, 92300 Levallois (France).

As for Q's family, there is only his son Jean-Marie who is a painter.
[Handwritten; with the addressee's heirs.]

To Guido Almansi—Norwich

Paris 27.2.78

Dear Guido,

The fox-hedgehog system would lead me to very different classifications from yours.[39] If the hedgehog is the writer who has one unshakeable conceptual and stylistic unity, whereas the fox adapts his strategy to the circumstances, Moravia is a hedgehog in that he is tenaciously consistent with himself whatever he writes, both in terms of poetics and of his vision of the world. Whereas I change my method and field of reference from book to book because I can never believe in the same thing two times running, therefore I am a fox, even though I dream of being a hedgehog in all my dreams, and even though I try to write hedgehog books if you take each of them one by one. Pasolini is a fox, yes, because he adopts different strategies (worldly novels written in dialect, poems with the virtuoso effects of classical rhetoric) but he is also a hedgehog (and not a super-fox) because in all his incarnations his conceptual world is at its core compact and unchangeable. It seems to me that your classification tends to be polarized along the extrovert-introvert axis and in my view this is beside the point.

Gadda is a hedgehog, I'd say, if it is the case that one can reconstruct his unitary philosophy as Roscioni has done, and even his plurilingualism is a consistent not a contradictory system. It's more difficult classifying poets: Ungaretti I'd say is a hedgehog, Montale too, though with unexpected vulpine moments, but here I'm not so sure.

Maybe the system doesn't work with contemporary Italian authors. I see that I am tempted to define as "hedgehogness" the limited means used (which can also be a strength, in that it is an immersion in one's own nature) and to see experimentalism as "foxness" (which can be motivated by serious anxieties) but maybe that is not the way that

Berlin's move should be understood—his system works for the great classics and defines categories of greatness and not limits: the hedgehog must know "one *big* thing" and the fox must identify with the Shakespearean variety of the world.

Ciao,

Italo

[Handwritten; in the Archivio della Radio della Svizzera Italiana, Lugano Besso (and a handwritten draft in the Calvino Archive).]

To Daniele Ponchiroli—Viadana (Mantua)

Pineta di Roccamare
58043 Castiglione della Pescaia

3 July 1978

Dear Daniele,

Instead of *Incipit* I could use as the title for the book a typical opening phrase from a nineteenth-century novel, for instance:

If a Traveler at Nightfall

What do you think? It is difficult to find anything briefer because it has to convey a hint of suspense.[40]

This kind of title harks back to the moment when I had the first idea for this book: next to my desk I had a Peanuts poster with Snoopy the dog typing and the phrase "It was a dark and stormy night . . ."

Best wishes,

Italo

[Handwritten; with the addressee's heirs.]

To Michele Rago—Rome

Castiglione della Pescaia 12.8.78

Dear Michele,

I READ YOUR ARTICLE WITH GREAT INTEREST. YOUR INTERpretations of the Eurydice myth, its literary fortunes and my reversal of it are relevant and very sophisticated.[41] Precisely because my text develops lyrical and polyvalent images following their own internal logic, it lends itself to many kinds of reading. The crucial point in your discourse where you consider the two possible symbolic ways of reading "the deep," the psychological and the historical, and you opt for the historical reading, is convincing. The network of allegories you weave around the images allows a dialog to take place between my story and your political discourse (which is very serious and important in itself) where both sides bring something of their own to the dialog: in your case a post-1968 general examination of conscience.

The only point which I feel your analysis does not take account of is that the representation of the subterranean world does not come from myth or the lyrical-unconscious imagination, but is meant to be "scientific." In other words it is meant to correspond to the various zones of the cross-section of the earth (the mantle, core etc.) and to the phases of the earth's formation. This story, written still in the wake of *Cosmicomics*, had like those other stories a background of scientific reading behind it: in this case geology seismology vulcanology.

As for the best outcome in terms of publishing both things, I am not yet in a position to say. Since my story was originally intended to accompany Matta's drawings, that remains the most appropriate solution. Otherwise doing a small self-standing volume of my text and yours would only highlight the disproportion between my 10 pages and your 34. But the real reason why the idea does not convince me is that if it comes out in a small volume that seems to come from my initiative and not from a publishing occasion, it would look as if it was I who was imposing on the reader the importance you attribute to this story (and which for me was a nice surprise, and it convinced me as I reread my own text). It would seem that I was inviting the reader to read the most committed meanings into this story.

This would not happen if my story came out in a book of short stories of mine and at the same time or shortly afterwards your article appeared in a volume of your essays. In this case your important critical discourse—even though it draws its origins and its conclusion from my text—would be presented with its own autonomy, which would also justify its length. In order to go down this route I would need to have other similar stories ready (already your verdict is encouraging me to think along those lines), and probably you would have the same problem.

In short, I'll think about it and let you know.

I saw that in the first volume of the enormous and slightly crazy *La sapienza dei Greci* (*The Wisdom of the Greeks*) by Giorgio Colli, which Adelphi has recently published, there is a huge section devoted to Orpheus and I looked to see if I could find some new elements to update your bibliography. But it seems to me that here we are far from our theme (that book deals with Orpheus the poet, who perhaps really did exist, the founder of Orphism): however, there is the tradition that Orpheus was the author of a hymn on the rape of Kore-Proserpina, which would establish a link between the two myths.

We were pleased to have you here with Ninetta and I hope to see you both soon. Meanwhile thank you very much.

Italo

[Handwritten; with the addressee.]

To Daniele Ponchiroli—Viadana (Mantua)

Pineta di Roccamare
Castiglione della Pescaia

15.8.78

Dear Daniele,

THANKS FOR THE CROSSWORD.

My book is going one step forward and one step backwards, like Penelope's web.

I'm still not sure about the title.

If a Traveler at Nightfall seems too much of a mouthful and too difficult to remember. I had thought of something simpler along the same lines:

It Was a Moonless Night

I've now had the idea for a different kind of title:

Under False Pretenses

What do you think?

Best wishes to all of you

Italo

[Handwritten; with the addressee's heirs.]

To Angelo Tamborra—Rome

Pineta di Roccamare
Castiglione della Pescaia

20 August 1978

Dear Prof. Tamborra,

THANK YOU VERY MUCH FOR THE PAGES FROM YOUR BOOK where you talk about the case of the "fake Calvino."[42]

The stolen passport was the official version of the facts that my father gave to the authorities who suspected him of being complicit with the Russian revolutionary. In fact my father had given his passport to the astronomer Lebedintzev to allow him to get back to Russia secretly.

When Lebedintzev was arrested in Russia under the name of Mario Calvino and the "Calvino Case" broke in the international press, my father went into hiding so that the campaign could be launched for the Italian government to intervene on behalf of this "citizen,"

When the attempts to stop him being executed failed, my father made his appearance at a conference of agricultural technicians in Rome, causing a huge sensation. He was summoned by the minister Tittoni to whom he explained the case in the "official" version.

My father had in fact had offers to go to Georgia to teach olive-growing, and that was why he had obtained a passport with a visa for Russia. I don't know whether this Lebedintzev was involved in these negotiations or whether, as seems more likely, my father had said so to justify his relations with the Russian revolutionary and his version of the disappearance of the passport. The most likely reconstruction of what happened seems to me that when the Georgia project did not come off, my father found himself in possession of a passport for Russia, and decided to make it available to Russian revolutionaries.

My memories of how my father told this story are unfortunately fragmentary and confused. I don't know how Lebedintzev came to know my father. He talked of him as a rather naïve idealist, who when in Paris had fallen into the hands of a Tzarist agent-provocateur, who had given him a bomb hidden in a book for an attempt on the Tzar's life, but the bomb was immediately discovered by the Tzarist police as soon as the Calvino impostor set foot in Russia. This is what I remember of how my father told the story when I was a boy.

On the other hand, I have no idea about the political environment where the idea could have been hatched to allow the Russian astronomer to take the identity of a Ligurian agronomist. Although my father (1875–1951) had been an anarchist or close to the anarchists when he was a student at Pisa, I think that at the time of the "Calvino Case" he could have been defined as a reforming socialist. His closest friends were his fellow-citizen Orazio Raimondo, a famous lawyer and socialist member of parliament, and Giovanni Canepa, the editor of *Il Lavoro*, who was also a native of our area. In short, the environment was that of Masonic socialists; and I note that Lebedintzev had connections with free-masonry, according to evidence given in your book.

Once my father told me (in the last years of his life) that he had sent his passport to Switzerland; and he wondered whether it wasn't Lenin who had acted as the go-between. From this bit of evidence, I would deduce that his relationship with Lebedintzev came about through an organization.

I remember other stories my father told me about being followed after his name had appeared in the international press. At Porto Maurizio he was under close watch not just by the Italian police but also by unknown characters that he thought belonged to the Tzarist police.

The "Calvino Case" rekindled hostilities against my father in conservative and clerical circles (he was someone who was very typical of those times: he was an apostle of agrarian education, founder of oil-press cooperatives, editor of the journal *L'Agricoltura Ligure*, and staunchly anti-clerical). Life in Porto Maurizio became difficult for him and in 1909 he left for Mexico, where he had been offered the post of Director of the Mexican Agronomy Institute. He stayed in Mexico until 1917, taking part in the first phase of the Revolution with Madero, but then settled in Cuba and later returned to San Remo in 1925 (where his friend Orazio Raimondo had died, leaving his land and property so that my father could found an experimental institute in floriculture they had planned together).

I recently discovered in our house in San Remo the clippings from the newspapers of 1908 with the ongoing news and theories on the "Calvino Case" up to the execution of the martyr and discovery of his false identity. If they might be of use to you, I can let you have photocopies.

I remember an Italian novel that came out in the Thirties (*Borea* by Noemi Carelli) on the Russian exiles in Italy, which talked about the Calvino impostor (it said that the passport was stolen from my father in a train).

This is more or less all I know. My father told many stories when I was young and I was not able to understand and hang on to the details that were most interesting in historical terms. When he got older he talked much less; I had the idea of making him talk in detail about his adventurous life (that could have given me material for more than one novel!) but I delayed too long in carrying out this plan also because I was no longer living in San Remo and I rarely saw him. At the age of seventy-five he had an attack of thrombosis and it was already too late. I've been left with the remorse of not having collected his memoirs.

Recently I learned from Rosellina Gosi's book that Giovanni Rossi,[43] who had already founded an anarchist branch in Brazil, was in

Porto Maurizio in those very years: my father had invited him to work with him in his peripatetic Chair (I later discovered that the Tuscan anarchist had worked on my father's journal as far back as his Brazil years) and I wondered whether it was not through Rossi that my father got to know the Russian revolutionary.

Certainly it would be worth studying the whole story in depth, in the Russian and Italian archives. I am at your complete disposal for what it is in my power to do.

Thank you very much and best wishes,
Yours,

Italo Calvino

[Typed letter with autograph signature; with Luca Baranelli, who thanks Prof. Angelo Tamborra for presenting him with the original copy of the letter.]

To Guido Neri—Bologna

Turin, 19 September 1978

Dear Guido,

I HEARD THE NEWS ABOUT YOUR HEALTH FROM FRIENDS AND I was a bit worried, but I know that you have now made a complete recovery. Please send me your news.

I started Paulhan's stories only the other day. I read *Progrès en amour assez lents* (*Progress in Love on the Slow Side*) and I find it extraordinary.[44] He has a clarity that no one else has ever managed to achieve in seeing everything that happens when you are young: this extreme sensitivity in the coolness and clearness of his observation seems to me something that is unparalleled. After reading this, everything else seems false and conventional (even Proust!). I had only glanced at Paulhan before and seeing that they were all stories set in the country, in the French countryside, I had decided that he didn't interest me and instead . . . Now

I will read the rest as well, but this story alone would justify the whole volume on its own.

Have you got the translation? Did you ever write to that woman, whose name I can't remember? Maybe given that I've let a couple of years go by without replying to her, she'll have sent the proposal to another publisher.

Write to me with news about yourself. I'm fine. I'm writing but I don't know. I saw Gianni this summer.

Best wishes,
Yours,

Italo

Chichita phoned me last night and summarized the contents of your letter which arrived in Paris yesterday. You are in my thoughts and I send best wishes for the operation. I hope to see you soon in Paris.
[Typed letter on Einaudi headed paper, with autograph signature and postscript; with the addressee's heirs.]

To Franco Fortini—Milan

Turin 7 May 1979
(immediately after our telephone call)

Dear Fortini,
THE REASONS FOR MY FEELINGS OF DISTANCE FROM YOUR book on *The Dogs* can be quickly listed and I may as well say them to you now, since we've never mentioned them before.[45] They bear on something very deep and which has never been completely resolved: the relationship with one's father. I could also call them reasons that make me feel close to you, but that is also why they hurt. My father too was an old free-mason (born in 1875); his past, his values, his rhetoric all made him an anachronistic figure in Fascist Italy. My father too reached some compromises with the regime, not all of which were

dictated by necessity, and the only thing he got from them was unpleasantness and further confirmation of his status as an outsider. Then in the German period, cruel persecutions. Like you, but differently from you, I grew up having to come to terms with the good sides and the darker sides of this past. (Even though our conditions were much less ominous since we were not Jewish.) In your book I found, in a story that is in part also my own story, a pietas and also a ruthlessness different from the pietas and ruthlessness with which I look at my own father and the failure of the culture of humanitarian progress and socialism of the pre-Fascist era. In reading your book what touched me more were the notes of pietas and harmony. In enduring the reading in the screen version it was the pitiless judgments and irony (the Garibaldi monument) that offended me.[46]

The differences between us are profound and go back a long way. Any collaboration between the two of us that did not take account of this would be insincere. Just as every moment of enmity between us is a burden to me.

Calvino

[Handwritten; in the Franco Fortini Archive, Siena.]

To Giovanni Raboni—Milan

Pineta di Roccamare
Castiglione della Pescaia

2.7.79

Dear Raboni,

Now that almost all the critics have had their say, I can state with confidence that it is your article, Giovanni (if I may?), that has given me most pleasure, it is the one that says the things I wanted to be said.[47]

As for the other reviews, I can certainly not be anything but happy; on the contrary, I could not have hoped for more positive notices, but the general impression they give seems to be that of a difficult, complicated book, which revolves totally around the construction of the narrative mechanism. And this is precisely what I did not want because I did not intend it to be difficult to read. For this reason I find that you show a sensitivity in conveying the true substance of my work, the kind of communication I was trying to establish with the reader, and you display an impatience with hasty definitions, and these are qualities that are so rare as to be almost unique. Of course if the critics were accustomed to saying "Calvino is so human, Calvino is so warm," then I'd feel the need to warn them, "No, watch out, I'm actually cold and geometric." But since they all seem to go in the opposite direction,* the correction can be made only with the sense of measure and sophistication that you are capable of.

You say that it will be an important book in the coming decades, but we really cannot say so. Usually the books that become important subsequently are not recognizable as such at the time. But even if my book was the "final" book of something rather than the "initial" book of something, I would already be quite happy with that.

Thank you very much,

Italo Calvino

*Apart from Renato Barilli (*Il Giorno*, 23/6) for whom I'm too affable.
[Handwritten; with the addressee.]

To Arnold Cassola—St Andrew's (Malta)

[Pineta di Roccamare,] 10.7.79

Dear Mr Cassola,

I am replying to your letter of 8 June. The things I could tell you about *Cultura e Realtà* you certainly know already, seeing that you are studying this topic, and you will certainly have spoken at length with Franco Rodano and Mario Motta who, after the death of Felice Balbo, were the most important promoters of the journal.

You will clearly know everything about the group of Catholic Communists (or the "Christian Left") and their position within the PCI at that time, and about the anathemas invoked on their heads both by the Vatican and (when they tried to bring the journal to life) by the PCI; and about the different way each of them reacted.

It would take longer to explain how on earth I found myself involved with them, I whose ideal positioning was very different (if one can talk about ideal positioning in the case of a young man like me, who was at that stage at the beginning of his cultural education), belonging as I did to an atheist, anticlerical family and not having had any religious education nor any interests in that direction. (But actually other people outside the "Christian Left," such as Cesare Pavese, collaborated on the journal as well.) The principal reason was the fact that I was very friendly with Felice Balbo: Balbo's intellectual and human hold on people was such that only those who knew him personally can testify to it.[48] (His writings don't explain this except in minimal terms.) There was an atmosphere of very strong friendship that bound Pavese and Natalia Ginzburg to Balbo as well, and along with them it also included myself who was younger than they were. We worked all day at the Einaudi offices in Turin where we were editors; and we often spent the evening at Balbo's house. Through Balbo I got to know and became friends with the other "Catholic Communists" who lived in Rome and who took the initiative over the journal.

I don't remember much about the writings of mine that you quote, but I think the one on Paradise, in response to a review by Mario Motta of the famous book *The God That Failed*, is pretty representative of my position then.[49] The bitterness of the Cold War soon dissolved that climate of friendship (and Pavese's suicide was a tragic ordeal for all of us) and in the following years each of us went our separate ways.

Best wishes for your work.

Italo Calvino

[Photocopy of the handwritten letter; in the Calvino Archive. Previously in *Bozze 81*, 8–10 (August–October 1981), pp. 124–25.]

To Guido Neri—Paris

Pineta di Roccamare
Castiglione della Pescaia

20.8.79

Dear Guido,

Your letter of 8 August gave me great pleasure—first of all because it reassured me that your convalescence following your operation has been successfully completed—and also of course because of the depth of your critical reflections on my book, especially on its opening.[50]

It is true that waiting is the theme of the book—even though apart from the first micro-novel the theme is not in the forefront of all ten "novels."

The format I chose for the ten micro-novels is the one that I then summarize at the end in the pseudo-*Arabian Nights* episode: a man—who narrates the story in the first person—finds himself in a situation that does not fit his identity (or his role, or his intentions), a situation in which he becomes more and more entangled because of feeling attracted towards a female character, and which leads him to confront the threat posed by a mysterious collective enemy.

In each chapter the female reader articulates the type of novel she would like to read, or to put it another way, she excludes—from her previous choice—the kind of novel (the kind of fascination for the novel) that had come her way in the last novel that was interrupted, and she becomes more precise about what she now desires to read. Having given this statement of genre (which is connected with a system of successive eliminations) and provided the title (which later will have to form part of the novel opening provided by all the titles put together at the very end) and the plot I mentioned before, then comes the novel fragment. But rather than being an actual passage from it, the text should give an account of the *reading* of the micro-novel—this happens in the first two micro-novels, then (also because the procedure would get boring) direct narration prevails—but in every novel fragment there is at least one passage in which the written page comes into the foreground.

I am sending this by express post because normal mail is working very slowly. I hope you will get this when you're still in Paris. But I'll phone you in Bologna in September. Ciao. Look after yourself. I can't wait to see you.

Italo

PUBLISHING MATTERS

Leiris—my enthusiasm for Leiris has so far been based more on samples of reading than on the reading of a whole book at one sitting. In order to write about him I'd need to try to move to this second phase. Will I manage to do so? I hope so.

Schwob—I remember speaking about this at a meeting, months ago now. And seeing that there was no one at Einaudi able to say yes, or no, or but, we can take it that this is a yes. So in September I'll chase up the contract.

Zola—since the beginning of the summer I have had *Une page d'amour* (*A Love Episode*) on my bedside table. The fact that there are more urgent or attractive books jostling for attention still continues to work against him. I hope that some day soon Zola will manage to prevail over my anti-Zolan inertia.

Paulhan—the first thing to do is to get our Secretariat to ask for the rights (of those three stories you mentioned) and even before that to find out who we have to contact for the rights.

Did you see that I wrote a long article on Ponge in the *Corriere* (29/7)?[51] If you didn't see it, I'll send you a photocopy. I gave high praise to the fine introduction by J. R.[52] As for the translation, I preferred to retranslate almost everything for my quotations. I would have had a lot to say about the translation had I seen it in time. Apart from various debatable—though always just about defendable—linguistic choices and solutions, I found at least three factual errors in the interpretation of the French.

[Handwritten; with the addressee's heirs.]

To Lucio Lombardo Radice—Rome

Paris 13.11.79

Dearest Lucio,

YOUR LETTER OF 21 OCTOBER GAVE ME GREAT PLEASURE—first of all the pleasure of being read by you so carefully, and also the pleasure of knowing that you were then moved to write to me with the warmth of that friendship that we have maintained despite the years and the distance—and pleasure at the things you say, the acuteness of your observations.[53]

As far as the "sources" of the ten "novels" are concerned, I did not want to turn to any author in particular but rather to a type of narration, and of course in each instance this kind of narration carries with it echoes of readings that have remained in my memory. In short, my prime intention was not to mimic or parody anyone. Certainly, when I wanted to convey the revolutionary-existential atmosphere of so many Russian or German novels of the 1920s and '30s, Bulgakov's *The White Guard* was an obvious point of reference. In the same way, in setting my "erotic-perverted novel" in Japan I thought of Kawabata and Tanizaki; and in setting the "primordial-telluric" novel in Latin America I thought of many authors ranging from Juan Rulfo to Arguedas etc. etc. Similarly I thought of Borges in constructing that kind of logical-geometrical story full of learned allusions. Of the names that you mention the only one I had not thought of was [Bashevis] Singer, but some other critic has already mentioned his name, also in connection with that second "beginning."

I think it's true that for the whole book, as far as the narrative mechanism is concerned, one can cite, as you do, Chesterton's *The Man Who Was Thursday*.

Your point that the "beginnings" are in fact completed narrations seems right to me. You are one of the few to have spotted this; almost all the critics have overlooked this fact, which was imposed on me almost against my will as I gradually proceeded in the writing. The fact is that I have always been more a writer of short stories than a novelist, and it is second nature to me to *close*—both in formal and conceptual terms—even a story that remains *open*; to condense into a short narrative space all the elements that give a sense of completion to the story.

However, I do not mean by this that I am in favor only of short time-spans—or rather, there is no doubt that we are living in a period in which time has been shattered, there is no room to breathe, no possibility of foreseeing and planning ahead, and that this rhythm is imposed on what I write—but ideally I believe more and more that the only thing that counts is what moves in long, very long time-spans, both in geological eras and in the history of society. Trying to work out the directions in which these things are moving is very difficult; for that reason I feel more and more incapable of understanding what really is happening in a world which does nothing but prove each model wrong. Perhaps this book of mine can be read as a survey not only of different types of novel but of attitudes toward the world which one by one I end up eliminating, while always in the background there remains the impossibility of accepting the world as it is. Notwithstanding my basic skepticism, in each case I never stop asking myself and deciding what is good and what is bad.

Thus I empathize a lot with your various stances and I always consider your moral vitality as something precious in holding together what is left of the "legibility" of the world.

The image of relaxing readings that your letter evoked is consoling; less consoling is the event that caused the enforced leisure that you have had to undergo. With great affection I wish you long hours of reading but without the medical reasons for it, and I hope that you find the time and desire to write me soon another letter just as pleasant,

Yours,

Italo

[Handwritten; in the Archivio della Fondazione dell'Istituto Gramsci, Rome.]

To Vittorio Spinazzola—Milan

Pineta di Roccamare
58043 Castiglione della Pescaia

15.7.80

Dear Prof. Spinazzola,

YOUR ARTICLE ON MY ESSAYS WHICH APPEARED IN *L'UNITÀ* ON 6 July I would say is the best review my book has had, the most precise one too and one that takes account of the negative reactions and answers them.[54] I can tell you that I recognize myself in the portrait and outline that you trace. All of which confirms the impression that I've come to over the last few months, namely that the right readership for this book, given how I've constructed it, are those who have lived through the experiences of our times. But the book does not cross beyond the boundary of our generation, and it does not communicate—in the way I would have liked—the sense of a history to those who come after us.[55] In this sense I've missed my target: or rather, my first mistake was perhaps to delay so long before publishing the oldest essays in a volume, and the second that of believing it was now time to historicize them. (As for the decade 1945–55—or rather up to most of the 1950s—which as you observe I have left out, I initially intended to make them into a separate volume; but now I see it would be even more difficult to get people to understand their logic, without the context to which they belonged.)

I would now like to reread the review you wrote about a year ago of the *Traveler* (where it seemed to me the topic of distance was paramount) to connect it with your discourse of today, but I've not got it with me so I'll have to do it another time.[56]

Thank you and best wishes,
Yours,

Italo Calvino

[Handwritten; with the addressee.]

To Guido Neri—Bologna

Pineta di Roccamare 27.8.80

Dear Guido,

I READ YOUR LETTER WITH GREAT PLEASURE. I PUBLISHED that book of essays only because I wanted to defend myself from those who bring out posthumous books and I made it actually just like a posthumous book, but maybe I shouldn't have published it, just kept it there.[57] The thing is that for years people kept asking: why don't you reissue your essays? And now that I have published it, it's obvious that this is a book that marks a clear generational gap, because the young (and people like yourself who are more in sympathy with the culture of young people or at least of those whose roots do not go back to the early postwar years in Italy) react negatively, whereas my contemporaries or people who are older say bravo, well done. In short, I was right not to publish my essays. This was only a volume of general essays and I had left out, perhaps for later volumes, first and foremost the more party-political period, then the essays and articles on individual books and authors, and other thematic collections that I could assemble. Now perhaps I'll put together these other books all the same, because I am obsessed by the idea of these awful people who edit posthumous volumes and one must take action in good time to defend oneself by leaving them as little as possible; well, in the end, I'll prepare the books as though for publication but then won't deliver them.

As for your possible collaboration with Einaudi: at this point in time there does not exist an editorial board in Turin in the sense of a team of people who are there and with whom you can have an exchange of opinions. In other words, for much of your work you can have contacts with Fossati and this is certainly a big advantage, first because Fossati is alive and secondly because you can see him also in Bologna. But for the rest it seems to me impossible for you to keep contacts with the publishing house unless you go to Turin every now and again. But even if you do go to Turin it's not that you can "talk to the publishing house": you will speak with individuals who might be interested or not in individual questions, and the crucial thing that will make you want to talk to these people will be the human and intellectual interest these individuals display, not their publishing side. I myself go to Turin very rarely and apart from relationships with the friends I can meet there I have no interest in going there, except for the odd book which I have to follow personally through to publication. It may be that it won't be like that forever; but it seems that, despite all they say about unemployment amongst intellectuals, there aren't any bright young people who are attracted to work in publishing. So it's pointless you writing letters to Turin because there isn't anyone not just to reply to you but not even to read your letters. There is room to do things, but you have to go there and do them yourself, without saying anything beyond the strictly necessary to anyone.

As for Claudio R., he's going through a rough time because he has to stay at Varallo to look after his mother and other people in his family, and in addition his eyesight is still in danger;[58] but precisely because he lives in Varallo he often comes to Turin and you can easily meet up with him if you arrange your trip there in advance. There is no other way of contacting him because his psychological block regarding writing is total and no one has even seen any letters of his.

As soon as I go to Turin I'll pass on what you've told me about Leiris and Artaud, but it won't be that soon, because September and October will be hellish months for me because of logistical questions and the house move. I am very pleased at what you tell me about the SCHWOB project. As soon as the book is ready, and I hope that's soon, I'll get going for an appropriate relaunch of Schwob.

I am in a very complicated period because this transfer of the family from Paris, which I should have done years ago on obvious economic grounds, instead of simplifying my life, is complicating it horrendously for me (for us). And all this year I've been swamped by very serious property and financial problems which don't let me sleep at night, and which will go on for who knows how long yet. First: I have not been able to sell my house in San Remo and I don't know [if] I'll ever manage to sell it, and my hassles with the Council are exhausting, and this financial operation, which was to have been the one that allowed all the others to take place, has become extremely problematic. The buying of the house in Rome and the work on it have turned out to be much more expensive than we could have foreseen, and the time needed for the work and the permits for it from the Council (which I still have not received) are delaying our move for who knows how long yet. The sale of the Paris house and the purchase of a smaller apartment have turned out to be anything but simple operations and I don't know when or if I'll manage to solve these Paris problems. In short, my days are full of practical difficulties on one front or another, and I manage to do very little work. This summer the only thing I was able or rather obliged to do was to meet my commitments to *la Repubblica* but I'm always behind with them, and this jack-of-all-trades kind of writing does not give me any satisfaction at all, even though, yes, it is also a vocation of mine, but it is certainly the most time-consuming and least useful activity I could be doing, and what's more in recent times what I manage to come up with are only boring things and my conscience is only at peace if I manage to entertain people.

Publishing matters: I am laboriously revising the translation done by the eighty-year-old Sergio Solmi of Queneau's *Petite Cosmogonie*: it's fine in terms of versification but all or nearly all of the scientific conundrums still have to be worked out and rewritten in Solmi-style verse. I've recently contacted the German translator who has sent me pages of replies from Queneau to his queries. But these are elementary problems whereas the difficulties I have neither he nor Solmi have ever had. I'm writing a *Piccola guida alla Piccola cosmogonia* (*Small Guide to Queneau's Petite Cosmogonie*) which I would like to publish in an appendix to the volume, and so I would like to understand absolutely everything, which would mean tracking down the scientific books Queneau had to hand when he was writing, something that no one can help me with.[59]

Meanwhile I am finishing the project I've been dragging along now for years: Queneau's essays. I've discovered a really important essay that nobody ever cites: in the issue of *Critique* dedicated to Bataille—issue 195–196 (August–September 1963)—Queneau wrote "Premières confrontations avec Hegel" (First Confrontations with Hegel), which contains memories of the post-surrealist period in the thirties when he and Bataille went to Kojève's lectures on Hegel.[60] I'll add this text to my selection. However, I've noticed that in *Critique* there is a misprint, a line missed out, which happens in the middle of a quote from

Bataille. I wanted to ask you, if you have Bataille's works to hand, if you could fill in this lacuna. It is a text of 1929, published in *Documents*, no. 4: *Figure humaine*. The gap comes in the sentence that begins "Il est permis de supposer que, parmi les intellectuels les [. . .] sur le nez d'un orateur" etc. But if you could send me a photocopy of the whole article you would be doing me a great favor.

I am staying here at Roccamare until 12 September. After that my address will be the Rome one: Piazza Campo Marzio 5—00186 Rome—tel. 654.23.66 but we can only settle into the house in October because the work will not yet be finished, and for a month we will be in temporary accommodation.

I was very pleased to get your news and to realize—even though you don't mention it, or rather precisely because of that—that your health is good. Best wishes and get back to me about Bataille immediately if you can

Italo

[Handwritten; with the addressee's heirs.]

To Cesare Segre—Milan

[Rome,] 6.11 [1980]

Dear Segre,

When I reread your excellent article in printed form I was able to appreciate it even more in all its coherence: it goes from the initial observation of the "apparent characteristic" of the dialog with the reader through the diagram (but they've made a mistake with the dotted line!) and the parable about the Koran, and finally ends up condemning the novelist to holding capricious <sway> over the reader.[61] You define perfectly the mechanism which produces the articulation of "the kind of need that the next partial novel attempts to satisfy"—as you do with the reader's theorizations and the Marana-Flannery complementarity.

The frame: the move from the "very domestic opening" to the "novelistic and improbable" was already in my initial plan. The male reader had to become progressively more involved in events that were more and more novelistic and which remained cold and distant from him, whereas his real emotional tension became more and more concentrated on what he was reading. (But to give maximum force to this contrast I ought to have made him read more and more introspective novels, devoid of any events that were not internal. But the pleasure of variety drove me to look instead for other patterns, ones that can be illustrated by diagrams such as the one I suggested in *Alfabeta*.) And in terms of style the frame story (in other words, the "real" events) was meant to become more and more flat, written off the cuff, <almost> as in a comic strip, highlighting its contrast with the very <dense> and detailed subject matter of the novels, of "written" life.

In the inserted novels, rather than providing "outlines" or "summaries," my intention was to give not the text but the reading of it, to narrate the reader while he reads a novel that we perceive through this reading and whose text emerges only periodically. I stuck to this setup in chapters I and II. Chapter III, however, I decided to start as direct narration and I thought that to insist too much on that other technique would be monotonous, just repetitions of formulae. Thus in the novels that follow I was only concerned that there was at least one passage where the text faded into the background and the reading (or writing?) of it came to the fore.

The name Ataguitan[ia] literally does exist in the Encyclopedia Britannica. I'll send you the precise reference. I'm now in post-removal chaos and I won't emerge from it very quickly. My new address is the one at the top of the letter. The phone number is: . . .[62] If you come to Rome, call me. Thank you once more, and best wishes,

[Handwritten draft; in the Calvino Archive. The angled brackets indicate words that are difficult to read.]

To Umberto Eco—Milan

Piazza Campo Marzio 5
00186 Rome

29 Nov. 1980

Dear Umberto,

I'VE JUST FINISHED READING IT.[63] THE ELEMENTS OF INTEREST in my reading were, in the following order:

(1) The philosophy of laughter, which I fully endorse in its ethical, aesthetic, and epistemological dimension (I don't understand why on earth the critics I've read so far ignore or attach less importance to what is *the* theme of the book).*

(2) The medieval erudition: theology, the history and politics of the religious orders, bibliography, the encyclopedic knowledge systems, all this makes of your novel a genuine encyclopedia of the Middle Ages. At least that's the way I read it and I read it with the kind of curiosity that is aroused by a book written by a historian, full of footnotes.

(3) The semiotic and linguistic epistemology, which also seems convincing to me and I think can be linked to point (1), but in that case I would have to reread it to find this link.

(4) The Oulipo aspects, in other words the plot which is dictated by pre-existing fixed structures like the trumpets of the Apocalypse etc.

(5) The Zadig aspect under which I group all the more basic ethical-gnomic elements of William of Baskerville's wisdom.

(6) The coups-de-scène that I would say were à la Jules Verne, like the idea of the Fabriano paper which becomes the very key to the solution, allowing the pages to be stuck with poison, the book to be eaten etc.

(7) The in-house allusions, such as the non-writer Paolo and his maestro, but this I believe is only a marginal aspect.

(8) The political-ideological allegories in what happens to the splinter groups, autonomous factions etc., a more obvious aspect also for the majority of critics.

(9) The functioning of the complex narrative construction which proceeds skillfully with consistent writing and without any lapses, even though I would have preferred greater economy.

I stop at this number nine though maybe I could continue to other magic numbers. When you come to Rome, phone me on 654.23.66.

Ciao,

Italo

*The thing I don't understand is why the terrible enemy of laughter resembles and is called something like Borges. What has JLB got to do with that character? Maybe there you touch on a point that ought to be developed: the two levels of laughter, the corporeal, carnival-Bakhtinian, *Coena Cipriani* laughter, and mental laughter, Schopenhauer's laugh when he was thinking of who knows what geometric figure, Borges's laughter (and ours, I believe).
[Handwritten; with the addressee.]

1981–1985

To *Paese sera*—Rome

[Rome, 13–17 March 1981]

Sir,

In *Paese sera* on 13 March, on page three, an article (signed by Dario Bellezza) states in its headline that I hate poets, and in the body of the article that I have a "very poor opinion" of Italian poetry and that "deep down" I hate Montale, someone whom I have always stated is my favorite poet. No evidence is adduced to support such claims. The article, besides defining Montale in terms which seem to me to be not just incorrect but also uncivil, claims he is "magniloquent," something which is a first in sixty years of Montale criticism; and what's more it would seem that this opinion stems from a piece I wrote on Caproni.[1] I do not think I need to refute such unfounded accusations; I only wanted to say to you, Sir, how sorry I was to read such things in your newspaper.

Italo Calvino

[Published in *Paese sera* (18 March 1981), p. 3.]

To Claudio Milanini—Milan

Piazza Campo Marzio 5
00186 Rome

20 April 1981

Dear Prof. Milanini,

YOUR ARTICLE GAVE ME GREAT PLEASURE.[2] IF I DID NOT REPLY to you immediately it was because I was trying to find someone who knew your address; but I don't want to delay any longer and I hope that this letter reaches you via Spinazzola.

The account you give of the *Traveler* seems to me to be the finest and most complete ever given, and I recognize myself in it, precisely because you also say things that I would not have known how to think or say but which match my intentions, such as your decisive statement: "there is no inspiration outside communication." The same could be said of the key metaphor of the trap and escaping from the trap. In this sense it seems to me that your essay offers an effective response to Cesare Segre's objection that the male reader stops being the same as the real reader as soon as he meets the female reader in chapter II and gets transported into a fictitious adventure.[3] Written at the same time, the two most carefully thought out articles on this novel confront the same problem from a different angle, and your definition is the one that convinces me more.

The way you reconstruct the journey that has led me to my current situation, the journey of someone "tormented by a historical and political pessimism which is becoming ever more marked"—and you do so by comparing my successive declarations on the "ideal reader"—seems equally persuasive and accurate. I was also interested in your search for the common elements in the "micro-novels" (which partly coincides with my intentions in structuring the book but to a large extent emerges from my unconscious urges)—though at the same time bearing in mind that these are "fictional" novels where one must suppose that it is not my "voice" speaking but that of fictitious authors, in other words implied characters—and I also found intriguing the list of negative reflections on reality that link the "novels" and the frame.

Above all I was happy to see how much you valued the final story, the one about the Prospect, which I am very keen on, and which you connect with the finale of my "The Count of Montecristo" and of *Invisible Cities* (both finales I consider valid today). (And happy too to find Valéry in that conclusion: he is one of my authors, even though I did not know that passage.)

All in all, this is an article that is very useful to me, also because it charts lines of continuity that are anything but obvious between my position today and earlier phases. I am grateful to you, and to Spinazzola for having "sponsored" your essay and for having placed it in the context of his ever useful and sound annual volume. I would like to find out more about you and read other things you have written.

Italo Calvino

[Handwritten; with the addressee.]

To Luciano Berio—Milan

[Rome,] 10 December 1981

Dear Luciano,

You say: "Everything would need to begin suddenly, you see, with no prelude, a voice immediately starts singing, a very powerful voice, like an explosion, the orchestra would be heard later, but it is as if it had been playing for some time, you see, maybe there are two orchestras, one on the stage replying to the orchestra down in the pit, and a tremendous amount of activity on the stage, many things happening all at once, you see?"[4]

I reply: "Yes, I see, we agree about that, but in a certain way I was thinking about a silence, an effect of silence, no, wait, let me explain, let's say a silence-effect which nevertheless does not rule out what you say about the voice, the orchestra, the two orchestras and everything else, look I actually agree but the effect could be—now I'll tell you what I think then we'll see—the effect is that of waiting, waiting for the sound like someone singing and what does he sing? It's the wait for the song or rather its absence, I don't know if you get my idea."

You then reply something along these lines: "Yes, yes, in a certain sense it is the case that this, let's say that this is one of the elements, you see, the silence comes out in negative since everything is filled by the voice and the music, and then it is a bit as if inside the music there was silence, and also the music. The music would need to be heard within the music, you see, and that is why I thought that the scene has to emerge during the scene, inside the scene, I mean, I don't know if you follow me."

Then I reply: "I found this thing by Roland Barthes in the *Enciclopedia* there, and now I'll read it to you:[5] '*Hearing* is a physiological phenomenon; *listening* is a psychological act,' that's what he says. 'It is possible to define the physical conditions of hearing etc. with acoustics and the physiology of hearing; listening, on the other hand, can only be defined starting with its object or its objective. There are three types of listening . . . ' Listen to this."

And you: "Wonderful. The theater, the site of listening, could represent in active terms the act of listening, contain listening in all its forms . . ."

I continue to read: "'The first type of listening is based on *clues*. At this level, nothing distinguishes animals from men: the wolf listens for the approach of his prey, the hare has ears only for the dog's bark, the lover listens to the approaching steps, recognizes the signs that tell him that the person he loves is arriving . . .'"

A woman's voice sings an aria. The stage is a labyrinth. Outlines of men try to reach the woman singing but don't succeed.

"'Hearing seems connected essentially'—I'm still reading Barthes—'to spatio-temporal evaluation . . . from an anthropological point of view listening is the very sense of space and time captured through degrees of distance, and rhythms . . . the appropriation of space is sonorous. The house is the equivalent of an animal's territory, a space for familiar sounds, sounds that are *recognized*, domestic harmony . . .' "

Kafka's *Diary*, 5 November 1911: "I am seated in my bedroom, the headquarters of the uproar. I hear all the doors banging; only their noise prevents me from hearing the footsteps that run from one door to another . . . The bolt in the front door is slid along, it creaks as if it had a sore throat, it opens with the brief note of a female voice then it shuts with a deafening, masculine, crash that echoes without regard for anyone. My father has gone out; now the more delicate noise begins, dispersed, desperate, despairing, sung by the voices of the canaries. I would like to open a chink in the door and slither like a viper into the nearby room and from the ground ask my sisters and their governess to stay quiet a bit."

Me: "The libretto then could be this, listen. A king strains his ear in an empty palace. He fears a plot. He strains his ear to the sentinels' footsteps, to the trumpets' fanfares . . . Every unusual noise could be the enemies threatening . . ."

The King: "A king is accustomed to listening with others' ears . . . When he has to use his own ears catching the echoes of the ear-palace, nothing reassures him . . ."

Chorus: "Facts are as subtle as breaths . . . they can insinuate themselves, infiltrate, make their way . . . whispers, whistling, leaks, clues . . ."

Me: "The king confides only in his old squire who is deaf."

Squire: "The informers insinuate, however, . . ."

The King: "What?"

Squire: "I don't know . . . I hear that they were talking about the queen . . . I didn't hear properly . . ."

The King: "Doralice?"

Chorus: "You believe she's faithful . . . you believe she is . . . faithful as a wife . . . as a queen . . . There are leaks, clues, rumours . . ."

The King: "I hear her footsteps . . . They seemed to be getting closer . . . Now they're receding . . . Where is she going?"

The voice of a woman who appears and disappears in the labyrinth, pursued by men.

You: "This is fine as a situation, in a general sense, but now you should transport everything onto another plane, use a different language . . . You really can't do a libretto like an old melodrama, it doesn't make sense, do you see . . . I would like an image of contemporary power . . . For instance, the director of an opera theater . . . The whole action could take place in a theater . . ."

Kafka, *Diary*, 9 November 1911: "I dreamt this the day before yesterday. Everything was a theater; I was at times up in the balcony, at times on stage. The actress was a girl that had attracted me some months previously; I saw her lithe body just at the moment when she seized the back of a chair in terror . . . At a certain point the set was so big I did not see anything else anymore, no stage no stalls no darkness no footlights . . .There was an imperial festival going on and a revolution. At first nothing could be seen of the festival; however, it was the court people who had gone off to a festival; and in the meantime a revolution had broken out . . . the crowd had invaded the castle . . . Here they were, the courtiers' carriages coming back very fast through the Eisengasse. A crowd of people passed me by, mostly the theater audience . . . and in their midst a young girl I knew . . ."

You: "No, the festival, the revolution, we've already done that . . . in *La vera storia* (*The True Story*) . . ."[6]

Me: "Dreams repeat themselves . . ."

You: "A dream, a dream in a theater . . ."

Me: "That's it: the theater director has had a dream . . ."

The theatre director: "I dreamt of a theater, another theater, there is another theater outside my theater (this piece already written)."

Me: "He is dreaming of reaching a woman who is nothing other than the ghost of a voice."

Woman's voice: "There is a voice hidden amongst the voices (piece already written)."

You: "Yes, this could be a starting point . . . but at the same time there is everything that happens behind the set, in the wings, on the evening of a première . . . (action)."

Me: "A theater where there is ill feeling against the director. The wheels of the great mechanism grind to a halt. Threatening signs of disintegration can be seen (action)."

You: "And at the same time the opera too that gets represented on stage, where power appears such as the boyars in *Boris*, the Grandees of Spain in *Don Carlos* . . ."

Me: "At this point I foresaw a king listening to a voice coming from below the earth. The king keeps his predecessor, whose throne he has usurped, prisoner in the cellars. No, it is only the deaf squire who hears that voice. The king has no ears for the lament coming from the cell."

You: "I prefer the director's dream."

Director: "There is a door, the artists' door . . . the door that leads directly where? There is a passage (piece already written)."

Woman's voice: (duet already written)

Me: "I continue to quote from the *Enciclopedia*. 'The second kind [of listening] is *decipherment*; what you try to catch with your ears are *signs*, based on certain codes. Before writing, before rock paintings, there was the deliberate reproduction of a rhythm, which is characteristic of man. What is listened to is no longer the *possible* (threat, desire) but something *secret*, what is buried . . . the hidden world of the gods . . ."

The King: "The palace space is described by sounds, as is time too, the calm hours and the anxious ones."

The director: "Where is my place? Please forgive the interruption (piece already written)."

Me: " 'To conclude,' says Barthes, 'the third type of listening takes place in an inter-subjective space, where 'I listen' also means 'Listen to me', a 'meaning' deferred to infinity, into the subconscious . . ."

The King: "I strain my ear to the noise that comes from the city: fragmented, undecipherable sounds arrive; listening to them is relaxing. If I strain my ear perhaps I'll be able to catch a call, a presage, as from the mouth of an oracle."

Woman's voice: (she sings an aria).

You: "And then?"

Me: "That would be the end of the first act."

You: "You call that an act?"

Me: "Well let's say the end of the first letter. All it remains for me to do is to sign off with best wishes,"

Yours,

Italo

[Typed, with autograph signature. Published in *Un re in ascolto* (*A King Listens*) (Milan: Edizioni del Teatro alla Scala, 1986), pp. 28–33; later in *Berio*, ed. E. Restagno (Turin: EDT, 1995), pp. 135–38.]

To Sergio Pautasso—Milan

Rome, 18 February 1982

Dear Pautasso,

I am writing to you not about Landolfi but about another author—I don't know whether this is your domain or Gelli's or someone else's; in the latter case please forward this letter to the colleague concerned.

It's a novel in English:

Salman Rushdie, *Midnight's Children* (Jonathan Cape).

The author is Indian (born in Bombay in 1947 but he studied in London where he now lives). He is a man of great sophistication and intelligence also as a critic (he wrote an excellent article on my works in *The London Review of Books*) and is very highly regarded in London.[7]

Midnight's Children is a hilarious autobiography of an Indian born on the same night in 1947 that India gained Independence, a life that, going back to the story of his grandfather and various relations, is bound up with the history of the Indian nation, but always in a grotesque key. The influence of Naipaul but also of Günter Grass and perhaps of García Màrquez can be detected.

The book won a major British prize last year. It has obtained translation contracts everywhere except in Italy (where he is represented not by Linder but by an agent in Rome whose name escapes me).

Why don't I propose it to Einaudi? Because it is very long (445 pages) and I know already that even if our publishing house overcame its fears about this huge size in time to acquire the rights, this problem would crop up again subsequently with the time it would take to process it and who knows when it would get published. As a result (I have been asked by the author, who is a very good friend of mine, to do something for his book in Italy), I really think that Rizzoli would be the publisher best able to guarantee him success here.[8]

In recommending the book to you, I still have to tell you that this business of length is a negative factor, also because it reflects a rather overabundant though not prolix streak in Rushdie's writing, but I would also say that his fertile powers in invention and solutions makes it always an entertaining book.

That was all I wanted to say. Best wishes,

Yours,

Italo

[Handwritten; in the Archivio Rizzoli, Milan.]

To Luciano Berio—Milan

[Rome, April 1982?]

Dear Luciano,

IT'S BEEN A LONG TIME SINCE I LAST WROTE TO YOU. WE should take up that theme for the second act: that character who is following a song which for him is like the song of the Sirens . . .

The minute I say Sirens, you immediately say: "Yes, this could be the idea to develop, an idea that of course runs parallel to the other ones: Ulysses and the Sirens."

But I was only saying the Sirens just for something to say, don't make me lose the thread.

You: "What thread do you think you'll lose when I've been waiting for this letter of yours for six months. The second act opens with the Sirens' song, that's absolutely fine for me."

Me: "Wait. The first thing to do is to check in Homer's poem what precisely the Sirens say. Let me check this for a minute. *The Odyssey*, book twelve, line one hundred and eighty-four and following:

> Here, come quickly, o glorious Odysseus, the great boast of the Achaeans,
> Stop your ship, to listen to our voices.
> No one ever goes away from here with their black ship,
> Unless he hears first, the sound of honey, the voices from our lips;
> Then they depart full of joy, and knowing more things.

[...]
We know everything that happens on the all-nourishing earth."

You: "We could take just a few words: 'stop your ship,' 'sound of honey,' 'we know everything'."

Me: "But doing it like that makes the Sirens' song seem something straightforward, the song that they want people to believe . . . Whereas instead Homer had already explained how things stood, at line forty-four and following:

. . . but the Sirens seated on the meadow bewitched him
With their harmonious song; the shore all around swarms with wasting
Human skeletons; their flesh dissolves on their bones."

You: "Right 'the shore with skeletons' could work very well, but so could 'seated on the meadow': there are these two simultaneous moments, one a kind of watermark on the other, you see."

Me: "Everything depends on how we decide from what point of view we're looking at it; because it could also be the Sirens' song as Ulysses' companions imagine it with their ears blocked. Or the song as Ulysses tries to remember it, when the danger is past and he is untied, and he tries to sing the tune and realizes that he's already forgotten it, evanescent like the memory of a dream."

You: "He is a man of our time, everything has to be very contemporary, Ulysses is a man of today trying to remember the Sirens' song, but it's obvious he's never heard them except in his dreams, those Sirens never existed. And yet it is the Sirens' song that makes him go on; it's a song of the future that he has in his ears. This is the idea you should develop."

Me: "In that case this theme could be inserted in the plot we had started: the director would like to go back to the theater he dreamt, hear the perfect execution of that aria by that soprano. But in order to do this he has to identify with the spirit of that music, of those voices, of that theater, and give up everything he has become. He has to find within himself what he has lost and reach the voice of his desire."

You: "Yes, this is a nice idea, but I need something that is visible on stage, a dramatic situation. And then you must give me some words to be sung, I can't really set to music the thoughts that flit through your head."

Me: "If you look amongst your papers, there must be a page I wrote which maybe was not bad, it depends on what you want to do with it, it was the one numbered A.2.1, that begins:

Is there a door, the artists' door? The door
that leads directly where? There is a passage . . .

See if you can find it; in any case I have a copy."

You: "Yes, yes, that can work as well, but at the same time there has to be the opera being performed on the stage in that theater, and it has to be an action that is the same as the stage outside the theater. Something like in *Don Carlos*, do you know what I mean? Until finally there is a general musical involvement almost like a tempest. Now I am just saying that for the sake of it, I don't really want a tempest, I mean something involving the whole orchestra, maybe two orchestras so the two levels become one."

Me: "Well, you have to bear in mind that I had also worked out that story of the king going through the town incognito, with his deaf squire, mingling with the crowd. I would insert some choruses from the crowd enjoying themselves but underneath this a hint of menace, a growing violence. And on the other hand some choruses of revenge and destruction, which instead throb as though with songs of love."

You: "I was more interested in the idea you had about the song contest."

Me: "Oh yes, in order to find the woman he had heard singing in the first act, the king invites musicians and male and female singers to his palace and will offer a prize to the best voice. In this way he hopes to find her again, but he doesn't know that a voice that sings before a king can no longer be the voice of desire that he had heard. At this point there is a whole scene I had imagined; but there's no point in me repeating it to you; I've got all the drafts; if you need it get in touch. Then everything should end with a palace conspiracy and a popular revolution."

You: "This is absolutely fine for me, except that everything should be seen from inside the stage as it were, showing the obverse of an opera performance. All the nervousness, you see, that there is behind the curtains, an impatience, a real agitation that acts as counterpoint to the unread dramatic tension. All the things that go wrong at the last minute . . ."

Me: "The soprano whose voice goes . . ."

You: "No, not that."

Me: "What then?"

You: "Well, let's see, clothes that don't suit . . . the seamstress . . ."

Me: "No, I don't like the idea of the seamstress, I like firefighters. Why don't we put in the start of a fire? The firefighters rush in with their extinguishers . . ."

You: "I feel you are getting away from the main theme and we risk losing the plot. The theme we started out with was that of listening."

Me: "There's still that text by Barthes that we need for the conceptual framework. Look at this, for instance: 'Nature, with her sounds, is brimming with meaning: at least that was the way the ancient Greeks listened to her, according to Hegel. The oaks of Dodona expressed prophecies with the rustle of their leaves . . . ' Hey, what do you think? The oaks of Dodona could be the finale of the second act. A rustle that occupies all the space of sound."

You: "What Dodona, what leaves are you on about? That's not it, we've not got it yet. The Sirens were better, taking up again the theme of the Sirens at this point . . ."

Me: "But they are exactly the same thing! As Blanchot says: 'There was something marvelous in that real, common, secret song, a simple everyday song, which suddenly became recognizable . . . song of the abyss: which once heard, opened up an abyss in every word inviting us compellingly to disappear into it.'"

I had better stop on these words and let you reflect.

Yours,

Italo

[Typed, with autograph signature; in the Archivio Berio, Paul Sacher Stiftung, Basel (p. 1 is missing). Published in *Berio*, ed. E. Restagno (Turin: EDT, 1995), pp. 138–41.]

To Giovanni Falaschi—Florence

Rome, 1st December 1982

Dear Falaschi,

It's a difficult problem and I don't know if I can help you.[9]

The function of mediating between author and public which all publishers and newspaper editors ought to carry out exists so that the publication of a text is not an imposition of the single author's *auctoritas* but receives the appropriate amount of collective approval and checking to sanction the text's belonging to a culture and not just to individual whim. But nobody wants to exercise this function any more, manuscripts go straight to the printers without anyone daring to touch a comma, because the Author has become sacred and everyone has to accept every blunder he makes as though they were his religious followers. This is by now common practice, but it's not that things were very different before (it was just that there was more belief that there was a collective job to be done and that it was a duty toward the author as well as toward the readers), because even before now the people who had the patience to devote time and effort to other people's manuscripts, especially those by young authors, were very few in number. Vittorini was one of these, because he had an enthusiasm for literature as a common discourse, and every so often he would start working on a manuscript, even one in a very rough state by an unknown writer, but one where he saw a truth, and would prune everything that was just a superimposition of some *idée reçue* of literature. For instance, I remember what he said about Rigoni Stern: V. had received a manuscript with many digressions on that distant country, dreams, etc. and he persuaded the author to eliminate them all in order just to keep the bare account of the retreat from Russia.[10]

I don't think it is easy to find documents of this kind; you would have to conduct lengthy investigations author by author in order to find some examples. Niccolò Gallo was in contact for years with D'Arrigo, who would never stop rewriting (at proof stage) his *Horcynus Orca*, and he (Gallo) died before D'Arrigo returned the proofs. Certainly

Gallo was the most authoritative mentor in Italian literature of the fifties. (Not Vittorini who operated on the margins.) I can't really tell you anything else, except on the basis of what I remember.

Best wishes,
Yours,

Calvino

[Handwritten; with the addressee.]

To Elsa Morante—Rome

[Rome,] 14 April 1983

I STILL THINK ABOUT YOU WITH AFFECTION, DEAR ELSA, AS AN old friend, even though we have not seen each other for years. Only yesterday coming back from a trip I discovered that you were there[11] and I wanted to send you this note, full of so many things I don't know how to articulate, as happens when people have not spoken for some time, but I would only want to let you know that amongst the people who love you there is also, always

Calvino

[Handwritten; with the addressee's heirs.]

To Franco Rella—Rovereto

Castiglione Della Pescaia, 14 August 1983

Dear Rella,
I READ YOUR *METAMORFOSI* WITH GREAT INTEREST.[12] MY SUPport for it was wholehearted at the beginning (Valéry the essayist is one of the few maestros I recognize without reservations, and you define him very well) and I did not feel anything but satisfaction let's say for the first four chapters. After that I went on always finding interesting

points but seeing less clearly the coherence of your discourse, with a slight feeling of repetition and excess, in short, with the impression of a book where everything could come in, and where for that reason your most original and solid core of thought risks being lost. And I don't think your lyrical expansiveness helps; in any case, you yourself define very well the failure of the lyrical side of Nietzsche; so I cannot but subscribe to your reservations in the Epilogue regarding the mixing of the two languages.

There is one point which seems to me very important and original and which is very close to my heart and that is the bit about *figura-Gleichnis*, so much so that I would like to see it dealt with in such a way as to become the cornerstone of the book's argument. It would be worthwhile working more on this terminological and conceptual suggestion of yours, starting by making it very clear how you understand the difference between Bild and Gleichnis, Image and Figure (and later "metaphor" and in short distinguishing carefully all these contiguous semantic areas). (Several times I've found myself in lexical trouble trying to say something which I still felt was clear in my head about this tangle of "iconic" thought—most recently for the French translation of this word in an essay of mine.) It seems to me that this theme of the *figure* is the book's central theme (also going by your subtitle, *Images of Thought*) along with the other fundamental theme (or perhaps they are one and the same) namely that of the visuality of myth, as it is articulated at the start of chap. XII and exemplified in the most convincing way in the references to Kafka that occur throughout the volume (more than in the *erudite* interpretations of Narcissus). All in all, the impression is of a book that finishes where one would like it to start, and perhaps this fits in with the program and itinerary outlined in your Epilogue-Diary.

This is a letter on my reactions as a reader, not a publisher's letter.

When I resume contact with the publishing house in September I will present your typescript and support it, despite the reservations I have mentioned to you, and I will try to find some other Einaudi person with whom I can compare opinions. But the reactions of individual temperaments (and tastes) will be quite important, since your way of writing is addressed to this kind of reaction, rather than to any authority stemming from theoretical rigor.

I had read with great pleasure *Il silenzio e le parole*, but I do not think I ever saw your second book.[13] Could you let me have a copy?

With all good wishes,
Yours,

Italo Calvino

[Typed, with autograph signature; with the addressee.]

To Alfredo Giuliani—Rome

[Paris, December 1983]

Dear Giuliani,

Only today did I manage to get hold of *La Repubblica* for Friday the 9th, which never made it to Paris.[14] I am very pleased that the first article to come out on *Mr Palomar* was yours. It not only describes and understands perfectly everything that is in the book, but displays a close empathy with things that I thought during its composition, as though we had discussed them together: relationships[15] with *Monsieur Teste*, the near and the distant, the deconstructed autobiography, the problems with the human world. You highlight above all the descriptive gaze, the epistemological intent even though this is never conclusive, and the pathos that is perhaps present though hidden. These are three dimensions that Citati (whose article I had read before yours) denies me tout-court perhaps because the portrait he traces, which is based on reductions and impasses—though accurate in the main—forces him to simplify the design to such an extent that one can no longer see what is in the book. On one point your portrait (which is so much richer and more subtle) and Citati's agree and that is in the stress put on perplexity, uncertainty, emptiness. And I certainly cannot be surprised at this because one could say that this condition is asserted on every page of the book, but I have to say that as I wrote each piece I thought that this was just a bit of additional psychological <colouring>,[16] not the element that would most stand out. For a long time I thought that some philosophy of mine (even though I was not able to expound it intentionally) would emerge from this book (and would take on a shape also for me) from the juxtaposition and intersection of problems, like a figure taking shape from a puzzle or mosaic. But the minute I started to assemble the pieces to construct the book (in other words to discard and reduce the material I had accumulated down to its essentials), I realized that[17] by the end I knew less than at the beginning.

Best wishes to you and yours for the holidays and the New Year < . . . >

[Handwritten draft, undated; in the Calvino Archive. The angled brackets indicate words that are difficult to decipher.]

To Goffredo Fofi—Milan

Rome, 30 January 1984

Dear Fofi,

I READ MARIO BARENGHI'S ARTICLE ALMOST A MONTH AGO now and noted down at the time the things that I found most interesting and liked;[18] but immediately afterwards I was overtaken by a series of journeys one after the other, and they are still not over. Today, when we have a rest day in Rome, I found my notes and I'll give you the gist of them asking you to photocopy this letter of mine and send it to Barenghi with my thanks. I found his essay full of original ideas and with wide-ranging critical qualities: he really knows how to read.

So I'll start by listing the things that seemed most remarkable to me:

- The definition of the various and mutable, as distinct from the versatile;
- *Smog* = an allegory constructed on a kind of reticence (p.7);
- Searching for invisible cities in my other books (p. 7);
- The reading of *Marcovaldo* and *Invisible Cities* together;
- The shape of the grid and the network (p. 10) (though I would have something to say about his evaluation of the labyrinth);
- The bewilderment caused by duplicates which is already heralded in *Smog* (p. 16);

- The symbolic flexibility of objects but above all the desire to say something meaningful;
- The functionality of the folk-tale.

The danger that Barenghi needs to be careful of, in my view, is that of overestimating my "critical self-awareness." As a young man I felt the need constantly to make general programmatic pronouncements, which did not correspond (or corresponded only in part) with what I managed to achieve in practice. Nowadays I believe that an author's poetics must be derived a posteriori from his works, that is to say from what he has managed actually to *achieve*; declarations of intent merely document the options that in a given moment someone makes his own amidst the various possibilities that are offered by him by the range of intellectual, political-literary etc. positions.

For instance, a statement like "*Una pietra sopra* (*Moving On*) is without doubt one of the most notable books of the post-war period . . ." (p. 5), said like that, categorically, without giving any proof or arguments, does not seem convincing to me.

The first thing that comes to mind is to wonder whether one can really call *a book* something that is a retrospective collection of works written in different periods and collected with the intention of providing historical documentation, being quite honest right from the title which proclaims their lack of actuality. It would have been a book if I had collected into one volume or broadened my range of essays, let's say in the period 1955 and 196?: in other words when I believed they contained a proposal for their times. Today does Barenghi appreciate *Una pietra sopra* for its—let's say—Stoic and primacy-of-the-will phase, or for the later phase when such attitudes are—let's say—being rethought?

Thus (still on p. 5) the statement (even though it starts with "I suspect") that "the best thing written by Calvino is . . . the essay 'Pavese: essere e fare' (Pavese: Being and Doing)" is significant because certainly that is a kind of manifesto of that stoicism and historicism that I professed at that time; but it remains to be seen whether . . .

At the same time, while I approve of the importance attributed to Robbe-Grillet as a point of reference (from about 1959 onwards) for the problems I was dealing with, I wonder whether it is not taking "Il mare dell'oggettività" (The Sea of Objectivity) a little too literally to make me an antagonist of R.-G.: deep down I was merely locking myself up in my Italian historicism to protect myself from what was a stylistic option that was rigorous and taken to its extreme by a writer who was truly innovative like R.-G. In the end the value of that essay was the way I was able to see and link (in 1959) so many things that were moving in the international world, and to understand their significance, even though in the end my conclusions were defensive and argued a bit too insistently. Oh well!

Other minor points. (p. 5): the contrast Jekyll + Hyde/Utterson is Lucentini's (in the note to his translation); I merely emphasize it in my review.[19]

(p. 6): *The Argentine Ant* is not a Kafkian-oneiric story as all the critics have always said. It is the most realistic story I have written in my life; it describes with absolute exactness the situation that came about because of the invasion of the Argentine ants into the cultivated areas of San Remo and a large swathe of the Western Riviera during my childhood, in the twenties and thirties.[20]

I still really have a lot to say and discuss and a lot of things I approve of, but all in all it is an excellent essay full of new ideas and I will be happy to see it published in *Linea d'Ombra*, so my thanks to both Barenghi and Fofi.

Italo Calvino

[Handwritten; with Mario Barenghi. Previously in "Sei lettere di Italo Calvino" (Six Letters by Italo Calvino), *Nuova Corrente*, 100 (vol. 2 of special issue *Italo Calvino*, ed. Mario Boselli), (July–December 1987), pp. 416–18.]

To Mario Lavagetto—Parma

Pineta di Roccamare
Castiglione Della Pescaia

14.8.84

Dear Lavagetto,

THE PILE-UP OF UNANSWERED MAIL IS MAKING ME DESPAIR: I am years behind in replying to the letters I receive. In the summer I try to devote some hours every day to dealing with the biggest delays. That's how I found a letter of yours from 12 March that I would have liked to reply to immediately.

I am curious about what you say about the article for the American journal (it's for the *Review of Contemporary Fiction*: is it doing a special issue?), an article on the model from which all my books are derived. I wanted to say to you that *Mr Palomar* should not disturb your outline, since it is more outside than within the confines of fiction, it's a diary written in a special way, or an experiment in a particular kind of essayistic prose etc.

As for your proposal regarding rewritten stories for *Pratiche*, this is the kind of thing that demands immediate choices, reflections, ideas. What would I choose? Look, the first thing that comes to mind is Henry James, *The Jolly Corner*.[21] But when will I find the time? I foresee a very full program of work for the coming years. In short, I'll say that in principle I'll do it though then in practice it will be dependent on the accumulation of things to do and deadlines.

Another thing I support in principle is the proposal in your letter about a school for publishing. I agree, though I recommend that it is a school that is as practical and functional as possible. We do not need a specialist school for general ideas and problems.

I apologize once more for the lateness in replying; I await your article with great interest.

In all friendship,
Yours,

Italo Calvino

[Handwritten; with the addressee.]

To Claudio Varese—Florence

Rome 23.9.84

Dear Varese,

It is always a pleasure to receive your letters. But you'll have to excuse my delays in replying. I'm finding it more and more difficult to keep up with correspondence. I have here two letters of yours (5 May and 23 August) and I still have to thank you for the little volume on Foscolo and Sterne, a pairing that is close to my heart—because I feel myself more and more distant from the first name and closer and closer to the second.

For that letter of mine you would like to publish, I no longer remember what I wrote, but I certainly have no objection to publishing passages that relate to *Palomar*.[22]

As for Berio's opera at Salzburg, my input is the title and I don't think anything else.[23] Berio doesn't need libretti: he assembles words from various sources according to his needs. A couple of years ago he sent me a text to look at that had almost nothing of mine in it—after that there was no further contact. I didn't go to Salzburg because I don't like the way he insists on putting my name on things I have not taken part in. I've never heard the music, which they say is wonderful and I don't doubt it is, because as a composer Berio is magical, but his idea of theater is confused and stuck in the avant-garde movement of twenty years ago.

I apologize for the haste with which I'm writing to you, but I'm in a period of travels and of dealing with backlogs of work.

Best wishes,
Yours,

Italo Calvino

[Handwritten; with the addressee.]

TO GRAZIANA PENTICH—ROME

Paris 18-3-85

Dear Graziana,
YOUR LETTER WRITTEN ON THE EPIPHANY BROUGHT ME BACK a flood of memories. My memories of Alfonso belong above all to the period 1946–47, Milan, Genoa, maybe Venice but especially the months you two spent in Turin, in that room you rented in Via Garibaldi, memories of Alfonso and you together, the three of us walking for

hours and hours along those dreary streets discussing things, Alfonso with his eyebrows raised shouting out his invectives . . . Then also Rome, 1948, 1949 . . .[24]

For some time now I've been intending to write a long short story on those years, something autobiographical, part of which I already have in mind word for word and you two are in it right at the start. I've been held back by a certain reluctance to abandon myself to the promptings of autobiographical memory, but each year I put it amongst the things to be done.

I have fewer memories of Leone:[25] a party at the Casina Valadier (for the Zolla-Spaziani wedding) where Leone took the chair from under Ungaretti who landed on the ground . . . On another occasion Alfonso showed me Leone who was already grown up, saying: "Don't you recognize him?" When was that? Maybe at the Strega prize-giving when Alfonso supported me against the author who won, shouting— the winning novel was *Una spirale di nebbia* (*A Spiral of Mist*)—"The mist has won!" Then once I started spending most of my time in Paris, I also saw Alfonso only rarely. Once he came to see me in Paris, maybe a year before his death. But friendships are always linked to one particular period of one's life, and in our case it was linked to those years of postwar poverty: these memories are still manifold and very much alive although suspended in a cloud almost outside of time, like childhood memories. I will await impatiently for you to put together this collection.

Affectionately yours,

Italo

[Handwritten; in the Fondo Manoscritti del Centro di ricerca sulla tradizione manoscritta di autori moderni e contemporanei, University of Pavia.]

To Primo Levi—Turin

Rome 30 April 85

Dear Primo,

I WAS VERY PLEASED TO RECEIVE YOUR LETTER OF 6 APRIL.[26] I have a few hypotheses to put to you.

Leggere la vita (*Reading the riot act*).[27] The only doubt I have about your convincing reconstruction of the origin of that phrase is whether the monks' reading matter in the monasteries was really Leviticus, as the sources you cite claim. I went and read Leviticus, and it seems to me to be a very technical text about sacrifices, purificatory rites, and Jewish religious prohibitions: I cannot see how it could have been adapted to monastic rules. On the other hand, I remembered a line of Dante, and having looked it up—*Purg.* XVI, 130: "O Marco mio,"—diss'io,—"bene argomenti; / e or discerno perché dal retaggio / li figli di Levì furono esenti"" ("O Marco," I said, "you reason well; and now I see why the sons of Levi were excluded from inheriting goods")—I saw that the footnote gave as a source some Biblical verses (Numbers, 18:20) where the Levites are mentioned and there it says "In terra eorum nihil possidebitis etc. (You shall possess nothing in their land)," in other words a ban on the owning of material goods, which is perfectly suited to being inculcated into the friars' minds at night, to move them to an examination of conscience. So in my view the correct original formulation would have been "leggere i Leviti (reading the Levites)" in the sense of a Biblical passage where the Levites are named, and not "leggere il Levitico (reading Leviticus)."

Of course an expert in the history of monastic life could easily solve this question, but I don't know any.

Queneau-Mendel-Morse. The *P. C. P.* is from 1950, so before DNA, and before François Jacob wrote those things.[28] But I've recently discovered a much more promising lead. In Hans Blumenberg's very interesting book, *La leggibilità del mondo* (*The Legibility of the World*), Il Mulino, 1984, he talks of (Ch. XII, p. 375) the physicist Erwin Schrödinger who in a lecture given in Dublin in 1943 entitled *What Is*

Life? anticipated the concept of "genetic code," seeing it as analogous to Morse code.

Warmest good wishes.
Yours,

Italo

[Handwritten; with the addressee's heirs.]

Notes

Introduction

1. Italo Calvino, *The Literature Machine: Essays*, trans. Patrick Creagh (London: Secker & Warburg, 1987), pp. 16, 22.

2. *The Literature Machine*, p. 341 (translation slightly amended).

3. Luca Baranelli and Ernesto Ferrero, eds., *Album Calvino* (Milan: Mondadori, 1995), pp. 90–91. My translation.

4. Italo Calvino, *Invisible Cities*, trans. William Weaver (New York: Harcourt, 1974), pp. 165, 164.

5. Italo Calvino, *Hermit in Paris: Autobiographical Writings*, trans. Martin McLaughlin (New York: Vintage, 2003), pp. 203, 201.

6. Italo Calvino, *Numbers in the Dark*, trans. Tim Parks (New York: Pantheon, 1995), p. 12.

1941–1945

1. Calvino's best friend at school in San Remo was Eugenio Scalfari (1924–), who later became a major figure in Italian journalism, editor of the weekly magazine *L'Espresso* and founder of the daily *la Repubblica*. The other school-friends mentioned here are Emilio Maiga and Percivalle (known as Pasquale or Percy) Roero di Monticello.

2. The Ministero della Cultura Popolare (Ministry of Popular Culture), Minculpop for short, was the name of the Fascist Ministry of Culture.

3. The other school-friends mentioned in this paragraph are: Agostino Donzella, Gianni (Giovanni Battista) Pigati, Silvio Dian, Duilio Cossu, Piero Dentone (also called Godiasco from the small town near Pavia where he was born), Francesco (also called Francuccio) Kahnemann.

4. Scalfari was living in Rome, with an aunt of his, at 123 Viale Mazzini.

5. The titles all mock the Fascist culture of the time. The Tripartite Pact was signed by Italy, Germany, and Japan in September 1940.

6. Salvatore (Turi) Vasile was at the time a young author of plays for theater and radio.

7. In an earlier letter, of 17 February 1942, Scalfari had written that he had found himself amid "a talent pool of young writers on a rather good journal." In a later letter Scalfari would write: "I am trying to have articles published by a terrible journal run by Azione Cattolica."

8. The Italian playwright Ugo Betti (1892–1953).

9. Calvino was referring to some of the playwrights who were most active at the time: Guido Cantini, Cesare Giulio Viola, Vincenzo Tieri, Ugo Betti, Cesare Vico Ludovici (often spelled here and elsewhere as "Lodovici").

10. Pirandello's *Six Characters in Search of an Author*; Renzo Ricci was a well-known actor.

11. The Calvino's family home was the Villa Meridiana in San Remo, and they also had land in the countryside in the village of San Giovanni.

12. A nickname for Percivalle Roero (see note 1), whose brother Aimone had died in the war at the end of January. These events would be worked up in narrative form in the opening pages of the title story in Calvino's 1953 trilogy *Into the War*, trans. Martin McLaughlin (Harmondsworth: Penguin, 2011).

13. Edmond Rostand (1868–1919), the French playwright, Gabriele D'Annunzio (1863–1938), Italy's most famous Decadent novelist, poet, and dramatist, and Sem Benelli (1877–1949), often regarded as a minor D'Annunzio, but actually an anti-Fascist playwright whose plays were censured by the regime.

14. Cesare Vico Ludovici and Stefano Landi (pseudonym of Stefano Pirandello).

15. Eustachio Paolo Lamanna was the author of the most widely used school manual for teaching the history of philosophy.

16. Calvino presumably used terms such as "youknowwhat" to refer to the army, and "whatsitcalled" for the Fascist Party card, in order to avoid his letters arousing the suspicions of the censors.

17. Calvino also used this nickname when he fought with the partisans: it alludes to his place of birth, Santiago de las Vegas, near Havana in Cuba.

18. Adriano Tilgher (1887–1941), philosopher and critic, expert on Pirandello's plays.

19. Tullio Pinelli (1908–2009), playwright who later collaborated as scriptwriter on several Fellini films.

20. Julius Evola (1898–1974), a leading Fascist theorist.

21. The theater group of the Gioventù Universitaria Fascista (GUF).

22. See note 16.

23. Ente Italiano Audizioni Radiofoniche (EIAR) was the only public service broadcaster under Fascism, forerunner of what later would become RAI. Calvino had presumably submitted one of his plays to the radio.

24. The mention of Giacomo and the infinite in this poem show that it is parodying Giacomo Leopardi's famous poem "L'infinito" (The Infinite), whose first line mentions the "lonely hill" where the poet speculated about the infinite.

25. Ruggero Jacobbi (1920–81), poet and literary critic, was at the time a theater critic.

26. The proposal was to have "some story or piece of prose or criticism" published on the cultural page of the weekly *Nuovo Occidente*, on which Scalfari worked.

27. Elio Vittorini's *Conversazione in Sicilia* (*Conversations in Sicily*) was published by Bompiani in 1941.

28. Massimo Simili worked on the humorous fortnightly review *Bertoldo* (1936–43).

29. Johan Huizinga, "The Crisis of Civilization" was published in *The Shadow of Tomorrow* (Italian edition, Turin: Einaudi, 1937).

30. Karl Jaspers, *Philosophy of Existence* (Italian translation 1941), Nicola Abbagnano, *Introduzione all'esistenzialismo* (published 1943).

31. The journals *Nuovo Occidente* and *Roma Fascista* respectively.

32. A Fascist display for workers.

33. As Scalfari had said to Calvino in a letter dated 15 March, the theater director Lucio Chiavarelli had been booed at his last performance at the Teatroguf in Rome.

34. Professor Pacchiaudi had been their philosophy teacher in high school.

35. Scalfari had written saying that he had been "warned and rebuked" for his unorthodox positions, and that the publication of *Nuovo Occidente* had been temporarily suspended.

36. These were three "Apologues" entitled "Dieci soldi in plastilina" (Ten Cents in Plasticine), "Invece era un'altra" (It Was Another Woman Instead), "Passatempi" (Pastimes). They would be published in *Roma Fascista* (the journal of the GUF) on 29 April 1943, thanks to the sub-editor Giovanni Gigliozzi, to whom Scalfari had given *The People's Comedy*, despite the highly critical verdict of chief editor Garroni.

37. Giovanni Gigliozzi, author of radio plays, worked at the EIAR.

38. Calvino is referring to the texts and drawings that Fellini published in the humorous weekly *Marc'Aurelio*.

39. Giovanni Mosca (1908–83) also worked on *Bertoldo* as well as writing the plays mentioned here.

40. A famous line from Ungaretti's poem "Giunone" (Juno) from his 1931 collection *Sentimento del tempo* (*The Feeling of Time*).

41. This is the story "Chi si contenta" (Making Do)', written 17 May 1943, published posthumously: the English translation is in *Numbers in the Dark*, pp. 11–12.

42. The issue of *Pattuglia* dedicated to Ligurian writers (it was to have come out in July 1943) was never published because of the war and the upheaval following the removal of Mussolini from power on 25 July 1943.

43. After the Armistice between Italy and the Allied Forces announced on 8 September 1943, the Germans took control of most of the peninsula, apart from those parts (mostly Sicily and some areas in the South) that were under Allied control.

44. Calvino's brother Floriano (1927–88) was also with him in hiding. The two brothers had decided to take to the hills to avoid conscription under Mussolini's Fascist Republic of Salò, hence the brevity of the note. They would eventually join the partisans to fight in the Ligurian Alps above their home town of San Remo.

1946–1950

1. The Italian phrase for 'to read the riot act' ("leggere la vita") was one whose origins are discussed in the late letter to Primo Levi, of 30 April 1985, the last in this selection.

2. Giovanni Nicosia was a journalist on *l'Unità*, a writer and a translator from Russian.

3. Cesare Pavese (1908–50), major novelist, critic, and translator (of English and American fiction), he was also Calvino's mentor at the Einaudi publishing house. His most famous novel, *La luna e i falò* (*The Moon and the Bonfire*), was published in 1950, the year of his suicide.

4. Natalia Ginzburg (1916–91), author of many novels, also worked with Calvino at Einaudi. In 1946 she was writing the novel *È stato cosí* (*The Dry Heart*) which would be published in 1947.

5. Pavese was working on his novel *Il compagno* (*The Comrade*), which would be published in 1947.

6. This was Calvino's first novel, *Il sentiero dei nidi di ragno* (*The Path to the Spiders' Nests*), written November–December 1946 and published by Einaudi in 1947. For the English translation, see *The Path to the Spiders' Nests*, trans. Archibald Colquhoun, rev. Martin McLaughlin (London: Cape, 1998).

7. The editor of *Omnibus* was at that time Salvato Cappelli: on Calvino's failure to collaborate on the magazine, see the letter to Marcello Venturi of 19 January 1947.

8. In this and the next three paragraphs, Calvino seems to be imitating and parodying Micheli's Viareggio dialect.

9. "Fear on the Footpath'" had come out in the review *Darsena Nuova*, 4 (June–July 1946). The English translation can be found in *Adam, One Afternoon and Other Stories*, tr. Archibald Colquhoun and Peggy Wright (London: Minerva, 1992), pp. 47–53.

10. An allusion to Calvino's review of Riccardo Rangoni's *Uccidere il re*, published in the Communist daily, *l'Unità*, Turin edition, 27 October 1946.

11. Marcello Venturi (1925–2008) was a writer of neorealist fiction. He and Calvino were joint winners in 1946 of a prize for a short story put up by *l'Unità*: Calvino's winning story was "Going to Headquarters," in *Adam, One Afternoon*, pp. 61–67.

12. Giansiro Ferrata (1907–86) was a literary critic who worked for the Mondadori publishing house.

13. Calvino is talking about his first novel, *The Path to the Spiders' Nests*.

14. "Ultimo viene il corvo" (The Crow Comes Last) was published in the Milan edition of *l'Unità*, 5 January 1947. The English translation by Archibald Colquhoun can be read in *Adam, One Afternoon*, pp. 68–73.

15. Calvino's proposal never came to anything. *Il Politecnico* (1945–47) was a major left-wing cultural and literary journal.

16. Giodo Piovene (1907–74) was a major novelist and writer of short stories at this time; Alberto Moravia (1907–90) was the most famous and most translated Italian novelist of the second half of the twentieth century until the arrival on the scene of Calvino himself.

17. In *Agorà*, Calvino published the essay "Pavese in tre libri" (Pavese in three books) (8 August 1946) and the short story "Alba sui rami nudi" (Dawn on the bare branches) (1 January 1947) (no English translation of these exists).

18. Giansiro Ferrata, at the time editor of the culture pages of the Milan edition of *l'Unità*, had written to Calvino on 7 April, in his capacity as member of the jury, explaining why his novel, *The Path to the Spiders' Nests*, had failed in the Mondadori Prize.

19. The Mondadori Prize.

20. The Fronte della Gioventù (Youth Front) was at that time the youth organization of the Communist Party and its allies.

21. Hrand Nazariantz, Armenian writer and journalist who lived in Italy (d. 1962).

22. Aldo Capasso (1909–97), poet and critic.

23. Calvino would review Micheli's *Un figlio, ella disse* (*A Son, She Said*) in the Turin edition of *l'Unità* on 17 August 1947, now in *S*, I, 1176–78.

24. N. C. stands for the Einaudi series Narratori Contemporanei, but this ended in 1947. *The Path to the Spiders' Nests* would come out in the Coralli series in October 1947.

25. In fact Calvino's novel won the Premio Riccione: see Andrea Dini, *Il Premio Nazionale "Riccione" 1947 e Italo Calvino* (Cesena: Il Ponte Vecchio, 2007).

26. Alfonso Gatto (1909–76) was a poet and journalist who had also taken part in the Resistance. See the letter to Graziana Pentich of 18 March 1985.

27. Raf Vallone became famous as an actor in various Italian films, including *Riso amaro* (*Bitter Rice*): see the letter of 11 June 1948 to Silvio Micheli.

28. This refers to a piece (just over two typed pages with additional handwritten notes), now in the Calvino Archive, with the title "Notes on Hemingway." Calvino had just published this anonymously, in a slightly different and shorter form (without the references to Malraux and Koestler), under the title "Hemingway, o della felicità e della noia" (Hemingway, or On Happiness and Boredom): it appeared in the *Bollettino di informazioni culturali*, 12 (31 December 1947), 2–4. This *Bollettino* was a cyclostyled publication, edited by Calvino in 1947–48, with the aim of promoting Einaudi's new books to journalists, booksellers, cultural circles etc.

29. An allusion to the debate that had taken off in the final set of issues of *Politecnico* (nos. 31–32, July–August 1946) with Vittorini's editorial on "Politica e cultura" (Politics and Culture), and had continued in subsequent issues with letters and articles by Palmiro Togliatti, Fabrizio Onofri, etc. and with further interventions by Vittorini, amongst which was his reply to Togliatti (no. 35, January–March 1947).

30. A reference to Felice Balbo's article, "Cultura antifascista" (Anti-Fascist Culture), in issue 39 (December 1947): with that issue the monthly edition of *Politecnico* also ceased publication.

31. This was Calvino's second novel, the unpublished *Il Bianco Veliero* (*The White Schooner*). On 31 May he had written to Marcello Venturi: "For seven or eight months now I've been mucking about with a novel that I began in a moment of weakness and it's turning out to be very bad, causing me to waste lots of my time. But at least it'll get rid of my desire to write novels for four or five years, which is what I dream of doing, and will allow me to study kind of seriously and learn to write decently."

32. The film was *Riso amaro* (*Bitter Rice*) (1949), with Raf Vallone, Walter Gassman, Doris Dowling, and Silvana Mangano.

33. Micheli's *Paradiso maligno* was published in 1948 by Einaudi.

34. Calvino had recently become editor of the cultural page of the Turin edition of *l'Unità*, which published new fiction.

35. On 17 January, Calvino had written to his parents: "In November the most popular Russian magazine *Ogonëk* (The Hearth) published my story 'Il sogno di un giudice' (The Judge's Dream); I knew nothing about it: the cultural attaché Franco Venturi wrote to me from Moscow to tell

me." The story can be found in English as "A Judgement," in Italo Calvino, *Adam, One Afternoon*, pp. 133–41.

36. *Prima che il gallo canti* (1949) contained two novels: *Il carcere* (*The Political Prisoner*) and *La casa in collina* (*The House on the Hill*).

37. Cicino was the nickname of Felice Balbo, a Catholic Communist who also worked at Einaudi: see the letter of 10 July 1979 to Arnold Cassola. Franco Rodano (1920–83) was a Catholic intellectual with Communist sympathies who worked on the Communist journal *Rinascita*. On 1 July 1949, his exclusion from the sacraments and from the liturgical life of the Church would be sanctioned by a decree from the Holy Office, which also threatened with excommunication any Catholics who, like Rodano, belonged to the Italian Communist Party.

38. Pavese's novel was published that year with the title *Tra donne sole* in a volume in the Supercorallo series entitled *La bella estate* (*The Beautiful Summer*): it contained *Il diavolo sulle colline*, *La bella estate*, *Tra donne sole*.

39. This was Ewald Volhard's work, whose Italian translation was published by Einaudi in 1949 in the "Collezione di studi religiosi, etnologici e psicologici" series, the "purple" series run by Pavese.

40. Calvino jokingly alludes to his friends and colleagues at Einaudi: Natalia Ginzburg, Felice Balbo, Bruno Fonzi, Ubaldo Scassellati. He uses the ending in "–ame" to parody the term "culturame" (culturage), used by the Home Secretary Mario Scelba to describe those left-wing intellectuals who, when voting in the election of 18 April 1948, had aligned themselves "in ambiguous alliances with those who deny culture and freedom."

41. Pampaloni had reviewed Calvino's collection of short stories *Ultimo viene il corvo* (*The Crow Comes Last*) (Turin: Einaudi, 1949) in "Il secondo libro di Calvino," in *Comunità* (September–October 1949). Many of the stories in the collection are available in English in *Adam, One Afternoon and Other Stories*.

42. *Il Bianco Veliero*, which had been announced in the notice launching *The Crow*: see also the letters to Elsa Morante of 2 March 1950, and 9 August 1950.

43. In a postcard to his parents dated 5 January, Calvino had written: "I was already hoping I wouldn't have to answer the call-up for military service under the new rules, but as a graduate I have to go along anyway. Let's hope it goes well."

44. The journal was *Cultura e realtà*, which appeared once every two months, edited by Motta and published in Rome. Three issues appeared between May 1950 and March '51. On the editorial board were Fedele d'Amico, Augusto del Noce, Gerardo Guerrieri, Nino Novacco, and Cesare Pavese (the latter only for the first issue). Calvino published two "notes" in it: "Necessità di una critica letteraria" (The Necessity for Literary Criticism) and "Moravia e l'Occidente" (Moravia and the "West") as well

as an open letter to the editor, "Una lettera sul 'Paradiso'" (in this volume, letter of July 1950 to Motta). For an overall account of his experience of *Cultura e realtà*, see the letter to Arnold Cassola of 10 July 1979.

45. Ubaldo Scassellati, a friend of Motta, at this time an editor at the Einaudi publishing house.

46. Valentino Gerratano edited the collection of Giaime Pintor's writings, *Il sangue d'Europa* (*The Blood of Europe*), which was published by Einaudi in 1950.

47. Henry de Montherlant (1895–1972), French writer and dramatist, who like Hemingway was fond of traveling, but who was suspected of being a collaborator for works written during the Second World War.

48. This was an essay by Cesare Pavese collected in his *Letteratura americana e altri saggi*, edited by Calvino (Turin: Einaudi, 1951).

49. Calvino would eventually write a substantial essay on the American author, making some of these points: entitled "Hemingway e noi" ("Hemingway and Ourselves"), it appeared in *Il Contemporaneo* 1:33 (1954), English translation in *Why Read the Classics?*, trans. Martin McLaughlin (London: Cape, 1999), pp. 223–29.

50. The reference is to the essay by Joseph W. Beach, "Tecnica del romanzo novecentesco" (The Technique of the Twentieth-Century Novel), in *Prospettiva della letteratura inglese*, ed. Mario Praz (Milan: Bompiani, 1946).

51. Calvino had already reviewed a book by Anna Seghers, *La rivolta dei pescatori di Santa Barbara* (*Revolt of the Fishermen of Santa Barbara*) (Turin: Einaudi, 1949) in the Piedmont edition of *l'Unità* of 30 July 1949. The other two books were *I sette della miniera* (*The Seventh Cross*) and *I morti non invecchiano* (*The Dead Stay Young*) (Turin: Einaudi, 1950 and 1952).

52. Elsa Morante (1912–85), one of the most important novelists of the postwar period, author of the bestseller *La storia. Romanzo* (*History. A Novel*) (1974).

53. In September 1949, after his spell in the editorial office of the Turin edition of *l'Unità*, Calvino had gone back to work at Einaudi.

54. Alberto Moravia was Morante's husband at the time.

55. Andrea da Barberino's chivalric romance *Guerrin Meschino* (*Miserable Guerrin*), written in the fifteenth century, followed a hero through a series of bizarre adventures.

56. See the letter of 9 August 1950 to Elsa Morante.

57. This letter was published in *Cultura e realtà*, 1 (May–June 1950), pp. 111–12. In the book *The God That Failed*, ed. Richard H. S. Crossman (1950), translated as *Il Dio che ha fallito* (Milan: Edizioni di Comunità, 1950), six writers who had been militants or sympathizers with the Communist Party in the 1930s and '40s (André Gide, Louis Fischer, Arthur Koestler, Ignazio Silone, Stephen Spender, and Richard Wright) recounted their

political experiences and explained the reasons for their rejection of Communism.

58. In the manuscript copy of this letter there follows a sentence which Calvino, in a letter dated 4 September 1950, will ask Motta to add: "Dear Mario, I now discover that Lenin really did use the phrase 'paradise on earth.' [. . .] since I want to remove any pretext for polemic (in the end my job is that of a writer, not an ideological polemicist), I would ask you to add to my piece on paradise, at the end of the fourth (I think) paragraph, where it says " . . . amidst things, in the world of history," immediately after the full stop, the following sentence: "The expression 'paradise on earth', used on one occasion by Lenin (with polemical intent), seems to me to be in this sense new and active and constantly relevant.' [. . .] As long as you think this seems OK, and that this is not making things worse." In the end Motta convinced Calvino it was better not to add the sentence.

59. The manuscript here reads: "but rather than a single point of arrival—one of many—what counts etc."

60. In the manuscript the phrase after the colon reads: "the 'paradisiacal' are all those with whom I have a few scores to settle, the 'non-paradisiacal' are those I can now consider brothers and fathers."

61. In the manuscript the sentence continues: "in any case tomorrow I'm going to the beach, and will be back on Monday."

62. In the manuscript the paragraph ended as follows: " . . . that in oral discussions with you (you who found a theistic basis in all of the various strands of modern atheism) I would maintain, as the truest human position (you say that it does not hold philosophically, but what does that matter? We have so many centuries ahead of us to think about it), defining it as *atheistic atheism*."

63. In the manuscript this is followed by the following phrase in brackets: "(a proverb coined by me on the spur of the moment)."

64. Calvino quotes "sedendo e mirando" (sitting and gazing) from the fourth line of Leopardi's famous poem "L'infinito" (The Infinite).

65. On 27 April 1950, in thanking Dario Puccini for his review of *The Crow Comes Last*, he had written: "I am well aware that my 'cold and detailed approach' and 'mechanical technique' are my most serious dangers. I reached a point of no return along this route in the novel I finished a year ago and which I have not yet decided to publish. Now I will try other routes, but it is not easy."

66. On 25 August he would write to Valentino Gerratana: "I wanted to spend three weeks of holidays alone and in peace, to escape from the distracting rhythm of life I'd got used to. I got a bit bored, but all in all I'm happy. I've not 'produced' much but I've recovered a little bit of the urge to write for myself." See also the letters to Isa Bezzera of 16 July and to Elsa Morante of 9 August.

67. It appeared with the title "Un cannone per i fichi" (A cannon for the figs) in the Turin edition of *l'Unità*, 17 August 1950, now in *RR*, III, 882–88.

68. Published in *l'Unità* on 6 August 1950 with the title "Cent'anni di Maupassant" (Maupassant's Centenary), it is now in *S*, I, 871–74.

69. This is the first quatrain of "Le mort joyeux" (*Les Fleurs du mal*, *Spleen et idéal*, LXXII).

70. In 1950, Natalia Ginzburg married Gabriele Baldini (1919–69), an eminent scholar of English literature as well as cinema critic.

71. The word is missing in the manuscript. The rough copy in the Calvino archive uses the word "desperation."

72. Massimo Bontempelli (1878–1960), an important novelist from the Fascist era, at first a supporter then a critic of the regime.

73. See the letter to Mario Motta of July 1950.

74. Calvino is referring to an earlier letter to Gerratana of 15 September 1950 and to his article "Malvagità degli ignoranti" (The wickedness of the ignorant), in the Turin edition of *l'Unità*, 10 September 1950, and to his piece on Pavese for the *Bollettino del Sindacato nazionale degli scrittori*, 2 (September 1950), pp. 5–6.

75. "la maglia rotta nella rete" (the broken mesh in the net) is a well-known phrase from the opening poem of Montale's famous collection *Ossi di seppia* (*Cuttlefish Bones*) (1924).

76. The two phrases refer to Pirandellian notions about existence.

77. "Delitti che pochi immaginano" and "Bestialità da SS" in *l'Unità* (Turin ed.), 8 and 10 October 1950.

78. Emilio Sereni (1907–77) was a leading Communist thinker and writer. An anti-Fascist and partisan, after the war he was a minister under De Gasperi's government: he was also head of the Communist Party's Cultural Commission.

1951–1955

1. Pampaloni's articles had all come out in *Il Ponte*: "I nomi e le lagrime di Elio Vittorini" (December 1950); "Ritratto sentimentale di George Orwell" (May 1951); "Povero cuore che sussulti" (June 1951).

2. *Verrà la morte e avrà i tuoi occhi* was a collection of Pavese's final poems.

3. Vittorini had written his favorable verdict on *The Cloven Viscount* to Calvino in a letter dated 11 December 1951: see Elio Vittorini, *Gli anni del "Politecnico". Lettere 1945–1951* (Turin: Einaudi, 1977), p. 393.

4. This will be "La formica argentina" (The Argentine Ant), *Botteghe Oscure*, 10 (1952), 406–41. English translation by Archibald Colquhoun in *Adam, One Afternoon*, pp. 155–90.

5. Rago had been commissioned to translate Rousseau's *Confessions*, which would be published by Einaudi in 1955.

6. *I giovani del Po* (Youth in Turin), a novel written 1950–51, but never published by Calvino in book form because he was unsatisfied with it. The Italian text is now in *RR*, III, 1011–1126, but no English translation is available. See also the letter to Carlo Salinari of 22 December 1952.

7. On 12 July he would write to Rago: "As for *I giovani del Po*, my corrections can only maybe be stylistic pruning. But please do have Pratolini read the manuscript, and Salinari and Puccini. In short, if I see there is a platform of consensus that is broad enough, I'm prepared to publish it."

8. See the letter to Rago of 7 June 1952 and note 5 above.

9. In the manuscript in the Calvino Archive the sentence goes on after a comma to say: "valiant defenders of the freedom of their people, who will also have their own line of conduct and influence on these events."

10. Leader of the Brazilian Communist Party.

11. The manuscript contains a phrase after "To conclude" not included here: "my first instinct, and I believe that of many readers of *l'Unità*, was one of solidarity with the rebels: perhaps this is not warranted, but as we wait for fuller information . . .".

12. A review of *Il visconte dimezzato* (*The Cloven Viscount*).

13. Salinari's review of *Il visconte dimezzato* came out in *l'Unità* on 6 August 1952. It is interesting to note that on 20 February 1956, Calvino would write a letter, containing almost identical arguments and words, to René Lacote, who had reviewed the French translation of *Il visconte* in *Lettres Françaises*.

14. The square brackets are in the manuscript; in the typescript the brackets are round.

15. In the typescript "completely" is missing.

16. The letter to Rago referred to here is that of 27 June 1952; see also the letter to Salinari of 22 December 1952.

17. Carocci had written to Calvino on 6 October inviting him to collaborate on the journal he was putting together with Alberto Moravia; and he had asked him to write an article for the first issue, on the theme of "Art and Communism."

18. In the second issue of the journal (May–June 1953), Calvino would publish the short story "Gli avanguardisti a Mentone" (The Avanguardisti in Menton).

19. See the letter to Michele Rago of 27 June 1952.

20. The Communist Party of Italy's publishing house.

21. The Piccola Biblioteca Scientifica Letteraria was an Einaudi series started in 1950.

22. Aldo De Jaco's stories *Le domeniche di Napoli* (*Neapolitan Sundays*) would be published by Einaudi in the Gettoni series in 1954. V. is Elio Vittorini.

23. After "Gli avanguardisti a Mentone" (The Avanguardisti in Menton), which came out in the second issue of *Nuovi Argomenti* (May–June 1953), Carocci would have to wait until issue 34 (September–October 1958) for "another story," namely "La nuvola di smog" (Smog). "The Avanguardisti in Menton" would be the second story in the autobiographical trilogy *L'entrata in guerra*, published by Einaudi in 1953—for an English version see Calvino, *Into the War*, pp. 25–60.

24. *Sagapò*, published that year in the Gettoni series.

25. Paolo Spriano, at that time on the editorial board of *l'Unità*.

26. The project never came to fruition.

27. Cesare Pavese.

28. G. Lukács, *Il marxismo e la critica letteraria* (*Marxism and Literary Criticism*), ed. C. Cases (Turin: Einaudi, 1953). On 30 September, Calvino would write also to Valentino Gerratana: "I have something sensational to tell you. I've been unexpectedly bowled over by reading Lukács: all my aesthetic ideas have been thrown overboard, I found that book (I'm talking especially about the second part) more stimulating and clarifying than I'd ever have believed, and I can only think now by starting out from his categories."

29. The Giuseppe Pitré Ethnographical Museum in Palermo, of which Cocchiara was director at that time.

30. Francesco Novati (1859–1915), historian and critic.

31. One of Cocchiara's proposals to Einadi had been "to think about a collection of the best folk tales of the Italian people."

32. Einaudi had published Afanasiev's collection of Russian tales as *Antiche fiabe russe* in 1953.

33. Vittorio Imbriani, *La novellaja fiorentina* (Livorno: F. Vigo, 1871) was the major source of Tuscan folktales.

34. On 16 April, Calvino would reply to Cocchiara who had declared himself opposed to Vidossi's "mixed criterion": "all of us here are in agreement with you on opting to go down the route of a collection of creative texts, completely rewritten, and with no philological scruples. And I am in agreement too [. . .] the prospect [of being the "narrator"] is too attractive to turn down." He added that "Einaudi would be happy to entrust to you" the work of collecting, philologically cataloguing, and translating the folktales, and once that work was "finished or at an advanced stage, I would be released from my publishing duties as an employee and, for a period of about nine months, I would be seconded to work solely on the folktales. I would study the project with you, then I would go off somewhere quiet on my own, with all the material; while remaining in constant touch with you for philological questions, I would ruminate on my folktales until I've completed the definitive new version."

35. The article had been printed in *l'Unità* on which Pistoi was the art critic.

36. At the time Sesa Tatò and Paolo Spriano worked as editors on the Turin edition of *l'Unità*.

37. Rea had used this expression in a letter to Calvino of 1 March 1954, in which he asked why he was "so laconic".

38. This letter, addressed to Carlo Salinari, Antonello Trombadori, Marco Cesarini Sforza, and Valentino Gerratana, documents Calvino's initial reaction on examining issue no. 1 of the weekly *Il Contemporaneo* (dated 27 March 1954): the addressees were the weekly's editors and writers.

39. A cultural weekly edited by Monsignor Pietro Barbieri.

40. In the draft of the letter, this is followed by the following sentences: "Don't you know that different sizes of typeface were invented for a reason? Don't you realize that you need something interesting on the first page, something that attracts attention?"

41. The draft has "is a novice's error, which gives the whole review an air of Arcadian ennnui."

42. The minute reads: "The rubrics, the famous rubrics that were to denounce and inform and thus give a particular tone to the journal, that were meant to be like machine-gun fire, volleys of shots, a kind of Annamaria Caglio, something which people go and read immediately, are instead non-existent, miserable, weak." Annamaria Moneta Caglio was quite a well-known figure at the time in the high-life and legal news.

43. The draft continues: "This is where you see an editorial board that is either working or is simply scratching its balls. Surely you should have dealt immediately with some major cultural problem, some burning issue? There's none of this visible."

44. In the draft the following paragraph appears: "And putting the novel on the last page is further proof of the lack of material in the paper."

45. In the draft, in place of this last sentence we read: "Vicari's *Il Caffè* has just reached me. Now I have no sympathy for student humor, but at least his journal gives the idea of having a certain kind of life—superficial café life, as the rest of life in Rome is anyway—whereas ours is just boring."

46. The draft has the following two sentences: "Right, if we don't start firing insults at each other we won't make any progress. I'll go first."

47. In the editorial entitled "Reciprocità del silenzio" (Reciprocity of Silence) the journal denounced the Scelba government for having passed measures "aimed at limiting, and in practice suffocating, cultural relations with the USSR."

48. The acronym of the European Defense Community, which had been promoted in 1952 by Belgium, France, Italy, Luxembourg, the Low

Countries, and the Federal German Republic with the aim of creating a European army connected with NATO. The EDC never came into being, because of the failure of France to ratify it (August 1954). The Italian Communist Party put up strong opposition in those years to the EDC and German rearmament.

49. Amerigo Bartoli: he and Mino Maccari were the authors of the drawings and cartoons in the weekly *Il Mondo*.

50. Calvino is referring to one of the stories in *Marcovaldo*, which had appeared in *l'Unità* on 5 July 1953: English translation in *Marcovaldo*, trans. William Weaver (London: Minerva, 1994), pp. 40–44.

51. On 21 August Elsa Morante had sent a postcard from Sils (in Engadin, Switzerland) in order "to tell you how much I liked *L'entrata in guerra* (*Into the War*)."

52. Calvino and Alberto Moravia had been at the Lido di Venezia to attend the cinema festival (Calvino as a special correspondent for the magazine *Cinema nuovo*).

53. The piece was "Cronache scolastiche" (School Chronicles) by Leonardo Sciascia, which Carocci would publish in *Nuovi Argomenti*, 12 (January–February 1955), and would later form part of *Le parrocchie di Regalpietra* (*Salt in the Wound*) (Bari: Laterza, 1956; later Milan: Adelphi, 1991).

54. These were printed by the Salvatore Sciascia publishing house in Caltanissetta.

55. I. Pizzetti, "Un addio a Hemingway" (A Farewell to Hemingway), *Società*, 1 (February 1955).

56. Two lines omitted here.

57. See the letter of 15 January 1954 to Cocchiara.

58. The first issue of *Officina* (which described itself as "a two-month fascicle of poetry") had just come out in Bologna. The editors of the first twelve issues of the first series were: Francesco Leonetti, Pier Paolo Pasolini, Roberto Roversi. The two issues of the second series were published by Bompiani with the editorial board enlarged to include Franco Fortini, Angelo Romanò, and Gianni Scalia.

59. Calvino is referring to Pasolini's "Pagine introduttive alla poesia popolare italiana" (Introduction to Italian Popular Poetry), *Nuovi Argomenti*, 12 (January–February 1955), 55–79. This was an extract from his lengthy introduction to *Il canzoniere italiano. Antologia della poesia popolare* (*The Italian Song-Book. An Anthology of Italian Popular Poetry*) (Parma: Guanda, 1955; later Milan: Garzanti, 1972); and to his "Poesia popolare e poesia d'avanguardia" (Popular and Avant-Garde Poetry), *Paragone* (*Letteratura*), 64 (April 1955), 98–104.

60. P. P. Pasolini, M. Dell'Arco, eds., *Poesia dialettale del Novecento* (*Twentieth-Century Dialect Poetry*) (Parma: Guanda, 1952).

61. Piero Jahier (1884–1966), poet and translator.

62. Pavese's first collection of poetry (1936) appeared in English with the title *Hard Labor*, trans. William Arrowsmith (New York: Grossman, 1976).

63. Luigi Comencini's very successful 1953 film, with Vittorio De Sica and Gina Lollobrigida.

64. Giovanni Verga (1840–1922), the Sicilian realist novelist and writer of short stories.

65. The draft reads: "the semi-proletariat in hotels."

66. In the draft the reference is more explicit: "Some of my partisan stories in *Ultimo viene il corvo* (*The Crow Comes Last*) are stories I heard being told in the evening in the partisan detachments." And in 1959 Calvino will be more precise: "When I started out as an author, writing was easy. There was no difference between words and things, between the power of the facts and style, between the objective and subjective worlds. Life around us swarmed with stories. Many of the stories that I and others wrote were 'tales of hearsay,' stories we heard being told in the partisan bivouacs or in the third-class train compartments in the early postwar years" ("I racconti che non ho scritto") (The Stories I never Wrote), in Calvino, *I racconti* (*The Short Stories*) (Milan: Mondadori, 1993), p. vii.

67. The draft has "Marxism-Leninism."

68. Ippolito Pizzetti and Filippo Di Pasquantonio.

69. Mario Spinella: at the time he worked on *Società*, but after the resignations of Manacorda and Muscetta in 1956, he would be editor of the new series of the journal (1957–61) which would no longer be run by Einaudi.

70. Referring to the English analytical philosopher Gilbert Ryle's *The Concept of Mind* (1949); Einaudi had published the Italian translation by Ferruccio Rossi-Landi, in its "Biblioteca di cultura filosofica" series in 1955.

71. Carlo Bertelli and Enrico Castelnuovo.

72. Aldemaro Ossella and Guido Donadio were functionaries at Einaudi.

73. There is a gap of half a page in the photocopy.

74. Calvino's verdict on this novel can be found in the letter to Pavese of 27 July 1949.

75. The screenplay was written by Antonioni himself along with Suso Cecchi d'Amico and the writer Alba de Céspedes.

1956–1960

1. See the letter to Pasolini of 9 May 1955.

2. Gianfranco Contini (1912–90), regarded as one of the most sophisticated Italian literary critics of the twentieth century.

3. Pietro Citati and Cesare Garboli were literary critics as well as friends and correspondents of Calvino's. The Giubbe Rosse was a famous literary café in Florence between the wars, frequented by Montale and others.

4. Renato Solmi was a friend and colleague of Calvino at Einaudi.

5. Further evidence of Calvino's interest in Pasolini's poetry can be found in a note from 28 June 1957: "I read "La terra di lavoro" (The land of toil) in *Nuovi Argomenti* and I liked it a lot"; and in a letter of 10 July 1958, talking of Pasolini's "Usignolo della Chiesa Cattolica" (The Catholic Church's nightingale) which had just been published by Longanesi: "A reading of your new book of old poems suggests that there has been a redistribution of literary genres: today what was originally the subject matter of autobio-Bildung-psycho-ideological novels now belongs to poetry, whereas narrative prose now deals with that translation of the writer's own subjective world into objective images, musical rhythm and linguistic codes which was once the theme of poetic verse. Which is perfectly right."

6. Jacopo Pirona was the author of a Friulan-Italian dictionary.

7. Calvino is referring to an editorial by the editors of *Il Contemporaneo*, published in issue 25 (23 June 1956) in reply to a long letter from Pasolini. In it Pasolini contested the critical remarks made by Vann'Antò (pseudonym of Giovanni Antonio Di Giacomo, a Sicilian poet and a lecturer in the traditions of popular literature) regarding his *Canzoniere italiano. Antologia della poesia popolare* in a review entitled "La Baronessa di Carini," in *Il Contemporaneo*, 23 (9 June 1956).

8. Sciascia's short story "La morte di Stalin" (The death of Stalin), later included in *Gli zii di Sicilia* (*Sicilian Uncles*), published in the Gettoni series (Turin: Einaudi, 1958).

9. Carlo Cassola (1917–87), realist novelist who took part in the Resistance, and was also among Calvino's correspondents.

10. *L'isola di Arturo* (*Arturo's Island*) (Turin: Einaudi, 1957): Calvino had clearly read the original typescript. The "Torpidiniera delle Antille" (The Torpedo-boat of the Antilles), mentioned at the end of the letter, is Arturo's boat.

11. An article published in *Paragone* (*Arte*), 86 (September 1956); later in Arcangeli's *Dal romanticismo all'informale*, II: *Il secondo dopoguerra* (Turin: Einaudi, 1977), pp. 338–76. Francesco Arcangeli (1915–74), an art historian and pupil of Roberto Longhi, was an expert on seventeenth-century painting in Emilia Romagna as well on contemporary art.

12. Cesare Brandi (1906–88), an art critic of the time.

13. Here there are one or two words which Arcangeli could not decipher in his transcription and which he marked with question marks.

14. Mattia Moreni (1920–99), Italian artist and sculptor.

15. Giovanni Testori (1923–93), Milanese writer of novels and plays.

16. The heads of the Italian Communist Party, in particular those in charge of the Cultural Commission, of which Calvino had been a member from 1956.

17. Giorgio Amendola (1907–80), writer and member of the Italian Communist Party from 1948 till his death.

18. Carlo Muscetta (1912–2004), Marxist literary critic.

19. On 14 November 1956, in the midst of the crisis caused within the Italian Communist Party by the Soviet invasion of Hungary, Calvino had voiced similar feelings to his translator in Buenos Aires, Attilio Dabini: "We lead a life fragmented between a thousand tasks and worries (for three years now I have not been able to write for myself) and these last few weeks of political anxieties which show no sign of ending are even more corrosive of any concrete activity."

20. On 19 April 1957 he would write to Paolo Spriano: "I am following the ups and downs of *Il Contemporaneo*, but without any passion or hope now."

21. P. P. Pasolini, "La confusione degli stili" (The confusion of styles), *Ulisse* (September 1956); later in his *Passione e ideologia 1948–1958* (*Passion and Ideology*) (Milan: Garzanti, 1960).

22. His unpublished novel, *I giovani del Po* (*Youth in Turin*) would appear in the Bolognese journal *Officina*: see the following letter to Francesco Leonetti of 19 February 1957 and the earlier ones to Michele Rago of 27 June 1952, and to Carlo Salinari of 22 December 1952.

23. Mario Soldati (1906–99), prolific novelist and short-story writer as well as film director.

24. The story seems to be about the inaccuracies surrounding Pasolini: he had published a work entitled *La meglio gioventù*, but the American film *Rebel without a Cause* arrived in Italy about this time, entitled *Gioventù bruciata*, so the priest seems to have confused the two titles; furthermore, Pasolini was published by Garzanti, not Mondadori, and he was an Italian writer whose works therefore should not have been in a series for foreign authors.

25. The novel Calvino had given to Pasolini was *I giovani del Po* (see the previous letter). It was published in four extracts in *Officina* (issue 8, January 1957; issue 9–10, June 1957; issue 11, November 1957; issue 12, April 1958), with an introductory note signed "i.c." at the foot of the first page of the first extract. Part of the note states: "*Officina* is aimed at those who are interested in literature as an area of research and as something problematic, so in accepting its invitation, I am publishing here in instalments this short novel of mine, written between January 1950 and July 1951, but which has always remained in the drawer. In this work I wanted finally to express also in narrative form that area of my interests and experience which I have so far managed to bring to life only in a few pages

of non-fiction, namely: the city, industrial civilization, the workers. At the same time, however, I wanted to articulate that other part of reality and of my interests (from which it was however always easier for me to extract narrative symbols) that is nature, adventure, the tough search for a natural happiness today. My objective was to provide an image of human integration with the world. Instead I ended up with a work that was uncharacteristically grey for me: although it contained much talk about the fullness of life, little of that comes across: that was why I have never wanted to publish it as a book."

26. Citati's letter offered comments on *Il barone rampante* (*The Baron in the Trees*): Calvino had sent him the typescript of the novel to read.

27. It would be published a few months later in issue 20 of *Botteghe Oscure*, then in a shortened version in Calvino's collected *Racconti*, and finally in a definitive version, published by Einaudi, in 1963.

28. After the book's publication, Calvino would write to Vittorini on 8 July: "Dear Elio, I am delighted to read your verdict after your second reading, just as your first reading had already provided me with the first satisfaction I got from the book. And very happy that Ginetta liked it: she, I know, is a reader who does not get enthusiastic easily. I thank both of you. Very best wishes, Yours, Calvino."

29. In a letter of 21 June 1956, Calvino had written to Fortini: "Dear Fortini, you are quite right, my goodness! But this is a widespread phenomenon. Books that contain ideas, that start a discussion, all fall into the void. The impressive series of Saggi (Essays) that we brought out this year has barely stirred up an echo. The thing is if a book is not strictly relevant to the 'literary critic' or to the various specialists in papers and journals, but is a problematic book both in literary and political terms—Nehru, Angelopoulos, Auerbach, Lukács, your book—it fails to find the right reviewer. The problem we are up against here is finding a new type of criticism, for the key books will be more and more of this kind." Calvino was referring to Tibor Mende, *Conversations with Nehru*; Angelos Angelopoulos, *Will the Atom Unite the World?*; Erich Auerbach, *Mimesis. Realism in Western Literature*; György Lukács, *Brief History of German Literature from the Eighteenth Century to the Present*; Franco Fortini, *Asia maggiore. Viaggio in Cina* (*Asia Major. Journey to China*).

30. Carlo Bo (1911–2001), major literary critic and academic; Franco Antonicelli (1902–74), an anti-Fascist who set up his own publishing house, De Silva, which published the first edition of Primo Levi's *Se questo è un uomo* (*If This Is a Man*) in 1947.

31. Jean Giono, *Le hussard sur le toit* (*The Hussar on the Roof*), published in 1951.

32. Ippolito Nievo (1831–61): Calvino admitted to having modeled some characters and episodes in *Il barone rampante* on Nievo's novel *Le confessioni di un italiano* (*The Confessions of an Italian Man*), published posthu-

mously in 1867. In a letter to Luigi Santucci of 28 June, Calvino had written, amongst other things, "In particular I am glad to hear that you liked the story of Viola's loves. (And your reference to la Pisana is absolutely spot on: and it is not the only Nievo reference in the book; the *Confessions* are one of my favorite books, and I continually discover that they bear fruit in my work without me noticing it.)"

33. Antonio Giolitti, who had left the Communist Party: his resignation letter was dated 20 July.

34. Dionys Mascolo, French writer, and head of the Gallimard publishing house.

35. See the letter published in *Nuova Stampa* and the *Gazzetta del popolo* on 10 January 1957.

36. In the earlier typewritten draft of the letter, after "younger leaders" the following words were scored out: "who felt more strongly the need for new perspectives."

37. In the first draft, after the semicolon there is this scored out sentence: "I continue to believe that the figure of the militant intellectual is—when he succeeds and is allowed to fulfil himself fully—superior to that of the isolated intellectual; I know well that seeing oneself forced to quit the Party ranks as a defeat, and unfortunately not just my defeat."

38. In the first draft Calvino had written "my decision."

39. He is referring to the letter of 25 July, published on 1 August in *Avanti!* in which Carlo Muscetta resigned from the PCI.

40. Carlo Salinari and Antonello Trombadori were the editors of *Il Contemporaneo*.

41. *La speculazione edilizia* (*A Plunge into Real Estate*). English translation in *Difficult Loves*, trans. William Weaver (London: Picador, 1985), pp. 161–250.

42. He is referring to the financial difficulties of the Einaudi publishing house.

43. Rossana Rossanda (1924–), prominent Communist intellectual and writer.

44. Eugenio Reale, a leading figure in the PCI, had resigned from the party in 1956 and was editor of the periodical *Corrispondenza socialista*, which was considered a "social-democratic" organ also by Calvino.

45. A novel by Roger Vailland (1957).

46. The editorial "Il giorno della disfatta" (The day of defeat) which appeared in *Il Contemporaneo* on 3 August 1957 and had already been mentioned at the beginning of the letter.

47. The Partito d'Azione (Action Party), a non-Communist anti-Fascist group during the Second World War, which also formed part of the first postwar government, but then splintered in 1946.

48. This was a collection entitled *Roma e i nostri anni* (*Rome and our Time*) (Milan: Feltrinelli, 1957), which Socrate had proposed unsuccessfully to

Einaudi and about which Calvino had written a long letter on 19 February (it can be read in *ILDA*, pp. 210–11).

49. "La gran bonaccia della Antille" (Becalmed in the Antilles), Calvino's allegory attacking the Communist leadership's lack of mobility, was published in *Città Aperta* (March 1957). An English translation is in *Numbers in the Dark*, pp. 115–21.

50. Dario Puccini, another of the founding editors of *Città aperta*.

51. Calvino had been given a banning order from France for having participated in a congress of the Partisans for Peace in Paris in April 1949.

52. The Communist monthly journal *Rinascita*.

53. On 19 October, Togliatti would reply to Calvino with a letter (in the Calvino Archive) which amongst other things says: "Dear Calvino, the "ill-wishers" you mention at the start of your letter are partly right and partly wrong. I did not mention your name in my report to the C. C. Speaking of 'the man of letters etc.' I meant rather to identify a type: that of the man of letters who yesterday considered commitment to a cause—even in a work of literature—as something contemptible, but today is himself totally committed to producing works or ensuring that works are produced that are aimed solely at disseminating slanderous opinions of our Party and to promoting defeatism etc. etc. I find in this type some traits which unfortunately were traditionally typical of too many Italian literati: court jesters not real characters. [. . .] Whether you too, to some extent and for some reason, come under this category, is a question of fact that is of less interest. But the letter you wrote when you resigned from the party certainly comes into that category."

54. Calvino is referring to the proof of a draft editorial, containing the journal's program, written collectively by the editors of *Città aperta*.

55. In a villa in Capocotta, near Rome, a certain Wilma Montesi had died in circumstances that were unclear (probably an overdose). She was a young woman whose body was then found on 11 April 1953 on the beach at Tor Vaianica: the scandal that then ensued in the press, in 1954, led to some prominent Christian Democrat figures also being involved in judicial proceedings. Suor Pasqualina, whose real name was Pascalina Lehnert, was a Bavarian nun, a powerful and scheming maid-cum-factotum of Pius XII throughout the whole period of his papacy.

56. Calvino's proposal was accepted in its entirety and constituted the first paragraph of an editorial entitled "Questioni per un programma" (Questions for a program), signed by Calvino and another twenty-five intellectuals, which would open the new series of *Città aperta*, 6 (March 1958).

57. Arrigo Benedetti (1910–76), writer and journalist, founder of the weekly magazine *L'Espresso*.

58. Georgij S. Breitburd, scholar of Italian literature and translator, was the Secretary of the Foreign Commission of the Union of Soviet Writers.

59. Romano Bilenchi (1909–89), Tuscan novelist.

60. Vitaliano Brancati (1907–54), Sicilian writer of ironic and sometimes erotic novels.

61. Carlo Bernari (1909–93), Neapolitan novelist. In a letter of 16 January 1958, Calvino wrote to Veršinin: "I realize that you are more interested in short stories to publish in magazines rather than in novels. So I will send you Giorgio Bassani's *Cinque storie ferraresi* (*Five Stories of Ferrara*). Bassani is one of our most interesting young writers both on account of his style and for the ethical problems he deals with: his world is the Jewish middle classes in Ferrara in the Fascist and postwar periods. I will also get them to send you Anna Maria Ortese's *Il mare non bagna Napoli* (*The Bay Is Not Naples*), one of the foremost works of Italian documentary realism. [. . .] Amongst the most recent Italian works I would highlight a vast collection of short stories by Mario Soldati, which has just been published by Garzanti. Soldati is an Italian writer concerned with the "bourgeois" world and its problems, but really quite important. However, I do not know if his work could be of interest in the USSR except as evidence of another world." On 12 July 1961 he would write to him: "I will send you *L'Adalgisa*, by our most bizarre writer, C. E. Gadda, in which you will find some pieces for your collection of humorous stories."

62. Armando Bozzoli worked at the Biblioteca Comunale di San Felice sul Panaro.

63. In a letter of 22 November 1957, Calvino had written to Caretti to say he was "very happy that it will be you who in '58 will be talking about Italian books on the Third Programme"; and on 17 January: "I am impatient to hear what you will say about me on the radio. I do not have a radio and I think it will be impossible for me to hear the broadcast, but I look forward to seeing the text."

64. Calvino is referring to the review of *Il barone rampante* that Leonardo Sciascia had just published (*Il Ponte*, 12 December 1957), in which among other things he wrote: "we are convinced that, in a process of natural and constant evolution and enrichment, Calvino remains essentially faithful to his own poetic world whether he takes on current, "real" subject matter, like the partisan war and *Into the War*, or whether he moves in the dimension of a past that is genuinely fable-like. Because above all else, Calvino is faithful to history." In a letter of 13 June 1958 Calvino would write to Marco Forti: "Some months ago Leonardo Sciascia, in a review in *Il Ponte*, wrote things that I would like to think are true."

65. Calvino is referring to the negative verdict on the first edition of the novel (which came out in the Gettoni series in 1952) which he had made

clear to Cassola in a letter dated 12 July 1951 (in *ILDA*, pp. 50–52). The new edition was published in the Supercoralli series in 1958.

66. Opposing attitudes to modern art and literature had already emerged in Calvino's epistolary exchanges with Cassola. On 10 October 1956, for instance, Calvino had replied in the following terms to Cassola's dismissive verdict on Simone de Beauvoir's *The Mandarins*, when he claimed the intellectuals were "represented as monsters," devoid of the "most basic human substance": "The problem is whether one has to believe in a 'basic human substance,' as you confidently think exists also in our times; or in a variety of possibilities of monsters, either horrible or marvelous, in all epochs of human history, as I sometimes am inclined to believe." And on 12 February 1958, replying to a letter in which Cassola had polemically championed the claims of a literature "with human features," Calvino wrote: "We are both fully in agreement that we are against the literature of the 'intellectuals' in which everything is an ideological puppet. This was in fact my first polemical starting point in writing: against Gide and the literature of intellectualism I chose Hemingway and the literature of facts. But actually part of the literature that you condemn had the merit of articulating, with a coldness amounting to poetry (and morality, there exists also a *moral* cynicism), the cruelty and monstrosity of the contemporary world. Camus's *L'étranger* (*The Outsider*) neither philosophizes nor ideologizes; and as for Sartre, at least his story *Le mur* is like that" (*ILDA*, p. 248).

67. Cesare Cases's article "Storia di un cane" (Story about a dog) on Tibor Déry's short novel *Niki* (Turin: Einaudi, 1957)—which would come out in *Passato e Presente*, 3 (May–June 1958)—ended thus: "If by chance someone [the critic on *Il Contemporaneo*, Rino dal Sasso] finds in *Niki* an 'anxious Crepuscularism,' it is clear that he will project onto it, as people do, his own decadent nostalgia. And if the same critic assures us that in order to tell us about 'the contradictions of that tormented country' what is needed is 'a higher, less prejudiced intellectual stance' than Déry offers, this position must with all probability be that of Carlo Emilio Gadda, the new model for realism, whom our writer very much admires. And indeed, if instead of 'bringing back to life a tranquil, crepuscular world, worthy of being alive certainly, but marginal,' Déry had recounted to us some terrible deed from the lurid pages of the papers, in a mixture of something typical of Budapest and something typically Roman, not only would he have caught those contradictions much better, but nobody would ever have thought of criticizing him. He would have killed two birds with one stone: socialist realism 'of the new type' and personal freedom. He would have his place in the sun instead of seeing it from behind bars. That little place in the sun that is always there for those who happily don't give a damn about truth, socialism, man, and in general, everything (except of course

'literature')." For Calvino's defense of Gadda's *Il pasticciaccio* (*That Awful Mess on Via Merulana*), see the next letter to Cases.

68. He is referring to Carlo Emilio Gadda's important novel, *Quer pasticciaccio brutto de via Merulana* (*That Awful Mess on Via Merulana*) (Milan: Garzanti, 1957).

69. Calvino's article "Pasternak e la rivoluzione" (Pasternak and the Revolution) would come out in *Passato e Presente*, 3 (May–June 1958), pp. 360–74; English translation in *Why Read the Classics?*, pp. 179–96.

70. The reading of this word is difficult: Calvino had at first written then cancelled out "and abandons realism."

71. Calvino's reference is to a sentence in a letter to him from Cases of 27 February: "I was not attacking G. directly, but rather Rino dal Sasso who wrote that despicable review of *Niki*, and in general the line taken by *Il Contemporaneo* which uses Gadda in order not to confront the real problems (so not an attack on G. himself, but on G. being used as our answer to and alibi for Déry and Pasternak, mutatis mutandis)." See also the previous letter.

72. Cases had cited this passage from Giacomo Leopardi's letter to his brother Carlo of 20 February 1820, in which he describes the road leading to Tasso's tomb, which is "all lined with houses that have been designated for manufacturing": "In a leisurely, dissipated city, devoid of purpose, as capital cities are, it is still wonderful to consider the image of the quiet, ordered life, one that busies itself with useful professions. Even the features and manners of the people one meets in that street have something more simple and humane than the features and manners of others, and they display the habits and character of people whose life is founded on truth not falsehood, that is to say they live on labour and not on intrigue, imposture and deceit, unlike the majority of the population."

73. A. Asor Rosa, "Calvino dal sogno alla realtà" (Calvino from Dream to Reality), *Mondo Operaio*, 3–4 (March–April 1958), Supplemento scientifico-letterario. Asor Rosa had read *La speculazione edilizia* (*A Plunge into Real Estate*) in *Botteghe Oscure*, 20 (Autumn 1957), where it first appeared.

74. Vasco Pratolini (1913–91), Florentine neo-realist writer whose novels had a strong local setting.

75. Calvino is probably thinking of the first-person protagonist in Levi's *Cristo si è fermato a Eboli* (*Christ Stopped at Eboli*).

76. There had been threats of and preparations for subversion coming both from clandestine organizations of the far right and from the more extremist sections of French settlers and soldiers in Algeria headed by General Jacques Massu. As a result, on 1 June 1958, the President of the French Republic, René Coty, in an exceptional procedure had given full powers (confirmed by the French parliament for six months) to General

Charles de Gaulle. On Calvino's worries regarding the French situation, see his statements quoted by Cesare Pillon in his article "Per combattere il fascismo in Francia bisogna anche vigilare in casa nostra" (To combat Fascism in France we must also be vigilant at home), *l'Unità* (Turin), 11 June 1958.

77. Calvino is referring with all probability to the military coup d'état in Iraq, of 14 July 1958, which overthrew the monarchy (King Faisal II was killed) and established a republic.

78. This was a book by Michel Save, translated and published by Einaudi in 1959 as *Lo splendore del deserto*.

79. The exact title of I. Meszaros's book was *La rivolta degli intellettuali in Ungheria* (*The Revolt of the Intellectuals in Hungary*).

80. The writer Marguerite Duras, and Giulio Einaudi.

81. In a similar letter to Pietro Citati of 2 September, in which he shows doubts and asks him advice on the shape of the volume (in *ILDA*, pp. 262–64), Calvino wrote: "So out of all my fiction of any importance the only thing that would be excluded would be the trilogy of stories in *L'entrata in guerra* (*Into the War*). This is perhaps a pity because if I put them in, the volume would end up containing all of Calvino's short stories, from '45 to '58. But they would stick out like a sore thumb. I could insert them in *La vita difficile*, after the *Formica* (*The Argentine Ant*), and never mind about the harmony of the whole. Or create a separate "book": *Le memorie difficili* (*Difficult Memories*), and put in there "Pomeriggio coi mietitori" (Afternoon with the harvesters), "I figli poltroni" (The lazy sons), and "Pranzo con un pastore" (Goatherd at luncheon), three quite good stories from the *Crow* with an autobiographical slant. But where will I put this book of "difficult memories"? Between the *Idilli* and the *Amori*? That would ruin the progression in the titles of the three books. Everything is still too complicated and a bit of a mess. Maybe it's better not to include them, best to keep them for another possible collection, if I ever write autobiographical stories in that vein again." In the end Calvino would include in the collection the book of *Memorie difficili*, using the criterion and the stories mentioned in the letter to Citati, and inserting them between *Difficult Idylls* and *Difficult Loves*.

These doubts about the shape of *I racconti* are in evidence also in a letter of 27 January 1961 to Attilio Dabini, who was translating the book for an Argentinian publisher: "As far as I am concerned, I agree about dividing the stories into two volumes. We can do as you suggest (Volume I: *Idilli* and *Amori*; Volume II: *Memorie* and *Vita*). Either that or: Volume I: *Idilli*, *Amori*, *Memorie*; Volume II: the three stories of *La vita*, which are perhaps long enough to constitute a volume on their own. Or another alternative: Volume I: short stories (*Idilli*, *Amori*, and the shorter tales from *Memorie*); Volume II: longer stories (the three tales from *L'entrata in guerra* plus the three from *La vita difficile*). That's enough: it's a disaster if I start to think about how to structure a book of short stories. I spent more than a year full of doubts thinking about the architecture of that volume."

82. On the cover of the book, Calvino defined *I racconti* as "a *Novellino* of contemporary Italy." The *Novellino* (c. 1300) is one of the earliest collections of short stories in Italian literature.

83. On 14 October he wrote a letter to Citati asking him to tell him "at once what you think of this title: *Racconti verdi e grigi* (Green and Grey Stories). It came to me last night and it seems to have a wealth of meanings, but lots of people like it and lots don't; others still (but they are just a few) associate it with the grey-green of our soldiers' uniforms."

84. Fortini's contribution to a "Debate on *Dr Zhivago*," *Il Ponte*, 7 (July 1958).

85. L. Santucci, *La letteratura infantile* (*Children's Literature*) (Milan: Fabbri, 1958).

86. Paul Hazard (1878–1944), French historian and critic whose 1932 work *Les Livres, les enfants et les hommes* (*Books, Children and Men*) was one of the first studies of children's literature.

87. This was an Einaudi project that never came to fruition for an anthology of Christian legends which Santucci was to edit.

88. Cases had written a long letter to Calvino thanking him for the copy of *I racconti* which had just been published, and commenting on the three stories that made up Book IV (*La vita difficile*): *La formica argentina* (*The Argentine Ant*), *La speculazione edilizia* (*A Plunge into Real Estate*), and *La nuvola di smog* (*Smog*).

89. E. Zolla, "I racconti di Calvino," *Tempo Presente* (December 1958). Calvino had also received from Giovanni Arpino a verdict that was meant to be negative, but which he claimed to appreciate: "I approve entirely of the verdict you pass on my stories. It is precisely what I was aiming to do and what I believe is right to do: to give a style—that is to say a sense and a moral—to the false pretexts and dissatisfactions of life. Cold as an icicle? That would be the nicest compliment that anyone has ever paid me: unfortunately I am miles away from that. Start again, change? I have never done anything else in my life" (Letter to G. Arpino of 5 March 1958, in *ILDA*, p. 301).

90. Maria Luisa Spaziani (1924–), poet born in Turin, who began her output with poems in the Montale style.

91. Letter written in French.

92. Lombardo Radice was obviously referring to the ten Marcovaldo stories that had been included in *I racconti*. *Marcovaldo* would eventually be published as a single volume containing twenty tales in 1963.

93. Fortini's work had appeared in *La Situazione*, 9 (May 1959).

94. The novels were by Giuseppe Tomasi di Lampedusa (Milan: Feltrinelli, 1958) and Mario Soldati (Milan: Mondadori, 1959), respectively.

95. A. Paolini, "L'inquietudine di Calvino," *La Situazione*, 9 (May 1959).

96. "Etica e estetica di Trotzkij" (Trotsky's ethics and aesthetics), *Passato e Presente*, 7 (January–February 1959), pp. 970–74.

97. The book in question here was Bertolt Brecht's *Poesie e canzoni*, ed. R. Leiser and F. Fortini, with musical bibliography by Giacomo Manzoni (Turin: Einaudi, 1959).

98. Pasolini's *Una vita violenta* (*A Violent Life*) (Milan: Garzanti, 1959). Calvino expressed the same positive opinion in a letter to Pietro Citati of 8 June 1959: "The Pasolini is a beautiful book. Beautiful. One of the finest Italian books of the postwar period, one of the best books of recent years *tout court*. Those nights, that aimless wandering around. I have only read three quarters of it up to now, so I can't talk about the much discussed finale. The first chapter of the book is awful, though, and should have been cut, and nothing would have been lost" (*ILDA*, p. 314).

99. "T." [standing for Tommaso] is an addition made on the autograph copy of the third paragraph which is in the Calvino Archive.

100. The reference is to the anthology of Christian legends which Santucci was to have edited for Einaudi, already mentioned in the letter of 15 November 1958 (and see also the letter of 3 August 1960, in *ILDA*, pp. 336–39).

101. Giuseppe Giacosa (1847–1906), famous playwright and author of libretti for Puccini such as *La Bohème*, *Tosca*, and *Madame Butterfly*.

102. Letter written in English. Lettunich was in charge of the Arts Division of the Institute of International Education (I.I.E.) in New York, and was the American referee for the six-month trip to the United States which Calvino would shortly undertake thanks to a grant from the Ford Foundation.

103. This was the introduction commissioned by Einaudi from Moravia for an edition of *I promessi sposi* (*The Betrothed*) in the I Millenni series (Turin, 1960).

104. On 28 October, responding to a point made by Moravia, Calvino would write: "Your distinction between propaganda that is done consciously and propaganda that is carried out having others believe you are writing a work of art is spot on, and very well formulated. Try to include it using this formulation in your article as well."

105. Elsa Morante, who was traveling in the United States. On 29 October, he would write to her: "Dear Elsa, I see in a letter from Alberto that you have returned and I welcome you back to Italy just as I too am about to leave. I am sorry not to see you and hear your views on America. It means that we will have to wait till I return before exchanging our American impressions. Best wishes from your Calvino."

106. Calvino had clearly read it before came out in *Nuovi Argomenti*, 42–43 (January–April 1960).

107. Both Calvino and Einaudi lived near the river Po in Turin.

108. Actually Calvino is mistaken: Riverside Drive is not on the East River but on the Hudson, which is on the other (West) side of Manhattan.

109. Ivrea was the Piedmont town dominated by the Olivetti firm throughout most of the twentieth century.

110. Nickname of the Turin architect Franco Berlanda.

111. Alberto Mondadori and Giacomo Debenedetti were respectively the founder (1958) and the main consultant of the Milan publishing house Il Saggiatore. The "Biblioteca delle Silerchie," a sophisticated series of short texts from all over the world, was typical of its activities right from the start.

112. Bobi or Roberto Bazlen, at the time an adviser at Einaudi (before becoming consultant and the inspiration behind the Adelphi publishing house), had obviously drafted the program for a "collana di morale dell'uomo moderno" (series of moral texts for modern man). About two months later Calvino would come up with his own counter-proposal for this Einaudi project, which was in the end never realized: "Notes and general ideas for a small collection of texts of moral enquiry for modern man." Later the title was changed to "Appunti per una collana di ricerca morale" (Notes for a series on moral research), for which Calvino wrote an outline in 1960, now in *S*, II, 1705–9.

113. Simone de Beauvoir, major French existentialist novelist and philosopher, author of one of the founding texts of twentieth-century feminism, *The Second Sex* (1949).

114. Michael Kamenetzki (1919–95), better known by his pseudonym of Ugo Stille, who was for more than forty years the U.S. correspondent for the *Corriere della sera*.

115. Actually Calvino meant Gustav Mahler: the slip was perhaps due to the fact that the protagonist of Luchino Visconti's film *Senso* was called Lieutenant Franz Mahler.

116. This was the first line of the seven verses of *Sul verde fiume Po*, a song written by Calvino with music by Fiorenzo Carpi. The Momiglianos mentioned immediately afterwards are Franco Momigliano and his wife, Luciana Nissim.

117. Vando Aldrovandi (called Al) was Renata Einaudi's brother and owner of the Einaudi Bookshop in Milan.

118. Giacomo Devoto (1897–1974), one of Italy's leading linguistics experts.

119. Adriano Olivetti (1901–60) was an innovative entrepreneur, son of the founder of the Olivetti firm.

120. "La Nuova Libreria," a series that never materialized, was to have been a substantial collection of texts of an encyclopaedic nature. Renato Solmi in particular worked on the planning of it in 1959–61: see Luisa

Mangoni, *Pensare i libri. La casa editrice Einaudi dagli anni trenta agli anni sessanta* (Turin: Bollati Boringhieri, 1999), pp. 881–82.

121. This was a new literary journal set up by Vittorini with help from Calvino: it lasted from 1959 until 1967.

122. This was Claude Ollier's *La mise en scène* (1958), which Einaudi would publish in translation as *La messa in scena* in 1962.

123. In a letter of 21 January, Luciano Foà had asked Calvino to tell Einaudi about Paul Goodman's novel, *The Empire City*, published by Bobbs-Merrill in 1959.

124. Raymond Queneau (1903–76) was a French novelist, poet, and founder of the Ouvroir de Littérature Potentielle (Oulipo): Calvino became an admirer, friend, and translator of some of his works.

125. On 29 January, Caretti had written to Calvino to thank him for the complimentary copies of Pavese's *Racconti* and Calvino's *Il cavaliere inesistente* (*The Non-Existent Knight*), published by Einaudi in December 1959 ("my new novel," which Calvino talks about later).

126. A letter of 20 March to Daniele Ponchiroli and the other colleagues at Einaudi ends with these words: "Life in New York has started to become ferociously pleasant again. I must be daft, but I am more in love than ever with this horrendous city. New York is the only true love of my life."

127. In the letter dated 20 March to Daniele Ponchiroli and the other Einaudi colleagues, Calvino complained that they had not "said anything about an article that came out in *Mondo Nuovo* on 31 January where *The Non-Existent Knight* was interpreted in a crazily arbitrary way as an anti-Communist allegory, and mention was made of my anti-Communism as though this were fact. We must immediately head off these charges made by provocateurs in bad faith. I will write a letter to the editor but meanwhile two months have already elapsed."

128. In the typescript there followed a paragraph that was later deleted: "When I have a political discourse that I want to make, I have always tried to do so clearly, in political terms; when I wanted to write political satire, against the reactionaries, war-mongerers or philistines of the bourgeoisie, and—in a few clearly defined cases—when involved in an internal polemic within the movement I am part of, I have used a specific and easily recognizable literary genre, the political apologue."

129. On this, see the letter about "paradise" to Mario Motta of July 1950.

130. The interview (2 June 1960) was about the French translation of *The Baron in the Trees*. On the same day as this letter, 5 July, Calvino wrote to Paul Flamand of Les Éditions du Seuil in French: "Nearly all the interviews went well, and served their purpose. In my last few days in Paris some people recognized me in the street, because they had seen me on

TV or in *Le Figaro*: this is the maximum level of celebrity a writer can hope for!"

131. The negotiations by the Prime Minister Fernando Tambroni to form a Christian Democrat government with the support of the neo-fascists in the Movimento Socialista Italiano (MSI) had sparked a vast wave of protests and demonstrations in the streets from left-wing supporters.

132. This was the review of *Our Ancestors* published in the Milan edition of *l'Unità*, on 13 August 1960.

133. The director Luigi Vanzi, who was to have made the film on Marco Polo for Franco Cristaldi's Vides company. The statement by Mario Monicelli, who was the originator of the project and was first choice as director, is interesting. After recalling his collaboration with Calvino in the screenplay for *Renzo e Lucia*, an episode in the film *Boccaccio '70*, Monicelli goes on: "I had already worked with Calvino prior to this. At that time there had been a boom in exotic documentaries, like Napolitano's *Magia verde* (*Green Magic*) and those by Quilici and Jacopetti. I had this wonderful idea and told Cristaldi about it: to retrace Marco Polo's route from Venice to Peking, travelling along the same roads today and seeing what was left and what had changed. [. . .] In short, to retrace his steps in a way that was part documentary, part fantasy. [. . .] Talking with Cristaldi and Suso Cecchi d'Amico we thought: 'Who can provide an outline story for Marco Polo that hovers between the magical, the documentary, and the evocative?' And Suso said: 'Let's try Calvino.' We asked him and he said yes. After a while he turned up with about fifty absolutely extraordinary pages which maybe were no use for the film but which could have been published as a small book" (Mario Monicelli, *L'arte della commedia* (*The Art of Comedy*), ed. L. Codelli (Bari: Dedalo, 1986), pp. 71–73).

134. *I briganti* was the Italian title of the Chinese historical novel known in English as *All Men Are Brothers* in Pearl S. Buck's 1933 translation.

135. The substantial treatment written by Calvino (105 typewritten pages) for this *Marco Polo* that was never made into a film was published in *RR*, III, 509–86; see also Mario Barenghi's "notizia sul testo" (ibid., 1263–67).

136. Wahl's brief article had come out in *La Revue de Paris*, 67 (November 1960), as a presentation of the French translation of Calvino's story "Adventure of a Poet"; the story had been translated into French by Pierre Denivelle, to whom Calvino refers later on. The English version is in *Difficult Loves*, pp. 103–8.

137. The story was "Adventure of the Married Couple," in *Difficult Loves*, pp. 99–102.

138. Claude Simon's book, translated by Guido Neri, would come out with Einaudi in 1962 as *La strada delle Fiandre*.

139. Jean-René Huguenin, *La Côte sauvage* (Paris: Seuil, 1960).

140. Moravia's novel *La noia* (*The Empty Canvas*) was published by Bompiani.

1961–1965

1. This was the cinema version of Calvino's "Adventure of the Married Couple": see *Difficult Loves*, pp. 99–102. The story was part of the film *Boccaccio '70* (1962): see the next note.

2. On 19 March, Calvino would write to her: "Dear Suso, I am happy if my ideas turn out to be useful to you and Monicelli for the marriage-firm episode. What can I ask for it? Well, you can judge that. I, like Signor Bonaventura, would say: a million. Without having the foggiest idea of what the budget is for screenplay-writers for a film like this." The reference to the "marriage-firm episode" suggests that this was the "11-page typewritten text narrating the ups and downs of a couple of young workers who want to get married," mentioned by Mario Barenghi in *RR*, III, p. 1259. Out of the episodes that make it up—amongst which were "A Factory That Forbids Marriage," "The Secret Wedding" "A Honeymoon on Foot" etc.—the last one ("Incompatible Working-Hours") was the subject matter both of the short story "Adventure of the Married Couple" and of the song "Canzone triste" and also of a scene in *La panchina*, an opera libretto based by Calvino on one of the stories from *Marcovaldo*: "Park-Bench Vacation" in *Marcovaldo*, pp. 5–12. The screenplay of "Adventure of the Married Couple" became part of a film in four parts entitled *Boccaccio '70*, co-directed by Vittorio De Sica, Federico Fellini, Mario Monicelli, and Luchino Visconti, which would be completed in 1961 and would be released in 1962. The third "act," entitled "Renzo e Luciana," would be directed by Monicelli with screenplay by the director along with Suso Cecchi d'Amico, Calvino, and Giovanni Arpino.

3. M. Socrate, *Favole paraboliche* (*Parabolic Fables*) (Milan: Feltrinelli, 1961).

4. It was to have been directed by Folco Quilici with screenplay by Quilici, Augusto Frassineti, and Calvino. The first part of the story written for this film would come out with the title "Tikò e il pescecane" (Tikò and the Shark) in the weekly magazine *ABC*, 9 September 1962 (later in *RR*, III, pp. 587–603 and 1268–69).

5. On 26 April, Calvino would write to Armanda Giambrocono Guiducci: "But as for the book about my travels in America—after working on it for many months and tying up all the loose ends—I've destroyed it. The older I get, the less sure I am about things." The book was the diary of his

travels and stay in the United States (1959–60), which was to have come out with Einaudi in the spring of 1961 with the title *Un ottimista in America* (An Optimist in America), but which Calvino decided not to publish when it was already at proof stage.

6. Ginzburg's *Le voci della sera* (*Voices in the Evening*), to be published by Einaudi around this time. On the cover of the book the blurb (anonymous but written by Calvino) contains almost the same words and phrases as in this letter.

7. Alessandra Tornimparte was the pseudonym adopted by Natalia Ginzburg when in 1942 she published her first novel with Einaudi, *La strada che va in città* (*The Road to the City*).

8. Oreste Molina, in charge of production (the "technical department") in the publishing house.

9. This was an article published as the first item in *Nuovi Argomenti*, 46 (September–October 1960); it would later be included as the title piece in Ginzburg's collection of essays *Le piccole virtù* (*The Little Virtues*) (Turin: Einaudi, 1962).

10. Letter in French.

11. Giovanni Arpino (1927–87), popular novelist who also started off as a writer of the Resistance.

12. Raffaele La Capria (born 1922) achieved major success with his novel *Ferito a morte* (*The Mortal Wound*) (1961).

13. Entitled "Temi industriali della narrativa italiana" (Industrial Themes in Italian Fiction), it would be published in *Il Menabò di letteratura*, 4 (1961). The dating of this letter is hypothetical, and the only chronological indication for it is the date of publication of this number of *Il Menabò*, 4 September 1961.

14. G. Buzzi, *Il senatore* (Milan: Feltrinelli, 1958).

15. G. Bufalari, *La masseria* (Milan: Lerici, 1960).

16. This paragraph reads almost identically in Forti's article (pp. 219–20).

17. These paragraphs too are repeated almost verbatim in Forti's article (pp. 221–22).

18. Several months previously, in a letter of 16 May, Calvino had written to Veršinin: "And I am very pleased to hear that Breitburd wants to translate *La speculazione edilizia* (*A Plunge into Real Estate*). I consider this *povest*, as you would say, my best effort in terms of *realism*, and I think it gives quite an important idea of Italy today."

19. These sentences, which Calvino requests Veršinin not to cut, are cited from the first edition of his *Racconti* (Turin: Einaudi, 1958); the passages in English translation are from *Difficult Loves*, pp. 153–54.

20. The typescript has "from." The letter to which Calvino is referring was published in *ILDA*, pp. 376–77.

21. This story can be found in *Adam One Afternoon*, pp. 97–104.

22. Cecilia Kin, an Italian expert and Russian translator.

23. Primo Levi, using the pseudonym Damiano Malabaila, would publish these stories under the title *Storie naturali* (Turin: Einaudi, 1966): some of them are available in English translation in *The Sixth Day and Other Tales*, trans. Raymond Rosenthal (New York: Simon & Schuster, 1990).

24. Son of the playwright Edmond Rostand, Jean Rostand (1894–1977) was a famous biologist and effective popularizer of science. Calvino knew his books also because of his own publishing work: *Piccola storia della biologia* had been published by Einaudi in 1949 and *L'uomo artificiale* in 1959.

25. The references are to the two stories "L'amico dell'uomo" (Man's Friend) and "Quaestio de Centauriis" (The Question of Centaurs): the former is in English translation in *The Sixth Day and Other Tales*.

26. The story is "Il mnemagogo" (The Mnemagogue), not available in English.

27. Calvino is alluding to Arpino's previous novel, *Un delitto d'onore* (*A Crime of Honor*) (Milan: Mondadori, 1961).

28. Arpino's novel was published by Mondadori in Milan in 1962.

29. Arpino's *Gli anni del giudizio* (*The Years of Wisdom*) was published by Einaudi in 1958.

30. Umberto Eco, "Del modo di formare come impegno sulla realtà" (On the manner of giving form as a committed way of acting on reality), *Il menabò di letteratura*, 5 (1962).

31. The reference is to Cecilia, protagonist of the eponymous novel by Elémire Zolla, and her symbiotic relationship with the car, for which Eco claims there is an analogy with primitive man's relationship with stone tools.

32. Ingmar Bergman, *Quattro film* (*Four Films*) (Turin: Einaudi, 1961).

33. In the letter to Antonioni of 12 October 1962, Calvino would clarify the problems that needed to be overcome in order to publish the book.

34. Sciascia's historical "inchiesta" (enquiry) would be published by Einaudi in 1963.

35. The letter of 3 October 1962.

36. In a brief letter of 30 October 1962, Calvino would write: "Dear Antonioni, I've read the screenplays. I think they work very well: they make attractive reading, which readers will naturally supplement with their memories of the images from the films. The book can come out very quickly if you send us the preface." The volume—*Sei film* (*Le amiche. Il grido. L'avventura. La notte. L'eclisse. Deserto rosso*)—would come out in 1964.

37. It had appeared in RAI's quarterly magazine *Terzo Programma*, 3 (1962).

38. This was the article "Le poesie politiche di Pavese" (Pavese's Political Poems), which appeared in the collaborative volume, *Miscellanea per le nozze di Enrico Castelnuovo e Delia Frigessi. 24 Ottobre 1962* (Turin: Einaudi, 1962), pp. 31–41.

39. Several years after this letter, Donald Heiney would translate into English a short story by Calvino that at the time was still unpublished in Italian: "The Other Eurydice," in *The Iowa Review* (Fall 1971), now in *The Complete Cosmicomics*, trans. Martin McLaughlin, Tim Parks, and William Weaver (Harmondsworth: Penguin, 2009), pp. 393–402.

40. This was almost certainly the novel *La penombra che abbiamo tutti attraversato* (*The Penumbra We Have All Crossed*), which would be published by Einaudi in 1964.

41. Probably an allusion to the novel which she later abandoned: *Senza i conforti della religione* (*Without Religious Comfort*).

42. Ginzburg's *Lessico famigliare* (*Family Sayings*) would come out in 1963.

43. Letter written in English.

44. This letter is followed by Calvino's responses to a questionnaire sent to him by Mateo Lettunich (there is no trace of it in the Calvino Archive but it can be reconstructed from Calvino's replies). Lettunich was in charge of the Arts Program of the Institute of International Education, and had helped organize Calvino's trip to the United States in 1959–60 with the aid of a grant from the Ford Foundation.

45. In this brief reply about his stay in the United States (1959–60), Calvino alludes to three very well known books about America and Americans from the 1950s: David Riesman, *The Lonely Crowd*, Vance Packard, *The Hidden Persuaders*, William H. Whyte, *The Organization Man*; he also refers to the novel by Eugene Burdick and William J. Lederer, *The Ugly American*.

46. Rago's "Uno scrutatore al Cottolengo" (A Scrutineer at the Cottolengo), *l'Unità*, 20 March 1963, was a review of Calvino's *La giornata d'uno scrutatore* (*The Watcher*) (1963).

47. The book was *La giornata d'uno scrutatore*.

48. In a letter to Silvio Guarnieri of 26 May, Calvino would say this about *The Watcher*: "You found that my story lacked the 'aggressive peremptoriness' I once had. And with good reason. I am very far from the style you mention. If I tried today to express anything other than my tentativeness, I would not be sincere and would not write anything good. Is this maybe just a period when I rethink things? I would prefer it to be a definite sign of a maturity I had reached."

49. This was probably the new edition of Monti's *Tradimento e fedeltà* (*Betrayal and Fidelity*) (1949), which came out in 1963 with the title *I Sansôssi* (*The Sans Soucis*).

50. Aldo Camerino, "Lo scrutatore di Italo Calvino" (Italo Calvino's Scrutineer), *Il Gazzettino*, 14 May 1963.

51. Calvino is alluding to his membership of the jury for the Premio Formentor, which took place in Corfu that year; and to the Premio Internazionale Charles Veillon, which he was awarded on 18 May in Lausanne for *The Watcher*; he was to have been in the jury for the Premio Conegliano, sponsored by the journal *Il Caffè*, but this year did not go.

52. Renato Poggioli had died on 3 May in a car accident while he was driving from Palo Alto to Portland for a conference. Calvino would write to his widow on 23 July: "Dear Signora Renata, it is hard to go back to talking about work with our thoughts still on what happened. After the tragedy, I did not know how to get in touch with you. We were very worried about the news of your health. Eventually Dante Della Terza wrote to me to say that you had come back to Cambridge, and that your daughter had recovered; I wrote her a letter which maybe you found on your return. When I received your letter of 19 June I discovered that you were still at Palo Alto, and that with great force of mind had started working on Renato's writings."

53. In an unpublished piece that we can date to the period 1963–64, Calvino would write: "Poggioli was in a phase of extraordinary creativity and activity. He was full of happiness at being at Palo Alto, at meeting the people in that Center for Advanced Studies, happy with his work, with the many projects he had begun or completed. Latterly he was writing to me almost every week: and with every letter he enclosed, with that typical methodical and programmatic clarity of his, an outline of work in progress, providing for each book the point he had reached and who it was for, or a summary of a book he had planned, or a list of essays. (That same methodical clarity that he displayed, when you went to see him in Boston, in giving you all the train times, stations and connections.) And I would continually receive off-prints of his writings, on Slav and non-Slav subjects such as the final canti of the *Purgatorio*, or Virgil and Goethe.

Apart from being a great scholar and expert in poetry, he was also a great worker and organizer of his own work. I said that this was an extraordinary period for him, but in fact I always found Poggioli like this, both in letters and in person. What struck one was his vitality, his calm in the midst of activity, the way he moved with unflagging satisfaction in that kind of Utopia of learning and intelligence that is Harvard University, or in that super-elite of the land of Utopia that is the Society of Fellows, his love for intellectual quality, his Tuscan partisanship, and his incisive verdicts.

Studies in comparative literature seemed ideally suited to his insatiable intelligence, an intelligence that was able to systematize knowledge in a sophisticated way: from an analysis of a brief Kavafy poem he would outline a concept of Decadence, or from a monograph on Rozanov he would provide an overview of the concept of individuality from the eighteenth century to today."

54. In a letter to Giambattista Vicari of 29 October 1963, Calvino would write amongst other things: "one reader, Antonella Santacroce, [. . .] has sent me an essay which is both an apologia for my fantasy fiction and an invective against my realistic work, a bit naïve in both areas, but also

nicely engaged as young people are (she must be—as I can see also from her letters—a student from the provinces, totally isolated) and—what is more important—with several accurate and original insights. I enclose it for you (I've eliminated the odd rhetorical flourish here and there) so you can include it, if you want, in the famous *dossier*, or publish it now without waiting for the 'special issue.' In any case, if it makes a good impression on you, you might write to Miss Santacroce and ask her if she wants to collaborate on *Il Caffè*."

55. The date is based on what Calvino writes to Adriana Motti in a letter of 28 October 1963. Published, with the title *Sulla traduzione* [On Translation], in *Paragone (Letteratura)*, 168 (December 1963), pp. 112–18; later in *S*, II, pp. 1776–86.

56. *A Passage to India* had been published in Italian by Einaudi in 1962 under the title *Passaggio in India*. The critique by Claudio Gorlier to which Calvino refers was contained in Gorlier's "Forster, Firbank, e i rischi delle riscoperte" (Forster, Firbank, and the Dangers of Rediscoveries), *Paragone (Letteratura)*, 164 (August, 1963).

57. The English original, not quoted by Calvino, is in E. M. Forster, *A Passage to India* (Harmondsworth: Penguin, 1977), p. 315.

58. Ibid., pp. 219–20.

59. Varese's review of *La giornata d'uno scrutatore* (*The Watcher*) had appeared in *La Nuova Antologia* (May 1963).

60. This was a review of *La giornata d'uno scrutatore*.

61. Calvino had come to Cuba with Esther "Chichita" Singer two days before the date of this letter and had immediately sent a telegraph to his mother: "Arrived safely. Full summer."

62. On the same day, 27 January, Calvino sent another telegram to his mother: "Wonderful visit Santiago de las Vegas. Emotional welcome Roig. Everyone remembers you, says hello. Love Italo." Mario Calvino had for several years run an experimental agricultural center in Santiago de las Vegas, and it was there that Italo had been born on 15 October 1923.

63. In a handwritten transcription of this letter, done by Eva Mameli Calvino and conserved in the Archivio Calvino along with the original manuscript, instead of "Conjea" we find "Congea."

64. On 13 February, Calvino would telegram his mother from Havana: "Back from wonderful trip to Oriente. Maybe leave for Mexico next week." And on 19 February, announcing his marriage to Chichita that day, would inform her that the departure for Mexico was scheduled for 20 February.

65. Calvino's letter followed a discussion—and an initial letter from Lucentini—on the preface that Carlo Fruttero and Franco Lucentini had written for *La verità sul caso Smith. Antologia della nuova narrativa Americana* (*The Truth about the Case of Mr Smith. An Anthology of New American Fiction*)

(Milan: Mondadori, 1963): the two men became famous later as a team that wrote successful crime fiction.

66. Vittorini had edited an important collection of American writers in the late 1930s which came out with this title in censored form, but only in 1942.

67. *Storie di fantasmi. Antologia di racconti anglosassoni del soprannaturale* (*Ghost Stories. A Collection of English Tales of the Supernatural*), ed. Carlo Fruttero and Franco Lucentini, Preface by Carlo Fruttero (Turin: Einaudi, 1960).

68. Lucentini would reply by return of post with the following letter: "Dear Calvino, Thank you for your reply and I quite agree about regarding the split as not having happened. As for the ideological discrepancy, I had never considered it negligible, though not excessive either; and of course after that kind phone-call of yours the whole thing seemed to me (despite so much intensification in tones and coloring elsewhere) happily reduced in dimensions. Hence my total bewilderment at finding the split increased and almost total, the other evening at Einaudi. I reacted with a version of the facts that was emotionally ambivalent: you, from whom I expected something better ideologically, out of generic opportunism back-tracked on this better something etc. On the ideological level (which for me is always the same as the emotional one, nor does it reflect in anything other than transitory terms the private vices and virtues of each person, their good or bad manners), I then, in this version, was keeping a friend; disgustingly opportunist, but still a friend. If instead I now accepted your explanations, I would do so losing out on everything, I would be giving up our unshaken friendship for a resentment that has now vanished; and consequently, however rational they are, I prefer not to accept your explanations. It still is the case that now that the emotion has subsided, for me too there is no trace of the split. Yours, Lucentini."

69. On 29 November 1963, Calvino had written: "As for your linguistic analysis of *Smog* I had thought so much about what I wanted to say to you that at a certain point I must have convinced myself that I actually had written to you; now your letter proves that this is not the case. Please excuse me, and now accept my sincere if rather belated thanks. But the letter I wanted to write to you is not this one: it is a much longer letter, since your analysis of my work inevitably leads me on to discuss the critical method you use. It is a method which I am very fond of, opposed as I am to criticism "without opening the book," as practiced by the majority of Italian critics. Consequently I promise that as soon as I have a free day and am in the mood I will write you a long letter to discuss these things." The English translation of *Smog*, from which the quotations in this letter come, is in *Difficult Loves*, pp. 111–60. Calvino's page references in the letter are to the edition of "La nuvola di Smog" in his *I racconti* (Turin: Einaudi, 1958), pp. 521–67.

70. *Difficult Loves*, p. 111.
71. *Difficult Loves*, p. 111.
72. *Difficult Loves*, p. 111.
73. *Difficult Loves*, p. 113.
74. These four passages are in *Difficult Loves*, pp. 139, 144, 152, 135–36.
75. *Difficult Loves*, p. 113.
76. A famous line (line 7) from Leopardi's "La quiete dopo la tempesta" (The Calm After the Storm).
77. *Difficult Loves*, pp. 149–50, 152–53.
78. *Difficult Loves*, p. 115.
79. *Difficult Loves*, p. 116.
80. A few days later, on 27 April, Calvino would write to Paola Gagliardi, a student from Padua who had to write a graduating thesis on him: "Dear Miss Gagliardi, if you want my advice, never try to get to know writers in person. If a writer is worth anything, it is in what he has written. Knowing the person does not add anything. Furthermore, authors are the people least qualified to speak about their own works. It is for precisely this reason that literary studies work much better when they deal with dead rather than with living authors. [. . .] I apologize for being so brusque, but this business of studying contemporary authors at university is something I really cannot stand, and every time I hear about it I get angry. Probably none of today's Italian writers will last in the memory of posterity. It is almost certain that in fifty years' time when they discover that nowadays people wrote theses on X or Y or myself, they will all fall about laughing" (*ILDA*, p. 469).
81. It seems that Antonella Santacroce had also contacted Michele Rago, conscious of the fact that in 1957, when he was an editor on *Il Contemporaneo*, he had had some of her short stories published.
82. The pupils in the second year (II Media) of a middle school in Milan had told Calvino of their "immense pleasure at seeing *I promessi sposi* (*The Betrothed*) being replaced as their text book for Italian by *The Baron in the Trees*."
83. Bobbio (1909–2004) was an influential philosopher: he had written to Calvino, attributing this position to him after reading "L'antitesi operaia" (The working-class as antithesis), *Il Menabò*, 7 (1964).
84. Calvino is alluding to Nikita Khruschev, then head of the Communist Party and of the USSR.
85. Some years later, in a letter of 18 November 1969 to Alberto Filippi, who was planning an anthology from *Il Menabò*, that never materialized, Calvino would define in a moment of auto-criticism, "L'antitesi operaia" as "a banal and now antiquated account of the problems."
86. In a letter of 8 May 1964, Calvino had written to her: "I am very pleased that a collection of my stories is to be published in Romania and I am very grateful to you for your work in translating them. You will

certainly have found some difficult points: every now and again my writings contain dialect expressions that are not to be found in dictionaries, or unclear phrases which all translators bang their heads against. I will be grateful to you if you would let me have all your doubts. For languages I do not know this is the only way I can help translators. And I believe that only those who ask their author many questions are good translators."

87. Presumably the Romanian translation of "Viaggio con le mucche," one of the Marcovaldo stories: see *Marcovaldo*, pp. 45–50.

88. This theatrical piece would be published the following year in Einaudi's "Collezione di teatro" series.

89. Ferretti's article "Il lungo sentiero di Calvino" (Calvino's long path), in *l'Unità*, 1 November 1964, was a piece that analyzed the "Author's Preface" to the new edition of *Il sentiero dei nidi di ragno* (*The Path to the Spiders' Nests*) (Turin: Einaudi, 1964).

90. Michele Tondo, *Itinerario di Cesare Pavese* (Padua: Liviana, 1965).

91. Davide Lajolo, *Il "vizio assurdo". Storia di Cesare Pavese* (Milan: Il Saggiatore, 1960) was an influential study of the author, reprinted several times.

92. "Le poesie politiche di Pavese" (Pavese's Political Poems), in *Miscellanea per Enrico Castelnuovo e Delia Frigessi, 24 October 1962* (Turin: Einaudi, 1962), pp. 31–41. See the postscript to this letter.

93. In a letter of 16 February 1965, Calvino would confirm to Tondo Einaudi's decision not to publish his *Itinerario di Cesare Pavese* (it would come out that year with Liviana, in Padua), and amongst other things he would write: "You will have received the special issue of the journal *Sigma*, dedicated to Pavese. Some of the articles seem to me to signal a new phase in Pavese studies: specialist studies conducted with scholarly rigor are starting to appear. (And also with a certain ruthlessness: something I cannot criticize, when it is based on facts.) So far I have seen four interesting articles: the two on language (Grassi, although it is strictly technical, and Beccaria) and the two on the culture of "myth" (Jesi, terrible in its tendentiousness but I think relevant; and Corsini, rather naughty but serious). Also Gorlier's piece on the translations makes some serious points, others more debatable, but it ought to be contextualized in an overall evaluation of what counted and what counts in the general overview of Pavese as a translator."

94. In the manuscript Calvino had added here and then cancelled: "Pavese's Stoicism."

95. The 45 days from the fall of the Fascist government on 25 July 1943 and the signing of the armistice with the Allies on 8 September 1943.

96. On Turinese Nietzscheanism, and in particular on Pavese's version of it, see the letter to Grazia Marchianò, of 21 December 1965.

97. "Calvino, scrittore 'rampante'," *Il Caffè*, 5 (December 1964) later in her book *La mutevole forma* (Naples: Senna, 1979).

98. Giovanni Sercambi was a writer of novelle of the fourteenth century; the story referred to here is "De Simplicitate."

99. One of Calvino's earliest short stories, trans. Martin McLaughlin as "Waiting for Death in a Hotel," *The New Yorker*, 12 June 2006, pp. 104–10.

100. Roland Barthes, *Sur Racine* (Paris: Seuil, 1963).

101. Bergman's *The Silence* came out in 1963, Antonioni's *Red Desert* and Pasolini's *The Gospel According to Saint Matthew* in 1964.

102. In a note written to Pasolini on 3 July 1964, his praise of the poet ("*Vittoria* is excellent, one of your finest poems") was followed by the curt final phrase about Pasolini as director: "When are you going to stop making films?"

103. This verdict was attached to the letter, and later published in "I migliori film dell'anno" (The Best Films of the Year), in *Cinema nuovo*, 174 (March–April 1965), p. 113.

104. Cesare Lupo, a highly placed operative in RAI (the Italian state broadcaster), had proposed that Calvino do a series of radio broadcasts on the *Orlando furioso*.

105. The formal contract would be given to Calvino two years later; and Cetra would issue the records of the Ariosto programs by Calvino in the "Collana Letteraria Documenti Cetra."

106. Calvino is referring to the "Ricerca letteraria" series, launched by Einaudi in 1965; in that year the first volumes in the "Foreign Writers" section came out, amongst which were Arno Schmidt's *Alessandro o della verità* (*Alexander or What Is Truth*), translated by Emilio Picco, and Samuel Beckett's *Come è* (*How It Is*) by Franco Quadri.

107. Queneau published under the pseudonym Sally Mara, *On est toujours trop bon avec les femmes* (1947) and *Journal intime* (1950).

108. Many years later Calvino would persuade Sergio Solmi to translate it for Einaudi as *Piccola cosmogonia portatile* (Turin: Einaudi, 1982).

109. On the translation of *Sally Mara* see also the letter to Quadri of 1 April 1965.

110. The French linguistics expert Georges Mounin dealt a lot with the question of translation: Einaudi published his *Teoria e storia della traduzione* in 1965.

111. Einaudi would in the end give up on *Il diario intimo di Sally Mara*, which would come out with Feltrinelli in 1991, translated by Leonella Prato Caruso. As is well known, Calvino would translate Queneau's *Les fleurs bleues* (Einaudi, 1967), and would collaborate with Sergio Solmi on the Italian edition of *Piccola cosmogonia portatile* (Einaudi, 1982).

112. Leonetti, "L'eversione costruita" (Constructed subversion), *Il Menabò*, 8 (1965).

113. C. Lévi-Strauss and R. Jakobson, "*Les Chats* de Charles Baudelaire," *L'homme*, 1 (January–April 1962), Italian translation in L. Rosiello (ed.), *Letteratura e strutturalismo* (Bologna: Zanichelli, 1974), pp. 99–117.

114. On 27 September 1963, Calvino had written to her: "Dear Miss Alenius, I am pleased to know that in Stockholm there is someone writing a thesis on me. Thank you very much. And I am happy that you are dealing with my links with Ariosto."

115. For this 1965 Einaudi edition, Calvino used the anagrammatic pseudonym Tonio Cavilla (the latter name plays on the notion of a commentator who "cavils" at pedantic questions).

116. "Hemingway e noi" (Hemingway and Ourselves), *Il Contemporaneo*, 33 (13 November 1954), English translation now in *Why Read the Classics?* pp. 223–29.

117. Calvino's newly born daughter, Giovanna.

118. Two lines have been omitted here.

119. This sentence is from the penultimate paragraph of Chapter X of *The Watcher*, trans. William Weaver (San Diego-New York-London: Harcourt, Brace & Company, 1971), pp. 42–43.

120. The quote from Marx comes in Chapter XI, just a few pages after the sentence from Chapter X explained by Calvino to Wahl.

121. The screenplay in question, loosely based on the story "Las babas del diablo" by Julio Cortázar—from his 1959 collection *Las armas secretas* (in English in *Blow-Up and Other Stories*)—is that of the film which would come out in 1966 as *Blow-Up*.

122. These are the stories later published as *Cosmicomics* (1965 in Italy), now in *The Complete Cosmicomics*, pp. 1–151.

123. Tonino Guerra (1920–2012), novelist and screenwriter.

124. The book had been published in Rome, by Officina in 1963.

125. On 25 November, Calvino would write to Garroni, amongst other things: "I have received your letter and I am partly sorry that I made that critique of your 'quoting everyone' since you only dwell on that point; but I am also partly glad because the arguments that you have come back with seem convincing to me, so that I now have the chance to go in for some self-criticism for an attitude that was too much about taste or even downright snobbish."

126. Now in *The Complete Cosmicomics*, pp. 32–42.

127. *A ciascuno il suo* (*To Each His Own*), which would be published by Einaudi in 1966.

128. Grazia Marchianò had sent Calvino something she had written on contemporary fiction by Piedmontese writers, asking him for an opinion.

129. Elémire Zolla (1926–2002), Turinese writer and philosopher of religion.

130. Zolla's *Minuetto all'inferno* (*Minuet in Hell*) had been published by Einaudi in its Gettoni series in 1956.

131. Alberto Arbasino (b. 1930), avant-garde novelist; Lucio Mastronardi (1930–79) wrote novels about his home town Vigevano; the Scapigliatura was a nineteenth-century avant-garde movement that emerged in Milan in the 1860s.

1966–1970

1. In the end Maria Livia Serini did not give permission for Pavese's letters to her to be published.

2. Ferretti's letter, dated 29 December 1965, in which he conveyed his impressions on *Cosmicomics*, can be found in *ILDA*, pp. 559–60.

3. Giansiro Ferrata's review, "Le due strade di Italo Calvino" (The two paths of Italo Calvino), had appeared in *Rinascita*, on 22 January 1966.

4. Calvino's mentor, Elio Vittorini, had died in Milan on 12 February 1966.

5. The title was "The Canto of Lili Toffler." It was included in the Italian translation of Peter Weiss, *L'istruttoria. Oratorio in undici canti* (*The Trial. Oratorio in Eleven Canti*) (Turin: Einaudi, 1966) but appeared initially in *Il Menabò*, 9 (1966).

6. Letter written in French.

7. Gruppo 63 was the name of a group of writers of the Neo-avanguardia: it originally met in Palermo in June 1963, hence its name.

8. *Cahiers du Cinéma*, 185 (December 1965), 87–99; it appeared in English translation as "Cinema and the Novel: Problems of Narrative," in Calvino, *The Literature Machine: Essays*, trans. Patrick Creagh (London: Secker & Warburg, 1987), pp. 74–80.

9. Afer Vittorini's death, only one more issue of *Il Menabo* would appear, issue 10 (1967), solely devoted to Vittorini and edited by Calvino.

10. *A floresta é jovem e cheja de vida*, for voices, clarinet, copper-plates and magnetic tape, had had its premiere at the Festival of Contemporary Music in Venice on 7 September 1966.

11. Calvino is alluding to Picasso's *Guernica*, Vittorini's *Conversazione in Sicilia*, and Arnold Schönberg's 1947 opera.

12. Calvino would end up by replying to Ferretti's survey in *Rinascita*: see the letter to Ferretti of 22 October 1967. It appeared in English as "Whom Do We Write For? Or The Hypothetical Bookshelf," in *The Literature Machine*, pp. 81–88.

13. Woodhouse had asked Calvino in which Italian region he felt most at home.

14. The question concerned his university studies.

15. Woodhouse had asked Calvino what the theoretical basis to his political commitment was: see also note 17.

16. Having noted Calvino's religious agnosticism, Woodhouse had asked him if he felt he was a "humanist" à la Bertrand Russell.

17. The article—entitled "Un'infanzia sotto il fascismo" (A Childhood under Fascism)—contained his replies to the survey "La generazione degli anni difficili" (The Generation that Lived through Difficult Times), *Il Paradosso*, 23–24 (September–December 1960), pp. 11–18. Calvino totally rewrote the replies for the Laterza book of 1962. Both essays are in "Political Autobiography of a Young Man," *Hermit in Paris*, pp. 130–56.

18. Sergio Pacifici, *A Guide to Contemporary Italian Literature* (New York: Meridian Books, 1962).

19. For the English version of this story, see Calvino, *The Road to San Giovanni*, trans. Tim Parks (London: 1993), pp. 3–34.

20. The title of the English version of the article was "Main Currents in Italian Fiction Today," and it appeared on pp. 3–14 of the issue mentioned by Calvino; the Italian version, "Tre correnti del romanzo italiano oggi," came out in the *Annuario del Liceo-Ginnasio G.D.Cassini di Sanremo* (San Remo: Gandolfi, 1960), 123–33; it was then reprinted in *Una pietra sopra* (Turin: Einaudi, 1980), pp. 46–57, and in *S*, I, pp. 60–75.

21. W. Saroyan, *Che ve ne sembra dell'America?* (Milan: Mondadori, 1960).

22. Woodhouse had asked Calvino if the model for Pietrochiodo in *The Cloven Viscount* was by chance a bizarre but real inventor.

23. Calvino, "Vittorini: progettazione e letteratura," *Il menabò di letteratura*, 10 (1967), later in *Una pietra sopra*, pp. 127–49 (and *S*, I, pp. 160–87).

24. Terracini's article appeared in *Archivio Glottologico Italiano* (1966), and later in his volume of essays *I segni, la storia*, ed. Gian Luigi Beccaria (Naples: Guida, 1976), pp. 359–63.

25. Letter written in French.

26. The first part of the letter, dealing with matters strictly relating to publishing, has been omitted.

27. Between mid-April and June 1967, Calvino wrote three "deductive tales": "L'inseguimento" (The Chase), "La memoria del mondo" (World Memory), and "Il guidatore notturno" (The Night Driver). The last story was the most experimental one and is probably the one Calvino is referring to here. The first and last of these tales were included in *Ti con zero* (*Time and the Hunter*) (Turin: Einaudi, 1967). The middle one was the title story in *La memoria del mondo e altre storie cosmicomiche*. All are now available in English in *The Complete Cosmicomics*. For the dates of composition

see Calvino, *Tutte le cosmicomiche*, ed. Claudio Milanini (Milan: Mondadori, 1997), p. 415; and in English, see Martin McLaughlin, "Introduction" to *The Complete Cosmicomics*, pp. vii–xxiv.

28. The "Six Day War" (5–10 June 1967), which began with a surprise attack by the Israeli air-force on twenty-five airports in Arab countries, and which ended with the occupation of Sinai, the Gaza Strip, the West Bank, and the Golan Heights.

29. The Calvino family did in fact move from Rome to Paris on that date.

30. This was probably a petition concerning the Six Day War (see the previous letter to François Wahl).

31. The Calvino family was moving to Paris.

32. Pietro Citati, "Goethe" (I: Return to Weimar; II: The French Campaign), *Paragone*, 208 (June 1967): these were "the introductory chapters from a forthcoming book."

33. Calvino, "Philosophy and Literature," *Times Literary Supplement*, 28 September 1967, pp. 871–72; later in *The Literature Machine*, pp. 39–49; Italian version in *Una pietra sopra*, pp. 150–56 (and *S*, I, pp. 188–96).

34. "Lo scaffale ipotetico" (The Hypothetical Bookshelf), *Rinascita*, 24 November 1967, p. 24; later with the title "Per chi si scrive? (Lo scaffale ipotetico)," in *Una pietra sopra*, pp. 159–63 (and *S*, I, pp. 199–204); in English in *The Literature Machine*, pp. 81–88. See the letter of 15 March 1967 to Ferretti.

35. When he sent his piece to Cecchi the same day, he wrote to him: "Perhaps I'll encounter more opposition than approval but this is something I've reflected on a lot, churning it over for several months—from the moment you asked me to write on 'commitment'—and I think that on some points I've come to new formulations of the problem."

36. Pavese, *La letteratura americana e altri saggi*.

37. Lorenzo Mondo, who had edited the first volume of Pavese's letters: *Lettere 1924–1944* (Turin: Einaudi, 1966).

38. This was a handwritten sheet of paper headed "Outline for the New Edition of Pavese's Complete Works: 1. *Lavorare stanca*; 2. *Paesi tuoi. La spiaggia. Il compagno* (or two volumes); 3. *Feria d'agosto*; 4. *Dialoghi con Leucò*; 5. *Prima che il gallo canti*; 6. *La bella estate*; 7. *La luna e i falò*; Posthumous Works: 8. *Il mestiere di vivere*; 9. *Verrà la morte* and other poems; 10. *Essays* (still to do); 11. *Short Stories* (all the ones not in *Feria d'ag.*, with the addition of the chapters in *Fuoco grande* that were written by P.); 12. *Letters* (abridged); Non-Essential Volumes: 13. *Ciau Masino* and other youthful writings (still to be done); 14. *Translations from Homer etc.* (still to do); 15. *Walt Whitman* (graduating thesis) (do we do this???)." This edition, comprising 14 titles in 16 volumes, would be published by Einaudi in 1968.

39. *Paesi tuoi*, *La spiaggia*, and *Il compagno* would all be published in separate volumes.

40. The English version of the story is in *Adam, One Afternoon*, pp. 19–23.

41. See the letter to John Woodhouse of 5 April 1967.

42. M. David, "Les délires logiques d'Italo Calvino" (Italo Calvino's Logical Delirium), *Le Monde*, 27 December, 1967, p. vii, was David's review of *Cosmicomics* and *Time and the Hunter*, which had not yet been translated into French.

43. Michel Butor (born 1926), French novelist often associated with the *nouveau roman*.

44. David's allusion to Massimo Bontempelli was cut from the article published in *Le Monde*. For Bontempelli's influence on Calvino, see also the letter to Luigi Baldacci of 15 January 1968.

45. Dino Buzzati (1906–72), novelist most famous for short stories and his novel *The Tartar Steppe* (1940); Nicola Lisi (1893–1975) was a Tuscan writer of novels and plays; Cesare Zavattini (1902–89), major screenwriter for a number of Italian Neo-realist directors.

46. Michel David, *La psicoanalisi nella cultura italiana* (*Psychoanalysis in Italian Culture*) (Turin: Boringhieri, 1966). In a letter dated 26 November 1967 Calvino had written to David: "I am always amazed at your knowledge of twentieth-century Italian culture, and often agree with your judgments, but also I would often like to discuss them with you and argue against them; I hope we'll have the chance to do so."

47. Milanese's article on *Time and the Hunter* (split into "Guide to Reading" and "A Few Notes of a General Character") was published in the December 1967 issue of *Il Caffè*.

48. The third section of *Time and the Hunter* was entitled "t zero" and contained the tales "t zero," "The Chase," "The Night Driver," and "The Count of Monte Cristo": see *The Complete Cosmicomics*, pp. 243–93.

49. This was Rago's review of *Time and the Hunter*, which came out on 13 December 1967 in *l'Unità* (Milan and Rome editions).

50. This appeared in *l'Unità* on 29 November 1967.

51. Luigi Baldacci, "Nei racconti di Calvino la vita diventa un'ipotesi" (In Calvino's Stories Life Becomes a Hypothesis), in *Epoca*, 31 December 1967.

52. *The Complete Cosmicomics*, p. 287.

53. Alice Ceresa, *La figlia prodiga* (Turin: Einaudi, 1967).

54. See the letter to Michel David of 13 December 1967.

55. In a letter to Gianni Sofri of 10 July 1968, Calvino would write: "In the envelope I sent you on Monday you will have found three pieces from the *Novellino* which I have 'translated.' (The language of the *Novellino* is full of problems; perhaps I will add some other stories to these three, but

here I do not have the dictionaries to do the work properly nor the encyclopaedias or historical reference works which I need: nearly every story is based on the relationships of feudal classes.)"

56. *I quaderni di San Gersolé*, ed. M. Maltoni and G. Venturi, preface by Calvino (Turin: Einaudi, 1959).

57. This section on novels was edited solely by Calvino, who presented and anthologized Swift's *Gulliver's Travels* (in volume 1), Defoe's *Robinson Crusoe* and Cervantes' *Don Quixote* (volume 2), and Nievo's *Confessions of an Italian* (volume 3). Calvino had also prepared a selection of extracts from Manzoni's *The Betrothed*, but they were not in the end included in the anthology.

58. Helen Wolff had written to Calvino on behalf of the publishers, Harcourt Brace & World, Inc.

59. These were the three "long short stories" or "short novels," *A Plunge into Real Estate*, *Smog*, and *The Watcher*.

60. Guido Fink, "*Ti con zero*" (*Time and the Hunter*), *Paragone* (*Letteratura*), 216 (February 1968).

61. The telegram began with these words: "Believing that the period of literary prizes is now definitely over, I do not accept this award because I do not feel I can continue to prop up with my consensus institutions that are now devoid of any meaning." The book that won the prize was *Time and the Hunter*.

62. Marcelo Weil, Chichita Calvino's son.

63. J. R. Woodhouse, *Italo Calvino: A Reappraisal and an Appreciation of the Trilogy* (Hull: University of Hull Publications, 1968).

64. Calvino had expressed analogous concepts at greater length in the blurb written by him for the Italian translation of Michel Tournier's novel, *Venerdí o il limbo del Pacifico* (Turin: Einaudi, 1968); Tournier's book appeared in English as *Friday and Robinson*, transl. Ralph Manheim (New York: Knopf, 1972).

65. D.M. was Dionys Mascolo.

66. The discussions about a journal to be called *Alí Babà* would continue in subsequent years. On 29 December Calvino had written to Paolo Valesio, who had recently moved from Bologna to Harvard University: "Celati and I have continued writing to each other and meeting, and along with him and Guido Neri we are setting up a launch-pad for a new journal. We will keep you informed. In fact, Gianni, who has a more eloquent pen than mine, could start writing to you, so that you can give us your opinion from the Harvard angle, in other words from that very special continent—that is neither Europe nor America—where you now live." See now Italo Calvino, Gianni Celati, Carlo Ginzburg, Enzo Melandri, Guido Neri, "*Alí Babà*": *Progetto di un rivista 1968–1972*, ed. Mario Barenghi and Marco Belpoliti, special issue of *Riga*, 14 (1998).

67. G. C. Ferretti, *La letteratura del rifiuto* (Milan: Mursia, 1969).

68. Francesco Jovine (1902–50), Southern Italian Neo-realist writer.

69. Lorenzo Mondo, Turinese literary critic who wrote for *La Stampa*.

70. Lorenzo Gigli, the literary critic on *La Gazzetta del Popolo*.

71. Calvino is referring to the preface written by Celati to Northrop Frye, *Anatomia della critica. Quattro saggi* (*Anatomy of Criticism*) (Turin: Einaudi, 1969) but which was not published with the book; it appeared, in an adapted form, as a separate article in *Libri nuovi* (5 August 1969) with the title "Anatomie e sistematiche letterarie" (Literary Anatomies and Systemizing).

72. Maud Bodkin, *Archetypal Patterns in Poetry: Psychological Studies of Imagination* (London: Oxford University Press, 1934).

73. As Calvino will make clear a little later, he is referring to Michail Bachtin, *Dostoevskij. Poetica e stilistica* (*Problems of Dostoievsky's Poetics*) (Turin: Einaudi, 1968).

74. Here Calvino is summarizing the plot of his novel fragment, *La decapitazione dei capi* (*Beheading the Heads*), which he would publish in *Il Caffè*, 4 (August [but really December] 1969), pp. 3–14; English translation in *Numbers in the Dark*, pp. 142–55.

75. In *Metodi e fantasmi* (Milan: Feltrinelli, 1969), pp. 15–39, Maria Corti had collected the studies she had written on Beppe Fenoglio up to that point, in a chapter entitled "Trittico per Fenoglio" (Triptych for Fenoglio): "Il partigiano capovolto," "Un nuovo anello della catena," "Costanti e varianti narrative." Corti would later return to Fenoglio's *Il partigiano Johnny* (*Johnny the Partisan*) in Alberto Asor Rosa, ed., *Letteratura italiana. Le Opere*. IV: *Il Novecento*, II: *La ricerca letteraria* (Turin: Einaudi, 1996), pp. 811–34.

76. See, in this connection, the letter to Maria Corti of 28 May 1969.

77. Calvino had written, and then deleted: "I recommended it."

78. In fact Calvino's letter to Vittorini is dated 8 November 1950.

79. Published with the title *I ventitré giorni della città di Alba* (1952).

80. Calvino is alluding to the reservations expressed by Vittorini on the cover of the 1954 edition in the Gettoni series.

81. On 8 September 1943, Italy declared an armistice with the Allied forces.

82. This was followed by a sentence later deleted: "What is certain is that after *Primavera di bellezza* came out and rather disappointed everyone, he started working again on the sequel."

83. Calvino had originally written "from which F. drew."

84. Here there was a word scored out.

85. As emerges from what follows ("expressions and nuances that could be slightly modified"), this was the original text of Maria Corti's introductory note for Beppe Fenoglio, *La paga del sabato* (Turin: Einaudi, 1969).

86. Despite Natalia Ginzburg's and Calvino's favorable opinions, Vittorini did not want Fenoglio's book for the Gettoni series.

87. Beatrice Solinas Donghi, "Il ballo dilazionato" ("The Extended Ball"), *Paragone (Letteratura)*, 228 (1969). On 16 January 1973, after receiving her book *Fiabe a Genova (Fables in Genoa)* (Genoa: Sagep, 1972), Calvino would write to her: "Dear Beatrice, Thank you very much for sending me the present of the Genoese folktales. There now, at a distance of many years my compilation of folktales is beginning to serve the purpose I had hoped for it: to encourage original collections of our patrimony of oral narrative, where that is still possible! Your book is intelligent and carefully edited, like all your work. [. . .] I should let you know that *La gran fiaba intrecciata (The Great Intertwined Fairy Tale)* was one of the first autonomous reading choices of my seven-year old daughter."

88. These two offprints were: Calvino's preface to S. A. Guastella, *Le parità e le storie morali dei nostri villani* (Palermo: Regione Siciliana, 1969); and "Appunti sulla narrativa come processo combinatorio," *Nuova Corrente*, pp. 46–47 (1968, [but really 1969]), later in *Una pietra sopra*, pp. 164–81 (and *S*, I, pp. 205–25); English version, "Cybernetics and Ghosts," in *The Literature Machine*, pp. 3–27.

89. *La letteratura beat americana* (Rome-Bari: Laterza, 1969).

90. Calvino is alluding to his article "Letteratura come proiezione del desiderio" (Literature as Projection of Desire), on Frye's *Anatomy of Criticism* (the Italian translation had been published by Einaudi). His article appeared in *Libri nuovi*, 5 (August 1969), p. 5; later reprinted in *Una pietra sopra*, pp. 195–203 (and *S*, I, pp. 242–51); English translation in *The Literature Machine*, pp. 50–61.

91. Einaudi would publish Vito Ventrella's *Il gatto Pik* (1971) and *Affabilità* (1979).

92. Mario Boselli, "*Ti con zero* o la precarietà del progetto" (*Time and the Hunter* or the Precariousness of the Project), *Nuova Corrente*, 49 (1969).

93. "The Count of Montecristo" was the final story in *Time and the Hunter*, now in *The Complete Cosmicomics*, pp. 280–93.

94. Mario Boselli, "Un continuum di progettazione" (A Continuum of Planning), *Il Caffè*, pp. 2–3 (1969).

95. The reference is to H. Heissenbüttel's book, *Testi 1/2/3* (Turin: Einaudi, 1968), and to his article, "Sulla definizione del concetto di letteratura sperimentale" (On the Definition of the Concept of Experimental Literature), *Il menabò di letteratura*, 7 (1964).

96. Juan Gelman.

97. Vanna Gentili, *Le figure della pazzia nel teatro elisabettiano* (*Figures of Madness in Elizabethan Theatre*) (Lecce: Milella, 1969); a second, enlarged edition, *La recita della follia. Funzioni dell'insania nel teatro dell'età di Shakespeare* (*Acting Madness. The Functions of Insanity in the Theatre of Shakespeare's*

Age), was published by Einaudi in 1978. Calvino wrote his impressions of the book in a letter to Vanna Gentili of 4 August 1970 (not in this selection). See the letter to Paolo Valesio of 16 December 1971 for another letter touching on the theme of madness in Elizabethan theater.

98. Mario Socrate, *Manuale di retorica in ultimi esempi* (Venice: Marsilio, 1973).

99. Charles Fourier, *Teoria dei Quattro Movimenti, Il Nuovo Mondo Amoroso e altri scritti sul lavoro, l'educazione, l'architettura nella società d'Armonia* (*The Theory of the Four Movements and the General Destinies*), published by Einaudi in 1971.

100. A left-wing monthly journal founded in 1969 that became a daily newspaper in 1970.

101. Francesca was the daughter of Vanna Gentili and Mario Socrate.

102. Sebastiano Timpanaro, "Engels, materialismo, 'libero arbitrio'" (Engels, Materialism, "Free Will"), *Quaderni piacentini*, 39 (November 1969).

103. Calvino is referring to Citati's *Goethe* (Milan: Mondadori, 1970).

104. This was almost certainly the proposal that Calvino write the introduction for an edition of Ovid's *Metamorphoses* in Mondadori's Fondazione Valla series, of which Citati was the editor. Calvino later wrote it for the Einaudi edition of the *Metamorphoses* (Turin, 1979), in English as "Ovid and Universal Contiguity," *Why Read the Classics?* pp. 25–35.

105. Stefano is Citati's son.

106. Calvino is referring to Citati's article on Conrad, published in *Il Giorno* and later collected in Citati's volume of essays, *Il tè del cappellaio matto* (*The Mad-Hatter's Tea-Party*) (Milan: Mondadori, 1972).

107. Calvino is alluding to two other pieces by Citati: the opening of a review of Graham Greene's *Travels with My Aunt*, which appeared in *Il Mondo* on 29 August 1970; and to a polemic with Carlo Cassola on the plot-based novel which was also published in *Il Giorno*.

108. The result of this project would be *Le città invisibili* (*Invisible Cities*) (Turin: Einaudi, 1972).

1971–1975

1. Calvino edited and wrote an introduction for a selection of Charles Fourier's works: see note 99 of the previous section.

2. Goethe's *Faust* in Fortini's translation had come out in 1970 in the Mondadori Meridiani series.

3. Ruth Leiser, Fortini's wife.

4. Esther Benítez was preparing a selection of Pavese's *Letters* for a Spanish publisher.

5. In 1979, the French journal *L'Arc* would devote a special issue to Leonardo Sciascia, and Calvino would collaborate on the project with some of his letters to the Sicilian writer. The original texts of these letters would be published later, in the spring of 1981, in the American journal *Forum Italicum*, preceded by this short introduction by Calvino, dated 27 August 1979, and already published in *L'Arc*: "When *L'Arc* asked me for something for the issue on Sciascia, I tried to remember if there was any suitable work of mine that had been published in Italy but was unavailable in France, but nothing came to mind. And yet I was one of the first people to read almost all of Sciascia's books: he sent them to me in manuscript form, as I was a reader at the publisher Einaudi and also I was a friend, so I could tell him what I thought of them. [. . .] Then I remembered I had written letters to Leonardo about his books, some of them quite long [. . .] Maybe I could find some of those letters [. . .] In fact it was Leonardo who found them: they went back twenty-three years. Seeing them all together I realize I have written almost a complete guide to Sciascia. [Unfortunately, I can't find the letter on *Il contesto* (*Equal Danger*), which I remember as rather long and with a series of detective solutions like the one I did for *Todo modo* (*One Way or Another*).] Reading through this correspondence again, I find it is a kind of personal diary in which my ideas develop through a dialog with the works of an author who is also a friend. I see the trenchant confidence of my judgments, typical of youth, slowly giving way to an attitude of general perplexity, an attitude I had learnt to adopt over the years partly from reading Sciascia and partly from looking at the spectacle of the world." The letter on *Il contesto* (*Equal Danger*), which Sciascia had been unable to find and whose absence Calvino bemoans here, was found by Maria Andronico Sciascia, whom Luca Baranelli thanks warmly for having forwarded it to him.

6. Calvino was referring to Giovanni Falaschi, "Calvino tra 'realismo' e razionalismo" (Calvino between "Realism" and Rationalism), *Belfagor*, 4 (31 July 1971).

7. Falaschi's book would be published by Einaudi in 1976 with the title *La resistenza armata nella narrativa italiana* (*The Armed Resistance in Italian Fiction*): chapter 5, devoted to Calvino, would develop this 1971 article, "Calvino tra 'realismo' e razionalismo" (Calvino between "Realism" and Rationalism).

8. Calvino had reviewed Levi's *Paura della libertà* (*Of Fear and Freedom*) in the Turin edition of *l'Unità*, on 15 December 1946.

9. Calvino's survey, "La letteratura italiana sulla Resistenza" (Italian Resistance Literature), possibly written in 1948, had come out in 1949 in

the first issue of the journal *Il movimento della liberazione in Italia* (*The Liberation Movement in Italy*), now in *S*, I, pp. 1492–1500.

10. This article was entitled "Abbiamo vinto in molti" (Many of us were winners), now in *S*, I, pp. 1476–79. The prize, 50,000 lire, was divided equally between Calvino, for the story "Campo di mine" (Minefield), and Marcello Venturi, for "Cinque minuti di tempo" (Five Minutes of Time).

11. The Partito Socialista Italiano di Unità Proletaria (Italian Socialist Party of Proletariat Unity).

12. The English translation of the story is in *Adam, One Afternoon*, pp. 61–67.

13. Franco Fortini, "Piú velenoso di quanto pensiate. Considerazioni non 'marxiste'" (More Poisonous than You Think. Some non-"Marxist" Reflections), and "Pasolini non è la poesia" (Pasolini is Not Poetry), *Quaderni Piacentini*, 44–45 (October 1971).

14. This last sentence "Now I am not thinking . . . of class" was added on the left margin of the sheet of paper, at this point in the paragraph.

15. These verses in German, Greek, Italian, Spanish, and French were declaimed by Cosimo in chapter 22 of *The Baron in the Trees*.

16. Valesio's article, lent to Calvino by Gianni Celati, was "The Language of Madness in the Renaissance," *Yearbook of Italian Studies*, 1 (1971), pp. 199–234.

17. Vanna Gentili, *Le figure della pazzia nel teatro elisabettiano* (*Figures of Madness in Elizabethan Theatre*) (Lecce: Milella, 1969): see note 97 of the previous section.

18. Gertrude Moakley, *The Tarot Cards Painted by Bonifacio Bembo for the Visconti-Sforza Family: An Iconographic and Historical Study* (New York: New York Public Library, 1966).

19. In the introductory note to *Gli amori difficili* (*Difficult Loves*) (Turin: Einaudi, 1970), Calvino had said of himself: "In the same period [1954–55] he found particularly significant the discussions he had with the Hegelian Marxists in Milan, Cesare Cases and especially Renato Solmi, and behind them Franco Fortini, who had been and would continue to be an implacable interlocutor for Calvino" (p. viii).

20. This was one of Calvino's earliest stories, first published in *Il Politecnico*, 19 January 1946; in English in *Adam, One Afternoon*, pp. 61–67.

21. Giuseppe Bonura, *Invito alla lettura di Calvino* (Milan: Mursia, 1972).

22. Germana Pescio Bottino, *Calvino* (Florence: Il Castoro, 1967).

23. Here Calvino replaces a couple of lines he had crossed out: "and a dialogue with what happens also outside of literature, even though in a mediated way."

24. Cesare Cases, "Calvino o il pathos della distanza" (Calvino or the Pathos of Distance), was an article Cases had written on *The Baron in the Trees* in 1958, now in Cases, *Patrie lettere* (Turin: Einaudi, 1978), pp. 160–66.

25. Voltaire's *Zadig* would be published in Einaudi's Centopagine series (of which Calvino was series editor) in 1974.

26. The story of the peasant Bertoldo at the court of King Alboino was the subject of works by G. C. Croce and Goldoni.

27. This was a conference on Italian literature that was to have been held in the spring of 1973.

28. Ferrucci had suggested to Calvino for the Centopagine series Constant's *Adolphe*, Melville's *Bartleby*, and Bunyan's *Pilgrim's Progress*. On 20 March 1973, Calvino would write to Ferrucci, who had sent him an introduction to Chekhov's *The Steppe* way ahead of schedule: "Your introduction is a fine piece from the diary of a reader. For our purposes (in a popularizing series like Centopagine) it is a little bit impressionistic (almost a short story to introduce another short story), a little bit allusive (it does not have the explanatory thrust of your introduction to the Voltaire, in other words it presumes a more refined kind of reader), and it has a little bit too much of Manzoni lost in the steppes. Now it is my turn to demand a more 'historical' approach to the text, more of a 'frame' along the lines: the story was written in . . . when Chekhov had already . . . etc. I know that in asking you to try to produce a more calibrated piece I run the risk of losing the spontaneity of your off the cuff writing, still . . . If you do not feel you can do it, never mind, but I would like you to bear it in mind when it comes to the Tolstoy that I still hope you will do for me." *The Steppe* would not be published, and the collaboration with Ferrucci would be limited to his introduction to *Zadig*.

29. Giovanni Falaschi, "Italo Calvino," *Belfagor*, 5 (30 September 1972).

30. The new book was *Le città invisibili* (*Invisible Cities*). He had written to Fortini on 18 September 1972: "A new book of mine will come out shortly, a totally decadent book."

31. "The Count of Montecristo" was the last story in *Time and the Hunter*.

32. This article had come out in *Il Menabò*, 7 (1964): see the letter to Norberto Bobbio of 28 April 1964.

33. In his article "Calvino tra 'realismo' e razionalismo" (Calvino between "Realism" and Rationalism), *Belfagor*, 4 (31 July 1971).

34. Guido Almansi, "Il mondo binario di Italo Calvino" (Italo Calvino's Binary World), *Paragone (Letteratura)*, 258 (August 1971).

35. Falaschi was obviously referring to the Resistance novel by Ubaldo Bertoli, *La quarantasettesima* (*The Forty-Seventh Brigade*) (Parma: Guanda, 1961; new, revised edition: Turin: Einaudi, 1976).

36. In 1975, Einaudi would publish in the series "Letture per la scuola media" Vittorini's *Conversazione in Sicilia*, ed. Giovanni Falaschi.

37. This was Pampaloni's review of *Invisible Cities*, *Corriere della sera*, 26 November 1972. See also the letter to Pampaloni of 16 May 1973. The "very

fine pages [. . .] in the Garzanti *History*" alluded to in the next paragraph refers to the chapter by Pampaloni on Calvino in *Storia della letteratura italiana*, ed. Emilio Cecchi and Natalino Sapegno, vol. IX: *Il Novecento* (Milan: Garzanti, 1969).

38. *La Ronda* was a literary journal which in its short life (1919–23) favored a classical style as opposed to the Futurist vogue.

39. Vittorio Spinazzola, "Catalogo del caos" (Catalogue of Chaos), *l'Unità* (14 December 1972).

40. Vittorini's *Le città del mondo* (*The Cities of the World*) had been published in 1969.

41. Antonio Faeti, *Guardare le figurine. Gli illustratori italiani dei libri per l'infanzia* (*Looking at Pictures. Italian Illustrators of Children's Books*) (Turin: Einaudi, 1972).

42. On 8 September 1943, Italy signed an armistice with the Allied forces, and on 23 September, Mussolini, freed from prison by German paratroops, set up his "Italian Social Republic" based in the Northern town of Salò.

43. Faeti, "Dormi tranquillo e asciutto" (Sleep Soundly), *Inchiesta* (Summer 1972).

44. *Nuova Corrente*.

45. The book referred to is *Le città invisibili* (*Invisible Cities*).

46. " . . . cercare e saper riconoscere chi e che cosa, in mezzo all'inferno, non è inferno, e farlo durare, e dargli spazio" (seek and learn to recognize who and what, in the midst of the inferno, are not inferno, then make them endure, give them space): see *Invisible Cities*, p. 165.

47. This was "Literature as Projection of Desire. On Northrop Frye's *Anatomy of Criticism*," in *The Literature Machine*, pp. 50–61.

48. This was Pasolini's review of *Invisible Cities*, published in the weekly *Tempo*, 28 January 1973; later included in Pier Paolo Pasolini, *Descrizioni di descrizioni*, ed. G. Chiarcossi (Turin: Einaudi, 1979), pp. 34–39.

49. Pasolini had written: "Poi Calvino ha cessato di sentirsi vicino a me" (Then Calvino stopped being close to me).

50. Guido Nobili, *Memorie lontane*, with an introduction by Pampaloni would appear in the Centopagine series in 1075.

51. See the letter to Mario Lavagetto of 18 May 1973.

52. Geno Pampaloni, "Nel cuore dell'ambiguità" (In the Heart of Ambiguity) (on *Invisible Cities*), in *Libri Nuovi*, 12 (March 1973). See also the letter to Pampaloni of 28 November 1972.

53. Mario Lavagetto, "Le carte visibili di Italo Calvino" (Italo Calvino's Visible Cards), *Nuovi Argomenti*, 31 (January–February, 1973).

54. See the letter to Geno Pampaloni of 16 May 1973.

55. Calvino replied to some of these letters, clearing up doubts and giving explanations. One of his most wide-ranging and interesting replies seems to be the one that he wrote on 12 January 1972 to the pupils of a middle school in Santa Maria a Monte near Pisa. This letter was published minus a page in *ILDA* (pp. 585–86), but it has not been possible to track down the complete letter either in the school or in the Einaudi Archive. In this letter one can read amongst other things: "Almost all of you have got it in for *paradoxes* without giving examples of these paradoxes you don't like. I could reply for a start that paradoxes exist in reality, in the world around us, long before they exist in my book. But if you mean that I should not have written a book of funny little stories (even though they have a bitter edge) but a serious book, then that is like saying that I should have written another book, I should have tried to compete with the many serious and weighty books that exist, amongst which are many masterpieces. But maybe I am not a writer of serious and weighty books: what *I* want to say is that one can use humor, irony, caricature, and maybe paradox to try to make people think about so many things that otherwise would escape their notice, make their minds work more quickly and reason more efficiently. [. . .] For this reason I will leave your curiosity about the *author* unsatisfied: the author is someone who sits at his desk and writes, but as he does so he has in mind—maybe without thinking about it—his public, his past and future readers. So you are authors too, especially now that I have had this direct correspondence with you. So I consider you my collaborators. There now, you'll say: that Calvino never stops with his paradoxes. But actually I am speaking seriously. And though I often joke, it is with all my heart that I tell you how grateful I am to you and to your excellent teacher." Calvino had written about the use and reception of *Marcovaldo* in Italian middle schools in the article "Prime Conclusioni" (First conclusions), *Rendiconti*, 22–23 (April 1971).

56. Morante's *La storia. Romanzo* (*History: A Novel*) would be published by Einaudi in 1974. See the letter to Elsa Morante of 6 August 1974.

57. In a letter to Mario Socrate of 18 August, Calvino had written: "We are spending a very busy summer because we've had a summer house built in this pine-wood which is an oasis of solitude and silence, something extremely rare on our coastlines, and we are having to deal with all the problems of settling into a new house."

58. Ferdinando Camon, *Il mestiere di scrittore* (Milan: Garzanti, 1973).

59. The words "the three dark stories" are a correction for "in *The Castle.*" Calvino is probably alluding to "Tre storie di follia e distruzione" (Three Tales of Madness and Destruction) in *Il castello dei destini incrociati*: for an English version, see *The Castle of Crossed Destinies*, trans. William Weaver (London: Secker & Warburg, 1977), pp. 113–20. They now appear

as the final chapter in *The Tavern of Crossed Destinies* but it appears from this letter that Calvino had initially thought of placing the three stories in *The Castle of Crossed Destinies*.

60. The phrase is a correction for "this would be subsequently followed."

61. Correction for "commented through the Grail."

62. These words were scored out: "not the grammatical 'I' of the [*Taverna*]."

63. A line was cancelled after this: "I am sorry about all these years when we have not se[en] each other."

64. Calvino initially published *The Castle of Crossed Destinies* as a text to accompany the Franco Maria Ricci edition of the Visconti Tarot cards in 1969; later he added *The Tavern of Crossed Destinies*, a text to accompany illustrations of the standard Tarot pack of cards, and the two texts were published together as a single volume by Einaudi in 1973, entitled *Il castello dei destini incrociati*.

65. These words are very hard to decipher, and they correct the original phrase "from my stories."

66. In fact Almansi had published what he called "Imimitations," coining the term from the idea of imitating imitative works such as Robert Lowell's *Imitations*: see "Imimitations da Montale e da Lowell," *Il Caffè*, 20:2–3 (luglio–agosto, 1973), pp. 36–42, later in Guido Almansi, Guido Fink, *Quasi come* (Milan: Bompiani, 1976), pp. 348–58.

67. This was Almansi's review of *Invisible Cities*, contained in "Trittico Calviniano" (A Calvinian Triptych), and published in the journal *Il Bimestre*, 26–29 (1973).

68. Corinna Salvadori Lonergan was the lecturer in Italian at Trinity College who had been given the task of organizing the lectures. In the "hesitant" letter of 9 February, Calvino had written to her amongst other things: "Dear Mrs Lonergan, Please accept my apologies for this late reply but making decisions about travel months in advance is so difficult that I end up turning down all invitations. Another thing that terrifies me is preparing lectures because I am not capable of speaking if I do not have a written text before my eyes. [. . .] The only lecture in Italian that I have ready is on Manzoni. I realize that the Manzoni centenary is over, and the Ariosto centenary has started but I have nothing new on Ariosto, unless I read some extracts from that little edition I did of the *Orlando furioso*." The edition was *Orlando furioso di Ludovico Ariosto raccontato da Italo Calvino. Con una scelta del poema* (Turin: Einaudi, 1970).

69. Vidal's review "Fabulous Calvino" was published in *The New York Review of Books* on 30 April 1974.

70. Morante, *La storia. Romanzo* (*History: A Novel*) (Turin: Einaudi, 1974). See the letter to Elsa Morante of 5 August 1973.

71. Milanese's article was published as "Saggio di letteratura pitagorica. Il numero segreto delle *Città invisibili* di Italo Calvino" (A Sample of Pythagorean Literature. The Secret Number in Italo Calvino's *Invisible Cities*, *Il Caffè*, 5–6 (June, 1975).

72. *Luca Ronconi e la realtà del teatro* (Milan: Feltrinelli, 1973).

73. Sciascia, *Todo modo* (*One Way or Another*) (Turin: Einaudi, 1974).

74. Calvino is alluding to his letter to Sciascia of 14 September 1971.

75. The book would be published by Einaudi in 1975 in the new series of Supercoralli.

76. Falaschi had reviewed *Invisible Cities* and *The Castle of Crossed Destinies* in *Belfagor*, 5 (30 September 1974).

77. Carlo Levi (1902–75), author of *Christ Stopped at Eboli* (1945), died in Rome on Sunday, 5 January 1975. This is the draft of a letter Calvino sent to his widow. The sentence after this was deleted: "Words are becoming more and more difficult/laborious: the spoken word but now also the written word too."

78. Corrected from "muttering to myself."

79. Correction from "opening *Le Figaro* on Monday."

80. Corrected from "at the funeral."

81. The phrase "with those who really knew him" was deleted.

82. The following sentence was deleted: "I do not know when I will be able to write about him; the written word is becoming as difficult for me as speaking."

83. The word "through" was deleted here but it makes sense.

84. Corrected from "an unrealizable model."

85. The following phrase was deleted: "in a world which [on] days like this seems to be more and more impoverished."

86. Manganelli's "Risposta a Pasolini" was the first in a series of articles replying to Pasolini's article "Sono contro l'aborto" (I Am against Abortion) which had been published on the front page of the *Corriere della sera* on 19 January 1975. The abortion debate was raging at this time in Italy: the abortion law was passed in May 1978. On this topic see also the letter to Claudio Magris from early February 1975.

87. Magris's article had appeared in the *Corriere della sera* on 3 February 1975. Calvino would reply to it with "Che cosa vuol dire 'rispettare la vita'" (What "Respect for Life" Means) in *Corriere della sera* of 9 February 1975 (reprinted in Calvino's *S*, II, pp. 2262–67): the article includes phrases and expressions that are identical to those in this letter, which must then be dated somewhere between 3 and 8 February. See also the letter to Manganelli of 22 January 1975.

88. This was followed by a deleted paragraph: "Also the first part of your article, on children who cannot be cured, seems seriously superficial,

taking for granted a sacredness of life in all its forms which does not mean anything and which ends up by diminishing the heroism of the many cases I know of lives that have been sacrificed for children with Down Syndrome or paralysis."

89. Good relations between Magris and Calvino would later be restored.

90. A slip by Calvino here turned "Pier Paciugo" into "Gian Paciugo."

91. On 7 May 1975, Calvino would reply to Esther Benítez: "*El vizconde trunco* I don't like. If I'm not mistaken, *trunco* gives the notion of something sliced horizontally, or without legs. So in that case I prefer *Las dos mitades del vizconde*." The translation into Castilian came out later with the title *El vizconde demediado*.

92. On 21 March 1975, in answer to a request for clarification from Esther Benítez, Calvino would reply amongst other things: "*Barbetti*: in Piedmont, during the Napoleonic period (when Piedmont was annexed to France) the guerrillas who remained loyal to the king and fought against the French invasion were called 'barbet.' (Traditionally this popular Piedmontese term *barbét* was used to refer to the Protestants of the ancient sect of Valdensians from the Val Pellice; nobody knows what connection there is between one meaning and the other; maybe the use of a beard.) (It is a word few readers know, even amongst Italians, I believe; you must pardon these erudite preciosities of the then young author.)"

93. Letter in French.

94. One sentence deleted here was: "(Amongst the writers of this period Aldo Palazzeschi (1885–1973) would deserve a place, but he would have to be better known in France first of all.)"

95. In a letter of 9 October 1975, Cassola had proposed to Calvino that he collaborate on a weekly journal of political debate, "not belonging to any political tendency," which never saw the light of day (he also sent Calvino a copy of the plan but this has not been found in the Calvino Archive). In a letter written on 11 November he thanked Calvino for his "promise to collaborate" and asked him to be "one of the editors of the journal. [. . .] I thought of an editorial board made up of Bobbio, Calvino, Cancogni, Cassola, Fortini, Geymonat, Moravia. [. . .] The world can only be saved by individualists who manage to come together in a common cause."

1976–1980

1. Along with a letter dated 1975–76, Zanzotto had sent Calvino two sonnets in manuscript—"Sonetti di sterpi e limiti" (Sonnet about Thorns and Limits) and "Sonetto di Linneo e Dioscoride" (Sonnet about Lin-

naeus and Dioscorides)—which would be published subsequently in his *Galateo del bosco* (Milan: Mondadori, 1978).

2. The article Calvino is referring to is probably "Poesia?" (Poetry?), published in *Il Verri*, 1 (1976), later in Andrea Zanzotto, *Le poesie e prose scelte*, ed. S. Dal Bianco and G. M. Villata (Milan: Mondadori, 1999), pp. 1200–1204.

3. Calvino had written then crossed out: "does not come to my mind."

4. A movement of avant-garde Italian poets that began in the 1960s.

5. Juan Rulfo (1918–86), important Mexican novelist whose two major works were the collection of short stories *El llano en llamas* (*The Burning Plain and Other Stories*) (1953), and the novel *Pedro Páramo* (1955). Calvino later admitted to being partly influenced by the latter in the penultimate story of *If on a Winter's Night a Traveler*.

6. Carlo Minoia was entrusted with editing the second of the three planned volumes of Vittorini's letters: *Gli anni del "Politecnico". Lettere 1945–1951* (Turin: Einaudi, 1977).

7. See the reconstruction in C. Minoia, "Una polemica non innocente" (A not so Innocent Polemic), *Il Belpaese*, 6 (Milan: Camunia, 1987).

8. A line has been omitted here regarding Vittorini's private life.

9. Letter written in English.

10. At the behest of Robert B. Silvers, Calvino had written a political article for *The New York Review of Books*, but it was never published.

11. These explanations were part of a letter to Danièle Sallenave, who had contacted Calvino on 27 August 1976 in order to get some "suggestions" and "advice" for her French translation, which she also sent him, of *Dall'opaco* (published in *Adelphiana* 1971). The translation was to appear in issue 10 of the periodical *Digraphe* (December 1976). English translation in *The Road to San Giovanni*, pp. 129–55.

12. R. Oliva and A. Portelli, *Conrad: l'imperialismo imperfetto*, ed. Giorgio Melchiore (Turin: Einaudi, 1973).

13. Joseph Conrad, *Cuore di tenebra*, introductory note by Giuseppe Sertoli (Turin: Einaudi, 1973).

14. Emma Grimaldi, "Storia di Pin. Virtualità e azione nel *Sentiero dei nidi di ragno*" (The Story of Pin: Virtuality and Action in *The Path to the Spiders' Nests*), *Misure Critiche*, 18 (January–March 1976).

15. This was followed by a deleted phrase: "proof that there is something in the terrain in which the book has its roots that takes me back etc."

16. Fortini's letter of 19 May 1977—which can be read in Italo Calvino—Franco Fortini, "Lettere scelte 1951–1977," ed. Giuseppe Nava and Elisabetta Nencini, *L'ospite ingrato*, Annuario del Centro Studi Franco Fortini (Macerata: Quodlibet, 1998), p. 116—contained his enthusiastic reaction to "La poubelle agréée," which came out in *Paragone* (*Letteratura*), 324 (February 1977), pp. 3–20; now in English in *The Road to San Giovanni*,

pp. 91–126. Calvino had sent Fortini an offprint of it with the dedication: "For Fortini, this spiritual testament by Calvino—May 77."

17. In a letter of 23 October 1976, Calvino had written to Fortini: "For months now I have been carrying around with me in the folder of urgent things to write the photocopy of your 'I silenzi di Ariosto' (Ariosto's silences) (in *La Rassegna della letteratura italiana*, 79:1–2 (1975), 12–14), a wonderful piece which I really feel is a crucial intervention in this dialog with you, and which forces me to reflect on so many things, on the Ferrarese road to Taoism, on the non-exchangeability of human beings; and for months now I've been meaning to write you a letter which is becoming more and more important and demanding, so much so that I still have not written it. I really have gone into my cocoon, and my dialogs are all in my head, so these days I spend a lot of time debating with you [. . .]. When you write to me it really makes me very, very happy."

18. The Finnish journalist's questions were: "1. What do you think of the Nobel Prize in general? 2. Under what criteria and for what achievements would you award it? 3. Are you satisfied with the way the jury works and its competence, or do you think it should be more broadly based and have perhaps an international dimension? 4. Who are the writers no longer alive who in your view deserved to win the Prize in the past, but were overlooked by the Swedish Academy? 5. Finally, can you suggest the names of 5–6 living writers and poets who in your view ought to be candidates for the Prize?"

19. In his letter Guido Calogero was discussing Calvino's article on the neutron bomb, in particular Calvino's statement that "as well as the 'right men' there are also the 'right things.' It has always seemed to me that Socrates established clearly once and for all that there are never right things and wrong things but only right or wrong uses that man makes of things."

20. At the end of his article Calvino had written: "Our responsibility towards things and towards our fellow humans through things still remains. The ideal towards which one should aim is to construct the just city, one endowed with many right things which can be used in the right way."

21. Ponchiroli had pointed out to Calvino the book by Rosellina Gosi, *Il socialism utopistico. Giovanni Rossi e la colonia anarchica Cecilia* (*Utopian Socialism. Giovanni Rossi and the Anarchist Group Cecilia*) (Milan: Moizzi, 1977) which alluded to the links between the anarchist Rossi and Mario Calvino in the early decades of the twentieth century.

22. The real name of the Russian astronomer and revolutionary whom Calvino mentions was actually Vsevelod Vladimirovič Lebedintzev. On Mario Calvino, Lebedintzev (and Giovanni Rossi), see the letter to Angelo Tamborra of 20 August 1978, as well as the richly documented account

in Stefano Adami, "L'ombra del padre. Il caso Calvino," *California Italian Studies Journal*, 1:2 (2010). Retrieved from: http://escholarship.org/uc/item/8qm3b0q3.

23. As is clear from what follows, Calvino was reading either in manuscript or in proofs the short story that would come out in the book entitled *La famiglia* (Turin: Einaudi, 1977), which also contained another story "Borghesia." In English as Ginzburg, *Two Novellas: Famiglia and Borghesia*, trans. Beryl Stockman (Manchester: Carcanet, 1988).

24. Via del Vantaggio was a street and Ciaccia Oppi a character in "La famiglia."

25. Franco Di Bella was editor of the *Corriere della sera* at the time.

26. See the previous letter.

27. "Borghesia" had come out in seven installments in the *Corriere della sera* (14 August–18 September 1977).

28. "Borghesia" (1972), words and music by Claudio Lolli: "Vecchia piccola borghesia / per piccina che tu sia / io non so se mi fai piú rabbia, pena, schifo o malinconia" (Little old bourgeoisie, petite as you are, I don't know whether you cause me more anger, grief, disgust or sadness).

29. Calvino had clearly read, either in manuscript or at proof stage, Carmelo Samonà's novel *Fratelli* (Turin: Einaudi, 1978).

30. This was the provisional title of *Se una notte d'inverno un viaggiatore* (*If on a Winter's Night a Traveler*).

31. Gianni is Gianni Celati.

32. This was the interview with Daniele Del Giudice, "Colloquio con Italo Calvino. Un altrove da cui guardare l'universo" (Interview with Italo Calvino. An Elsewhere to Look at the Universe from), *Paese sera*, 7 January 1978; now in *S*, II, 2828–32.

33. This was Giorgio Agamben: Guido Neri and Calvino supported him being taken on as publishing adviser, and Einaudi agreed. The essays on "Il Presepio" and on "Esperienza" were included in Agamben's book, *Infanzia e storia. Distruzione dell'esperienza e origine della storia* (Turin: Einaudi, 1978). The journal to which Calvino alludes at the start of the next paragraph was also an idea of Agamben's.

34. This was the journal *Alí Babà*; see Italo Calvino, Gianni Celati, Carlo Ginzburg, Enzo Melandri, and Guido Neri, *"Alí Babà": Progetto di una rivista 1968–1972*.

35. Calvino is referring to a small collection of poems (with a foreward by Guido Neri) by Nicola Muschitiello, a young student and friend of Neri.

36. Ippolito Simonis.

37. These were the upheavals involving the student movement in Italy which lasted for months in 1977, up to the conference in September on repression in Italy.

38. Calvino is alluding to a plan drawn up by Emilio Panaitescu to translate and edit a selection of Paul Valéry's scientific and epistemological works.

39. In all probability Calvino is referring to a piece by Almansi on Isaiah Berlin's *Russian Thinkers*, a collection of essays published in 1978, which would later be translated into Italian as *Il riccio e la volpe e altri saggi* (Milan: Adelphi, 1986). The Italian title draws on one of the main essays in the book, which in turn was inspired by a line from Archilochus: "The fox knows many things, but the hedgehog knows one big thing."

40. See also the letter of 15 August 1978 to Ponchiroli.

41. The reference is to "The Other Eurydice," a rewriting of "The Stone Sky": the latter had been published in *La memoria del mondo e altre storie cosmicomiche* (*World Memory and Other Cosmicomic Stories*) (Milan: Club degli Editori, 1968), whereas the former came out first in English translation in 1971, then would appear in Italian in *Gran Bazaar*, 10 (September–October 1980). Both stories are now in English in *The Complete Cosmicomics*, pp. 332–39, 393–402.

42. Angelo Tamborra, *Esuli russi in Italia dal 1950 al 1917* (*Russian Exiles in Italy from 1905 to 1917*) (Rome-Bari: Laterza, 1977), pp. 188–90.

43. Rosellina Gosi, *Il socialismo utopistico. Giovanni Rossi e la colonia anarchica Cecilia*.

44. This story by Jean Paulhan would be translated into Italian and published by Il Melangolo (Genoa, 1992) with the title *Lenti progressi in amore*.

45. Franco Fortini, *I cani del Sinai* (*The Dogs of Sinai*) (Bari: De Donato, 1967).

46. Calvino is referring to the extracts from *I cani del Sinai* read aloud in the film *Fortini/Cani* made by Jean-Marie Straub and Danièle Huillet.

47. Raboni's review of *If on a Winter's Night a Traveler* had appeared in the *Tuttolibri* section of *La Stampa* on 30 June under the title "Calvino racconta al lettore un romanzo di tutti i romanzi" (Calvino Tells the Reader a Novel about All Novels)." Calvino later intervened in the discussion of his book, prompted by Angelo Guglielmi's review, and wrote a lengthy open letter to Guglielmi published in *Alfabeta*, in December 1979, with the title "Se una notte d'inverno un narratore" (If on a Winter's Night a Novelist) (later in *RR*, II, pp. 1388–97).

48. Calvino would mention on other occasions his friendship with Balbo: see, for instance, "Testimonianza su Felice Balbo" (Statement concerning Felice Balbo), *Dimensioni*, 18 (March 1981), 103–4; and "Dialoghi con Cicino" (Talking with Cicino), *la Repubblica* (4 February 1984), now in *S*, II, pp. 2892–99.

49. This was the letter to Mario Motta of July 1950, published in *Cultura e Realtà*, 2 (July–August 1950), under the title "Una lettera sul 'Paradiso'" (A Letter on "Paradise"), in this volume at pp. 55–60.

50. *If on a Winter's Night a Traveler*.

51. "Felice tra le cose (Gli ottant'anni del poeta Francis Ponge)" (Happy amidst Things. For the Poet Francis Ponge's 80th Birthday), now in *S*, I, pp. 1401–7; in English in *Why Read the Classics?* pp. 231–35.

52. Jacqueline Risset, editor of the Italian version of Ponge's book, *Il partito preso delle cose* (*The Voice of Things*) (Turin: Einaudi, 1979).

53. Lombardo Radice's letter was about *If on a Winter's Night a Traveler*.

54. Vittorio Spinazzola, "Vi dico i mali della nostra cultura" (I'll Tell You What's Wrong with Our Culture), *l'Unità*, 6 July 1980, was a review of Calvino's book of essays *Una pietra sopra* (*Moving On*) (Turin: Einaudi, 1980).

55. Almost identical ideas are expressed in Calvino's letter to Guido Neri of 27 August 1980.

56. Vittorio Spinazzola, "Un uomo e una donna per dieci racconti" (A Man and a Woman for Ten Stories), *l'Unità*, 22 July 1979, later in Spinazzola's *Dopo l'avanguardia* (*After the Avant-Garde*) (Ancona-Rome: Transeuropa, 1989).

57. Calvino had expressed the same sense of perplexity in a letter to Gian Carlo Ferretti of 25 July 1980: "I must thank for you for your review of *Una pietra sopra*, to the point as always. In any case, I'm already regretting having published this book: for many years I refused to publish my essays in a collected volume; I ought to have stuck to that line."

58. Claudio Rugafiori: see the letter to Guido Neri of 31 January 1978.

59. Calvino's *Piccola guida allla Piccola cosmogonia* would appear as an appendix in Raymond Queneau, *Piccola cosmogonia portatile*, trans. Sergio Solmi (Turin: Einaudi, 1982).

60. Calvino wrote about this in his essay "La filosofia di Raymond Queneau," now in *S*, I, pp. 1410–30; in English as "The Philosophy of Raymond Queneau," in *Why Read the Classics?* pp. 245–61.

61. Cesare Segre, "Se una notte d'inverno uno scrittore sognasse un aleph di dieci colori" (If on a Winter's Night a Writer Dreamt an Aleph of Ten Colours), *Strumenti critici*, pp. 39–40 (October 1979); later republished with the title "Se una notte d'inverno un romanziere sognasse un aleph di dieci colori" (If on a Winter's Night a Novelist Dreamt an Aleph of Ten Colours)," in his *Teatro e romanzo* (Turin: Einaudi, 1984), pp. 135–73. As can be deduced from this first sentence, Calvino had already read the original typescript of the article sent to him by the author. A few months later, shortly after his move from Paris, he reread Segre's article in the issue of *Strumenti critici* which came out many months after the date on the issue of "October 1979."

62. Since this is just the draft of a letter, Calvino omits both the new address and the Rome phone number.

63. Eco's novel *Il nome della rosa* (*The Name of the Rose*) (Milan: Bompiani, 1980).

1981–1985

1. Calvino, "Nel cielo dei pipistrelli" (In the Bats' Sky), *la Repubblica*, 19 December 1980, p. 17; later published under the title "Il taciturno ciarliero" (The Taciturn Chatterbox), in *Genova a Giorgio Caproni*, ed. G. Devoto and S. Verdino (Genoa: Edizioni di San Marco dei Giustiniani, 1982), pp. 247–50. Now in *S*, I, pp. 1023–27.

2. C. Milanini, "Calvino, un'utopia discontinua" (Calvino, a Discontinuous Utopia), *Pubblico*, ed. V. Spinazzola (Milan: Milano Libri, 1981); the article was later recast in Milanini's book, *L'utopia discontinua. Saggio su Italo Calvino* (Milan: Garzanti, 1990).

3. Cesare Segre, "Se una notte d'inverno uno scrittore sognasse un aleph di dieci colori" (If on a Winter's Night a Writer Dreamt an Aleph of Ten Colours), *Strumenti critici*, pp. 39–40 (October 1979): see the letter of 6 November 1980 and note 61 in the previous section.

4. Calvino was collaborating on an opera entitled *Un re in ascolto* (*A King Listens*) with the avant-garde composer Luciano Berio: but see the letter to Claudio Varese of 23 September 1984 where Calvino says he played only a small role in the work which was premiered at Salzburg in 1984. The idea also led to a short story written in 1984 which became part of the posthumous collection *Sotto il sole giaguaro* (Milan: Garzanti, 1986); for the English translation, see *Under the Jaguar Sun*, trans. William Weaver (London: Vintage, 1992), pp. 31–64.

5. Here and later Calvino quotes rather loosely sentences from the entry "Ascolto" (Listening) written by Roland Barthes and Roland Havas for the *Enciclopedia Einaudi*, vol. I (Turin: Einaudi, 1977), pp. 982–84.

6. Calvino had written the libretto for this Berio opera, which was premiered in Milan in 1982.

7. Calvino is referring to a review article published in the issue for 17–30 September 1981, in which Rushdie reviewed *The Path to the Spiders' Nests*, *Our Ancestors*, *Cosmicomics*, *The Castle of Crossed Destinies*, *Invisible Cities*, and *If on a Winter's Night a Traveler*.

8. In the end the Italian translation would be published by Garzanti (Milan, 1984) with the title *I figli della mezzanotte*.

9. Falaschi had asked him for information about important cases of editorial intervention by editors in the literature section of Einaudi.

10. Mario Rigoni Stern (1921–2008), novelist and author of *Il sergente nella neve* (*The Sergeant in the Snow*) (1953), the account of his experiences on the Russian front, which is the book referred to here.

11. Elsa Morante had been in the Villa Margherita clinic in Rome for some months.

12. Rella's book, *Metamorfosi. Immagini del pensiero* (*Metamorphosis. Images of Thought*), would be published not by Einaudi but by Feltrinelli (Milan, 1984).

13. Actually Rella believes that Calvino had read not *Il silenzio e le parole. Il pensiero nel tempo della crisi* (*Silence and Words. Thought in the Time of Crisis*) (Milan: Feltrinelli, 1981), but the book he published after that, *Miti e figure del moderno* (*Myths and Figures of the Modern*) (Parma: Pratiche, 1981).

14. A. Giuliani's review of *Palomar*, "Signor Telescopio" (Mr Telescope), came out in *la Repubblica*, 9 December 1983.

15. Correction for "differences and affinities."

16. Correction for "a marginal element."

17. Here Calvino had written then crossed out "from so many questions no reply emerged."

18. M. Barenghi, "Italo Calvino e i sentieri che s'interrompono" (Italo Calvino and the Interrupting Paths) was written for *Linea d'ombra* but it would come out in *Quaderni piacentini*, 15 (1984).

19. This was Calvino's review of Robert Louis Stevenson's *Lo strano caso del Dr. Jekyll e del Sig. Hyde* (translated by C. Fruttero and F. Lucentini, and published in Einaudi's "Scrittori tradotti da scrittori" series in 1983). The review came out in *la Repubblica* on 18 June 1983, with the newspaper title "Tra Jekyll e Hyde è meglio Utterson" (Between Jekyll and Hyde Utterson is Better), now in *S*, I, pp. 981–88.

20. Calvino insisted on this authentic interpretation of *The Argentine Ant*, as is evident from the letter to Cesare Cases of 20 December 1958.

21. This is the story that Calvino says he "would like to have written": see his reply to the survey "I would have liked to have written . . ." *The New York Times Book Review* (6 December 1981), p. 7.

22. This was a letter written to Varese on 4 April 1984, part of which was quoted by Claudio Varese in "Lettera a Calvino su *Palomar*" (A Letter to Calvino about *Palomar*), *Otto/Novecento*, 5–6 (September–December 1984).

23. *Un re in ascolto* (*A King Listens*), "a musical action in two parts by Luciano Berio and Italo Calvino," whose premiere took place at the Salzburg Festival on 7 August 1984.

24. Alfonso Gatto (1909–76), poet and journalist who took part in the Resistance, and was a member of the Communist Party until 1951.

25. The son of Graziana Pentich and Alfonso Gatto, Leone died at age twenty-six in 1976, a few months after the death of his father. Graziana Pentich, as can be deduced from Calvino's final wish in this letter, wanted to collect and publish testimonials and memoirs of her son from friends who had known him.

26. In the letter Levi had thanked Calvino for his review of Levi's *L'altrui mestiere* (*Other People's Trades*) (in *la Repubblica* of 6 March 1985) in the following terms: "one of the best reviews I have ever had: both as a verdict on the book and in terms of quality." The review can be found in *S*, I, pp. 1138–41.

27. "*Leggere la vita*" is a chapter in *L'altrui mestiere* (Turin: Einaudi, 1985) where Levi advanced an hypothesis on the origin and meaning ("to blame,

reproach") of this "curious expression whose use, restricted to the North of Italy, though not strictly dialectal, is slowly dying out." For Calvino's use of the phrase, see the letter to Silvio Micheli of 8 November 1946.

28. The pairing of Mendel and Morse was one of the "riddles" that Sergio Solmi and Calvino had come across when the former was translating Queneau's *P[etite] C[osmogonie] P[ortative]* (*The Little, Portable Cosmogony*) (book II, lines 108ff.). Calvino had written to Solmi on 7 February 1978: "I am wracking my brains over your last question but I can't get to the bottom of it. [. . .] *morse / et la breve et la longue* makes me instantly think of Morse code, but that is still a long way from helping us understand what the lines mean [. . .]. From the lines before it looks as if he is talking about a genetic process." And in a letter of 28 May 1978 he had said to Solmi: "the lines on p. 40 that gave us so many problems (*le semeur endurci*) were to do with Mendel's laws. Mendel experimented with garden peas and in drawing up his genealogical laws of heredity he probably used symbols like the shorts and longs of Morse code in order to designate small plants and bigger ones. (Having said that, those lines still remain very obscure.)" In his letter to Calvino of 6 April 1985, à propos these lines, Levi had hypothesized that Queneau had gotten the idea from a text by François Jacob contained in his *Evoluzione e bricolage* (Turin: Einaudi, 1978).

Index